Meeting the
Ethical Challenges
of Leadership

4
edition

To my students

Meeting the
Ethical Challenges
of Leadership
Casting Light or Shadow

4 edition

Craig E. Johnson
George Fox University

SAGE

Los Angeles | London | New Delhi
Singapore | Washington DC

Los Angeles | London | New Delhi
Singapore | Washington DC

FOR INFORMATION:

SAGE Publications, Inc.
2455 Teller Road
Thousand Oaks, California 91320
E-mail: order@sagepub.com

SAGE Publications Ltd.
1 Oliver's Yard
55 City Road
London EC1Y 1SP
United Kingdom

SAGE Publications India Pvt. Ltd.
B 1/I 1 Mohan Cooperative Industrial Area
Mathura Road, New Delhi 110 044
India

SAGE Publications Asia-Pacific Pte. Ltd.
33 Pekin Street #02-01
Far East Square
Singapore 048763

Acquisitions Editor: Lisa Cuevas Shaw
Development Editor: Julie Nemer
Editorial Assistant: MaryAnn Vail
Production Editor: Eric Garner
Copy Editor: Melinda Masson
Typesetter: C&M Digitals (P) Ltd.
Proofreader: Sally Jaskold
Indexer: Judy Hunt
Cover Designer: Anupama Krishnan
Graphic Designer: Helen Salmon
Permissions Editor: Karen Ehrmann

Printed in the United States of America

Library of Congress Cataloging-in-Publication Data

Johnson, Craig E. (Craig Edward), 1952-

Meeting the ethical challenges of leadership : casting light or shadow / Craig E. Johnson. — 4th ed.

p. cm.
Includes bibliographical references and index.

ISBN 978-1-4129-8222-1 (pbk.)

1. Leadership—Moral and ethical aspects. I. Title.

HM1261.J64 2012 303.3′4—dc22 2011001690

This book is printed on acid-free paper.

11 12 13 14 15 10 9 8 7 6 5 4 3 2 1

Contents

Preface

This edition of *Meeting the Ethical Challenges of Leadership,* like previous versions, is guided by seven principles. First, there are few topics as important as leadership ethics. To highlight that fact, I've adopted Parker Palmer's metaphor of light or shadow as the book's central metaphor. Palmer reminds us that leaders have the power to do significant benefit or harm. In extreme cases, leaders literally make the difference between life and death.

Second, we need to recognize the reality of bad leadership. Understanding why and how leaders cast shadows can help us prevent destructive behaviors and promote positive leadership.

Third, there are important ethical demands associated with the leadership role. Those who want to serve as leaders have a responsibility to exercise their authority on behalf of others. There are also ethical challenges associated with the follower role.

Fourth, the study of leadership ethics must draw from a wide variety of academic disciplines and traditions. Philosophers have been interested in the moral behavior of leaders for centuries. In the modern era they have been joined by social scientists. As a consequence, material for this text is drawn not only from philosophy but also from political science, psychology, management, business ethics, communication, education, sociology, and other fields. This multidisciplinary approach introduces readers to (1) how moral decisions are made (what scholars describe as the descriptive perspective on ethics) and (2) how to lead in a moral manner (the prescriptive or normative perspective).

Fifth, both theory and practice are essential to learning. I try to balance presentation of important concepts and research findings with opportunities for application through self-assessments, case analyses, and exploration exercises.

Sixth, texts should be readable. My objective is to write in an informal, accessible style. I don't hesitate to bring in my own experiences and, in some cases, my biases, in hopes of engaging readers and sparking discussion and disagreement.

Seventh, improvement is the bottom line. The ultimate goal of teaching and writing about ethics is to produce more ethical leaders. I believe that ethical development is part of leadership (and followership) development. Leaders and followers can develop their ability to make and follow through on their moral decisions, just as they develop their other competencies. *Meeting the Ethical Challenges of Leadership* is designed to help students build their ethical expertise through theoretical understanding, skill development, case and film analysis, group and class discussions, personal assessment and reflection, research projects, and writing assignments.

Key Features

Examples and Case Studies

Whatever the specific context, leaders face similar kinds of ethical choices. For that reason, I draw examples from a wide variety of settings: business, coaching, education, government, nonprofit organizations, and the military. Cases continue to play an important role in this edition. Three cases are included in each chapter (with the exception of Chapter 7, which has two). Discussion probes at the end of each case encourage students to reflect on key ethics concepts and apply what they have learned from the chapter to the situations under consideration. Students are also asked to consider what additional leadership ethics lessons can be drawn from these narratives.

Leadership Ethics at the Movies

You'll also find a feature called "Leadership Ethics at the Movies." Each of these short summaries introduces a feature film that illustrates principles from the chapter. This feature is designed to encourage students to (1) identify the important ethical principles portrayed in the film, (2) analyze and evaluate how the characters respond to moral dilemmas, and (3) draw ethical implications and applications from the movie. I have also provided three discussion questions with each film to get you and your students started.

Self-Assessments

The next feature, "Self-Assessment," is designed to help students measure their performance with respect to an important behavior, skill, or concept discussed in the chapter.

Focus on Follower Ethics

This feature addresses the ethical challenges facing followers. Followers are critical to the success of any enterprise. The "Focus on Follower Ethics" box in each chapter helps students recognize and master the ethical demands of the follower role.

Implications and Applications

This section, found immediately after the body of each chapter, reviews key ideas and their ramifications for readers.

For Further Exploration, Challenge, and Self-Assessment

This feature encourages interaction with chapter content. Activities include brainstorming exercises, small-group discussions, conversational dyads, debates, self-analysis, personal reflection, and application and research projects.

What's New to This Edition?

Readers of previous editions will note a new chapter on ethical crisis leadership. Crises are major, unexpected events that pose significant threats to groups and organizations. Chapter 11 describes the stages of crises and introduces principles and strategies for ethically managing these traumatic events.

Examples throughout the text have been updated, and there is new and expanded coverage of the following:

- Ethical expertise
- Unhealthy motivations
- Moral identity
- Followership ethics
- Moral hypocrisy
- The ethics of care
- Responsible leadership
- Authentic leadership
- Servant leadership
- Moral emotions and intuition
- Emotional intelligence
- Universal psychological values patterns
- Appreciative inquiry

- Organizational justice
- Cosmopolitanism
- Cross-cultural ethical decision making

Many of the cases from previous editions have been replaced. New cases in this edition include descriptions of AIG, Washington Mutual, DNA databases, paying college athletes, the Peanut Corporation of America, Microsoft, the Columbine school shooting, Turnitin, Bernie Madoff, and Siemens Global. Cases retained from the third edition have been updated, including those dealing with the genocide in Darfur, Pat Tillman, Google in China, incentives for organ donations, and the *Columbia* space shuttle crash.

Ancillaries

Instructor Teaching Site

A password-protected instructor's manual is available at **www.sagepub .com/johnsonmecl4e** to help instructors plan and teach their courses. These resources have been designed to help instructors make the classes as practical and interesting as possible for students.

- **Overview for the Instructor** offers the author's insights on how to most effectively use this book in a course on leadership ethics.
- **Chapter tests** offer a variety of questions to assist with assessment of student learning.
- **PowerPoint slides** capture key concepts and terms for each chapter for use in lectures and review.
- **Sample Course Syllabus** provides a model for structuring your course.
- **Leadership Seminar Syllabus** is an additional course option for a seminar format.
- **Teaching Strategies** offers ideas and insights into various approaches to teaching and learning.
- **Assignments and Projects** provide unique and highly creative activities for meaningful involvement in learning.

Student Study Site

An open-access student study site can be found at **www.sagepub.com/johnsonmecl4e**. The site offers **Learning From SAGE Journal Articles**, with access to recent, relevant full-text articles from SAGE's leading research journals. Each article supports and expands on the concepts presented in the book. This feature also provides discussion questions to focus and guide student interpretation.

Acknowledgments

Colleagues and students provided practical and emotional support during the writing of this edition, just as they did for earlier versions. Much of the work on this revision was completed during a sabbatical leave granted by George Fox University's Academic Affairs Office. I am grateful for the generosity of Provost Patrick Allen and former School of Business Dean Ken Armstrong who provided me with valuable released time to work on the project. Research librarian Janis Tyhurst and her colleagues helped locate sources and double-check facts. Phil Smith clarified my understanding of several philosophical theories. Student assistants, ably supervised by Kelly Borror, picked up books and photocopied materials. Rebecca Jensen provided editorial and reference assistance. Students enrolled in my leadership seminar, doctoral leadership seminar, business ethics, and leadership communication classes shaped this and earlier editions by responding to chapter content, exercises, and cases. My special thanks go to instructors from around the country who adopted the first three editions of *Meeting the Ethical Challenges of Leadership,* which made this fourth edition possible. Three anonymous reviewers provided input that guided my revisions. Kristina Findley supplied material for a scenario in Chapter 7. Editor Lisa Shaw ably picked up where her predecessors at SAGE left off. Finally, I want to once again thank my wife, Mary, who continues to encourage my writing efforts.

Introduction

Leaders: The Bad News and the Good News

When it comes to leaders, there is both bad news and good news. The bad news is that wherever we turn—business, military, politics, medicine, education, or religion—we find leaders toppled by ethical scandals. Nearly all have sacrificed their positions of leadership and their reputations. Many face civil lawsuits, criminal charges, and jail time. The costs can be even greater for followers. Consider, for example:

- A global economic crisis was triggered by leaders in the financial industry who downplayed risks and engaged in fraud in order to generate short-term profits.
- Investors lost billions in the greatest scam in history run by financier Bernie Madoff.
- Thousands of former Enron and WorldCom employees may never recover from the loss of their jobs and their retirement savings.
- Consumers in 44 states and one Canadian province were sickened by peanut butter products allegedly shipped after plant officials knew they were contaminated with salmonella.
- Members of the British Parliament used public funds to remodel their personal residences.
- Hundreds of children in the United States, Ireland, and Europe suffered sexual abuse at the hands of Catholic clergy. Victims' lawsuits bankrupted some dioceses.
- Over 200,000 women caught in Congo's civil war have been raped as military leaders engage in a campaign of sexual terrorism.
- Patients taking the popular pain medication Vioxx faced a much greater risk of heart attack because Merck officials hid information about the drug's side effects in order to get it approved.
- Executives at Toyota were slow to respond to safety concerns, putting the lives of hundreds of thousands of drivers in danger.

- The Gulf of Mexico oil spill, one of the greatest environmental disasters in U.S. history, was the product of a series of poor decisions by leaders at BP who apparently ignored safety warnings and had no strategy in place for capping deepwater oil leaks.

The misery caused by unethical leaders drives home an important point: Ethics is at the heart of leadership.[1] When we assume the benefits of leadership, we also assume ethical burdens. I believe that we must make every effort to act in such a way as to benefit rather than damage others, to cast light instead of shadow. Doing so will significantly reduce the likelihood that we will join the future ranks of fallen leaders.

Fortunately, we can also find plenty of examples of leaders who brighten the lives of those around them. That's the good news. Consider these examples:

- The leaders of hundreds of relief organizations immediately responded to the devastating earthquakes in Haiti and Chile.
- Dr. Paul Farmer, a world expert on infectious diseases, founded Partners in Health, which operates a clinic in Haiti and fights drug-resistant tuberculosis in prisons and slums around the world.
- On his 81st birthday, CEO Robert Moore gave his company, Bob's Natural Foods, to his 200 Oregon employees.
- Greg Mortenson and the Central Asia Institute have helped over 50,000 Pakistani and Afghan girls attend school.
- Former CEO Maurice Myers led Waste Management's recovery from a billion-dollar accounting scandal and helped the company create an ethical culture; Tyco's executive team led a similar ethical turnaround after former CEO Dennis Kozlowski diverted company funds to support his lavish lifestyle.
- Eunice Kennedy Shriver founded the Special Olympics, a sports competition for adults with mental challenges that draws 2.5 million participants annually.
- US Airways pilot Captain Chesley Sullenberger saved the lives of all of his crew and passengers by safely landing his damaged plane in New York's Hudson River.
- Government leaders in Rwanda introduced affordable universal health care for all citizens, no matter their income.
- Muhammad Yunus started Bangladesh's Grameen Bank, which makes small (micro) loans to poor women who operate their own businesses.
- Officials at Britain's HALO Trust work to eliminate land mines in former war zones around the world.

Researchers report that if we take our ethical responsibilities seriously, we too can create a variety of positive group and organizational outcomes.[2] These include lower stress levels, less turnover, and less absenteeism; higher employee job satisfaction, commitment, and willingness to give extra effort;

better decision making; greater levels of trust and collaboration; positive public image; and, in many cases, higher performance (productivity, profitability).[3]

You should find this book helpful if you are a leader or an aspiring leader who (1) acknowledges that there are ethical consequences associated with the leadership role, (2) wants to exert positive influence over others, (3) seeks to make more informed ethical choices and to follow through on your decisions, and (4) desires to foster ethical behavior in others. You'll also find useful insights if you are a follower who wants to behave ethically and bring out the best in your leaders.

There is no guarantee that after reading this book you will act in a more ethical fashion in every situation. Nor can you be sure that others will reach the same conclusions as you do about what is the best answer to an ethical dilemma or that you will succeed in improving the ethical climate of your group or organization. Nevertheless, you can increase your ethical competence and encourage others to do the same. This book is dedicated to that end.

Defining Terms

Because this is a book about leadership ethics, we need to clarify what both of these terms mean. Leadership is the exercise of influence in a group context.[4] Want to know who the leaders are? Look for the people having the greatest impact on the group or organization. Leaders are change agents engaged in furthering the needs, wants, and goals of leaders and followers alike. They are found wherever humans associate with one another, whether in a social movement, sports team, task force, nonprofit agency, state legislature, military unit, or corporation.

No definition of leadership is complete without distinguishing between leading and following. Generally leaders get the most press. The newfound success of a college football team is a case in point. A head coach gets most of the credit for changing a losing team into a winner, but the turnaround is really the result of the efforts of many followers. Assistant coaches work with offensive and defensive lines, quarterbacks, and kicking teams; trainers tend to injuries; academic tutors keep players in school; athletic department staff members solicit contributions for training facilities; and sports information personnel draw attention to the team's accomplishments. (In Chapter 5 we will see that followers in all fields are more important than ever.)

In truth, leaders and followers function collaboratively, working together toward shared objectives. They are relational partners who play complementary roles.[5] Whereas leaders exert a greater degree of influence and take more responsibility for the overall direction of the group, followers are more involved in implementing plans and doing the work. During the course of a day or week, we typically shift between leader and follower roles, heading up a project team at work, for example, while taking the position of follower as a student in a night class. As a result, we need to know how to behave ethically as both leaders and followers.

Moving from a follower role to a leadership role brings with it a shift in expectations. Important leader functions include establishing direction, organizing, coordinating activities and resources, motivating, and managing conflicts. Important follower functions include carrying out group and organizational tasks (engineering, social work, teaching, accounting), generating new ideas about how to get jobs done, teamwork, and providing feedback.[6]

Viewing leadership as a role should put to rest the notion that leaders are born, not made. The fact that nearly all of us will function as leaders if we haven't already done so means that leadership is not limited to those with the proper genetic background, income level, or education. Many ordinary people emerged as leaders during the horrific events of September 11, 2001, for example. Office workers in the World Trade Center calmed victims and bandaged their wounds. They formed human chains to walk down the stairs in the smoke and darkness, assisting those who had difficulty navigating the steps. While these workers were headed down, firefighters of all ranks were rushing up the staircases to help. A paramedic driving near the Pentagon took his bag out of his car, doused burn victims with saline, and got others to drag victims to safety. Passengers on hijacked United Airlines Flight 93 rushed the attackers and prevented the plane from striking its intended target.

Leadership should not be confused with position, although leaders often occupy positions of authority. Those designated as leaders, such as a disillusioned manager nearing retirement, don't always exert much influence. On the other hand, those without the benefit of a title on the organizational chart can have a significant impact. Václav Havel was a Czech playwright who served time in prison for opposing the government. Later he went on to help lead the Velvet Revolution that overthrew the country's communist regime and became the nation's first democratic president. Erin Brockovich was a poor single mother in California without legal training who helped victims of chemical poisoning reach a multimillion-dollar legal settlement with Pacific Gas and Electric.

Human leadership differs in important ways from the pattern of dominance and submission that characterizes animal societies. The dominant female hyena or male chimpanzee rules over the pack or troop through pure physical strength. Each maintains authority until some stronger rival (often seeking mates) comes along. Unlike other animals, which seem to be driven largely by instinct, humans consciously choose how they want to influence others. We can rely on persuasion, rewards, punishments, emotional appeals, rules, and a host of other means to get our way. Freedom of choice makes ethical considerations an important part of any discussion of leadership. The term *ethics* refers to judgments about whether human behavior is right or wrong. We may be repulsed by the idea that a male lion will kill the offspring of the previous dominant male when he takes control of the pride. Yet we cannot label his actions as unethical because he is driven by a genetic drive to start his own bloodline. We can and do condemn the actions of leaders who decide to lie, belittle followers, and enrich themselves at the expense of the less fortunate.

Some philosophers distinguish between *ethics*, which they define as the systematic study of the principles of right or wrong behavior, and *morals*, which they describe as specific standards of right and wrong ("thou shall not steal," "do unto others as they would do unto you"). Just as many scholars appear to use these terms interchangeably, I will follow the latter course.

The practice of *ethical leadership* is a two-part process involving personal moral behavior and moral influence.[7] Ethical leaders earn that label when they act morally as they carry out their duties and shape the ethical contexts of their groups, organizations, and societies. Both components are essential. Leaders must demonstrate such character traits as justice, humility, optimism, courage, and compassion; make wise choices; and master the ethical challenges of their roles. In addition, they are also responsible for the ethical behavior of others. These dual responsibilities intertwine. As we'll see later in the book, leaders act as role models for the rest of the organization. How followers behave depends in large part on the example set by leaders. Conversely, leaders become products of their own creations. Ethical climates promote the moral development of leaders as well as followers, fostering their character and improving their ability to make and follow through on ethical choices. Ethical organizational environments are marked by integrity, justice, a concern for how goals are achieved, and a sense of social responsibility. They also have safeguards that keep both leaders and followers from engaging in destructive behaviors.

Overview of the Book

Part I of this book examines the important topic of "The Shadow Side of Leadership." Chapter 1 outlines common shadows cast by leaders: abuse of power and privilege, mismanagement of information, misplaced and broken loyalties, inconsistency, and irresponsibility. Chapter 2 explores the reasons why leaders often cause more harm than good and then outlines strategies for stepping out of the shadows and into the light.

After identifying the factors that cause us to cast shadows as leaders, we will then begin to master them. To do so we will need to look inward; Part II, "Looking Inward," focuses on the inner dimension of leadership. Chapter 3 examines the role of character development in overcoming our internal enemies and faulty motivations, and Chapter 4 explores the nature of evil, forgiveness, and spirituality.

Part III, "Ethical Standards and Strategies," addresses ethical decision making and provides the theory and tactics we need to move beyond our status as ethical novices. Chapters 5 and 6 survey a wide range of perspectives, both general and leader-focused, that can help us set moral priorities. Chapter 7 then describes the process of moral action as well as formats that we can use to make better ethical choices and follow through on our decisions.

Part IV, "Shaping Ethical Contexts," looks at ways in which leaders can shed light in a variety of situations. Chapter 8 examines ethical group decision making. Chapter 9 describes the creation of ethical organizational climates. Chapter 10 highlights the challenges of ethical diversity. Chapter 11 provides an overview of ethical leadership in crisis situations.

Expect to learn new terminology along with key principles, decision-making formats, and important elements of the ethical context. This information will be drawn from a number of different fields of study—philosophy, communication, theology, history, psychology, sociology, political science, and organizational behavior—because we need insights from many different disciplines if we're to step out of the shadows. You can anticipate reading about and then practicing a variety of skills, ranging from information gathering to listening and conflict management.

With these preliminaries out of the way, let's begin by taking a closer look at some of the ethical hurdles faced by leaders in Chapter 1.

Notes

1. See Ciulla, J. (Ed.). (2004). *Ethics: The heart of leadership.* Westport, CT: Praeger.

2. Johnson, C. E. (2007). Best practices in ethical leadership. In J. A. Conger & R. E. Riggio (Eds.), *The practice of leadership: Developing the next generation of leaders* (pp. 150–171). San Francisco: Jossey-Bass; Brown, M. E., Trevino, L. K., & Harrison, D. A. (2005). Ethical leadership: A social learning perspective for construct development and testing. *Organizational Behavior and Human Decision Processes, 97,* 117–134.

3. See Waddock, S. A., & Graves, S. B. (1997). The corporate social performance–financial performance link. *Strategic Management Journal, 18,* 303–319.

4. Bass, B. M. (1990). *Bass and Stogdill's handbook of leadership* (3rd ed.). New York: Free Press.

5. Hollander, E. P. (1992, April). The essential interdependence of leadership and followership. *Current Directions in Psychological Science,* 71–75.

6. Johnson, C. E., & Hackman, M. Z. (1997). *Rediscovering the power of followership in the leadership communication text.* Paper presented at the National Communication Association convention, Chicago.

7. Brown, M. E., & Trevino, L. K. (2006). Ethical leadership: A review and future directions. *The Leadership Quarterly, 17,* 595–616.

PART I

The Shadow Side of Leadership

1

The Leader's Light or Shadow

We know where light is coming from by looking at the shadows.

—Humanities scholar Paul Woodruff

WHAT'S AHEAD

This chapter introduces the dark (bad, toxic) side of leadership as the first step in promoting good or ethical leadership. The metaphor of light and shadow dramatizes the differences between moral and immoral leaders. Leaders have the power to illuminate the lives of followers or to cover them in darkness. They cast light when they master ethical challenges of leadership. They cast shadows when they (1) abuse power, (2) hoard privileges, (3) mismanage information, (4) act inconsistently, (5) misplace or betray loyalties, and (6) fail to assume responsibilities.

A Dramatic Difference

In an influential essay titled "Leading From Within," educational writer and consultant Parker Palmer introduces a powerful metaphor to dramatize the distinction between ethical and unethical leadership. According to Palmer, the difference between moral and immoral leaders is as sharp as the contrast between light and darkness, between heaven and hell.

3

> A leader is a person who has an unusual degree of power to create the conditions under which other people must live and move and have their being, conditions that can be either as illuminating as heaven or as shadowy as hell. A leader must take special responsibility for what's going on inside his or her own self, inside his or her consciousness, lest the act of leadership create more harm than good.[1]

For most of us, leadership has a positive connotation. We have been fortunate enough to benefit from the guidance of teachers or coaches, for example, or we admire noteworthy historical leaders. However, Palmer urges us to pay more attention to the shadow side of leadership. Political figures, parents, clergy, and business executives have the potential to cast as much shadow as they do light. Refusing to face the dark side of leadership makes abuse more likely. All too often, leaders "do not even know they are making a choice, let alone how to reflect on the process of choosing."[2]

Recently other scholars have joined Palmer in urging us to pay more attention to the dark or negative dimension of leadership. Claremont Graduate University professor Jean Lipman-Blumen uses the term *toxic leaders* to describe those who engage in destructive behaviors and who exhibit dysfunctional personal characteristics.[3] These behaviors and qualities (summarized in Table 1.1 on page 6) cause significant harm to followers and organizations. A group of Norwegian researchers points out that destructive organizational leadership undermines the group's success and/or the well-being of followers. Destructive leaders can be antiorganization, antisubordinates, or both. *Tyrannical leaders* reach organizational goals while abusing followers. *Supportive-disloyal leaders* care for the welfare of subordinates at the expense of organizational goals. They may tolerate loafing or stealing, for example. *Derailed leaders* act against the interests of subordinates and the organization. At the same time they bully, manipulate, deceive, and harass followers, they may be stealing from the organization, engaging in fraudulent activities, and doing less than expected. *Constructive leaders,* on the other hand, care about subordinates and help the organization achieve its goals while using resources wisely.[4]

Harvard professor Barbara Kellerman believes that limiting leadership solely to good leadership ignores the reality that a great many leaders engage in destructive behaviors.[5] Overlooking that fact, Kellerman says, undermines our attempts to promote good leadership: "I take it as a given that we promote good leadership not by ignoring bad leadership, nor by presuming that it is immutable, but rather by attacking it as we would a disease that is always pernicious and sometimes deadly."[6]

According to professor Kellerman, bad leaders can be ineffective, unethical, or ineffective and unethical. She identifies seven types of bad leaders:

Incompetent. These leaders don't have the motivation or ability to sustain effective action. They may lack emotional or academic intelligence, for example, or be careless, distracted, or sloppy. Some can't function under stress, and their communication and decisions suffer as a result. Former International Olympic Committee President Juan Antonio Samaranch (1961–2000) is one example of an incompetent leader. Toward the end of his tenure he turned a blind eye to commercialism, drug scandals, and corruption in the Olympic movement.

Rigid. Rigid leaders may be competent, but they are unyielding, unable to accept new ideas, new information, or changing conditions. Thabo Mbeki is one such leader. After becoming president of South Africa in 1999, he insisted that HIV did not cause AIDS and withheld antiretroviral drugs from HIV-positive women. These medications would have dramatically cut the transmission of the disease to their babies.

Intemperate. Intemperate leaders lack self-control and are enabled by followers who don't want to intervene or can't. Marion Barry, Jr.'s political career demonstrates intemperate leadership in action. Barry served as mayor of Washington, DC, from 1979 to 1991. He ignored widespread corruption in his administration, perhaps in part because he was busy cheating on his wife and doing drugs. Barry was convicted of possessing crack cocaine and served 6 months in jail. After being released from prison, he was elected to the city council in 1992 and was reelected as mayor in 1994. During his administrations, the district's schools and public services deteriorated while the murder rate soared.

Callous. The callous leader is uncaring or unkind, ignoring or downplaying the needs, wants, and wishes of followers. Former hotel magnate Leona Helmsley personifies the callous leader. She earned the title "The Queen of Mean" by screaming at employees and firing them for minor infractions such as having dirty fingernails. Helmsley later served time for tax evasion. (She once quipped, "Only the little people pay taxes.")

Corrupt. These leaders and at least some of their followers lie, cheat, and steal. They put self-interest ahead of public interest. Former United Way of

Table 1.1   The Behaviors and Personal Characteristics of Toxic Leaders

Destructive Behaviors	Toxic Qualities
Leaving followers worse off	Lack of integrity
Violating human rights	Insatiable ambition
Feeding followers' illusions; creating dependence	Enormous egos
Playing to the basest fears and needs of followers	Arrogance
Stifling criticism; enforcing compliance	Amorality (unable to discern right from wrong)
Misleading followers	Avarice (greed)
Subverting ethical organizational structures and processes	Reckless disregard for the costs of their actions
Engaging in unethical, illegal, and criminal acts	Cowardice (won't make tough choices)
Building totalitarian regimes	Failure to understand problems
Failing to nurture followers, including successors	Incompetent in key leadership situations
Setting constituents against one another	
Encouraging followers to hate or destroy others	
Identifying scapegoats	
Making themselves indispensable	
Ignoring or promoting incompetence, cronyism, and corruption	

SOURCE: Adapted from Lipman-Blumen, J. (2005). *The allure of toxic leaders: Why we follow destructive bosses and corrupt politicians—and how we can survive them.* Oxford, UK: Oxford University Press, pp. 19–23.

America chief William Aramony is an exemplar of this type of leader. Aramony used United Way funds to buy and furnish an apartment for his girlfriend and to pay for vacations. His top financial officers helped him hide his illegal actions. Aramony and his colleagues were convicted on fraud-related charges.

Insular. The insular leader draws a clear boundary between the welfare of his or her immediate group or organization and outsiders. Former President Bill Clinton behaved in an insular manner when he didn't intervene in the Rwandan genocide that took the lives of 800,000–1 million people in 1994. He later traveled to Africa to apologize for failing to act even though he had reliable information describing how thousands of Tutsis were being hacked to death by their Hutu neighbors.

Evil. Evil leaders commit atrocities, using their power to inflict severe physical or psychological harm. Foday Sankoh is one example of an evil leader. He started a civil war in Sierra Leone in 1991. His army, which included many boy soldiers, carried out a campaign of rape and murder. The rebels were also known for chopping off the legs, hands, and arms of innocent civilians.

The Leader's Shadows

When we function as leaders, we take on a unique set of ethical burdens in addition to a set of expectations and tasks. These dilemmas involve issues of power, privilege, information, consistency, loyalty, and responsibility. How we handle the challenges of leadership determines whether we cause more harm than good or, to return to Palmer's metaphor, whether we cast light or shadow. Unless we're careful, we're likely to cast one or more of the shadows described in this section.

The Shadow of Power

Power is the foundation for influence attempts. The more power we have, the more likely others are to comply with our wishes. Power comes from a variety of sources. The most popular power classification system identifies five power bases.[7] *Coercive power* is based on penalties or punishments such as physical force, salary reductions, student suspensions, or embargoes against national enemies. *Reward power* depends on being able to deliver something of value to others, whether tangible (bonuses, health insurance, grades) or intangible (praise, trust, cooperation). *Legitimate power* resides in the position, not the person. Supervisors, judges, police officers, instructors, and parents have the right to control our behavior within certain limits. A boss can require us to carry out certain tasks at work, for example, but in most cases he or she has no say in what we do in our free time. In contrast to legitimate power, *expert power* is based on the characteristics of the individual regardless of her or his official position. Knowledge, skills, education, and certification all build expert power. *Referent (role model) power* rests on the admiration one person has for another. We're more likely to do favors for a supervisor we admire or to buy a product promoted by our favorite sports hero.

Leaders typically draw on more than one power source. The manager who is appointed to lead a task force is granted legitimate power that enables her to reward or punish. Yet in order to be successful, she'll have to demonstrate her knowledge of the topic, skillfully direct the group process, and earn the respect of task force members through hard work and commitment to the group. ("Leadership Ethics at the Movies: *Doubt*" describes one leader who skillfully uses her power to achieve a worthy objective.)

There are advantages and disadvantages of using each power type. For instance, rewards are widely accepted in Western culture but can be counterproductive if they promote the wrong behaviors (see Chapter 9) or go to the wrong people. Researchers report that U.S. workers are more satisfied and productive when their leaders rely on forms of power that are tied to the person (expert and referent) rather than on forms of power that are linked to the position (coercive, reward, and legitimate).[8] In addition, positional power is more susceptible to abuse. Coercive tactics have the potential to do the most damage, threatening the dignity as well as the physical and mental health of followers. Leaders, then, have important decisions to make about the types of power they use and when.

The fact that leadership cannot exist without power makes some Americans uncomfortable. Harvard business professor Rosabeth Kanter goes so far as to declare that power is "America's last dirty word."[9] She believes that for many of us talking about money and sex is easier than discussing power. We admire powerful leaders who act decisively but can be reluctant to admit that we have and use power.

Our refusal to face up to the reality of power can make us more vulnerable to the shadow side of leadership. Cult leader Jim Jones presided over the suicide–murder of 909 followers in the jungles of Guyana. Perhaps this tragedy could have been avoided if cult members and outside observers had challenged Jones's abuse of power.[10] Conversely, ignoring the topic of power prevents the attainment of worthy objectives, leaving followers in darkness. Consider the case of the community activist who wants to build a new shelter for homeless families. He can't help these families unless he skillfully wields power to enlist the support of local groups, overcome resistance of opponents, raise funds, and secure building permits.

I suspect that we treat power as a dirty word because we recognize that power has a corrosive effect on those who possess it. We've seen how Richard Nixon used the power of his office to order illegal acts against his enemies and how George W. Bush authorized warrantless wiretaps to listen in on the conversations of U.S. citizens.[11] Many corporate leaders have been intoxicated by their power, using their positions to abuse their subordinates. One such boss kept an employee in an all-day meeting even as her mother was dying. Another called the paramedics when an employee had a heart attack and then ordered everyone else to go back to work even as the victim was still lying on the floor. Yet another berated and humiliated a subordinate who suffered an emotional breakdown and had to be hospitalized. His response? "I can't help it if she is overly sensitive."[12]

LEADERSHIP ETHICS AT THE MOVIES

DOUBT

Key Cast Members: Meryl Streep, Philip Seymour Hoffman, Amy Adams

Synopsis: Sister Aloysius Beauvier (Streep) is the no-nonsense principal of Saint Nicholas Catholic School in the early 1960s. Being sent to her office for talking in class, chewing gum, or any number of other minor offenses is a terrifying experience. She clashes with charismatic priest Father Flynn (Hoffman) who wants the school and parish church to be more welcoming and friendly. Their conflict escalates when Sister James (Adams), the school's youngest teacher, reports that Flynn is paying special attention to a troubled young boy. The priest denies making sexual advances to the student, but Sister Beauvier and Sister James have their doubts. The principal has less power than Flynn and other males in the Catholic hierarchy, but is determined to get the priest to confess his sin and resign.

(Continued)

(Continued)

Rating: PG-13 for adult themes

Themes: types of power, use and abuse of power, abuse of privilege, betrayal, deception, inconsistency, responsibility and irresponsibility, compassion, courage

Discussion Starters

1. What types of power does Father Flynn use to protect himself and his position? How does Sister Beauvier wield power?

2. What leadership shadows are cast by Father Flynn? By Sister Beauvier?

3. How should followers respond when they have doubts about the behaviors of their leaders?

Unfortunately, abuse of power is an all too common fact of life in modern organizations. In one survey, 90% of those responding reported that they had experienced disrespect from a boss some time during their working careers. Twenty percent of the sample said they currently work for an abusive leader. (Complete "Self-Assessment: The Brutal Boss Questionnaire" to determine whether your supervisor is abusive or just tough.) "Brutal" bosses regularly engage in the following behaviors, some of which will be discussed in more detail later in the chapter.[13]

- *Deceit.* Lying and giving false or misleading information.
- *Constraint.* Restricting followers' activities outside work, such as telling them whom they can befriend, where they can live, with whom they can live, and the civic activities they can participate in.
- *Coercion.* Inappropriate or excessive threats for not complying with the leader's directives.
- *Selfishness.* Blaming subordinates and making them scapegoats.
- *Inequity.* Supplying unequal benefits or punishments based on favoritism or criteria unrelated to the job.
- *Cruelty.* Harming subordinates in such illegitimate ways as name-calling or public humiliation.
- *Disregard.* Ignoring normal standards of politeness; obvious disregard for what is happening in the lives of followers.
- *Deification.* Creating a master–servant relationship in which bosses can do whatever they want because they feel superior.

The cost of the petty tyranny of bad bosses is high. Victims suffer low self-esteem and psychological distress, are less satisfied with their jobs and lives, are less productive, and are more likely to quit. The work unit as a whole is less trusting and cohesive, reducing collective performance.[14] The majority of employees in one study reported spending 10 or more hours every month complaining about abusive and other kinds of bad bosses or listening to the complaints of fellow workers.[15] In addition to complaining, workers respond to tyranny by surrendering their personal beliefs, keeping a low profile, engaging in revenge fantasies, taking indirect revenge (i.e., not supporting the boss at a critical moment), challenging the supervisor directly, or bringing in outsiders like the human resources department or the boss's boss to get help in dealing with the abusive leader.[16]

The greater a leader's power, the greater the potential for abuse. This prompted Britain's Lord Acton to observe that "power corrupts, and absolute power corrupts absolutely." The long shadow cast by absolute power, as in the case of North Korea's Kim Jong Il and the military junta in Burma, can be seen in censorship, repression, torture, imprisonment, murder, and starvation. Psychologists offer several explanations for why concentrated power is so dangerous.[17] First, power makes it easier for impulsive, selfish people to pursue their goals without considering the needs of others. They are likely to justify their actions by claiming that their personal rights and interests take priority over obligations to others. Second, those in power protect their positions by attacking those they perceive as threats. Third, powerful leaders are prone to biased judgments.[18] They generally make little attempt to find out how followers think and feel. As a result, they are more likely to hold and act on faulty stereotypes that justify their authority. Powerful people believe that they deserve their high status because powerless people aren't as capable as they are. Fourth, possessing power makes individuals more resistant to feedback from others.

Power deprivation exerts its own brand of corruptive influence.[19] Followers with little power become fixated on what minimal influence they have, becoming cautious, defensive, and critical of others and new ideas. In extreme cases, they may engage in sabotage, such as when one group of fast-food employees took out their frustrations by spitting and urinating into the drinks they served customers.

SELF-ASSESSMENT

THE BRUTAL BOSS QUESTIONNAIRE

For an assessment of your current experience of abuse by superior(s) and its possible consequences for your health, well-being, and work productivity, complete the questionnaire that follows. Then find your personal rating using the scoring information, which is provided on the reverse side.

Rate your boss on the following behaviors and actions. If you agree that a statement categorizes your boss, write a number from 1 to 4, depending on the extent of your agreement. If you disagree with a statement in reference to your boss, write a number from 5 to 8, depending on the extent of your disagreement.

1	2	3	4	5	6	7	8
Strongly Agree							Strongly Disagree

1. My boss deliberately provides me with false or misleading information. _____

2. My boss treats me unfairly at times for no apparent reason. _____

3. My boss deceives me sometimes. _____

4. My boss deliberately withholds information from me
   that I need to perform my job. _____

5. My boss criticizes low-quality work from me. _____

6. My boss tells me how I should be spending my time when not at work. _____

7. My boss will "get" me if I don't comply with her or his wishes. _____

8. My boss humiliates me in public. _____

9. My boss calls me unflattering names. _____

10. My boss requires that her or his standards be met
    before giving a compliment. _____

11. My boss believes that I am generally inferior and blames me
    whenever something goes wrong. _____

12. My boss acts as if she or he can do as she or he pleases to me,
    because she or he is the boss. _____

13. My boss treats me like a servant. _____

14. My boss expects me to dress appropriately at all times. _____

15. My boss treats me unjustly. _____

16. My boss steals my good ideas or work products and
    takes credit for them. _____

17. My boss will make me "pay" if I don't carry out her or his demands. _____

18. My boss displays anger publicly toward me by shouting, cursing, or slamming objects. _____

19. My boss criticizes me on a personal level rather than criticizing my work. _____

20. My boss demands that I give my best effort all the time. _____

21. My boss is tougher on some subordinates because she or he dislikes them regardless of their work. _____

22. My boss is discourteous toward me. _____

23. My boss is dishonest with me. _____

24. My boss shows no regard for my opinions. _____

25. My boss is deliberately rude to me. _____

26. My boss lies to me. _____

27. My boss misleads me for her or his own benefit. _____

28. My boss insists that I work hard. _____

29. My boss places blame for her or his failures on me. _____

30. My boss openly degrades and personally attacks me. _____

31. My boss mistreats me because of my lifestyle. _____

32. My boss demands that I constantly do high-quality work. _____

33. My boss reprimands me in front of others. _____

34. My boss deliberately makes me feel inferior. _____

35. My boss is not honest with the people who rank beneath her or him. _____

36. My boss threatens me in order to get what she or he wants. _____

Scoring

Total your responses to the following questions:

#5: _____

#10: _____

#14: _____

#20: _____

#28: _____

#32: _____

TOUGH BOSS TOTAL: _____

Now total your response to the remaining 30 questions.

BAD BOSS TOTAL: _____

Continued: Self-Assessment Key

Tough boss total	+	Bad boss total	=	Assessment of boss
Less than 36		Less than 90		Not particularly tough
Between 36 and 48		Less than 90		Tough, but not abusive
Between 36 and 48		Between 90 and 195		Tough, with instances of abuse. Adverse effects on work and well-being may very well occur.
Any		Greater than 195		Abusive. Deteriorating mental and physical health and lowered productivity are associated with this level of mistreatment.

SOURCE: "The Brutal Boss Questionnaire" from *Brutal Bosses and Their Prey* by Harvey A. Hornstein, copyright © 1996 by Harvey A. Hornstein. Used by permission of Riverhead Books, an imprint of Penguin Group (USA) inc.

To wield power wisely, leaders have to wrestle with all the issues outlined here. They have to consider what types of power they should use and when and for what purposes. They also have to determine how much power to keep and how much to give away. Finally, leaders must recognize and resist the dangers posed by possessing too much power while making sure that followers aren't corrupted by having too little. Fortunately, there is evidence, when it comes to power, that a number of leaders are casting light rather than shadow. They recognize that sharing power prevents power abuses and improves organizational performance. Top officials at Johnsonville Sausage, Harley-Davidson, McCormick & Company, and other successful organizations have relinquished much of their legitimate, coercive, award, and expert power bases to lower-level leaders. At a great many other companies, self-directed work teams have taken over functions (hiring, scheduling, quality control) that used to be the province of mid- and lower-level managers.[20]

The Shadow of Privilege

Leaders almost always enjoy greater privileges than followers do. The greater the leader's power, generally the greater the rewards he or she receives. Consider the perks enjoyed by corporate CEOs, for example. Top business leaders in the United States are the highest paid in the world. Over the past 30 years, the average pay for chief executives of large U.S. firms skyrocketed to $10.5 million (including salary, bonuses, stock, and stock option grants). The paycheck of the average American was left in the dust. The typical U.S. worker now makes less, when adjusted for inflation, than he or she did in the 1970s.[21] CEOs also eat in private dining rooms and travel around in chauffeured limousines and corporate jets.

Abuse of privilege is particularly evident in the financial industry.[22] U.S. banking executives continued to receive generous pay packages even during the worst financial crisis since the Great Depression. Nine banks paid out an estimated $32 billion in bonuses at the same time they were being bailed out with $175 billion from the federal government. Five thousand employees received bonuses of $1 million or more. Merrill Lynch paid out $3.6 billion just before declaring $15 billion in losses and merging with Bank of America. Goldman Sachs awarded nearly $1 billion to 200 of its workers. (Turn to Case Study 1.1 for a closer look at how one recipient of federal bailout money became the target of public scorn for its bonus program.) Executives weren't shy about spending on themselves either. Citigroup planned to purchase a $50 million jet until word got out and it cancelled its order. Former Merrill Lynch CEO John Thain spent $1.2 million to redecorate executive offices in Manhattan, including $87,000 for an area rug, $1,400 for a trash receptacle, and $11,000 for a "Roman shade."[23]

CASE STUDY 1.1

PAYING FOR FAILURE AT AIG

American International Group (AIG) was the largest recipient of federal bailout money designed to prop up the U.S. financial system in 2008–2009. The company received $182 billion from the Troubled Asset Relief Program (TARP) after it got in trouble by insuring financial derivatives that were tied to the real estate market. When the subprime mortgage market crashed, the company—which did not set aside enough reserves to cover potential losses—was unable to meet its obligations. Federal regulators then determined that AIG (America's largest health and life insurer, the second largest property and casualty insurer, and a major player in the airplane leasing business) was "too big to fail." They worried that bankruptcy would destabilize the insurance industry, shrink the credit market, undermine the world economy, and dramatically reduce purchases of planes and parts from companies like Boeing and General Electric.

(Continued)

(Continued)

The decision to bail out AIG came under heavy criticism. Some analysts doubted that the firm's failure would have been devastating to the world economy. Others noted that at least $20 billion of taxpayer money distributed to AIG was passed on to European banks. However, these complaints paled in comparison to the furor generated by the firm's decision to pay retention bonuses that, for the most part, went to executives in the Financial Products division who were responsible for most of the losses. These bonuses were designed to keep high-ranking employees on the job as the firm reduced its toxic asset portfolio. Seventy-three employees received at least $1 million; the highest payout was $6.4 million. Thirty-three employees receiving the bonuses had already left the company by the time the money was paid out.

Americans took issue with the AIG bonus program, which appeared to reward the very same overpaid executives who bankrupted the company in the first place. Revelations that company officials continued to hold conferences and retreats at expensive resorts after the bailout further aggravated taxpayers who were now footing the bill. Of those polled, 86% were angered by the bonuses, and 76% supported trying to get the money back. President Barack Obama referred to the bonus program as an "outrage." Then–New York Attorney General Andrew Cuomo declared that the idea of giving performance bonuses to AIG employees was "adding insult to injury" and issued subpoenas for the names of recipients.[1] At a hostile congressional hearing, Boston Representative Stephen Lynch compared AIG leaders to the captain and crew of a ship who took the lifeboats and said "to hell with the passengers."[2] Congress threatened to "claw back" the money by imposing high tax rates on the payouts.

AIG President Edward Liddy defended the bonuses, arguing that they could not be rescinded because they were written into the contracts of employees with the approval of the Treasury Department. Breaking the contracts could spur lawsuits. He noted that the amount of the payouts was small when compared to the company's exposure to $1.6 trillion in potential derivative losses. Further, current employees were best equipped to clean up the mess. "I am trying desperately to prevent an uncontrolled collapse of that business," said Liddy. "This is the only way to improve AIG's ability to pay taxpayers back quickly and completely."[3] Nevertheless, Liddy urged those receiving the largest bonuses to return the money, and most did.

The New York attorney general backed off his subpoena threat after much of the money was returned. Congress shifted its attention to other matters. However, the fallout from the taxpayer bailout and bonus scandal continued. CEO Liddy resigned. In response to the firestorm of negative publicity, the company removed the AIG name and logo from its buildings. Employees were encouraged not to display their company ID cards and not to wear AIG-branded apparel in public. The Obama administration appointed a "pay czar" to impose limits on compensation for the top 100 executives at AIG and other firms receiving TARP funds.

Discussion Probes

1. Do you agree with government leaders that some companies, like AIG, are too big to fail? If so, should there be a limit on how large companies can grow?

2. Did the AIG bonuses reward failure, or were they necessary to retain the experienced executives who were best equipped to clear up the toxic assets of AIG?

3. If you had been the president of AIG, would you have refused to pay these bonuses? Why or why not?

4. If you had received one of the AIG bonuses, would you have returned the money? Why or why not?

5. Should the government regulate compensation at taxpayer-supported firms? At all large U.S. companies?

6. What leadership ethics lessons do you take from this case?

Notes

1. Kennedy, H. (2009, March 17). Enough is enough! *Daily News (New York)*, p. 6.
2. McAuliff, M., & Kennedy, H. (2009, March 19). Give it back! AIG's chief begs execs. *Daily News*, p. 7.
3. Brune, T. (2009, March 19). Not his fault but now his problem. *Newsday*, p. A7.

Sources

AIG bonuses; only part of the mess. (2009, March 19). *The Philadelphia Inquirer*, p. A14.

Barron, J., & Buettner R. (2009, March 20). Scorn trails A. I. G. executives, even in their own driveways. *The New York Times*, p. A1.

H.R. 1577: To require the Secretary of the Treasury to pursue every legal means to stay or recoup certain . . . (2009, July 12). *GovTrack.us*. Retrieved from http://www.govtrack.us/congress/bill.xpd?bill=h111-1577

(Continued)

(Continued)

Labaton, S. (2009, June 11). Treasury to set executives' pay at 7 ailing firms. *The New York Times*, p. A1.

Peddie, S. (2009, March 24). Top AIG execs return bonuses. *Newsday*, p. A03.

Puzzanghera, J., Simon, R., & Kristof, K. M. (2009, June 11). Financial crisis; plans to rein in exec pay announced. *Los Angeles Times*, p. B1.

Saporito, B., Calabresi, M., Duffy, M., Newton-Small, J., Schere, M., Thompson, M., Zagorin, A. (2008, March 30). *How AIG became too big to fail*. Retrieved from http://www.time.com/time/business/article/0,8599,1886275,00.html

Son, H. (2009, June 19). AIG tries to keep a low profile. *The Boston Globe*, Business, p. 7.

Nonprofit leaders can also abuse the perks that come from their positions of influence. British citizens were shocked to learn that members of Parliament (MPs) had billed the government for such expenses as purchasing a chandelier and a floating duck island, maintaining a helipad, cleaning a moat, plumbing a tennis court, repairing a swimming pool boiler, and reimbursement for interest on nonexistent mortgages.[24] A number of MPs decided to resign or not stand for reelection. For the first time in 300 years, the Speaker of the House of Commons (who was supposed to monitor MP expenses) was forced to step aside.

Leader excess is not a new phenomenon. Ancient Chinese philosophers criticized rulers who lived in splendor while their subjects lived in poverty. Old Testament prophets railed against the political and social elites of the nations of Israel and Judah, condemning them for hoarding wealth, feasting while the poor went hungry, and using the courts to drive the lower classes from their land.

The passage of time hasn't lessened the problem but has made it worse. There are an estimated 950 billionaires in the world, with a combined wealth of $3.5 trillion. At the same time, the poorest of the poor are deprived of such basic necessities as food, shelter, clean water, and health care. The AIDS epidemic is fueled in large part by poverty. Little money is available in the developing world for prevention efforts or AIDS medicines. While wealthy nations generally provide AIDS medications for their citizens, approximately 12 million individuals in poor countries are unable to get the drugs they need to save their lives. The problem appears to be getting worse as governments and nongovernmental organizations cut back on funding for AIDS programs as a result of the worldwide recession. The Joint United Nations Programme on HIV/AIDS estimates that, by the year 2025, the disease will take the lives of 31 million people in India, 18 million in China, and as many as 100 million in Africa.[25]

Most of us would agree that leaders deserve more rewards because they assume greater risks and responsibilities, and some leaders get more than they deserve. Beyond this point, however, our opinions are likely to diverge. Americans are divided over such questions as "How many additional privileges should leaders have?" "What should be the relative difference in pay and benefits between workers and top management?" and "How do we close the large gap between the world's haves and have-nots?" We'll never reach complete agreement on these issues, but the fact remains that privilege is a significant ethical burden associated with leadership. Leaders must give questions of privilege the same careful consideration as questions of power. The shadow cast by the abuse of privilege can be as long and dark as that cast by the misuse of power. Conversely, sharing privilege can cast significant light. Every year, for example, thousands of Americans (often members of religious congregations) leave their comfortable homes to spend their vacations serving in developing nations. There they build schools and homes, dig wells, and provide medical care.

The Shadow of Mismanaged Information

Leaders have more access to information than do others in an organization. They are more likely to participate in the decision-making processes, network with managers in other units, have access to personnel files, and formulate long-term plans. Knowledge is a mixed blessing. Leaders must be in the information loop in order to carry out their tasks, but possessing knowledge makes life more complicated. Do they reveal that they are in the know? When should they release information and to whom? How much do they tell? Is it ever right for them to lie?

No wonder leaders are tempted to think ignorance is bliss! If all these challenges weren't enough, leaders face the very real temptation to lie or hide the truth to protect themselves. For instance, tobacco executives swore before Congress that smoking was safe even though they had sponsored research that

SOURCE: Dilbert: @Scott Adams/United Features Syndicate, Inc.

said otherwise. Prominent pastor Ted Haggard tried to salvage his ministry by denying that he had sex with a male prostitute. (Case Study 1.2 on page 32 describes another example of how leaders tried to cover up the truth.)

The issues surrounding access to information are broader than deciding whether to lie or to tell the truth. Although leaders often decide between lying and truth telling, they are just as likely to be faced with the questions related to the release of information. Take the case of a middle manager who has learned about an upcoming merger that will mean layoffs. Her superiors have asked her to keep this information to herself for a couple of weeks until the deal is completed. In the interim, employees may make financial commitments (home and car purchases) that they would postpone if they knew that major changes were in the works. Should she voluntarily share information about the merger despite her orders? What happens when a member of her department asks her to confirm or deny the rumor that the company is about to merge?

Privacy issues raise additional ethical concerns. E-commerce firms routinely track the activity of Internet surfers, collecting and selling information that will allow marketers to better target their advertisements. Supermarkets use courtesy cards to track the purchases of shoppers. Hundreds of thousands of video cameras track our movements at automated teller machines, in parking lots, at stores, and in other public places. Employers are also gathering more and more information about employee behavior both on and off the job.[26] Technology allows supervisors to monitor computer keystrokes and computer screens, phone calls, website use, voicemail, and e-mail. Employers also monitor worker behavior outside the workplace. Employees have been fired for comments and pictures posted on blogs and social networking sites. Personal information placed on Facebook and other social networking sites is used to screen out job applicants.

Companies have a right to gather information in order to improve performance and eliminate waste and theft. Organizations are also liable for the inappropriate behavior of members, such as when they send sexist and racist messages using the company's e-mail system. However, their efforts to monitor employee behavior are often done without the knowledge of workers and are inconsistent with organizational values like trust and community. Invading privacy takes away the right of employees to determine what they reveal about themselves; unwanted intrusion devalues their worth as individuals.[27]

In sum, leaders cast shadows not only when they lie but also when they mismanage information and engage in deceptive practices. Unethical leaders

- deny having knowledge that is in their possession,
- withhold information that followers need,
- use information solely for personal benefit,
- violate the privacy rights of followers,

- release information to the wrong people, and
- put followers in ethical binds by preventing them from releasing information that others have a legitimate right to know.

Patterns of deception, whether they take the form of outright lies or hiding or distorting information, destroy the trust that binds leaders and followers together. Consider the popularity of conspiracy theories, for example. Many citizens are convinced that the U.S. Air Force is hiding the fact that aliens landed in Roswell, New Mexico. They also believe that law enforcement officials are deliberately ignoring evidence that John F. Kennedy and Martin Luther King, Jr., were the victims of elaborate assassination plots. Over one third of Americans polled (and the majority of respondents between the ages of 18 and 29) believe that the Bush administration either planned the attacks on the World Trade Center in 2001 or did nothing after learning of the terrorist plot. These theories may seem illogical, but they flourish in part because government leaders have created a shadow atmosphere through deceit. It wasn't until after the first Gulf War that we learned that our "smart bombs" weren't really so smart and missed their targets. The president and other cabinet officials overstated the danger posed by Saddam Hussein in order to rally support for the second Gulf War.

University of California–Davis history professor Kathryn Olmsted argues that many Americans believe that the government is out to get them in large part because government officials have previously engaged in secret conspiracies.[28] In 1962, for example, the Joint Chiefs of Staff cooked up a plan to get citizens to support a war on Castro's Cuba by sending a drone plane painted to look like a passenger airliner over the island to be shot down. Fortunately, this plot (dubbed "Operation Northwoods") never went into effect. However, many others were implemented. According to Olmsted,

> By the height of the cold war, government agents had consorted with mobsters to kill a foreign leader, dropped hallucinogenic drugs into the drinks of unsuspecting Americans in random bars, and considered launching fake terrorist attacks on Americans in the United States. Public officials had denied potentially life-saving treatment to African American men in medical experiments, sold arms to terrorists in return for American hostages, and faked documents to frame past presidents for crimes they had not committed . . . Later, as industrious congressmen and journalists revealed these actual conspiracies by the government, many Americans came to believe that the most outrageous conspiracy theories about the government could be plausible.[29]

Leaders must also consider ethical issues related to the image they hope to project to followers. In order to earn their positions and to achieve their objectives, leaders carefully manage the impressions they make on others.

Impression management can be compared to a performance on a stage.[30] Leader–actors carefully manage everything from the setting to their words and nonverbal behaviors in order to have the desired effect on their follower audiences. For example, presidential staffers make sure that the chief executive is framed by visual images (Mount Rushmore, the Oval Office) that reinforce his messages and his presidential standing. Like politicians, leaders in charge of such high-risk activities as mountain climbing and whitewater kayaking also work hard to project the desired impressions. In order to appear confident and competent, they stand up straight, look others in the eye, and use an authoritative tone of voice.

Impression management is integral to effective leadership because followers have images of ideal leaders called prototypes.[31] We expect that the mountain climbing guide will be confident (otherwise we would cancel the trip!), that the small-group leader will be active in group discussions, and that the military leader will stay calm under fire. The closer the person is to the ideal, the more likely it is that we will select that person as leader and accept her or his influence. Nonetheless, a number of students find impression management ethically troubling. They value integrity and see role playing as insincere because the leader may have to disguise his or her true feelings in order to be successful.

There is no doubt that impression management can be used to reach immoral ends. Disgraced financier Bernie Madoff, for example, convinced investors that he was a financial genius even as he was stealing their money. (More information on Madoff's gigantic fraud scheme can be found in Chapter 2.) Careerists who are skilled at promoting themselves at the expense of others are all too common.[32] It would be impossible to eliminate this form of influence, however. To begin, others form impressions of us whether we are conscious of that fact or not. They judge our personality and values by what we wear, for instance, even if we don't give much thought to what we put on in the morning. Most of us use impression management to accurately convey our identities, not to conceal them or to manipulate others.

When considering the morality of impression management, we need to consider its end products. Ethical impression managers meet group wants and needs, not just the needs of the leaders. They spur followers toward highly moral ends. These leaders use impression management to accurately convey information, to build positive interpersonal relationships, and to facilitate good decisions. Unethical impression managers produce the opposite effects, subverting group wishes and lowering purpose and aspiration. These leaders use dysfunctional impression management to send deceptive messages, to undermine relationships, and to distort information, which leads to poor conclusions and decisions.[33]

The Shadow of Inconsistency

Leaders deal with a variety of constituencies, each with its own set of abilities, needs, and interests. In addition, they like some followers better than others. The Leader–Member Exchange (LMX) theory is based on the notion that leaders develop closer relationships with one group of followers.[34] Members of the "in-group" become advisors, assistants, and lieutenants. High levels of trust, mutual influence, and support characterize their exchanges with the leader. Members of the "out-group" are expected to carry out the basic requirements of their jobs. Their communication with the leader is not as trusting and supportive. Not surprisingly, members of in-groups are more satisfied and productive than members of out-groups. For that reason, LMX theorists have begun to explore ways in which leaders can develop close relationships with all of their followers.

Situational variables also complicate leader–follower interactions. Guidelines that work in ordinary times may break down under stressful conditions. A professor may state in her syllabus that five absences will result in flunking a class, for instance. However, she may have to loosen her standard if a flu epidemic strikes the campus.

Diverse followers, varying levels of relationships, and elements of the situation make consistency an ethical burden of leadership. Should all followers be treated equally even if some are more skilled and committed or closer to us than others? When should we bend the rules and for whom? Shadows arise when leaders appear to act arbitrarily and unfairly when faced with questions such as these, as in the case of a resident assistant who enforces dormitory rules for some students but ignores infractions committed by friends. Of course, determining whether a leader is casting light or shadow may depend on where you stand as a follower. Star NFL quarterback Brett Favre had his own dressing area after being traded from the Green Bay Packers to the New York Jets. The next year he was allowed to join the Minnesota Vikings well after training camp had begun. Favre was comfortable with these arrangements, but some teammates took issue with this special treatment.

Issues of inconsistency can also arise in a leader's relationships with those outside the immediate group or organization. Misgivings about the current system of financing political elections stem from the fact that large donors can buy access to elected officials and influence their votes. Laws often favor those who have contributed the most, as in the case of climate change legislation. Midwestern congressional representatives who received significant contributions from the Farm Bureau and ethanol producers were able to weaken a climate change bill by exempting farmers, ranchers, and biodiesel refineries from cutting greenhouse gas emissions and by making other changes to the proposed legislation. This group (dubbed the "Agracrats") has been successful in keeping farm subsidies as well.[35] The power of political donations can also be seen in the battle over health care reform. Many of the senators and representatives who opposed health care revisions were major recipients of money from pharmaceutical companies and health care providers.

The Shadow of Misplaced and Broken Loyalties

Leaders must weigh a host of loyalties or duties when making choices. In addition to their duties to employees and stockholders, they must consider their obligations to their families, their local communities, their professions, the larger society, and the environment. Noteworthy leaders put the needs of the larger community above selfish interests. For example, outdoor clothing manufacturer Timberland receives praise for its commitment to community service and social responsibility. Company leaders pay employees for volunteer service, partner with community groups, and support nonprofit organizations through the sale of selected products. In contrast, those who appear to put their interests first are worthy of condemnation. Executives at United Airlines were harshly criticized for profiting at the expense of employees and travelers. The company filed for bankruptcy, which allowed executives to dump pension funds, void labor contracts, and cut costs. A quarter of the workforce was laid off, and those remaining took significant pay cuts. Customer service suffered as a result. When United emerged from bankruptcy, 400 executives (some of whom had helped mismanage the airline into bankruptcy) ended up with 8% of the new firm, estimated to be worth more than $300 million. CEO Glenn Tilton alone received $40 million in stock and stock options.[36]

Loyalties can be broken as well as misplaced. If anything, we heap more scorn on those who betray our trust than on those who misplace their loyalties. Many of history's villains are traitors: Judas Iscariot, Benedict Arnold, Vidkun Quisling (he sold out his fellow Norwegians to the Nazis), and Tokyo Rose, a U.S. citizen who broadcast to American troops on behalf of the Japanese in World War II. More recent examples of leaders who violated the trust of followers include Enron CEO Kenneth Lay, who assured workers that the firm was in good shape even as it was headed toward collapse (see Case Study 1.3 on page 34), and the leaders of Lehman Brothers, who told investors that the firm was strong even as it was struggling to raise money to stave off bankruptcy during the financial crisis.[37]

Employees are often victimized by corporate betrayal motivated by the bottom line. Individuals commonly develop deep loyalties to their coworkers and to their employers. As a consequence, they may do more than what is required in their job descriptions, turn down attractive job offers from other employers, and decide to invest their savings in company stock.[38] Unfortunately, companies and their leaders often fail to respond in kind. During economic downturns they are quick to slash salaries and benefits and to lay off even the most loyal workers. Even if business is good, they don't hesitate to shut down domestic plants and research facilities in order to open up new operations overseas. No wonder that leaders who stick by their workers shine so brightly. Aaron Feuerstein kept paying his Malden Mills employees after the textile manufacturer's plant burned down. Bob Moore turned over ownership of his Red Mill Natural Foods company to his employees on his 81st birthday.[39]

As egregious as corporate examples of betrayal appear, they pale in comparison to cases where adults take advantage of children. Catholic priests in Boston; Portland, Oregon; New Mexico; Brazil; Ireland; Germany; and elsewhere used their positions as respected spiritual authorities to gain access to young parishioners for sexual gratification.[40] Bishops and cardinals failed to stop the abusers. In far too many instances they let offending priests continue to minister and to have contact with children. Often church officials transferred pedophiles without warning their new congregations about these priests' troubled pasts. In another example involving the betrayal of children, described in more detail in Chapter 6, two Pennsylvania juvenile court judges sentenced undeserving young offenders to for-profit detention centers in return for cash payments.

The fact that I've placed the loyalty shadow after such concerns as power and privilege should not diminish its importance. Philosopher George Fletcher argues that we define ourselves through our loyalties to families, sports franchises, companies, and other groups and organizations.[41] Philosopher Josiah Royce contends that loyalty to the right cause produces admirable character traits like justice, wisdom, and compassion.[42] Loyalty is a significant burden placed on leaders. In fact, well-placed loyalty can make a significant moral statement. Such was the case with Pee Wee Reese. The Brooklyn Dodger never wavered in his loyalty to Jackie Robinson, the first Black player in the major leagues. In front of one especially hostile crowd in Cincinnati, Ohio, Reese put his arm around Robinson's shoulders in a display of support.[43]

Pay particular attention to the shadow of loyalty as you analyze the feature films highlighted in each chapter. In most of these movies, leaders struggle with where to place their loyalties and how to honor the trust others have placed in them.

The Shadow of Irresponsibility

Earlier we noted that the breadth of responsibility is one of the factors distinguishing between the leader and follower roles. Followers are largely responsible for their own actions or, in the case of a self-directed work team, for those of their peers. This is not the case for leaders. They are held accountable for the performance of their entire department or unit. However, determining the extent of a leader's responsibility is far from easy. Can we blame a college coach for the misdeeds of team members during the off-season or for the excesses of the university's athletic booster club? Are clothing executives responsible for the actions of their overseas contractors who force workers to work in sweatshops? Do employers owe employees a minimum wage level, a certain degree of job security, and safe working conditions? If military officers are punished for following unethical orders, should their supervisors receive the same or harsher penalties? Rabbis and pastors encourage members of their congregations to build strong marriages. Should they lose their jobs when they have affairs?

Leaders act irresponsibly when they fail to make reasonable efforts to prevent followers' misdeeds, ignore or deny ethical problems, don't shoulder responsibility for the consequences of their directives, deny their duties to followers, or hold followers to higher standards than themselves. We don't hold coaches responsible for everything their players do. Nonetheless, we want them to encourage their athletes to obey the law and to punish any misbehavior. Most of us expect the Gap, Old Navy, and Banana Republic to make every effort to treat their overseas labor force fairly, convinced that the companies owe their workers (even the ones employed by subcontractors) decent wages and working conditions. We generally believe that officers giving orders are as culpable as those carrying them out, and we have little tolerance for religious figures and others who violate their own ethical standards. For that reason, a number of well-known politicians from both parties have been labeled as hypocrites for preaching family values while cheating on their spouses. The list includes (but is not limited to) (1) former vice presidential candidate John Edwards, who had an affair with a campaign videographer while his wife battled cancer; (2) Eliot Spitzer, former New York attorney general and governor who prosecuted prostitution rings while regularly meeting with a hooker; (3) conservative Christian Nevada Senator John Ensign, who had an extramarital affair with a staffer; and (4) South Carolina Governor Mark Sanford, who, as a congressman, urged

Bill Clinton to resign for moral reasons but then remained on the job as governor after spending five days in Argentina with his lover. (He told his staff and the public that he was hiking the Appalachian Trail.)[44]

Many corporate scandals demonstrate what can happen when boards of directors fail to live up to their responsibilities. Far too many boards in the past were rubber stamps. Made up largely of friends of the CEO and those doing business with the firm, they were quick to approve executive pay increases and other management proposals. Some directors appeared interested only in collecting their fees and made little effort to understand the company's operations or finances. Other board members were well intentioned but lacked expertise. Now federal regulations require that the chair of the audit committee be a financial expert. The compensation, audit, and nominating committees must be made up of people who have no financial ties to the organization. These requirements should help prevent future abuses, but only if directors take their responsibilities seriously.

These, then, are some of the common shadows cast by leaders faced with the ethical challenges of leadership. Identifying these shadows raises two important questions: (1) *Why is it, when faced with the same ethical challenges, that some leaders cast light and others cast shadows?* (2) *What steps can we take as leaders to cast more light than shadow?* In the next chapter, we'll explore the forces that contribute to the shadow side of leadership and outline ways to meet those challenges. But first read "Focus on Follower Ethics: The Ethical Challenges of Followership" to learn about the ethical demands facing followers.

FOCUS ON FOLLOWER ETHICS

THE ETHICAL CHALLENGES OF FOLLOWERSHIP

Followers, like leaders, face their own set of ethical challenges. Followers walk on the dark side when they fail to meet the moral responsibilities of their roles. Important ethical challenges confronted by followers include the following.

The Challenge of Obligation. Followers contribute to a shadowy atmosphere when they fail to fulfill their minimal responsibilities by coming to work late, taking extended breaks, not carrying out assignments, undermining the authority of their leaders, stealing supplies, and so on. However, they can also contribute to an unethical climate by taking on too many obligations.

(Continued)

(Continued)

Employees forced to work mandatory overtime and salaried staff at many technology and consulting firms work 70–80 hours a week, leaving little time for family and personal interests. They experience stress and burnout, and their family relationships suffer.

Followers also have ethical duties to outsiders. Carpenters and other tradespeople have an obligation to buyers to build high-quality homes and to meet construction deadlines, for example. Government employees owe it to taxpayers to spend their money wisely by working hard while keeping expenses down. These questions can help sort out the obligations we owe as followers.

- Am I doing all I reasonably can to carry out my tasks and further the mission of my organization? What more could I do?
- Am I fulfilling my obligations to outsiders (clients, neighbors, community, customers)? Are there any additional steps I should take?
- Am I giving back to the group or organization as much as I am taking from it?
- Am I carrying my fair share of the workload?
- Am I serving the needs of my leaders?
- Am I earning the salary and benefits I receive?
- Can I fulfill my organizational obligations and, at the same time, maintain a healthy personal life and productive relationships? If not, what can I do to bring my work and personal life into balance?

The Challenge of Obedience. Groups and organizations couldn't function if members refused to obey orders or adhere to policies, even the ones they don't like. As a result, followers have an ethical duty to obey. However, blindly following authority can drive followers to engage in illegal and immoral activities that they would never participate in on their own. Obeying orders is no excuse for unethical behavior. Therefore, deciding when to disobey is critical. To make this determination, consider the following factors: Does this order appear to call for unethical behavior? Would I engage in this course of action if I weren't ordered to? What are the potential consequences for others, and for myself, if these directions are followed? Does obedience threaten the mission and health of the organization as a whole? What steps should I take if I decide to disobey?

The Challenge of Cynicism. There is a difference between healthy skepticism, which prevents followers from being exploited, and unhealthy cynicism, which undermines individual and group performance. Followers darken the atmosphere when they become organizational cynics. That's because cynicism destroys commitment and undermines trust. Collective performance suffers as a result. Few give their best effort when they are disillusioned with the group. Cynical employees feel less identification with and commitment to their employers while being more resistant to change. The greater the degree of cynicism, the more effort is directed toward attacking the organization at the expense of completing the task at hand.

The Challenge of Dissent. Expressing disagreement is an important ethical duty of followership. Followers should take issue with policies and procedures that are inefficient, harmful, or costly and with leaders who harm others or put the organization at risk. Doing so serves the mission of the organization while protecting the rights of its members and the larger community. Although followers contribute to the shadowy environment when they fail to speak up, they can go too far by generating a constant stream of complaints. Ethical followers know when to speak up (not every issue is worth contesting) and when to wait until a more important issue comes along. They must also determine whether the problem is significant enough to justify going outside the organization (becoming a whistle-blower) if leaders don't respond.

The Challenge of Bad News. Delivering bad news is risky business. Followers who tell their bosses that the project is over budget, that sales are down, or that the software doesn't work as promised may be verbally abused, demoted, or fired. Organizations and leaders pay a high price when followers hide or cover up bad news, deny responsibility, or shift blame. Leaders can't correct problems they don't know exist. Failure to address serious deficiencies such as accounting fraud, cost overruns, and product contamination can destroy an organization. Leaders who don't get feedback about their ineffective habits (micromanaging, poor listening skills, indecisiveness) can't address these behaviors. When leaders deny accountability and shift blame, this undermines trust and diverts people's focus from solving problems to defending themselves.

To avoid contributing to a shadowy environment, followers must deliver bad news and accept responsibility for their actions. They also need to pay close attention to how they deliver bad tidings, selecting the right time, place, and message channel. Significant problems should be brought to the leader's attention immediately, when he or she is most receptive, and delivered face-to-face whenever possible, not through e-mail, faxes, and other less personal channels.

SOURCE: Adapted from Johnson, C. E. (2007). *Ethics in the workplace: Tools and tactics for organizational transformation.* Thousand Oaks, CA: SAGE, Ch. 7.

(Continued)

(Continued)

Additional Sources

Bedian, A. G. (2007). Even if the tower is "ivory," it isn't "white": Understanding the consequences of faculty cynicism. *Academy of Management Learning and Education, 6,* 9–32.

Dean, J. W., Brandes, P., & Dharwadkar, R. (1998). Organizational cynicism. *Academy of Management Review, 23,* 341–352.

Hajdin, M. (2005). Employee loyalty: An examination. *Journal of Business Ethics, 59,* 259–280.

Roloff, M. E., & Paulson, G. D. (2001). Confronting organizational transgressions. In J. M. Darley, D. M. Messick, & T. R. Tyler (Eds.), *Social influences on ethical behavior in organizations* (pp. 53–68). Mahwah, NJ: Erlbaum.

Schrag, B. (2001). The moral significance of employee loyalty. *Business Ethics Quarterly, 11,* 41–66.

Stanley, D. J., Meyer, J. P., & Topolnytsky, L. (2005). Employee cynicism and resistance to organizational change. *Journal of Business and Psychology, 19,* 429–459.

Implications and Applications

- Understanding the dark (bad, toxic) side of leadership is the first step in promoting good or ethical leadership.
- The contrast between ethical and unethical leadership is as dramatic as the contrast between light and darkness.
- "Toxic" or "bad" leaders engage in destructive behaviors. They may be ineffective, unethical, or both. Common types of bad leaders include incompetent, rigid, intemperate, callous, corrupt, insular, and evil.
- Certain ethical challenges or dilemmas are inherent in the leadership role. If you choose to become a leader, recognize that you accept ethical burdens along with new tasks, expectations, and rewards.
- *Power* may not be a dirty word, but it can have a corrosive effect on values and behavior. You must determine how much power to accumulate, what forms of power to use, and how much power to give to followers.
- If you abuse power, you'll generally overlook the needs of followers as you take advantage of the perks that come with your position.
- Leaders have access to more information than followers. In addition to deciding whether or not to tell the truth, you'll have to determine when to reveal what you know and to whom, how to gather and use information, and so on.
- A certain degree of inconsistency is probably inevitable in leadership roles, but you'll cast shadows if you are seen as acting arbitrarily and unfairly.
- As a leader you'll have to balance your needs and the needs of your small group or organization with loyalties or duties to broader communities. Expect condemnation if you put narrow, selfish concerns first.

- Leadership brings a broader range of responsibility, but determining the limits of accountability may be difficult. You'll cast a shadow if you fail to make a reasonable attempt to prevent abuse or to shoulder the blame, deny that you have a duty to followers, or hold others to a higher ethical standard than you are willing to follow.
- Followers face their own set of ethical challenges. When filling a follower role, you will need to determine the extent of your obligations to the group, decide when to obey or disobey, combat cynicism, offer dissent, and deliver bad news to your leaders.

For Further Exploration, Challenge, and Self-Assessment

1. Create an ethics journal. In it, describe the ethical dilemmas you encounter as a leader and as a follower, how you resolve them, how you feel about the outcomes, and what you learn that will transfer to future ethical decisions. You may also want to include your observations about the moral choices made by public figures. Make periodic entries as you continue to read this text.

2. Harvard professor Rosabeth Kanter argues that "powerlessness corrupts and absolute powerlessness corrupts absolutely." Do you agree? What are some of the symptoms of powerlessness?

3. What do your scores on the Brutal Boss Questionnaire reveal about your leader? How can you use this information to become a more effective follower?

4. What factors do you consider when determining the extent of your loyalty to an individual, a group, or an organization?

5. Debate the following propositions in class.
   - The federal government should set limits on executive compensation.
   - Married politicians who have extramarital affairs should be forced to resign.
   - Employers have the right to monitor the behavior of workers when they are not on the job.

6. Evaluate the work of a corporate or nonprofit board of directors. Is the board made up largely of outside members? Are directors qualified? Does the board fulfill its leadership responsibilities? Write up your findings.

7. Which shadow are you most likely to cast as a leader? Why? What can you do to cast light instead? Can you think of any other ethical shadows cast by leaders?

8. Look for examples of unethical leadership behavior in the news and classify them according to the six shadows. What patterns do you note? As an

alternative, look for examples of ethical leadership. How do these leaders cast light instead of shadow?

9. What is the toughest ethical challenge of being a follower? How do you meet that challenge?

CASE STUDY 1.2

HIDING THE TRUTH

Friendly Fire and the Death of Pat Tillman

In war, truth is the first casualty.

—Greek playwright Aeschylus

Former National Football League star Pat Tillman was an authentic American hero. Tillman turned down a 3-year, $3.6-million contract extension with the Arizona Cardinals to join the Army with his brother Kevin after the September 11 terrorist attacks. His determination to defend his country earned him a letter of thanks from then–Secretary of Defense Donald Rumsfeld and praise from talk show hosts and ordinary citizens.

Tillman took part in the invasion of Iraq and then was transferred to Afghanistan. On April 22, 2004, the two Tillman brothers were part of a patrol that came under enemy fire in a canyon in southeastern Afghanistan. The unit split into two sections (Kevin in one group, Pat in the other) during the battle. In the confusion, soldiers from Kevin's section began firing at Pat's group. Pat Tillman was killed while trying to stop the shooting.

Attempts to cover up the fact that Tillman died due to friendly fire began almost immediately. Fellow soldiers were ordered not to tell Kevin what happened and to burn Pat's equipment, including his protective vest. (These items are supposed to be preserved as evidence in friendly fire cases.) After the first reports about the incident went out on military radio, phone and Internet service was cut off to prevent anyone from discussing the incident. The initial casualty report said that Tillman died by enemy fire. A doctor at a field hospital reported that Tillman received cardiopulmonary resuscitation and intensive care before his life ended (even though the bullets had gone through his head). The initial press release implied that enemy forces had killed the Army Ranger, claiming that he died "when his patrol vehicle came under attack."[1]

The most blatant distortions came in Tillman's Silver Star commendation, the third most prestigious military honor. "Above the din of battle, Cpl. Tillman was heard issuing fire commands to take the fight to the enemy," the recommendation claims.[2] It also praises Tillman for getting his group through the ambush, which ignores the fact that Tillman and another soldier were killed while two others were wounded. At Tillman's well-publicized funeral, top military officials kept silent as speakers declared that the former football star had died at the hands of the Taliban.

Eventually the truth about Tillman's death came out. Army coroners refused to certify that the death was from enemy fire and asked Army criminal investigators to examine the case. The Tillman family began pressing for the facts. An Army inspector general's investigation found a "series of mistakes" in how the incident was reported but no organized attempt at a cover-up. Four soldiers were given minor punishments, and one had his military pay reduced. The inspector general criticized three generals for their actions, and one was censured for giving a false report and failing to demonstrate leadership. In congressional hearings on the matter, House committee members released an e-mail suggesting that the top-ranking general in Iraq and Afghanistan, General John Abizaid, as well as Defense Secretary Rumsfeld, knew the true cause of Tillman's death within days. (Abizaid testified that he learned a week later, and Rumsfeld claimed that he didn't get word until three weeks after the generals.)

Tillman perished at a bad time for the military, which is probably what prompted the deceit. The war in Iraq was going badly, and the prison abuse scandal at Abu Ghraib was headline news. Officials apparently hoped to stir up patriotism and support for the war while avoiding bad publicity. They used the story of Private Jessica Lynch in much the same way. The Pentagon claimed that Lynch fought back when captured by Iraqi forces and was rescued in a dramatic hospital raid. In truth, she never fired a shot (she was knocked unconscious by the crash of her vehicle), and hospital staff offered no resistance. "The story of the little girl Rambo from the hills who went down fighting is not true," Lynch says. "The bottom line is, the American people are capable of determining their own ideas for heroes, and they don't need to be told elaborate lies."[3]

Pat Tillman's Silver Star medal will not be taken back, although the wording of the commendation will be rewritten. A Pentagon spokesperson acknowledged mistakes in the case and has apologized on behalf the U.S. Army. However, members of the Tillman family remain bitter about the Pentagon's dishonesty and how the tragedy of Pat's death was turned into an "inspirational message" designed to bolster U.S. foreign policy.[4] They point out that when the truth was revealed, "Pat was no longer of use as a sales asset."[5]

(Continued)

(Continued)

Discussion Probes

1. Were Army leaders justified in trying to conceal the real cause of Tillman's death? Why or why not?

2. Does Pat Tillman remain a hero despite the fact that he died by friendly fire?

3. Was this a case of a series of mistakes by Army officials or an organized cover-up?

4. Would you punish high-ranking officers and officials, including the Secretary of Defense, for what happened in this case?

5. What leadership and followership ethics lessons do you take from this case?

Notes

1. Colle, Z. (2007, April 21). Evidence of cover-up key to Tillman hearings. *The San Francisco Chronicle*, p. A1.

2. Colle, Z., & Collier, R. (2007, April 25). Lawmakers see cover-up, vow to probe Tillman death. *The San Francisco Chronicle*, p. A1.

3. Cornwell, R. (2007, April 26). Secrets and lies: How war heroes returned to haunt Pentagon. *The Independent* (London).

4. Collier, R., & Epstein, E. (2007, March 27). Tillmans assail Pentagon report. *The San Francisco Chronicle*, p. A1.

5. Krakauer, J. (2009). *Where men win glory: The odyssey of Pat Tillman.* New York: Doubleday, p. 319.

CASE STUDY 1.3

CASTING SHADOWS AT ENRON

In the 1990s, Enron was one of the fastest-growing, most admired companies in the United States. From its humble origins as a regional natural gas supplier, the Houston, Texas, firm grew to become the seventh largest company of the *Fortune 500*. In 2000, the company employed 21,000 people, and its stock hit an all-time high of $90 per share.

Enron appeared regularly on lists of the nation's best companies, receiving accolades for its innovative climate. The firm focused on energy transportation, trading, and financing and developed new ways to market nontraditional commodities. Founder and CEO Kenneth Lay was profiled in a number of business magazines, gave generously to local charities, and golfed regularly with Presidents Bill Clinton and George W. Bush.

Rising stock values and revenues were the glue that held the company together. To keep debt (which would lower the price of the stock by lowering earnings) off the books, Chief Financial Officer Andrew Fastow created special-purpose entities. These limited partnerships with outside investors enable firms to share risks while hiding deficits. Although special purpose entities are legal and used in many industries, Enron's partnerships didn't have enough outside investors. In essence, the company was insuring itself. Employees who managed these investments made millions while acting against the best interests of the firm.

In 2001, losses in overseas projects and a major subsidiary caused a financial meltdown. Enron's stock price dropped, and the company was unable to back its guarantees. Financial analysts and journalists who had previously sung the company's praises began to question Enron's financial statements. In the midst of the unfolding disaster, Chairman Lay repeatedly assured employees that the stock was solid. At one point he declared, "Our performance has never been stronger; our business model has never been more robust; our growth has never been more certain." At the same time he was making these optimistic pronouncements, Lay and other officials were calling Bush cabinet members to ask them to intervene on the firm's behalf. Arthur Andersen auditors then forced the company to restate earnings, and the Securities and Exchange Commission began to investigate.

Enron filed for bankruptcy in December 2001, and in January 2002 Lay resigned. Both Fastow and his deputy pled guilty for their roles in creating and managing the illegal partnerships. Enron energy traders also entered guilty pleas for manipulating electricity markets. In 2006, both Lay and Jeffrey Skilling (Lay's short-term replacement) were convicted of conspiracy and fraud for lying about the company's financial health and condoning illegal accounting practices. Lay died of a heart attack before entering jail. Skilling is currently serving a 24-year sentence, but the length of his jail term may be reduced after appeal. A judge ruled that Lay's conviction was void after his death because he had not had a chance to appeal his conviction. As a result, the government cannot seek restitution for victims of his crime from his estate (though individuals can pursue claims through civil court proceedings).

Greed, pride, lack of internal controls, pressure to make quarterly earnings projections, and other factors all played a role in Enron's collapse.

(Continued)

(Continued)

However, most of the blame must go to the firm's executives, who failed to meet each of the challenges of leadership described in this chapter. Leaders at Enron cast shadows in the following ways:

Abuse of Power. Both Lay and Skilling wielded power ruthlessly. Lay routinely demoted vice chairs who disagreed with him, and Skilling frequently intimidated subordinates.

Excess Privilege. Excess typified top management at Enron. Lay told a friend, "I don't want to be rich; I want to be world-class rich." At another point he joked that he had given his wife, Linda, a $2 million decorating budget for a new home in Houston, which she promptly exceeded. Lay and other executives were able to unload their shares even as the 401(k) accounts of employees (made up largely of Enron stock) were wiped out.

Mismanaged Information. Enron officials manipulated information to protect their interests and to deceive the public. Both executives and board members claimed that they weren't aware of the company's off-the-books partnerships and shaky financial standing. However, both Skilling and Lay were warned that the firm's accounting tactics were suspect, and the Senate Permanent Subcommittee on Investigations concluded, "Much that was wrong with Enron was known to the board."

Inconsistent Treatment of Internal and External Constituencies. Five hundred Enron officials received "retention bonuses" totaling $55 million after the firm filed for bankruptcy. At the same time, laid-off workers received only a fraction of the severance pay they had been promised. Outsiders also received inconsistent treatment. The company was generous with its friends. As the top contributor to the Bush campaign, Enron used this leverage to nominate friendly candidates to serve on the Securities and Exchange Commission and the Federal Energy Regulatory Commission. Company representatives also helped set federal energy policy that deregulated additional energy markets for Enron's benefit. In contrast, critics of the company could expect retribution. Investment bankers who expressed the least bit of doubt about Enron lost underwriting business from the firm. Critical stock analysts lost their jobs.

Misplaced and Broken Loyalties. Leaders at Enron put their loyalty to themselves above everyone else with a stake in the company's fate:

stockholders, business partners, ratepayers, local communities, and foreign governments. They also abused the trust of those who worked for them. Employees felt betrayed in addition to losing their jobs and retirement savings.

Irresponsibility. Enron's leaders acted irresponsibly by failing to take needed action, failing to exercise proper oversight, and failing to shoulder responsibility for the ethical miscues of their organization. CEO Lay downplayed warnings of financial improprieties, and some board members didn't understand the company's finances or operations. Too often managers left employees to their own devices, encouraging them to achieve financial goals by any means possible. Neither CEO stepped forward to accept blame for what happened after the firm's collapse. Lay invoked Fifth Amendment privileges against self-incrimination; Skilling claimed ignorance.

Discussion Probes

1. Which attitudes and behaviors of Enron's leaders do you find most offensive? Why?

2. Did one shadow caster play a more important role than the others in causing the collapse of Enron? If so, which one and why?

3. How much responsibility should the board of directors assume for what happened at Enron?

4. Should laws be changed to allow the government to seek restitution from the estate of those, like Lay, who are convicted of a crime but die before they have a chance to appeal their convictions?

5. What similarities do you see between what happened at Enron and what happened at other well-known companies accused of ethical wrongdoing?

6. What can be done to prevent future Enrons?

7. What leadership and followership ethics lessons do you draw from this case?

SOURCES: Adapted from Johnson, C. E. (2002). *Enron's ethical collapse: Lessons from the top.* Paper delivered at the National Communication Association convention, New Orleans, LA; Johnson, C. E. (2003). Enron's ethical collapse: Lessons for leadership educators. *Journal of Leadership Education, 2.*

(Continued)

(Continued)

Additional Sources

Conviction of Enron's Lay is vacated by judge. (2006, October 18). *The Wall Street Journal.*

Hays, K. (2007, May 24). Linda Lay files against forfeiture. *The Houston Chronicle,* Business, p. 3.

Jones, A. (2009, January 7). Executives on trial: Enron's Skilling to be resentenced. *The Wall Street Journal,* p. C7.

Mulligan, T. S. (2006, May 26). The Enron verdicts. *Los Angeles Times,* p. A1.

Weidlich, T., & Calkins, L. B. (2006, October 24). Skilling jailed 24 years. *National Post,* p. FP1.

Notes

1. Palmer, P. (1996). Leading from within. In L. C. Spears (Ed.), *Insights on leadership: Service, stewardship, spirit, and servant-leadership* (pp. 197–208). New York: Wiley, p. 200.

2. Palmer, p. 200.

3. Lipman-Blumen, J. (2005). *The allure of toxic leaders: Why we follow destructive bosses and corrupt politicians and how we can survive them.* Oxford, UK: Oxford University Press.

4. Einearsen, S., Schanke Aasland, M., & Skogstad, A. (2007). Destructive leadership behavior: A definition and conceptual model. *The Leadership Quarterly, 18,* 207–216.

5. Kellerman, B. (2004). *Bad leadership: What it is, how it happens, why it matters.* Boston: Harvard Business School Press; Kellerman, B. (2008). Bad leadership—and ways to avoid it. In J. V. Gallos (Ed.), *Business leadership* (pp. 423–432). San Francisco: Jossey-Bass.

6. Kellerman (2004), p. xvi.

7. French, R. P., & Raven, B. (1959). The bases of social power. In D. Cartwright (Ed.), *Studies in social power* (pp. 150–167). Ann Arbor: University of Michigan, Institute for Social Research.

8. Hackman, M. Z., & Johnson, C. E. (2009). *Leadership: A communication perspective* (5th ed.). Prospect Heights, IL: Waveland, Ch. 5.

9. Kanter, R. M. (1979, July–August). Power failure in management circuits. *Harvard Business Review, 57,* 65–75.

10. Pfeffer, J. (1992, Winter). Understanding power in organizations. *California Management Review, 34,* 29–50.

11. Ritchey, W. (2009, January 14). Bush pushed the limits of presidential power. *Christian Science Monitor,* p. 11.

12. Examples taken from Caudron, S. (1995, September 4). The boss from hell. *Industry Week,* pp. 12–16; Terez, T. (2001, December). You could just spit: Tales of bad bosses. *Workforce,* pp. 24–25.

13. Hornstein, H. A. (1996). *Brutal bosses and their prey.* New York: Riverhead.

14. Ashforth, B. E. (1997). Petty tyranny in organizations: A preliminary examination of antecedents and consequences. *Canadian Journal of Administrative Sciences, 14*(2), 126–140; Burton, J. P., & Hoobler, J. M. (2006). Subordinate self-esteem and abusive supervision. *Journal of Managerial Science, 3,* 340–355; Tepper, B. J. (2000). Consequences of abusive supervision. *Academy of Management Journal, 43*(2), 178–190.

15. Bad bosses drain productivity. (2005, November). *Training & Development,* p. 15.

16. For a complete typology of responses to abusive supervisors, see Bies, R. J., & Tripp, T. M. (1998). Two faces of the powerless: Coping with tyranny in organizations. In R. M. Kramer & M. A. Neale (Eds.), *Power and influence in organizations* (pp. 203–219). Thousand Oaks, CA: Sage.

17. Keltner, D., Langner, C. A., & Allison, M. L. (2006). Power and moral leadership. In D. L. Rhode (Ed.), *Moral leadership: The theory and practice of power, judgment, and policy* (pp. 177–194). San Francisco: Jossey-Bass; Kipnis, D. (1972). Does power corrupt? *Journal of Personality and Social Psychology, 24,* 33–41.

18. Bailon, R. R., Moya, M., & Yzerbyt, V. (2000). Why do superiors attend to negative stereotypic information about their subordinates? Effects of power legitimacy on social perception. *European Journal of Social Psychology, 30,* 651–671; Fiske, S. T. (1993). Controlling other people: The impact of power on stereotyping. *American Psychologist, 48,* 621–628.

19. Smith, P. K., Jostmann, N. B., Galinsky, A. D., & van Dijk, W. W. (2008). Lacking power impairs executive functions. *Psychological Science, 19*(5), 441–447.

20. Hackman & Johnson.

21. Anderson, S., Cavanagh, J., Collins, C., Pizzigati, S., & Lapham, M. (2008). *Executive excess 2008.* Retrieved from http://www.faireconomy.org/files/executive_excess_2008.pdf

22. Dickson, D. M. (2009, July 31). Doing well—regardless; billions in bonuses paid employees despite losses. *The Washington Times,* p. A10; Hamilton, W. (2009, July 31). Payouts lavish despite bailout. *Los Angeles Times,* p. A1; Story, L. (2008, December 18). Wall St. profits were a mirage, but huge bonuses were real. *The New York Times,* p. A1.

23. Gonzalez, J. (2009, January 9). Top execs still live like kings. *Daily News,* p. 6.

24. Totaro, P. (2009, June 20). After the MP blitz, a $4m blackout. *Sydney Morning Herald,* International News, p. 15; Wilson, P. (2009, May 16). Dark day for British parliament. *Weekend Australian,* World, p. 11.

25. Income disparity statistic taken from Sachs, J. (2007, May 27). Sharing the wealth. *Time,* p. 81. Data about the AIDS epidemic taken from Seston, A. (2006, December 6). AIDS day draws attention to epidemic. *The Daily Cardinal;* York, G. (2009, July 20). Recession, broken promises posing health disaster. *The Globe and Mail,* p. A1.

26. Armour, S. (2006. November 8). Employers look closely at what workers do on job. *USA Today,* pp. B1, B2.

27. Hubbartt, W. S. (1998). *The new battle over workplace privacy.* New York: AMACOM.

28. Olmsted, K. S. (2009). *Real enemies: Conspiracy theories and American democracy, World War I to 9/11.* Oxford, UK: Oxford University Press.

29. Olmsted, pp. 8–9.

30. Brissett, D., & Edgley, C. (Eds.). (1990). The dramaturgical perspective. In D. Brissett & C. Edgley (Eds.), *Life as theater: A dramaturgical sourcebook* (2nd ed., pp. 1–46). New York: Aldine de Gruyter.

31. Brown, D. J., Scott, K. A., & Lewis, H. (2004). Information processing and leadership. In J. Antonakis, A. T. Cianciolo, & R. J. Sternberg (Eds.), *The nature of leadership* (pp. 125–147). Thousand Oaks, CA: Sage.

32. Bratton, V. K., & Kacmar, K. M. (2004). Extreme careerism: The dark side of impression management. In W. Griffin & K. O'Reilly (Eds.), *The dark side of organizational behavior* (pp. 291–308). San Francisco: Jossey-Bass.

33. Rosenfeld, P., Giacalone, R. A., & Riordan, C. A. (1995). *Impression management in organizations: Theory, measurement, practice.* London: Routledge.

34. For more information on LMX theory, see Graen, G. B., & Graen, J. A. (Eds.). (2007). *New multinational network sharing.* Charlotte, NC: Information Age Publishing; Graen, G. B., & Uhl-Bien, M. (1998). Relationship-based approach to leadership. Development of leader–member exchange (LMX) theory of leadership over 25 years: Applying a multi-level multi-domain perspective. In F. Dansereau & F. J. Yammarino (Eds.), *Leadership: The multiple-level approaches* (pp. 103–158). Stamford, CT: JAI Press; Schriesheim, C. A., Castor, S. L., & Cogliser, C. C. (1999). Leader-member exchange (LMX) research: A comprehensive review of theory, measurement, and data-analytic practices. *The Leadership Quarterly, 10*(1), 63–114; Vecchio, R. P. (1982). A further test of leadership effects due to between-group variation and in-group variation. *Journal of Applied Psychology, 67,* 200–208.

35. Morgan, D. (2009, August 16). Democratic dissenters. *The Oregonian,* p. D5.

36. Shared sacrifice? Not for these airline executives. (2006, February 2). *USA Today,* p. 14A.

37. Berman, D. K. (2008, October 28). The game: Post-Enron crackdown comes up woefully short. *The Wall Street Journal,* p. C2.

38. Rosanas, J. M., & Velilla, M. (2003). Loyalty and trust as the ethical bases of organizations. *Journal of Business Ethics, 44,* 49–59.

39. Seeger, M. W., & Ulmer, R. R. (2001). Virtuous responses to organizational crisis: Aaron Feuerstein and Milt Cole. *Journal of Business Ethics, 31,* 369–376; Tims, D. (2010, February 17). Bob gives Red Mill to workers. *The Oregonian,* pp. A1, A5.

40. Ghosh, B. (2010, March 29). Sins of the fathers. *Time,* pp. 34–37; Pogatchnik, S. (2010, March 14). Abuse scandals hit Catholic Church across Europe. *The Oregonian,* p. A11.

41. Fletcher, G. (1993). *Loyalty: An essay on the morality of relationships.* New York: Oxford University Press.

42. Royce, J. (1920). *The philosophy of loyalty.* New York: Macmillan.

43. Rampersad, A. (1997). *Jackie Robinson.* New York: Alfred A. Knopf.

44. The cheat sheet. (2009, July 9). *The Boston Globe,* p. G23.

2

Stepping Out of the Shadows

Darkness is most likely to get a "hold" when you are safely settled in the good and righteous position, where nothing can assail you. When you are absolutely right is the most dangerous position of all, because, most probably, the devil has already got you by the throat.

—Psychotherapist Edward Edinger

WHAT'S AHEAD

In this chapter, we look at why leaders cast shadows instead of light and how they can master these forces. Shadow casters include (1) unhealthy motivations, (2) faulty decision making caused by mistaken assumptions and failure of moral imagination, (3) lack of ethical expertise, and (4) contextual (group, organizational, societal) pressures that encourage people to set their personal standards aside. To address these shadow casters, we need to look inward to address our motivations, improve our moral decision making, acquire ethical knowledge and skills, and resist negative situational influences as we create healthy ethical environments. Ethical development, like other forms of leader development, incorporates assessment, challenge, and support. We can track our progress by adopting the skills and strategies used by ethical experts.

Only humans seem to be troubled by the question "Why?" Unlike other creatures, we analyze past events (particularly the painful ones) to determine their causes. The urge to understand and to account for the ethical failures of leaders has taken on added urgency with the recent spate of corporate and political scandals. Observers wonder, why would bright, talented CEOs make fraudulent loans, lie to investors, and engage in insider trading? Why can't multimillionaire executives be satisfied with what they already have? Why do they feel they need more? Why do politicians lose sight of the fact that they are public servants? How can they urge others to behave ethically at the same time they enrich themselves at taxpayer expense and cheat on their spouses? (See Box 2.1 for one set of answers to these questions.)

Coming up with an explanation provides a measure of comfort and control. If we can understand *why* something bad has happened (broken relationships, cruelty, betrayal), we may be able to put it behind us and move on. We are also better equipped to prevent something similar from happening again. Such is the case with shadows. If we can identify the reasons for our ethical failures (what I'll call "shadow casters"), we can then step out of the darkness they create.

The first section of this chapter identifies common shadow casters; the second section outlines strategies for meeting these challenges. Keep in mind that human behavior is seldom the product of just one factor. For example, leaders struggling with insecurities are particularly vulnerable to external pressures. Faulty decision making and inexperience often go hand in hand; we're more prone to make poor moral choices because we haven't had much practice. To cast more light and less shadow, we'll need to address all the factors that undermine ethical performance.

Shadow Casters

Unhealthy Motivations

Internal Enemies or Monsters

Parker Palmer believes that leaders project shadows out of their inner darkness. That's why he urges leaders to pay special attention to their motivations lest "the act of leadership create more harm than good." Palmer identifies five internal enemies or "monsters" living within leaders that produce unethical behavior.[1] I'll include one additional monster to round out the list.

Monster 1: Insecurity. Leaders often are deeply insecure people who mask their inner doubts through extroversion and by tying their identity to their roles as leaders. Who they are is inextricably bound to what they do. Leaders project their insecurities on others when they use followers to serve their selfish needs.

Monster 2: Battleground Mentality. Leaders often use military images when carrying out their tasks, speaking of "wins" and "losses," "allies" and "enemies," and "doing battle" with the competition. For example, former IBM chief Lou Gerstner inspired hatred of Microsoft by projecting a picture of Bill Gates on a large screen and telling his managers, "This man wakes up hating you."[2] (A leader driven by an extremely destructive competitive spirit is described in "Leadership Ethics at the Movies: *There Will Be Blood.*") Acting competitively becomes a self-fulfilling prophecy; competition begets competitive responses in return. This militaristic approach can be counterproductive. More often than not, cooperation is more productive than competition (see Chapter 8). Instead of pitting departments against each other, for instance, a growing number of companies use cross-functional project teams and task forces to boost productivity.

BOX 2.1 THE DARK SIDE OF SUCCESS: THE BATHSHEBA SYNDROME

Management professors Dean Ludwig and Clinton Longenecker believe that top managers often become the victims of their successes, leading even highly moral individuals to abandon their principles. After achieving their goals after years of service and hard work, these competent, popular, and ethical leaders destroy their careers by engaging in behavior they know is wrong. The authors refer to this pattern as the Bathsheba syndrome based on the story of King David reported in both the Bible and the Torah. King David, described as a "man after His [God's] own heart" in I Samuel 13:14, expanded the national borders of ancient Israel by vanquishing the country's enemies. Yet, at the height of his powers, he began an affair with Bathsheba. After she got pregnant, he tried to cover up his actions by calling her husband Uriah back from the battlefield to sleep with her. When Uriah refused to enjoy the comforts of home while his comrades remained in battle, David sent Uriah back to the front

(Continued)

(Continued)

lines to be killed. As Ludwig and Longenecker note, "David's failings as a leader were dramatic even by today's standards and included an affair, the corruption of other leaders, deception, drunkenness, murder, the loss of innocent lives . . ." (p. 265). The fallout from David's immoral behavior was devastating. He lost the child he fathered with Bathsheba, his top military commander Joab betrayed him, and one of his sons temporarily drove him from office.

There are four by-products of success that put otherwise ethical leaders in a downward spiral. First, personal and organizational success encourages leaders to become complacent and to lose their strategic focus. They begin to shift their attention to leisure, entertainment, and other self-centered pursuits and fail to provide adequate supervision. David's problems began, for example, when he stayed home instead of going to war with his men. Second, success leads to privileged access to information and people, which the leader uses to fulfill personal desires (like having sex with Bathsheba) instead of serving the organization. Third, success leads to the control of resources, which are then used selfishly. David used his power to begin the affair, to call Uriah back from the battlefield, and then to order Joab to put Uriah in the thick of the battle and to withdraw, leaving Uriah and his colleagues to be killed. Fourth, control of resources is often tied to an inflated belief in one's ability to control the outcomes of a situation. David was confident that he could cover up his actions, but the prophet Nathan later revealed his sins.

Professors Ludwig and Longenecker offer advice to successful leaders to keep them from becoming victims of the Bathsheba syndrome. Be humble—what happened to David and to other successful leaders can happen to any leader no matter how smart or skilled. Keep in touch with reality by living a balanced life filled with family, relationships, and interests outside of work. Never be satisfied with current direction and performance. Recognize that privilege and status equip leaders for providing a strategic vision and executing strategy; they are not the reward for past performance or for personal gratification. Assemble a team of ethical managers to provide challenge or support as needed. Finally, recognize that ethical leadership is a component of good leadership. Ethical, effective leaders serve as role models, make wise use of resources, build trust, and make good decisions.

SOURCE: Ludwig, D. C., & Longenecker, C. O. (1993). The Bathsheba syndrome: The ethical failure of successful leaders. *Journal of Business Ethics, 12*, 265–273.

Monster 3: Functional Atheism. Functional atheism is a leader's belief that she or he has the ultimate responsibility for everything that happens in a group or an organization. "It is the unconscious, unexamined conviction within us that if anything decent is going to happen here, I am the one who needs to make it happen."[3] This shadow destroys both leaders and followers. Symptoms include high stress, broken relationships and families, workaholism, burnout, and mindless activity.

Monster 4: Fear. Fear of chaos drives many leaders to stifle dissent and innovation. They emphasize rules and procedures instead of creativity and consolidate their power instead of sharing it with followers. (To see how fear motivates followers, see both "Focus on Follower Ethics: Follower Motivations and the Dangers of Toxic Leadership" and Case Study 2.2 page 67.)

Monster 5: Denying Death. Our culture as a whole denies the reality of death, and leaders, in particular, don't want to face the fact that projects and programs should die if they're no longer useful. Leaders also deny death through their fear of negative evaluation and public failure. Those who fail should be given an opportunity to learn from their mistakes, not be punished. Only a few executives display the wisdom of IBM founder Thomas Watson. A young executive entered his office after making a $10 million blunder and began the conversation by saying, "I guess you want my resignation." Watson answered, "You can't be serious. We've just spent $10 million educating you!"[4]

Monster 6: Evil. There are lots of other demons lurking in leaders and followers alike—jealousy, envy, rage—but I want to single out evil for special consideration. Palmer doesn't specifically mention evil as an internal monster, but it is hard to ignore the fact that some people seem driven by a force more powerful than anxiety or fear. Evil may help us answer the question "Why?" when we're confronted with monstrous shadows such as those cast by the Holocaust and the genocides in Serbia and Sudan.

Selfishness

A great deal of destructive leadership behavior is driven by self-centeredness, which manifests itself through pride, greed, narcissism, and Machiavellianism. Self-centered leaders are proud of themselves and their accomplishments. They lack empathy for others and can't see other points of view or learn from followers. They are too important to do "little things" such as making their own coffee or standing in line, so they hire others to handle these tasks for them.[5] Their focus is on defending their turf and maintaining their status instead of on cooperating with other groups to serve the common good. Ego-driven leaders ignore creative ideas and valuable data that come from outside their circle of influence.

 LEADERSHIP ETHICS AT THE MOVIES

THERE WILL BE BLOOD

Key Cast Members: Daniel Day-Lewis, Paul Dano, Kevin J. O'Connor, Dillon Freasier

Synopsis: Daniel Day-Lewis won an Academy Award for his portrayal of Daniel Plainview, an early 20th-century oil baron who will stop at nothing to best his rivals. Driven by greed, insecurity, competition, and disdain for other people, he lies, cheats, bribes, and intimidates his way into control of a major oil field in California. Plainview doesn't hesitate to use his adopted son as a prop to soften his image, though he is torn between his ambition and his desire to be a father figure. The main obstacle to the oilman's plans is a young preacher (Dano) who turns out to be just as ambitious and devious as he. The oilman makes his fortune and vanquishes his enemies but ends up totally isolated and consumed by his demons. Loosely based on the novel *Oil!* by Upton Sinclair.

Rating: R for violence

Themes: inner monsters, selfishness, deceit, abuse of power, betrayal, toxic leadership, toxic followership

Discussion Starters

1. What unhealthy motivations do you see in Plainview? In the young preacher?

2. Do you see any desirable qualities in the oilman? Why was he unable to overcome the shadow side of his nature?

3. How does the film's title reflect the themes and message of the movie?

Greed is another hallmark of self-oriented leaders. They are driven to earn more (no matter how much they are currently paid) and to accumulate additional perks. Greed focuses attention on making the numbers—generating more sales, increasing earnings, boosting the stock price, collecting more donations. In the process of reaching these financial goals, the few often benefit at the expense of the many, casting the shadow of privilege described in Chapter 1.

The recent international financial crisis, based on the collapse of the U.S. housing market, can largely be attributed to greed.[6] Mortgage brokers generated higher commissions and profits by making risky and fraudulent loans. (See Chapter 11 for a closer look at how one major mortgage lender came to financial ruin.) Borrowers often took on too much credit, buying homes they couldn't afford or consumer items. Wall Street banks, eager to make money off of the mortgage market, repackaged mortgages and sold them to investors as "low risk" products in the United States, in Europe, and elsewhere. AIG and other insurers generated revenue by guaranteeing what turned out to be toxic investments. The financial system nearly collapsed when housing prices dropped and consumers defaulted on their loans, putting lenders, investment bankers, investors, and insurers at risk. (Another example of greed can be found in Case Study 2.3 on page 71.)

Narcissism is another manifestation of self-centeredness. The word *narcissism* has its origins in an ancient Greek fable. In this tale, Narcissus falls in love with the image of himself he sees reflected in a pond. Like their ancient namesake, modern-day narcissists are self-absorbed. They like attention, constantly seek positive feedback, and feel entitled to their power and positions. They also have an unrealistic sense of what they can accomplish.[7]

Narcissistic leaders engage in a wide range of unethical behaviors. They claim special privileges, demand admiration and obedience, abuse power for their personal ends, ignore the welfare of others, and have an autocratic leadership style. In extreme cases (Hitler and Stalin, for example), they can be hyperaggressive, exploitive, and sadistic. Narcissists put their groups, organizations, and countries at risk because their dreams and visions are unrealistic and can't be implemented. For example, Napoleon stretched France's resources beyond the breaking point. Jean-Marie Messier, a modern French business leader, followed in Napoleon's footsteps by overextending his financial empire.[8] Messier spent $100 billion trying to build Vivendi (originally a French water and sewage provider) into the number-one (or largest) media and entertainment company in the world by buying phone companies, Internet ventures, cable networks, and Seagram's (which owned Universal Studios and Universal Records). His grandiose ambitions outstripped his ability to bring them to fruition. Losses from his collection of mismatched companies mounted, and he was forced out. The result was the greatest financial loss in French corporate history.

Machiavellianism is the fourth indication that a leader is more self than other focused. Psychologists Richard Christie and Florence Geis first identified this personality factor in 1970. Christie and Geis named this trait after Italian philosopher Niccolo Machiavelli who argued in *The Prince* that political leaders should maintain a virtuous public image but use whatever means necessary (ethical or unethical) to achieve their ends.[9] Highly Machiavellian individuals are skilled at manipulating others for their own ends. They have a better grasp of their abilities and reality than narcissists but, like their narcissistic colleagues, engage in lots of self-promotion, are emotionally cold, and are prone to aggressive behavior. Machiavellian leaders often engage in deception because they want to generate positive impressions while they get their way. They may pretend to be concerned for others, for example, or assist in a project solely because they want to get in good with the boss. Machiavellians often enjoy a good deal of personal success (organizational advancement, higher salaries) because they are so skilled at manipulation and at disguising their true intentions. Nonetheless, Machiavellian leaders put their groups in danger. They may be less qualified to lead than others who are not as skilled as they in impression management. They are more likely to engage in unethical practices that put the organization at risk because they want to succeed at any cost. If followers suspect that their supervisors are manipulating them, they are less trusting and cooperative, which can make the organization less productive.[10]

 FOCUS ON FOLLOWER ETHICS

FOLLOWER MOTIVATIONS AND THE DANGERS OF TOXIC LEADERSHIP

Leadership expert Jean Lipman-Blumen argues that followers have deep-seated psychological needs and fears that make them seek leaders. However, we need to make sure that these motivations, which can drive us toward good leaders, don't drive us into the arms of toxic leaders instead.

A Need for Parent Figures. As children, we depend heavily on caretakers who have far more power than we do. Obedience to these authorities keeps us safe and feeling loved. As adults, we may look for other authority figures to meet our needs and obey their directives. If we haven't resolved our issues with our parents, we are likely to have similar issues with our leaders. Negative role models (authoritative, abusive, demeaning) often encourage followers to seek out similar toxic leaders later in life.

Exchanging Freedom for Security. Reaching adulthood is both liberating and frightening. Freedom allows people to be themselves but can produce a sense of isolation. Insecure followers often give up their freedom in order to join unethical leaders and destructive causes.

The Need to Feel Chosen. Feeling special is a powerful motivator. Bad leaders take advantage of that fact by convincing followers that they are part of a unique organization or cause that is better than all others. Joining with these leaders becomes "a route not simply to safety but to victory and glory" (p. 37). Driven by a feeling of superiority, group members may convert outsiders, dominate them, absorb them into the group, or even kill them.

The Need for Community. The need to belong is intertwined with the need to feel special. Humans are social animals, defined in large part by their communities. Group membership provides security and meaning and equips individuals to deal with their fears. People will sacrifice a great deal to maintain their group memberships. They will endure abusive treatment from their leaders, obey unethical orders, accept low wages, and so on.

Fear of Ostracism, Isolation, and Social Death. Speaking out against an unethical leader, organization, or cause brings ostracism ("social death") that keeps followers from dissenting. Whistle-blowers, those who go public with complaints or concerns, can expect a hostile reaction as peers, friends, and even family members turn against them. They may be demoted, fired, shunned by neighbors, and threatened with violence.

A Sense of Personal Weakness and Powerlessness. Followers who otherwise feel competent find it intimidating to challenge a toxic leader. Instead, they try to adapt, change themselves, or escape from the situation, not realizing that expressing dissent might empower others to do the same. Toxic leaders play on follower fears by isolating dissenters and rewarding their backers. They reinforce their powerful images by mobilizing displays of support while attacking and eliminating those they identify as enemies.

SOURCE: Adapted from Lipman-Blumen, J. (2005). *The allure of toxic leaders: Why we follow destructive bosses and corrupt politicians—and how we can survive them.* Oxford, UK: Oxford University Press, Ch. 2.

CASE STUDY 2.1

THE PIRATE DILEMMA

In recent years Somali pirates have been doing a booming business in the Indian Ocean, along one of the busiest shipping routes in the world. The pirates track the progress of commercial vessels using satellite phones and GPS monitoring devices and then launch their attacks armed with pistols, grenade launchers, and AK-47s. Due to international law, most ships are unarmed, making them easy targets for groups of raiders who board them from small speedboats. The pirates then take crews hostage and demand ransom before returning sailors and cargos.

In 2008 alone, 120 vessels were seized in the region, and shipping companies paid an estimated $150 million for their return. (The ransom for a large ship typically runs between $3 million and $5 million.) That same year 889 hostages were taken in piracy incidents worldwide. Eleven hostages were killed, 232 were injured, and 21 were reported missing and presumed dead. The average hijacking incident lasted two months.

Failure to meet pirate demands puts the lives of captured employees in danger and results in the loss of oil, food, and other cargo. That's why shippers typically negotiate with the pirates. In fact, they sometimes purchase ransom insurance policies and hire security consultants to negotiate on their behalf. However, the U.S. and British governments urge shipping companies not to pay ransom. U.S. Secretary of State Hillary Clinton called the pirates "nothing more than criminals."[1] Britain's Foreign Secretary David Miliband said, "There is a strong view of the British government, and actually the international community, that payments for hostage taking are only an encouragement to further hostage-taking."[2] In one well-publicized incident, U.S. Navy sharpshooters killed three Somalis holding the captain of the *Maersk Alabama,* the first American ship to be captured by pirates in 200 years. But even U.S. Navy officials admitted that killing the three men might escalate violence against other crews in future pirate attacks.

Imagine that you are the CEO of a shipping company and pirates have captured one of your vessels. Would you pay ransom for the return of your crew?

Notes

1. Mazzetti, M. (2009, April 10). Navy's standoff with pirates shows U.S. power has limits. *The New York Times,* p. A1.

2. Hughes, C. (2008, November 21). Pirates: We want pounds 17M within 10 days . . . or else. *The Mirror,* p. 31.

Sources

Krieger, F. (2009, May 28). Owners turn to kidnap and ransom cover. *Lloyd's List*, p. 9.
McCrummen, S., & Tyson, A. S. (2009, April 13). Navy kills 3 pirates, rescues ship captain. *The Washington Post*, p. A01.
Pile, J. (2009, May 29). *Piracy: Murky waters to navigate.* Retrieved from http://free .financialmail.co.za/report09/deneysmay09/bden.htm

Faulty Decision Making

Identifying dysfunctional motivations is a good first step in explaining the shadow side of leadership. Yet well-meaning, well-adjusted leaders can also cast shadows, as in the case of Shell UK. In 1995 company officials decided to dispose of the Brent Spar, a large floating oil storage buoy in the North Sea, by sinking it in deep water.[11] This was the least expensive option for disposing of the structure, and the British government signed off on the project. However, Shell and British government leaders failed to adequately consider the environmental impact of their proposal. Greenpeace activists, who were trying to curb the dumping of waste and other contaminants into the world's oceans, argued that deepwater disposal set a bad precedent. They worried that the sinking of the Brent Spar would be the first of many such sinkings, and Greenpeace members twice occupied the Brent Spar in protest. Consumers in continental Europe began boycotting Shell petrol stations, and representatives of the Belgian and German governments protested to British officials. Shell withdrew its plan to sink the buoy, and it was towed to Norway instead, where it was cut apart and made part of a quay. Shell later noted that this was a defining event in the company's history, one that made it more sensitive to outside groups and possible environmental issues.

Blame for many ethical miscues can be placed on the way in which ethical decisions are made. Moral reasoning, though focused on issues of right and wrong, shares much in common with other forms of decision making. Making a wise ethical choice involves many of the same steps as making other important decisions: identifying the issue, gathering information, deciding on criteria, weighing options, and so on. A breakdown anywhere along the way can derail the process. Problems typically stem from (1) unsound assumptions and (2) failure of moral imagination.

Mistaken Assumptions

Decision-making experts David Messick and Max Bazerman speculate that many unethical business decisions aren't the product of greed or callousness but stem instead from widespread weaknesses in how people process information and make decisions. In particular, executives have faulty theories about how the world operates, about other people, and about themselves.[12]

Theories About How the World Operates. These assumptions have to do with determining the consequences of choices, judging risks, and identifying causes. Executives generally fail to take into account all the implications of their decisions (see Box 2.2). They overlook low-probability events, fail to consider all the affected parties, think they can hide their unethical behavior from the public, and downplay long-range consequences. In determining risk, decision makers generally fail to acknowledge that many events happen by chance or are out of their control. America's involvement in Vietnam, for example, was predicated on the mistaken assumption that the United States could successfully impose its will in the region. Other times, leaders and followers misframe risks, thus minimizing the dangers. For instance, a new drug seems more desirable when it is described as working half of the time rather than as failing half of the time.

The perception of causes is the most important of all our theories about the world because determining responsibility is the first step to assigning blame or praise. In the United States, we're quick to criticize the person when larger systems are at fault. Consider the Sears automotive repair scandal, for example. Investigators discovered that Sears automotive technicians, who were paid commissions based on the number and cost of the repairs they ordered, charged customers for unnecessary work. Although the mechanics ought to be held accountable for their actions, the commission system was also at fault. Executives should be blamed for creating a program that rewarded dishonesty. Messick and Bazerman also point out that we're more likely to blame someone else for acting immorally than for failing to act. We condemn the executive who steals. However, we are less critical of the executive who doesn't disclose the fact that another manager is incompetent.

Theories About Other People. These are "our organized beliefs about how 'we' differ from 'they'" (competitors, suppliers, managers, employees, ethnic groups). Such beliefs, which we may not be aware of, influence how we treat other people. Ethnocentrism and stereotyping are particularly damaging. *Ethnocentrism* is the tendency to think that we are better than they, that our way of doing things is superior to theirs. We then seek out (socialize with, hire) others who look and act like us. Military leaders often fall into the trap of ethnocentrism when they underestimate the ability of the enemy to resist hardships. For example, commanders have no trouble believing that their own citizens will survive repeated bombings but don't think that civilian populations in other nations can do the same. Such was the case in World War II. The British thought that bombing Berlin would break the spirit of the Germans, forgetting that earlier German air raids on London had failed to drive Britain out of the war. Similar reasoning fed into the decision to storm the Branch Davidian compound in Waco, Texas, in 1993. FBI officers underestimated the commitment of cult leader David Koresh and his followers to their cause. They thought that Koresh was afraid of physical harm and would surrender rather than risk injury. Instead, he led his followers in a mass suicide when federal authorities rushed the compound.[13]

BOX 2.2 DECISION-MAKING BIASES

Theories of the World

- Ignoring low-probability events even when they could have serious consequences later
- Limiting the search for stakeholders and thus overlooking the needs of important groups
- Ignoring the possibility that the public will find out about an action
- Discounting the future by putting immediate needs ahead of long-term goals
- Underestimating the impact of a decision on a collective group (e.g., industry, city, profession)
- Acting as if the world is certain instead of unpredictable
- Failure to acknowledge and confront risk
- Framing risk differently than followers
- Blaming people when larger systems are at fault
- Excusing those who fail to act when they should

Theories About Other People

- Believing that our group is normal and ordinary (good) whereas others are strange and inferior (bad)
- Giving special consideration and aid to members of the in-group
- Judging and evaluating according to group membership (stereotyping)

(Continued)

(Continued)

Theories About Ourselves

- Rating ourselves more highly than other people
- Underestimating the likelihood that negative things will happen to us, such as divorce, illness, accidents, and addictions
- Believing that we can control random events
- Overestimating our contributions and the contributions of departments and organizations
- Overconfidence, which prevents us from learning more about a situation
- Concluding that the normal rules and obligations don't apply to us

SOURCE: Messick, D. M., & Bazerman, M. H. (1996, Winter). Ethical leadership and the psychology of decision making. *Sloan Management Review, 37*(2), 9–23. See also Bazerman, M. H. (1986). *Management in managerial decision making.* New York: Wiley. Table reprinted from Hackman, M. Z., & Johnson, C. E. (2008). *Leadership: A communication perspective* (5th ed.). Prospect Heights, IL: Waveland. Reprinted by permission.

Stereotypes, our beliefs about other groups of people, are closely related to ethnocentrism. These theories (women are weaker than men, the mentally challenged can't do productive work) can produce a host of unethical outcomes, including sexual and racial discrimination. (We'll take a closer look at ethnocentrism and stereotyping in Chapter 10.)

Theories About Ourselves. These faulty theories involve self-perceptions. Leaders need to have a degree of confidence to make tough decisions, but their self-images are often seriously distorted. Executives tend to think they (and their organizations) are superior, are immune to disasters, and can control events. No matter how fair they want to be, leaders tend to favor themselves when making decisions. Top-level managers argue that they deserve larger offices, more money, and stock options because their divisions contribute more to the success of the organization. Overconfidence is also a problem for decision makers because it seduces them into thinking that they have all the information they need, so they fail to learn more. Even when they do seek additional data, they're likely to interpret new information according to their existing biases.

Unrealistic self-perceptions of all types put leaders at ethical risk. Executives may claim that they have a "right" to steal company property because they are vital to the success of the corporation. Over time they may come to believe that they aren't subject to the same rules as everyone else.

University of Richmond leadership studies professor Terry Price argues that leader immorality generally stems from such mistaken beliefs.[14] Leaders know right from wrong but often make exceptions for (justify) their own behavior. They are convinced that their leadership positions exempt them from following traffic laws or from showing up to meetings on time, for example. They may justify immoral behavior such as lying or intimidating followers on the grounds that it is the only way to protect the country or to save the company. Unethical leaders may also decide (with the support of followers) that the rules of morality apply only to the immediate group and not to outsiders. Excluding others from moral considerations (from moral membership) justified such unethical practices as slavery and colonization in the past. In recent times, this logic has been used to deny legal protections to suspected terrorists.

The loftier a leader's position, the greater the chances that he or she will overestimate his or her abilities. Powerful leaders are particularly likely to think they are godlike, believing they are omniscient (all knowing), omnipotent (all powerful), and invulnerable (safe from all harm).[15] Top leaders can mistakenly conclude they know everything because they have access to many different sources of information and followers look to them for answers. They believe that they can do whatever they want because they have so much power. Surrounded by an entourage of subservient staff members, these same officials are convinced that they will be protected from the consequences of their actions. Former President Clinton's affair with Monica Lewinsky demonstrates the impact of these delusions. Caught up in the power of his position, Clinton didn't expect to be found out or to face negative repercussions from his actions.

Failure of Moral Imagination

According to many ethicists, moral imagination—sensitivity to moral issues and options—is key to ethical behavior and works hand in hand with moral reasoning in the decision-making process.[16] University of Virginia professor Patricia Werhane offers a three-part definition of moral imagination. *Reproductive imagination* is being aware of elements of the context (participants, setting, etc.), what schemas (scripts, ways of thinking) are operating, and what ethical conflicts are present. *Productive imagination* is reframing the problem from a variety of perspectives and revamping one's current schemas. *Creative imagination* is coming up with new and morally sound solutions that can be justified to outsiders. Those with moral imagination are sensitive to ethical dilemmas but can also detach themselves from the immediate situation in order to see the bigger picture. They recognize their typical ways of thinking and set aside these normal operating rules to come up with creative solutions that are "novel, economically viable, and morally justifiable."[17] (To test your level of moral imagination, complete the "Self-Assessment: Moral Imagination Scale.")

Werhane cites former Merck CEO Roy Vagelos as one example of a leader with a vivid moral imagination. He proceeded with the development of the drug Mectizan, which treats the parasite that causes river blindness in Africa and South America, even though developing the product would be expensive with little hope that patients in poor countries could pay for it.[18] When relief agencies didn't step forward to fund and distribute the drug, Merck developed its own distribution systems in poor nations. Lost income from the drug totaled more than $200 million, but the number of victims (who are filled with globs of worms that cause blindness and death) dropped dramatically. In contrast, NASA engineer Roger Boisjoly recognized the ethical problem of launching the *Challenger* shuttle in cold weather in 1985 but failed to generate a creative strategy for preventing the launch. He stopped objecting and deferred to management (normal operating procedure). Boisjoly made no effort to go outside the chain of command to express his concerns to the agency director or to the press. The *Challenger* exploded upon liftoff, killing all seven aboard. (Turn to Chapter 8 for a description of the more recent *Columbia* shuttle disaster.)

Moral imagination facilitates ethical reasoning because it helps leaders step away from their typical mental scripts or schemas and to recognize the moral elements of events. Unfortunately, our scripts can leave out the ethical dimension of a situation. Shell officials failed to adequately consider the ethical considerations of their decision to sink the Brent Spar, for instance. To them, this was a routine business decision, largely based on cost, that would solve an oil industry problem—how to cheaply dispose of outdated equipment. Or consider the case of Ford Motor's failure to recall and repair the gas tanks on Pintos manufactured between 1970 and 1976. Gas tanks on these subcompacts were located behind the rear axle and ruptured during low-speed rear-end collisions. Sparks ignited the fuel, engulfing the car in flames. Fixing the problem would have only cost $11 per vehicle, but Ford refused to act. The firm believed that all small cars were inherently unsafe and that customers weren't interested in safety. Furthermore, Ford managers conducted a cost–benefit analysis and determined that the costs in human life were less than the costs to repair the problem.

The National Highway Traffic Safety Administration finally forced Ford to recall the Pinto in 1978. By that time the damage had been done. The company lost a major lawsuit brought by a burn victim. In a trial involving the deaths of three Indiana teens in a rear-end crash, Ford became the first major corporation to face criminal, not civil, charges for manufacturing faulty products. The automaker was later acquitted, but its image was severely tarnished.

Business professor Dennis Gioia, who served as Ford's recall coordinator from 1973 to 1975, blames moral blindness for the company's failure to act.[19] Ethical considerations weren't part of the safety committee's script. The group made decisions about recalls based on the number of incidents and cost–benefit analyses. Because there were only a few reports of gas tank explosions and the expense of fixing the tank didn't seem justified, members decided not to act. At no point did Gioia and his colleagues question the morality of putting a dollar value on human life and of allowing customers to die in order to save the company money.

Moral imagination also enhances moral reasoning by encouraging the generation of novel alternatives. Recognizing our typical problem-solving patterns frees us from their power. We are no longer locked into one train of thought but are better able to generate new options. However, Werhane cautions that moral imagination must always be grounded in solid logic and reasoning and have an evaluative component. In fact, she notes creative imagination can become overactive when leaders and followers focus on novelty at the expense of ethical common sense. For example, managers and employees at personal computer disk manufacturer MiniScribe tried to meet impossible sales goals in the 1980s by double shipping to customers, making up accounts, altering auditors' reports, and, at one point, shipping bricks in disk drive cartons. These were highly creative but highly immoral responses to an ethical dilemma. Audi had to recall its 5000 series German automobile when drivers and the media claimed that the vehicle suffered from an acceleration problem. As it turned out, deaths linked to a mechanical defect were really the product of drivers accidentally putting their feet on the accelerator instead of the brake. Hyperactive moral imagination created a false scenario that cost Audi 80% of its market share.

SELF-ASSESSMENT

MORAL IMAGINATION SCALE

The following survey is designed to provide you with feedback on all three components of moral imagination: reproductive, productive, and creative. Respond to each of the following items on a scale of 1 (*strongly disagree*) to 7 (*strongly agree*).

Response choices: 1 = Not at all;   2 = Somewhat;   3 = Very much;   4 = Exactly

1. I like to imagine how the consequences of
    my behavior affect others.   1   2   3   4

2. I anticipate any moral problems that threaten our organization.   1   2   3   4

3. I am not able to imagine similarities and differences
    between the situation at hand and other situations
    where I could apply the same rule.*   1   2   3   4

4. I have the ability to recognize which ideas are morally
    worth pursuing and which are not.   1   2   3   4

5. When I find myself uncertain about how to act in a
    morally ambiguous situation, I change my understanding
    of the moral concepts that might be involved.   1   2   3   4

6. I resist any regulations detrimental to the environment,
    even if I have to risk my current position in the organization.   1   2   3   4

7. I have systematically investigated the factors that
    may affect the moral decisions of my organization.   1   2   3   4

8. I am careful about condemning past decisions made
    under entirely different circumstances.   1   2   3   4

9. I accept new regulations of the organization
    without any justification.*   1   2   3   4

10. In general, when there is a discussion about moral
    issues, everyone tends to listen to me.   1   2   3   4

11. My moral imagination heightens my ability to
    perceive morally relevant situations.   1   2   3   4

12. I have the ability to revise my existing moral beliefs
    so as to adapt to changing conditions.   1   2   3   4

13. My imagination enables me to look at myself from the point of view of another person.   1 2 3 4

14. It would be a waste of time for me to ask the opinion of those who disagree with me when I make a decision.*   1 2 3 4

15. It is difficult for me to bridge the gap between sensory data and intelligent thought.*   1 2 3 4

16. I can put myself in the place of others.   1 2 3 4

17. I do not have enough ability to compare and contrast my own culture with that of others.   1 2 3 4

18. I can create alternative solutions to new moral situations.   1 2 3 4

19. I discipline all my capacities and inclinations in order to achieve self-control.   1 2 3 4

20. Personal commitment, not personal reward, makes me willing to envision novel and possible alternatives toward moral issues.   1 2 3 4

21. Once I have generated reasons supporting my belief, I find it difficult to generate contradictory reasons.*   1 2 3 4

22. I have trouble understanding others' culture and values.*   1 2 3 4

Scoring

Reverse scoring on items marked with an *.

Reproductive imagination. Add up scores for items 1, 2, 4, 5, 7, 10, 12, 13, 18, 19 (Range 10–70)

Productive imagination. Add up scores for items 6, 11, 14, 16, 17, 22 (Range 6–36)

Creative imagination. Add up scores for items 3, 8, 9, 15, 20, 21 (Range 6–36)

SOURCE: Moral Imagination Scale. Yurtsever, G. (2006). Measuring moral imagination. *Social Behavior and Personality, 34*, pp. 212–213. Used by permission.

Lack of Expertise

Leaders may unintentionally cast shadows because they lack the necessary knowledge, skills, and experience. Many of us have never followed a formal, step-by-step approach to solving an ethical problem in a group. Or we may not know what ethical perspectives or frameworks can be applied to ethical dilemmas. When you read and respond to Case Study 2.1 on page 50, for example, you will likely have strong opinions about whether or not you would pay ransom (my students overwhelmingly say they would). You may be less clear about the standards you use to reach your conclusions, however. You might use a common ethical principle ("Human life is more important than money"; "Paying ransom will cause more damage in the long run") but not realize that you have done so.

Emotions can play an important role in ethical decision making and action, as we'll see in Chapter 7. And it's possible to blunder into good ethical choices. Nevertheless, it is far more likely that we'll make wise decisions when we are guided by some widely used ethical principles and standards. These ethical theories help us define the problem, highlight important elements of the situation, force us to think systematically, encourage us to view the problem from a variety of perspectives, and strengthen our resolve to act responsibly.

Contextual Pressures

Not all shadow casters come from individual forces like unhealthy motivations, faulty decision making, and lack of expertise. Ethical failures are the product of group, organizational, and cultural factors as well. Conformity is a problem for many small groups. Members put a higher priority on cohesion than on coming up with a well-reasoned choice. They pressure dissenters, shield themselves from negative feedback, keep silent when they disagree, and so on.[20] Members of these shadowy groups engage in unhealthy communication patterns that generate negative emotions while undermining the reasoning process.

Organizations can also be shadow lands. For instance, car dealerships are known for their deceptive practices, and computer retailers have largely earned the same reputation. Although working in such environments makes moral behavior much more difficult, no organization is immune to ethical failure. Top managers at some organizations may fire employees who talk about ethical issues so that they can claim ignorance if followers do act unethically. This "don't ask, don't tell" atmosphere forces workers to make ethical choices on their own without the benefit of interaction. They seldom challenge the questionable decisions of others and assume that everyone supports the immoral acts. Division of labor allows low-level employees to assert that they just follow orders and upper-level employees to claim that they only set broad policies and therefore can't be held accountable for the illegal acts of their subordinates.[21] When tasks are broken down in small segments, workers may not even know that they are engaged in an improper activity. For example, the secretary who shreds documents may not realize that the papers are wanted in a civil or criminal investigation. The pressures of organizational moral decision making can create a kind of *ethical segregation*. Leaders and followers may have strong personal moral codes that regulate their personal lives but act much less ethically while at work.

Socialization is another process that encourages employees to set their personal codes aside. Organizations use orientation sessions, training seminars, mentors, and other means to help new hires identify with the group and absorb the group's culture. Loyalty to and knowledge of the organization are essential. Nonetheless, the socialization process may blind members to the consequences of their actions. This may have happened at Microsoft. A federal judge ruled that the company used unfair tactics in order to monopolize software and web browser markets. Many Microsoft executives and employees refused to acknowledge any wrongdoing. Instead they claimed that the court's ruling was just the latest in a series of unfair attacks against the company.

There are organizations that deliberately use the socialization process to corrupt new members through co-option, incrementalism, and compromise.[22] In *co-option*, organizational leaders use rewards to reduce new employees' discomfort with immoral behaviors. Targets may not realize that these incentives are warping their judgment, making it easier to justify destructive behavior. For example, salespeople rewarded for selling expensive products (copiers, televisions, computers) with more features than consumers need may convince themselves that these items are good values. *Incrementalism* gradually leads new members up the "ladder of corruption." Newcomers are first persuaded to engage in a practice that is only mildly unethical, such as accepting free meals from company vendors. After the first practice becomes normal, employees are then encouraged to move on to increasingly more corrupt activities such as steering contracts to vendors in return for cash payments. Eventually they find themselves participating in acts that they would have rejected when they first joined the organization. *Compromise* backs members into corruption as they deal with dilemmas and conflicts. For instance, politicians enter into many compromises in order to secure votes for their pet projects. Cutting deals and forming political networks make it harder for them to take ethical stands. In the end they find themselves supporting causes and people they would normally avoid, which has led to the adage "Politics makes strange bedfellows."

Cultural differences, like group and organizational forces, can also encourage leaders to abandon their personal codes of conduct. (We'll examine this topic in more depth in Chapter 10.) A corporate manager from the United States may be personally opposed to bribery. Her company's ethics code forbids such payments, and so does federal law. However, she may bribe customs officials and government officials in her adopted country if such payments are an integral part of the national culture and appear to be the only way to achieve her company's goals.

So far our focus has been on how external pressures can undermine the ethical behavior of leaders and followers. However, this picture is incomplete, as we will explore in more depth in the last section of the text. Leaders aren't just the victims of contextual pressures but are the architects of the unethical climates, structures, policies, and procedures that cause groups and organizations to fail in the first place. Corporate scandals, as we'll see in Chapter 9, are typically the direct result of leaders who not only engage in immoral behavior but also encourage their followers to follow their example. They are poor role models, pursue profits at all costs, punish dissenters, reward unethical practices, and so on.

Stepping Out of the Shadows

Now that we've identified the factors that cause us to cast shadows as leaders, we can begin to master them. To do so we will need to look inward to address our motivations; improve our ethical decision making; acquire ethical knowledge, strategies, and skills; and resist negative contextual influences at the same time we create healthy ethical climates. I hope you will view your ethical development as part of your overall development as a leader. According to researchers at the Center for Creative Leadership (CCL), we can expand our leadership competence, and the skills and knowledge we acquire (including those related to ethics) will make us more effective in a wide variety of leadership situations, ranging from business and professional organizations to neighborhood groups, clubs, and churches.[23] CCL staff members report that leader development is based on assessment, challenge, and support. Successful developmental programs provide plenty of feedback that lets participants know how they are doing and how others are responding to their leadership strategies. Assessment data provoke self-evaluation ("What am I doing well?" "How do I need to improve?") and provide information that helps answer these questions. Simply put, a leader learns to identify gaps between current performance and where he or she needs to be and then closes those gaps. The most powerful leadership experiences also stretch or challenge people. As long as people don't feel the need to change, they won't. Difficult and novel experiences, conflict situations, and high goals force leaders outside their comfort zones and give them the opportunity to practice new skills. To make the most of feedback and challenges, leaders need support. Supportive comments ("I appreciate the effort you're making to become a better listener"; "I'm confident that you can handle this new assignment") sustain the leader during the struggle to improve. The most common source of support is other people (family, coworkers, bosses), but developing leaders can also draw on organizational cultures and systems. Supportive organizations believe in continuous learning and staff development, provide funds for training, reward progress, and so on.

All three elements—assessment, challenge, and support—should be part of your plan to increase your ethical competence. You need feedback about how well you handle ethical dilemmas, how others perceive your character, and how your decisions affect followers. You need the challenges and practice that come from moving into new leadership positions. Seek out opportunities to influence others by engaging in service projects, chairing committees, teaching children, or taking on a supervisory role. You also need the support of others to maximize your development. Talk with colleagues about ethical choices at work, draw on the insights of important thinkers, and find groups that will support your efforts to change.

University of Notre Dame psychologist Darcia Narvaez offers the novice–expert continuum as one way to track our ethical progress.[24] She argues that the more we behave like moral experts, the greater our level of ethical development. Ethical authorities, like experts in other fields, think differently than novices. First, they have a broader variety of schemas to draw from, and they know more about the ethical domain. Their networks of moral knowledge are more developed and connected than those of beginners. Second, they see the world differently than novices. While beginners are often overwhelmed by new data, those with expertise can quickly identify and act on the relevant information, such as what ethical principles might apply in this situation. Third, experts have different skill sets. They are better able to define the moral problem and then match the new dilemma with previous ethical problems they have encountered. "Unlike novices," Narvaez says, "they know *what* information to access, *which* procedures to apply, *how* to apply them, and *when* it is appropriate."[25] As a result, they make faster, better moral decisions.

Narvaez argues that to become an ethical expert, you should learn in a well-structured environment (like a college or university) where correct behaviors are rewarded, and where you can interact with mentors and receive feedback and coaching. You will need to master both moral theory and skills (see Box 2.3). You should learn how previous experts have dealt with moral problems and how some choices are better than others. As you gain experience, you'll not only get better at solving ethical problems but be able to better explain your choices. Finally, you will have to put in the necessary time and focused effort. Ethical mastery takes hours of practice wrestling with moral dilemmas.

It's important to note that making and implementing ethical decisions takes communication as well as critical thinking skills, as Box 2.3 illustrates. We must be able to articulate our reasoning, convince other leaders of the wisdom of our position, and work with others to put the choice into place. For instance, a manager who wants to eliminate discriminatory hiring practices will have to listen effectively, gather information, formulate and make arguments, appeal to moral principles, and build relationships. Failure to develop these skills will doom the reform effort.

BOX 2.3 ETHICAL SKILLS: A SAMPLER

Darcia Narvaez developed the following sampling of ethical skills that should be incorporated into ethical education programs. They are also abilities we will need to develop as leaders and are addressed in this text. Narvaez developed the list after surveying moral exemplars like Martin Luther King, Jr., and virtue theory, as well as scholarship in morality, moral development, positive psychology, and citizenship. Taken together, these skills help us function well in a pluralistic democracy while promoting the health of society as a whole.

Ethical sensitivity (recognition of ethical problems)

Understanding emotional expression

Taking the perspective of others

Connecting to others

Responding to diversity

Controlling social bias

Interpreting situations

Communicating effectively

Ethical judgment (decision making)

Understanding ethical problems

Using codes and identifying judgment criteria

Reasoning generally

Reasoning ethically

Understanding consequences

Reflecting on process and outcome

Coping and resiliency

Ethical focus (motivation to act ethically)

Respecting others

Cultivating conscience

Acting responsibility

Helping others

Finding meaning in life

Valuing traditions and institutions

Developing ethical identity and integrity

Ethical action (following through on moral decisions)

Resolving conflicts and problems

Asserting respectfully

Taking initiative as a leader

Implementing decisions

Cultivating courage

Persevering

Working hard

SOURCE: Narvaez, D. Integrative ethical education. In M. Killen & J. G. Smetana (Eds.), *Handbook of moral development* (p. 717). Used by permission of the publisher.

Implications and Applications

- Unethical or immoral behavior is the product of a number of factors, both internal and external. All of these elements must be addressed if you want to cast light rather than shadow.
- Unhealthy motivations that produce immoral behavior include internal enemies (insecurity, battleground mentality, functional atheism, fear, denial of death, evil) and selfishness (pride, ego, narcissism, Machiavellianism).
- "Good" leaders can and do make bad ethical decisions because of defective reasoning.
- Beware of faulty assumptions about how the world operates, other people, and yourself. These can lead you to underestimate risks and overestimate your abilities and value to your organization. Avoid the temptation to excuse or justify immoral behavior based on your leadership position.
- Exercise your moral imagination: Be sensitive to ethical issues, step outside your normal way of thinking, and come up with creative solutions.
- Leaders may unintentionally cast shadows because they lack the necessary knowledge, skills, and experience.
- Contextual or situational pressures encourage leaders and followers to set aside their personal standards to engage in unethical behavior. Conformity will encourage you to put cohesion above ethical choices. Your organization may undermine your personal moral code by discouraging discussion of ethical issues, diffusing responsibility through division of labor, and promoting socialization processes that corrupt new members.
  Leaders not only have to resist contextual pressures; they have to create healthy environments that encourage ethical behavior in others.
- Make your ethical development part of your larger leader development plan. The three key elements of any development strategy are (1) assessment or feedback that reveals any gaps between current and ideal performance, (2) challenging (difficult, new, demanding) experiences, and (3) support in the form of resources and other people. To become more of an ethical expert, learn in a well-structured environment, master moral theory and skills, and devote the necessary time and effort to the task of ethical improvement.

For Further Exploration, Challenge, and Self-Assessment

1. In a group, identify unhealthy motivations to add to the list provided in the chapter.

2. Evaluate a well-publicized ethical decision you consider to be faulty. Determine if mistaken assumptions and/or lack of moral imagination were operating in this situation. Write up your analysis.

3. Find a partner and compare your scores on the "Self-Assessment: Moral Imagination Scale." Which component of moral imagination is most developed, and least developed, in each of you? What steps can you take to improve your ability to exercise your moral imagination?

4. Rate your ethical development based on your past experience and education. Where would you place yourself on the continuum between novice and expert? What in your background contributes to your rating?

5. Analyze a time when you cast a shadow as a leader. Which of the shadow casters led to your unethical behavior? Write up your analysis.

6. Why do followers support toxic leaders? How do your reasons compare to those offered in "Focus on Follower Ethics: Follower Motivations and the Dangers of Toxic Leadership"?

7. Does your employer pressure you to abandon your personal moral code of ethics? If so, how? What can you do to resist this pressure?

8. Create a plan for becoming more of an ethical expert. Be sure that it incorporates assessment, challenge, and support. Revisit your plan at the end of the course to determine how effective it has been.

CASE STUDY 2.2

DEATH BY PEANUTS

Nothing scares consumers more than the thought that the food they eat may not be safe. And rightfully so. Every year, 325,000 people are hospitalized in the United States from eating contaminated food; 5,000 die. Some survivors suffer organ damage. In recent years, recalls have been issued for tainted almonds, jalapeño peppers, tomatoes, spinach, pistachios, and other food products.

One of the most serious breaches of U.S. food safety to date involved the Peanut Corporation of America (PCA) with plants in Georgia and Texas. The firm's peanut paste and peanut butter were used in an estimated 4,000 products ranging from Thai food, granola bars, and peanut butter crackers to frozen cookie dough and ice cream. General Mills, Kellogg's, PetSmart, Kroger, Nutrisystem, and Clif Bar & Co. used PCA as a supplier. PCA shipped directly to schools and nursing homes as well. In fact, authorities issued a recall of all products using PCA ingredients when an elderly woman in a rehabilitation facility in Minnesota died after eating tainted peanut butter.

(Continued)

(Continued)

The form of salmonella found in the Peanut Corporation of America products comes from the feces of rats and birds and causes diarrhea, fever, and abdominal cramps lasting four to seven days. After eating the contaminated products, 644 consumers in 44 states and one Canadian province reportedly fell ill, and 8 died. As many as 20,000 may have been sickened but did not get tested or see a physician.

Food and Drug Administration (FDA) inspectors discovered a host of unsanitary conditions at Peanut Corporation of America's Blakely, Georgia, facility, including leaky roofs, moldy walls and ceilings, and holes that allowed birds, rodents, and other animals into the plant. Raw and roasted products were stored together, which increased the likelihood of cross-contamination, and workers washed their hands in the same sink that was used for cleaning utensils and mops.

Further investigation revealed that plant owner Stewart Parnell and plant manager Sammy Lightsey knowingly shipped contaminated products. On 12 separate occasions they received positive test results for salmonella. If they received word that a sample had tested positive for the bacteria, Parnell and Lightsey would forward it to another laboratory in hopes of getting a negative result. (Regulators recommend that products be destroyed after one positive test.) Five times the plant managers shipped the product even before additional test results came back, according to the FDA.

Parnell's primary concern was keeping costs down by getting product out the door as quickly as possible. In one instance, after being alerted that a sample had tested positive, he sent an e-mail replying that "the time lapse, besides the cost is costing us huge $$$$$ and causing obviously a huge lapse in time ..."[1] In another instance plant worker Mary Wilkerson wrote, "This lot is presumptive on SALMONELLA!!!!" Parnell replied, "Thanks Mary, I go thru this about once a week...I will hold my breath...again."[2] Later Parnell would tell employees that the firm had "never found any salmonella at all."[3]

Parnell and Lightsey face criminal charges for deliberately putting contaminated products into the nation's food system, and the Peanut Corporation of America has since gone out of business as a result of the recall. State and private inspectors, along with the FDA, have come under fire for failing to identify the problems at the plant. Congress is considering stricter safety and enforcement standards to prevent outbreaks. (The current system is inadequately funded and depends heavily on manufacturers policing themselves.) Much less attention has been focused on the culpability of employees. Workers at the PCA plant in Georgia were well aware of the deplorable conditions. Employees told reporters that they had to step over puddles of water after rainstorms and saw roaches and rats every day. They only deep cleaned the plant before scheduled inspections and had little time to clean after completing their regular tasks. Buckets of outdated product received updated labels and then were shipped. According to David James, who worked in the shipping department, "It was filthy and nasty all around the place."[4] One cook at the plant refused to eat the peanut butter he made or serve it to his kids.

Employees apparently talked about the plant's failings among themselves but were afraid to complain to management or to inspectors for fear of losing their jobs. Employment is hard to come by in rural Georgia, and even minimum wage positions like those at the plant are coveted in an area with an average household income of $26,000. PCA also relied heavily on part-time workers and often left important positions, like quality manager, unfilled for long periods of time. Since the plant passed inspections, some employees convinced themselves that their concerns were overblown.

While workers may have had good reasons for keeping their concerns to themselves, lives might have been saved if they had spoken up. Former employee James acknowledges that keeping silent had tragic consequences. "I'm not surprised this [the outbreak] happened," he said. "I just hate that people died."[5]

Discussion Probes

1. What factors described in the chapter contributed to top management's decision to ship contaminated products?

2. What factors encouraged plant workers to keep silent about conditions at the plant?

3. Were employees justified in keeping their concerns to themselves?

4. Should former PCA employees face criminal charges for failing to report the conditions at the plant to outside authorities? Why or why not?

5. How can leaders encourage followers to report unethical and illegal behavior?

6. What advice would you offer to employees who must decide whether or not to report unethical behavior or situations?

7. What leadership/followership ethics lessons do you take from this case?

(Continued)

(Continued)

Notes

1. Owner won't talk. (2009, February 12). *Newsday*, p. A08.
2. Owner won't talk.
3. Harris, G. (2009, February 12). Peanut foods shipped before testing came in. *The New York Times*, p. A24.
4. Glanton, D. (2009, February 9). Ex-peanut plant workers tell of rats, filth, mold. *The Oregonian*, p. A1.
5. Glanton, p. A4.

Sources

Charges possible in outbreak. (2009, February 15). *Newsday*, p. A50.

Glanton, D. (2009, February 8). Peanut recall puts town "in hot water." *Los Angeles Times*, p. A28.

Harris, G. (2009, January 31). Peanut plant recall leads to criminal investigation. *The New York Times*, p. A17.

Layton, L. (2009, January 29). Every peanut product from Ga. plant recalled. *The Washington Post*, p. A01.

Layton, L. (2009, April 3). FDA hasn't intensified inspections at peanut facilities, despite illness. *The Washington Post*, p. A04.

Layton, L. (2009, May 28). House calls for closer watch on food supply. *The Washington Post*, p. A17.

Making the food supply safer. (2009, August 10). *The Oregonian*, p. A10.

Maugh, T. H., & Engel, M. (2009, February 7). FDA says firm lied about peanut butter. *Los Angeles Times*, p. A1.

Moss, M. (2009, February 9). Peanut case shows holes in food safety net. *The New York Times*, p. A1.

Moss, M., & Martin, A. (2009, March 6). Food safety problems elude private inspectors. *The New York Times*, p. A1.

Ricks, D. (2009, January 22). Salmonella scare spreads. *Newsday*, p. A10.

Salmonella shipped. (2009, February 7). *Newsday*, p. A09.

Schmit, J. (2009, April 27). Broken system hid peanut plants' risks. *USA Today*, p. 1B.

Schmit, J., & Weise, E. (2009, January 29). Peanut butter recall grows. *USA Today*, p. 1B.

Weise, E. (2009, April 2). Nuts. *USA Today*, p. 1B.

Weise, E., & Schmit, J. (2009, February 10). Health risks may reach far beyond reported victims. *USA Today*, p. 1A.

Zhang, U. (2009, February 14). Peanut corporation files for bankruptcy. *Wall Street Journal Abstracts*, p. A3.

CASE STUDY 2.3

BERNIE MADOFF AND THE
BIGGEST SWINDLE IN HISTORY

For decades Bernard (Bernie) Madoff was one of the most respected figures on Wall Street. He chaired the NASDAQ electronic trading system and the National Association of Securities Dealers, the regulatory body assigned to prevent investment fraud. He conducted business from a multistory office building in Manhattan and owned a penthouse in New York, a mansion in Florida, and a villa in France. Madoff ran an investment fund that consistently reported steady, high returns (10%–12%) even during recessions. Potential clients eagerly sought the privilege of investing with him. All that changed, however, in December 2008, when Madoff confessed to running a pyramid or Ponzi scheme. Instead of making legitimate investments, Bernie used contributions from new victims to pay back old victims, underwrite losses in his legitimate brokerage business, and finance his lavish lifestyle. The financier cheated victims out of $65 billion, which likely makes this the largest swindle in history. While billions were funneled into his fund through U.S. and European banks and hedge funds, a number of Madoff's friends and associates were also caught in the scam, along with many charities that trusted him with their money. Even Carl Shapiro, a close friend of Madoff who loaned him $250,000 to start his business, lost $1.7 million in the scheme.

The disgraced con artist pled guilty to a number of criminal charges. In his statement to the court, he said he was "deeply sorry and ashamed" for his acts.[1] Judge Denny Chin then sentenced Madoff to 150 years in prison, well in excess of what the parole board had recommended. He called Madoff's scam "extraordinarily evil" after hearing victims describe how Bernie had destroyed their lives by stealing their life savings. He noted that the sentence was largely symbolic because Madoff (age 71 at the time of his sentencing) would die after only finishing a portion of his sentence. However, Chin argued that such symbolism was important because it would not only serve as a form of retribution and deterrence, but the sentence itself would provide some measure of justice for victims.

(Continued)

(Continued)

It will take years for law enforcement officials, regulators, lawyers, victims, and others to sort through the wreckage Madoff left behind. To begin, there are questions about how the fraud went on so long without being detected, despite at least one whistle-blower's repeated attempts to convince the Securities and Exchange Commission that Madoff was engaged in fraud. (The head of the SEC division assigned to monitor money managers resigned after the scandal broke.) Like Madoff, many victims were also driven by greed. They seemed all too willing to believe that the fund could consistently outperform the market no matter the economic climate. Prosecutors are also trying to determine if others participated in the deceit. Bank and hedge fund officials who steered billions to Madoff through feeder funds may have suspected or known of the fraud but kept sending money in return for high fees. There are suspicions that at least some of the 200 employees of the fund knew what was going on. Further, the Madoffs appear to be a close-knit family. Some observers find it hard to believe that Bernie's wife Ruth, his brother, and his sons (who worked in the firm's legitimate brokerage division) did not know of his illegal activities. Nevertheless, Madoff claims to have acted alone, and his guilty plea means he doesn't have to testify against anyone else.

Settling financial claims will be particularly difficult. The trustee appointed to shut down the business "unearthed a labyrinth of interrelated international funds, institutions and entities of almost unparalleled complexity and breadth."[2] Recovered assets will only cover a small portion of the claims, and victims can only expect limited reimbursement from the Securities Investor Protection Corporation. The trustee is also trying to recover money from those who withdrew their "profits" before the investment fund collapsed. According to an attorney assisting in this effort, Madoff clients need to "share the pain" and realize that they have got "somebody else's money."[3] Those fortunate enough to cash in before the collapse are naturally reluctant to reimburse other investors.

Many victimized by Madoff will probably never recover. Not only were they swindled out of their retirement and college savings; in many cases they were betrayed by someone they trusted. Bernie continued to betray those closest to him until the very end. Just weeks before his arrest he convinced a longtime friend, a recent widow, to invest her entire life savings in his fund.

Discussion Probes

1. What unhealthy motivations drove Madoff to defraud investors and betray his friends?

2. Was Madoff's scheme "extraordinarily evil" as the judge claimed?

3. Was his punishment excessive? Will it deter other possible criminals?

4. Are the victims partially to blame for the success of this swindle?

5. Do you think Madoff acted alone, or did he have help from employees and/or family members?

6. Should clients who got their money out before the fund collapsed be forced to return these funds to help reimburse less fortunate investors?

7. What leadership and followership ethics lessons do you take from this case?

Notes

1. McCoy, K. (2009, July 10). Madoff won't appeal sentence. *USA Today*, p. 3B.
2. McCoy, Madoff won't appeal sentence.
3. McCoy, K. (2009, March 4). Madoff clients' lawsuits look to others for recompense. *USA Today*, p. 1B.

Sources

Avedlund, E. (2009). *Too good to be true: The rise and fall of Bernie Madoff.* New York: Portfolio.

Chernow, R. (2009, March 23). Madoff and his models; where are the snow jobs of yesteryear? *The New Yorker*, p. 28.

Doran, J. (2009, March 14). The biggest swindle in history. *The Irish Times*, Weekend, p. 2.

Hamilton, W. (2009, March 13). "Sorry" is not enough, Madoff's victims say. *Los Angeles Times*, p. A1.

Healy, B., & Syre, S. (2009, July 6). Uneasy times for the Shapiro family. *The Boston Globe*, Metro, p. 1.

Henriques, D. B. (2009, June 30). Madoff, apologizing, is given 150 years. *The New York Times*, pp. A1, B4.

Kouwe, Z. (2009, June 30). Waiting to see Madoff, an angry crowed is disappointed. *The New York Times*, pp. B1, B5.

McLean, B. (2009, March 14). If only there were a Madoff to blame for the meltdown. *The Guardian*, p. 30.

Petruno, T. (2009, July 9). SEC division chief to resign. *Los Angeles Times*, p. B5.

Seib, C. (2009, March 16). Investors who made money from Madoff try to prevent clawback in aid of victims. *The Times*, p. 46.

Sibon, J. (2009, March 13). Did he work alone? Questions over fraudster's family unanswered. *The Daily Telegraph*, City, p. 5.

Notes

1. Palmer, P. (1996). Leading from within. In L. C. Spears (Ed.), *Insights on leadership: Service, stewardship, spirit and servant-leadership* (pp. 197–208). New York: Wiley.

2. Bing, S. (2000). *What would Machiavelli do? The ends justify the meanness.* New York: HarperBusiness.

3. Palmer, p. 205.

4. Garvin, D. A. (1993, July–August). Building a learning organization. *Harvard Business Review*, pp. 78–91.

5. Nash, L. L. (1990). *Good intentions aside: A manager's guide to resolving ethical problems.* Boston: Harvard Business School Press.

6. Michaelson, A. (2009). *The foreclosure of America: The inside story of the rise and fall of Countrywide Home Loans, the mortgage crisis, and the default of the American dream.* New York: Berkley Books; Wilmers, R. G. (2009, July 27). Where the crisis came from. *The Washington Post*, p. A19.

7. Higgs, M. (2009). The good, the bad and the ugly: Leadership and narcissism. *Journal of Change Management, 9,* 165–178; Lubit, R. (2002). The long-term organizational impact of destructively narcissistic managers. *Academy of Management Executive, 18,* 127–183; Padilla, A., Hogan, R., & Kaiser, R. B. (2007). The toxic triangle: Destructive leaders, susceptible followers, and conducive environments. *The Leadership Quarterly, 18,* 176–194.

8. Johnson, J., & Orange, M. (2003). *The man who tried to buy the world: Jean-Marie Messier and Vivendi Universal.* New York: Portfolio.

9. Christie, R., & Geis, F. L. (1970). *Studies in Machiavellianism.* New York: Academic Press.

10. Becker, J. A. H., & O'Hair, H. D. (2007). Machiavellians' motives in organizational citizenship behavior. *Journal of Applied Communication Research, 35,* 246–267; Paulus, D. L., & Williams, K. M. (2002). The dark triad of personality: Narcissism, Machiavellianism, and psychopathy. *Journal of Research in Personality, 36,* 556–563.

11. Jourdan, G. (1998). Indirect causes and effects in policy change: The Brent Spar case. *Public Administration, 76,* 713–770; Zyglidopoulos, S. C. (2002). The social and environmental responsibilities of multinationals: Evidence from the Brent Spar case. *Journal of Business Ethics, 36,* 141–151.

12. Messick, D. M., & Bazerman, M. H. (1996, Winter). Ethical leadership and the psychology of decision-making. *Sloan Management Review, 37*(2), 9–23.

13. Verhovek, S. H. (1993, April 22). Death in Waco: F.B.I. saw the ego in Koresh, but not a willingness to die. *The New York Times*, p. A1.

14. Price, T. L. (2006). *Understanding ethical failures in leadership.* Cambridge, UK: Cambridge University Press.

15. Sternberg, R. J. (2002). Smart people are not stupid, but they sure can be foolish. In R. Sternberg (Ed.), *Why smart people can be so stupid* (pp. 232–242). New Haven, CT: Yale University Press.

16. See Guroian, V. (1996). Awakening the moral imagination. *Intercollegiate Review, 32,* 3–13; Johnson, M. (1993). *Moral imagination: Implications of cognitive science for ethics.* Chicago: University of Chicago Press; Kekes, J. (1991). Moral imagination, freedom, and the humanities. *American Philosophical Quarterly, 28,* 101–111; Tivnan, E. (1995). *The moral imagination.* New York: Routledge, Chapman, and Hall.

17. Werhane, P. (1999). *Moral imagination and management decision-making.* New York: Oxford University Press, p. 93. See also: Bowie, N. E., & Werhane, P. H. (2005). *Management ethics.* Malden, MA: Blackwell.

18. Useem, M. (1998). *The leadership moment: Nine stories of triumph and disaster and their lessons for us all.* New York: Times Books.

19. Gioia, D. A. (1992). Pinto fires and personal ethics: A script analysis of missed opportunities. *Journal of Business Ethics, 11,* 379–389.

20. Janis, I. (1971, November). Groupthink: The problems of conformity. *Psychology Today,* pp. 271–279; Janis, I. (1982). *Groupthink* (2nd ed.). Boston: Houghton Mifflin; Janis, I. (1989). *Crucial decisions: Leadership in policymaking and crisis management.* New York: Free Press; Janis, I., & Mann, L. (1977). *Decision making.* New York: Free Press.

21. Conrad, C., & Poole, M. S. (1998). *Strategic organizational communication: Into the twenty-first century* (4th ed.). Fort Worth, TX: Harcourt Brace, Ch. 12; Darley, J. M. (1996). How organizations socialize individuals into evildoing. In D. M. Messick & A. E. Tenbrunsel (Eds.), *Codes of conduct: Behavioral research into business ethics* (pp. 12–43). New York: Russell Sage Foundation.

22. Anand, V., Ashforth, B. E., & Joshi, M. (2004). Business as usual: The acceptance and perpetuation of corruption in organizations. *Academy of Management Executive, 18,* 39–53.

23. McCauley, C. D., & Van Velsor, E. (Eds.). (2004). *The Center for Creative Leadership handbook of leadership development* (2nd ed.). San Francisco: Jossey-Bass, p. 4.

24. Narvaez, D., & Lapsley, D. K. (2005). The psychological foundations of everyday morality and moral expertise. In D. K. Lapsley & F. C. Power (Eds.), *Character psychology and character education* (pp. 140–165). Notre Dame, IN: Notre Dame Press.

25. Narvaez & Lapsley, p. 151.

PART II

Looking Inward

3

The Leader's Character

The course of any society is largely determined by the quality of its moral leadership.

> —Psychologists Anne Colby and William Damon

Virtue is better than wealth.

> —Kenyan proverb

WHAT'S AHEAD

This chapter addresses the inner dimension of leadership ethics. To shed light rather than shadow, we need to develop strong, ethical character made up of positive traits or virtues. We promote our character development through direct interventions or indirectly by finding role models, telling and living collective stories, learning from hardship, establishing effective habits, determining a clear sense of direction, and examining our values.

Elements of Character

In football, the best defense is often a good offense. When faced with high-scoring opponents, coaches often design offensive game plans that run as much time as possible off the clock. If they're successful, they can rest their defensive players while keeping their opponent's offensive unit on the sidelines. Building strong, ethical character takes a similar proactive approach to dealing with our shadow sides. To keep from projecting our internal enemies and selfishness on others, we need to go on the offensive, replacing or managing our unhealthy motivations through the development of positive leadership traits or qualities called virtues. Interest in virtue ethics dates at least as far back as Plato, Aristotle, and Confucius. The premise of virtue ethics is simple: Good people (those of high moral character) make good moral choices. Despite its longevity, this approach has not always been popular among scholars. Only in recent years have modern philosophers turned back to it in significant numbers.[1] They've been joined by positive psychologists who argue that there is more value in identifying and promoting the strengths of individuals than in trying to repair their weaknesses (which is the approach of traditional psychologists).[2]

Character plays an important role in leadership. CEOs Howell Raines (Fannie Mae), John Thain (Merrill Lynch), Anthony Mozilo (Countrywide Financial), and Martha Stewart (Martha Stewart Living Omnimedia) cast shadows due to greed, arrogance, dishonesty, ruthlessness, and other character failings. Their lack of virtue stands in sharp contrast to such widely admired leaders as Costco cofounder Jim Sinegal, Southwest Airlines President Emeritus Colleen Barrett (described in more detail in Chapter 6), and Patagonia CEO Yvon Chouinard. These leaders serve followers and customers and create organizational climates that foster caring and equality.

Proponents of virtue ethics start with the end in mind. They develop a description or portrait of the ideal person (in this case a leader) and identify the admirable qualities or tendencies that make up the character of this ethical role model. They then suggest ways in which others can acquire these virtues.

There are four important features of virtues. First, virtues are woven into the inner life of leaders. They are not easily developed or discarded but persist over time. Second, virtues shape the way leaders see and behave. Being virtuous makes them sensitive to ethical issues and encourages them to act morally. Third, virtues operate independently of the situation. A virtue may be expressed differently depending on the context (what's prudent in one situation may not be in the next). Yet a virtuous leader will not abandon his or her principles to please followers. Fourth, virtues help leaders live better (more satisfying, more fulfilled) lives.[3] Important virtues for leaders include the following:

Courage

Of all the virtues, courage is no doubt the most universally admired.

—Philosopher Andre Comte-Sponville

Courage is overcoming fear in order to do the right thing.[4] Courageous leaders acknowledge the dangers they face and their anxieties. Nonetheless, they move forward despite the risks and costs. The same is true for courageous followers (see "Focus on Follower Ethics: Courageous Followership"). Courage is most often associated with acts of physical bravery and heroism such as saving a comrade in battle or running dangerous river rapids. Nevertheless, most courageous acts involve other forms of danger, such as the school principal who faces the wrath of parents for suspending the basketball team's leading scorer before the state tournament or the manager who could lose his job for confronting the boss about unauthorized spending.[5]

People must have courage if they are to fulfill the two components of ethical leadership: acting morally and exerting moral influence. Ethical leaders recognize that moral action is risky but continue to model ethical behavior despite the danger. They refuse to set their values aside to go along with the group, to keep silent when customers may be hurt, or to lie to investors. They strive to create ethical environments even when faced with opposition from their superiors and subordinates.

 ## FOCUS ON FOLLOWER ETHICS

COURAGEOUS FOLLOWERSHIP

Ira Chaleff, who acts as a management consultant to U.S. senators and representatives, believes that courage is the most important virtue for followers. Exhibiting courage is easier if followers recognize that their ultimate allegiance is to the purpose and values of the organization, not to the leader. Chaleff outlines five dimensions of courageous followership that equip subordinates to meet the challenges of their role.

The Courage to Assume Responsibility

Followers must be accountable both for themselves and for the organization as a whole. Courageous followers take stock of their skills and attitudes, consider how willing they are to support and challenge their leaders, manage themselves, seek feedback and personal growth, take care of themselves, and care passionately about the organization's goals. They take initiative to change organizational culture by challenging rules and mind-sets and by improving processes.

(Continued)

(Continued)

The Courage to Serve

Courageous followers support their leaders through hard, often unglamorous work. This labor takes a variety of forms, such as helping leaders conserve their energies for their most significant tasks, organizing communication to and from the leader, controlling access to the leader, shaping a leader's public image, presenting options during decision making, preparing for crises, mediating conflicts between leaders, and promoting performance reviews for leaders.

The Courage to Challenge

Inappropriate behavior damages the relationship between leaders and followers and threatens the purpose of the organization. Leaders may break the law, scream at or use demeaning language with employees, display an arrogant attitude, engage in sexual harassment, abuse drugs and alcohol, and misuse funds. Courageous followers need to confront leaders acting in a destructive manner. In some situations, just asking questions about the wisdom of a policy decision is sufficient to bring about change. In more extreme cases, followers may need to disobey unethical orders.

The Courage to Participate in Transformation

Negative behavior, when unchecked, often results in a leader's destruction. Leaders may deny the need to change, or they may attempt to justify their behavior. They may claim that whatever they do for themselves (e.g., embezzling, enriching themselves at the expense of stockholders) ultimately benefits the organization. To succeed in modifying their behavior patterns, leaders must admit they have a problem and acknowledge that they should change. They need to take personal responsibility and visualize the outcomes of the transformation: better health, more productive employees, higher self-esteem, restored relationships. Followers can aid in the process of transformation by drawing attention to what needs to be changed; suggesting resources, including outside facilitators; creating a supportive environment; modeling openness to change and empathy; helping contain abusive behavior; and providing positive reinforcement for positive new behaviors.

The Courage to Leave

When leaders are unwilling to change, courageous followers may take principled action by resigning from the organization. Departure is justified when the leader's behaviors clash with the leader's self-proclaimed values or the values of the group, or when the leader degrades or endangers others. Sometimes leaving is not enough. In the event of serious ethical violations, followers must bring the leader's misbehavior to the attention of the public by going to the authorities or the press.

SOURCE: Chaleff, I. (2003). *The courageous follower: Standing up to & for our leaders* (2nd ed.). San Francisco: Berrett-Koehler.

Prudence (Practical Wisdom)

. . . the goal of human life is to be good. Prudence assists us in getting there.

—Baldwin-Wallace College professors
Alan Kolp and Peter Rea

Prudence is the ability to discern or select the best course of action in a given situation.[6] Thomas Aquinas argued that this virtue governs the others, determining when and how the other qualities should be used. For example, prudence reveals what situations call for courage or compassion and determines how to act justly. Foresight and caution are important elements of practical wisdom. Prudent leaders keep in mind the long-term consequences of their choices. As a result, they are cautious, trying not to overextend themselves and their organizations or to take unnecessary risks. Billionaire investor Warren Buffett is one example of a prudent leader. Buffett, the head of Berkshire Hathaway, sticks to a basic investment strategy, searching for undervalued companies that he can hold for at least 10 years. His lifestyle is modest as well (he still lives in the home he bought for $31,500 and earns $100,000 a year). When Buffett and his wife die, 99% of his estate will go to a charitable foundation.

Optimism

Hope is not the conviction that something will turn out well, but the certainty that something makes sense, regardless of how it turns out.

—Former Czechoslovakian president Václav Havel

Optimists expect positive outcomes in the future even if they are currently experiencing disappointments and difficulties.[7] They are more confident than pessimists, who expect that things will turn out poorly. People who are hopeful about the future are more likely to persist in the face of adversity. When faced with stress and defeat, optimists acknowledge the reality of the situation and take steps to improve. Their pessimistic colleagues, on the other hand, try to escape the problem through wishful thinking, distractions, and other means.

Optimism is an essential quality for leaders. As we'll see later in the chapter, nearly every leader experiences hardships. Those who learn and grow from these experiences will develop their character and go on to greater challenges. Those who ignore unpleasant realities stunt their ethical growth and may find their careers at an end. At the same time, leaders need to help followers deal constructively with setbacks, encouraging them to persist. Followers are more likely to rally behind optimists who appear confident and outline a positive image or vision of the group's future. (See "Leadership Ethics at the Movies: *Happy-Go-Lucky*" for one example of a highly optimistic leader.)

 LEADERSHIP ETHICS AT THE MOVIES

HAPPY-GO-LUCKY

Key Cast Members: Sally Hawkins, Eddie Marsan, Alexis Zegerman

Synopsis. Sally Hawkins stars as Poppy, a free-spirited 30-year-old British primary school teacher who takes a positive approach to life no matter the circumstances. Whether dealing with troubled students in her role as a leader or managing her everyday encounters with an obsessive driving instructor, a rude clerk, a homeless man, or a distraught dance instructor, Poppy looks for the best in other people. Physical pain and disappointments can't derail her optimism, which is her key to a happy life.

Rating: R for language

Themes: optimism, compassion, courage, integrity, values, personal mission

Discussion Starters

1. How does Poppy function as a leader?

2. Besides optimism, what other character traits does Poppy demonstrate and how?

3. Is it possible to be too optimistic? Does Poppy take her optimism too far?

Integrity

Integrity lies at the very heart of understanding what leadership is.

—Business professors Joseph Badaracco
and Richard Ellsworth

Integrity is wholeness or completeness. Leaders possessing this trait are true to themselves, reflecting consistency between what they say publicly and how they think and act privately. In other words, they practice what they preach. They are also honest in their dealings with others.

Nothing undermines a leader's moral authority more quickly than lack of integrity. Followers watch the behavior of leaders closely. One untrustworthy act can undermine a pattern of credible behavior. Trust is broken, and cynicism spreads. In an organizational setting, common "trust busters" include inconsistent messages and behavior, inconsistent rules and procedures, blaming, dishonesty, secrecy, and unjust rewards.[8] (You can determine the integrity of one of your leaders by completing the "Self-Assessment: Perceived Leader Integrity Scale.") Employees at United Airlines were particularly outraged by the bonuses given to executives described in Chapter 1 because these officials had consistently promoted "shared sacrifice" during the bankruptcy. Performance suffers when trust is broken. Trust encourages teamwork, cooperation, and risk taking. Those who work in trusting environments are more productive and enjoy better working relationships.[9] (I'll have more to say about trust in Chapter 6.)

SELF-ASSESSMENT

PERCEIVED LEADER INTEGRITY SCALE

You can use this scale to measure the integrity of your immediate supervisor or, as an alternative, ask a follower to rate you. The higher the score (maximum 124), the lower the integrity of the leader rated.

The following items concern your immediate supervisor. You should consider your immediate supervisor to be the person who has the most control over your daily work activities. Circle responses to indicate how well each item describes your immediate supervisor.

Response choices: 1 = Not at all;   2 = Somewhat;   3 = Very much;   4 = Exactly

1. Would use my mistakes to attack me personally   ① 2 3 4

2. Always gets even   ① 2 3 4

3. Gives special favors to certain "pet" employees but not to me   ① 2 3 4

4. Would lie to me   1 ② 3 4

5. Would risk me to protect himself or herself in work matters   ① 2 3 4

6. Deliberately fuels conflict among employees   ① 2 3 4

7. Is evil   ① 2 3 4

8. Would use my performance appraisal to criticize me as a person   ① 2 3 4

9. Has it in for me   ① 2 3 4

10. Would allow me to be blamed for his or her mistake   ① 2 3 4

11. Would falsify records if it would help his or her work reputation   ① 2 3 4

12. Lacks high morals   ① 2 3 4

13. Makes fun of my mistakes instead of coaching me as
    to how to do my job better   1 ② 3 4

14. Would deliberately exaggerate my mistakes to make me look
    bad when describing my performance to his or her superiors   ① 2 3 4

15. Is vindictive   ① 2 3 4

16. Would blame me for his or her own mistake   ① 2 3 4

17. Avoids coaching me because she or he wants me to fail   ① 2 3 4

18. Would treat me better if I belonged to a different ethnic group   ① 2 3 4

19. Would deliberately distort what I say   1 ② 3 4

20. Deliberately makes employees angry at each other   ① 2 3 4

21. Is a hypocrite   ① 2 3 4

22. Would limit my training opportunities
    to prevent me from advancing   ① 2 3 4

23. Would blackmail an employee if she or he could get away with it   ① 2 3 4

24. Enjoys turning down my requests   ① 2 3 4

25. Would make trouble for me if I got on his or her bad side   ① 2 3 4

26. Would take credit for my ideas   1 ② 3 4

27. Would steal from the organization   ① 2 3 4

28. Would risk me to get back at someone else   1 ② 3 4

29. Would engage in sabotage against the organization   ① 2 3 4

30. Would fire people just because she or he doesn't like
    them if she or he could get away with it   ① 2 3 4

31. Would do things that violate organizational policy
    and then expect subordinates to cover for him or her   ① 2 3 4

Total Score ___36___

SOURCE: Bartholomew, C. S., & Gustafson, S. B. (1998). Perceived leader integrity scale: An instrument for assessing employee perceptions of leader integrity. *The Leadership Quarterly, 9,* 143–144. Used by permission.

Humility

Let us be a little humble; let us think that the truth may not be entirely with us.

—Jawaharlal Nehru

The failure of many celebrity CEOs is a strong argument for encouraging leaders to be humble. In the 1990s, many business leaders, such as Carly Fiorina of Hewlett-Packard (see Chapter 9), Revlon's Ron Perelman, Disney's Michael Eisner, WorldCom's Bernie Ebbers, and Tyco's Dennis Kozlowski, seemed more like rock stars than corporate executives.[10] These charismatic figures became the public faces of their corporations, appearing on magazine covers and cable television shows and in company commercials. Within a few years, however, most of these celebrity leaders were gone because of scandal (some are in jail) or poor performance. Quiet leaders who shun the spotlight replaced them and, in many instances, produced superior results.

Management professors J. Andrew Morris, Celeste Brotheridge, and John Urbanski argue that true humility strikes a balance between having an overly low and having an overly high opinion of the self.[11] It does not consist of low self-esteem, as many people think, or of underestimating our abilities. Instead, humility is made up of three components. The first component is self-awareness. A humble leader can objectively assess her or his strengths and limitations. The second element is openness, which is a product of knowing one's weaknesses. Possessing humility means being open to new ideas and knowledge. The third component is transcendence. Humble leaders acknowledge that there is a power greater than the self. This prevents them from developing an inflated view of their importance while increasing their appreciation for the worth and contributions of others.

Humility has a powerful impact on ethical behavior. Humble leaders are less likely to be corrupted by power, claim excessive privileges, engage in fraud, abuse followers, and pursue selfish goals. They are more willing to serve others instead, putting the needs of followers first while acting as role models. Humility encourages leaders to build supportive relationships with followers that foster collaboration and trust. Because they know their limitations and are open to input, humble leaders are more willing to take advice that can keep them and their organizations out of trouble.

Reverence

It's not wise To lift our thoughts too high; We are human and our time is short.

—Ancient Greek playwright Euripides

University of Texas humanities professor Paul Woodruff argues that reverence, which was highly prized by the ancient Greeks and Chinese, is an important virtue for modern leaders.[12] Reverence has much in common with humility. It is the capacity to feel a sense of awe, respect, and even shame when appropriate. Awe, respect, and shame are all critical to ethical leadership, according to Woodruff. Ethical leaders serve higher causes or ideals. They are concerned not about power struggles or about winners or losers but with reaching common goals. They respect the input of others, rely on persuasion rather than force, and listen to followers' ideas. Ethical leaders also feel shame when they violate group ideals. Such shame can prompt them to self-sacrifice—accepting the consequences of telling the truth, for example, or of supporting unpopular people or ideas.

Compassion (Kindness, Generosity, Love)

All happiness in the world comes from serving others; all sorrow in the world comes from acting selfishly.

—Leadership expert Margaret Wheatley

Compassion and related terms such as *concern, care, kindness, generosity,* and *love* all describe an orientation that puts others ahead of the self.[13] Those with compassion value others regardless of whether they get anything in return from them. Compassion is an important element of altruism, an ethical perspective we'll describe in more detail in Chapter 5. An orientation toward others rather than the self separates ethical leaders from their unethical colleagues.[14] Ethical leaders recognize that they serve the purposes of the group. They seek power and exercise influence on behalf of followers. Unethical leaders put their self-interests first. They are more likely to control and manipulate followers and subvert the goals of the collective. In extreme cases, this self-orientation can lead to widespread death and destruction.

Eunice Shriver provides an outstanding model of compassionate leadership.[15] Born into the wealthy and powerful Kennedy family, which included brother John, who became president, and brothers Robert and Ted, who became senators, she used her money and political clout on behalf of those with mental limitations. When Jack Kennedy became president, she convinced him to set up a committee to study developmental disabilities, which led to the creation of the National Institute of Child Health and Human Development. She started a camp for the intellectually disabled at her estate and cofounded the Special Olympics. The first Special Olympics meet had 1,000 contestants. Now more than 2.5 million athletes in 80 countries take part. Shriver's efforts played a major role in changing public attitudes toward those facing Down syndrome, mental retardation, and other intel-lectual challenges. They used to be viewed as outcasts and warehoused in mental facilities. Shriver encouraged Americans to see that, with adequate training, those with intellectual limitations could live productive lives and contribute to society.

Justice

> *And what does the Lord require of you? To act justly, and to love mercy. And to walk humbly with your God.*
>
> —Old Testament prophet Micah

Justice has two components.[16] The first component is a sense of obligation to the common good. The second element is treating others as equally and fairly as possible. Just people feel a sense of duty and strive to do their part as a member of the team, whether that team is a small group, an organization, or society as a whole. They support equitable rules and laws. In addition, those driven by justice believe that everyone deserves the same rights even if they have different skills or status.

Although justice is a significant virtue for everyone, regardless of her or his role, it takes on added importance for leaders. To begin, leaders who don't carry out their duties put the group or organization at risk. Furthermore, leaders have a moral obligation to consider the needs and interests of the entire group and to take the needs of the larger community into account. The rules and regulations they implement should be fair and benefit everyone. Leaders also need to guarantee to followers the same rights they enjoy. They should set personal biases aside when making choices, judg-ing others objectively and treating them accordingly. Leaders also have a responsibility to try to correct injustice and inequality caused by others. (For an example of an unjust leader, see Case Study 3.1.)

CASE STUDY 3.1

SENATE SEAT FOR SALE

After Abraham Lincoln and Barack Obama, Rod Blagojevich may be the most famous politician ever to come from the state of Illinois. Unfortunately, Blagojevich is known for his character failings rather than for his political suc-cesses. In late 2008 the governor made national and international headlines after being charged with trying to sell Obama's vacated Illinois Senate seat to the highest bidder. The federal prosecutor in the case said that he acted because "we were in the middle of a corruption crime spree, and we wanted to stop it."[1] In addition to the accusation that he tried to sell the Senate seat to the highest bidder, the Democratic governor was charged with (1) pressuring a racetrack owner into making contributions in return for legislation that would benefit the horse racing industry, (2) threatening to withdraw state help to the Chicago Tribune Company if it didn't fire the paper's editorial writers, (3) shaking down a children's hospital administrator by holding back $8 million in pediatric care until the executive gave $50,000 to Blagojevich's campaign fund, and (4) aggressively seeking campaign contributions from those doing business with the state. Later Blagojevich was impeached and removed from office by a 117-to-1 vote of the Illinois Senate (his sister-in-law cast the lone dissenting vote).

Much of the federal case against the former governor is based on FBI tapes of his telephone conversations. Speaking of the vacant Senate seat, Blagojevich says, "I've got this thing, it's [expletive] golden . . . I'm just not giving it up for [expletive] nothing."[2] He told the owner of the *Chicago Tribune* to "get rid of those guys" (the editorial writers) and, at another point, is heard arranging for a bill signing when a donation is received. Blagojevich does not appear to be happy with his job or financial situation, complaining about being "stuck" as governor and proclaiming, "I want to make money." These factors appear to be behind his desire to auction off the Senate seat. He hoped to use the Senate opening either to raise campaign contributions, to procure an appointment to a cabinet post (which could lead to a high-paying position in private industry), to become an ambassador, or to secure lucrative jobs for him and his spouse. On the recordings Blagojevich contemplates appointing himself to the Senate in order to avoid impeachment.

Concern about the ex-governor's character began well before his federal indictments for bribery and corruption. Blagojevich refused to move to the state capital in Springfield but worked instead out of his Chicago office (office mates report that he was seldom there). Instead of cooperating with state lawmakers, he periodically circumvented the state legislature to institute new programs and tried to bully representatives. He called the legislature into special session during the holidays and, on one occasion, insisted that the lawmakers stay in session while he went to a professional hockey game. The former governor was known for being late to nearly all appointments and

(Continued)

(Continued)

meetings, and aides could expect his wrath if they made even minor mistakes, like misplacing the hairbrush he used on his signature black hair.

Blagojevich is not the first Illinois governor to run afoul of the law. In fact, four out of the eight state governors before Blagojevich were indicted, and George Ryan, Blagojevich's Republican predecessor, is currently serving a federal sentence for racketeering. Both Democratic and Republican office-holders hope that the governor's removal from office will spur political reform. The new governor Pat Quinn appointed a commission to offer suggestions for making government more transparent, tightening up campaign finance rules, and regulating relationships with state contractors. For his part, Blagojevich maintains his innocence. During his impeachment battle, he claimed that many of his taped comments were taken out of context and appeared on a number of talk shows to defend his actions. However, his decision not to resign cost the state millions in legal fees and paralyzed state government when it was in the midst of a fiscal crisis brought on by a national recession.

Discussion Probes

1. What character traits did the governor lack while in office?

2. How did the governor act unjustly?

3. What can be done to change a culture of political corruption like that found in Illinois state government?

4. What similarities do you see between this case and other cases of political corruption?

5. What leadership ethics lessons do you learn from this case?

Notes

1. Saulny, S. (2008, December 11). Calls for governor to quit in scandal on Senate seat. *The New York Times*, p. A1.

2. Thomas, E., Smalley, S., & Wolffe, R. (2008, December 22). Being Rod Blagojevich. *Newsweek*, p. 30.

Sources

Curl, J. (2009, January 28). Blagojevich tapes aired at impeachment trial. *The Washington Times*, p. A08.

Davey, M. (2008, December 15). 2 sides of a troubled governor, sinking deeper. *The New York Times*, p. A1.

Davey, M. (2009, January 13). Uneasy times for Blagojevich and his colleagues. *The New York Times*, p. A13.

Davey, M. (2009, January 30). On his way out, Blagojevich makes a day of it. *The New York Times*, p. A1.

Davey, M. (2009, February 1). A governor's removal spurs (the latest) calls for political reform in Illinois. *The New York Times*, p. A16.

From the complaint: "You just don't give it away for nothing." (December 10, 2008). *The New York Times*, p. A32.

Maag, C. (2008, December 23). Illinois impeachment panel hears of fund-raising. *The New York Times*, p. A20.

Perez-Pena, R. (2008, December 10). Governor threatened Tribune over criticism, prosecutors says. *The New York Times*, p. A33.

Identifying important leadership virtues is only a start. We then need to blend desirable qualities together to form a strong, ethical character—to develop what moral psychologist Augusto Blasi calls a *moral identity*.[17] Those with moral identity place ethics at the center of their being. They are motivated to take moral action (e.g., be just, demonstrate compassion) because they want to act in a way that is consistent with their core identity. Developing ethical character or moral identity is far from easy, of course. At times, our personal demons will overcome even our best efforts to keep them at bay, and we will fail to live up to our ideals. We're likely to make progress in some areas while lagging in others. We may be courageous yet arrogant, reverent yet pessimistic, optimistic yet unjust. No wonder some prominent leaders reflect both moral strength and weakness. Martin Luther King, Jr., showed great courage and persistence in leading the civil rights movement but engaged in extramarital relationships. Franklin Roosevelt was revered by many of his contemporaries but had a long-standing affair with Lucy Mercer. In fact, Mercer (not Eleanor Roosevelt) was present when he died.

The poor personal behavior of political and business leaders has sparked debate about personal and public morality. One camp argues that the two cannot be separated. Another camp makes a clear distinction between the public and private arenas. According to this second group, we can be disgusted by the private behavior of politicians such as those who engage in extramarital affairs (e.g., Bill Clinton, Rudy Giuliani, former New York Governor Eliot Spitzer, Nevada Senator John Ensign) but vote for them anyway based on their performance in office.

I suspect that the truth lies somewhere between these extremes. We should expect contradictions in the character of leaders, not be surprised by them. Private lapses don't always lead to lapses in public judgment. On the other hand, it seems artificial to compartmentalize private and public ethics. Private tendencies can and do cross over into public decisions. Arizona State business ethics professor Marianne Jennings points out that many fallen corporate leaders (e.g., Richard Scrushy, Dennis Kozlowski, Scott Sullivan, Bernie Ebbers) cheated on their wives or divorced them to marry much younger women.[18] She suggests that executives who are dishonest with the most important people in their lives—their spouses—are likely to be dishonest with others who aren't as significant: suppliers, customers, and stockholders. Furthermore, the energy devoted to an affair distracts a leader from his or her duties and provides a poor role model for followers. That's why the Boeing board fired CEO Harry Stonecipher when it discovered that he was having an affair with a high-ranking employee.[19]

In the political arena, Franklin Roosevelt tried to deceive the public as well as his wife and family. He proposed expanding the number of Supreme Court justices from 9 to 15, claiming that the justices were old and overworked. In reality, he was angry with the Court for overturning many New Deal programs and wanted to appoint new justices who would support him. Roosevelt's dishonest attempt to pack the Supreme Court cost him a good deal of his popularity. Bill Clinton's personal moral weaknesses overshadowed many of his political accomplishments.

Fostering character is a lifelong process requiring sustained emotional, mental, and even physical effort. Strategies for developing leadership virtues can be classified as direct or indirect. Direct approaches are specifically designed to promote virtues. For example, many schools have character education programs.[20] Instead of deliberate moralizing (telling children how to behave), the best of these programs foster character development though debate, dialogue, case studies, self-evaluation, and problem solving. In psychological interventions, therapists help clients become less egocentric (and therefore more humble) by encouraging them to develop a more realistic assessment of their strengths and weaknesses. Counselors suggest that their counselees convert pessimism into optimism by identifying their negative cognitions ("I am a failure") and then converting them into more positive thoughts ("I may have failed, but I can take steps to improve"). Psychologists have also found ways to help people deal with their fears (and build their courage). They first expose clients to low levels of threat. Once they have mastered their initial fears, therapists then introduce clients to progressively greater dangers.[21]

Although direct methods can build character, more often than not virtues develop indirectly, as a by-product of other activities. In the remainder of this chapter, I'll introduce a variety of indirect approaches or factors that encourage the development of leadership virtues. These include identifying role models, telling and living out shared stories, learning from hardship, cultivating good habits, creating a personal mission statement, and clarifying values.

Character Building

Finding Role Models

Character appears to be more caught than taught. We often learn what it means to be virtuous by observing and imitating exemplary leaders. That makes role models crucial to developing high moral character.[22] US Airways Captain Chesley (Sully) Sullenberger is one such role model.[23] Immediately after takeoff from New York's LaGuardia Airport, Sullenberger's Airbus A320 hit a flock of birds, shutting down both engines. Unable to get back to LaGuardia or to another airport, Captain Sully avoided densely populated areas and landed the plane safely on the Hudson River. He then walked through the cabin twice to make sure that no passengers were left as the plane settled in the river. All 150 passengers and five crew members were rescued with the only seriously injured passenger suffering two broken legs. The landing (which could have resulted in multiple deaths had the pilot not set the plane down perfectly level) was dubbed "the miracle on the Hudson." Sullenberger deflected praise about the successful emergency landing, declaring "that's what we are trained to do."

Government ethics expert David Hart argues that it is important to differentiate between different types of moral examples or exemplars.[24] Dramatic acts, such as rescuing a child from danger or landing a plane safely, capture our attention. However, if we're to develop worthy character, we need examples of those who demonstrate virtue on a daily basis. Hart distinguishes between *moral episodes* and *moral processes*. Moral episodes are made up of *moral crises* and *moral confrontations*. Moral crises are dangerous, and Hart calls those who respond to them "moral heroes." Oskar Schindler, a German industrialist, was one such hero. He risked his life and fortune to save 1,000 Jewish workers during World War II. Moral confrontations aren't dangerous, but they do involve risk and call for "moral champions." Marie Ragghianti emerged as a moral champion when, as chair of the parole board in Tennessee, she discovered that the governor and his cronies were selling pardons and reported their illegal activities to the FBI.

Moral processes consist of *moral projects* and *moral work*. Moral projects are designed to improve ethical behavior during a limited amount of time and require "moral leaders." A moral leader sets out to reduce corruption in government, for example, to introduce a more effective medical treatment, or to improve the working conditions of migrant farmworkers. In contrast to a moral project, moral work does not have a beginning or an end but is ongoing. The "moral worker" strives for ethical consistency throughout life. This moral exemplar might be the motor vehicle department employee who tries to be courteous to everyone who comes to the office or the neighbor who volunteers to coach youth soccer.

Hart argues that the moral worker is the most important category of moral exemplar. He points out that most of life is lived in the daily valleys, not on the heroic mountain peaks. Because character is developed over time through a series of moral choices and actions, we need examples of those who live consistent moral lives. Those who engage in moral work are better able to handle moral crises. For instance, André and Magda Trocmé committed themselves to a life of service and nonviolence as pastors in the French village of Le Chambon. When the German occupiers arrived, the Trocmés didn't hesitate to protect the lives of Jewish children and encouraged their congregation to do the same. This small community became an island of refuge to those threatened by the Holocaust.[25] (Turn to Case Study 3.2 on page 108 for a closer look at another outstanding moral exemplar.)

Anne Colby and William Damon studied 23 moral workers to determine what we can learn from their lives.[26] They found three common characteristics in their sample:

- *Certainty.* Moral exemplars are sure of what they believe and take responsibility for acting on their convictions.
- *Positivity.* Exemplars take a positive approach to life even in the face of hardship. They enjoy what they do and are optimistic about the future.
- *Unity of self and moral goals.* Exemplars don't distinguish between their personal identity and their ethical convictions. Morality is central to who they are. They believe they have no choice but to help others and consider themselves successful if they are pursuing their mission in life.

What sets exemplars apart from the rest of us is the extent of their engagement in moral issues. We make sure that our children get safely across the street. Moral exemplars, on the other hand, "drop everything not just to see their own children across the street but to feed the poor children of the world, to comfort the dying, to heal the ailing, or to campaign for human rights."[27]

Colby and Damon offer some clues about how we might develop broader moral commitments like the exemplars in their study. They note that moral capacity continues to develop well beyond childhood. Some in their sample didn't take on their life's work until their 40s and beyond. As a result, we should strive to develop our ethical capacity throughout our lives. The researchers also found that working with others on important ethical tasks or projects fosters moral growth by exposing participants to different points of view and new moral issues. We too can benefit by collaborating with others on significant causes such as working for better children's health care, building affordable housing, or fighting AIDS. The key is to view these tasks not as a burden but as an opportunity to act on what we believe. Adopting a joyful attitude will help us remain optimistic in the face of discouragement.

Telling and Living Collective Stories

Character building never takes place in a vacuum. Virtues are more likely to take root when nurtured by families, schools, governments, and religious bodies. These collectives impart values and encourage self-discipline, caring, and other virtues through the telling of narratives or stories. Shared narratives both explain and persuade. They provide a framework for understanding the world and, at the same time, challenge us to act in specified ways. For example, one of the most remarkable features of the American political system is the orderly transition of power between presidents.[28] George Washington set this precedent by voluntarily stepping down as the country's first leader. His story, told in classrooms, books, and films, helps explain why the current electoral system functions smoothly. Furthermore, modern presidents and presidential candidates follow Washington's example, as in the case of the 2000 election. Al Gore garnered more popular votes than George W. Bush but conceded defeat after the Supreme Court rejected his court challenge.

Character growth comes from living up to the roles we play in the story. According to virtue ethicist Alasdair MacIntyre, "I can only answer the question 'What am I to do?' if I can answer the prior question, 'Of what story or stories do I find myself a part?'"[29] Worthy narratives bring out the best in us, encouraging us to suppress our inner demons and to cast light instead of shadow.

In the introduction to this text, I argued that we could learn about leadership ethics from fictional characters as well as from real-life ones. Ethics professor C. David Lisman offers several reasons why the ethical models contained in literature can provide a moral education that helps us to nurture our virtues.[30] Lisman focuses on literature, but his observations also apply to other forms of fiction (films, plays, television shows). In Lisman's estimation, fiction helps us understand our possibilities and limits. We can try to deny the reality of death, the fact that we're aging, and that there are factors outside our control. However, novels and short stories force us to confront these issues.

Literature explores many common human themes, such as freedom of choice, moral responsibility, conflict between individual and society, conflict between individual conscience and society's rules, and self-understanding. Fiction writers help us escape our old ways of thinking and acting. Their best works expand our emotional capacity, enabling us to better respond to the needs of others. They also provide us with an opportunity to practice moral reflection and judgment by evaluating the actions of important characters.[31] In sum, almost any story about leaders, whether real or fictional, can teach us something about ethical and unethical behavior. Moral exemplars can be found in novels, television series, and feature films as well as in news stories, biographies, documentaries, and historical records.

Learning From Hardship

Hardship and suffering also play a role in developing character. The leaders we admire the most are often those who have endured the greatest hardships. Nelson Mandela, Václav Havel, and Aleksandr Solzhenitsyn served extended prison terms, for instance, and Moses endured 40 years in exile and 40 in the wilderness with his people.

Perhaps no other American leader has faced as much hardship as did Abraham Lincoln. He was defeated in several elections before winning the presidency. Because of death threats, he had to slip into Washington, DC, to take office. He presided over the slaughter of many of his countrymen and women, lost a beloved son, and was ridiculed by Northerners (some in his cabinet) and Southerners alike. However, all these trials seemed to deepen both his commitment to the Union and his spirituality. His second inaugural address is considered to be one of the finest political and theological statements ever produced by a public official. (Turn to Case Study 3.3 on page 110 for another example of a leader who faced and overcame hardship.)

Trainers at the Center for Creative Leadership (CCL) have identified hardship as one of the factors contributing to leadership development. Leaders develop the fastest when they encounter situations that stretch or challenge them. Hardships, along with novelty, difficult goals, and conflict, challenge people. CCL staffers Russ Moxley and Mary Lynn Pulley believe that hardships differ from other challenging experiences because they are unplanned, are experienced in an intensely personal way, and involve loss.[32]

Research conducted by the CCL reveals that leaders experience five common categories of hardship events. Each type of hardship can drive home important lessons.

- *Business mistakes and failures.* Examples of this type of hardship event include losing an important client, failed products and programs, broken relationships, and bankruptcies. These experiences help leaders build stronger working relationships, recognize their limitations, and profit from their mistakes.

- *Career setbacks.* Missed promotions, unsatisfying jobs, demotions, and firings make up this hardship category. Leaders faced with these events lose control over their careers, their sense of self-efficacy or competence, and their professional identity. Career setbacks function as wake-up calls, providing feedback about weaknesses. They encourage leaders to take more responsibility for managing their careers and to identify the type of work that is most meaningful to them.
- *Personal trauma.* Examples of personal trauma include divorce, cancer, death, and difficult children. These experiences, which are a natural part of life, drive home the point that leaders (who are used to being in charge) can't run the world around them. As a result, they may strike a better balance between work and home responsibilities, learn how to accept help from others, and endure in the face of adversity.
- *Problem employees.* Troubled workers include those who steal, defraud, can't perform, or perform well only part of the time. In dealing with problem employees, leaders often lose the illusion that they can turn these people around. They may also learn how important it is to hold followers to consistently high standards and become more skilled at confronting subordinates.
- *Downsizing.* Downsizing has much in common with career setbacks, but in this type of hardship leaders lose their jobs through no fault of their own. Downsizing can help leaders develop coping skills and force them to take stock of their lives and careers. Those carrying out the layoffs can also learn from the experience by developing greater empathy for the feelings of followers.

Being exposed to a hardship is no guarantee that you'll learn from the experience. Some ambitious leaders never get over being passed over for a promotion, for instance, and become embittered and cynical. Benefiting from adversity takes what Warren Bennis and Robert Thomas call "adaptive capacity." Bennis and Thomas found that, regardless of generation, effective leaders come through *crucible moments* that have a profound impact on their development.[33] These intense experiences include failures such as losing an election but also encompass more positive events such as climbing a mountain or finding a mentor. The successful leaders they sampled experienced just as many crises as everyone else but were able to learn important principles and skills from their struggles. This knowledge enabled them to move on to more complex challenges.

Successful leaders see hard times as positive high points of their lives. In contrast, less successful leaders are defeated and discouraged by similar events. To put it another way, effective leaders tell a different story than their ineffective counterparts. They identify hardships as stepping-stones, not as insurmountable obstacles. We too can enlarge our adaptive capacity by paying close attention to our personal narratives, defining difficult moments in our lives as learning opportunities rather than as permanent obstacles. To see how you can learn from a specific failure, take the following steps:

1. Identify a significant failure from your professional or personal life and summarize the failure in a sentence (be sure to use the word *failure*).

2. Describe how you felt and thought about the failure immediately after it happened.

3. Move forward in time to identify any positive outcomes that came out of the failure, including skills you acquired, lessons you learned, and any relationships you established.

4. Identify how the failure changed or shaped you as a person, noting any new traits or attitudes you have adopted and whether you are any more mature now than before the failure event.[34]

Developing Habits

One of the ways in which we build character is by doing well through the development of habits.[35] Habits are repeated routines or practices designed to foster virtuous behavior. Examples of good habits include working hard, telling the truth, giving to charity, standing up to peer pressure, and always turning in original work for school assignments. Every time we engage in one of these habits, it leaves a trace or residue. Over time, these residual effects become part of our personality and are integrated into our character. We also become more competent at demonstrating virtues. Take courage, for example. To develop the courage and skill to confront our bosses about their unethical behavior, we may first need to practice courage by expressing our opinions to them on less critical issues such as work policies and procedures.[36]

Business consultant Stephen Covey developed the most popular list of habits. Not only is he the author of the best-selling book *The Seven Habits of Highly Effective People,* but thousands of businesses, nonprofit groups, and government agencies have participated in workshops offered by the Covey Center for Leadership.[37] Covey argues that effectiveness is based on such character principles as integrity, fairness, service, excellence, and growth. The habits are the tools that enable leaders and followers to develop these characteristics. Covey defines a habit as a combination of knowledge (what to do and why to do it), skill (how to do it), and motivation (wanting to do it). Leadership development is an "inside-out" process that starts within the leader and then moves outward to affect others. The seven habits of effective and ethical leaders are as follows:

Habit 1. Be Proactive. Proactive leaders realize that they can choose how they respond to events. When faced with a career setback, they try to grow from the experience instead of feeling victimized by it. Proactive people also take the initiative by opting to attack problems instead of accepting defeat. Their language reflects their willingness to accept rather than avoid responsibility. A proactive leader makes such statements as "Let's examine our options" and "I can create a strategic plan." A reactive leader makes comments such as "The organization won't go along with that idea," "I'm too old to change," and "That's just who I am."

Habit 2. Begin With the End in Mind. This habit is based on the notion that "all things are created twice." First we get a mental picture of what we want to accomplish, and then we follow through on our plans. If we're unhappy with the current direction of our lives, we can generate new mental images and goals, a process Covey calls rescripting. Creating personal and organizational mission statements is one way to identify the results we want and thus control the type of life we create. (I'll talk more about how to create a mission statement in the next section.) Covey urges leaders to center their lives on inner principles such as fairness and human dignity rather than on such external factors as family, money, friends, or work.

Habit 3. Put First Things First. A leader's time should be organized around priorities. Too many leaders spend their days coping with emergencies, mistakenly believing that urgent means important. Meetings, deadlines, and interruptions place immediate demands on their time, but other less pressing activities, such as relationship building and planning, are more important in the long run. Effective leaders carve out time for significant activities by identifying their most important roles, selecting their goals, creating schedules that enable them to reach their objectives, and modifying plans when necessary. They also know how to delegate tasks and have the courage to say no to requests that don't fit their priorities.

Habit 4. Think Win–Win. Those with a win–win perspective take a cooperative approach to communication, convinced that the best solution benefits both parties. The win–win habit is based on these dimensions: character (integrity, maturity, and a belief that the needs of everyone can be met); trusting relationships committed to mutual benefit; performance or partnership agreements that spell out conditions and responsibilities; organizational systems that fairly distribute rewards; and principled negotiation processes in which both sides generate possible solutions and then select the one that works best.

Habit 5. Seek First to Understand, Then to Be Understood. Ethical leaders put aside their personal concerns to engage in empathetic listening. They seek to understand, not to evaluate, advise, or interpret. Empathetic listening is an excellent way to build a trusting relationship. Covey uses the metaphor of the emotional bank account to illustrate how trust develops. Principled leaders make deposits in the emotional bank account by showing kindness and courtesy, keeping commitments, paying attention to small details, and seeking to understand. These strong relational reserves help prevent misunderstandings and make it easier to resolve any problems that do arise.

Habit 6. Synergize. Synergy creates a solution that is greater than the sum of its parts and uses right-brain thinking to generate a third, previously undiscovered alternative. Synergistic, creative solutions are generated in trusting relationships (those with high emotional bank accounts) where participants value their differences.

Habit 7. Sharpen the Saw. Sharpening the saw refers to continual renewal of the physical, mental, social or emotional, and spiritual dimensions of the self. Healthy leaders care for their bodies through exercise, good nutrition, and stress management. They encourage their mental development by reading good literature and writing thoughtful letters and journal entries. They create meaningful relationships with others and nurture their inner or spiritual values through study or meditation and time in nature. Continual renewal, combined with the use of the first six habits, creates an upward spiral of character improvement.

Developing Mission Statements

Developing a mission statement is the best way to keep the end or destination in mind. Leaders who cast light have a clear sense of what they hope to accomplish and seek to achieve worthwhile goals. For example, Abraham Lincoln was out to preserve the Union, Nelson Mandela wanted to abolish apartheid, Mother Teresa devoted her whole life to reducing suffering, and Eunice Shriver was determined to meet the needs of individuals who are mentally challenged.

Author and organizational consultant Laurie Beth Jones believes that useful mission statements are short (no more than a sentence long), easily understood and communicated, and committed to memory.[38] According to Jones, developing a personal mission statement begins with personal assessment. Take a close look at how your family has influenced your values and interests. Identify your strengths and determine what makes you unique (what Jones calls your "unique selling point"). Once you've isolated your gifts and unique features, examine your motivation. What situations make you excited or angry? Chances are, your mission will be related to the factors that arouse your passion or enthusiasm (teaching, writing, coaching, or selling, for example).

Jones outlines a three-part formula for constructing a mission statement. Start with the phrase "My mission is to" and record three action verbs that best describe what you want to do (e.g., *accomplish, build, finance, give, discuss*). Next, plug in a principle, value, or purpose that you could commit the rest of your life to (joy, service, faith, creativity, justice). Finish by identifying the group or cause that most excites you (real estate, design, sports, women's issues). Your final statement ought to inspire you and should direct all your activities, both on and off the job.

Leadership consultant Juana Bordas offers an alternative method or path for discovering personal leadership purpose based on Native American culture. Native Americans discovered their life purposes while on vision quests. Vision cairns guided members of some tribes. These stone piles served both as directional markers and as a reminder that others had passed this way before. Bordas identifies nine cairns or markers for creating personal purpose.[39]

Cairn 1: Call Your Purpose; Listen for Guidance. All of us have to be silent in order to listen to our intuition. Periodically you will need to withdraw from the noise of everyday life and reflect on such questions as "What am I meant to do?" and "How can I best serve?"

Cairn 2: Find a Sacred Place. A sacred place is a quiet place for reflection. It can be officially designated as sacred (e.g., a church or meditation garden) or merely a spot that encourages contemplation, such as a stream, park, or favorite chair.

Cairn 3: See Time as Continuous; Begin With the Child and Move With the Present. Our past has a great impact on where we'll head in the future. Patterns of behavior are likely to continue. Bordas suggests that you should examine the impact of your family composition, gender, geography, cultural background, and generational influences. A meaningful purpose will be anchored in the past but will remain responsive to current conditions such as diversity, globalization, and technological change.

Cairn 4: Identify Special Skills and Talents; Accept Imperfections. Take inventory by examining your major activities and jobs and evaluating your strengths. For example, how are your people skills? Technical knowledge? Communication abilities? Consider how you might further develop your aptitudes and abilities. Also take stock of your significant failures. What did they teach you about your limitations? What did you learn from them?

Cairn 5: Trust Your Intuition. Sometimes we need to act on our hunches and emotions. You may decide to turn down a job that doesn't feel right, for instance, in order to accept a position that seems to be a better fit.

Cairn 6: Open the Door When Opportunity Knocks. Be ready to respond to opportunities that are out of your control, such as a new job assignment or a request to speak or write. Ask yourself whether this possibility will better prepare you for leadership or fit in with what you're trying to do in life.

Cairn 7: Find Your Passion and Make It Happen. Passion energizes us for leadership and gives us stamina. Discover your passion by imagining the following scenarios: If you won the lottery, what would you still do? How would you spend your final 6 months on Earth? What would sustain you for a hundred more years?

Cairn 8: Write Your Life Story; Imagine a Great Leader. Turn your life into a story that combines elements of reality and fantasy. Imagine yourself as an effective leader and carry your story out into the future. What challenges did you overcome? What dreams did you fulfill? How did you reach your final destination?

Cairn 9: Honor Your Legacy, One Step at a Time. Your purpose is not static but will evolve and expand over time. If you're a new leader, you're likely to exert limited influence. That influence will expand as you develop your knowledge and skills. You may manage only a couple of people now, but in a few years you may be responsible for an entire department or division.

Identifying Values

If a mission statement identifies our final destination, then our values serve as a moral compass to guide us on our journey. Values provide a frame of reference, helping us to set priorities and to determine right or wrong. There are all sorts of values. For example, I value fuel economy (I like spending less on gas), so I drive a small, fuel-efficient pickup truck. However, ethical decision making is concerned primarily with identifying and implementing moral values. Moral values are directly related to judgments about what's appropriate or inappropriate behavior. I value honesty, for instance, so I choose not to lie. I value privacy, so I condemn Internet retailers who gather personal information about me without my permission.

There are two ways to identify or clarify the values you hold. You can generate a list from scratch or rate a list of values supplied by someone else. If brainstorming a list of important values seems a daunting task, you might try the following exercise, developed by James Kouzes and Barry Posner. The credo memo asks you to spell out the important values that underlie your philosophy of leadership.

> Imagine that your organization has afforded you the chance to take a six-month sabbatical, all expenses paid. You will be going to a beautiful island where the average temperature is about eighty degrees Fahrenheit during the day. The sun shines in a brilliant sky, with a few wisps of clouds. A gentle breeze cools the island down in the evening, and a light rain clears the air. You wake up in the morning to the smell of tropical flowers.

You may not take any work along on this sabbatical. And you will not be permitted to communicate to anyone at your office or plant—not by letter, phone, fax, e-mail, or other means. There will be just you, a few good books, some music, and your family or a friend.

But before you depart, those with whom you work need to know something. They need to know the principles that you believe should guide their actions in your absence. They need to understand the values and beliefs that you think should steer their decision making and action taking. You are permitted no long reports, however. Just a one-page memorandum.

If given this opportunity, what would you write on your one-page credo memo? Take out one piece of paper and write that memo.[40]

Examples of values that have been included in credo memos include "operate as a team," "listen to one another," "celebrate successes," "seize the initiative," "trust your judgment," and "strive for excellence." These values can be further clarified through dialogue with coworkers. Many discussions in organizations (e.g., how to select subcontractors, when to fire someone, how to balance the needs of various stakeholders) have an underlying value component. Listen for the principles that shape your opinions and the opinions of others.

Working with a list of values can also be useful. Psychologist Gordon Allport identified six major value types. People can be categorized based on how they organize their lives around each of the following value sets.[41] Prototypes are examples of occupations that fit best into a given value orientation.

- *Theoretical.* Theoretical people are intellectuals who seek to discover the truth and pride themselves on being objective and rational. Prototypes: research scientists, engineers.
- *Economic.* Usefulness is the most important criterion for those driven by economic values. They are interested in production, marketing, economics, and accumulating wealth. Prototype: small business owners.
- *Aesthetic.* Aesthetic thinkers value form and harmony. They enjoy each event as it unfolds, judging the experience based on its symmetry or harmony. Prototypes: artists, architects.
- *Social.* Love of others is the highest value for social leaders and followers. These "people persons" view others as ends, not means, and are kind and unselfish. Prototype: social workers.
- *Political.* Power drives political people. They want to accumulate and exercise power and enjoy the recognition that comes from being in positions of influence. Prototypes: senators, governors.
- *Religious.* Religious thinkers seek unity through understanding and relating to the cosmos as a whole. Prototypes: pastors, rabbis, Muslim clerics.

Identifying your primary value orientation is a good way to avoid situations that could cause you ethical discomfort. If you have an economic bent, you will want a job (often in a business setting) where you solve real-life problems. On the other hand, if you love people, you may be uncomfortable working for a business that puts profits first.

Some well-meaning writers and consultants make values the end-all of ethical decision making. They assume that groups will prosper if they develop a set of lofty, mutually shared values. However, having worthy values doesn't mean that individuals, groups, or organizations will live by these principles. Other factors—time pressures, faulty assumptions, corrupt systems—undermine their influence. Values, though critical, have to be translated into action. Furthermore, our greatest struggles come from choosing between two good values. Many corporate leaders value both customer service and product quality, but what do they do when reaching one of these goals means sacrificing the other? Pushing to get a product shipped to satisfy a customer may force the manufacturing division into cutting corners in order to meet the deadline. Resolving dilemmas such as these takes more than value clarification; we also need some standards for determining ethical priorities. With that in mind, I'll identify ethical decision-making principles in Chapters 5 and 6. But first we need to confront one final shadow caster—evil—in Chapter 4.

Implications and Applications

- Character is integral to effective leadership, often making the difference between success and failure.
- Virtues are positive leadership qualities or traits that help us manage our shadow sides.
- Important virtues to develop as a leader include courage (overcoming fear in order to do the right thing), prudence (practical wisdom), optimism (expectation of positive outcomes in the future), integrity (wholeness, completeness, consistency), humility (self-awareness, openness, a sense of transcendence), reverence (a sense of awe, respect, and shame), compassion (kindness, generosity, love), and justice (obligation to the common good; treating others equally and fairly).
- Strive for consistency but don't be surprised by contradictions in your character or in the character of others. Become more tolerant of yourself and other leaders. At the same time, recognize that a leader's private behavior often influences his or her public decisions.
- Indirect approaches that build character include identifying role models, telling and living out shared stories, learning from hardship, cultivating habits, creating a personal mission statement, and clarifying values.
- Never underestimate the power of a good example. Be on the lookout for real and fictional ethical role models.

- Shared narratives nurture character development, encouraging you to live up to the role you play in the collective story.
- Hardships are an inevitable part of life and leadership. The sense of loss associated with these events can provide important feedback, spur self-inspection, encourage the development of coping strategies, force you to reorder your priorities, and nurture your compassion. However, to benefit from them you must see challenges as learning opportunities that prepare you for future leadership responsibilities.
- Adopting habits can speed the development of character. Seek to be proactive, begin with the end in mind, organize around priorities, strive for cooperation, listen for understanding, develop synergistic solutions, and engage in continual self-renewal.
- Having an ultimate destination will encourage you to stay on your ethical track. Develop a personal mission statement that reflects your strengths and passions. Use your values as a moral compass to keep you from losing your way.

For Further Exploration, Challenge, and Self-Assessment

1. Which virtue is most important for leaders? Defend your choice.

2. Can the private and public morals of leaders be separated? Try to reach a consensus on this question in a group.

3. What steps can you take to develop a more positive outlook about future events?

4. Brainstorm a list of moral exemplars. What does it take to qualify for your list? How would you classify these role models according to the types described in the chapter?

5. Reflect on the ways in which a particular shared narrative has shaped your worldview and behavior. Write up your conclusions.

6. Interview a leader you admire. Determine his or her crucible moment and capacity to learn from that experience.

7. Rate yourself on each of the seven habits of effective people and develop a plan for addressing your weaknesses. Explore the habits further through reading and training seminars.

8. Develop a personal mission statement using the guidelines provided by Jones or Bordas.

9. Complete the credo memo exercise on page 104 if you haven't already done so. Encourage others in your work group or organization to do the same and compare your statements. Use this as an opportunity to dialogue about values.

CASE STUDY 3.2

THE GREATEST REFORMER IN HISTORY

Finding a moral exemplar who has had more impact than English politician and philanthropist William Wilberforce (1759–1833) would be hard to
do. The son of a wealthy merchant, Wilberforce spent his entire career as a
member of the British parliament. There he labored tirelessly for the abolition of slavery and the reformation of British society. His efforts paid off.
During his lifetime, Britain abolished slaveholding throughout the empire.
Few in England tried to help the poor and suffering before Wilberforce.
Under his direction, hundreds of groups sprung up to deal with social ills
such as child labor, prisoner abuse, orphanhood, and cruelty to animals.
(Wilberforce belonged to 69 such groups himself.) Great Britain developed
a social conscience where none had existed before. Americans Thomas
Jefferson, Abraham Lincoln, Harriet Beecher Stowe, Henry David Thoreau,
and John Greenleaf Whittier looked to him for inspiration. In recognition of
his impact, Wilberforce has been called the "greatest social reformer of the
history of the world."[1]

Wilberforce was an unlikely candidate to become a reformer. His parents
went to great lengths to keep him from the clutches of religion and encouraged him to adopt an extravagant lifestyle instead, one filled with trips to
the theater, elegant balls, and card parties. He wasted much of his college
career drinking and partying. When he first came to Parliament, he focused
solely on the interests of his district and was known to use his wit and sarcasm to belittle his opponents. Then Wilberforce underwent a gradual religious conversion he called "the Great Change." After this change, he
wanted to drop out of politics but was dissuaded by close friend William
Pitt, who was to become prime minister. At age 27, Wilberforce decided to
take on the major missions or goals of his life: the abolition of the slave
trade (and of slavery) and the "reformation of manners" (morals). He then
put his superior intelligence and eloquence (he was considered one of the
greatest orators of his day) to work in pursuit of these objectives.

Wilberforce had to overcome great odds to reach his goals, beginning
with his physical condition. Short of stature (5-foot-3), he suffered ulcerative
colitis throughout his life. This condition nearly killed him on several occasions, and he treated it with daily doses of morphine. Wilberforce's antislav-
ery efforts met with stiff resistance from powerful merchants and politicians.
He was mocked by opponents and in the popular press. Captains of slave
ships threatened him with violence and death. Every year he introduced
legislation to ban the slave trade, which cost the lives of hundreds of slaves

who died en route to the West Indies. Every year he was defeated. It took 20 years to get the slave trade banned and another 26 years after that (within a few days of his death) to abolish slaveholding. Wilberforce's campaign to improve the lot of the poor had to overcome apathy on the part of the middle and upper classes, who felt no obligation to care for the less fortunate.

Wilberforce was sustained in his long battle for social justice by his religious faith and by his friends and fellow reformers. He took his inspiration from Christian scripture and regularly renewed his faith through private study and worship. (Wilberforce was also an avid reader of philosophy and almost any other literature he could get his hands on.) He had a large circle of friends who visited him regularly. Wilberforce and other like-minded people formed the Clapham Circle, a group that met together to share ideas and strategies for social change. Pastor Thomas Clarkson, politician Granville Sharp, John Newton (writer of the hymn "Amazing Grace"), and poet William Cowper worked with him in the campaign to abolish slavery.

By the end of his life, many of those who had opposed Wilberforce joined with him. His character won many over. Not only was he cheerful and compassionate, giving as much as one fourth of his income away some years, he was also extremely humble. Wilberforce turned down the chance to become a British lord and was uncomfortable with celebrity and acclaim. When one friend praised him for his generosity, he replied, "With regard to myself, I have nothing whatsoever to urge, but the poor publican's plea, 'God be merciful to me a sinner.'"[2] Wilberforce was gentle in his dealings, choosing first to look for the good in others (even slave traders and owners) to see whether he could establish common ground. He tried to mix mercy with grace. For instance, he agreed to plans to reimburse slave owners in the West Indies even though other abolitionists believed that doing so could be seen as a reward for their bad behavior.

All the members of Parliament, the Duke of Wellington, and huge crowds attended Wilberforce's funeral. Though a commoner, he was buried with royalty in Westminster Abbey. African freemen in the United States honored his memory by wearing a badge of mourning for 30 days. In a public eulogy for Wilberforce delivered in New York City, African American Benjamin Hughes described him as "the Philanthropist" and "the Hercules of Abolition."

Discussion Probes

1. What do you learn from the example of William Wilberforce?

2. What steps can you take to follow his example?

(Continued)

(Continued)

3. What does Wilberforce have in common with other moral exemplars?

4. Do you think Wilberforce was the "greatest social reformer in history"? Whom would you nominate for this honor?

5. What leadership ethics lessons do you take from this case?

Notes

1. Metaxas, E. (2007). *Amazing grace: William Wilberforce and the heroic campaign to end slavery.* San Francisco: Harper San Francisco, p. xvii.
2. Metaxas, p. 273.

Sources

Belmonte, K. (2007). *William Wilberforce: A hero for humanity.* Grand Rapids, MI: Zondervan.

Metaxas, E. (2007). *Amazing grace: William Wilberforce and the heroic campaign to end slavery.* San Francisco: Harper San Francisco.

CASE STUDY 3.3

LEADING WITH A BLINK OF THE LEFT EYE

Jean-Dominique Bauby lived a charmed life. The 43-year-old editor of the French fashion magazine *Elle* moved in the highest levels of society, attended fashion shoots, dined at the best restaurants, drove fine automobiles, traveled extensively, attracted the attention of beautiful women, and was the doting father of two children. All that changed in December 1995 when Bauby (nicknamed Jean-Do by his friends) had a massive stroke. After 20 days of intensive treatment he awoke in a hospital to find out that he suffered from "locked-in syndrome." In this rare condition, the mind remains healthy but is locked into a body that no longer works. Bauby could only move his neck and communicate by blinking his left eye (the other was sewn shut). He was fed through an intravenous tube, and this once active, proud, handsome, and highly independent man was reduced to a drooling shadow of his former self, totally dependent on others. This is how Jean-Dominique describes what he saw when he noticed his reflection in a glass case:

> Reflected in the glass I saw the head of a man who seemed to have emerged from a vat of formaldehyde. His mouth was twisted, his nose

damaged, his hair tousled, his gaze full of fear. One eye was sewn shut, the other goggled like the doomed eye of Cain. For a moment I stared at that dilated pupil, before I realized it was only mine.

Whereupon a strange euphoria came over me. Not only was I exiled, paralyzed, mute, half deaf, deprived of all pleasures, and reduced to the existence of a jellyfish, but I was also horrible to behold. (p. 25)

A speech therapist introduced Bauby to an alphabet based on frequency of usage (the letters *E*, *S*, and *A* appear first in this system). Each letter was given a number (*E* = 1, *S* = 2, *A* = 3), and Bauby would blink the assigned number of times to select the letters he wanted to use. He employed this system to construct words and sentences when conversing with visitors and to create letters he mass mailed to friends and acquaintances. Later, with the help of a book editor, Bauby went on to write his memoir. He would wake early in the morning, mentally compose and rehearse what he wanted to say, and then blink out the text when the editor arrived. (The project took an estimated 200,000 blinks to complete.)

Bauby titled his work *The Diving Bell and the Butterfly.* The diving bell describes the feeling of being shut up in his body, and the butterfly refers to his imagination. Bauby's imagination set him free to sample delicious meals, to travel to distant locations, and to move back and forth in time despite all of his physical limitations. He was motivated to write about his experience, in part, because of reports that gossips in Paris called him a "total vegetable," relegating him to "a vegetable stall and not to the human race." Bauby concluded, "I would have to rely on myself if I wanted to prove that my IQ was still higher than a turnip's" (p. 82).

The former editor's testament reveals a man who had been deepened by his tragic circumstances. Bauby, as many observers have noted, was far from a saint before his stroke. Quick-tempered, he had a number of mistresses and left the mother of his children to live with a fellow journalist. He speaks of his regrets and admits that he was ashamed of "playing at being editor in chief in the frothy world of fashion magazines" when a journalistic colleague was held hostage for several years in the Middle East. He makes peace with his current condition, however, noting, "I have indeed begun a new life, and life is here, in this bed, that wheelchair, and those corridors. Nowhere else" (p. 129).

Bauby died of heart failure caused by pneumonia just two days after his book was released and 10 years before the film based on his memoir brought

(Continued)

(Continued)

his story to the attention of a wider international audience. Millions have been moved by his experience. The stricken editor demonstrated that it is possible to lead with the blink of an eye. He provided insight into the inner lives of those who are locked into their bodies and helped the rest of us better meet their needs. A month before he died he established the Association for Locked-in Syndrome to help patients and their families deal with this condition and search for a cure. This society reflects the hope found in the final words of Jean-Dominique's memoir: "Does the cosmos contain keys for opening up my diving bell? A subway line with no terminus? A currency strong enough to buy my freedom back? We must keep looking" (p. 132).

Discussion Probes

1. What virtues does Bauby demonstrate?

2. What do you think Bauby learned from undergoing this personal tragedy?

3. What do you learn from his example?

4. What other leaders have undergone significant hardships that have helped them become more ethical and effective?

5. What leadership ethics lessons do you take from this case?

Note

All quotations come from Bauby, J.-D. (1997). *The diving bell and the butterfly: A memoir of life in death.* New York: Vintage Books.

Sources

Mallon, T. (1997, June 15). *In the blink of an eye.* Retrieved from http://www.nytimes.com/books/97/06/15/reviews/970615.mallon.html

Swardson, A. (2007, March 11). A tale of courage, told in a blink of an eye. *The Washington Post,* p. A01.

Webster, P. (1997, March 7). Memoir unlocks medical enigma. *The Guardian,* p. 15.

Notes

1. Johannesen, R. L. (2002). *Ethics in human communication* (5th ed.). Prospect Heights, IL: Waveland, Ch. 1.

2. Snyder, C. R., & Lopez, S. J. (2005). *Handbook of positive psychology.* Oxford, UK: Oxford University Press; Aspinwall, L. G., & Staudinger, U. M. (Eds.). (2002). *A psychology of human strengths: Fundamental questions about future directions for a positive psychology.* Washington, DC: American Psychological Association.

3. Johannesen, R. L. (1991). Virtue ethics, character, and political communication. In R. E. Denton (Ed.), *Ethical dimensions of political communication* (pp. 69–90). New York: Praeger; Annas, J. (2006). Virtue ethics. In D. Copp (Ed.), *The Oxford handbook of ethical theory* (pp. 515–536). Oxford: Oxford University Press; Timmons, M. (2002). *Moral theory: An introduction.* Lanham, MD: Rowman & Littlefield.

4. Peterson, C., & Seligman, M. E. P. (2004). *Character strengths and virtues: A handbook and classification.* Oxford, UK: Oxford University Press; Comte-Sponville, A. (2001). *A small treatise on the great virtues: The uses of philosophy in everyday life.* New York: Metropolitan.

5. Kidder, R. M. (2005). *Moral courage.* New York: William Morrow.

6. Kolp, A., & Rea, P. (2006). *Leading with integrity: Character-based leadership.* Cincinnati, OH: AtomicDog; Comte-Sponville.

7. Carver, C. S., & Scheier, M. F. (2005). Optimism. In C. R. Snyder & S. J. Lopez (Eds.), *Handbook of positive psychology* (pp. 231–243). Oxford, UK: Oxford University Press.

8. See Bruhn, J. G. (2001). *Trust and the health of organizations.* New York: Kluwer/Plenum; Elangovan, A. R., & Shapiro, D. L. (1998). Betrayal of trust in organizations. *Academy of Management Review, 23,* 547–566.

9. See Dirks, K. T. (1999). The effects of interpersonal trust on work group performance. *Journal of Applied Psychology, 84,* 445–455; Kramer, R. M., & Tyler, T. L. (1996). *Trust in organizations: Frontiers of theory and research.* Thousand Oaks, CA: Sage.

10. Crosariol, B. (2005, November 21). The diminishing allure of rock-star executives. *The Globe and Mail,* p. B12; Varachaver, N. (2004, November 15). Glamour! Fame! Org charts! *Fortune,* pp. 76-85.

11. Morris, J. A., Brotheridge, C. M., & Urbanski, J. C. (2005). Bringing humility to leadership: Antecedents and consequences of leader humility. *Human Relations,* pp. 1323–1350. See also Tangney, J. P. (2000). Humility: Theoretical perspectives, empirical findings and directions for future research. *Journal of Social and Clinical Psychology, 19,* 70–82.

12. Woodruff, P. (2001). *Reverence: Renewing a forgotten virtue.* Oxford, UK: Oxford University Press.

13. Peterson & Seligman.

14. Howell, J., & Avolio, B. J. (1992). The ethics of charismatic leadership: Submission or liberation? *Academy of Management Executive, 6,* 43–54.

15. Smith, J. Y. (2009, August 12). The Olympian force behind a revolution. *The Washington Post,* p. A07; Hodgson, G. (2009, August 12). Eunice Kennedy Shriver; Mental health campaigner who founded the Special Olympics. *The Independent,* Obituaries, p. 26.

16. Peterson & Seligman; Comte-Sponville; Smith, T. (1999). Justice as a personal virtue. *Social Theory & Practice, 25,* 361–384; Solomon, R. C. (1990). *A passion for justice: Emotions and the origins of the social contract.* Reading, MA: Addison-Wesley.

17. Blasi, A. (1984). Moral identity: Its role in moral functioning. In W. M. Kurtines & J. L. Gewirtz (Eds.), *Morality, moral behavior, and moral development* (pp. 128–139). New York: Wiley.

18. Jennings, M. M. (2006). *The seven signs of ethical collapse: How to spot moral meltdowns in companies . . . before it's too late.* New York: St. Martin's Press.

19. Wayne, L. (2005, March 8). Boeing chief is ousted after admitting affair. *The New York Times,* p. A1.

20. Devine, T., Seuk, J. H., & Wilson, A. (2001). *Cultivating heart and character: Educating for life's most essential goals.* Chapel Hill, NC: Character Development Publishing.

21. Tangney; Carver & Scheier; Cavanagh, G. F., & Moberg, D. J. (1999). The virtue of courage within the organization. In M. L. Pava & P. Primeaux (Eds.), *Research in ethical issues in organizations* (Vol. 1, pp. 1–25). Stamford, CT: JAI Press.

22. MacIntyre, A. (1984). *After virtue: A study in moral theory* (2nd ed.). Notre Dame, IN: University of Notre Dame Press; Hauerwas, S. (1981). *A community of character.* Notre Dame, IN: University of Notre Dame Press.

23. McFaddon, R. D. (2009, January 16). All 155 aboard safe as crippled jet crash-lands in Hudson. *The New York Times,* p. A1; Rivera, R. (2009, January 17). In a split second, a pilot becomes a hero years in the making. *The New York Times,* p. A21.

24. Hart, D. K. (1992). The moral exemplar in an organizational society. In T. L. Cooper & N. D. Wright (Eds.), *Exemplary public administrators: Character and leadership in government* (pp. 9–29). San Francisco: Jossey-Bass.

25. Hallie, P. (1979). *Lest innocent blood be shed: The story of the village of Le Chambon and how goodness happened there.* New York: Harper & Row.

26. Colby, A., & Damon, W. (1992). *Some do care: Contemporary lives of moral commitment.* New York: Free Press; Colby, A., & Damon, W. (1995). The development of extraordinary moral commitment. In M. Killen & D. Hart (Eds.), *Morality in everyday life: Developmental perspectives* (pp. 342–369). Cambridge, UK: Cambridge University Press.

27. Colby & Damon (1995), p. 363.

28. Burns, J. M. (2003). *Transforming leadership: A new pursuit of happiness.* New York: Atlantic Monthly Press, Ch. 5.

29. MacIntyre, p. 216.

30. Lisman, C. D. (1996). *The curricular integration of ethics: Theory and practice*. Westport, CT: Praeger.

31. Lisman's arguments are echoed by Goldberg, M. (1997). Doesn't anybody read the Bible anymo'? In O. F. Williams (Ed.), *The moral imagination: How literature and films can stimulate ethical reflection in the business world* (pp. 19–32). Notre Dame, IN: Notre Dame Press; Ellenwood, S. (2006). Revisiting character education: From McGuffey to narratives. *Journal of Education, 187,* 21–43.

32. Moxley, R. S., & Pulley, M. L. (2004). Hardships. In C. D. McCauley & E. Van Velsor (Eds.), *The Center for Creative Leadership handbook of leadership development* (2nd ed., pp. 183–203). San Francisco: Jossey-Bass.

33. Bennis, W. G., & Thomas, R. J. (2002). *Geeks and geezers: How era, values, and defining moments shape leaders*. Boston: Harvard Business School Press.

34. Dotlich, D. L., Noel, J. L., & Walker, N. (2008). Learning for leadership: Failure as a second chance. In J. Gallos (Ed.), *Business leadership* (2nd ed., pp. 478–485). San Francisco: Jossey-Bass.

35. Aristotle. (350 B.C.E./1962). *Nichomachean ethics* (Martin Ostwald, Trans.). Indianapolis, IN: Bobbs-Merrill.

36. Cavanagh, G. F., & Moberg, D. J. (1999). The virtue of courage within the organization. In M. L. Pava & P. Primeaux (Eds.), *Research in ethical issues in organizations* (Vol. 1, pp. 1–25). Stamford, CT: JAI Press.

37. Covey, S. (1989). *The seven habits of highly effective people*. New York: Simon & Schuster.

38. Jones, L. B. (1996). *The path: Creating your mission statement for work and for life*. New York: Hyperion.

39. Bordas, J. (1995). Becoming a servant-leader: The personal development path. In L. Spears (Ed.), *Reflections on leadership* (pp. 149–160). New York: Wiley.

40. Kouzes, J. M., & Posner, B. Z. (2003). *Credibility: How leaders gain and lose it, why people demand it*. San Francisco: Jossey-Bass, pp. 62–63. Used by permission of the publisher.

41. Allport, G. (1961). *Pattern and growth in personality*. New York: Holt, Rinehart & Winston; Guth, W. D., & Tagiuri, R. (1965, September–October). Personal values and corporate strategy. *Harvard Business Review*, pp. 123–132.

4

Combating Evil

Evil, in whatever intellectual framework, is by definition a monster.

—Essayist Lance Morrow

Without forgiveness there is no future.

—South African Archbishop Desmond Tutu

WHAT'S AHEAD

In this chapter, we wrestle with the most dangerous of all unhealthy motivations: evil. The first section surveys some of the forms or faces of evil. The second section examines the role of forgiveness in breaking cycles of evil. The third section probes the relationship between spirituality and leadership, highlighting how spiritual practices can equip us to deal with evil and foster more ethical, productive workplaces.

The Faces of Evil

The attacks on the World Trade Center, Madrid commuter trains, and the London Underground; the systematic rape of thousands of women in the

117

Congo; suicide bombings and prisoner abuse (see "Leadership Ethics at the Movies: *Taxi to the Dark Side*") in the Middle East; and genocide in Darfur (see Case Study 4.1) have heightened national and international awareness of the existence of evil. While recognizing the presence of evil is an important first step, we can't combat this powerful force until we first understand our opponent. Contemporary Western definitions of evil emphasize its destructiveness.[1] Evil inflicts pain and suffering, deprives innocent people of their humanity, and creates feelings of hopelessness and despair. Evildoers do excessive harm, going well beyond what is needed to achieve their objectives. The ultimate product of evil is death. Evil destroys self-esteem, physical and emotional well-being, relationships, communities, and nations.

We can gain some important insights into the nature of evil by looking at the various forms or faces it displays. In this section, I'll introduce six perspectives on evil and then talk about how each approach can help us better deal with this powerful, destructive force.

CASE STUDY 4.1

RESPONDING TO THE REMNANTS OF GENOCIDE

Darfur is a barren, mountainous region in western Sudan, which is south of the Sahara. Arabs (largely nomads) and Black villagers (some of whom are also Muslim) generally lived in peace until non-Arab tribes joined together to rebel against the Sudanese government in 2003. Sudanese authorities in the capital of Khartoum retaliated by arming militias—the Janjaweed—and turning them loose to empty the region of African civilians. The Janjaweed, equipped with machine guns and rocket-propelled grenades, overwhelmed local patrols armed with bows and arrows and spears. They then engaged in an orgy of rape, killing, and looting, leaving nothing but corpses and smoldering ashes in their wake. Between 300,000 and 400,000 people died in the region, and 3 million fled to refugee camps. The number of deaths dropped dramatically after six years, not due to the intervention of world governments, but largely because there were so few civilians left to murder. "Remnants of genocide" remain, however, as displaced Sudanese struggle to survive and rival Arab militias and rebel groups battle one another. At the same time, civil war in southern Sudan (ended through a peace settlement) threatens to reignite.

The humanitarian crisis in Darfur sparked a massive relief effort. Ten thousand aid workers from the United Nations and 13 other humanitarian groups, including Doctors Without Borders, Oxfam, and Save the Children, supplied food, water, medical care, and other services to the refugee camps. But when the International Criminal Court (ICC) indicted Sudanese President Omar Hassan al-Bashir of war crimes, al-Bashir ordered all international aid groups except the United Nations out of the country. (United Nations aid workers remained but were threatened with expulsion.) Death rates due to malnutrition, meningitis, and contaminated water rose immediately after the relief agencies departed.

Al-Bashir's indictment (the first to be brought against a sitting head of state) pitted human rights and humanitarian groups against one another. One side wanted to vigorously pursue al-Bashir's conviction, fearing that failure to do so would undermine the ICC and allow the architect of the genocide to remain free. On the other side were those who feared that pressing legal action would make the crisis in Darfur worse and threaten the lives of hundreds of thousands of refugees. They argued that humanitarian concerns should take priority over justice. Said one Darfur advocate, "Who are we to say that Darfuris must pay the price of international justice?"[1]

Members of the Obama administration also debated whether to take a tough or softer approach to Sudan, finally settling on the latter. Instead of pushing for al-Bashir's conviction and implementing a no-fly zone over the country, federal officials decided to try a mix of incentives (e.g., reducing sanctions), pressure, and direct negotiation. They noted that the country was no longer a haven for al-Qaida and other terrorists and that they did not want to endanger the peace agreement between Khartoum and rebels in southern Sudan. Officials hoped that a friendlier approach, along with the diplomatic efforts of nations like France and Egypt, would convince al-Bashir to let humanitarian workers return and set the stage for disarming militias and returning displaced persons to their homes. Of course, this strategy requires dealing directly with the regime behind the mass murders. U.S. ambassador to the United Nations Susan Rice argued that engagement with al-Bashir and other Sudanese officials should be seen not as a reward but as the only way to bring peace and security to the region. U.S. special Sudan envoy General Scott Gration defended the government's new policy by quoting an old African proverb. "If you want to go fast, go alone. If you want to go far, you have to go with someone. We want to go far and to do that we are going to have to go with Khartoum."[2]

(Continued)

(Continued)

Discussion Probes

1. Should humanitarian concerns take priority over justice in Darfur? Why or why not?

2. What are the dangers of delaying prosecution of al-Bashir?

3. Did the U.S. government make the right choice in deciding to take a softer approach to the Sudanese government?

4. Do you think that the United States and other governments will restore peace and security ("go far") by working directly with the government of Sudan?

5. Is it ethical to engage in direct negotiations with evil leaders? Why or why not?

6. What leadership ethics lessons do you take from this case?

Notes

1. Sudan; be tough on Al-Bashir, activists tell Obama. (2009, September 14). *Africa News*.

2. Thompson, G. (2009, October 18). Sudan's critics relieved that Obama chose a middle course. *The New York Times*, p. A10.

Sources

Addario, L., & Polgreen, L. (2009, March 23). In aid groups' expulsion, fears of more misery engulfing Darfur. *The New York Times*, p. A6.

Baker, P. (2009, March 18). Adding pressure to Sudan, Obama will tap retired general as special envoy. *The New York Times*, p. A6.

Gettleman, J. (2007, September 3). Chaos in Darfur on rise as Arabs fight with Arabs. *The New York Times*, p. A1.

Hoge, W. (2007, September 7). Sudan officials and rebels to discuss peace in Darfur. *The New York Times*, p. A12.

Leader of Darfur peacekeeping mission resigns. (2009, August 26). *The New York Times*, p. A10.

MacFarquhar, N. (2009, August 28). As Darfur fighting diminishes, U.N. officials focus on the south of Sudan. *The New York Times*, p. A4.

Perry, A. (2007, March 19). A war without end gets worse. *Time*.

Perry, A. (2007, May 7). How to prevent the next Darfur. *Time*.

Petrou, M., & Savage, L. (2006, December 11). Genocide in slow motion. *Maclean's*, pp. 35–41.

Reeves, E. (2007, Summer). Genocide without end? The destruction of Darfur. *Dissent*, pp. 9–13.
Sudan; be tough on Al-Bashir, activists tell Obama. (2009, September 14). *Africa News*.
Thompson, G. (2009, October 18). Sudan's critics relieved that Obama chose a middle course. *The New York Times*, p. A10.

Evil as Dreadful Pleasure

University of Maryland political science professor C. Fred Alford defines evil as a combination of dread and pleasure. Alford recruited 60 respondents from a variety of ages and backgrounds to talk about their experiences with evil. He discovered that people experience evil as a deep sense of uneasiness, "the dread of being human, vulnerable, alone in the universe and doomed to die."[2] They do evil when, instead of coming to grips with their inner darkness, they try to get rid of it by making others feel "dreadful." Inflicting this pain is enjoyable. Part of the pleasure comes from being in charge, of being the victimizer instead of the victim.

Evil can also be a product of chronic boredom.[3] Boredom arises when people lose their sense of meaning and purpose. They no longer enjoy life and try to fill the emptiness they feel inside. Ordinary distractions such as television, movies, surfing the Internet, shopping, and sports don't fill the void, so people turn to evil instead. Evil is an attractive alternative because it engages the full energy and attention of perpetrators. For example, a serial killer has to plan his crimes, locate victims, keep his actions secret, and outsmart law enforcement.

Evil as Deception

Psychiatrist Scott Peck identifies evil as a form of narcissism or self-absorption.[4] Mentally healthy adults submit themselves to something beyond themselves, such as God or love or excellence. Submission to a greater power encourages them to obey their consciences. Evil people, on the other hand, refuse to submit and try to control others instead. They consider themselves above reproach and project their shortcomings, attacking anyone who threatens their self-concepts. Evil people are consumed with keeping up appearances. Peck calls them "the people of the lie" because they deceive themselves and others in hopes of projecting a righteous image. Peck believes that truly evil people are more likely to live in our neighborhoods than in our jails. They generally hide their true natures and appear to be normal and successful. Inmates, on the other hand, land in prison because they've been morally inconsistent or stupid.

LEADERSHIP ETHICS AT THE MOVIES

TAXI TO THE DARK SIDE

Key Cast Members: Alex Gibney (narrator), Moazzam Begg, Donald Rumsfeld, Dick Cheney, Tim Golden, John McCain, Lawrence Wilkerson, military jailers

Synopsis: This Oscar-winning documentary examines the torture policies of the Bush administration in Afghanistan, at Guantánamo Bay, and in Iraq following the September 11 attacks. In 2002 a young taxi driver was falsely accused of terrorist activities and sent to Bagram Air Base in Afghanistan. Three days later he died from injuries inflicted by American military police and interrogators. The driver was a victim, not only of his jailers, but also of policy set at the highest levels of the U.S. government. The president, vice president, defense secretary, and other federal officials sanctioned sleep deprivation, waterboarding, stress positions, and other "enhanced" interrogation methods that violated international law. Many of the victims of these tactics were falsely imprisoned. Much of the information gleaned through torture and sexual humiliation turned out to be false, as prisoners told their captors what they wanted to hear in hopes of avoiding further suffering.

Rating: R for extremely graphic images of torture and sexual humiliation

Themes: sanctioned evil, dehumanization, evil as ordinary, cycle of evil

Discussion Starters

1. Which of the faces of evil do you see in this story?

2. Was the use of torture justified after the September 11 attacks? Is it ever justified?

3. Who was most to blame for the prisoner abuse—the jailers or the high-level leaders who sanctioned the use of severe interrogation methods?

Evil as Bureaucracy

The 20th century was the bloodiest period in history. More than 100 million people died as the direct or indirect result of wars, genocide, and other violence. According to public administration professors Guy Adams and Danny Balfour, the combination of science and technology made the 1900s so destructive.[5] Scientific and technological developments (tanks, airplanes, chemical warfare, nuclear weapons) made killing highly efficient. At the same time, belief in technological progress encouraged government officials to take a rational approach to problems. The integration of these factors produced administrative evil. In administrative evil, organizational members commit heinous crimes while carrying out their daily tasks. Balfour and Adams argue that the true nature of administrative evil is masked or hidden from participants. Officials are rarely asked to engage in evil; instead they inflict pain and suffering while fulfilling their job responsibilities.

The Holocaust provides the most vivid example of administrative evil in action. Extermination camps in Germany would not have been possible without the willing cooperation of thousands of civil servants engaged in such functions as collecting taxes, running municipal governments, and managing the country's social security system. These duties may seem morally neutral, but in carrying them out public officials condemned millions to death. Government authorities defined who was undesirable and then seized their assets. Administrators managed the ghettos, built concentration camp latrines, and employed slave labor. Even the railway authority did its part. The Gestapo had to pay for each prisoner shipped by rail to the death camps. Railroad officials billed the SS at third-class passenger rates (one way) for adult prisoners, with discounts for children. Guards were charged round-trip fares.

Evil as Sanctioned Destruction

Social scientists Nevitt Sanford and Craig Comstock believe that widespread evil occurs when victimizers are given permission or sanction to attack groups that have been devalued or dehumanized.[6] Such permission opens the door for such crimes as mass murder and genocide. Sanctions can be overt (a direct statement or order) or disguised (a hint, praise for others engaging in aggressive behavior). Once given, sanctions open the door to oppression because targeted groups no longer enjoy the protections given to the rest of society. American history is filled with examples of devalued peoples. Native Americans were targeted for extinction; African Americans were routinely lynched for, among other reasons, public entertainment; and Chinese laborers were denied citizenship. Recently the entire U.S. population has become the target of dehumanization. Some Muslims consider the United States to be the "Great Satan," populated by infidels. Such reasoning accounts for the spontaneous celebrations that broke out on the streets of some Islamic nations on news of the 9/11 attacks. (Of course, far too many Americans were quick to label all Muslims as "terrorists.")

Evil as a Choice

Any discussion of good and evil must consider the role of human choice. Just how much freedom we have is a matter of debate, but a number of scholars argue that we become good or evil through a series of small, incremental decisions. In other words, we never remain neutral but are moving toward one pole or another. Medieval scholar C. S. Lewis draws on the image of a road to illustrate this point.[7] On a journey, we decide which direction to take every time we come to a fork in the road. We face a similar series of decisions throughout our lives. We can't correct poor decisions by continuing on but must go back to the fork and take the other path.

Psychologist Erich Fromm makes the same argument as Lewis. Only those who are very good or very bad do not have a choice; the rest of us do. However, each choice we make reduces our options.

> Each step in life which increases my self-confidence, my integrity, my courage, my conviction also increases my capacity to choose the desirable alternative, until eventually it becomes more difficult to choose the undesirable rather than the desirable action. On the other hand, each act of surrender and cowardice weakens me, opens the path for more acts of surrender, and eventually freedom is lost. Between the extreme when I can no longer do a wrong act and the other extreme when I have lost my freedom to right action, there are innumerable degrees of freedom of choice. In the practice of life the degree of freedom to choose is different at any given moment. If the degree of freedom to choose the good is great, it needs less effort to choose the good. If it is small, it takes a great effort, help from others, and favorable circumstances.[8]

Fromm uses the story of Israel's exodus from ancient Egypt to illustrate what happens when leaders make a series of evil choices. Moses repeatedly asks Pharaoh to let his people go, but the Egyptian ruler turns down every request. Eventually the king's heart is "hardened," and he and his army are destroyed.

Evil as Ordinary

The evil-as-ordinary perspective focuses on the situational factors that cause otherwise ordinary or normal people to become evildoers. Although it is comforting to think that evildoers must be heartless psychopaths or deranged killers, in many cases perpetrators look and act a lot like the rest of us. Social philosopher Hannah Arendt pointed this out in her analysis of the trial of Adolf Eichmann in 1961.[9] Eichmann was responsible for deportation of millions of Jews to concentration and extermination camps. What struck Arendt was how ordinary Eichmann seemed. Half of a dozen psychiatrists examined him and certified him as "normal." Arendt used the phrase the "banality of evil" when describing Eichmann to point out that the sources of evil are not mysterious or demonic but commonplace. If that is the case, then any one of us can commit heinous crimes. The Rwandan genocide supports Arendt's thesis. Thousands of ordinary Rwandan Hutus literally went next door or across the street to hack and beat their Tutsi neighbors to death with machetes and other farm implements. Interviews with one group of young killers revealed a chilling routine. They would have a hearty breakfast (running down Tutsis took a lot of energy), meet at the soccer field to get their assignments to kill or loot, march off singing, find and murder victims until the final whistle blew, and then relax with beer and food after a hard day's work.[10]

Philip Zimbardo and other social psychologists have identified a number of situational factors that can turn otherwise "nice" people into torturers and murderers.[11] Zimbardo discovered firsthand the power of the system to promote unethical behavior through his famous Stanford Prison Experiment. He created a mock prison in the basement of the psychology department and randomly assigned student volunteers to roles as prisoners and guards. It didn't take long for both groups to get caught up in their roles. Soon the prisoners revolted and the guards retaliated. The jailers strip-searched prisoners, forced them into prolonged exercise, put them into solitary confinement, denied them bathroom privileges (they had to urinate and defecate in their cells), and made them clean toilets by hand. Two prisoners suffered significant emotional trauma and had to be immediately released from the experiment. Zimbardo, who served as the prison warden, also got caught up in the role-play. At one point, he tried to transfer the experiment to an empty cell at the local police station to ensure more security. He got angry when the police refused his request. Zimbardo ended the experiment early after a visitor (who would later become his wife) complained about the disgusting conditions at the "jail." Of the 50 outsiders who visited the experiment, she was the only person to object.

Zimbardo went on to analyze the role of situational variables in real-life cases of evil such as the widespread torture of political opponents in Brazil and prisoner abuse at Iraq's Abu Ghraib prison. According to Zimbardo, ordinary people, such as the military guards at Abu Ghraib, are motivated to do evil when they feel peer pressure to participate in such acts, obey authority, remain anonymous, are given permission to engage in antisocial behavior, and dehumanize others (treat them as less than fully human). Evil is likely to continue when others fail to intervene to stop it.

Facing Evil

Each of the perspectives just described provides insights into how we as leaders can come to grips with evil. The dreadful pleasure approach highlights both the origins of evil and the attraction of doing evil, forcing us to examine our motivations. We need to ask ourselves, "Am I projecting my insecurities onto others?" "Am I punishing a subordinate because of her or his poor performance or because exercising coercive power makes me feel strong?" "Am I making a legitimate request or merely demonstrating that I have the authority to control another person?" "Am I tempted to harm others just to fill the emptiness I feel inside?"

The evil-as-deception viewpoint makes it clear that people aren't always as they seem. On the surface, evil people appear to be successful and well adjusted. In reality, they exert tremendous energy keeping up appearances. (Turn to Case Study 4.2 on page 141 for a chilling example of how two young evildoers were able to mislead their families and authorities until it was too late.) Deceit and defensiveness can serve as warning signs. If we routinely lie to protect our images, refuse constructive feedback, and always blame others, we may be engaged in evil. The same may be true of other leaders and followers who display these behaviors. Peck, like Parker Palmer, believes that to master our inner demons we must first name them. Once we've identified these tendencies, we can begin to deal with them by examining our will. We should determine whether we're willing to submit to a positive force (an ideal, authority) that is greater than we are. Peck urges us to respond to the destructive acts of others with love. Instead of attacking evildoers, we can react with goodness and thereby "absorb" the power of evil.

The administrative evil perspective introduces a new type of evil, one based on technology and logic. Modern evil has greater capacity for destruction. Its impact, once contained by distance and technological limitations, now extends to the entire world. Globalization and the miniaturization of nuclear and biochemical weapons mean that just one person can wreak as much havoc as infamous world leaders such as Caligula and Stalin did in the past.[12] Furthermore, the face of evil may be masked or hidden from those who participate in it. We need to be aware of how our activities contribute to good or evil. Claiming that we were "just following orders" is no excuse.

The evil-as-sanction approach should alert us to the danger of dehumanizing any segment of the population. Language is one of the evildoers' most powerful tools. It is much easier to persecute others who have been labeled as "nerds," "radicals," "scum," "Muslim extremists," or "tree huggers." We need to challenge and eliminate these labels (whether we use them or someone else does). Also, we must be alert to disguised sanctions. If we don't respond to racial slurs, for example, we legitimize these behaviors and encourage future attacks.

Evil as a choice puts the ethical burden squarely on our shoulders. Group and organizational pressures may contribute to our wrongdoing. However, we make the decision to participate in evil acts. Furthermore, the choices we make now will limit our options in the future. Every moral decision, no matter how insignificant it seems at the time, has lasting consequences.

The final perspective, evil as ordinary, is a sobering reminder that we all have the potential to become evildoers. Not only do we as followers need to resist situational influences that can turn us into brutes (see "Focus on Follower Ethics: Resisting Situational Pressures to Do Evil"), but also as leaders we should eliminate conditions that promote evil behavior in our subordinates. It is our ethical duty to intervene when we see evil behavior and to reward others who do the same.

Making a Case for Forgiveness

Breaking the Cycle of Evil

Scott Peck is not alone in arguing that loving acts can overcome evil. A growing number of social scientists believe that forgiving instead of retaliating can prevent or break cycles of evil. In a cycle of evil, aggressive acts provoke retaliation followed by more aggression. When these destructive patterns characterize relations between ethnic groups (e.g., Turks vs. Armenians, Serbs vs. Croats), they can continue for hundreds of years. Courageous leaders can end retaliatory cycles through dramatic acts of reconciliation, however. Former Egyptian Prime Minister Anwar al-Sadat engaged in one such conciliatory gesture when he traveled to Jerusalem to further the peace process with Israel. Pope John Paul II went to the jail cell of his would-be assassin to offer forgiveness. Archbishop Desmond Tutu and Nelson Mandela prevented a bloodbath in South Africa by creating the Truth and Reconciliation Commission. This body, made up of both Blacks and Whites, investigated crimes committed during the apartheid era and allowed offenders to confess their guilt and ask for pardon. Similar commissions were created after widespread torture and murder in Argentina, Peru, and Rwanda.

 FOCUS ON FOLLOWER ETHICS

**RESISTING SITUATIONAL PRESSURES TO DO EVIL:
A 10-STEP PROGRAM**

Philip Zimbardo offers the following 10-step program designed to help followers resist situational forces that promote evildoing.

(Continued)

(Continued)

"I made a mistake!" Admit your mistakes. (Say, "I'm sorry"; "I apologize"; "Forgive me.") Vow to learn from your errors and move on. Don't stay the course if you are engaged in an immoral activity.

"I am mindful." Don't rely on scripts from the past. They can blind you to the tactics of influencers and key elements of the situation. Instead, pay close attention to (be mindful of) the here and now. In addition, think critically. Ask for evidence, imagine future consequences, and reject simple solutions to complex problems. Encourage others to do the same.

"I am responsible." Maintaining personal accountability increases your resistance to conformity pressures. Take charge of your decisions and actions rather than spreading responsibility to your group, coworkers, or military unit. Remember that claiming "everyone else was doing it" is no defense in a court of law.

"I am me, the best I can be." Don't let others take away your individuality, making you anonymous. State your name, credentials, and unique features.

"I respect just authority but rebel against unjust authority." Distinguish between those in authority who deserve your respect and those who are leading others astray or promoting their own interests. Critically evaluate and disobey destructive leaders.

"I want group acceptance but value my independence." Group acceptance is a powerful force but shouldn't overpower your sense of right and wrong. Resist social pressure by stepping out of the group, getting other opinions, and finding new groups more in line with your values.

"I will be more frame-vigilant." Frames (words, pictures, slogans, logos) shape our attitudes toward issues and people, often without our being aware of their impact. For example, many politicians use the colors of the flag—red, white, and blue—on their campaign signs and other materials. Be vigilant, noting the way that the frame is designed to shape your thoughts and emotions.

"I will balance my time perspective." Living in the present increases the power of situational influences that promote evil. You are less likely to go along with abusive behavior if you consider the long-term consequences of such actions and remember the values and standards you developed in the past.

"I will not sacrifice personal or civic freedoms for the illusion of security." Reject any offer that involves sacrificing even small freedoms for the promise of future security. Such sacrifices (e.g., loss of privacy, legal protections, and freedom of speech) are immediate and real, but the promised security is often a distant illusion.

"I can oppose unjust systems." Join with others to resist systems that promote evil. Try to bring about change, blow the whistle on corruption, get away from the group or organization, resist groupthink, draw on the resources of outsiders, and so on.

SOURCE: Adapted from Zimbardo, P. G. (2007). *The Lucifer effect: Understanding how good people turn evil.* New York: Random House, pp. 451–456.

The concept of forgiving evildoers is controversial.[13] (See Case Study 4.3 on page 144 for a closer look at some of the issues raised by forgiveness.) Skeptics worry that (1) guilty parties will get off without acknowledging they have done wrong or paying for their crimes, (2) forgiveness is a sign of weakness, (3) forgiveness is impossible in some situations, (4) forgiveness can't be offered until the offender asks for it, and (5) no leader has the right to offer forgiveness on behalf of other victims. Each of these concerns is valid. You will have to decide whether forgiveness is an appropriate response to evil deeds. However, before you make that determination, I want to describe the forgiveness process and identify some of the benefits that come from extending mercy to others.

The Forgiveness Process

There are many misconceptions about what it means to forgive another person or group of people. According to Robert Enright, professor of educational psychology and president of the International Forgiveness Institute at the University of Wisconsin, forgiveness is *not* the following:[14]

- Forgetting past wrongs to "move on"
- Excusing or condoning bad, damaging behavior
- Reconciliation or coming together again (forgiveness opens the way to reconciliation, but the other person must change or desire to reconcile)
- Reducing the severity of offenses
- Offering a legal pardon

- Pretending to forgive in order to wield power over another person
- Ignoring the offender
- Dropping our anger and becoming emotionally neutral

Enright and his colleagues define forgiveness as "a willingness to abandon one's right to resentment, negative judgment, and indifferent behavior toward one who unjustly injured us, while fostering the undeserved qualities of compassion, generosity, and even love toward him or her."[15] This definition recognizes that the wronged party has been unjustly treated (slandered, betrayed, imprisoned); the offended person willingly chooses forgiveness regardless of the offender's response; forgiving involves emotions, thoughts, and behavior; and forgiveness is a process that takes place over time. (To measure your likelihood to forgive others, complete the "Self-Assessment: Tendency to Forgive Scale.")

Enright and his fellow researchers offer a four-stage model to help people forgive. (A list of the psychological factors that go into each stage is found in Box 4.1 on page 132.) In the first phase, *uncovering*, a victim may initially deny that a problem exists. However, when the person does acknowledge the hurt, he or she may experience intense feelings of anger, shame, and betrayal. The victim invests a lot of psychic energy in rehashing the offense and comparing his or her condition with that of the offender. Feeling permanently damaged, the person may believe that life is unfair.

During the second phase, *decision*, the injured party recognizes that he or she is paying a high price for dwelling on the injury, considers the possibility of forgiveness, and commits himself or herself to forgiving.

Forgiveness is accomplished in the third stage, *work*. The wronged party tries to understand (not condone) the victimizer's background and motivation. He or she may experience empathy and compassion for the offender. Absorbing pain is the key to this stage. The forgiver decides to endure suffering rather than pass it on, thereby breaking the cycle of evil. Viewed in this light, forgiveness is a gift of mercy to the wrongdoer.

SELF-ASSESSMENT

TENDENCY TO FORGIVE SCALE

Instructions: Respond to each of the following items on a scale of 1 (*strongly disagree*) to 7 (*strongly agree*).

1	2	3	4	5	6	7
Strongly Agree						Strongly Disagree

1. "I tend to get over it quickly when someone hurts my feelings."   _____

2. "If someone wrongs me, I often think about it a lot afterward."   _____

3. "I have a tendency to harbor grudges."   _____

4. "When people wrong me, my approach is just to forgive and forget."   _____

Scoring:

Reverse your scores on items 2 and 3 and then add up your responses to all four statements. The higher the score (possible scores range from 4 to 28), the more likely you are to forgive others and the less likely you are to bring up offenses from the past.

SOURCE: Brown, R. P. (2003). Measuring individual differences in the tendency to forgive: Construct validity and links with depression. *Personality and Social Psychology Bulletin, 29,* p. 770. Published by SAGE Publications on behalf of the Society for Personality and Social Psychology., Inc.

The fourth and final phase, *deepening*, describes the outcomes of forgiving. A forgiver may find deeper meaning in suffering, realize his or her own need for forgiveness, and come to a greater appreciation for support groups (friends, congregations, classmates). In the end, the person offering forgiveness may develop a new purpose in life and find peace.

The four-stage model has been used successfully with a variety of audiences: survivors of incest, inmates, college students deprived of parental love, heart patients, substance abusers, and elderly women suffering from depression. In each case, forgivers experienced significant healing. Enright emphasizes that personal benefits should be a by-product, not the motivation, for forgiving. Nonetheless, a growing body of evidence suggests that forgiveness can pay significant psychological, physical, and relational dividends.[16] Those who forgive are released from resentments and experience less depression and anxiety. Overall, they enjoy a higher sense of well-being. By releasing their grudges, forgivers experience better physical health. Reducing anger, hostility, and hopelessness lowers the risks of heart attack and high blood pressure while increasing the body's resistance to disease. Acting mercifully toward transgressors also maintains relationships between friends and family members.

BOX 4.1 PSYCHOLOGICAL ELEMENTS OF FORGIVENESS

PSYCHOLOGICAL VARIABLES THAT MAY BE INVOLVED WHEN WE FORGIVE

Uncovering Phase

- Evaluation of psychological defenses.
- Confrontation of anger; the point is to release, not harbor, the anger.
- Admittance of shame, when this is appropriate.
- Awareness of cathexis.
- Awareness of cognitive rehearsal of the offense.
- Insight that the injured party may be comparing self with the injurer.
- Realization that one may be permanently and adversely changed by the injury.
- Insight into a possibly altered "just world" view.

Decision Phase

- A change of heart, conversion, new insights that old resolution strategies are not working.
- Willingness to consider forgiveness as an option.
- Commitment to forgive the offender.

Work Phase

- Reframing, through role taking, who the wrongdoer is by viewing him or her in context.
- Empathy toward the offender.
- Awareness of compassion, as it emerges, toward the offender.
- Acceptance and absorption of the pain.

Deepening Phase

- Finding meaning for self and others in the suffering and in the forgiveness process.
- Realization that self has needed others' forgiveness in the past.
- Insight that one is not alone (universality, support).
- Realization that self may have a new purpose in life because of the injury.
- Awareness of decreased negative affect and, perhaps, increased positive affect, if this begins to emerge, toward the injurer; awareness of internal, emotional release.

SOURCE: Enright, R. D., Freedman, S., & Rique, J. (1998). The psychology of interpersonal forgiveness. In R. D. Enright & J. North (Eds.), *Exploring Forgiveness* © 1998 by the Board of Regents of the University of Wisconsin System. Reprinted by permission of The University of Wisconsin Press.

The social-scientific study of forgiveness is continuing, and results are extremely encouraging. Forgiving does appear to absorb or defuse evil. If this is the case, then as leaders we should practice forgiveness when treated unjustly by followers, supervisors, peers, or outsiders. When we give offense ourselves, we will need to apologize and ask for mercy. At times, though, we will need to go further and follow the example of Anwar al-Sadat and Nelson Mandela by offering forgiveness on behalf of followers in hopes of reconciling with a long-standing enemy. We may also need to offer a collective apology in order to facilitate reconciliation between our group and those we have offended. Such political apologies are becoming increasingly common.[17] For example:

- Former British Prime Minister Tony Blair apologized for his country's inaction during the Irish potato famine.
- The Belgian prime minister apologized to Rwandans for not stepping in to prevent the 1994 genocide.
- Germany's Chancellor Gerhard Schroeder requested forgiveness from the Russian people for the damage done by his nation during World War II.
- Bill Clinton expressed regret to Ugandans for African slavery.
- The Natal Law Society apologized for excluding Mohandas K. Gandhi from the practice of law in South Africa.
- The U.S. Senate passed a resolution apologizing for not enacting legislation that would have made lynching a federal crime.
- The Oregon state legislature held a public session to revoke and to express regret about an 1849 law that prohibited African Americans from entering Oregon territory.

Donald Shriver uses the metaphor of a cable to explain how warring groups can overcome their mutual hatred and bind together to restore fractured relationships.[18] This cable is made up of four strands. The first strand is *moral truth*. Forgiveness starts with recalling the past and rendering a moral judgment. Both parties need to agree that one or both engaged in behavior that was wrong (see the discussion of political apologies above) and unjust and caused injury. Refusal to admit the truth makes reconciliation impossible. That's why South Africa's Truth and Reconciliation Commission began the process of national healing after apartheid by publicly airing Black victims' statements and requests for amnesty by White police officers.

The second strand of the cable is *forbearance*. Forbearance means rejecting revenge in favor of restraint. Moral indignation often fuels new crimes as offended parties take their vengeance. Forbearance breaks this pattern and may soften enemies who expect retaliation.

The third strand is *empathy* for the enemies' humanity. Empathy doesn't excuse wrongs but acknowledges that offender and offended share much in common. This recognition opens the way for both sides to live together in peace. Ulysses S. Grant demonstrated how to combine the judgment of wrong with empathy at Appomattox. When Southern troops surrendered to end the Civil War, Grant wrote the following in his journal. "I felt . . . sad and depressed at the downfall of a foe who had fought so long and valiantly, and had suffered so much for a cause, though that cause was, I believe, one of the worst for which a people ever fought."[19]

The fourth and final strand of the forgiveness cable is *commitment* to restore the broken relationship. Forgivers must be prepared to live and interact with their former enemies. At first, the two parties probably will coexist in a state of mutual toleration. Later, they may fully reconcile, as the United States and Germany have done since the end of World War II.

In sum, I believe that forgiveness is one of a leader's most powerful weapons in the fight against evil. Or, to return to the central metaphor of this text, forgiving is one of the ways in which leaders cast light rather than shadow. We must face our inner darkness, particularly our resentments and hostilities, in order to offer genuine forgiveness. By forgiving, we short-circuit or break the shadowy, destructive cycles that poison groups, organizations, or societies. Offering forgiveness brightens our lives by reducing our anxiety levels and enhancing our sense of well-being. Requesting forgiveness opens the door for reconciliation.

Spirituality and Leadership

Coming to grips with evil is hard work. We must always be on the lookout for evil whatever form it takes, continually evaluate our motivations and choices, and make a conscious effort to forgive by reshaping our thoughts, emotions, and behaviors. A great number of leaders turn to spirituality to help equip themselves for these tasks. If spirituality seems to be a strange topic to discuss in a book about leadership ethics, consider the recent explosion of interest in spirituality in the workplace. More and more academics are studying the link between spiritual values and practices and organizational performance. One of the fastest-growing interest groups in the Academy of Management, for example, focuses on the connection between spirituality and managerial practice and publishes the *Journal of Management, Spirituality & Religion*. A number of other scholarly journals (*Journal of Managerial Psychology, Journal of Organizational Change Management, Journal of Management Education, The Leadership Quarterly*, and *Journal of Management Inquiry*) have devoted special issues to the topic. According to one survey, 1,598 articles with the word *spirituality* in the title appeared in social science journals between 1991 and 2008 (232 dealt specifically with workplace spirituality).[20] Approximately 80% of these articles appeared after the year 2000. The publication rate for books on workplace spirituality also demonstrates that interest in the topic continues to accelerate. Of 72 books published on the topic over the past two decades, nearly half were written in the last five years.

Popular interest in spirituality is also surging. Meditation rooms and reflective gardens are part of many company headquarters. Some organizations sponsor groups for spiritual seekers, hire chaplains, and send employees to business and spirituality workshops. Tom's of Maine, Toro, BioGenex, and Medtronic integrate spiritual values into their organizational cultures. David Whyte, James Autry, and Thomas Chappell are a few of the popular writers who encourage spiritual development at work.

The recent surge of interest in spirituality in the workplace has been fueled in large part by the growing importance of organizations. For better or worse, the organization has replaced other groups (family, church, social groups) as the dominant institution in society. Work takes up increasing amounts of our time and energy. As a result, we tend to develop more friendships with coworkers and fewer with people outside the organization. Many of us want a higher return on this investment of time and energy, seeking meaningful tasks and relationships that serve higher purposes. At the same time, downsizing, restructuring, rapid change, and information overload have generated fear and uncertainty in the workplace, which prompts us to seek stability and to reexamine our lives.[21] Baby boomers, in particular, are reevaluating their priorities, shifting their focus from individual achievement toward purpose and community. For their part, organizations hope to benefit from more connected members. Investigators have discovered that spirituality enhances the following:[22]

- Commitment to mission, core values, and ethical standards
- Organizational learning and creativity
- Morale
- Productivity and profitability
- Collaboration
- Loyalty
- Willingness to mentor others
- Job effort
- Job satisfaction
- Social support
- Sensitivity to ethical issues

Donde Ashmos Plowman and Dennis Duchon define workplace spirituality as "the recognition that employees have an inner life that nourishes and is nourished by meaningful work that takes place in the context of community."[23] The *inner life* refers to the fact that employees have spiritual needs (their core identity and values) just as they have emotional, physical, and intellectual wants, and they bring the whole person to work. Even industrialist Henry Ford, who only wanted human cogs for his automobile assembly line, noted this fact. "Why is it that I always get the whole person," he complained, "when all I really want is a pair of hands?"[24] *Meaningful work* describes the fact that workers typically are motivated by more than material rewards. They want their labor to be fulfilling and to serve the needs of society. *Community* refers to the fact that organization members desire connection to others. A sense of belonging fosters the inner life. It should be noted that religion and spirituality overlap but are not identical. Religious institutions encourage and structure spiritual experiences, but spiritual encounters can occur outside formal religious channels.[25]

Interest in spiritual leadership is an offshoot of the larger workplace spirituality movement. Many leaders report that spirituality has played an important role in their character development, giving them the courage to persist in the face of obstacles, remain optimistic, demonstrate compassion, learn from hardship, and clarify their values.[26] Spiritual leadership expert Laura Reave reviewed more than 150 studies and found that leaders who see their work as a calling demonstrate a higher degree of integrity (honesty) and humility, key virtues described in Chapter 3. These character traits, in turn, build trust with followers and foster honest communication.[27] Reave also found that leaders who engage in common spiritual practices are both more ethical and more effective. These behaviors, emphasized in a variety of belief systems, include the following:

- *Demonstrating respect for others' values.* Many spiritual traditions emphasize respect for the individual. Ethical leaders demonstrate their respect for followers by including them in important decisions. By doing so, they empower followers and bring individual, group, and organizational values into alignment. When values are aligned, an organization is more likely to enjoy long-term success.

- *Treating others fairly.* Fairness is a natural outcome of viewing others with respect. Employees are very concerned about how fairly they are treated, particularly when it comes to compensation. Followers are more likely to trust leaders who act justly. Subordinates who believe that their supervisors are fair also go beyond their job descriptions to help coworkers.

- *Expression of caring and concern.* Spirituality often takes the form of supportive behavior. Caring leaders typically have more satisfied and productive followers. Concerned leaders are also more likely to build positive relationships that are the key to their personal success. Furthermore, demonstrating care and concern for the community pays dividends. Employees working for firms known for their corporate philanthropy rate their work environments as excellent and ethical, get a greater sense of achievement from their work, and take more pride in their companies.

- *Listening responsively.* Listening and responding to the needs of others is another practice promoted in many spiritual paths. Good listeners are more likely to emerge as group leaders; organizational leaders who demonstrate better listening skills are rated as more effective. Ethical leaders also respond to what they hear by acting on feedback and suggestions.

- *Appreciating the contributions of others.* Most of the world's faith traditions encourage adherents to treat others as creations of God who are worthy of praise. Praise of God's creation, in turn, becomes an expression of gratitude to God. In the workplace, recognizing and praising employee contributions generates goodwill toward the organization, creates a sense of community, and fosters continuing commitment and contribution.

- *Engaging in reflective practice.* Spiritual practice doesn't end with demonstrating fairness, caring, and appreciation to others. It also incorporates individual self-examination or communication with God. Meditation, prayer, journaling, and spiritual reading not only deepen spirituality; they also pay practical dividends.[28] Leaders who engage in such activities are more effective because they experience less stress, enjoy improved mental and physical health, and develop stronger relationships with others. They are better equipped to rebound from crises and see a greater (transcendent) meaning in even the most stressful circumstances. Self-reflective leaders also manage their emotions more effectively and exercise greater self-discipline.

Spiritual values help leaders create ethical organizational climates. Spiritual leaders develop a vision that helps organization members experience a sense of calling, the belief that life has meaning and makes a difference.[29] This vision builds hope and faith in the future, which encourages group members to put forth their best efforts and to persevere. Spiritually focused leaders also establish a culture based on altruistic love that fosters a sense of membership and connection. (I'll have more to say about altruism in Chapter 5.) Leaders and followers enjoy a sense of "ethical well-being" in which their behavior reflects their inner values. Members of such groups are more likely to be committed, productive, and socially responsible.

The path to individual and organizational spiritual transformation will have its ups and downs. After the initial excitement of discovering the benefits of spirituality, individuals and organizations will typically hit obstacles—frustration, financial challenges, feelings of emptiness—that demand new spiritual practices and a renewed commitment to a greater purpose if growth is to continue.[30] With this in mind, the following framework can be used for measuring the spiritual climate of a workplace.[31] You can use the following values or characteristics to determine your organization's spiritual progress.

Benevolence: kindness toward others; desire to promote the happiness and prosperity of employees.

Generativity: long-term focus; concern about future consequences of actions for this and future generations.

Humanism: policies and practices that respect the dignity and worth of every employee; opportunity for personal growth when working toward organizational goals.

Integrity: adherence to a code of conduct; honesty; sincerity; candor.

Justice: even-handed treatment of employees; impartiality; unbiased rewards and punishments.

Mutuality: employees feel interconnected and mutually dependent; work together to complete projects and achieve goals.

Receptivity: flexible thinking; open-mindedness; take calculated risks; reward creativity.

Respect: treat employees with esteem and value; show consideration and concern.

Responsibility: members independently follow through on goals despite obstacles; are concerned with what is right.

Trust: members and outsiders have confidence in the character and truthfulness of the organization and its representatives.

To this point our focus has been on the positive benefits of spirituality. However, before ending our discussion of the topic, it should be noted that spiritual leadership has a potential dark side. Noting these pitfalls can keep us from falling victim to them as leaders or followers. To begin, some leaders view spirituality solely as a tool for increasing follower commitment (obedience) and productivity, losing sight of the fact that spirituality has value in and of itself, helping organizational members find meaning and establish connections. Other leaders try to impose their particular religious and spiritual views on followers. In the worst-case scenario, authoritarian leaders engage in spiritual abuse.[32] They use spirituality to reinforce their power, to seek selfish (often fraudulent) goals, and to foster dependency in followers. Spiritual abuse is a danger in business organizations as well as religious ones. Common abusive tactics include (1) overemphasizing spiritual authority and forbidding challenges from followers; (2) demanding unquestioning obedience as a sign of follower loyalty, which takes away the right of subordinates to make their own choices; (3) keeping members apart from outsiders and dismissing external critics while, at the same time, hiding character flaws and unethical practices from the public; (4) insisting on rigid beliefs and behavior while demanding conformity and perfection; (5) suppressing follower dissent through humiliation, deprivation, and other means; and (6) using nearly absolute power to engage in fraud, sexual immorality, and other unethical practices.

Implications and Applications

- Evil takes a variety of forms or faces, including a sense of dreadful pleasure, deception, rational administration, sanctioned devaluation, a series of small but fateful decisions, and the product of situational forces that convert ordinary people into evildoers. Whatever face it displays, evil is a destructive force that inflicts pain and suffering and ends in death.

- Ultimately, the choice of whether to do or participate in evil is yours.
- Work to eliminate the situational factors—peer pressure, obedience to authority, anonymity, and dehumanization—that turn leaders and followers into evildoers. Intervene to stop evil behavior.
- Forgiveness is one way to defuse or absorb evil. As a leader, you need to seriously consider the role of forgiveness in your relations with followers, peers, supervisors, and outsiders.
- Forgiving does *not* mean forgetting or condoning evil. Instead, forgivers hold offenders accountable for their actions at the same time they offer mercy. Forgiving takes a conscious act of will, unfolds over time, and replaces hostility and resentment with empathy and compassion.
- Forgiveness breaks cycles of evil and restores relationships. However, you may gain the most from extending mercy. Forgiving can heighten your sense of wellbeing, give you renewed energy, and improve your health.
- Warring groups can overcome their mutual hatred by facing and judging the past, rejecting revenge in favor of restraint, feeling empathy for their enemies' humanity, and being committed to restoring the broken relationship. As a leader, you may need to offer an apology for the offenses of your group in order to foster reconciliation.
- Spiritual resources can equip you for the demanding work of confronting evil by contributing to your character development.
- Common spiritual practices that can make you more effective and ethical as a leader include (1) demonstrating respect for others' values, (2) treating others fairly, (3) expressing caring and concern, (4) listening responsively, (5) appreciating the contributions of others, and (6) engaging in reflective practice.
- You can foster an ethical organizational climate by acting as a spiritual leader who creates a vision that helps members experience a sense of calling and establishes a culture based on altruistic love.
- Recognize that there is a potential dark side to spiritual leadership. Be careful not to use spirituality solely as a tool to boost productivity, to force your particular beliefs onto followers, or to reinforce your power.

For Further Exploration, Challenge, and Self-Assessment

1. Which of the perspectives on evil described in the chapter is most useful to you? How does it help you better understand and prevent evil?

2. Develop your own definition of forgiveness. Does your definition set boundaries that limit when forgiveness can be offered? What right do leaders have to offer or accept forgiveness on behalf of the group?

3. Consider a time when you forgave someone who treated you unjustly. Did you move through the stages identified by Enright and his colleagues? What

benefits did you experience? Conversely, describe a time when you asked ᵢ.
and received forgiveness. What process did you go through? How did you
and the relationship benefit?

4. Develop your own forgiveness case study based on the life of a leader who
   prevented or broke a cycle of evil through an act of apology, mercy, or
   reconciliation.

5. What should be the role of spirituality in leadership? Try to reach a consensus
   on this question in a group.

6. Define spiritual leadership. How does it differ from other forms of leadership? How can abuse of spiritual leadership be prevented?

7. Evaluate the spiritual climate of an organization using the values presented
   on page 138. Share your findings with the rest of the class.

CASE STUDY 4.2

EVIL IN THE BASEMENT: THE ATTACK ON COLUMBINE HIGH

On April 20, 1999, two teens dressed in trench coats and armed with bombs,
shotguns, and semiautomatic rifles launched an assault on Columbine High
School in suburban Denver, Colorado. For 48 minutes seniors Eric Harris and
Dylan Klebold set off homemade pipe bombs and napalm while shooting at
students and teachers. At the end of their killing spree, 14 students (including
the shooters) and one faculty member were dead (23 others were seriously
injured). The carnage could have been much worse. The killers wanted to
inflict a higher death toll than the Oklahoma City bombing, but their most
powerful explosive devices failed to detonate. In addition, they seemed to get
bored with murder and killed themselves well before law enforcement officials
entered the building.

Many other school attacks have occurred since the Columbine tragedy,
but this event remains the most infamous. Other school shooters have
adopted the dress and tactics of the Columbine killers and looked to them
for inspiration. Virginia Tech killer Seung-Hui Cho, for example, mentioned
Harris and Klebold twice in the manifesto he left after murdering 32 students and faculty. Further, the motives of Harris and Klebold are harder to
explain. Unlike a number of other school shooters who could clearly be
labeled as mentally ill (like Cho) or as social outcasts, the Columbine killers

(Continued)

(Continued)

were highly intelligent, mainstream students from privileged backgrounds who had bright futures after graduation. The horrific acts of these adolescents, who held part-time jobs, bowled regularly, and attended the prom, brought the reality of evil far too close to home.

Reporter and author David Cullen spent several years reconstructing what happened before, during, and after the killing spree. In his book *Columbine*, he describes the evolution of the Columbine shooters and how outward appearances can be deceiving. Drawing upon the tapes and journals of the teens and interviews with an FBI profiler, the author concludes that Eric Harris, the duo's leader, was a psychopath who "just enjoyed being bad" (p. 240). He boasted of his superiority to the rest of the human race and demonstrated a total lack of empathy. He spewed forth hate on his website and on Internet chat rooms as well as in his private journal. For his part, Dylan Klebold struggled with depression and low self-worth, feeling cut off from humanity. Columbine for him was a form of murder–suicide. He took his own life after taking out his anger and self-loathing on others.

Harris and Klebold evolved into killers over time. Their criminal activities escalated from vandalism against those they particularly detested, to computer hacking, to breaking in to school lockers and a vehicle, to making and setting off pipe bombs, to the final assault. While they hinted at their plans to friends and on websites, their skill at deceiving school officials, law enforcement authorities, and their parents ultimately kept them from being stopped. Like other psychopaths, Eric was a master of deception. He confessed just enough of his crimes to appear sincere. For example, he admitted to his parents that he had been drinking a few times but hid the fact that he often got drunk and used pot. For his part, Dylan Klebold kept his despair to himself. His parents didn't discover the depth of his pain until after he was dead.

The duo's behavior after being arrested for stealing equipment from a van illustrates their success in fooling adults. When faced with a felony conviction, they managed to convince a judge to approve them for a diversion program instead. They made a very positive impression on the magistrate by dressing up, acting well behaved, and treating him with respect. The judge thought they were going to do well in the program. After the murders, he would admit that he had been misled. "What's mind-boggling is the amount of deception," the judge noted. "The ease of their deception. The coolness of their deception" (p. 220). Harris, in particular, manipulated the counselors in the diversion program. He was humorous and clever, kept his grades and work performance up, and pretended to have concern for the victim of his crime. As a result, he was released early, which is achieved by only 5% of those enrolled in the program. All the while Eric recorded his contempt for the legal system, his counselors, the van owner, and human-kind in his personal notebook. He took a great deal of pleasure in conning his parents and the authorities.

Despite the duo's efforts to hide their plans, authorities came agoniz-ingly close to preventing the massacre, according to author Cullen. Parents of a former friend of Harris and Klebold complained repeatedly about the threats they made against their son. The Jefferson County sheriff's office investigated, copied Eric's webpages, and found evidence that he was mak-ing pipe bombs. The investigator on the case drafted an affidavit for a search warrant for the Harris residence 13 months before the attack, but the affidavit was never presented to a judge. (After the assault, sheriff's officials would also engage in deception by denying that they had ever investigated the complaints or drafted an affidavit.)

The Harrises missed several opportunities to prevent the assault as well. They believed Eric's lies. When his father discovered evidence that he was making pipe bombs, Eric promised to stop and did a better job of hiding his activities from that point on. (Police did discover bomb-making materials in the Harris home after the attack.) As the day for carrying out the plot grew near, Eric and Dylan created the "Basement Tapes" while the Harris family slept upstairs. On the tapes the killers vented their rage, insulted those they considered inferior (Blacks, Latinos, women, gays), identified victims they were going to shoot, and offered apologies (but then excused their behav-ior). They also described how they were going to die in the final battle they called NBK after the movie *Natural Born Killers.* Tragically, the Harrises never awoke to discover the evil festering in their suburban basement.

Discussion Probes

1. What, if anything, do you remember about the Columbine attack? Why do you think it has inspired other school shooters?

2. What forms of evil do you see reflected in the Columbine murders?

3. What steps could parents and authorities have taken to prevent Harris and Klebold from evolving into killers?

4. How do we keep from being deceived by evildoers?

(Continued)

(Continued)

5. Should Harris and Klebold be forgiven for their assault on Columbine High School? Should their parents be forgiven for not stopping the attack?

6. What leadership ethics lessons do you take from this case?

SOURCE: Cullen, D. (2009). *Columbine.* New York: Twelve.

CASE STUDY 4.3

FORGIVING DR. MENGELE?

Russian soldiers liberated Poland's Auschwitz-Birkenau German concentration camp in January 1945. A film clip of the event shows two little girls holding hands leading a line of survivors out through the barbed wire. The girls, Eva and Miriam Mozes, were identical twins from Romania. Their parents and two older siblings went to the gas chambers immediately upon arrival at the camp in May 1944. Eva and Miriam were kept alive to serve as subjects for the genetic experiments of Dr. Josef Mengele. The Mozes sisters were one set of approximately 1,400 pairs of twins who were forced to endure a variety of deadly tests, including being subjected to extreme cold and receiving injections of poison and bacteria. The shots that Miriam received prevented her kidneys from growing. Eva was infected with a virus or bacteria that kept her near death for weeks. If either had died, Mengele would have immediately murdered the other twin and performed simultaneous autopsies. Eva's strong determination to survive kept her alive and helped save her sister's life as well.

Following the war both Eva and Miriam immigrated to Israel. Eva married an American (Michael Kor) and then moved to Terre Haute, Indiana, where she became a real estate agent, founded the CANDLES (Children of Auschwitz Nazi Deadly Lab Experiment Survivors) Holocaust Museum, and began speaking to student groups about her experiences. In 1993 Miriam died, perhaps as a result of the injections she received at Auschwitz. Eva set out to track down Mengele's medical records to find out the dangers she and other twin survivors faced. Though she never located the records, she met Dr. Hans Münch during her search. Münch was a doctor at Auschwitz who was later acquitted of war crimes. As a result of their meeting, Eva wrote a letter of forgiveness to Münch. In 1995, during the 50th anniversary of the liberation of Auschwitz, Münch signed a letter testifying to the horrors of the camp, and Eva issued a declaration of amnesty and forgiveness to Mengele and to all Nazis. Eva also began to incorporate her message of forgiveness into her presentations.

Eva Mozes Kor's declaration of forgiveness alienated her from most of her fellow twin survivors and generated criticism from Jewish theologians and Holocaust experts, much of it captured in the documentary *Forgiving Dr. Mengele,* the story of Eva's life and controversial decision to forgive her tormentors. Her critics argue that no forgiveness can be offered unless the Nazi perpetrators ask for it first, that forgiveness means forgetting the horror that was the Holocaust, and that forgiveness cannot be offered on behalf of other Holocaust victims. In response, Eva points to forgiveness as one of the paths to healing. Forgiving means she is no longer a helpless victim but has power over her victimizers. Now she can live without dwelling on the hurt of the past. "I felt as though an incredibly heavy weight of suffering had been lifted," she told an interviewer. "I never thought I could be so strong."[1] As for the charge that she is helping to erase the memory of the Holocaust, she points to her museum and speaking engagements as evidence that she is keeping this history alive. Forgiving does not mean forgetting. According to Eva, "What the victims do does not change what happened."[2]

Do you agree with Eva Moses Kor's decision to forgive Dr. Mengele and the Nazis? Why or why not?

Notes

1. Heflick, R. (2005, December 9). Forgiving Josef Mengele. *Der Spiegel.*
2. Heflick.

Sources

Hercules, B. (Producer), & Pugh, C. (Producer). (2005). *Forgiving Dr. Mengele* [Documentary film]. (Available from First Run Features, The Film Center Building, 630 Ninth Ave., Suite 1213, New York, NY 10036, or from firstrunfeatures .com)

Mozes Kor, E., & Wright, M. (1995). *Echoes from Auschwitz. Dr. Mengele's twins. The story of Eva and Miriam Moses.* Terre Haute, IN: CANDLES, Inc.

Stevens, D. (2006, May 18). Forgiving Dr. Mengele. Letting go of the death camps in "Forgiving Dr. Mengele." *The New York Times,* p. E5.

Notes

1. Definitions of evil can be found in the following sources. Of course, a host of other definitions are offered by major religions and philosophical systems.

> Hallie, P. (1997). *Tales of good and evil, help and harm*. New York: HarperCollins.
>
> Katz, F. E. (1993). *Ordinary people and extraordinary evil: A report on the beguilings of evil*. Albany: State University of New York Press.
>
> Kekes, J. (2005). *The roots of evil*. Ithaca, NY: Cornell University Press.
>
> Peck, M. S. (1983). *People of the lie: The hope for healing human evil*. New York: Touchstone.
>
> Sanford, N., & Comstock, C. (Eds.). (1971). *Sanctions for evil*. San Francisco: Jossey-Bass.
>
> Vetelson, A. J. (2005). *Evil and human agency: understanding collective evildoing*. Cambridge, UK: Cambridge University Press.

2. Alford, C. F. (1997). *What evil means to us*. Ithaca, NY: Cornell University Press, p. 3.

3. Kekes.

4. Peck.

5. Adams, G. B., & Balfour, D. L. (1998). *Unmasking administrative evil*. Thousand Oaks, CA: Sage.

6. Sanford & Comstock. For a closer look at the role of sanctions in genocide, see Staub, E. (1989). *The roots of evil: The origins of genocide and other group violence*. Cambridge, UK: Cambridge University Press.

7. Lewis, C. S. (1946). *The great divorce*. New York: Macmillan.

8. Fromm, E. (1964). *The heart of man: Its genius for good and evil*. New York: Harper & Row, p. 136.

9. Arendt, H. (1964). *Eichmann in Jerusalem: A report on the banality of evil*. New York: Viking.

10. Hatzfeld, J. (2005). *Machete season: The killers in Rwanda speak* (L. Coverdale, Trans.). New York: Farrar, Straus and Giroux.

11. Zimbardo, P. G. (2007). *The Lucifer effect: Understanding how good people turn evil*. New York: Random House; Zimbardo, P. G. (2005). A situationist perspective on the psychology of evil. In A. G. Miller (Ed.), *The social psychology of good and evil* (pp. 21–50). New York: Guilford. See also Waller, J. (2007). *Becoming evil: How ordinary people commit genocide and mass killing* (2nd ed.). Oxford, UK: Oxford University Press.

12. Morrow, L. (2003). *Evil: An investigation*. New York: Basic Books.

13. See the following:

> Murphy, J. G. (2003). *Getting even: Forgiveness and its limits*. Oxford, UK: Oxford University Press.
>
> Ransley, C., & Spy, T. (Eds.). (2004). *Forgiveness and the healing process: A central therapeutic concern*. New York: Brunner-Routledge.

14. Material on the definition and psychology of forgiveness is taken from the following:

Enright, R. D., Freedman, S., & Rique, J. (1998). The psychology of interpersonal forgiveness. In R. D. Enright & J. North (Eds.), *Exploring forgiveness* (pp. 46–62). Madison: University of Wisconsin Press.

Enright, R. D., & Gassin, E. A. (1992). Forgiveness: A developmental view. *Journal of Moral Education, 21,* 99–114.

Freedman, S., Enright, R. D., & Knutson, J. (2005). A progress report on the process model of forgiveness. In E. L. Worthington, Jr. (Ed.), *Handbook of forgiveness* (pp. 393–406). New York: Routledge.

McCullough, M. E., Pargament, K. I., & Thoresen, C. E. (2000). The psychology of forgiveness: History, conceptual issues, and overview. In M. E. McCullough, K. I. Pargament, & C. E. Thoresen (Eds.), *Forgiveness: Theory, research, and practice* (pp. 1–14). New York: Guilford.

Thomas, G. (2000, January 10). The forgiveness factor. *Christianity Today,* pp. 38–43.

15. Enright et al.
16. For information on the by-products of forgiveness, see the following:

Casarjian, R. (1992). *Forgiveness: A bold choice for a peaceful heart.* New York: Bantam.

Enright et al.

Freedman et al.

McCullough, M. E., Sandage, S. J., & Worthington, E. L. (1997). *To forgive is human: How to put your past in the past.* Downers Grove, IL: InterVarsity Press.

Thoresen, C. E., Harris, H. S., & Luskin, F. (2000). Forgiveness and health: An unanswered question. In M. E. McCullough, K. I. Pargament, & C. E. Thoresen (Eds.), *Forgiveness: Theory, research and practice* (pp. 254–280). New York: Guilford.

Worthington, E. L., Jr. (2005). Initial questions about the art and science of forgiving. In E. L. Worthington (Ed.), *Handbook of forgiveness* (pp. 1–13). New York: Routledge.

Waltman, M. A., Russell, D. C., Coyle, C. T., Enright, R. D., Holter, A. C., & Swoboda, C. M. (2009). The effects of a forgiveness intervention on patients with coronary artery disease. *Psychology and Health, 24*(1), 11–27.

17. Lowenheim, N. (2009). A haunted past: Requesting forgiveness for wrongdoing in international relations. *Review of International Studies, 35,* 531–555; Shriver, D. W. (2001). Forgiveness: A bridge across Abysses of revenge. In R. G. Helmick & R. L. Peterson (Eds.), *Forgiveness and reconciliation: Religion, public policy, & conflict transformation* (pp. 151–167). Philadelphia: Templeton Foundation Press; Griswold, C. L. (2007). *Forgiveness: A philosophical exploration.* Cambridge, UK: Cambridge University Press.

18. Shriver, D. W. (1995). *An ethic for enemies: Forgiveness in politics*. New York: Oxford University Press. See also:

> Wilmot, W. W., & Hocker, J. L. (2001). *Interpersonal conflict* (6th ed.). New York: McGraw-Hill Higher Education, Ch. 1.

19. Shriver, p. 8.

20. Oswick, C. (2009). Burgeoning workplace spirituality? A textual analysis of momentum and directions. *Journal of Management, Spirituality & Religion, 6,* 15–25.

21. King, S., Biberman, J., Robbins, L., & Nicol, D. M. (2007). Integrating spirituality into management education in academia and organizations: Origins, a conceptual framework, and current practices. In J. Biberman & M. D. Whitty (Eds.), *At work: Spirituality matters* (pp. 243–256). Scranton, PA: University of Scranton Press.

22. Information on the benefits of workplace spirituality is taken from the following:

> Craigie, F. C. (1999). The spirit and work: Observations about spirituality and organizational life. *Journal of Psychology and Christianity, 18,* 43–53.
>
> Fairholm, G. W. (1996). Spiritual leadership: Fulfilling whole-self needs at work. *Leadership & Organization Development Journal, 17*(5), 11–17.
>
> Garcia-Zamor, J. C. (2003). Workplace spirituality and organizational performance. *Public Administration Review, 63,* 355–363.
>
> Giacalone, R. A., & Jurkiewicz, C. L. (2003). Right from wrong: The influence of spirituality on perceptions of unethical business activities. *Journal of Business Ethics, 46,* 85–97.
>
> Giacalone, R. A., & Jurkiewicz, C. L. (2003). Toward a science of workplace spirituality. In R. A. Giacalone & C. L. Jurkiewicz (Eds.), *Handbook of workplace spirituality and organizational performance* (pp. 3–28). Armonk, NY: M. E. Sharpe.
>
> Jurkiewicz, C. L., & Giacalone, R. A. (2004). A values framework for measuring the impact of workplace spirituality on organizational performance. *Journal of Business Ethics, 49,* 129–142.
>
> Mirvis, P. H. (1997). "Soul work" in organizations. *Organization Science, 8,* 193–206.
>
> Rego, A., & Pina e Cunha, M. (2008). Workplace spirituality and organizational commitment: An empirical study. *Journal of Organizational Change Management, 21*(1), 53–75.

23. Ashmos, D. P., & Duchon, D. (2000). Spirituality at work: A conceptualization and measure. *Journal of Management Inquiry, 9,* 134–145, p. 137; see also Duchon, D., & Plowman, D. A. (2005). Nurturing the spirit at work: Impact on work unit performance. *The Leadership Quarterly, 16,* 807–833.

24. Pollard, C. W. (1996). *The soul of the firm*. Grand Rapids, MI: HarperBusiness.

25. See Zinnbauer, B. J., & Pargament, K. I. (2005). Religiousness and spirituality. In R. F. Paloutzian & C. L. Park (Eds.), *Handbook of the psychology of religion and spirituality* (pp. 21–42). New York: Guilford.

26. See Judge, W. Q. (1999). *The leader's shadow: Exploring and developing executive character*. Thousand Oaks, CA: Sage.

27. Reave, L. (2005). Spiritual values and practices related to leadership effectiveness. *The Leadership Quarterly, 16,* 655–687.

28. One detailed list of personal and collective spiritual practices can be found in Foster, R. J. (1978). *Celebration of discipline: The path to spiritual growth*. New York: Harper & Row.

29. Fry, L. W. (2003). Toward a theory of spiritual leadership. *The Leadership Quarterly, 14,* 693–727; Fry, L. W., Vitucci, S., & Cedillo, M. (2005). Spiritual leadership and army transformation: Theory, measurement, and establishing a baseline. *The Leadership Quarterly, 16,* 835–862; Fry, L. W. (2005). Toward a theory of ethical and spiritual well-being, and corporate social responsibility through spiritual leadership. In R. A. Giacalone, C. L. Jurkiewicz, & C. Dunn (Eds.), *Positive psychology in business ethics and corporate responsibility* (pp. 47–84). Greenwich, CT: Information Age Publishing.

30. Benefiel, M. (2005). *Soul at work: Spiritual leadership in organizations*. New York: Seabury Books; Benefiel, M. (2005). The second half of the journey: Spiritual leadership for organizational transformation. *The Leadership Quarterly, 16,* 723–747.

31. Jurkiewicz & Giacalone.

32. Boje, D. (2008). Critical theory approaches to spirituality in business. In J. Biberman & L. Tischler (Eds.), *Spirituality in business: Theory, practice, and future directions* (pp. 160–187). New York: Palgrave Macmillan.

PART III

Ethical Standards and Strategies

5

General Ethical Perspectives

Leaders are truly effective only when they are motivated by a concern for others.

—Business professors Rabindra Kanungo
and Manuel Mendonca

WHAT'S AHEAD

This chapter surveys widely used ethical perspectives that can be applied to the leadership role. These approaches include utilitarianism, Kant's categorical imperative, Rawls's justice as fairness, communitarianism, and altruism. I provide a brief description of each perspective along with a balance sheet that identifies the theory's advantages and disadvantages.

Learning about well-established ethical systems can help us expand our ethical expertise. The moral dilemmas we face as leaders may be unique. However, we can meet these challenges with the same tools that we apply to other ethical problems. I've labeled the ethical approaches or theories described in this chapter as "general" because they were developed for all kinds of moral choices. Yet as we'll see, they have much to say to those of us in leadership positions.

Utilitarianism: Do the Greatest Good for the Greatest Number of People

Utilitarianism is based on the premise that ethical choices should be based on their consequences. People probably have always considered the likely outcomes of their decisions when determining what to do. However, this process wasn't formalized and given a name until the 18th and 19th centuries. English philosophers Jeremy Bentham (1748–1832) and John Stuart Mill (1806–1873) argued that the best decisions generate the most benefits as compared with their disadvantages and benefit the largest number of people.[1] In sum, utilitarianism is attempting to do the greatest good for the greatest number of people. Utility can be based on what is best in a specific case (act utilitarianism) or on what is generally best in most contexts (rule utilitarianism). For example, we can decide that telling a specific lie is justified in one situation (to protect someone's reputation) but, as a general rule, believe that lying is wrong because it causes more harm than good.

There are four steps to conducting a utilitarian analysis of an ethical problem.[2] First, clearly identify the action or issue under consideration. Second, specify all those who might be affected by the action (e.g., the organization, the local community, a professional group, society), not just those immediately involved in the situation. Third, determine the good and bad consequences for those affected. Fourth, sum the good and the bad consequences. The action is morally right if the benefits outweigh the costs. (Turn to Case Study 5.1 on page 156 for an example of a decision that involves choosing the less costly of two alternatives.)

Political leaders often take a utilitarian approach to ethical decision making. For instance, security screening procedures at American airports have been tightened based on utilitarian considerations. In response to the World Trade Center attacks, security personnel began x-raying bags and carry-on items, patting down some passengers, and sending travelers through metal detectors. When a Nigerian airline passenger set off a packet of chemicals hidden in his underwear on Christmas Day in 2009, the Transportation Security Administration began to expand its use of body imaging devices. These screening technologies reveal metal and nonmetal objects hidden beneath clothing but can also produce graphic images of the human body. All these measures are costly. They are expensive, time consuming, inconvenient, and intrusive. But so far federal officials and the majority of passengers believe that these costs are justified because they prevent attacks and save lives.

Balance Sheet

Advantages (Pros)

- Is easy to understand
- Is frequently used
- Forces us to examine the outcomes of our decisions
- Supersedes personal interests

Disadvantages (Cons)

- Consequences are difficult to identify, measure, and evaluate
- May have unanticipated outcomes
- May result in decision makers reaching different conclusions

The notion of weighing outcomes is easy to understand and to apply. We create a series of mental balance sheets for all types of decisions, such as determining whether an item, a car, or a vacation package is worth the price; considering a job offer; or evaluating the merits of two political candidates. Focusing on outcomes encourages us to think through our decisions, and we're less likely to make rash, unreasoned choices, which is particularly important when it comes to ethical dilemmas. The ultimate goal of evaluating consequences is admirable: to maximize benefits to as many people as possible (not just ourselves). Utilitarianism is probably the most defensible approach in emergency medical situations involving large numbers of injured victims. Top priority should go to those who are most likely to survive. It does little good to spend time with a terminal patient while another victim who would benefit from treatment dies.

Identifying possible consequences can be difficult, particularly for leaders who represent a variety of constituencies or stakeholders. Take the case of a college president who must decide what academic programs to cut in a budget crisis. Many different groups have a stake in this decision, and each probably will reach a different conclusion about potential costs and benefits. Every department believes that it makes a valuable contribution to the university and serves the mission of the school. Powerful alumni may be alienated by the elimination of their majors. Members of the local community might suffer if the education department is terminated and no longer supplies teachers to area schools or if plays and concerts end because of cutbacks in the theater and music departments. Unanticipated consequences further complicate the choice. If student enrollments increase, the president may have to restore programs that she eliminated earlier. Yet failing to make cuts can put the future of the school in jeopardy.

Even when consequences are clear, evaluating their relative merits can be daunting. It is hard to compare different kinds of costs and benefits, for example. The construction of a housing development provides new homes but takes farmland out of production. How do we weigh the relative value of urban housing versus family farms? Also, utilitarianism says little about how benefits are to be distributed. Doing the greatest good may mean putting one group at a serious disadvantage so that everyone else will benefit. In World War II, for example, Japanese Americans were warehoused in camps based on the mistaken belief that the nation as a whole would be safer. Conversely, utilitarian calculations may benefit the few at the expense of the majority. Many medical donors focus their contributions in developing countries on one disease, such as malaria, hoping to have a major impact on that illness. Such an approach benefits those who suffer from a particular malady but ignores the needs of everyone else suffering from other medical problems like HIV/ AIDS, tuberculosis, cancer, kidney disease, dysentery, and cholera. As I noted in Chapter 2, we also tend to favor ourselves when making decisions. Thus, we are likely to put more weight on consequences that most directly affect us. It's all too easy to confuse the "greatest good" with our selfish interests.

Based on the difficulty of identifying and evaluating potential costs and benefits, utilitarian decision makers sometimes reach different conclusions when faced with the same dilemma. Americans are still debating the merits of heightened airport security measures. Many argue that the costs of stricter security are justified because no further attacks have succeeded in causing serious damage to planes or passengers. On the other hand, privacy groups and some in Congress oppose the use of body imaging devices, labeling them as "digital strip searches."[3] A number of potential air travelers, turned off by the hassle of going through security checkpoints at airports, have opted to drive to their destinations instead.

CASE STUDY 5.1

DECIDING BETWEEN TWO EVILS: THE INVASION OF THE ASIAN CARP

The Asian carp is one scary species of fish. Bighead, black, silver, and grass carp can consume nearly 40% of their body weight in food every day, growing to be 4 feet long and weighing 100 pounds. They can leap 4 feet out of the water when threatened (by a motor, for instance) and seriously injure boaters, fishermen, and Jet Skiers. However, the greatest danger they pose is to the environment. Asian carp eat plankton and other food needed to sustain native fish and reproduce rapidly with no natural predators. Soon they become the dominant species, and the ecosystem collapses.

Southern catfish farmers imported Asian carp into the United States during the 1970s to eat algae in their ponds. However, the fish escaped during flooding and began moving up the Mississippi River. Now they are poised to enter Lake Michigan via the Illinois River, which reportedly has the highest concentration of Asian carp in the world. Officials in states bordering the Great Lakes, as well as leaders in Canada, fear an environmental disaster if the carp enter the lake. Not only would they destroy "an American treasure," threatening a $7 billion fishing industry and tourism, but the invaders could then spread up tributaries and to the other Great Lakes.[1]

The U.S. Army Corps of Engineers installed an electric barrier to prevent the carp from moving from the Illinois River to Lake Michigan through the Chicago Sanitary and Ship Canal, which connects the lake with the Mississippi River system. Concerned that this would not be enough to deter the fish, Michigan, Wisconsin, Minnesota, Ohio, New York, Pennsylvania, and the province of Ontario sued to close the locks between the lake and the canal. However, the state of Illinois and barge owners, who use the canal to ship gravel, sewage, commercial goods, wastewater, petroleum, and other products, argued that the costs of shutting the locks outweighed the potential damage from keeping them open. They asserted that closing the locks would "have a devastating effect" on the regional economy, dramatically driving up shipping rates and costing thousands of jobs.[2] The Supreme Court (which rules on cases involving competing states) sided with the shippers. Fisheries experts and regional governors aren't about to give up, though. Some have gone so far as to suggest that the canal be permanently closed.

The fight over the Asian carp is typical of battles over invasive species. In these cases, leaders must select between unattractive alternatives. Letting unwelcome plant or animal species remain is costly, but so is removing the offenders. Officials in the Florida Everglades, for example, must decide whether it is worth the financial cost and effort to remove the Burmese pythons that have moved into the area. They eat alligators, endangered pumas, and birds, and are perfectly capable of eating humans. However, the pythons are difficult to find, and making a significant dent in their population would consume much of Florida's entire budget for fighting invasive species. In these cases, leaders use a form of utilitarian reasoning to decide which option is less costly than the other. In other words, they must choose between the lesser of two evils.

What is the lesser of two evils? Shutting down the canal locks to prevent the spread of the Asian carp or keeping the locks open? Why?

(Continued)

(Continued)

Notes

1. Guarino, M. (2009, December 29). Minnesota, Ohio join lawsuit against Illinois over Asian carp. *The Christian Science Monitor.* Retrieved from http://www.csmonitor.com/USA/2009/1229/Minnesota-Ohio-join-lawsuit-against-Illinois-over-Asian-carp

2. Eilperin, J. (2010, February 7). Fight over invasive species turns into fight over lesser of two evils. *The Oregonian,* p. A2.

Sources

Barry, D. (2008, September 15). On an infested river, battling invaders eye to eye. *The New York Times,* p. A13.

Bilger, B. (2009, April 20). Swamp things; Florida's uninvited predators. *The New Yorker,* p. 80.

Cauchon, D. (2009, December 1). Invasive carp threatens Great Lakes. *USA Today,* p. 17A.

Davey, M. (2009, December 13). Be careful what you fish for. *The New York Times,* p. WK3.

Hammer, K. (2009, October 14). Asian carp just one flop away from Great Lakes. *The Globe and Mail,* p. A3.

Petry, C. (2010, January 22). Chicago locks will stay open, Supreme Court rules. *Metal Bulletin.*

Kant's Categorical Imperative: Do What's Right No Matter the Cost

In sharp contrast to the utilitarians, European philosopher Immanuel Kant (1724–1804) argued that people should do what is morally right no matter the consequences.[4] (The term *categorical* means "without exception.") His approach to moral reasoning is the best-known example of deontological ethics. Deontological ethicists argue that we ought to make choices based on our duty (*deon* is the Greek word for duty). Fulfilling our obligations may run contrary to our personal interests. For example, revealing a product defect to a potential customer might cost us a sale but is nevertheless the ethical course of action.

According to Kant, what is right for one is right for all. We need to ask ourselves one question: "Would I want everyone else to make the decision I did?" If the answer is yes, the choice is justified. If the answer is no, the decision is wrong. Based on this reasoning, certain behaviors such as truth telling and helping the poor are always right. Other acts, such as lying, cheating, and murder, are always wrong. Testing and grading would be impossible if everyone cheated, for example, and cooperation would be impossible if no one could be trusted to tell the truth.

Kant lived well before the advent of the automobile, but violations of his decision-making rule could explain why law enforcement officials have to crack down on motorists who run red lights. So many Americans regularly disobey traffic signals (endangering pedestrians and other drivers) that some communities have installed cameras at intersections to catch violators. Drivers have failed to recognize one simple fact: They may save time by running lights, but they shouldn't do so because the system breaks down when large numbers of people ignore traffic signals.

Kant also emphasized the importance of respecting persons, which has become a key principle in Western moral philosophy.[5] According to Kant, "Act so that you treat humanity, whether in your own person or that of another, always as an end and never as a means only." Although others can help us reach our goals, they should never be considered solely as tools. Instead, we should respect and encourage the capacity of others to think and choose for themselves. Under this standard, it is wrong for companies to expose citizens living near manufacturing facilities to dangerous pollutants without their knowledge or consent. Coercion and violence are immoral because such tactics violate freedom of choice. Failing to assist a neighbor is unethical because ignoring this person's need limits his or her options.

Balance Sheet

Advantages (Pros)

- Promotes persistence and consistency
- Is highly motivational
- Promotes the health of society as a whole
- Demonstrates respect for others

Disadvantages (Cons)

- Exceptions exist to nearly every "universal" law
- Moral obligations may conflict with one another
- Is demonstrated through unrealistic examples
- Is hard to apply, particularly under stress

Emphasis on duty encourages persistence and consistent behavior. Those driven by the conviction that certain behaviors are either right or wrong no matter the situation are less likely to compromise their personal ethical standards. They are apt to "stay the course" despite group pressures and opposition and to follow through on their choices. (See "Leadership Ethics at the Movies: *Defiance*" for an example of a leader who took his ethical duties seriously.) Transcendent principles serve as powerful motivational tools.

Seeking justice, truth, and mercy is more inspiring than pursuing selfish concerns. Society as a whole benefits when citizens tell the truth, honor their commitments, help others, and so on. Respecting the right of others to choose is an important guideline to keep in mind when making moral choices. This standard promotes the sharing of information and concern for others while condemning deception, coercion, and violence.

Most attacks on Kant's system of reasoning center on his assertion that there are universal principles that should be followed in every situation. In almost every case, we can think of exceptions. For instance, many of us believe that lying is wrong yet would lie or withhold the truth to save the life of a friend. Countries regularly justify homicide during war. Then, too, moral obligations can conflict. It may be impossible to keep promises made to more than one group, for example. Raises promised to employees may have to be set aside in order to pay dividends promised to stockholders. Or satisfying one duty may mean violating another, as in the case of a whistle-blower who puts truth telling above loyalty to the organization. (See Chapter 7 for more information on ethical dilemmas involving two right values.)

Despite the significant differences between the categorical and utilitarian approaches, both theories involve the application of universal rules or principles to specific situations. Dissatisfaction with rule-based approaches is widespread.[6] Some contemporary philosophers complain that these ethical guidelines are applied to extreme situations, not the types of decisions we typically make. Few of us will be faced with the extraordinary scenarios (stealing to save a life or lying to the secret police to protect a fugitive) that are often used to illustrate principled decision making. Our dilemmas are less dramatic. We have to determine whether to confront a coworker about a sexist joke or tell someone the truth at the risk of hurting his or her feelings. We also face time pressures and uncertainty. In a crisis, we don't always have time to carefully weigh consequences or to determine which abstract principle to follow.

 LEADERSHIP ETHICS AT THE MOVIES

DEFIANCE

Key Cast Members: Daniel Craig, Liev Schreiber, Jamie Bell, Alexa Davalos, Allan Corduner

Synopsis: Tells the true story of the Bielski brothers who become the reluctant protectors of over 1,000 of their fellow Belarusian Jews during World War II. Smugglers before the war, they take to the forest where they are joined by others fleeing German extermination squads. Tuvia (Daniel Craig) must put aside his desire for revenge against the Nazis and local collaborators in order to feed and shelter his new flock. His brother Zus (Schreiber), on the other hand, opts to fight back by joining the Russian partisans. Under Tuvia's leadership, the band of survivors manages to build a community while avoiding German troops and battling brutal winters.

Rating: R for violence and language

Themes: duty, justice, human dignity and rights, utilitarianism, communitarianism, altruism, evil, revenge, character, emergent leadership

Discussion Starters

1. What ethical issues do Tuvia and Zus face?

2. What ethical principles do the brothers follow when making ethical decisions? What virtues do they display?

3. How do the other survivors contribute to building this community?

Justice as Fairness: Guaranteeing Equal Rights and Opportunities Behind the Veil of Ignorance

Many disputes in democratic societies center on questions of justice or fairness. Is it just to give more tax breaks to the rich than to the poor? What is equitable compensation for executives? Should a certain percentage of federal contracts be reserved for minority contractors? Is it fair that Native Americans are granted special fishing rights? Why should young workers have to contribute to the Social Security system that may not be around when they retire?

In the last third of the 20th century, Harvard philosopher John Rawls addressed questions such as these in a series of books and articles.[7] He set out to identify principles that would foster cooperation in a society made up of free and equal citizens who, at the same time, must deal with inequalities (e.g., status and economic differences, varying levels of talent and abilities). Rawls rejected utilitarian principles because, as we noted earlier, generating the greatest number of benefits for society as a whole can seriously disadvantage certain groups and individuals. Cutting corporate taxes is another case of how utilitarian reasoning can undermine the interests of some groups at the expense of others. This policy may spur a region's overall economic growth, but most of the benefits of this policy go to the owners of companies. Other citizens have to pay higher taxes to make up for the lost revenue. Those making minimum wage, who can barely pay for rent and food, are particularly hard hit. They end up subsidizing wealthy corporate executives and stockholders.

Instead of basing decisions on cost–benefit analyses, Rawls argues that we should follow these principles of justice and build them into our social institutions:

> *Principle 1:* Each person has an equal right to the same basic liberties that are compatible with similar liberties for all.

> *Principle 2:* Social and economic inequalities are to satisfy two conditions: (A) They are to be attached to offices and positions open to all under conditions of fair equality of opportunity. (B) They are to provide the greatest benefit to the least advantaged members of society.

The first principle, the "principle of equal liberty," has priority. It states that certain rights, such as the right to vote, the right to hold property, and freedom of speech, are protected and must be equal to what others have. Attempts to deny voting rights to minorities would be unethical according to this standard. Principle 2A asserts that everyone should have an equal opportunity to qualify for offices and jobs. Discrimination based on race, gender, or ethnic origin is forbidden. Furthermore, everyone in society ought to have access to the training and education needed to prepare for these roles. Principle 2B, "the difference principle," recognizes that inequalities exist but that priority should be given to meeting the needs of the poor, immigrants, minorities, and other marginalized groups.

Rawls introduces the "veil of ignorance" to back up his claim that his principles provide a solid foundation for a democratic society such as the United States. Imagine, he says, a group of people who are asked to come up with a set of principles that will govern society. These group members are ignorant of their characteristics or societal position. Standing behind this veil of ignorance, these people would choose (a) equal liberty, because they would want the maximum amount of freedom to pursue their interests; (b) equal opportunity, because if they turned out to be the most talented members of society, they would probably land the best jobs and elected offices; and (c) the difference principle, because they would want to be sure they were cared for if they ended up disadvantaged.

Balance Sheet

Advantages (Pros)

- Nurtures both individual freedom and the good of the community
- Highlights important democratic values and concern for the less fortunate
- Encourages leaders to treat followers fairly
- Provides a useful decision-making guide

Disadvantages (Cons)

- Principles can be applied only to democratic societies
- Groups disagree about the meaning of justice and fairness
- Lack of consensus about the most important rights

Rawls offers a system for dealing with inequalities that encompasses both individual freedom and the common good. More talented, skilled, or fortunate people are free to pursue their goals, but the fruits of their labor must also benefit their less fortunate neighbors. His principles also uphold important democratic values such as equal opportunity, freedom of thought and speech, and the right to own and sell property. Following Rawls's guidelines would ensure that everyone receives adequate health care, decent housing, and a high-quality education. At the same time, the glaring gap between the haves and have-nots would shrink. Using such principles in the organizational setting could help resolve disputes over how to allocate limited organizational resources such as bonuses, corner offices, computers, and departmental budgets and ensure more equitable treatment of employees. (We will take a closer look at organizational justice in Chapter 9.)

The justice-as-fairness approach is particularly relevant to leaders who, as we noted in Chapter 1, cast shadows by acting inconsistently. Inconsistent leaders violate commonly held standards of fairness, arbitrarily giving preferential treatment to some followers while denying the same benefits to others who are equally deserving (or more so). Rawls encourages leaders to be fair. They have a responsibility to guarantee basic rights to all followers; to ensure that followers have equal access to promotion, training, and other benefits; and to make special efforts to help followers who have unique needs.

Stepping behind a veil of ignorance is a useful technique to use when making moral choices. Behind the veil, wealth, education, gender, and race disappear. The least advantaged usually benefit when social class differences are excluded from the decision-making process. Our judicial system is one example of an institution that should treat disputants fairly. Unfortunately, economic and racial considerations influence the selection of juries, the determination of guilt and innocence, the length of sentences (and where they are served), and nearly every other aspect of the judicial process.

Rawls's theory of justice as fairness has come under sharp attack. Rawls himself acknowledged that his model applies only to liberal democratic societies. It would not work in cultures governed by royal families or religious leaders who are given special powers and privileges denied to everyone else. In addition, the more diverse democratic nations become, the more difficult it is for groups to agree on common values and principles.[8]

Rawls's critics note that definitions of justice and fairness vary widely, a fact that undermines the usefulness of his principles. What seems fair to one group or individual often appears grossly unjust to others. Evidence of this fact is found in disputes over college admission criteria. Minorities claim that they should be favored in admission decisions to redress past discrimination and to achieve equal footing with Whites. Caucasians, on the other hand, feel that such standards are unfair because they deny equal opportunity and ignore legitimate differences in abilities.

Some philosophers point out that there is no guarantee that parties who step behind the veil of ignorance would come up with the same set of principles as Rawls. Rather than emphasize fairness, these people might choose to make decisions based on utilitarian criteria or to emphasize certain rights. For example, libertarians hold that freedom from coercion is the most important human right. Every person should be able to produce and sell as he or she chooses regardless of impact on the poor. Capitalist theorists believe that benefits should be distributed based on the contributions each person makes to the group. They argue that helping out the less advantaged rewards laziness while discouraging productive people from doing their best. Because decision makers may reach different conclusions behind the veil, skeptics contend that Rawls's guidelines lack moral force. Other approaches to managing society's inequities are just as valid as the notion of fairness.

Communitarianism: Shoulder Your Responsibilities and Seek the Common Good

Rawls and many other Western philosophers, legal experts, and political theorists emphasize the importance of individual autonomy and personal rights. However, focusing on the individual ignores the fact that humans are social creatures. Personal identities are shaped through interactions with others in particular communities.[9] Community members, in turn, have significant obligations to their fellow citizens and to the group as a whole.

In 1990 sociologist Amitai Etzioni convened 15 ethicists, social scientists, and philosophers in Washington, DC, to express their concerns about the state of American society. Members of this gathering took the name *communitarian* to highlight their desire to shift the attention of citizens from individual rights to communal responsibilities. The next year the group started a journal and organized a teach-in that produced the communitarian platform. In 1993, Etzioni published the communitarian agenda in a book titled *The Spirit of Community: The Reinvention of American Society*.[10] The communitarian platform suggests a moratorium on the generation of new individual rights; recognition that citizenship means accepting civic responsibilities (serving on a jury) along with rights and privileges (the right to a trial by jury); acknowledgment that certain duties may not bring any immediate payoffs; and reinterpretation of some legal rights in order to improve public safety and health. For example, sobriety checkpoints, like airport security checkpoints, mean less personal freedom but are justified because they can significantly reduce traffic deaths. In addition to Etzioni, other writers associated with communitarianism include Robert Bellah, Charles Taylor, Michael Walzer, Michael Sanford, and Alasdair MacIntyre.

Contemporary communitarianism is not a cohesive philosophy but rather a movement based on several themes. Communitarians differ among themselves on a number of issues, such as how much freedom to give to individuals and how much control the community should exercise over its members. One wing of communitarianism is evangelistic, out to recruit followers to communitarian tenets that promote moral revival. U.S. society is fragmenting and in a state of moral decline, these communitarians proclaim. Evidence of this decay is all around us in the form of high divorce and crime rates, campaign attack ads, and the growing influence of special interest groups in politics. The United States needs renewal that can come only through the creation of healthy local, regional, and national communities. According to John Gardner, founder of the public interest group Common Cause, healthy or responsive communities are made up of the following:[11]

- *Wholeness incorporating diversity.* The existence of community depends on sharing some vision of a common good or purpose that makes it possible for people to live and work together. Yet at the same time, segments of the system are free to pursue their diverse and often competing interests.
- *A reasonable set of shared values.* Responsive communities agree on a set of core values that are reflected in written rules and laws, unwritten customs, a shared view of the future, and so on. Important ideals include justice, equality, freedom, the dignity of the individual, and the release of human talent and energy.

- *Caring, trust, and teamwork.* Healthy communities foster cooperation and connection at the same time they respect individual differences. Citizens feel a sense of belonging as well as a sense of responsibility. They recognize the rights of minorities, engage in effective conflict resolution, and work together on shared tasks.
- *Participation.* To function effectively, large, complex communities depend on the efforts of leaders dispersed throughout every segment of society.
- *Affirmation.* Healthy collectives sustain a sense of community through continuous reaffirmation of the history, symbols, and identity of the group.
- *Institutional arrangements for community maintenance.* Responsive communities ensure their survival through such structures as city and regional governments, boards of directors, and committees.

Creation of the kinds of communities envisioned by Gardner and others requires citizens to shoulder a number of collective responsibilities. Communitarian citizens should stay informed about public issues and become active in community affairs. They must serve on juries, work with others on common projects, care for the less fortunate, clean up corruption, provide guidance to children, and so forth. These tasks are often accomplished through voluntary associations such as environmental groups, churches, neighborhood patrols, youth sports leagues, and service organizations.

Concern for the common good may be the most important ethical principle to come out of the communitarian movement. Considering the needs of the broader community discourages selfish, unethical behavior. Lying, polluting, or manufacturing dangerous products may serve the needs of a leader or an organization, but such actions are unethical because they rarely benefit society as a whole. Furthermore, if each group looks out only for its own welfare, the larger community suffers. Communitarians address the problems posed by competing interests by urging leaders and followers to put the needs of the whole above the needs of any one individual, group, or organization. (Turn to "Focus on Follower Ethics: The Growing Influence of Followers: Engaging With and Resisting Leaders" for a closer look at how followers should engage with leaders and serve the public interest.) By promoting the common good, the communitarian movement encourages dialogue and discussion within and between groups. Consensus about ethical choices may come out of these discussions.

Balance Sheet

Advantages (Pros)

- Discourages selfish individualism
- Fosters dispersed leadership and ethical dialogue

- Encourages collaborative leadership strategies
- Promotes character development

Disadvantages (Cons)

- May repress individual rights and freedoms
- Evangelistic fervor of some proponents
- Promotes one set of values in a pluralistic society
- Formation of exclusive communities
- Fails to resolve competing community standards

Communitarianism is a promising approach to moral reasoning, particularly for leaders. First, communitarianism addresses selfishness head-on, encouraging us to put responsibilities above rights and to seek the common good. We're less tempted to abuse power or to accumulate leadership perks, for instance, if we remember that we have obligations both to our immediate followers and to the entire communities in which we live.

Second, communitarianism promotes the benefits of dispersed leadership and ethical dialogue. Healthy nations are energized networks of leaders operating in every segment of society: business, politics, health care, unions, social service, religion, and education. Leaders in these countries create a framework (characterized by equality, openness, and honesty) that encourages discussion of moral questions.

Third, communitarianism encourages collaborative leadership, a new way of solving public problems based on partnership.[12] Collaborative leaders bring together representatives of diverse groups to tackle civic problems such as failing schools, substandard housing, lack of minority leadership, public health problems, economic blight, and uncontrolled development. They focus on the decision-making process rather than promote a particular solution. Collaborative leaders have little formal power but function as "first among equals," convening discussions, providing information, finding resources, helping the group reach agreement, and seeing that the solution is implemented. Collaborative efforts have produced concrete, tangible results in a number of U.S. cities. Perhaps just as important, these efforts change the way in which communities do business. Trust is created, new communication networks form, the focus shifts from serving special interests to serving a common vision, and citizens are more likely to collaborate again in the future.

Fourth, the rise of communitarianism coincides with renewed interest in virtue ethics, which was our focus in Chapter 3. Both are concerned with the development of moral character. The communitarian movement fosters the development of the virtues by supporting strong families, schools, religious congregations, and governments. A "virtue cycle" is created. Virtuous citizens build moral communities that, in turn, encourage further character formation.

The communitarian movement has its share of detractors. Some critics fear that focusing on the needs of the collective will suppress individual freedoms. Others worry about the evangelistic fervor of some communitarians and object to promoting one set of values in a pluralistic society. For example, who decides which values are taught in the public schools? Christians want the Ten Commandments displayed in courtrooms, but Buddhists, Muslims, and other religious groups object. Still other critics point out that many communities (gated residential neighborhoods, for example) exclude outsiders.[13]

Competing community standards may pose the greatest threat to communitarianism. Communities often have conflicting moral guidelines. For example, the National Collegiate Athletic Association (NCAA) has banned Indian nicknames, mascots, and logos from championship competition and refuses to stage championship events at schools that keep these symbols. The organization calls Indian mascots at 18 schools "hostile and abusive." Many fans and alumni oppose the ban, claiming that their mascots are an integral part of school tradition and honor Native Americans, not defame them. On the other hand, many tribal leaders support the NCAA, arguing that these symbols degrade native peoples and reinforce racist stereotypes. The University of Illinois retired its 81-year-old Indian mascot, Chief Illiniwek, in response to NCAA pressure.[14]

Communitarians turn first to community agreement when resolving conflicts such as these.[15] Local values should be respected because they reflect the unique history of the group. Community standards can be oppressive, however. After all, Native Americans have been the continuing victims of discrimination since Whites first arrived on the continent. Communitarian thinkers turn next to societal values and then to global principles in such cases. Local preferences must be accountable to the larger society and to universal values. Based on this reasoning, Native American mascots should be retired because they undermine such national and international principles as equality, tolerance, respect, and diversity.

Applying societal and global norms does not always resolve intercommunity moral conflicts. This is the case with Oregon's "Death With Dignity Act," which sanctions physician-assisted suicide. Twice state voters approved this measure despite strong opposition from medical and religious groups. The U.S. attorney general tried to outlaw the use of painkillers for medically assisted suicide under the federal Controlled Substances Act. However, he was prevented from doing so by a federal court ruling.[16] Both sides in the dispute claim that their positions are based on widely shared moral principles. Proponents of death with dignity believe that suicide is justified by such values as compassion, quality of life, free will, and self-determination. Opponents give more priority to the sanctity of life and argue that extending life is more compassionate than prematurely ending it.

 FOCUS ON FOLLOWER ETHICS

THE GROWING INFLUENCE OF FOLLOWERS: ENGAGING WITH AND RESISTING LEADERS

Harvard University political scientist Barbara Kellerman believes that followers are gaining power at the expense of leaders. "It's clear the gap between leaders and followers is closing," she asserts (p. 46). "Leaders need followers more than followers need leaders" (p. 242). Followers led the antiwar, civil rights, and women's movements in the United States, for example, and toppled Communism and the Berlin Wall. Shareholders are becoming more active in corporate governance, and a number of autocratic CEOs and orchestra conductors have been replaced with friendlier, more approachable leaders. Kellerman attributes the growing influence of followers to the equalitarian spirit of the 1960s and the ongoing information revolution, which makes data accessible to everyone, not just leaders, and flattens organizational structures.

Professor Kellerman offers a follower typology based on the level of involvement that followers have with their leaders. *Isolate* followers are the least engaged, completely withdrawn and detached. *Bystander* followers observe and remain neutral. *Participant* followers are invested in helping or resisting their leaders. *Activist* followers are even more engaged in working on behalf of or against their leaders. *Die-hard* followers take great risks because they are strongly devoted to, or strongly opposed to, their leaders.

Kellerman argues that, at a minimum, ethical followers engage with their leaders. Isolates and bystanders therefore demonstrate bad followership. However, engagement alone is not enough to make followers "good." Participants, activists, and die-hards can support unethical leaders. Kellerman notes that the question then becomes "Willingness to engage to what end, for what purpose?" (p. 229). She concludes that good followers are not only involved; they are motivated to serve the public good, not selfish interests. To encourage followers to serve the greater good by resisting bad leaders, she offers a number of guidelines. Among them are the following:

- Be informed.
- Be engaged.

(Continued)

(Continued)

- Be independent.
- Be a watchdog.
- Be prepared to analyze and judge the situation, the leader, and the other followers.
- Be open to allies and to forming coalitions.
- Be prepared to be different.
- Be prepared to take a stand.
- Be loyal to the group, not to any single individual.
- Know the slippery slope—bad leaders who over time become more deeply embedded and more difficult to uproot.
- Know your options.
- Know the risk of doing something—and of doing nothing.
- Check your moral compass. (pp. 257–258)

SOURCE: Kellerman, B. (2008). *Followership: How followers are creating change and changing leaders.* Boston: Harvard Business School Press.

Altruism: Love Your Neighbor

Advocates of altruism argue that love of neighbor is the ultimate ethical standard. Our actions should be designed to help others whatever the personal cost. The altruistic approach to moral reasoning, like communitarianism, shares much in common with virtue ethics. Many of the virtues that characterize people of high moral character, such as compassion, hospitality, empathy, and generosity, reflect concern for other people. Clearly, virtuous leaders are other-centered, not self-centered.

Altruism appears to be a universal value, one promoted in cultures from every region of the world. The Dalai Lama urges followers to practice an ethic of compassion, for instance, and Western thought has been greatly influenced by the altruistic emphasis of Judaism and Christianity. The command to love God and to love others as we love ourselves is our most important obligation in Judeo-Christian ethics. Because humans are made in the image of God and God is love, we have an obligation to love others no matter who they are and no matter their relationship to us. Jesus drove home this point in the parable of the Good Samaritan.

A man was going down from Jerusalem to Jericho when he fell into the hands of robbers. They stripped him of his clothes, beat him, and went away, leaving him half dead. A priest happened to be going down the same road, and when he saw the man, he passed by on the other side. So too, a Levite, when he came to the place and saw him, passed by on the other side. But a Samaritan, as he traveled, came where the man was; and when he saw him, he took pity on him. He went to him and bandaged his wounds, pouring on oil and wine. Then he put the man on his own donkey, took him to an inn, and took care of him. The next day he took out two silver coins and gave them to the innkeeper. "Look after him," he said, "and when I return, I will reimburse you for any extra expense you may have." Which of these three do you think was a neighbor to the man who fell into the hands of robbers? The expert replied, "The one who had mercy on him." Jesus told him, "Go and do likewise." (Luke 1:3–35, New International Version)

Hospice volunteers provide a modern-day example of the unconditional love portrayed in the story of the Good Samaritan. They meet the needs of the dying regardless of a person's social or religious background, providing help at significant personal cost without expecting anything in return. (An ethical approach specifically based on caring for others is described in Box 5.1.)

Concern for others promotes healthy social relationships. Society as a whole functions more effectively when people help one another in their daily interactions. Researchers from social psychology, economics, political science, and other fields have discovered that altruistic behavior is more often than not the norm, not the exception.[17] Every day we help others by pitching in to help finish a project, shoveling the driveway of an elderly neighbor, listening to a roommate's problems, and so on. Altruism is the driving force behind all kinds of movements and organizations designed to help the less fortunate and to eliminate social problems. Name almost any nonprofit group, ranging from a hospital or medical relief team to a youth club or crisis hotline, and you'll find that it was launched by someone with an altruistic motive. (See Case Study 5.2 on page 179, for example.) In addition, when we compare good to evil, altruistic acts generally come to mind. Moral heroes and moral champions shine so brightly because they ignore personal risks to battle evil forces.

From this discussion, it's easy to see why altruism is a significant ethical consideration for all types of citizens. However, management professors Rabindra Kanungo and Manuel Mendonca believe that concern for others is even more important for leaders than it is for followers.[18] By definition, leaders exercise influence on behalf of others. They can't understand or articulate the needs of followers unless they focus on the concerns of constituents. To succeed, leaders may have to take risks and sacrifice personal gain. According to Kanungo and Mendonca, leaders intent on benefiting followers will pursue organizational goals, rely on referent and expert power bases, and give power away. Leaders intent on benefiting themselves will focus on personal achievements; rely on legitimate, coercive, and reward power bases; and try to control followers.

Followers prefer selfless leaders to selfish ones.[19] Self-focused leaders destroy loyalty and trust and are more likely to lead their communities into disaster. On the other hand, leaders who sacrifice on behalf of the group demonstrate their commitment to its mission. They set a powerful example that encourages followers to do the same. Higher performance often results. *Individual-focused* leader altruistic behaviors include providing training, technical assistance, and mentoring. *Group-focused* leader altruistic behaviors include team building, participative group decision-making, and minority advancement programs. *Organizational-focused* leader altruistic attitudes and actions include demonstrating commitment and loyalty, protecting organizational resources, and whistle-blowing. *Societal-focused* leader altruistic behaviors include making contributions to promote social welfare, reducing pollution, ensuring product safety, and maintaining customer satisfaction.[20] ("Self-Assessment: Organizational Citizenship Behavior Scale" tests your willingness to engage in altruistic behavior on the job.)

BOX 5.1 THE ETHIC OF CARE

The altruistic ethic of care developed as an alternative to what feminists label as the traditional male-oriented approach to ethics. The categorical imperative and justice-as-fairness theories emphasize the importance of acting on abstract moral principles, being impartial, and treating others fairly. Carol Gilligan, Nel Noddings, and others initially argued that women take a different approach (have a "different voice") to moral decision making based on caring for others. Instead of expressing concern for people in abstract terms, women care for others through their relationships and tailor their responses to the particular needs of the other individual. Subsequent research revealed that the ethic of care is not exclusive to women. Men as well as women may prefer care to justice.

Philosopher Virginia Held identifies five key components of the care ethic:

1. *Focuses on the importance of noting and meeting the needs of those we are responsible for.* Most people are dependent for much of their existence, including during childhood, during illness, and near the end of life. Morality built on rights and autonomy overlooks this fact. The ethic of care makes concern for others central to human experience and puts the needs of specific individuals (a child, an elderly relative) first.

2. *Values emotions.* Sympathy, sensitivity, empathy, and responsiveness are moral emotions that need to be cultivated. This stands in sharp contrast to ethical approaches that urge decision makers to set aside their feelings in order to make rational, impartial determinations. However, emotions need to be carefully monitored and evaluated to make sure they are appropriate. For instance, caregivers caught up in empathy can deny their own needs or end up controlling the recipients of their care.

3. *Specific needs and relationships take priority above universal principles.* The ethic of care rejects the notion of impartiality and believes particular relationships are more important than universal moral principles like rights and freedom. For example, the needs of the immediate family take precedence over the needs of neighbors or society as a whole. Persons in caring relationships aren't out to promote their personal interests or the interests of humanity; instead they want to foster ethical relationships with each other. Family and friendships have great moral value in the ethic of care, and caregiving is a critical moral responsibility.

4. *Breaks down the barriers between the public and private spheres.* In the past, men were dominant in the public sphere while relegating women to the "private" sphere. Men largely made decisions about how to exercise political and economic power while women were marginalized and dependent. The ethic of care argues that the private domain is just as important as the public domain and that problems faced in the private sphere, such as inequality and dependency, also arise in the public sphere.

5. *Views persons as both relational and interdependent.* Each of us starts life depending on others, and we depend on our webs of interpersonal relationships throughout our time on Earth. In the ethic of care, individuals are seen as "embedded" in particular families, cultures, and historical periods. Being embedded means that we need to take responsibility for others, not merely leave them alone to exercise their individual rights.

Adopting the ethic of care would significantly change national priorities. Child rearing, education, elder care, and other caring activities would consume a greater proportion of governmental budgets. Societal leaders would ensure that caregivers receive more money, recognition, and status. More men would take on caregiving responsibilities. Organizational leaders would help employees strike a

(Continued)

(Continued)

better balance between work and home responsibilities and provide more generous family leave policies. Corporations would devote more attention to addressing societal problems.

Sources

Gilligan, C. (1982). *In a different voice: Psychological theory and women's development.* Cambridge, MA: Harvard University Press.

Held, V. (2006). The ethics of care. In D. Copp (Ed.), *The Oxford handbook of ethical theory* (pp. 537–566). Oxford, UK: Oxford University Press.

Larrabee, M. J. (Ed.) (1993). *An ethic of care: Feminist and interdisciplinary perspectives.* New York: Routledge.

Noddings, N. (2003). *Caring: A feminine approach to ethics and moral education.* Berkeley: University of California Press.

Tronto, J. C. (1993). *Moral boundaries: A political argument for an ethic of care.* New York: Routledge.

Balance Sheet

Advantages (Pros)

- Ancient yet contemporary
- Important to society and leaders
- Powerful and inspiring

Disadvantages (Cons)

- Impossible to meet every need
- Failure of many who profess to love their neighbor to act as if they do
- Takes many different, sometimes conflicting, forms

Altruism is an attractive ethical perspective for several reasons. First, concern for others is an ancient yet contemporary principle. Two thousand years have passed since Jesus told the story of the Good Samaritan. However, we're still faced with the same type of dilemma as the characters in the story. Should we stop to help a stranded motorist or drive on? Should we give our spare change to the homeless person on the street or ignore him? Do we help a fallen runner in a marathon race or keep on running? Second, as I noted earlier, altruism is essential to the health of society in general and leaders in particular. Third, altruism is both powerful and inspiring. Acting selflessly counteracts the effects of evil and inspires others to do the same.

Although attractive, love of neighbor is not an easy principle to put into practice. The world's needs far exceed our ability to meet them. How do we decide whom to help and whom to ignore? Far too many people who claim to follow the Christian ethic fail miserably. They come across as less, not more, caring than those who don't claim to follow this approach. Some of the bitterest wars are religious ones, fought by believers who seemingly ignore the altruistic values of their faiths. There's also disagreement about what constitutes loving behavior. For example, committed religious leaders disagree about the legitimacy of war. Some view military service as an act of love, one designed to defend their families and friends. Others oppose the military, believing that nonviolence is the only way to express compassion for others.

SELF-ASSESSMENT

ORGANIZATIONAL CITIZENSHIP BEHAVIOR SCALE

Instructions

Take the following test to determine your willingness to engage in altruistic behavior in the work setting. Respond to each item on a 4-point scale ranging from 1 (*never engage in this behavior*) to 4 (*nearly always engage in this behavior*). Reverse the scale where indicated so that it ranges from 4 (*never engage in this behavior*) to 1 (*nearly always engage in this behavior*). Generate a total by adding up your scores. Maximum possible score: 80.

Response choices: 1 = Not at all;   2 = Somewhat;   3 = Very much;   4 = Exactly

1. Help other employees with their work when they
    have been absent.   1   2   3   4

2. Exhibit punctuality in arriving at work on time in the morning
    and after lunch and breaks.   1   2   3   4

3. Volunteer to do things not formally required by the job.   1   2   3   4

4. Take undeserved work breaks. (Reverse)   1   2   3   4

5. Take the initiative to orient new employees to the
    department even though it is not part of the job description.   1   2   3   4

6. Exhibit attendance at work beyond the norm; for example, take
    fewer days off than most individuals or fewer than allowed.   1   2   3   4

7. Help others when their workload increases (assist others until
    they get over the hurdles).   1   2   3   4

8. Coast toward the end of the day. (Reverse)   1   2   3   4

9. Give advance notice if unable to come to work.   1   2   3   4

10. Spend a great deal of time in personal telephone
    conversations. (Reverse)   1   2   3   4

11. Do not take unnecessary time off work.   1   2   3   4

12. Assist others with their duties.   1   2   3   4

13. Make innovative suggestions to improve the overall
    quality of the department.   1   2   3   4

14. Do not take extra breaks.   1   2   3   4

15. Willingly attend functions not required by the organization
    but that help its overall image.   1   2   3   4

16. Do not spend a great deal of time in idle conversation. 1   2   3   4

SOURCE: From *Organizational Citizenship Behavior: The Good Soldier Syndrome* by Organ, D. W. Copyright ©1988 by Lexington Books. Reproduced with permission of Lexington Books via Copyright Clearance Center.

Ethical Pluralism

I've presented these five ethical perspectives as separate and sometimes conflicting approaches to moral reasoning. In so doing, I may have given you the impression that you should select one theory and ignore the others. That would be a mistake. Often you'll need to combine perspectives (practice *ethical pluralism*) in order to resolve an ethical problem. I suggest that you apply all five approaches to the same problem and see what insights you gain from each one. You might find that a particular perspective is more suited to some kinds of ethical dilemmas than others. For example, when discussing Case Study 5.3 on page 183, you may conclude that communitarianism is less helpful than utilitarianism or the categorical imperative.

Implications and Applications

- Well-established ethical systems and values can help you set your ethical priorities as a leader.
- Utilitarianism weighs the possible costs and benefits of moral choices. According to this approach, seek to do the greatest good for the greatest number of people.
- Kant's categorical imperative urges us to do what's right no matter the consequences. By this standard, some actions (truth telling, helping others) are always right while others (lying, cheating, murder) are always wrong. Kant also urges us to treat followers with respect, never using them as tools for reaching our goals.
- The justice-as-fairness approach guarantees the same basic rights and opportunities to everyone in a democratic society. When these basic requirements are met, your responsibility as a leader is to give special consideration to the least advantaged.
- Communitarians focus attention on responsibility to the larger community and the need to make decisions that support the common good.
- Altruism encourages you to put others first, no matter the personal cost. The ethic of care is an altruistic approach to ethics based on meeting the needs of specific individuals.
- Don't expect perfection from any ethical perspective. Ethical approaches, like leaders themselves, have their strengths and weaknesses.
- Two well-meaning leaders can use the same ethical theory and reach different conclusions.
- Whenever possible, you should practice ethical pluralism by applying more than one perspective to the same problem.

For Further Exploration, Challenge, and Assessment

1. Can you think of any absolute moral laws or duties that must be obeyed without exception?

2. Reflect on one of your recent ethical decisions. What ethical system(s) did you follow? Were you satisfied with your choice?

3. What items can you add to each of the balance sheets in this chapter?

4. Given that inequalities will always exist, what is the best way to allocate wealth, education, health care, and other benefits in a democratic society? In organizations?

5. In a group, create a list of the characteristics of healthy and unhealthy communities. Then evaluate a town or city of your choice based on your list. Overall, how would you rate the health of this community?

6. Create your own ethics case based on your personal experience or on current or historical events. Describe the key ethical issues raised in the case and evaluate the characters in the story according to each of the five ethical standards.

7. Apply each of the five perspectives to Case Study 5.3 to determine whether you would support the inclusion of more genetic samples and familial DNA searches. Write up your conclusions.

CASE STUDY 5.2

FROM MOUNTAIN CLIMBER TO HUMANITARIAN

For several years Greg Mortenson was a self-described "dirtbag climber." The California nurse scrimped on living expenses so he could finance mountain climbing expeditions to some of the highest peaks in the world. That all changed in 1993, when he attempted to climb K2 in the Himalayas. He was forced to turn back 2,000 feet from the summit. Exhausted and dehydrated, Mortenson stumbled into the remote Pakistani village of Korphe at the base of the mountain. There the Balti villagers nursed him back to health, saving his life. While recuperating the climber noticed that the local children had to study outdoors because there was no school building. Mortenson vowed to build a school for the villagers.

Unlike a lot of other mountaineers who soon forget their promises when they return home, Mortenson followed through on his pledge. But it wasn't

(Continued)

(Continued)

easy. Broke and sleeping in his ancient Buick, Mortenson had to figure out how to raise $12,000 for construction. He sent 580 letters to celebrities, but only one (Tom Brokaw) responded with a check for $100. His fund-raising efforts got a boost when children at his mother's elementary school collected 62,400 pennies and a high-tech entrepreneur contributed most of the rest of the cost. Mortenson then sold his climbing gear and beloved car to raise additional cash and headed back to Pakistan.

When he arrived at Korphe, the village elders put his plans on hold, noting that they first needed a stone bridge built across the river gorge that cut off their town from neighboring villages. Greg then returned to the United States to raise an additional $10,000. It wasn't until 1996 that the Korphe School was completed. However, Mortenson, who took on the role of project supervisor, had another important lesson to learn. Village chief Haji Ali took him aside and told him he had to change his approach.

> If you want to thrive in Baltistan, you must respect our ways. The first time you share tea with a Balti, you are stranger. The second time you take tea, you are an honored guest. The third time you share a cup of tea, you become family... Doctor Greg, you must take time to share three cups of tea. We may be uneducated. But we are not stupid. We have lived and survived here for a long time.[1]

Once Greg stepped back from the role of foreman to become an observer, work proceeded much more quickly. He took away three lessons from this experience: (1) slow down and listen, (2) building relationships is critical, and (3) he had far more to learn from the villagers than he could ever hope to teach them.

The school at Korphe was only the beginning. Other village leaders in Pakistan and Afghanistan approached Mortenson for help, and he formed the Central Asia Institute (CAI) to build additional schools and to support other projects like building wells and libraries and underwriting teacher training. Mortenson's efforts received international attention when he was featured in a *Parade* magazine cover story and, more important, after the publication of the paperback version of his book (coauthored with David Relin) *Three Cups of Tea*, which has sold over 2.5 million copies and has been adopted for use in a number of colleges and universities. At last count, CAI has helped villagers to build 131 secular schools in Pakistan and 48 in Afghanistan.

The lessons Greg learned in Korphe serve as the cornerstone of the Central Asia Institute operating philosophy. All projects are initiated and managed by local people. Village committees oversee them, and residents must contribute resources and labor. Mortenson and his Western colleagues honor local customs and values. The CAI logo includes a crescent moon and star (Islamic symbols), for example, and Mortenson and his staff dress in traditional garb while in the field.

CAI is committed to educating females, noting that women's education is closely linked to economic development. The organization's leadership believes in the African proverb, "If you educate a boy, you educate an individual—if you educate a girl, you educate a community."[2] Girls who receive an education marry later, have fewer children, are less likely to die during childbirth, and have higher incomes.

Mortenson argues that education is also the most effective tool for promoting peace. "To fight terrorism with only war and not compassion is futile."[3] Ignorance and poverty are the breeding grounds for jihadists. Illiterate villagers must depend entirely on the local Muslim cleric, who may advocate violence, to interpret the Koran. A number of suicide bombers have been educated in madrassa schools in Pakistan, which are funded by the fundamentalist Sunni sect that is the state religion of Saudi Arabia. Secular education, in contrast, helps to raise the standard of living and promotes tolerance. Secularly educated women pass tolerant attitudes on to their sons. They are less likely to let their boys become insurgents or militants.

Mortenson seems uniquely qualified to carry out CAI's mission of promoting community-based education (particularly for girls) in one of the remotest, poorest, and most dangerous regions in the world. He grew up in a foreign culture, Tanzania, where his parents founded the nation's first teaching hospital. His experiences as a mountain climber, as well as living out of his car, helped prepare him for the Spartan conditions of Central Asia. Greg learns languages quickly. He is also undeterred by danger. Armed conflicts are common in the region, pitting India versus Pakistan, Pakistan versus the Taliban, and the U.S. and Afghan governments against the Taliban and al-Qaida. Mortenson was held hostage for eight days in Afghanistan and survived a gun battle between rival opium gangs by hiding under goatskins in the back of a truck. Then there are the natural dangers of the area. The region suffered from a major earthquake in 2005. Narrow roads, deep mountain gorges, and high mountain passes pose significant risks to travelers.

(Continued)

(Continued)

Above all, "Doctor Greg" sees his work as a calling. Part of his passion for educating girls comes from his relationship with his sister Christa. Christa suffered from epilepsy and brain damage; Greg was her protector. She died of a brain seizure just before Mortenson's K2 climb, which he dedicated to her. The children he saw in Korphe brought Christa to mind: "Everything about their life was a struggle. They reminded me of the way Christa had to fight for the simplest things."[4] The schools he builds serve as a tribute to her memory.

CAI's leader pays a high price for fulfilling his mission. He works for a modest salary and spends several months in the field every year, leaving behind his wife and two children. Even when back in the United States, Mortenson travels constantly. In one eight-month period this self-described introvert (who doesn't enjoy speaking in public) delivered over 400 presentations in 140 cities and gave 350 media interviews. His growing notoriety could put him in even greater danger in Central Asia as the target of the Taliban who oppose his efforts.

Greg's sacrifices have paid dividends. Fifty-one thousand have enrolled in CAI schools, and CAI continues to add supporters, staff, and projects. In recognition of his work, the Pakistani government awarded Mortenson its highest civilian medal, the Star of Pakistan, which is rarely given to a foreigner. Others are beginning to acknowledge that education, not war, is the key to establishing peace in the region. The U.S. military has asked Greg to speak to officer groups and is looking to CAI, with its emphasis on building relationships and carrying out humanitarian projects, as a model of how to combat the Taliban and extremists. The Chairman of the Joint Chiefs of Staff gave out books at the opening of a girls' school in the Hindu Kush mountains.

In the future the mountaineer-turned-humanitarian pledges to spend more time with his family. Doing so will be difficult as his commitment to the people of Central Asia and passion for his mission remain as strong as ever.

Discussion Probes

1. Why do you think Mortenson kept his promise to the Pakistani villagers when so many Western mountain climbers have not?

2. Should the CAI philosophy be the model for providing humanitarian aid in all regions of the world?

3. What are the potential risks to Mortenson and CAI that come from advising the military? The potential benefits?

4. Should the military shift its focus to humanitarian projects in Central Asia and elsewhere?

5. Can peace be created one school at a time?

6. Can CAI survive as an organization when Mortenson is no longer around? Can it be as effective?

7. What leadership ethics lessons do you take from this case?

Notes

1. Mortenson, G., & Relin, D. O. (2006). *Three cups of tea: One man's mission to promote peace . . . One school at a time.* New York: Penguin Group.

2. Maggin, A. (2009, March 27). *ABC News with Charles Gibson: Person of the week: Greg Mortenson.* Retrieved from https://www.ikat.org/2009/03/27/abc-mar-27-09/

3. Wilkinson, T. (2003, January 21). To fight terror, Montanan builds schools in Asia. *Christian Science Monitor,* USA, p. 1.

4. Blake, J. (2008, March 3). CNN special projects. *CNN International TV.* Retrieved from https://www.ikat.org/2008/03/03/cnn-special-projects/

Sources

Bly, L. (2009, January 2). "Three Cups of Tea" author finds new mountains to climb. *USA Today,* p. 4D.

Dreazen, Y. J. (2008, December 26). Military finds an unlikely adviser in school-building humanitarian. *The Wall Street Journal,* p. A9.

Friedman, T. L. (2009, July 19). Teacher, Can we leave now? No. *The New York Times,* WK, p. 10.

Maggin, A. (2009, March 27). Person of the week: Greg Mortenson. *ABC News.*

Mortenson, G. (2009). *Stones into schools: Promoting peace with books, not bombs, in Afghanistan and Pakistan.* New York: Viking.

Ronnow, K. (2008). Educate girls, change the world. *Journey of Hope,* pp. 21–26.

Ronnow, K. (2009, March 24). *Mortenson receives Star of Pakistan.* Retrieved from http://www.bozemandailychronicle.com/news/article_ccff0e98-0c8e-5fc9-857d-b5a639ef7a25.html

CASE STUDY 5.3

EXPANDING DNA DATABASES

DNA testing has become an indispensable crime-fighting tool. Using skin cells, hair, saliva, and other biological material, forensic experts can identify some individuals as suspects while eliminating other people from consideration. When presented with DNA evidence, juries are usually quick to convict.

(Continued)

(Continued)

The effectiveness of DNA profiling has encouraged law enforcement authorities to increase the size of their DNA databases. At first databases in the United Kingdom and the United States generally only included samples taken from those convicted of crimes. But now police in Britain collect DNA from anyone "suspected, charged or convicted of a 'recordable offense.'"[1] Samples stay in the system even if the individual is never charged or convicted of a crime. The United States is following suit. The FBI has joined a number of states in collecting genetic material from those awaiting trial as well as from immigrants who have been detained. Some local authorities will collect samples from minors and from adults picked up for misdemeanors like shoplifting or writing an insufficient funds check. Some U.S. databanks are also collecting samples from crime victims and lab workers.

Expanding DNA databases raises important ethical concerns. Forcing U.S. residents not convicted of crimes to provide their genetic material appears to violate the Fourth Amendment of the Constitution that protects citizens from arbitrary searches. Collection of the material also implies that individuals are guilty until proved innocent. Information in databanks could be abused. For example, if employers and insurers get access to the genetic samples, they might use the information to screen out applicants for jobs and insurance policies. Currently a much higher percentage of African American males are in the system than members of other ethnic groups, raising concerns about racial genetic profiling. British police have been accused of arresting individuals solely to collect their DNA.

In response to these concerns, the United Nations Educational, Scientific and Cultural Organization (UNESCO) has declared that genetic data policies should protect human rights. Materials should only be collected and stored for medical, criminal, and research purposes, according to UNESCO. Informed consent would be required for collection, and genetic material would be destroyed if a person was not charged with or convicted of a crime. The European Court of Human Rights ruled that Britain's policy of keeping DNA from innocent parties violated their right to privacy.

Those who want more inclusive DNA databases point to a variety of potential benefits. Investigators could quickly eliminate innocent suspects, free those who have been falsely convicted, and use DNA evidence in more trials. Knowing their genetic material was on file might deter potential criminals. Including samples from more people would reduce the racial disparity found in the current system.

"Familial searching" has raised the ethical stakes in the debate over the size of DNA databases. Authorities can now identify suspects by using DNA collected from family members. For example, Wichita's infamous BTK (Bind, Torture, Kill) serial murderer was identified from genetic material collected from his daughter. She provided the sample while a student at Kansas State University. Not all states allow familial DNA searching. Complained one New York state district attorney, forbidding familial searching "is insanity. It's disgraceful. If I've got something of scientific value that I can't share because of imaginary privacy concerns, it's crazy. That's how we solve crimes."[2] Opponents of familial searching argue that the procedure makes family members into "genetic informants." According to the science advisor to the American Civil Liberties Union, "If practiced routinely we would be subjecting hundreds of thousands of innocent people who happen to be relatives of individuals in the FBI database to lifelong genetic surveillance."[3]

Discussion Probes

1. Can you think of any other advantages to expanding DNA databases? Disadvantages?

2. Should DNA databases be expanded beyond those convicted of a crime? Who else should be included? Excluded?

3. What limits, if any, should be placed on how long genetic material is kept?

4. Would you voluntarily provide your DNA to a database? Why or why not?

5. How can law enforcement and government officials ensure that genetic information isn't used for the wrong purposes?

6. Should DNA familial searching be prohibited? Why or why not?

7. What leadership/followership ethics lessons do you take from this case?

Notes

1. Williams, R., & Johnson, P. (2006). Inclusiveness, effectiveness and intrusiveness: Issues in developing uses of DNA profiling in support of criminal investigations. *Journal of Law, Medicine & Ethics, 34,* 234–247

2. Nakashima, E. (2008, April 21). From DNA of family, a tool to make arrests. *The Washington Post,* p. A01.

3. Nakashima.

(Continued)

(Continued)

Sources

Bosch, X. (2003). UN agency sets out global rules for protecting genetic data. *The Lancet,* p. 45.

Moore, S. (2009, April 19). F.B.I. and states vastly expanding databases of DNA. *The New York Times,* p. A1.

Moore, S. (2009, May 12). In a lab, an ever-growing database of DNA profiles. *The New York Times,* p. D3.

Police targeting people for their DNA. (2009, November 24). *The Independent,* News, p. 6.

Simoncelli, T. (2006). Dangerous excursions: the case against expanding forensic DNA databases to innocent persons. *Journal of Law, Medicine & Ethics,* 390–397.

Smith, M. E. (2006). Let's make the DNA identification database as inclusive as possible. *Journal of Law, Medicine & Ethics,* 385–389.

Throw it out: A court decision limits the scope of police DNA databases. (2008, December 4). Retrieved from http://www.economist.com/node/12726053

Notes

1. See the following:

    Barry, V. (1978). *Personal and social ethics: Moral problems with integrated theory.* Belmont, CA: Wadsworth.

    Bentham, J. (1948). *An introduction to the principles of morals and legislation.* New York: Hafner.

    Gorovitz, S. (Ed.). (1971). *Utilitarianism: Text and critical essays.* Indianapolis, IN: Bobbs-Merrill.

    Timmons, M. (2002). *Moral theory: An introduction.* Lanham, MD: Rowman & Littlefield.

    Troyer, J. (2003). *The classical Utilitarians: Bentham and Mill.* Indianapolis, IN: Hackett Publishing.

    West, H. R. (2004). *An introduction to Mill's utilitarian ethics.* Cambridge, UK: Cambridge University Press.

2. De George, R. T. (1995). *Business ethics* (4th ed.). Englewood Cliffs, NJ: Prentice Hall, Ch. 3.

3. Savage, D. G. (2010, January 13). Scanners put privacy against security. *Los Angeles Times,* p. A11.

4. Kant, I. (1964). *Groundwork of the metaphysics of morals* (H. J. Ryan, Trans.). New York: Harper & Row; Christians, C. G., Rotzell, K. B., & Fackler, M. (1999). *Media ethics* (3rd ed.). New York: Longman; Leslie, L. Z. (2000). *Mass communication ethics: Decision-making in postmodern culture.* Boston: Houghton Mifflin; Velasquez, M. G. (1992). *Business ethics: Concepts and cases* (3rd ed.). Englewood Cliffs, NJ: Prentice Hall, Ch. 2; Sucher, S. J. (2008). *The moral leader: Challenges, tools, and insights.* London: Routledge; Timmons.

5. Graham, G. (2004). *Eight theories of ethics.* London: Routledge, Ch. 6.

6. Meilander, G. (1986). Virtue in contemporary religious thought. In R. J. Nehaus (Ed.), *Virtue: Public and private* (pp. 7–30). Grand Rapids, MI: Eerdmans; Alderman, H. (1997). *By virtue of a virtue.* In D. Statman (Ed.), *Virtue ethics* (pp. 145–164). Washington, DC: Georgetown University Press.

7. Material on Rawls's theory of justice and criticism of his approach are taken from Rawls, J. (1971). *A theory of justice.* Cambridge, MA: Belknap. See also the following:

> Rawls, J. (1993). Distributive justice. In T. Donaldson & P. H. Werhane (Eds.), *Ethical issues in business: A philosophical approach* (pp. 274–285). Englewood Cliffs, NJ: Prentice Hall.
>
> Rawls, J. (2001). *Justice as fairness: A restatement* (E. Kelly, Ed.). Cambridge, MA: Belknap.
>
> Velasquez.
>
> Warnke, G. (1993). *Justice and interpretation.* Cambridge, MA: MIT Press, Ch. 3.

8. Rawls, J. (1993). *Political liberalism.* New York: Columbia University Press.

9. Etzioni, A. (2006, Summer). A communitarian approach: A viewpoint on the study of the legal, ethical and policy considerations raised by DNA tests and databases. *Journal of Law, Medicine & Ethics,* 214–221; Sucher.

10. Etzioni, A. (1993). *The spirit of community: The reinvention of American society.* New York: Touchstone. See also the following:

> Bellah, N., Madsen, R., Sullivan, W. M., Swidler, A., & Tipton, S. M. (1991). *The good society.* New York: Vintage.
>
> Eberly, D. E. (1994). *Building a community of citizens: Civil society in the 21st century.* Lanham, MD: University Press of America.
>
> Etzioni, A. (Ed.). (1995). *New communitarian thinking: Persons, virtues, institutions, and communities.* Charlottesville: University Press of Virginia.
>
> Etzioni, A. (Ed.). (1995). *Rights and the common good: A communitarian perspective.* New York: St. Martin's, pp. 271–276.
>
> Etzioni, A. (2006, July–September). A neo-communitarian approach to international relations: Rights and the good. *Human Rights Review,* 69–80.
>
> Johnson, C. E. (2000). Emerging perspectives in leadership ethics. *Proceedings of the International Leadership Association, USA,* pp. 48–54.
>
> Tam, H. (1998). *Communitarianism: A new agenda for politics and citizenship.* New York: New York University Press.

11. Gardner, J. (1995). Building a responsive community. In A. Etzioni (Ed.), *Rights and the common good: The communitarian perspective* (pp. 167–178). New York: St. Martin's.

12. Chrislip, D. D., & Larson, C. E. (1994). *Collaborative leadership: How citizens and civic leaders can make a difference.* San Francisco: Jossey-Bass; Chrislip, D. D. (2002). *The collaborative leadership fieldbook.* San Francisco: Jossey-Bass;

Crosby, B. C., & Bryson, J. M. (2005). A leadership framework for cross-sector collaboration. *Public Management Review, 7,* 177–201; Alexander, J. A., Comfort, M. E., Weiner, B. J., & Bogue, R. (2001). Leadership in collaborative community health partnerships. *Nonprofit Management & Leadership, 12,* 159–175.

13. Zablocki, B. D. (2000). What can the study of communities teach us about community? In E. W. Lehman (Ed.), *Autonomy and order: A communitarian anthology* (pp. 71–88). Lanham, MD: Rowman & Littlefield.

14. Illinois yields to NCAA, will retire mascot. *The Washington Post,* p. E02.

15. Etzioni, A. (1996). *The new golden rule: Community and morality in a democratic society.* New York: Basic Books.

16. Liptak, A. (2002, April 18). Judge blocks U.S. bid to ban suicide law. *The New York Times,* p. A16.

17. Piliavin, J. A., & Chang, H. W. (1990). Altruism: A review of recent theory and research. *American Sociological Review, 16,* 27–65; Batson, C. D., Van Lange, P. A. M., Ahmad, N., & Lishner, D. A. (2003). Altruism and helping behavior. In M. A. Hogg & J. Cooper (Eds.), *The Sage handbook of social psychology* (pp. 279–295). London: Sage; Flescher, A. M., & Worthen, D. L. (2007). *The altruistic species: Scientific, philosophical, and religious perspectives of human benevolence.* Philadelphia: Templeton Foundation Press.

18. Kanungo, R. N., & Mendonca, M. (1996). *Ethical dimensions of leadership.* Thousand Oaks, CA: Sage.

19. Avolio, B. J., & Locke, E. E. (2002). Contrasting different philosophies of leader motivation: Altruism versus egoism. *The Leadership Quarterly, 13,* 169–191.

20. Kanungo, R. N., & Conger, J. A. (1990). The quest for altruism in organizations. In S. Srivastra & D. L. Cooperrider (Eds.), *Appreciative management and leadership* (pp. 228–256). San Francisco: Jossey-Bass.

6

Normative Leadership Theories

The whole point of studying leadership is to answer the question "What is good leadership?"

—Philosopher and ethicist Joanne Ciulla

WHAT'S AHEAD

In this chapter, we continue to look at ethical perspectives but narrow our focus to approaches that directly address the behavior of leaders and followers. These include transformational leadership, servant leadership, authentic leadership, responsible leadership, and Taoism. As in the last chapter, I'll describe each theory and then offer a balance sheet outlining some of its advantages and disadvantages.

In Chapter 5, we looked at well-established ethical systems or theories. I referred to them as general perspectives because they can be applied to any situation or role in which we find ourselves. In this chapter, we'll examine what philosopher and ethicist Joanne Ciulla of the University of Richmond calls "normative leadership theories."[1] Normative leadership theories tell leaders how they ought to act. They are built on moral principles or norms, but unlike general ethical perspectives, they specifically address leader behavior. In this chapter I won't cover every theoretical approach to leadership; I will cover only those that have a clear ethical foundation.

Transformational Leadership: Raising the Ethical Bar

Interest in transformational leadership began in 1978 with the publication of the book titled *Leadership* by James MacGregor Burns, a former presidential advisor, political scientist, and historian.[2] Burns contrasted traditional forms of leadership, which he called "transactional," with a more powerful form of leadership he called "transforming." Transactional leaders appeal to lower-level needs of followers—that is, the need for food, shelter, and acceptance. They exchange money, benefits, recognition, and other rewards in return for the obedience and labor of followers; the underlying system remains unchanged. In contrast, transformational leaders speak to higher-level needs, such as esteem, competency, self-fulfillment, and self-actualization. In so doing, they change the very nature of the groups, organizations, or societies they guide. Burns points to Franklin Roosevelt and Mahatma Gandhi as examples of leaders who transformed the lives of followers and their cultures as a whole. In a more recent work, *Transforming Leadership,* Burns argues that the greatest task facing transformational leaders is defeating global poverty, which keeps the world's poorest people from meeting their basic needs for food, medicine, education, and shelter.[3]

Moral commitments are at the heart of Burns's definition of transforming leadership. "Such leadership," states Burns, "occurs when one or more persons *engage* with others in such a way that leaders and followers raise one another to higher levels of motivation and morality."[4] Transformational leaders focus on terminal values such as liberty, equality, and justice. These values mobilize and energize followers, create an agenda for action, and appeal to larger audiences.[5] Transforming leaders are driven by duty, the deontological ethical approach described in the previous chapter.[6] They are guided by universal ethical principles, feel a sense of obligation to the group, and treat followers with respect. They are also altruistic, making sacrifices for followers, empowering others, and focusing on shared goals and objectives.

In contrast to transformational leaders, transactional leaders emphasize instrumental values, such as responsibility, fairness, and honesty, which make routine interactions go smoothly. They take a utilitarian approach, judging the morality of actions based on their outcomes. They use their power and position to convince followers to comply so that both they and their subordinates will benefit. More focused on the self, transactional leaders are concerned with protecting their interests rather than in promoting the interests of the group. They are more likely to be controlling than empowering. (One example of a self-focused, controlling leader is described in "Leadership Ethics at the Movies: *Frost/Nixon*.")

 LEADERSHIP ETHICS AT THE MOVIES

FROST/NIXON

Key Cast Members: Michael Sheen, Frank Langella, Sam Rockwell, Kevin Bacon, Matthew MacFadyen

Synopsis: Following Richard Nixon's resignation, British talk show host David Frost arranges a series of interviews with the former president in 1977. Frost, played by Michael Sheen, is seen as an intellectual lightweight and struggles to attract financial backing for the project. He appears to be hopelessly outmatched by the former president, who is dead set on sidestepping tough questions about his involvement in Vietnam and the Watergate break-in and subsequent cover-up. However, Frost, with the help of his support team, rises to the occasion in the final interview session. Nixon (Langella) admits his guilt and expresses regret for his actions. Based on the Broadway play, the film offers a look at the tortured psyche of the former president who was willing to break the law in an attempt to punish his political enemies.

Rating: R for language

Themes: transactional and transformational leadership, ethical group decision making, abuse of power, loyalty, character, greed, insecurity

Discussion Starters

1. What factors enabled Frost to meet the challenge of interviewing Nixon? What role did his team play?

2. What accounts for Nixon's involvement in Watergate? His decision to admit his guilt?

3. Do Nixon's crimes totally discredit his presidency?

In a series of studies, leadership experts Bernard Bass and his colleagues identified the factors that characterize transactional and transformational forms of leadership.[7] They found that transactional leadership has both active and passive elements. Active transactional leaders engage in *contingent reward* and *management-by-exception*. They provide rewards and recognition contingent on followers' carrying out their roles and reaching their objectives. After specifying standards and the elements of acceptable performance, active transactional leaders then discipline followers when they fall short. *Passive–avoidant* or *laissez-faire* leaders wait for problems to arise before taking action, or they avoid taking any action at all. These leaders fail to provide goals and standards or to clarify expectations.

According to Bass and Avolio, transformational leadership is characterized by the following:

- *Idealized influence.* Transformational leaders become role models for followers who admire, respect, and trust them. They put followers' needs above their own, and their behavior is consistent with the values and principles of the group.
- *Inspirational motivation.* Transformational leaders motivate by providing meaning and challenge to the tasks of followers. They arouse team spirit, are enthusiastic and optimistic, and help followers develop desirable visions for the future.
- *Intellectual stimulation.* Transformational leaders stimulate innovation and creativity. They do so by encouraging followers to question assumptions, reframe situations, and approach old problems from new perspectives. Transforming leaders don't criticize mistakes but instead solicit solutions from followers.
- *Individualized consideration.* Transformational leaders act as coaches or mentors who foster personal development. They provide learning opportunities and a supportive climate for growth. Their coaching and mentoring are tailored to the individual needs and desires of each follower.

Burns believed that leaders display either transactional or transformational characteristics, but Bass found otherwise. Transforming leadership uses both transactional and transformational elements. Explains Bass, "Many of the great transformational leaders, including Abraham Lincoln, Franklin Delano Roosevelt, and John F. Kennedy, did not shy away from being transactional. They were able to move the nation as well as play petty politics."[8] The transformational leader uses the active elements of the transactional approach (contingent reward and management-by-exception) along with idealized influence, inspirational motivation, intellectual stimulation, and individualized consideration.[9]

The popularity of the transformational approach probably has more to do with practical considerations than with ethical ones. Evidence from more than 100 empirical studies establishes that transforming leaders are more successful than their transactional counterparts.[10] Their followers are more committed, form stronger bonds with colleagues, work harder, and persist in the face of obstacles. As a result, organizations led by transforming figures often achieve extraordinary results: higher quality, greater profits, improved service, military victories, and better win–loss records. James Kouzes, Barry Posner, Tom Peters, Warren Bennis, and Burt Nanus are just some of the popular scholars, consultants, and authors who promote the benefits of transformational leadership.[11]

Burns originally believed that the transforming leader is a moral leader because the ultimate product of transformational leadership is higher ethical standards and performance. However, his definition didn't account for the fact that some leaders can use transformational strategies to reach immoral ends. A leader can act as a role model, provide intellectual stimulation, and be passionate about a cause. Yet the end product of her or his efforts can be evil. Hitler had a clear vision for Germany but left a trail of unprecedented death and destruction.

Acknowledging the difference between ethical and unethical transformational leaders, Bass adopted the terms *authentic* and *pseudo-transformational* to distinguish between the two categories.[12] Authentic transformational leaders are motivated by altruism and marked by integrity. They don't impose ethical norms but allow followers free choice, hoping that constituents will voluntarily commit themselves to moral principles. Followers are viewed as ends in themselves, not as a means to some other end. Pseudo-transformational leaders are self-centered. They manipulate followers in order to reach their personal goals. Envy, greed, anger, and deception mark the groups they lead. Mahatma Gandhi and Martin Luther King, Jr., deserve to be classified as transformational because they promoted universal brotherhood. Iran's President Mahmoud Ahmadinejad appears to be pseudo-transformational because he encourages followers to reject those who hold different beliefs. A list of the products of transformational and pseudo-transformational leadership is found in Box 6.1 on page 197. You can use this list to determine whether or not the leader described in Case Study 6.1 is transformational.

CASE STUDY 6.1

TRANSFORMING CLEAR LAKE COLLEGE

Clear Lake College was in serious trouble in 1996.[1] Enrollment at the Midwestern school had dropped from 650 to 600 undergraduates. Because it had no emergency endowment fund, Clear Lake counted on tuition revenue to pay its bills. The loss of so many students threatened to close the 90-year-old school. The college's president, who seemed unable to respond to the crisis, resigned.

(Continued)

(Continued)

The school's board of directors appointed Samuel (Sam) Thomas as the next president. Thomas had a PhD in higher education but came to Clear Lake directly out of a marketing position in business. Unlike his predecessor, Thomas didn't hesitate to make bold, sometimes risky decisions. He hired a new admissions staff, convinced faculty to agree to a salary and benefit freeze, and spent several hundred thousand dollars to launch the college's first graduate degree program.

The 1998 school year saw a surge in new students. The graduate program was a big success, and Sam used his marketing background to improve the college's visibility. An entrepreneur at heart, he encouraged faculty and staff to develop additional programs for new markets. In the next 10 years, enrollment grew to nearly 2,000 students. The college added more graduate degrees and several new undergraduate majors. Clear Lake College earned a national listing as "one of America's hidden educational gems."

Thomas had many admirable leadership qualities. To begin, he was a "people person" who enjoyed mixing with donors, students, faculty, and administrators at other schools. No one would think of calling him "Dr. Thomas." He was "Sam" to everyone. Second, he was more than willing to tackle tough problems and fire those who weren't performing up to standards. Third, he kept his word to faculty and staff. When the financial picture of the school improved, he raised faculty salaries dramatically. Fourth, he had an uncanny ability to sense new educational markets. He never made a major miscalculation when it came to proposing additional programs.

Yet all was not well under Sam's leadership. His friendly exterior masked an explosive temper. He dressed down faculty and other employees in public meetings and made personnel decisions on his own, based on his instincts rather than on hard data. A number of employees were let go without warning, and many of his hires lasted less than a year. In several instances, the college had to offer generous severance packages to dismissed employees in order to avoid costly lawsuits. Sam's autocratic style wasn't limited strictly to personnel decisions. He would change the school's governance structure without consulting faculty, who expected to participate in these choices. In addition, Sam engaged in micromanagement. He read minutes from every department meeting held on campus, for example, and didn't hesitate to send scathing memos if he disagreed with the group's conclusions.

Sam received lots of accolades for his success at Clear Lake College. He was credited for the school's turnaround and was named as the area's outstanding citizen one year. He was popular with other university presidents, serving on national collegiate boards and commissions. The board of the college was eager to renew his contract despite the concerns of the faculty. Unfortunately, Sam's successes made him less, not more, flexible. Frustrated by faculty criticism, he made even fewer efforts to consult them when making decisions. He began to call students who had offended him into his office to berate them.

By the end of the first decade of the new century, it looked as if the college had "outgrown" Sam's leadership style. After all, the school was much bigger and more complex than it had been when he took over. Sam had no intention of stepping down, however. He referred to Clear Lake as "my college" and continued to be involved in every detail of college life. In fact, Sam had to be forced to resign when he contracted Parkinson's disease in 2009. The college has continued to grow under the leadership of a new president who, while maintaining a good deal of decision-making power, relies heavily on his vice presidents and has very little input in the day-to-day operations of most departments.

Discussion Probes

1. What elements of transactional and transforming leadership did Sam exhibit?

2. Was Sam a transformational or a pseudo-transformational leader?

3. Have you ever had to confront a leader about her or his behavior? What did you say or do? What was the outcome of the encounter? Would you do anything differently next time?

4. Does success make leaders more dangerous, more likely to cast shadows?

5. How do you determine when to remove a leader, particularly one who has a proven track record of success?

6. What leadership ethics lessons do you draw from this case?

Note

1. Fictional case inspired by actual events.

Balance Sheet

Advantages (Pros)

- Strives for higher morality
- Reflects higher-level ethical reasoning
- Is highly effective
- Is inspirational
- Recognizes that leaders are made, not born
- Is not bound by the context or culture

Disadvantages (Cons)

- Practitioners often overlook moral principles
- Is confused with charismatic leadership
- Is leader-centric
- Creates dependency

Transformational leadership rests on a clear ethical foundation. The goal of a transforming leader is to raise the level of morality in a group or an organization. Pursuit of this goal should increase the ethical competence of followers, create a more moral climate, foster independent action, and serve the larger good. Investigators have discovered that this is indeed the case. As theorized, transformational leadership does promote ethical behavior. Transformational leaders engage in higher-level moral reasoning, demonstrate greater integrity, are more successful at leading organizational ethical turnarounds, encourage the development of positive ethical climates, institutionalize ethical practices, and foster corporate social responsibility.[13] Transformational leaders, as noted earlier, also get results. Identify a successful corporation, team, or military unit, many experts say, and you'll find the guiding hand of a transformational leader. This combination of morality and pragmatism makes transformational leadership very attractive. After all, who wouldn't want to be an extraordinary leader who is both good and effective?

The transformational approach holds promise for those wanting to become better, more ethical leaders. If transforming leadership consists of a set of practices, then anyone can function as a transformational leader by adopting these behaviors. The same set of practices works in every context, ranging from small informal groups and military units to large complex organizations. Ethical, effective leaders display the same set of characteristics that they adapt to their particular context. Furthermore, transforming leadership appears to be effective in a variety of cultures. Researchers at the Global Leadership and Organizational Behavior Effectiveness (GLOBE) Research Project asked managers in 62 cultures to identify the characteristics of successful leaders. Nine transformational attributes were universally associated with outstanding leadership: motive arouser, foresight, encouraging, communicative, trustworthy, dynamic, positive, confidence builder, and motivational.[14]

BOX 6.1 PRODUCTS OF TRANSFORMATIONAL AND PSEUDO-TRANSFORMATIONAL LEADERSHIP

Transformational Leaders

Raise awareness of moral standards

Highlight important priorities

Increase followers' need for achievement

Foster higher moral maturity in followers

Create an ethical climate (shared values, high ethical standards)

Encourage followers to look beyond self-interests to the common good

Promote cooperation and harmony

Use authentic, consistent means

Use persuasive appeals based on reason

Provide individual coaching and mentoring

Appeal to the ideals of followers

Allow followers freedom of choice

Pseudo-transformational Leaders

Promote special interests at the expense of the common good

Encourage dependency of followers and may privately despise them

Foster competitiveness

Pursue personal goals

Foment greed, envy, hate, and deception

(Continued)

(Continued)

Engage in conflict rather than cooperation

Use inconsistent, irresponsible means

Use persuasive appeals based on emotion and false logic

Keep their distance from followers and expect blind obedience

Seek to become idols for followers

Manipulate followers

SOURCES: Bass, B. M. (1995). The ethics of transformational leadership. In J. B. Ciulla (Ed.), *Ethics: The heart of leadership* (pp. 169–192). Westport, CT: Praeger; Bass, B. M., & Steidlmeier, P. (1999). Ethics, character, and authentic transformational leadership behavior. *The Leadership Quarterly, 1,* 181–217.

Unfortunately, the ethical assumptions underlying transformational leadership have often been overlooked in the pursuit of greater results. Many writers and researchers appear more interested in what works than in what is right. To them, transformational leadership equates with successful or effective leadership; leaders are transforming because they achieve extraordinary, tangible results, such as rescuing failing corporations or winning battles. These theorists are less concerned with whether leaders foster higher moral standards or whether transforming tactics serve ethical ends. In fact, this focus on results has led some scholars to confuse transformational leadership with charismatic leadership. The two types of leadership do have much in common. Both describe leaders who have a powerful effect on followers and organizations and can greatly improve performance. Few, for example, would doubt the impact that charismatic leaders like Alexander the Great and Joan of Arc have had on history. Nevertheless, transformational leadership and charismatic leadership are not interchangeable terms.[15] Charismatic leadership is more person centered. Followers develop strong emotional connections with their charismatic leaders, which can approach idol worship. The success of the charismatic leader rests on his or her personal characteristics like high energy and self-confidence, risk taking, courage, and the possession of extraordinary talent (public speaking ability, for example). Such leaders often emerge in times of stress. The transforming leader, on the other hand, is more group centered, and appeals to the needs and values of followers. His or her success is dependent on engaging in the four types of transformational behavior described earlier. More important, transformational leadership is prescriptive while charismatic leadership is descriptive. Transformational leadership is designed to raise the morality of both leaders and followers and prescribes how leaders should act. Charismatic leadership, on the other hand, is more results focused, attempting to explain or describe why certain leaders exert extraordinary influence. Failing to distinguish between charismatic and transforming leaders further obscures the ethical foundation of transformational leadership theory.

One group of critics labels transformational theorists as "leader-centric" for paying too much attention to leaders while downplaying the contributions of followers. One critic describes the image presented by transformational theorists this way: "The picture is one in which extraordinary leaders exercise a unidirectional influence on more-or-less willing followers, who are presumably little more than empty vessels awaiting a transfusion of insight from their betters."[16] These skeptics have reason for concern. Burns, Bass, and other proponents of transformative leadership argue that leaders play the most important role in determining group morality and performance. Leaders craft the vision, challenge the status quo, and inspire. At times, they may decide to transform the organization in spite of, not because of, followers, as in the case of the CEO who overrules his staff in order to bring about change. Critics of transformational leadership argue that followers are just as important to the success of a group as leaders, if not more so. After all, followers do most of the work. Worse yet, transforming leaders can silence dissent and encourage subordinates to sacrifice their legitimate self-interests in order to meet the needs of the group.[17]

So much focus on the leader can create dependency and undermine such values as shared decision making and consensus. Followers won't act independently if they continually look to the leader for guidance. Leaders may also get an inflated sense of their own importance, tempting them to cast shadows. Bass believes that the distinction between pseudo-transformational and authentic transformational leadership addresses these concerns. Transforming leaders are much less prone to ethical abuses, he asserts, because they put the needs of others first, treat followers with respect, and seek worthy objectives. You'll need to decide for yourself whether transformational theorists have adequately responded to the dangers posed by their perspective.

Servant Leadership: Put the Needs of Followers First

Servant leadership has roots in both Western and Eastern thought. Jesus told his disciples that "whoever wants to become great among you must be your servant, and whoever wants to be first must be slave of all" (Mark 1:43–44, New International Version). As we'll see in the final section of this chapter, Chinese philosophers encouraged leaders to be humble valleys. Robert Greenleaf sparked contemporary interest in leaders as servants. Greenleaf, who spent 40 years in research, development, and education at AT&T and 25 years as an organizational consultant, coined the term *servant leader* in the 1970s to describe a leadership model that puts the concerns of followers first.[18] Later he founded a center to promote servant leadership. A number of businesses (The Container Store, AFLAC), nonprofit organizations, and community leadership programs have adopted his model.[19] Margaret Wheatley, Peter Block, Max DePree, and James Autry have joined Greenleaf in urging leaders to act like servants.

The basic premise of servant leadership is simple yet profound. Leaders should put the needs of followers before their own needs. In fact, what happens in the lives of followers should be the standard by which leaders are judged. According to Greenleaf, when evaluating a leader we ought to ask, "Do those served grow as persons? Do they, while being served, become healthier, wiser, freer, more autonomous, more likely themselves to become servants?"[20] (To determine if you are being led by a servant leader, complete the "Self-Assessment: Servant Leadership Questionnaire.")

SELF-ASSESSMENT

SERVANT LEADERSHIP QUESTIONNAIRE

Instructions

You can use this questionnaire to rate the servant leadership behaviors of one of your leaders or ask someone else to rate you. Respond to each question on the following scale: 1 = strongly disagree, 2 = somewhat disagree, 3 = somewhat agree, 4 = strongly agree. The scale rates five dimensions of servant leadership, which are described below. Add up the item ratings to come up with the total score for each component.

Add the component scores to come up with a total servant leadership rating (range 24–96).

Response choices: 1 = strongly disagree;   2 = somewhat disagree;
                    3 = somewhat agree;   4 = strongly agree

1. This person puts my best interests ahead of his/her own.   1 2 3 4

2. This person does everything he/she can do to serve me.   1 2 3 4

3. This person is one I would turn to if I had a personal trauma.   1 2 3 4

4. This person seems alert to what's happening.   1 2 3 4

5. This person offers compelling reasons to get me to do things.   1 2 3 4

6. This person encourages me to dream
"big dreams" about the organization.   1 2 3 4

7. This person is good at anticipating the
consequences of decisions.   1 2 3 4

8. This person is good at helping me with my emotional issues.   1 2 3 4

9. This person has great awareness of what is going on.   1 2 3 4

10. This person is very persuasive.   1 2 3 4

11. This person believes that the organization needs
to play a moral role in society.   1 2 3 4

12. This person is talented at helping me to heal emotionally.   1 2 3 4

13. This person seems in touch with what's happening.   1 2 3 4

14. This person is good at convincing me to do things.   1 2 3 4

15. This person believes that our organization
needs to function as a community.   1 2 3 4

16. This person sacrifices his/her own interests to meet my needs.   1   2   3   4

17. This person is one who could help me mend my hard feelings.   1   2   3   4

18. This person is gifted when it comes to persuading me.   1   2   3   4

19. This person is talented at helping me to heal emotionally.   1   2   3   4

20. This person sees the organization for its
    potential to contribute to society.   1   2   3   4

21. This person encourages me to have a community
    spirit in the workplace.   1   2   3   4

22. This person goes above and beyond the call of
    duty to meet my needs.   1   2   3   4

23. This person seems to know what is going to happen.   1   2   3   4

24. This person is preparing the organization to
    make a positive difference in the future.   1   2   3   4

Scoring

Altruistic Calling (Deep-rooted desire to make a positive difference)

Item 1 _____

Item 2 _____

Item 16 _____

Item 21 _____

Item 22 _____

Total _____ out of 16

Emotional Healing (Fostering spiritual recovery from hardship or trauma)

Item 3 _____

Item 8 _____

Item 12 _____

Item 17 _____

Item 19 _____

Total _____ out of 16

Wisdom (Awareness of surroundings and anticipation of consequences)

Item 4 _____

Item 7 _____

Item 9 _____

Item 13 _____

Item 23 _____

Total _____ out of 20

Persuasive Mapping (Use of sound reasoning and mental frameworks)

Item 5 _____

Item 6 _____

Item 10 _____

Item 14 _____

Item 18 _____

Total _____ out of 20

Organizational Development (Making a collective positive contribution to society)

Item 11 _____

Item 15 _____

Item 20 _____

Item 21 _____

Item 24 _____

Total _____ out of 20

Overall score _____ out of 96

SOURCE: Adapted from Babuto, J. E., & Wheeler, D. W. (2006). Scale development and construct clarification of servant leadership. *Group & Organization Management,* pp. 322–323. Used by permission. Published by SAGE Publications.

By continually reflecting on what would be best for their constituents, servant leaders are less likely to cast shadows by taking advantage of the trust of followers, acting inconsistently, or accumulating money and power. So far theorists have identified a number of attributes that characterize servant leaders—see Box 6.2 on page 206. While the lists of attributes vary, five related concepts appear central to servant leadership:

1. *Stewardship*. Being a servant leader means acting on behalf of others.[21] Leaders function as the agents of followers, who entrust them with special duties and opportunities for a limited time. (See Case Study 6.2 on page 224 for a description of two leaders who failed to carry out their stewardship responsibilities.) Servant leaders are charged with protecting and nurturing their groups and organizations while making sure that these collectives serve the common good. Stewardship implies accountability for results. However, stewards reach their objectives through collaboration and persuasion rather than through coercion and control.

2. *Obligation*. Servant leaders take their obligations or responsibilities seriously. Max DePree, former CEO of Herman Miller, a major office furniture manufacturer, offers one list of what leaders owe their followers and institutions.[22]

- *Assets*. Leaders need to ensure financial stability as well as the relationships and reputation that will ensure future prosperity. Leaders must also provide followers with adequate tools, equipment, and facilities.
- *A legacy*. When they depart, leaders ought to leave behind people who find more meaning, challenge, and joy in their work.
- *Clear institutional values*. Servant leaders articulate principles that shape both individual and organizational behavior.
- *Future leadership*. Current leaders are obligated to identify and then develop their successors.
- *Healthy institutional culture*. Servant leaders are responsible for fostering such organizational characteristics as quality, openness to change, and tolerance of diverse opinions.
- *Covenants*. Covenants are voluntary agreements that serve as reference points for organization members, providing them with direction. Leaders and followers who enter into a covenant are bound together in pursuit of a common goal.
- *Maturity*. Followers expect a certain level of maturity from their leaders. Mature leaders have a clear sense of self-worth, belonging, responsibility, accountability, and equality.
- *Rationality*. Leaders supply the reason and understanding that help followers make sense of organizational programs and relationships. A rational environment

builds trust, allows followers to reach their full potential, and encourages ongoing organizational learning.

- *Space.* Space is a sense of freedom that allows followers and leaders to be and express themselves. Leaders who create adequate space allow for the giving and receiving of such gifts as new ideas, healing, dignity, and inclusion.
- *Momentum.* Servant leaders help create the feeling that the group is moving forward and achieving its goals. Momentum arises out of a clear vision and strategy supported by productive research, operations, financial, and marketing departments.
- *Effectiveness.* Effectiveness comes from enabling followers to reach their personal and institutional potential. Servant leaders allow followers to assume leadership roles when conditions warrant.
- *Civility and values.* A civilized institution is marked by good manners, respect for others, and service. Wise leaders can distinguish between what is healthy for the organization (dignity of work, hope, simplicity) and what is superficial and unhealthy (consumption, instant gratification, affluence).

3. *Partnership.* Servant leaders view followers as partners, not subordinates. As a consequence, they strive for equity or justice in the distribution of power. Strategies for empowering followers include sharing information, delegating authority to carry out important tasks, and encouraging constituents to develop and exercise their talents. Concern for equity extends to the distribution of rewards as well. For example, both employees and executives receive bonuses when the company does well.

4. *Emotional healing.* Servant leaders help followers and organizations recover from disappointment, trauma, hardship, and broken relationships.[23] They are both empathetic and highly skilled as listeners. They create climates that facilitate the sharing of personal and work-related feelings and issues. Emotional healing restores a "sense of wholeness" to both individuals and organizations.

5. *Elevating purpose.* In addition to serving followers, servant leaders also serve worthy missions, ideas, and causes. Seeking to fulfill a high moral purpose and understanding the role one plays in the process make work more meaningful to leaders and followers alike. Consider the example of three bricklayers at work in the English countryside. When asked by a traveler to describe what they were doing, the first replied, "I am laying bricks." The second said, "I am feeding my family by laying bricks." The third bricklayer, who had a clearer sense of the purpose for his labor, declared, "Through my work of laying bricks, I am constructing a cathedral, and thereby giving honor and praise to God."

BOX 6.2 SERVANT LEADER ATTRIBUTES

listening	vision	empathy	altruistic calling
empathy	honesty	integrity/honesty	emotional healing
healing	integrity	competence	wisdom
awareness	trust	agreeableness	persuasive mapping
persuasion	service	(Washington, Sutton,	organizational
conceptualization	modeling	& Feild, 2006)	stewardship
foresight	pioneering		(Babuto & Wheeler,
stewardship	appreciation of others		2006)
commitment to the	empowerment		
growth of people	communication		
building community	credibility		
(Spears, 2004)	competence		
	visibility		
	influence		
	persuasion		
	listening		
	encouragement		
	teaching		
	delegation		
	(Russell & Stone, 2002)		

Sources

Babuto, J. E., & Wheeler, D. W. (2006). Scale development and construct clarification of servant leadership. *Group & Organization Management, 31*, 300–326.

Russell, R. F., & Stone, A. G. (2002). A review of servant leadership attributes: Developing a practical model. *Leadership & Organization Development Journal, 23*(3), 145–157.

Spears, L. C. (2004). The understanding and practice of servant leadership. In L. C. Spears & M. Lawrence (Eds.), *Practicing servant leadership: Succeeding through trust, bravery, and forgiveness* (pp. 9–24). San Francisco: Jossey-Bass.

Washington, R. R., Sutton, C. D., & Feild, H. S. (2006). Individual differences in servant leadership: The roles of values and personality. *Leadership & Organization Development Journal, 27*(8), 700–716.

Balance Sheet

Advantages (pros)

- Is altruistic
- Incorporates simplicity
- Promotes self-awareness
- Fosters moral sensitivity
- Ongoing development

Disadvantages (cons)

- Seems unrealistic
- May not work in every context
- Poses the danger of serving the wrong cause or offering unwise service
- Carries a negative connotation in the term *servant*

Altruism is the first strength of servant leadership. Concern for others, in this case followers, comes before concern for self. We can serve only if we commit ourselves to the principle that others should come first.

Simplicity is the second strength of servant leadership. We are far less likely to cast shadows if we approach our leadership roles with one goal in mind: the desire to serve. A great number of ethical abuses, as we emphasized in Chapter 2, stem from leaders putting their personal interests first. Instead, servant leaders act out of a sense of stewardship and obligation, promoting the growth of followers and the interests of the larger community. They share, rather than hoard, power, privilege, and information.

Self-awareness is the third strength of servant leadership. Servant leaders listen to themselves as well as to others, take time for reflection, and recognize the importance of spiritual resources.

Moral sensitivity is the fourth strength of servant leadership. Servant leaders are acutely aware of the importance of pursuing ethical purposes that bring meaning and fulfillment to work. Serving a transcendent goal means that every act of leadership has a moral dimension.

Ongoing development is the fifth strength of servant leadership. For much of the theory's history, support for servant leadership was anecdotal, consisting largely of lists of servant characteristics and examples of servant leaders. More recently, scholars have begun to subject servant leadership to empirical testing. Servant leadership questionnaires like the one in the "Self-Assessment" on page 201 have been developed, and researchers are exploring the impact of servant leadership on followers and organizational performance. So far they have discovered that servant leaders help satisfy follower needs and boost their job satisfaction and job performance. Followers also give servant leaders higher character ratings.[24]

Despite its strengths, servant leadership has not met with universal approval. Cynicism is often the first response when this model is presented. "Sounds good in principle," listeners respond, "but it would never work at my company, in my family, at my condominium association meeting, or _____" (fill in the blank). Skeptics report that they have been "walked on" whenever they've tried to be nice to poor performers at work, rebellious teenagers, or nasty neighbors. Others equate a servant attitude with passivity.

Skepticism about servant leadership may stem in part from a misunderstanding that equates service with weakness. Servant leaders need to be tough. Sometimes the best way to serve someone is to reprimand or fire that person. Nevertheless, there may be situations in which servant leadership is extremely difficult, if not impossible, to implement, such as in prisons, military boot camps, and emergencies.

Misplaced goals are problems for servant leaders and followers alike. The butler in the novel *The Remains of the Day*, by Kazuo Ishiguro, illustrates the danger of misspent service. He devotes his entire life to being the perfect servant who meets the needs of his English employer. Sadly, his sacrifice is wasted because the lord of the manor turns out to be a Nazi sympathizer. The desire to serve must be combined with careful reasoning and value clarification. We need to carefully examine who and what we serve, asking ourselves questions such as the following: Is this group, individual, or organization worthy of our service? What values are we promoting? What is the product of our service: light or darkness? (For a closer look at outstanding followership, see "Focus on Follower Ethics: Servant Followership.")

We are also charged with giving wise service. Lots of well-intentioned efforts to help others are wasted when leaders fail to do their homework. After the earthquake in Central Asia in 2005, for example, outdoor manufacturers donated high-tech mountaineering tents to victims. Unfortunately, these tents are highly flammable and caught fire from candles, kerosene lanterns, and cooking fires, burning and killing adults and children. After the Haiti earthquake, a group of Idaho church members was jailed after trying to take orphans out of the country. It turns out that the children weren't orphans after all. Some critics go so far as to argue that not only are some humanitarian efforts wasted; they can make problems worse and foster dependency in recipients.[25]

Finally, members of some minority groups, particularly African Americans, associate the word *servant* with a history of slavery, oppression, and discrimination. The negative connotations surrounding the word may keep you from embracing the idea of servant leadership. You may want to abandon this term and focus instead on related concepts such as altruism and the virtues of concern and compassion.

FOCUS ON FOLLOWER ETHICS

SERVANT FOLLOWERSHIP

Consultant and author Robert Kelley believes that servant followership is more important than servant leadership. He points out that most people spend most of their time in follower roles and that followers contribute the most to organizational success. From an ethical perspective, seeking to be a follower rather than a leader reduces the destructive competition and conflict that occur when people fight each other for leadership positions. Servant followers are more likely to build trust and keep the focus on organizational goals. They avoid the temptation to adopt authoritarian, self-centered styles when they do land in leader roles.

Kelley uses the term *exemplary* to describe ideal servant followers. The best followers score high in two dimensions: independent, critical thinking and active engagement. They think for themselves and, at the same time, take initiative. Outstanding followers contribute innovative ideas and go beyond what is required. Leaders can count on them to take on new challenges, follow through on projects without much supervision, disagree constructively, and think through the implications of their actions.

Kelley outlines five behavior patterns for those who hope to become exemplary followers.

- *Leading yourself.* Excellent followers know how to lead themselves. They step up to their responsibilities and view their work as equal in importance to that of leaders because they recognize that implementation is critical to success.
- *Commit and focus.* Exemplary followers are committed to ideas and causes bigger than themselves. They look beyond their personal careers and needs to serve an elevating purpose such as fighting illness or protecting the environment. Because they're committed to a broad principle, exemplary followers feel less need for status or titles.
- *Develop competence and credibility.* Exemplary followers set high personal standards that are more strenuous than those set by the leader or the organization as a whole. They are proactive, taking advantage of

(Continued)

(Continued)

continuing education and performance development opportunities. Outstanding followers also know their weaknesses and take steps to compensate by either acquiring the necessary skills or stepping aside to let others complete the task.

- *Use your courageous conscience.* Exemplary followers are very concerned about the ethics of their actions even if their leaders are not. Such followers serve as ethical watchdogs. They refuse to abandon personal principles but challenge immoral directives instead.

- *Disagree agreeably.* Servant followers work cooperatively with their leaders, recognizing that their responsibility is to make the job of the leader easier, not harder. However, when conflicts arise and decisions must be challenged, outstanding followers gather the facts, seek the advice of others, build coalitions, and work within established guidelines whenever possible (although they have the courage to go to higher authorities if absolutely necessary).

SOURCE: Kelley, R. (1998). Followership in a leadership world. In L. C. Spears (Ed.), *Insights on leadership: Service, stewardship, spirit and servant-leadership* (pp. 170–184). New York: Wiley. See also Johnson, C. E. (2007). *Ethics in the workplace: Tools and tactics for organizational transformation.* Thousand Oaks, CA: Sage, Ch. 7.

Authentic Leadership: Know Yourself and to Your Own Self Be True

Ancient Greek and Roman philosophers prized authenticity. "Know thyself" was inscribed on the frieze above the oracle of Delphi and appears in the writings of Cicero and Ovid.[26] Greek thinkers also exhorted listeners "to thine own self be true." Modern scholars have rediscovered the importance of this quality. Proponents of Authentic Leadership Theory (ALT) identify authenticity as the "root construct" or principle underlying all forms of positive leadership. The practice of authentic leadership leads to sustainable (long-term) and veritable (ethically sound) organizational performance.[27]

Authenticity has four components: self-awareness, balanced processing, internalized moral perspective, and relational transparency.[28] *Self-awareness* means being conscious of, and trusting in, our motives, desires, feelings, and self-concept. Self-aware people know their strengths and weaknesses, personal traits, and emotional patterns, and they are able to use this knowledge when interacting with others and their environments. *Balanced processing* describes remaining objective when receiving information. Inauthentic responses involve denying, distorting, or ignoring feedback we don't want to acknowledge. We may have to accept the fact that we aren't very good at certain activities (accounting, writing, playing basketball) or that we have problems managing our anger. *Internalized moral perspective* refers to regulating our behavior according to our internal standards and values, not according to what others say. We act in harmony with what we believe and do not change our behavior to please others or to earn rewards or avoid punishment. *Relational transparency* is presenting the authentic self to others, openly expressing true thoughts and feelings appropriate for the situation.

According to Bruce Avolio, Fred Luthans, and their colleagues at the Gallup Leadership Institute at the University of Nebraska at Lincoln and elsewhere, authentic leadership has a strong moral component. They make ethics a starting point for their theory, just as Burns did for transforming leadership. This moral element is reflected in their definition of authentic leaders as "those who are deeply aware of how they think and behave and are perceived by others as being aware of their own and others' values/moral perspectives, knowledge, and strengths; aware of the context in which they operate; and who are confident, hopeful, optimistic, resilient, and of high moral character."[29] Such leaders acknowledge the ethical responsibilities of their roles, can recognize and evaluate ethical issues, and take moral actions that are thoroughly grounded in their beliefs and values. In order to carry out these tasks, they draw on their courage and resilience—the ability to adapt when confronted with significant risk or adversity.[30]

Because authenticity is so critical to positive leadership performance, Avolio, Luthans, and others are interested in how leaders develop this quality. They report that critical incidents called *trigger events* play an important role in the development of the moral component of authentic leadership.[31] These events, like the crucible moments described in Chapter 3, can be positive or negative and promote introspection and reflection. Trigger experiences are often dramatic (facing racial hatred, visiting a third-world village) but can also be more mundane, such as reading a significant book. Sometimes a series of small events, such as several minor successes or failures, can have a cumulative effect, triggering significant thought. Leaders develop a clearer sense of who they are, including their standards of right and wrong, through these experiences. They build a store of moral knowledge that they can draw on to make better choices when facing future ethical dilemmas.

Authenticity can also be fostered through training and education. For example, trainers and educators can help leaders develop their moral capacity by (1) encouraging them to think about the possible consequences of their leadership decisions, (2) enhancing their perspective taking through discussion and training, (3) exposing them to common moral dilemmas to help them recognize the ethical issues they will face in their jobs, (4) building their belief in their ability to follow through on choices, (5) helping them develop strategies for adapting and coping with new ethical challenges, and (6) pairing them with moral leaders so they can observe authentic behavior firsthand.[32]

Authentic leadership produces a number of positive ethical effects in followers.[33] Followers are likely to emulate the example of authentic leaders who set a high ethical standard. They feel empowered to make ethical choices on their own without the input of the leader. They align themselves with the values of the organization and become authentic moral agents themselves. Leader authenticity also fosters feelings of self-efficacy (competence), hope, optimism, and resilience in followers. Authentic followers, for their part, provide feedback that reinforces the authentic behavior of leaders and increases the leaders' self-knowledge. They also reward their leaders by giving them more latitude to make difficult, unpopular choices. Authentic leadership and followership are more likely to develop in organizational climates that provide the information and other resources that employees need to get their work done, encourage learning, treat members fairly, and set clear goals and performance standards.

Proponents of ALT argue that authenticity pays practical as well as ethical dividends. They believe authenticity multiplies the effectiveness of leaders. Because authentic leaders are more predictable, followers have to waste less time and energy figuring out what their leaders will do next. Authentic leaders engender more trust, and trust, in turn, has been linked to higher organizational productivity and performance. Those who work in a trusting environment are more productive because they have high job satisfaction, enjoy better relationships, stay focused on their tasks, feel committed to the group, sacrifice for the greater organizational good, and are willing to go beyond their job descriptions to help out fellow employees.[34] The positive emotions fostered by leaders also enhance performance. Followers who believe in their abilities are more likely to take initiative and to achieve more, even in the face of difficult circumstances. Feelings of hope and optimism foster willpower. Resiliency enables followers to recover more quickly from setbacks.[35] (Read Case Study 6.3 on page 226 to learn how one authentic leader has helped foster these qualities in her followers.)

Balance Sheet

Advantages (Pros)

- Strong moral emphasis
- Developmental focus

- Is highly effective
- Incorporates followers and organizational climate
- Growing body of empirical support

Disadvantages (Cons)

- Overstates the importance of authenticity
- Equates authenticity with morality
- Differing interpretations of authentic behavior
- Authenticity can be defined as a personal characteristic or as a perception

Authentic leadership has much to offer, beginning with its strong moral emphasis. Its leading proponents incorporate values, moral perspectives, virtues, and character in their definition of authentic leadership. They have a worthy objective: to promote positive leadership behavior that makes a fundamental difference in the lives of organizations and their members. Their ultimate goal is not just to understand authenticity but also to help leaders become more authentic. ALT theorists make practical suggestions for helping leaders develop this strength. Furthermore, authentic leadership is effective as well as ethical. Authenticity multiplies the impact of leaders and lays the foundation for long-term organizational success. The theory acknowledges the role that followers and organizational culture and climate play in developing authentic leadership.

ALT has moved into the next stage of development. Most of the initial articles and chapters on authentic leadership offered propositions about ALT that were not supported by empirical research. But now an ALT scale has been developed and tested.[36] Validation of the scale demonstrates that authentic leadership, while sharing features with transformational and servant leadership, is a distinct construct.

The theory's underlying premise that authenticity is the source of all positive forms of leadership is subject to debate. There may be some other as yet undiscovered source instead. Or there may be multiple sources of ethical leadership. ALT theorists also seem to equate self-awareness with morality. The clearer we are about the self-concept, they claim, the more likely we are to act ethically. Yet the core values of some leaders promote self-seeking, destructive behavior. Then, too, expressing our "true" selves can produce undesirable consequences. Take the case of the boss who fails to temper his criticism of a subordinate. By accurately reflecting what he feels at that moment, he may do lasting damage to the self-concept of his employee. The critical boss believes he is acting authentically; the unfortunate employee and observers probably will conclude that he is callous instead.

Research into the effects of authentic leadership has identified a fundamental tension in the theory. On the one hand, authenticity has been tied to the personal traits described earlier—self-awareness, balanced processing, internal moral motivation, and relational transparency. On the other hand, for authenticity to have a positive influence on organizational behavior, observers must perceive that a leader's behavior is authentic.[37] Authenticity then becomes a product of perception, not of personal beliefs and behaviors. Leaders who hope to be successful must project an authentic image. In other words, *being* authentic is no longer enough. Leaders must also *appear* authentic. This could tempt some leaders to be untrue to themselves. They might fail to act on their values and self-understanding for fear that such behavior could be seen as inauthentic. In addition, inauthentic (pseudo-authentic) leaders could mislead followers by projecting an authentic image.[38] Further research and analysis are needed to resolve this apparent contradiction between the personal and perceptual dimensions of ALT.

Responsible Leadership: Promoting Global Good Through Ethical Relationships

Responsible leadership is an offshoot of global corporate social responsibility (CSR). Socially responsible corporations operating in a global economy try to improve social conditions and the environment in addition to making a profit. (Social responsibility is described in more detail in Chapter 9.) These businesses pay a living wage to workers in developing countries, for example, and adopt environmentally friendly practices like recycling and reducing energy use and pollution. Responding to the claims of stakeholders is an important element of CSR. Stakeholders consist of any group that is affected by the organization's operations. For a multinational corporation, stakeholders include, for example, domestic and foreign governments, nongovernmental organizations (NGOs), suppliers, customers, and employees in locations around the world.

European researchers Nicola Pless and Thomas Maak believe that leaders can help their corporations become a force for global good through exercising responsible leadership.[39] Responsible leaders build ethical relationships with stakeholders. These relationships then create a sense of shared purpose as well as motivation to address social and environmental problems. Maak and Pless define responsible leadership "as a values-based and principle-driven relationship between leaders and stakeholders who are connected through a shared sense of meaning and purpose through which they raise to higher ethical levels of motivation and commitment for achieving sustainable value creation and responsible change."[40]

Like transformational leadership, responsible leadership elevates the morality of the parties involved. However, responsible leadership incorporates all stakeholder groups affected by the leader and the organization, not just immediate followers. Responsible leaders establish a "web of inclusion" that connects with diverse constituencies. Relationship building can't be done from a position of authority. Instead, responsible leaders must function as equals who bring people together for a common purpose.

Character plays an important role in responsible leadership. Responsible leaders are authentic (see the previous section) and demonstrate such virtues as honesty, respect, service, and humility. They reflect moral maturity, practice reflection and critical thinking skills, and can generate creative ethical solutions. Drawing from this moral core, responsible leadership then manifests itself in the following roles:[41]

1. *The leader as steward.* Responsible leaders act as guardians of individual and organizational values, maintaining personal and collective integrity while helping the organization act responsibly. They are also custodians, protecting (and hopefully enriching) the values and resources they have been entrusted with. Stewardship incorporates a global perspective and considers the needs of the environment and future generations.

2. *The leader as servant.* Responsible leaders are focused on the needs of followers. They care for them through providing a safe and meaningful work environment, paying fair wages, listening to their concerns, and supporting their development. Responsible leaders also serve the needs of stakeholders through dialogue, by integrating the perspectives of many different groups, and by putting the good of the community above selfish concerns.

3. *The leader as coach.* Responsible leaders develop and support others, motivating diverse individuals and groups to work together to reach a common vision. This requires open communication, conflict management, coping with cultural differences, and providing culturally appropriate feedback. Moral development is an important element of coaching. Ethical leaders help others develop their moral reasoning and reflection skills.

4. *The leader as architect.* Responsible leaders focus on building integrity cultures, which are work environments that help diverse employees engage in meaningful labor; feel respected, included, and recognized; and reach their potential. Responsible leaders also engage in ongoing dialogue with external stakeholders.

5. *The leader as storyteller.* Responsible leaders communicate shared values and meaning through stories. Stories bring to life the organization's vision and values, help create meaning, and assist followers in making sense of the world. By sharing stories, leaders create a corporate identity, foster cooperation, and communicate their visions about their organization's social and environmental responsibilities.

6. *The leader as change agent.* Responsible leaders shape both the process and the product of change. They create a values-based vision, mobilize followers, keep change momentum going, and deal with the anxiety that always surrounds change efforts. In addition, they ensure that change helps create businesses that are founded on core values and sustainable over the long term.

7. *The leader as citizen.* Responsible leaders are just as concerned about the health of the community as they are about the health of their businesses. They recognize that private business and the public sphere are interdependent. Businesses need healthy communities in order to thrive, and healthy communities need the support of thriving businesses.

Maak and Pless have an ambitious agenda for responsible leadership. They believe that corporate leaders have a duty to act as agents of social change and as "agents of world benefit."[42] Multinational corporations exert greater and greater economic power and enjoy more and more privileges. Therefore, they have a moral obligation to promote social justice by trying to solve political and social problems. Responsible leaders join government and nonprofit leaders in promoting human rights, alleviating poverty and hunger, and fighting HIV/AIDS, malaria, and other illnesses. Such collaboration creates *social capital*—a network of structures, resources, and lasting positive relationships—which can then be used to address other social problems.[43]

Balance Sheet

Advantages (Pros)

- Explicit ethical emphasis
- Is altruistic/other-focused
- Incorporates the concerns of stakeholders
- Is global in scope

Disadvantages (Cons)

- Is new and still evolving
- Lacks empirical support
- Overlaps other theories
- Corporations are resistant to an expanded social role
- Focuses exclusively on business leadership

The developers of responsible leadership theory are very clear about the ethical basis of their model. Responsible leaders weave a web of relationships founded on ethical principles and values. Such leaders act out of high character and demonstrate sound moral reasoning, building relationships grounded in trust and integrity. They are concerned about the needs and development of others, both inside and outside the organization. Each of the roles they play has a strong moral component. Their efforts are aimed at a laudable ethical goal—the creation of a more just global society.

Of the theories discussed in this chapter, only responsible leadership incorporates globalization and stakeholder theory. It encourages leaders to work with others to solve difficult problems on every continent. This approach to leadership ethics highlights the fact that moral leaders must be concerned about all those who are impacted by their actions, not just immediate followers.

Responsible leadership theory is in the beginning stages of development, which accounts for many of its shortcomings. It is still evolving. Maak and Pless have modified their definition of responsible leadership from its original formulation and offer differing lists of the roles played by responsible leaders. To this point, only a few other scholars have joined them in exploring the implications of responsible leadership. Limited empirical evidence has been offered to support the theory's tenets. At the same time, the theorists incorporate elements of authentic leadership, transformational leadership, and servant leadership into their model. They need to further clarify how their theory relates to these other approaches.

Pless and Maak's bold assertion that corporations and their leaders need to be agents of social justice and world benefit is highly controversial. They advocate that businesses take on responsibilities usually associated with governments to address global problems, such as world hunger. A great number of observers are uneasy about multinational corporations acting as "quasi-states." Further, the traditional conception of social responsibility is much more limited than that advocated in responsible leadership. Corporate leaders typically tie their social efforts to their business goals, as in the case of an outdoor clothing manufacturer supporting the creation of wilderness areas. Then, too, multinational businesses generally target problems related to their operations and locations. For instance, a socially conscious manufacturer will focus on improving living conditions in the communities surrounding its plants. Few corporate leaders appear ready to tackle global issues like the shortage of clean water and widespread poverty, as proponents of responsible leadership urge them to do.

Additional theoretical development may address what is perhaps the greatest concern about responsible leadership, which is whether this perspective can serve as a general theory of leadership ethics. Maak and Pless developed their theory to foster greater social responsibility in multinational corporations. They specifically address business leaders. However, the components of responsible leadership would seem to apply to every type of organizational leader. Educators, agency heads, mayors, governors, and others also have to build values-based, principle-driven relationships with diverse stakeholder groups to achieve ethical objectives. They, too, need to act as stewards, servants, coaches, architects, storytellers, change agents, and citizens.

Taoism: Lead Nature's Way

Taoism (pronounced "Dowism") is one of the world's oldest philosophies, dating back to ancient China (600–300 B.C.). The nation had enjoyed peace and prosperity under a series of imperial dynasties but had become a patchwork of warring city-states. Groups of philosophers traveled from one fiefdom to another offering leaders advice for restoring harmony. The Taoists were one of these "100 Schools of Thought."[44]

The *Tao Te Ching* (usually translated as *The Classic of the Way and Its Power and Virtue*) is Taoism's major text. According to popular tradition, a royal librarian named Lao-tzu authored this book as he departed China for self-imposed exile. However, most scholars believe that this short volume (5,000 words) is a collection of the teachings of several wise men or sages.

Taoism divided into religious and philosophical branches by A.D. 200. Religious Taoists sought to extend their lives through diet and exercise and developed a priesthood that presided over elaborate temple rituals. Today Taoist religious practices are popular in both the East and the West, but those interested in Taoist leadership principles generally draw from the movement's philosophical roots. These principles are described for Western audiences in such books as *The Tao of Leadership*, *The Tao of Personal Leadership*, and *Real Power: Business Lessons From the Tao Te Ching*.

Understanding the "Way" or Tao is the key to understanding Taoist ethical principles. The Tao is the shapeless, nameless force or "nonbeing" that brings all things into existence, or being, and then sustains them. The Tao takes form in nature and reveals itself through natural principles. These principles then become the standards for ethical behavior. Ethical leaders and followers develop *te,* or character, by acting in harmony with the Tao, not by following rules and commandments. Laws reflect a distrust of human nature and create a new class of citizens—lawbreakers—instead of encouraging right behavior. Efforts to reduce crime, for example, seem to increase it instead:

> Throw away holiness and wisdom,
>
> And people will be a hundred times happier.
>
> Throw away morality and justice,

And people will do the right thing.

Throw away industry and profit, and there won't be any thieves.[45]

"Leave well enough alone" seems to capture the essence of Taoist ethics. Consistent with their hands-off approach, Taoist sages argue that he or she governs best who governs least. Leading is like cooking a small fish: Don't overdo it. The ideal Taoist leader maintains a low profile, leading mostly by example and letting followers take ownership.

> When the Master governs, the people
>
> Are hardly aware that he exists.
>
> Next best is a leader who is loved.
>
> Next, one who is feared.
>
> The worst is one who is despised.
>
> If you don't trust the people,
>
> You make them untrustworthy.
>
> The Master doesn't talk, he acts.
>
> When his work is done,
>
> The people say, "Amazing:
>
> We did it, all by ourselves!"[46]

Taoists rely on images or metaphors drawn from nature and daily life to illustrate the characteristics of model leaders. The first image is that of an uncarved block. An uncarved block of stone or wood is nameless and shapeless, like the Tao itself. Leaders should also be blocklike, avoiding wealth, status, and glory while they leave followers alone.

The second image is the child. Children serve as another reminder that wise leaders don't get caught up in the pursuit of power and privilege but remain humble. Mahatma Gandhi demonstrated childlike character. He dressed simply in clothes he made himself, owned almost nothing, and did not seek political office. Yet he emerged as one of history's most influential leaders.

The third image is water. Water provides an important insight into how leaders ought to influence others by illustrating that there is great strength in weakness. Water cuts through the hardest rock given enough time. In the same way, the weak often overcome the powerful.[47] Authoritarian governments in Soviet Russia, Argentina, and the Philippines were overthrown not by military means but through the efforts of ordinary citizens. Leaders who use "soft" tactics (listening, empowering, and collaborating) rather than "hard" ones, such as threats and force, are more likely to overcome resistance to change. Flexibility or pliability is an important attribute of water as well. Water seeks new paths when it meets resistance; leaders should do the same.

The fourth image is the valley. To the Taoists, the universe is made up of two forces: the yin (negative, dark, cool, female, shadows) and the yang (positive, bright, warm, male, sun). Creation operates as it should when these forces are in balance. Although both the yin and the yang are important, Taoists highlight the importance of the yin, or feminine side of leadership, which is represented by the valley metaphor. Leaders should seek to be valleys (which reflect the yin) rather than prominent peaks (which reflect the yang).

The fifth image is the clay pot, which celebrates emptiness by elevating nothing to higher status than something. The most useful part of a pot is the emptiness within. Similarly, the most useful part of a room is the empty space between the walls. Leaders ought to empty themselves, putting aside empty words, superficial thinking, technology, and selfishness. By being empty, leaders can use silence, contemplation, and observation to better understand the workings of the Tao and its ethical principles.

Balance Sheet

Advantages (Pros)

- Provides an alternative to Western approaches
- Is suited to the modern work environment
- Parallels trends in leadership studies
- Emphasizes inner peace, silence, contemplation, and service
- Focuses on character
- Addresses the leader's use of power and privilege and his or her relationship to nature

Disadvantages (Cons)

- Denies reason
- Rejects codes and laws
- Is ambiguous about many moral issues
- Promotes ethical pragmatism and ethical relativism
- Does not adequately explain evil

Nearly all the concepts presented in the typical Western leadership or ethics text are drawn from the United States, Great Britain, and Europe. Taoism is one of the few non-Western approaches to attract much attention. It's easy to see why Taoist thought is popular with some leaders and scholars.

Taoist principles provide an ethical framework for such important trends or themes in leadership studies as empowerment, innovation, teamwork, spirituality, and collaboration. Taoist philosophy seems particularly well suited to leaders working in fast-paced, rapidly changing, and decentralized work environments like those found in the high-tech industry. Taoist thinkers encourage us to be flexible and to use "soft" tactics such as listening and negotiation that facilitate teamwork in leaner, flatter organizations. They urge us to embrace silence and contemplation, to develop a sense of inner peace, to reject ambition, and to serve. Focusing on being rather than doing (being blocklike and childlike) encourages leaders to develop character, our focus in Chapter 3.

Taoism speaks most directly to the leader's use of power and privilege. The authors of the *Tao Te Ching* reject the use of force except as a last resort. They criticize the feudal lords of their day for living in splendor while their people sank into poverty and starvation. It is difficult to imagine that Taoist sages would approve of the vast difference in pay between American executives and employees, for example, or give their blessing to politicians who enjoy an extravagant lifestyle at taxpayer expense.

The Taoist perspective also addresses environmental issues. According to Taoists, we need to work with nature instead of controlling or managing it. The natural world seems to renew itself when left alone. When cows are kept out of streams, for instance, vegetation returns to the riverbank, providing shade that cools the water and encourages the return of native fish. On the other hand, attempts to manage the environment often end in disaster. Consider our attempts to suppress forest fires. Putting out wildfires allows tinder to build up over a period of years. When a blaze does take hold, it is much more likely to burn out of control. In addition, Taoists encourage us to look to nature for insights about leadership. Contemporary authors have begun to follow their lead, identifying leadership lessons that can be drawn from the natural world.[48]

There are some serious disadvantages to Taoist ethics. In their attempt to follow nature, Taoists encourage leaders to empty themselves of, among other things, reason. Intuition has its place, but we need to learn how to make more reasoned decisions, not to abandon logic. Taoists are rightly skeptical about the effectiveness of moral codes and laws. Nevertheless, laws can change society for the better. For example, civil rights legislation played a significant role in reducing racial discrimination and changing cultural norms. In organizations, reasonable rules, professional guidelines, and codes of conduct can and do play a role in improving ethical climate. (See Chapter 9.)

Although Taoism has much to say about the shadow of power and our relationship to the world around us, it is silent on many common ethical dilemmas, such as the case of the manager asked to keep information about an upcoming merger to herself (see Chapter 1). What does it mean to follow nature's example when faced with this decision? Perhaps the manager should keep quiet to keep from intruding into the lives of followers. Nonetheless, withholding information would put her in the position of a mountain instead of a valley, giving her an advantage.

Basing moral decision making on conformity to principles manifested in the natural world promotes ethical pragmatism and relativism. The Taoist is pragmatic, believing that the ethical action is the one that blends with natural rhythms to produce the desired outcome. In other words, what works is what is right. This pragmatic approach seems to ignore the fact that what may "work" (generate profits, create pleasure, ensure job security, earn a raise) may be unethical (result in an unsafe product, destroy public trust, exploit workers). The follower of the Tao also practices ethical relativism. Natural conditions are always changing: Seasons shift; plants and animals grow and die. The flexible leader adapts to shifting circumstances. However, this makes it impossible to come to any definite conclusion about right or wrong. What is the right moral choice in one context may be wrong in another.

One final concern should be noted: Taoism's firm conviction that humans, in their natural state, will act morally seems to deny the power of evil. My thesis has been that leaders and followers can and do act destructively, driven by their shadow sides.

Implications and Applications

- Contrary to popular belief, being ethical makes us more, not less, successful. Being a good leader means being both ethical *and* effective.
- Seek to be a transforming leader who raises the level of morality in a group or an organization. Transformational leaders speak to higher-level needs and bring about profound changes. They are motivated by duty and altruism and marked by personal integrity. Dimensions of transformational leadership include idealized influence, inspirational motivation, intellectual stimulation, and individualized consideration.
- Putting the needs of followers first reduces the likelihood that you'll cast ethical shadows. Servant leaders are stewards who have significant obligations to both their followers and their institutions, practice partnership, promote healing, and serve worthy purposes.
- Be careful who and what you serve. Make sure your efforts support worthy people and goals and are carefully thought out.
- Authentic leaders have an in-depth knowledge of themselves and act in ways that reflect their core values and beliefs. The four components of authenticity are self-awareness, balanced processing, internalized moral perspective, and

relational transparency. Authenticity multiplies the effectiveness of leaders and promotes ethical behavior in followers.

- Responsible leaders build ethical relationships with stakeholders both inside and outside the organization in order to address global problems. In order to act as a responsible leader, you will need to act as a steward, a servant, a coach, an architect, a storyteller, a change agent, and a citizen.
- Taoists argue that nature and elements of everyday life serve as a source of ethical leadership lessons. You can learn from uncarved blocks, children, water, valleys, and clay pots.

For Further Exploration, Challenge, and Self-Assessment

1. What additional advantages and disadvantages can you add for each approach described in the chapter? Which perspective do you find most useful? Why?

2. Brainstorm a list of pseudo-transformational and transformational leaders. What factors distinguish between the two types of leader? How do your characteristics compare with those presented in the chapter?

3. Discuss the following proposition in a group: "The most successful leaders are also the most ethical leaders." Do you agree? Why or why not? As an alternative, discuss the following assertion instead: "Business leaders have an ethical duty to address global problems like poverty and hunger."

4. Make a diligent effort to serve your followers for a week. At the end of this period, reflect on your experience. Did focusing on the needs of followers change your behavior? What did you do differently? What would happen if you made this your leadership philosophy?

5. Write a case study. Option 1 is to base your case on someone you consider to be an authentic leader. How does this person demonstrate authenticity? What impact has this person had on followers and her or his organization? What can we learn from this leader's example? Option 2 is to base your case on someone you consider to be a responsible leader. How does this individual play the roles of responsible leadership? How has his or her business been an agent of global good? What can we learn from this leader's example?

6. Which image from nature or daily life from Taoism do you find most interesting and helpful? Why? Can you think of additional natural metaphors that would be useful to leaders?

7. Read a popular book on transformational leadership or on a transformational leader. Write a review. Summarize the contents for those who have not read it. Next, evaluate the book. What are its strengths and weaknesses from an ethical point of view? Would you recommend it to others? Why or why not?

CASE STUDY 6.2

SENTENCING KIDS FOR CASH

Juvenile judges play a critical role in the judicial system. They deal with young, vulnerable offenders who are more likely to change than adults. As a result, juvenile judges are typically reluctant to sentence first-time defendants and those committing minor offenses to detention. They assign them instead to guidance counselors or probation officers. That was not the case in Luzerne County, Pennsylvania, however. From 2000–2007, juvenile justice Mark Ciavarella routinely incarcerated first-time defendants for such trivial crimes as slapping, throwing a sandal, fighting in school, possessing drug paraphernalia, stealing loose change from cars, and shoplifting a $4 jar of nutmeg.

An investigation into Ciavarella's harsh sentencing record began after he assigned a 14-year-old student with good grades and a clean record to three months of detention after she posted a MySpace page that poked fun at a school vice principal. She was led away in handcuffs after a trial lasting less than a minute. The probe revealed that Ciavarella and his friend and fellow judge, Michael Conahan, received $2.6 million in kickbacks from a construction contractor who built two private juvenile detention centers, and Robert Powell, who owned the facilities. Chief juvenile justice Conahan cut funding for the county juvenile facility. As a result, juveniles sentenced in Luzerne County entered the for-profit centers. Ciavarella then provided the centers with a steady stream of clients in return for cash. An audit later revealed that the private facilities overcharged the county and state $1.2 million. Much of the money paid to house county juveniles went to support the lavish lifestyle of Powell or was diverted to his other companies. By the time the scandal was revealed, the detention centers had to borrow money to pay their utility bills. The judges spent part of their proceeds from the kickbacks on a $785,000 condominium in Florida where Powell sometimes moored his yacht, "Reel Justice."

Judge Ciavarella sentenced approximately one quarter of defendants to detention during the scheme, more than double the national average and much higher than his previous 10% incarceration rate. Detention center officials were told how many teens to expect at the end of the day even before hearings were held. Ciavarella often overruled the recommendations of probation officers and didn't advise families that they could have legal representation, which kept some parents and children from knowing the consequences of pleading guilty. Even if defendants did hire attorneys, the judge often prevented them from speaking in court. On the other hand,

Judge Ciavarella could be kind to his friends. When a trooper testified that a high school friend of the magistrate had been going 80 miles per hour in a 55-mile-per-hour zone, the judge interrupted to say, "No, I think he was going 60" and dismissed the case.[1]

The two judges pled guilty to conspiracy and tax fraud and were originally sentenced to seven years in prison. However, a district judge threw out the plea deals because Conahan and Ciavarella did not accept full responsibility for their crimes. Ciavarella told a reporter that he innocently took the money and denied putting teens in custody in return for kickbacks. "Cash for kids? It never happened. People have jumped to conclusions—I didn't do any of these things."[2] Juvenile legal rights advocates beg to differ. The Juvenile Law Center of Philadelphia declared that "thousands of these children . . . were victims of a wave of unprecedented lawlessness" that significantly changed the direction of their lives. Noted one lawyer working with the center, "The people you are stepping on [in the kickback scheme] are the true, true little guys."[3]

Discussion Probes

1. What leadership shadows do you see cast in this case?

2. Prior to this scheme, the judges had good reputations. What do you think prompted them to engage in illegal activity?

3. Why do you think the judges were able to get away with their scheme despite indications that they were abusing their authority and violating the rights of defendants?

4. Why do you think judges Conahan and Ciavarella were unwilling to accept full responsibility for their actions despite pleading guilty?

5. What principles of servant leadership do you see violated in this case? Of transformational leadership?

6. What leadership and followership ethics lessons do you take from this case?

Notes

1. Urbina, I. (2009, March 28). Despite red flags about judges, a kickback scheme flourished. *The New York Times*, p. A1.

2. Pilkington, E. (2009, March 7). Jailed for MySpace parody, the student who exposed America's cash for kids scandal. *The Guardian*, International, p. 21.

3. Sullivan, J. (2009, February 27). Class-action suit filed in corrupt judges case. *The Philadelphia Inquirer*, p. A01.

(Continued)

(Continued)

Sources

Allen-Mills, T. (2009, March 9). Judges paid off to keep jails full in kids-for-cash scandal. *The Australian,* World, p. 12.

Bad judges: No deal. (2009, August 6). *The Philadelphia Inquirer,* p. A01.

Sullivan, J. (2009, February 12). Audit outlines high fees, spending. *The Philadelphia Inquirer,* p. A01.

Sullivan, J. (2009, March 14). Report submitted in juvenile-detention scandal. *The Philadelphia Inquirer,* p. B01.

CASE STUDY 6.3

THE AIRLINE EXECUTIVE AS "MOM IN CHIEF"

The career of Southwest Airlines executive Colleen Barrett demonstrates the power that comes from knowing yourself and living in harmony with your strengths and values. Barrett started work as a legal secretary for San Antonio attorney Herb Kelleher. When Kelleher founded Southwest Airlines in the early 1970s, she became his alter ego. Kelleher was the visionary; Barrett brought his visions to reality. According to Barrett, "Herb could have a dream in the middle of the night and say, 'Okay, this is what I want to do.' But he wouldn't have a clue, God love him, what steps have to be taken to get there. I'm not the most brilliant person in the whole world, but I can see systematically from A to Z, and I know what has to be done."[1]

Barrett's role at Southwest expanded as the company grew. She started as the secretary of the corporation, became vice president of administration, then became executive vice president of customers, and assumed the role of CEO and president in 2001 after Kelleher stepped aside. (She dropped her CEO duties in 2004.) During this period, Southwest went from a small startup serving three cities in Texas to the largest domestic air carrier in the United States, with 32,000 employees. The company went 34 years without losing money at the same time many of its competitors went into bankruptcy or out of business. In 2008, she stepped down as company president but continues to work for Southwest in her role as president emeritus.

Barrett is credited with being the architect of Southwest's culture, which emphasizes customer service, concern for employees, empowerment, and fun ("We take the competition seriously, but we don't take ourselves seriously"). She considers employees to be her "family," and they, in turn, consider her to be the company "mom." When she served as president (as "Mom in Chief"), for example, Barrett encouraged employees to put pictures of their families and pets on the walls. Over her years at the company she has handed out plenty of hugs and words of encouragement. Kelleher called her the "Heroine of Hearts." Following her retirement as president, the Transportation Workers Union made her an honorary lifetime member in appreciation for her support of unionized workers at Southwest.

Southwest's former president exemplifies authentic leadership. To begin, she gives the impression that she is much the same person now as she was when she worked in Kelleher's law practice. Barrett never aspired to become a top airline executive because she knew that her strengths were caring for people, not finance. (Besides, she loved being a legal secretary.) During her tenure as president, she dressed casually, in comfortable shoes, with her gray hair pulled back in a ponytail. Observers noted that she looked more like a neighborly grandmother than the most powerful woman in the airline industry and one of the 50 most powerful women in American business. She never used e-mail and didn't own a car.

Whatever her role at Southwest, Colleen Barrett has consistently lived out her respect for others, love, and forgiveness. The most vivid demonstration of her commitment to her values may have come after the events of September 11, 2001. Southwest was the only domestic air carrier not to lay off employees and paid workers for the days the airline was grounded. Barrett encourages her employees to express their individuality and gives them the power to make decisions that benefit the customer. Her decision to step down as company president was a reflection of her belief in her followers, allowing others to take the lead as she stepped back. "I have always thought," Barrett said, "that one of the best traits of a leader is to know when to follow."[2]

Discussion Probes

1. Would you like to work for Colleen Barrett? Why or why not?

2. Do you think Barrett's leadership style would work in other companies? Why or why not?

3. Do you agree that authenticity is the key to Barrett's effectiveness as a leader? What other factors might have contributed to her success?

4. Based on your experience with Southwest Airlines, does the culture of the company reflect Barrett's values?

(Continued)

(Continued)

5. Is one of the best traits of a leader knowing when to follow?

6. What leadership and followership ethics lessons do you take from this case?

Notes

1. Booker, K. (2001, May 28). The chairman of the board looks back. *Fortune*, p. 76.
2. Fisher, S. (2007, September). Flying off into the sunset. *Costco Connection*, p. 17.

Sources

Clark, K. (2001, December 31). Nothing but the plane truth. *U.S. News & World Report*.
Fitzpatrick, D. (2005, May 12). "Aw-shucks" president embodies Southwest style. *Pittsburgh Post-Gazette*.
Stewart, D. R. (2006, June 1). Southwest staff "family": The airline's corporate culture is tied to its success. *Tulsa World*.

Notes

1. Ciulla, J. B. (2004). Leadership ethics: Mapping the territory. In J. B. Ciulla (Ed.), *Ethics: The heart of leadership* (pp. 3–24). Westport, CT: Praeger.

2. Burns J. M. (1978). *Leadership*. New York: Harper & Row.

3. Burns, J. M. (2003). *Transforming leadership: A new pursuit of happiness.* New York: Atlantic Monthly Press.

4. Burns (1978), p. 2.

5. Burns (2003), Ch. 12.

6. Kanungo, R. N. (2001). Ethical values of transactional and transformational leaders. *Canadian Journal of Administrative Sciences, 18*, 257–265.

7. See the following:

> Bass, B. M. (1996). *A new paradigm of leadership: An inquiry into transformational leadership.* Alexandria, VA: U.S. Army Research Institute for the Behavioral and Social Sciences.
>
> Bass, B. M., Avolio, B. J., Jung, D. I., & Berson, Y. (2003). Predicting unit performance by assessing transformational and transactional leadership. *Journal of Applied Psychology, 88*, 207–218.

8. Bass, B. M. (1990). *Bass & Stogdill's handbook of leadership* (3rd ed.). New York: Free Press, p. 53.

9. See the following:

Bass, B. M., & Avolio, B. J. (1993). Transformational leadership: A response to critiques. In M. M. Chemers & R. Ayman (Eds.), *Leadership theory and research: Perspectives and directions* (pp. 49–60). San Diego: Academic Press.

Waldman, D. A., Bass, B. M., & Yammarino, F. J. (1990). Adding to contingent-reward behavior: The augmenting effect of charismatic leadership. *Group and Organizational Studies, 15,* 381–394.

10. For evidence of the effectiveness of transformational leadership, see Bass et al. (2003) and the following:

DeGroot, T., Kiker, D. S., & Cross, T. C. (2000). A meta-analysis to review organizational outcomes related to charismatic leadership. *Canadian Journal of Administrative Sciences, 17,* 356–371.

Fiol, C. M., Harris, D., & House, R. J. (1999). Charismatic leadership: Strategies for effecting social change. *The Leadership Quarterly, 1,* 449–482.

Lowe, K. B., & Kroeck, K. G. (1996). Effectiveness correlates of transformational and transactional leadership: A meta-analytic review. *The Leadership Quarterly, 7,* 385–425.

11. A few examples of popular leadership sources based on a transformational approach include the following:

Bennis, W., & Nanus, B. (2003). *Leaders: Strategies for taking charge.* New York: Harper Business Essentials.

Kotter, J. P. (1990). *A force for change: How leadership differs from management.* New York: Free Press.

Kouzes, J. M., & Posner, B. (2007). *The leadership challenge* (4th ed.). San Francisco: Jossey-Bass.

Nanus, B. (1992). *Visionary leadership.* San Francisco: Jossey-Bass.

Peters, T. (1992). *Liberation management.* New York: Ballantine.

12. Bass, B. M. (1995). The ethics of transformational leadership. In J. Ciulla (Ed.), *Ethics: The heart of leadership* (pp. 169–192). Westport, CT: Praeger.

13. Turner, N., Barling, J., Epitropaki, O., Butcher, V., & Milner, C. (2002, April). Transformational leadership and moral reasoning. *Journal of Applied Psychology, 87,* 304–311; Toor, S. R., & Ofori, G. (2009). Ethical leadership: Examining the relationships with full range leadership model, employee outcomes, and organizational culture. *Journal of Business Ethics, 90,* 533–547; Hood, J. N. (2003). The relationship of leadership style and CEO values to ethical practices in organizations. *Journal of Business Ethics, 43,* 263–273; Carlson, D. S., & Perrewe, P. L. (1995). Institutionalization of organizational ethics through transformational leadership. *Journal of Business Ethics, 14,* 829–838; Puffer, S. M., & McCarthy, D. J. (2008). Ethical turnarounds and transformational leadership: A global imperative for corporate social responsibility. *Thunderbird International Business Review, 50,* 304–314.

14. Den Hartog, D. N., House, R. J., Hanges, P. U., Ruiz-Quintanilla, S. A., & Dorfman, P. W. (1999). Culture specific and cross-culturally generalizable implicit

leadership theories: Are attributes of charismatic/transformational leadership universally endorsed? *The Leadership Quarterly, 10,* 219–257.

15. Lang, D. L. (1991). Transformational leadership is not charismatic leadership: Philosophical impoverishment in leadership continues. *Human Resource Development Quarterly, 2,* 397–402; Carlson & Perrewe.

16. Tourish, D. (2008). Challenging the transformational agenda: Leadership theory in transition? *Management Communication Quarterly, 21,* 522–528, p. 523.

17. Criticisms of transformational leadership can be found in the following:

    Kelley, R. (1992). *The power of followership.* New York: Doubleday/ Currency.

    Tourish, D., & Pinnington, A. (2002). Transformational leadership, corporate cultism and the spirituality paradigm: An unholy trinity in the workplace? *Human Relations, 55*(2), 147–172.

18. Greenleaf, R. K. (1977). *Servant leadership.* New York: Paulist Press.

19. Spears, L. (1998). Introduction: Tracing the growing impact of servant-leadership. In L. C. Spears (Ed.), *Insights on leadership* (pp. 1–12). New York: Wiley; Ruschman, N. L. (2002). Servant-leadership and the best companies to work for in America. In L. C. Spears & M. Lawrence (Eds.), *Focus on leadership: Servant-leadership for the twenty-first century* (pp. 123–139). New York: Wiley; Sendjaya, S., & Sarros, J. C. (2002). Servant leadership: Its origin, development, and application in organizations. *Journal of Leadership and Organization Studies, 9*(2), 57–64.

20. Greenleaf, pp. 13–14.

21. Block, P. (1996). *Stewardship: Choosing service over self-interest.* San Francisco: Berrett-Koehler; DePree, M. (2003). Servant-leadership: Three things necessary. In L. C. Spears & M. Lawrence (Eds.), *Focus on leadership: Servant-leadership for the 21st century.* (pp. 89–97). New York: Wiley.

22. DePree, M. (1989). *Leadership is an art.* New York: Doubleday.

23. Barbuto, J. E., & Wheeler, D. W. (2006). Scale development and construct clarification of servant leadership. *Group & Organization Management, 31,* 300–326; Spears, L. C. (2004). The understanding and practice of servant leadership. In L. C. Spears & M. Lawrence (Eds.), *Practicing servant leadership: Succeeding through trust, bravery, and forgiveness* (pp. 9–24). San Francisco: Jossey-Bass.

24. Barbuto & Wheeler; Russell, R. F., & Stone, A. G. (2002). A review of servant leadership attributes: Developing a practical model. *Leadership & Organization Development Journal, 23*(3), 145–157; Washington, R. R., Sutton, C. D., & Feild, H. S. (2006). Individual differences in servant leadership: The roles of values and personality. *Leadership & Organization Development Journal, 27,* 700–716; Mayers, D., Bardes, M., & Piccolo, R. F. (2008). Do servant-leaders help satisfy follower needs? An organizational justice perspective. *European Journal of Work and Organizational Psychology, 17*(2), 180–197; Jaramillo, F., Grisaffe, D. B., Chonko, L. B., & Roberts, J. A. (2009). Examining the impact of servant leadership on sales force performance. *Journal of Personal Selling & Sales Management, 24*(3), 257–275.

25. Kennedy, D. (2004). *The dark sides of virtue: Reassessing international humanitarianism.* Princeton, NJ: Princeton University Press.

26. Klenke, K. (2005). The internal theater of the authentic leader: Integrating cognitive, affective, conative and spiritual facets of authentic leadership. In W. L. Gardner, B. J. Avolio, & F. O. Walumbwa (Eds.), *Authentic leadership theory and practice: Origins, effects and development* (pp. 43–81). Amsterdam: Elsevier.

27. Avolio, B. J., & Gardner, W. L. (2005). Authentic leadership development: Getting to the root of positive forms of leadership. *The Leadership Quarterly, 16,* 315–340; Chan, A., Hannah, S. T., & Gardner, W. L. (2005). Veritable authentic leadership: Emergence, functioning, and impacts. In W. L. Gardner, B. J. Avolio, & F. O. Walumbwa (Eds.), *Authentic leadership theory and practice: Origins, effects and development* (pp. 3–41). Amsterdam: Elsevier.

28. Walumbwa, F. O., Avolio, B. J., Gardner, W. L., Wernsing, T. S., & Peterson, S. J. (2008). Authentic leadership: Development and validation of a theory-based measure. *Journal of Management, 34*(1), 89–126; Kernis, M. H. (2003). Toward a conceptualization of optimal self-esteem. *Psychological Inquiry, 14,* 1–26.

29. Avolio & Gardner, p. 321.

30. May, D. R., Chan, A. Y. L., Hodges, T. D., & Avolio, B. J. (2003). Developing the moral component of authentic leadership. *Organizational Dynamics, 32,* 247–260; Hanna, S. T., Lester, P. B., & Vogelgesang, G. R. (2005). Moral leadership: Explicating the moral component of authentic leadership. In W. L. Gardner, B. J. Avolio, & F. O. Walumbwa (Eds.), *Authentic leadership theory and practice: Origins, effects and development* (pp. 43–81). Amsterdam: Elsevier.

31. Gardner, W. L., Avolio, B. J., Luthans, F., May, D. R., & Walumbwa, F. O. (2005). "Can you see the real me?" A self-based model of authentic leader and follower development. *The Leadership Quarterly, 16,* 343–372.

32. May et al.; Ilies, R., Morgeson, F. P., & Nahrgang, J. D. (2005). Authentic leadership and eudemonic well-being: Understanding leader–follower outcomes. *The Leadership Quarterly, 16,* 373–394.

33. Gardner et al. (2005); Harvey, P., Martinko, M. J., & Gardner, W. L. (2006). Promoting authentic behavior in organizations: An attributional perspective. *Journal of Leadership and Organizational Studies, 12,* 1–11; Zhu, W., May, D. R., & Avolio, B. J. (2004). The impact of ethical leadership behavior on employee outcomes: The roles of psychological empowerment and authenticity. *Journal of Leadership and Organizational Studies, 11,* 16–26; Avolio, B. J., Gardner, W. L., Walumbwa, F. O., Luthans, F., & May, D. R. (2004). Unlocking the mask: A look at the process by which authentic leaders impact follower attitudes and behaviors. *The Leadership Quarterly, 15,* 801–823; Clapp-Smith, R., Vogelgesang, G. R., & Avey, J. B. (2009). Authentic leadership and positive psychological capital: The mediating role of trust at the group level of analysis. *Journal of Leadership & Organizational Studies, 15*(3), 227–240.

34. See the following:

   Bruhn, J. G. (2001). *Trust and the health of organizations.* New York: Kluwer/Plenum.

   Dirks, K. T. (1999). The effects of interpersonal trust on work group performance. *Journal of Applied Psychology, 84,* 445–455.

Driscoll, J. W. (1978). Trust and participation in organizational decision making as predictors of satisfaction. *Academy of Management Journal, 21*, 44–56.

Gilbert, J. A., & Tang, T. L (1998). An examination of organizational trust antecedents. *Public Personnel Management, 27*, 321–238.

Kramer, R. M., & Tyler, T. R. (1996). *Trust in organizations: Frontiers of theory and research.* Thousand Oaks, CA: Sage.

Mayer, R. C., & Gavin, M. B. (2005). Trust in management and performance: Who minds the shop while the employees watch the boss? *Academy of Management Journal, 48*, 874–888.

Shockley-Zalabak, P., Ellis, K., & Winograd, G. (2000). Organizational trust: What it means, why it matters. *Organization Development Journal, 18*, 35–47.

35. Clapp-Smith et al.

36. Walumbwa et al.

37. Clapp-Smith et al.

38. Chan et al.

39. Maak, T., & Pless, N. M. (2006). Responsible leadership in a stakeholder society—A relational perspective. *Journal of Business Ethics, 66*, 99–115; Maak, T., & Pless, N. M. (2006). Responsible leadership: A relational approach. In T. Maak & N. M. Pless (Eds.), *Responsible leadership* (pp. 33–53). London: Routledge; Pless, N. M. (2007). Understanding responsible leadership: Role identity and motivational factors. *Journal of Business Ethics, 85*, 437–456.

40. Maak, T., & Pless, N. M. (2009). Business leaders as citizens of the world. Advancing humanism on a global scale. *Journal of Business Ethics, 88*, 537–550, p. 539.

41. Maak & Pless, *Responsible leadership: A relational approach*; Pless, N. M. (2007). Understanding responsible leadership: Role identity and motivational drivers. *Journal of Business Ethics, 74*, 437–456.

42. Pless, N., & Maak, T. (2009). Responsible leaders as agents of world benefit: Learnings from "Project Ulysses." *Journal of Business Ethics, 85*, 59–71: Maak & Pless, Business leaders as citizens of the world.

43. Maak, T. (2007). Responsible leadership, stakeholder engagement, and the emergence of social capital. *Journal of Business Ethics, 74*, 329–343.

44. Material on key components of Taoist thought is adopted from:

Johnson, C. E. (1997, Spring). A leadership journey to the East. *Journal of Leadership Studies, 4*, 82–88.

Johnson, C. E. (2000). Emerging perspectives in leadership ethics. *Proceedings of the International Leadership Association*, pp. 48–54.

Johnson, C. E. (2000). Taoist leadership ethics. *Journal of Leadership Studies, 7*, 82–91.

For an alternative perspective on the origins of Taoism, see Kirkland, R. (2002). Self-fulfillment through selflessness: The moral teachings of the Daode Jing. In M. Barnhart (Ed.), *Varieties of ethical reflection: New directions for ethics in a global context* (pp. 21–48). Lanham, MA: Lexington.

45. Mitchell, S. (1988). *Tao te ching.* New York: Harper Perennial, p. 19.

46. Mitchell, p. 17.

47. Chan, W. (1963). *The way of Lao Tzu.* Indianapolis: Bobbs-Merrill, p. 236.

48. See the following:

Kiuchi, T., & Shireman, B. (2002). *What we learned in the rainforest: Business lessons from nature.* San Francisco: Berrett-Koehler.

White, B. J., & Prywes, Y. (2007). *The nature of leadership: Reptiles, mammals, and the challenge of becoming a great leader.* New York: AMACOM.

7

Ethical Decision Making
and Behavior

As we practice resolving dilemmas we find ethics to be less a goal than a pathway, less a destination than a trip, less an inoculation than a process.

—Ethicist Rushworth Kidder

WHAT'S AHEAD

This chapter surveys the components of ethical behavior—moral sensitivity, moral judgment, moral motivation, and moral character—and introduces systematic approaches to ethical problem solving. We'll take a look at four decision-making formats: Kidder's ethical checkpoints, the SAD formula, Nash's 12 questions, and the case study method. After presenting each approach, I'll discuss its relative advantages and disadvantages.

Understanding how we make and follow through on ethical decisions is the first step to making better choices; taking a systematic approach is the second. We'll explore both of these steps in this chapter. After examining the ethical decision-making process, we'll see how guidelines or formats can guide our ethical deliberations.

Components of Moral Action

There are a number of models of ethical decision making and action. For example, business ethics educators Charles Powers and David Vogel identify six factors or elements that underlie moral reasoning and behavior and that are particularly relevant in organizational settings.[1] The first is *moral imagination,* the recognition that even routine choices and relationships have an ethical dimension. The second is *moral identification and ordering,* which, as the name suggests, refers to the ability to identify important issues, determine priorities, and sort out competing values. The third factor is *moral evaluation,* or using analytical skills to evaluate options. The fourth element is *tolerating moral disagreement and ambiguity,* which arises when managers disagree about values and courses of action. The fifth is the ability to *integrate managerial competence with moral competence.* This integration involves anticipating possible ethical dilemmas, leading others in ethical decision making, and making sure any decision becomes part of an organization's systems and procedures. The sixth and final element is a sense of *moral obligation,* which serves as a motivating force to engage in moral judgment and to implement decisions.

James Rest of the University of Minnesota developed what may be the most widely used model of moral behavior. Rest built his four-component model by working backward. He started with the end product—moral action—and then determined the steps that produce such behavior. He concluded that ethical action is the result of four psychological subprocesses: (1) moral sensitivity (recognition), (2) moral judgment, (3) moral focus (motivation), and (4) moral character.[2]

Component 1: Moral Sensitivity (Recognition)

Moral sensitivity (recognizing the presence of an ethical issue) is the first step in ethical decision making because we can't solve a moral problem unless we first know that one exists. A great many moral failures stem from ethical insensitivity. The safety committee at Ford Motor decided not to fix the defective gas tank on the Pinto automobile (see Chapter 2) because members saw no problem with saving money rather than human lives. Wal-Mart was slow to respond to concerns raised by employees, labor groups, environmentalists, and others about wage violations, sexual discrimination, poor environmental practices, and other issues.[3] Many students, focused on finishing their degrees, see no problem with cheating. (You can test your ethical sensitivity by completing the "Self-Assessment: Moral Sensitivity Scenarios.")

According to Rest, problem recognition requires that we consider how our behavior affects others, identify possible courses of action, and determine the consequences of each potential strategy. Empathy and perspective skills are essential to this component of moral action. If we understand how others might feel or react, we are more sensitive to potential negative effects of our choices and can better predict the likely outcomes of each option.

A number of factors prevent us from recognizing ethical issues. We may not factor ethical considerations into our typical ways of thinking or mental models.[4] We may be reluctant to use moral terminology (*values, justice, right, wrong*) to describe our decisions because we want to avoid controversy or believe that keeping silent will make us appear strong and capable.[5] We may even deceive ourselves into thinking that we are acting morally when we are clearly not, a process called *ethical fading*. The moral aspects of a decision fade into the background if we use euphemisms to disguise unethical behavior, numb our consciences through repeated misbehavior, blame others, and claim that only we know the "truth."[6]

Fortunately, we can take steps to enhance our ethical sensitivity (and the sensitivity of our fellow leaders and followers) by doing the following:

- Active listening and role playing
- Imagining other perspectives
- Stepping back from a situation to determine whether it has moral implications
- Using moral terminology to discuss problems and issues
- Avoiding euphemisms
- Refusing to excuse misbehavior
- Accepting personal responsibility
- Practicing humility and openness to other points of view

In addition to these steps, we can also increase ethical sensitivity by making an issue more salient. The greater the moral intensity of an issue, the more likely it is that decision makers will take note of it and respond ethically.[7] We can build moral intensity by doing the following:

- Illustrating that the situation can cause significant harm or benefit to many people (magnitude of consequences)
- Establishing that there is social consensus or agreement that a behavior is moral or immoral (e.g., legal or illegal, approved or forbidden by a professional association)
- Demonstrating probability of effect, that the act will happen and will cause harm or benefit
- Showing that the consequences will happen soon (temporal immediacy)
- Emphasizing social, psychological, physical, or psychological closeness (proximity) with those affected by our actions
- Proving that one person or a group will greatly suffer due to a decision (concentration of effect)

Finally, paying attention to our emotions can be an important clue that we are faced with an ethical dilemma. Moral emotions are part of our makeup as humans.[8] These feelings are triggered even when we do not have a personal stake in an event. For example, we may feel angry when reading about mistreatment of migrant workers or sympathy when we see a picture of a refugee living in a squalid camp. Moral emotions also encourage us to take action that benefits other people and society as a whole. We might write a letter protesting the poor working conditions of migrant laborers, for instance, or send money to a humanitarian organization working with displaced persons.

Anger, disgust, and contempt are *other-condemning* emotions. They are elicited by unfairness, betrayal, immorality, cruelty, poor performance, and status differences. Anger can motivate us to redress injustices like racism, oppression, and poverty. Disgust encourages us to set up rewards and punishments to deter inappropriate behaviors. Contempt generally causes us to step back from others. Shame, embarrassment, and guilt are *self-conscious emotions* that encourage us to obey the rules and uphold the social order. These feelings are triggered when we violate norms and social conventions, present the wrong image to others, and fail to live up to moral guidelines. Shame and embarrassment can keep us from engaging in further damaging behavior and may drive us to withdraw from social contact. Guilt motivates us to help others and to treat them well.

Sympathy and compassion are *other-suffering emotions*. They are elicited when we perceive suffering or sorrow in our fellow human beings. Such feelings encourage us to comfort, help, and alleviate the pain of others. Gratitude, awe, and elevation are *other-praising (positive) emotions* that open us up to new opportunities and relationships. They are prompted when someone has done something on our behalf, when we run across moral beauty (acts of charity, loyalty, and self-sacrifice, for example), and when we read or hear about moral exemplars (see Chapter 3). Gratitude motivates us to repay others; awe and elevation encourage us to become better persons and to take steps to help others.

In sum, if we experience anger, disgust, guilt, sympathy, or other moral emotions, the chances are good that there is an ethical dimension to the situation that confronts us. We will need to look further to determine if this is indeed the case.

SELF-ASSESSMENT

MORAL SENSITIVITY SCENARIOS

Instructions

Read each vignette and consider the following statement:

There are very important ethical aspects to this situation. (1 = strongly disagree, 7 = strongly agree)

Then briefly explain your rating for each vignette in the space below it. For more information on the ethical issues raised by the scenarios, see Item 1 under "For Further Exploration, Challenge, and Self-Assessment."

Vignette 1

One of your most important customers, a medical clinic, called yesterday. The clinic had ordered a product 10 days ago (products are normally delivered within 7–10 days), but it had not arrived. Quickly, you traced the order to the shipping office. You asked the shipping clerk about the order, and she said, "I shipped it 2 days ago!" As you left the shipping office, you glanced at her desk and saw her shipping receipts. You could clearly see that the order was shipped this morning. You called the client back with the news that the product was on its way. As you talked with the client, you learned that the delay of the product had allowed the condition of some patients to worsen quite dramatically.

Vignette 2

Last Monday, you were sitting at your desk examining a request that a customer had just faxed to you. The customer was proposing a project that would make a tremendous amount of money for your company but had an extremely demanding time schedule. Just as you were about to call the customer and accept the project, one of your employees, Phil, knocked on the door. He entered your office, politely placed a letter of resignation on your desk, and told you he was sorry, but in two weeks, he would be moving to another state to be closer to his ailing parents. After he left, you thought about the proposed project and determined that even though Phil would be gone, you could still meet all of the customer's deadlines. You called the customer and accepted the project.

_____

_____

_____

_____

_____

Vignette 3

Earlier today, a salesman who works in Iowa called you and told you about an experience he had last week. One of his customers placed a small order of about $1,500 worth of product from corporate headquarters. The home office immediately shipped the package through a freight company, and it arrived the next day at the freight company's warehouse in Iowa. The salesman went to the warehouse just as it was closing and talked to one of the managers. The manager said that everyone had gone home for the day, but he assured him that the package would be delivered directly to his office the next day. The salesman knew that the customer did not need the materials for at least another 3 days, but he didn't want to wait. He placed a $20 bill on the counter and asked the warehouse manager one last time if there was anything he could do. The manager found the paperwork, got the product from the back of the warehouse, and brought it out to the salesman.

_____

_____

_____

_____

_____

SOURCE: Reynolds, S. J. (2006). Moral awareness and ethical predispositions: Investigating the role of individual differences in the recognition of moral issues. *Journal of Applied Psychology, 91,* 233–243. Published by the American Psychological Association.

Component 2: Moral Judgment

Once an ethical problem is identified, decision makers select a course of action from the options generated in Component 1. In other words, they make judgments about what is the right or wrong thing to do in this situation.

Moral judgment has generated more research than the other components of Rest's model. Investigators have been particularly interested in cognitive moral development, the process by which people develop their moral reasoning abilities over time. Harvard psychologist Lawrence Kohlberg argued that individuals progress through a series of moral stages just as they do physical ones.[9] Each stage is more advanced than the one before. Not only do people engage in more complex reasoning as they progress up the stages, but they also become less self-centered and develop broader definitions of morality.

Kohlberg identified three levels of moral development, each divided into two stages. Level I, *preconventional* thinking, is the most primitive and focuses on consequences. This form of moral reasoning is common among children who choose to obey to avoid punishment (Stage 1) or follow the rules in order to meet their interests (Stage 2). Stage 2 thinkers are interested in getting a fair deal: You help me, and I'll help you.

Conventional thinkers (Level II) look to others for guidance when deciding how to act. Stage 3 people want to live up to the expectations of those they respect, such as parents, siblings, and friends, and value concern for others and respect. Stage 4 individuals take a somewhat broader perspective, looking to society as a whole for direction. They believe in following rules at work, for example, and the law. Kohlberg found that most adults are Level II thinkers.

Level III, *postconceptual* or *principled* reasoning, is the most advanced type of ethical thinking. Stage 5 people are guided by utilitarian principles. They are concerned for the needs of the entire group and want to make sure that rules and laws serve the greatest good for the greatest number. Stage 6 people operate according to internalized, universal principles such as justice, equality, and human dignity. These principles consistently guide their behavior and take precedence over the laws of any particular society. According to Kohlberg, fewer than 20% of American adults ever reach Stage 5, and almost no one reaches Stage 6.

Critics take issue with both the philosophical foundation of Kohlberg's model and its reliance on concrete stages of moral development.[10] They contend that Kohlberg based his postconventional stage on Rawls's justice-as-fairness theory and made deontological ethics superior to other ethical approaches. They note that the model applies more to societal issues than to individual ethical decisions. A great many psychologists challenge the notion that people go through a rigid or "hard" series of moral stages, leaving one stage completely behind before moving to the next. They argue instead that a person can engage in many ways of thinking about a problem, regardless of age.

Rest (who studied under Kohlberg), Darcia Narvaez, and their colleagues responded to the critics by replacing the hard stages with a staircase of developmental schemas.[11] Schemas are networks of knowledge organized around life events. We use schemas when encountering new situations or information. You are able to master information in new classes, for instance, by using strategies you developed in previous courses. According to this "neo-Kohlbergian" approach, decision makers develop more sophisticated moral schemas as they develop. The least sophisticated schema is based on personal interest. People at this level are concerned only with what they may gain or lose in an ethical dilemma. No consideration is given to the needs of broader society. Those who reason at the next level, the maintaining norms schema, believe they have a moral obligation to maintain social order. They are concerned with following rules and laws and making sure that regulations apply to everyone. These thinkers believe that there is a clear hierarchy with carefully defined roles (e.g., bosses–subordinates, teachers–students, officers–enlisted personnel). The postconventional schema is the most advanced level of moral reasoning. Thinking at this level is not limited to one ethical approach, as Kohlberg argued, but encompasses many different philosophical traditions. Postconventional individuals believe that moral obligations are to be based on shared ideals, should not favor some people at the expense of others, and are open to scrutiny (testing and examination). Such thinkers reason like moral philosophers, looking behind societal norms to determine whether they serve moral purposes. (Refer to "Leadership Ethics at the Movies: *Michael Clayton*" for an example of a leader who shifts to a higher level of moral reasoning.)

Rest developed the Defining Issues Test (DIT) to measure moral development. Subjects taking the DIT (and its successor, the DIT-2) respond to six ethical scenarios and then choose statements that best reflect the reasoning they used to come up with their choices. These statements, which correspond to the three levels of moral reasoning, are then scored. In the best-known dilemma, Heinz's wife is dying of cancer and needs a drug he cannot afford to buy. He must decide whether to steal the drug to save her life.

Hundreds of studies using the DIT reveal that moral reasoning generally increases with age and education.[12] Undergraduate and graduate students benefit from their educational experiences in general and ethical coursework in particular. When education stops, moral development stops. In addition, moral development is a universal concept, crossing cultural boundaries.

Principled leaders can boost the moral judgment of a group by encouraging members to adopt more sophisticated ethical schemas.[13]

Models of cognitive development provide important insights into the process of ethical decision making. First, contextual variables play an important role in shaping ethical behavior. Most people look to others as well as to rules and regulations when making ethical determinations. They are more likely to make wise moral judgments if coworkers and supervisors encourage and model ethical behavior. As leaders, we need to build ethical environments. (We'll take a closer look at the formation of ethical groups and organizations in Chapters 8 and 9.) Second, education fosters moral reasoning. Pursuing a bachelor's, master's, or doctoral degree can promote your moral development. As part of your education, focus as much attention as you can on ethics (i.e., take ethics courses, discuss ethical issues in groups and classes, reflect on the ethical challenges you experience in internships). Third, a broader perspective is better. Consider the needs and viewpoints of others outside your immediate group or organization; determine what is good for the local area, the larger society, and the global community. Fourth, moral principles produce superior solutions. The best ethical thinkers base their choices on widely accepted ethical guidelines. Do the same by drawing on important ethical approaches such as utilitarianism, the categorical imperative, altruism, communitarianism, and justice-as-fairness theory.

 LEADERSHIP ETHICS AT THE MOVIES

MICHAEL CLAYTON

Key Cast Members: George Clooney, Tilda Swinton, Tom Wilkinson, Sydney Pollack

Synopsis: George Clooney stars as Michael Clayton, the "fixer" for a large New York City firm. Clayton takes care of any messes involving clients, like hit-and-run accidents and shoplifting charges. When the firm's top litigator (played by Wilkinson) begins to work for the other side in a $3 billion lawsuit, Clayton must get him back on his medications and under control. Karen Crowder (Swinton) is chief counsel for the conglomerate being sued for manufacturing a toxic chemical. She decides to permanently silence both the rogue lawyer and Clayton. The fixer, whose life and reputation have been tarnished by a series of poor ethical and business choices, must now decide how to respond to illegal wiretapping and murder. Swinton won a Best Supporting Actress Oscar for her

(Continued)

(Continued)

performance as the ambitious attorney who decides that corporate survival takes precedence over human life.

Rating: R for language, including sexual dialogue

Themes: moral reasoning, the dark side of leadership, corruption, greed, character, deception

Discussion Starters

1. What factors motivated Clayton to become a "fixer" and the conglomerate's chief counsel to protect her company at any cost?

2. Was it unethical for the law firm's top litigator to begin to work for the plaintiffs? Why or why not?

3. What accounts for Clayton's shift to a higher level of moral reasoning?

Component 3: Moral Focus (Motivation)

After concluding what course of action is best, decision makers must be focused (motivated to follow through) on their choices. Moral values often conflict with other significant values. For instance, an accounting supervisor who wants to blow the whistle on illegal accounting practices at her firm must balance her desire to do the right thing against her desire to keep her job, provide income for her family, and maintain relationships with her fellow workers. She will report the accounting abuses to outside authorities only if moral considerations take precedence over these competing priorities.

Psychologists report that self-interest and hypocrisy undermine moral motivation.[14] Sometimes individuals genuinely want to do the right thing, but their integrity is "overpowered" when they discover that they will have to pay a personal cost for acting in an ethical manner. Others never intend to follow an ethical course of action but engage in *moral hypocrisy* instead. These decision makers "want to appear moral while, if possible, avoiding the cost of actually being moral."[15] In experimental settings, they say that assignments should be distributed fairly but then assign themselves the most desirable tasks while giving less desirable chores to others. Both self-interest and hypocrisy encourage leaders to set their moral principles aside. For example, corporate executives may declare that lower-level employees deserve higher wages. However, whether they really want to help workers or just want to appear as if they do, these executives are not likely to pay employees more if it means that they will earn less as a result.

Rewards play an important role in ethical follow-through. People are more likely to give ethical values top priority when rewarded through raises, promotions, public recognition, and other means for doing so. Conversely, moral motivation drops when the reward system reinforces unethical behavior.[16] Unfortunately, misplaced rewards are all too common, as in the case of electronics retailers who reward employees for selling expensive extended warranties on new products. Such warranties are generally a bad deal for consumers.

Emotions also play a part in moral motivation.[17] As noted earlier, sympathy, disgust, guilt, and other moral emotions prompt us to take action. We can use their motivational force to help us punish wrongdoers, address injustice, provide assistance, and so on. Other researchers report that positive emotions such as joy and happiness make people more optimistic and more likely to live out their moral choices and to help others. Depression, on the other hand, lowers motivation, and jealousy, rage, and envy contribute to lying, revenge, stealing, and other antisocial behaviors.

To increase your moral motivation and the moral motivation of followers, seek out and create ethically rewarding environments. Make sure the reward system of an organization supports ethical behavior before joining it as an employee or a volunteer. Try to reduce the costs of behaving morally by instituting policies and procedures that make it easier to report unethical behavior, combat discrimination, and so on. Work to align rewards with desired behavior in your current organization. Be concerned about how goals are reached. If all else fails, reward yourself. Take pride in following through on your choices and on living up to your self-image as a person of integrity. Tap into moral emotions while making a conscious effort to control negative feelings and to put yourself in a positive frame of mind.

Component 4: Moral Character

Executing the plan of action takes character. Moral agents have to overcome opposition, resist distractions, cope with fatigue, and develop tactics and strategies for reaching their goals. This helps explain why there is only a moderate correlation between moral judgment and moral behavior. Many times deciding does not lead to doing.

The positive character traits described in Chapter 3 contribute to ethical follow-through. Courage helps leaders implement their plans despite the risks and costs of doing so while prudence helps them choose the best course of action. Integrity encourages leaders to be true to themselves and their choices. Humility forces leaders to address limitations that might prevent them from taking action. Reverence promotes self-sacrifice. Optimism equips leaders to persist in the face of obstacles and difficulties. Compassion and justice focus the attention of leaders on the needs of others rather than on personal priorities.

In addition to virtues, other personal characteristics contribute to moral action.[18] Those with a strong will, as well as confidence in themselves and their abilities, are more likely to persist. The same is true for those with an internal locus of control. Internally oriented people (internals) believe that they have control over their lives and can determine what happens to them. Externally oriented people (externals) believe that life events are beyond their control and are the product of fate or luck instead. Because they have personal responsibility for their actions, internals are more motivated to do what is right. Externals are more susceptible to situational pressures and therefore less likely to persist in ethical tasks.

Successful implementation also requires competence. For instance, modifying the organizational reward system may entail researching, organizing, arguing, networking, and relationship-building skills. These skills are put to maximum use when actors have an in-depth understanding of the organizational context: important policies, the group's history and culture, informal leaders, and so on.

Following the character-building guidelines presented in Chapter 3 will go a long way to helping you build the virtues you need to put your moral choices into action. You may also want to look at your past performance to see why you succeeded or failed. Believe that you can have an impact. Otherwise, you are probably not going to carry through when obstacles surface. Develop your skills so that you can better put your moral choice into action and master the context in which you operate.

Decision-Making Formats

Decision-making guidelines or formats can help us make better ethical choices. Taking a systematic approach encourages teams and individuals to carefully define the problem, gather information, apply ethical standards and values, identify and evaluate alternative courses of action, and follow through on their choices. They're also better equipped to defend their decisions. Four ethical decision-making formats are described in the pages to come. All four approaches are useful. You may want to use just one or a combination of all of them. The particular format you use is not as important as using a systematic approach to moral reasoning. You can practice these guidelines by applying them to Case Study 7.1 and the scenarios described at the end of the chapter.

You will probably find it difficult at first to follow a format. That's because using a format takes a significant amount of effort, and we are used to making rapid judgments mentally when faced with ethical choices.[19] Without being conscious of the fact, we quickly invoke decision-making rules we have learned though experience, such as "it is always good to obey authority" or "always be as fair as possible." Or we intuitively come to a rapid decision based on our emotions and cultural background. Often these quick responses are good ones. But not always. There may be times, for instance, when authority needs to be disobeyed or fairness must be set aside for compassion. Our intuitions are wrong when they are based on mistaken cultural beliefs. For example, many Americans used to immediately condemn interracial couples. As time passed, society recognized that this reaction was biased, unfounded, and unjust.

I suggest that, when confronted with ethical dilemmas like those in Case Study 7.1, you write down your initial reaction before using a format. Later compare your final decision to your immediate response. Your ultimate conclusion after following a series of steps may be the same as your first judgment. Or you might find that you come to a significantly different decision. In any case, you should be comfortable with your solution because your deliberations were informed both by your preconscious experiences, emotions, and intuitions as well as by your conscious reasoning.[20]

CASE STUDY 7.1

PARKING LOT SHOOTING

Over the past year several employees of a national fast-food chain have been shot or injured when intervening in fights or crimes occurring in the restaurant's parking lots. As a result, corporate headquarters drafted a new policy that forbids workers from leaving the building in such emergencies, instructing them instead to dial 911. Those who violate the policy will immediately be fired.

Imagine that you are day-shift manager at one of the company's locations where a shooting has occurred. You call 911 but notice that the victim, who is lying right outside the door, is bleeding profusely. No one else is stepping up to help the injured man. You have first-aid training and believe you can stabilize his condition before the ambulance arrives. The shooter has apparently fled the scene.

Would you disobey company policy and help the shooting victim?

Kidder's Ethical Checkpoints

Ethicist Rushworth Kidder suggests that nine steps or checkpoints can help bring order to otherwise confusing ethical issues.[21]

1. *Recognize that there is a problem.* This step is critically important because it forces us to acknowledge that there is an issue that deserves our attention and helps us separate moral questions from disagreements about manners and social conventions. For example, being late for a party may be bad manners and violate cultural expectations. However, this act does not translate into a moral problem involving right or wrong. On the other hand, deciding whether to accept a kickback from a supplier is an ethical dilemma.

2. *Determine the actor.* Once we've determined that there is an ethical issue, we then need to decide who is responsible for addressing the problem. I may be concerned that the owner of a local business treats his employees poorly. Nonetheless, unless I work for the company or buy its products, there is little I can do to address this situation.

3. *Gather the relevant facts.* Adequate, accurate, and current information is important for making effective decisions of all kinds, including ethical ones. Details do make a difference. In deciding whether it is just to suspend a student for fighting, for instance, a school principal will want to hear from teachers, classmates, and the offender to determine the seriousness of the offense, the student's reason for fighting, and the outcome of the altercation. The administrator will probably be more lenient if this is the offender's first offense and he was defending himself.

4. *Test for right-versus-wrong issues.* A choice is generally a poor one if it gives you a negative, gut-level reaction (the stench test), would make you uncomfortable if it appeared on the front page of tomorrow's newspaper (the front-page test), or would violate the moral code of someone that you care a lot about (the Mom test). If your decision violates any of these criteria, you had better reconsider.

5. *Test for right-versus-right values.* Many ethical dilemmas pit two core values against each other. Determine whether two good or right values are in conflict with one another in this situation. Right-versus-right value clashes include the following:
   o Truth telling versus loyalty to others and institutions. Telling the truth may threaten our allegiance to another person or to an organization, such as when leaders and followers are faced with the decision of whether to blow the whistle on organizational misbehavior (see Chapter 5). Kidder believes that truth versus loyalty is the most common type of conflict involving two deeply held values.

- o Personal needs versus the needs of the community. Our desire to serve our immediate group or ourselves can run counter to the needs of the larger group or community.
- o Short-term benefits versus long-term negative consequences. Sometimes satisfying the immediate needs of the group (giving a hefty pay raise to employees, for example) can lead to long-term negative consequences (endangering the future of the business).
- o Justice versus mercy. Being fair and even-handed may conflict with our desire to show love and compassion.

6. *Apply the ethical standards and perspectives.* Apply the ethical principle that is most relevant and useful to this specific issue. Is it communitarianism? Utilitarianism? Kant's categorical imperative? A combination of perspectives?

7. *Look for a third way.* Sometimes seemingly irreconcilable values can be resolved through compromise or the development of a creative solution. Negotiators often seek a third way to bring competing factions together. Such was the case in the deliberations that produced the Camp David peace accord. Egypt demanded that Israel return land on the West Bank seized in the 1967 War. Israel resisted because it wanted a buffer zone to protect its security. The dispute was settled when Egypt pledged that it would not attack Israel again. Assured of safety, the Israelis agreed to return the territory to Egypt.[22]

8. *Make the decision.* At some point we need to step up and make the decision. This seems a given (after all, the point of the whole process is to reach a conclusion). However, we may be mentally exhausted from wrestling with the problem, get caught up in the act of analysis, or lack the necessary courage to come to a decision. In Kidder's words,

> At this point in the process, there's little to do but decide. That requires moral courage—an attribute essential to leadership and one that, along with reason, distinguishes humanity most sharply from the animal world. Little wonder, then, that the exercise of ethical decision-making is often seen as the highest fulfillment of the human condition.[23]

9. *Revisit and reflect on the decision.* Learn from your choices. Once you've moved on to other issues, stop and reflect. What lessons emerged from this case that you can apply to future decisions? What ethical issues did it raise?

Balance Sheet

Advantages (Pros)

- Is thorough
- Considers problem ownership

- Emphasizes the importance of getting the facts straight
- Recognizes that dilemmas can involve right–right as well as right–wrong choices
- Encourages the search for creative solutions
- Sees ethical decision making as a learning process

Weaknesses (Cons)

- It is not easy to determine who has the responsibility for solving a problem
- The facts are not always available, or there may not be enough time to gather them
- Decisions don't always lead to action

There is a lot to be said for Kidder's approach to ethical decision making. For one thing, he seems to cover all the bases, beginning with defining the issue all the way through to learning from the situation after the dust has settled. He acknowledges that there are some problems that we can't do much about and that we need to pay particular attention to gathering as much information as possible. The ethicist recognizes that some decisions involve deciding between two "goods" and leaves the door open for creative solutions. Making a choice can be an act of courage, as Kidder points out, and we can apply lessons learned in one dilemma to future problems.

On the flip side, some of the strengths of Kidder's model can also be seen as weaknesses. As we'll see in Chapter 10, determining responsibility or ownership of a problem is getting harder in an increasingly interdependent world. Who is responsible for poor labor conditions in third-world countries, for instance? The manufacturer? The subcontractor? The store that sells the products made in sweatshops? Those who buy the items? Kidder also seems to assume that leaders will have the time to gather necessary information. Unfortunately, in situations like that described in Case Study 7.1, time is in short supply. Finally, the model seems to equate deciding with doing. As we saw in our earlier discussion of moral action, we can decide on a course of action but not follow through. Kidder is right to say that making ethical choices takes courage. However, it takes even more courage to put the choice into effect.

The SAD Formula

Media ethicist Louis Alvin Day of Louisiana State University developed the SAD formula in order to build important elements of critical thinking into moral reasoning. Critical thinking is a rational approach to decision making that emphasizes careful analysis and evaluation. It begins with an understanding of the subject to be evaluated; moves to identifying the issues, information, and assumptions surrounding the problem; and then concludes with evaluating alternatives and reaching a conclusion.[24]

Each stage of the SAD formula—situation definition, analysis of the situation, decision—addresses a component of critical thinking. (See Box 7.1.) To demonstrate this model, I'll use a conflict involving mandatory vaccinations of health care workers.[25]

Situation Definition

Health care professionals are at risk for contracting infectious diseases and spreading them to their patients. For that reason, the U.S. government determined that health care workers should be one of the first groups to receive flu vaccines such as the one designed to combat the H1N1 (swine flu) virus. Vaccination can reduce the likelihood of catching the flu by 70%–80% and is one of the best ways to prevent a pandemic. However, fewer than half of U.S. health workers get flu shots every year (rates are also low in Great Britain and Hong Kong). Medical personnel who fail to be vaccinated often do so for the same reasons as other Americans. They don't like shots, it is not convenient to get them, they claim they seldom get sick, or they believe the vaccine makes them ill (though scientists deny that this happens).

Health officials have tried a variety of strategies to increase the percentage of doctors and nurses receiving vaccinations, including promotional campaigns and prize drawings. However, these voluntary efforts have fallen short. Concerned about low participation rates, particularly in light of the danger posed by the swine flu, Hospital Corporation of America, MedStar Health (Maryland), Virginia Mason (Seattle, WA), BJC HealthCare (St. Louis, MO), and the state of New York began mandatory vaccination programs. A number of clinics and doctor's offices followed suit. Employees were told they would lose their jobs if they did not get the vaccine. Exceptions were made for those likely to have an allergic reaction (eggs are used in the production of the shots) or those with religious objections. Some health care workers and their unions immediately protested the stricter vaccination policies, labeling such programs as intrusive violations of individual rights.

Day says that the ethical question to be addressed should be as narrow as possible. In our example, we will seek to answer the following query: *Are mandatory flu-vaccination policies for health care workers ethically justified?*

BOX 7.1 THE MORAL REASONING PROCESS

Situation Definition

Description of facts

Identification of principles and values

Statement of ethical issue or question

↓

Analysis

Weighing of competing principles and values

Consideration of external factors

Examination of duties to various parties

Discussion of applicable ethical theories

↓

Decision

Rendering of moral agent's decision

Defense of that decision based on moral theory

SOURCE: From *Day.* Ethics in Media Communications: Cases and Controversies, 5E. Copyright © 2006 Wadsworth, a part of Cengage Learning, Inc. Reproduced by permission www.cengage.com/permissions.

Analysis

Evaluation of Values and Principles. Competing principles and values are clearly present in this situation. On the one side, medical administrators and public health officials put a high value on the responsibility of medical personnel to patients and argue that mandatory vaccinations will save lives, particularly those of vulnerable populations like the sick, those with compromised immune systems, pregnant women, the very young, and the elderly. In requiring mandatory vaccinations in New York, the state's health commissioner asserted: "The rationale begins with health-care ethics, which is: The patient's well-being comes ahead of the personal preferences of health-care workers."[26] (The commissioner later rescinded his edict when there was a shortage of the vaccine.) The chief medical officer of MedStar Health said the decision to require vaccinations "is all about patient safety." On the other side of the debate are individuals, employee unions, and groups who put their priority on individual rights. They believe that making flu shots a condition of employment takes away the right to make personal medical decisions, and they have concerns about the safety of the vaccines despite the assurances of medical experts. Opponents also worry that mandatory programs will spread from the health care sector into other areas of society. Said a representative of an organization wanting to limit government expansion, "You start with health-care workers but then expand that umbrella to make it mandatory for everybody. It's all part of an encroachment on our liberties."[27]

External Factors. Some influenza strains, like H1N1, pose greater risks than other strains and spread more rapidly, making vaccinations even more important. Medical employees already have to be inoculated for other conditions like mumps, measles, and tuberculosis, and there haven't been widespread protests about these requirements. In addition, medical personnel have to follow such mandatory safety procedures as washing their hands before surgery. Vaccinations appear to be a safety measure like hand washing. However, past inoculation programs have made some medical professionals skeptical about current efforts. Earlier vaccines did make recipients sore and could cause mild flu-like symptoms. The H1N1 vaccine seemed to be rushed into production, raising concerns that recipients were serving as "guinea pigs." Nurses, doctors, and home health givers, like other Americans, are increasingly worried about substances they put in their bodies.

Moral Duties or Loyalties. Professor Day borrows from theologian Ralph Potter for this part of his model. Potter believes we need to take into account important duties or loyalties when making ethical choices.[28] In this case, the following duties have to be kept in mind:

- Loyalty to self (individual conscience)
- Loyalty to patients
- Loyalty to vulnerable populations
- Loyalty to fellow employees
- Loyalty to others in the same profession
- Loyalty to the public

Medical officials seem primarily concerned for patients, vulnerable populations, and the larger community. Low vaccination rates threaten patients and clients and help the virus spread. Health care workers who refuse flu shots also damage the credibility of the medical profession. Why should patients be vaccinated if their doctors and nurses don't think it is safe or necessary to do so? Vaccination objectors are more concerned for their individual rights and, in some cases, their personal safety. They seem to overlook their primary duty, which is to serve their patients. Yet not all appear to be acting out of selfish motives. Some resistors are concerned about setting a precedent that could reduce the rights of their fellow citizens in the years to come.

Moral Theories. Each of the ethical perspectives outlined in Chapter 5 can be applied to this dilemma. From a utilitarian perspective, the benefit of protecting personal rights has to be weighed against the dangers of spreading the flu virus. However, the immediate benefits of slowing the virus also need to be weighed against the long-term costs—loss of individual rights and government intrusion. Based on Kant's categorical imperative, we could ask if we would want everyone to be vaccinated (probably) or if we would want everyone to refuse to be vaccinated (probably not). However, employees who resist the mandatory shots should carry through on their decision regardless of the consequences, such as losing their jobs. Rawls's theory could be applied to say that required vaccinations are justified because they protect the least advantaged members of society. Communitarianism also seems to support the mandatory vaccination position. Medical leaders put their emphasis on responsibility to patients, vulnerable groups, and the public. Objectors seem to emphasize individual rights rather than duties. Advocates of mandatory vaccinations have a stronger altruistic focus because such efforts are designed to reduce sickness and suffering. Opponents may argue, however, that they are demonstrating concern by protecting the rights of others.

Decision

Decisions often emerge out of careful definition and analysis of the problem. It may be clear which course of action is best after external constraints, principles, duties, and moral theories are identified and evaluated. In our example, mandatory flu vaccination programs for health care workers appear to be morally justified. Such programs put the needs of others first and reduce suffering and death. They seem consistent with other requirements placed on health care workers and support the patient-focused mission of the medical profession. Health care employees should prevent sickness, not spread it. This option also seems to be best supported by moral theory. Nonetheless, opponents of mandatory vaccination programs are right to point out that we should be cautious about requiring health treatments. Just because mandatory influenza vaccinations are justified for health care workers does not mean that we should require all citizens to be vaccinated (that's a different question for analysis) or force citizens into other medical treatments.

Balance Sheet

Advantages (Pros)

- Encourages orderly, systematic reasoning
- Incorporates situation definition, duties, and moral theories

Disadvantages (Cons)

- Failure to reach consensus
- Limits creativity
- Ignores implementation

The SAD formula does encourage careful reasoning by building in key elements of the critical thinking process. Following the formula keeps decision makers from reaching hasty decisions. Instead of jumping immediately to solutions, they must carefully identify elements of the situation, examine and evaluate ethical alternatives, and then reach a conclusion.

Three elements of the SAD formula are particularly praiseworthy. First, the formula recognizes that the keys to solving a problem often lie in clearly identifying and describing it. Groups are far less likely to go astray when members clearly outline the question they are to answer. Second, Day's formula highlights duties or loyalties. In the case of vaccinations, prioritizing loyalties is key to supporting or opposing mandatory vaccination programs. Third, the formula incorporates moral theories directly into the decision-making process.

The strengths of the SAD model must be balanced against some troubling weaknesses. Day implies that a clear choice will emerge after the problem is defined and analyzed. Nevertheless, that may not always be the case. Even in our example, there is room for dispute. While it appears as if mandatory vaccinations are morally justified, those who put a high value on personal freedoms will likely remain unconvinced. They raise valid concerns about the long-term impact of such programs as well. Focusing on a narrowly defined question may exclude creative options and make it hard to apply principles from one decision to other settings. Finally, the formula leaves out the important implementation stage.

Nash's 12 Questions

Ethics consultant Laura Nash offers 12 questions that can help businesses and other groups identify the responsibilities involved in making moral choices.[29] She argues that discussions based on these queries can be useful even if the group doesn't reach a conclusion. Managers who answer the questions surface ethical concerns that might otherwise remain hidden, identify common moral problems, clarify gaps between stated values and performance, and explore a variety of alternatives.

1. *Have you defined the problem accurately?* The ethical decision-making process begins with assembling the facts. Determine how many employees will be affected by layoffs, how much the cleanup of toxic materials will cost, or how many people have been injured by faulty products. Finding out the facts can help defuse the emotionalism of some issues (perhaps the damage is not as great as first feared).

2. *How would you define the problem if you stood on the other side of the fence?* Asking how others might feel forces self-examination. From a company's point of view, expanding a local plant may make good sense by increasing production and efficiency. Government officials and neighbors might have an entirely different perspective. A larger plant means more workers clogging already overcrowded roads and contributing to urban sprawl. For example, considering the company's point of view may impact the decision you reach in "Focus on Follower Ethics: Paying Back Microsoft" on page 258.

3. *How did this situation occur in the first place?* This question separates the symptoms from the disease. Lying, cheating customers, and strained labor relations are generally symptoms of deeper problems. Firing an employee for unethical behavior is a temporary solution. Probe to discover the underlying causes. For example, many dubious accounting practices are the result of pressure to produce high quarterly profits.

4. *To whom and to what do you give your loyalties as a person or group and as a member of the organization?* As we saw in Chapter 1, conflicts of loyalty are hard to sort through. However, wrestling with the problem of ultimate loyalty (Work group? Family? Self? Corporation?) can clarify the values operating in an ethical dilemma.

5. *What is your intention in making this decision?*

6. *How does this intention compare with the likely results?* These questions probe both the group's intentions and the likely products. Honorable motives

don't guarantee positive results. Make sure that the outcomes reflect your motivations.

7. *Whom could your decision or action injure?* Too often groups consider possible injury only after being sued. Try, in advance, to determine harmful consequences. What will happen if customers ignore label warnings and spread your pesticide indiscriminately, for example? Will the guns you manufacture end up in the hands of urban gang members? Based on these determinations, you may decide to abandon your plans to make these items or revise the way they are marketed.

8. *Can you engage the affected parties in a discussion of the problem before you make your decision?* Talking to affected parties is one way to make sure that you understand how your actions will influence them. Few of us would want other people to decide what's in our best interest. Yet we often push forward with projects that assume we know what's in the best interests of others.

9. *Are you confident that your position will be as valid over a long period of time as it seems now?* Make sure that your choice will stand the test of time. What seem like compelling reasons for a decision may not seem so important months or years later. Consider the U.S. decision to invade Iraq, for instance. American intelligence experts and political leaders tied Saddam Hussein to terrorist groups and claimed that he was hiding weapons of mass destruction. After the invasion, no solid links between Iraqis and international terrorists or weapons of mass destruction were discovered. Our decision to wage this war doesn't appear as justified now as it did in the months leading up to the conflict.

10. *Could you disclose without qualm your decision or action to your boss, your CEO, the board of directors, your family, or society as a whole?* No ethical decision is too trivial to escape the disclosure test. If you or your group would not want to disclose this action, then you'd better reevaluate your choice.

11. *What is the symbolic potential of your action if understood? Misunderstood?* What you intend may not be what the public perceives (see Questions 5 and 6). If your company is a notorious polluter, contributions to local arts groups may be seen as an attempt to divert attention from your firm's poor environmental record, not as a generous civic gesture.

12. *Under what conditions would you allow exceptions to your stand?* Moral consistency is critical, but is there any basis for making an exception? Dorm rules might require that visiting hours end at midnight on weekdays. Yet, as a resident assistant, is there any time when you would be willing to overlook violations? During finals week? On the evening before classes start? When dorm residents and visitors are working on class projects?

Balance Sheet

Advantages (Pros)

- Highlights the importance of gathering facts
- Encourages perspective taking
- Forecasts results and consequences over time

Disadvantages (Cons)

- Is extremely time consuming
- May not always reach a conclusion
- Ignores implementation

Like the ethical checkpoints, the 12 questions highlight the importance of problem identification and information gathering. They go a step further, however, by encouraging us to engage in perspective taking. We need to see the problem from the other party's point of view, consider the possible injury we might cause, invite others to give us feedback, and consider how our actions will be perceived. We also need to envision results and take a long-term perspective, imagining how our decisions will stand the test of time. Stepping back can keep us from making choices we might regret later. For example, the decision to test nuclear weapons on U.S. soil without warning citizens may have seemed justified to officials waging the Cold War. However, now even the federal government admits that these tests were immoral.

 FOCUS ON FOLLOWER ETHICS

PAYING BACK MICROSOFT?

Software giant Microsoft made an embarrassing error when it engaged in the first widespread layoffs in the firm's history. Company officials overpaid an average of $4,000–$5,000 to 25 out of the first 1,400 workers it furloughed. After discovering the error, the firm sent a letter asking for repayment from the 25 laid-off workers, requesting a check or money order and apologizing for the inconvenience.

Contents of the letter soon appeared on the Internet and in the national media. Microsoft officials then backed off their attempts to get the money back. According to a company spokesperson, "This was a mistake on our part. We should have handled this situation in a more thoughtful manner. We are reaching out to those impacted to relay that we will not seek any payment from those individuals."[1] While Microsoft decided to drop the matter because of negative publicity, the fact remains that some employees received more than they were promised. Except for a clerical error, the company did nothing wrong and has a legal right to ask for restitution. One outplacement expert noted that just because Microsoft is a large company doesn't mean it should have to automatically pay the cost for this mistake. "What if they'd put an extra three zeros on it?" he wondered. "Of course they'd expect to get it back."[2]

If you were one of the laid-off workers overpaid by Microsoft, would you give the money back? Why or why not? Would your response be different if the amount of the overpayment was much bigger and the company much smaller?

Notes

1. Microsoft will not seek overpaid severance. (2009, February 23). TECHWEB.
2. Microsoft will not seek overpaid severance.

Sources

Chan, S. P. (2009, May 6). Microsoft may not be done cutting jobs. *The Seattle Times*, p. A1.
Microsoft will not seek overpaid severance. (2009, February 23). TECHWEB.

I suspect that some groups will be frustrated by the amount of time it takes to answer the 12 questions. Not only is the model detailed, but discussing the problem with affected parties could take a series of meetings over a period of weeks and months. Complex issues such as determining who should clean up river pollution involve a variety of constituencies with very different agendas (government agencies, company representatives, citizens' groups, conservation clubs). Some decision makers may also be put off by the model's ambiguity. Nash admits that experts may define problems differently, that there may be exceptions to the decision, and that groups may use the procedure and never reach a conclusion. Finally, none of the questions use the ethical standards we identified in Chapter 5 or address the problem of implementing the choice once it is made.

The Case Study Method

The case study method is widely used for making medical diagnoses. At many hospitals, groups made up of doctors, nurses, and other staff members meet regularly to talk about particularly troublesome cases. They may be unable to determine the exact nature of the illness or how to best treat a patient. Many of these deliberations involve ethical issues such as whether to keep a terminally ill person on life support or how to respond to patients who demand unnecessary tests and procedures. The group solicits a variety of viewpoints and gathers as much information as possible. Members engage in analogical reasoning, comparing the specifics of a particular case with similar cases by describing the patient, her illness, and relationships with her family. Instead of focusing on how universal principles and standards can be applied in this situation, hospital personnel are more concerned with the details of the case itself. Participants balance competing perspectives and values, reach tentative conclusions, and look for similarities between the current case and earlier ones.

Medical ethicist and communication scholar David H. Smith argues that the case-based approach is a powerful technique because it is based on narrative or story.[30] When decision makers describe cases, they are telling stories. These narratives say as much about the storyteller as they do about the reality of the case. "Facts" are not objective truth but rather are reflections of what the narrator thinks is true and important. Stories knit these perceptions into a coherent whole. When discussing the fate of patients, it is not enough to know medical data. Hospital personnel need to learn about the patient's history, the costs and benefits of various treatment options, and other factors such as the wishes of relatives and legal issues. Smith outlines the following steps for case-based decision making:

1. *Foster storytelling.* Alert participants to the fact that they will be sharing their story about the problem. Framing the discussion as a storytelling session invokes a different set of evaluation criteria than is generally used in decision making. We judge evidence based on such factors as the quality of sources and logical consistency (see the discussion of argumentation in Chapter 8). We judge stories by how believable they seem to be, how well the elements of the story fit together and mesh with what we know of the world, and the values reflected in the narrative.[31]

2. *Encourage elaboration of essential events and characters.* Details are essential to the case study method. Additional details make it easier to draw comparisons with other examples.

3. *Encourage the sharing of stories by everyone with an interest in the problem.* Bringing more perspectives to bear on the problem reveals more details. In the end, a better, shared story emerges. Consider the case of an elderly man refusing a heart operation that could extend his life. Finding out why he is rejecting the surgery is an important first step to solving this ethical dilemma. As nurses, social workers, and doctors share information, they may discover

that the patient is suffering from depression or feels cut off from his family. Addressing these problems may encourage the patient to agree to the operation and thus resolve the moral issue.

4. *Offer alternative meanings.* Change the interpretation of the story by doing the following:
   - Providing additional expert information and pointing out where the facts of the story do not fit with other facts. The first diagnosis may not be correct. Press on when needed. In the case of our patient, claims that he is alienated from his family would be rejected if his children and grandchildren visit him daily.
   - Focusing attention on the characters in the story (the patient) rather than on some overarching ethical principle such as utilitarianism or the categorical imperative.
   - Examining analogies critically to make sure they really hold. Don't assume that the reasons one patient turns down treatment are the same as those of other patients, for example.
   - Offering alternative futures that might come to pass depending on decisions made by the group. In our case, what will be the likely outcome if treatment is delayed or never given? How much will the patient improve if he has the heart operation? Will attempts to persuade him backfire, locking him into his current position? What might happen if the hospital enlists his family to force him into compliance?

Balance Sheet

Advantages (Pros)

- Is unique
- Harnesses the power of narrative and analogical reasoning
- Avoids ethical polarization; allows for ethical middle ground

Disadvantages (Cons)

- Downplays the importance of objective reality
- Details are not always available to decision makers
- Consensus on the right course of action is not always possible

The case study method is significantly different from the others presented in this chapter. These other models outline a linear, step-by-step process for resolving ethical dilemmas that call for the application of universal ethical principles or standards. The case study approach is not linear but circular, calling on participants to share a variety of perspectives. Decision makers keep ethical principles in mind but don't try to invoke them to provide the resolution to a problem. They use them as general guides instead and focus on the case itself. Though unique, the case study method still requires decision makers to meet, systematically share information and analyze the problem, evaluate options, and reach a conclusion.

We often make choices based on stories. A good narrative is more persuasive than statistical evidence, for instance, and frequently uses the type of analogical reasoning reflected in the case study approach.[32] For example, when faced with an ethical decision about whether to tell your current employer about a job offer from another firm, you probably would consider the following: (1) the details of the situation (your relationship to your immediate supervisor, how hard it will be to replace you, your loyalty to the organization); (2) similar situations or cases in your past (what happened when you revealed this information before leaving your last job); and (3) what your friends did when facing similar circumstances. The case study method takes advantage of our natural tendency to reason through story and analogy.

As I noted in the discussion of character ethics in Chapter 3, universal principles can be difficult to apply to specific situations. There always seem to be exceptions to the rule. ("In general, don't lie, but it may be OK to lie if it protects someone else from danger.") A strength of the case study approach is that it acknowledges that specific circumstances often shape how a general principle can be used to resolve a particular dilemma. This approach also avoids polarization caused by invoking ethical absolutes. Take the abortion debate, for example. Proponents and opponents of abortion are locked into their positions by their interpretations of such values as freedom and the sanctity of life. The case study method suggests that some middle ground can be found by examining specific cases. After all, some pro-life advocates allow abortion in cases where the mother's life is in danger. Some in the pro-choice camp are uncomfortable with late-term abortions.

The case study approach has its downside. To begin, it minimizes objective reality. Although we always see ethical dilemmas through our perceptual filters, there do appear to be verifiable facts that ought to come into play in decision making. Crime scene evidence should be essential to determining a defendant's guilt or innocence, for instance. Some criticized the verdict of the O. J. Simpson murder trial in the mid-1990s because they thought that the jury overlooked factual DNA evidence and accepted the story of police misconduct instead. The same evidence was offered in a later civil trial. Jurors in that case concluded that the football star was indeed guilty of murdering his ex-wife and her friend and forced him to pay damages to the families.

A practical problem with the case study method is its dependence on detail. In real life, leaders may not have the luxury of being able to solicit stories and probe for additional information. They must make decisions quickly, particularly in crises. Students face a similar problem when discussing cases in class.

Short cases, such as the ones in this text, may leave out details you think are important. Yet you have to resolve them anyway.

Finally, consensus, though likely in this format, is not guaranteed. One overall story may emerge, but it may not. This is often the case in medical diagnoses. Two doctors may reach different conclusions about what is wrong with a patient. Differences in values, perspectives, and definitions of "facts" may keep ethical decision makers apart.

Implications and Applications

- Ethical behavior is the product of moral sensitivity, (recognition), moral judgment, moral focus (motivation), and moral character.
- Increase your sensitivity to potential ethical issues through perspective taking, using moral terminology, increasing the moral intensity of issues, and being sensitive to the presence of moral emotions like anger, disgust, guilt, or sympathy.
- Improve your ability to make moral judgments by creating an ethical environment that provides ethical role models and guidelines, continuing your education with a special focus on ethics, considering the needs and perspectives of broader audiences, and basing your decisions on widely accepted moral principles and guidelines.
- Foster your moral motivation and that of followers by rewarding ethical choices, responding to moral emotions, and controlling negative feelings.
- Your chances of following through on ethical decisions (moral character) are higher if you demonstrate virtue, believe you have some control over events in your life, and develop the necessary skills to put your plan into action.
- Decision-making guidelines can help you make better ethical choices. Possible ethical decision-making formats include Kidder's ethical checkpoints, the SAD formula, Nash's 12 questions, and the case study method. The particular format you choose is not as important as taking a systematic approach to ethical decision making.
- Your initial reaction to an ethical dilemma, based on emotions, cultural influences, past experiences, and intuitions, can inform the conclusion you reach using a decision-making format.
- Whatever format you follow, make every effort to gather in-depth, current, and accurate information.
- Creativity is as vital in making ethical decisions as it is in generating new products and programs. Sometimes you can come up with a "third way" that resolves ethical conflicts.
- Moral dilemmas often involve clashes between two core (good) values. Common right-versus-right dilemmas are truth versus loyalty, short term versus long term, individual versus community, and justice versus mercy.
- Think of ethical deliberation as an ongoing process. You may go through a sequence of steps and use them again. Return to your decision later to evaluate

and learn from it. As soon as one ethical crisis passes, there's likely to be another on the horizon.

- Don't expect perfection. As a leader, make the best choice you can after thorough deliberation but recognize that sometimes you may have to choose between two flawed alternatives.

For Further Exploration, Challenge, and Self-Assessment

1. Analyze your scores on the moral sensitivity test found in "Self-Assessment: Moral Sensitivity Scenarios." According to the investigator who developed these vignettes, you should have noted important ethical issues in Vignette 1, which involved significant harm to patients, and in Vignette 3, which involved bribery. Is this how you responded? Why did you answer the way you did? What do you learn from this assessment? How can you improve your sensitivity to the presence of ethical issues?

2. Apply the four-component model to the process you went through when faced with a moral dilemma. How successfully did you complete each stage? What would you do differently next time? Write up your analysis.

3. Develop a plan for improving your moral reasoning as part of your education. How can you take advantage of your college experiences to become more of a postconventional thinker?

4. Which of the four decision-making formats do you find most useful? Why?

5. In a group, brainstorm a list of possible ethical dilemmas faced by a college student. How many of these problems involve a clash between two important values (right versus right)? Identify which values are in conflict in each situation.

6. Apply each of the formats to one of the scenarios in Case Study 7.2. First reach your own conclusion based on your initial reactions without using a format and then discuss the situation in a group. See whether you can reach a consensus. Make note of the important factors dividing or uniting group members. Do you reach different conclusions depending on the system you follow?

7. Use a format from the chapter to analyze an ethical decision facing society (e.g., gay marriage or gay ordination, illegal music file sharing, illegal immigration). Write up your analysis and conclusions.

CASE STUDY 7.2

ETHICAL SCENARIOS FOR ANALYSIS

Scenario A: Clothing the Camp Counselors

You are a first-year counselor at a camp for needy children, which is subsidized through contributions from individuals and local businesses. Yours is the only camp experience that these disadvantaged kids will ever have. One afternoon, a few hours before the next batch of children is due to arrive, a semitruck stops by with a donated shipment of new shoes, shirts, and shorts for your campers. Immediately the other counselors (all of whom have more experience than you do) begin selecting items for personal use. They encourage you to do the same. When questioned, they argue that there is plenty to go around for both kids and counselors and that the clothes are a "fringe benefit" for underpaid camp staff.

Would you take any shoes or clothing to wear?

SOURCE: Kristina Findley, George Fox University.

Scenario B: Penalizing Timely Payments

You are the manager at a regional center that processes credit card payments. Company profits are down because of increased competition from other card issuers that charge lower interest rates. To boost income, the firm raised its penalties for late payments and reduced the length of the billing cycle. These changes were announced to cardholders. However, at the same time, company officials made an unofficial policy change. They instructed you and managers at the other processing centers to apply late penalties when checks arrive right before the due date. In these cases it will be difficult for cardholders to prove that their payments arrived on time. Some of your colleagues at other processing centers around the country have already begun this practice, knowing that failure to do so could cost them their jobs.

Will you institute this new policy at your processing center?

Scenario C: The Blowout

You are the coach of a high school girls' basketball team. This is your best season ever, and you are getting ready for the state play-offs. You teach an aggressive brand of basketball that involves playing full-court defense and fast-breaking at every opportunity. As a result, your team scores lots of points. You tell the young women on your squad that they may not always

(Continued)

(Continued)

win but that you want them to play hard and to always strive for excellence. Your last game of the regular season is with the worst team in your league, one with many starters who had not played basketball before this year. Not only are they less experienced and talented than your players; they are much shorter as well. Within minutes the game turns into a rout. By halftime the score is 50 to 4. Some state high school athletic associations have "mercy rules" that shorten or end lopsided games. Your state does not. This is the last chance your team will have to "tune up" before moving on to much stiffer competition.

In the second half will you deliberately try to keep the score down by changing how your team plays?

Sources:

Brady, E., & Halley, J. (2009, February 24). The blowup over blowouts. *USA Today,* p. 1C.
Coutts, M. (2009, January 27). Would Jesus run up the score? Christian school under fire for winning 100–0. *National Post,* p. A1.
Halley, J. (2009, January 29). Lopsided games are often pointless. *USA Today,* p. 4C.

Scenario D: Would You Run These Ads?

You are the sales manager for a local radio station that has seen a dramatic downturn in ads and revenue as the local economy loses industries and small businesses. One of your biggest advertisers has been MighTY Mortgage. MighTY Mortgage spots feature the company president, Tom Tyler promising to "save our friends lots of cash." In these commercials Tyler claims that his company offers the lowest mortgage rates and will pay to have homes appraised.

Two weeks ago state regulators charged MighTY Mortgage with a variety of unethical and illegal practices. The firm offers no proof that its loan rates are the lowest and charges enough in fees to more than cover the cost of the "free" appraisals. Investigators also found that, in most instances, MighTY failed to properly disclose loan terms to borrowers. The state wants to revoke the company's license, fine Tyler $250,000, and make sure the mortgage lender pays restitution to borrowers. However, final action has not been taken and won't be for several months.

After temporarily pulling his ads, Tom Tyler wants to go back on your station's airwaves with a new set of commercials. The new spots still promise to save listeners lots of money but no longer mention free appraisals. Instead of claiming to offer the lowest interest rate, MighTY Mortgage now says it offers a low interest rate.

Would you broadcast the new commercials for MighTY Mortgage?

SOURCE: Fictional case based on real-life events.

Notes

1. Powers, C. W., & Vogel, D. (1980). *Ethics in the education of business managers.* Hasting-on-Hudson, NY: Institute of Society, Ethics and the Life Sciences.

2. Rest, J. (1986). *Moral development: Advances in research and theory.* New York: Praeger; Rest, J. R. (1993). Research on moral judgment in college students. In A. Garrod (Ed.), *Approaches to moral development* (pp. 201–211). New York: Teachers College Press; Rest, J. R. (1994). Background: Theory and research. In J. R. Rest & D. Narvaez (Eds.), *Moral development in the professions: Psychology and applied ethics* (pp. 1–25). Hillsdale, NJ: Erlbaum.

3. Greenhouse, S., & Rosenbloom, S. (2008, December 24). Wal-Mart to settle suits over pay for $352 million. *The New York Times,* p. B1; Harris, J. (2009, October 16). Retail giant finds its green religion. *National Post,* p. FP12.

4. Werhane, P. (1999). *Moral imagination and management decision-making.* New York: Oxford University Press.

5. Bird, F. B. (1996). *The muted conscience: Moral silence and the practice of ethics in business.* Westport, CT: Quorum.

6. Tenbrunsel, A. E., & Messick, D. M. (2004). Ethical fading: The role of self-deception in unethical behavior. *Social Justice Research, 17,* 223–236.

7. Jones, T. M. (1991). Ethical decision making by individuals in organizations: An issue-contingent model. *Academy of Management Review, 15,* 366–395; Frey, B. F. (2000). The impact of moral intensity on decision making in a business context. *Journal of Business Ethics, 26,* 181–195; May, D. R., & Pauli, K. P. (2002). The role of moral intensity in ethical decision-making: A review and investigation of moral recognition, evaluation, and intention. *Business & Society, 41,* 84–117.

8. Haidt, J. (2003). The moral emotions. In R. J. Davidson, K. R. Scherer, & H. H. Goldsmith (Eds.), *Handbook of affective sciences* (pp. 852–870). Oxford, UK: Oxford University Press.

9. Kohlberg, L. A. (1984). *The psychology of moral development: The nature and validity of moral stages* (Vol. 2). San Francisco: Harper & Row; Kohlberg, L. A. (1986). A current statement on some theoretical issues. In S. Modgil & C. Modgil (Eds.), *Lawrence Kohlberg: Consensus and controversy* (pp. 485–546). Philadelphia: Palmer.

10. Rest, J., Narvaez, D., Bebeau, M. J., & Thoma, S. J. (1999). *Postconventional moral thinking: A neo-Kohlbergian approach.* Mahwah, NJ: Erlbaum; Trevino, L. K., & Weaver, G. R. (2003). *Managing ethics in business organizations: Social scientific perspectives.* Stanford, CA: Stanford University Press.

11. Rest, Narvaez, Bebeau, & Thoma; Thoma, S. J. (2006). Research on the defining issues test. In M. Killen & J. G. Smetana (Eds.), *Handbook of moral development* (pp. 67–91). Mahwah, NJ: Erlbaum.

12. See the following:

   Rest, J. R., & Narvaez, D. (1991). The college experience and moral development. In W. M. Kurtines & J. L. Gewirtz (Eds.), *Handbook of moral behavior and development. Vol. 2: Research* (pp. 229–245). Hillsdale, NJ: Erlbaum.

Rest (1993).

Thoma, S. J. (2006). Research on the defining issues test. In M. Killen & J. G. Smetana (Eds.), *Handbook of moral development* (pp. 67–91). Mahwah, NJ: Erlbaum.

13. Trevino & Weaver.

14. Batson, C. D., & Thompson, E. R. (2001). Why don't moral people act morally? Motivational considerations. *Current Directions in Psychological Science, 10,* 54–57; Batson, C. D., Thompson, E. R., & Chen, H. (2002). Moral hypocrisy: Addressing some alternatives. *Journal of Personality and Social Psychology, 83,* 330–339.

15. Batson & Thompson, p. 54.

16. James, H. S. (2000). Reinforcing ethical decision-making through organizational structure. *Journal of Business Ethics, 28*(1), 43–58; Werhane; O'Fallon, M. J., & Butterfield, K. D. (2005). A review of the empirical ethical decision-making literature: 1996–2003. *Journal of Business Ethics, 59,* 375–413.

17. See the following:

Connelly, S., Helton-Fauth, W., & Mumford, M. D. (2004). A managerial in-basket study of the impact of trait emotions on ethical choice. *Journal of Business Ethics, 51,* 245–267.

Eisenberg, N. (2000). Emotion, regulation, and moral development. *Annual Review of Psychology, 51,* 665–697.

Gaudine, A., & Thorne, L. (2001). Emotion and ethical decision-making in organizations. *Journal of Business Ethics, 31,* 175–187.

Griffin, R. W., & O'Leary-Kelly, A. M. (Eds.). (2004). *The dark side of organizational behavior.* San Francisco: Jossey-Bass.

18. Trevino & Weaver; O'Fallon & Butterfield.

19. Lapsley, D. K., & Hill, P. L. (2008). On dual processing and heuristic approaches to moral cognition. *Journal of Moral Education, 37,* 313–332; Haidt, J. (2001). The emotional dog and its rational tail: A social intuitionist approach to moral judgment. *Psychological Review, 108,* 814–834.

20. Seiler, S. (2009). *Developing responsible leaders.* Paper presented at the International Leadership Association Conference, Prague, Czech Republic.

21. Kidder, R. M. (1995). *How good people make tough choices: Resolving the dilemmas of ethical living.* New York: Fireside.

22. Fisher, R., & Ury, W. (1991). *Getting to yes* (2nd ed.). New York: Penguin.

23. Kidder, p. 186.

24. Day, L. A. (2006). *Ethics in media communications: Cases & controversies* (5th ed.). Belmont, CA: Wadsworth/Thomson Learning, Ch. 3.

25. Park, A. (2009, October 19). It's a jab or your job. *Time,* p. 55; Hartocollis, A., & Chan, S. (2009, October 23). Flu vaccine requirement for health workers is lifted. *The New York Times,* p. A30; Geracimos, A. (2009, September 29). Health workers spurn flu shot; for some, jobs depend on it. *The Washington Times,* p. A1;

Martin, R. (2009, September 17). Health care staff: Vaccinate thyself. *St. Petersburg Times*, p. 1A; McNeil, D. G., & Zrack, K. (2009, September 21). New York health care workers resist flu vaccine rule. *The New York Times*, p. A18; Blackwell, T. (2009, September 30). Mandatory flu shots rile health workers; "invasive procedure." *National Post*, p. A8.

26. Stein, (2009, September 26). Mandatory flu shots hit resistance. *The Washington Post*, p. A01.

27. Stein.

28. Potter, R. B. (1972). The logic of moral argument. In P. Deats (Ed.), *Toward a discipline of social ethics* (pp. 93–114). Boston: Boston University Press.

29. Nash, L. L. (1989). Ethics without the sermon. In K. R. Andrews (Ed.), *Ethics in practice: Managing the moral corporation* (pp. 243–257). Boston: Harvard Business School Press.

30. Smith, D. H. (1993). Stories, values, and patient care decisions. In C. Conrad (Ed.), *The ethical nexus* (pp. 123–148). Norwood, NJ: Ablex. For a history of the case study method, see Jonsen, A. R., & Toulmin, S. (1988). *The abuse of casuistry: A history of moral reasoning*. Berkeley: University of California Press.

31 Fisher, W. (1987). *Human communication as narration: Toward a philosophy of reason, value, and action*. Columbia: University of South Carolina Press.

32. Martin, J., & Powers, M. E. (1983). Truth or corporate propaganda: The value of a good story. In L. R. Pondy, P. J. Frost, G. Morgan, & T. C. Dandridge (Eds.), *Organizational symbolism* (pp. 93–107). Greenwich, CT: JAI Press.

PART IV

Shaping Ethical Contexts

8

Building an Effective, Ethical Small Group

Cooperation is the thorough conviction that nobody can get there unless everybody gets there.

—Author Virginia Burden Tower

Truth springs from argument amongst friends.

—Philosopher David Hume

WHAT'S AHEAD

This chapter examines ethical leadership in the small-group context. Groups are often charged with making ethical decisions because they have the potential to make better choices than individuals. To make the most of the small-group advantage, however, leaders must foster ethical accountability, resist groupthink and false consensus, and initiate productive (enlightening) communication patterns rooted in the pursuit of dialogue.

In his metaphor of the leader's light or shadow, Parker Palmer emphasizes that leaders shape the settings or contexts around them. According to Palmer, leaders are people who have "an unusual degree of power to create the conditions under which other people must live and move and have their being, conditions that can either be as illuminating as heaven or as shadowy as hell."[1] In this final section of the text, I'll describe some of the ways we can create conditions that illuminate the lives of followers in small-group, organizational, diverse, and crisis settings. Shedding light means both resisting and exerting influence. We must fend off pressures to engage in unethical behavior while actively seeking to create healthier moral environments.

The Leader and the Small Group

Leaders spend a great deal of their time in small groups, either chairing or participating in meetings. You can expect to devote more of your workday to meetings with every step up the organizational hierarchy. Some top-level executives spend as much as 21 weeks a year working in committees, task forces, and other small-group settings.[2] Meeting expert John Tropman points out that high-quality management is the product of high-quality meetings that render high-quality decisions. Meetings aren't distractions from our work, he argues; they *are* the work. Successful meetings are "absolutely central to the achievement of organizational goals."[3]

Groups meet for many different purposes: to coordinate activities, to pass along important information, to clarify misunderstandings, and to build relationships. In this chapter, however, I'll focus on the role of groups in making ethical decisions. Examples of ethical group dilemmas include the following:

- A congressional panel debating whether or not to expand health care coverage to all Americans
- Court justices determining the legal rights of terrorist suspects
- The board of the local United Way responding to a funding request from an abortion clinic or a Boy Scout troop that doesn't allow gay men to be leaders
- State department officials deciding whether to impose sanctions on a famine-stricken nation that is developing a nuclear weapons program
- Student officers disciplining a campus organization that has violated university and student government policies
- Corporate executives devising a plan to reduce the company's carbon footprint

Groups have significant advantages over lone decision makers when it comes to solving ethical problems such as those described above as well as the dilemma presented in Case Study 8.1. In a group, members can pool their information, divide up assignments, draw from a variety of perspectives, and challenge questionable assumptions. They are more likely to render carefully reasoned, defensible decisions as a result.[4] Of course, groups don't always make good moral choices, as in the case of executives who decide to hide product defects from the public or city officials who bypass regulations and award construction contracts to friends. Our task as leaders is to create the conditions that ensure that teams make the most of the small-group advantage. In particular, we must encourage members to take their ethical responsibilities seriously, prevent the problems of groupthink, and promote productive or "enlightening" communication patterns.

CASE STUDY 8.1

PAY FOR PLAY?

College athletics is very big business. The 1,000 member institutions of the National Collegiate Athlete Association (NCAA) spend $4 billion a year on their athletic programs. CBS recently signed a $6 billion deal with the NCAA to cover its Division I basketball tournament, and millions in payouts from college football bowl games go to NCAA athletic conferences every year. Schools also generate an estimated $4 billion annually through the sale of licensed merchandise. Lucrative television contracts and other income streams have boosted coaches' salaries. The average salary package for NCAA Division I football coaches is $950,000, not including such additional benefits as broadcast deals, shoe contracts, game tickets, luxury suites, and cuts of stadium revenue, as well as free cars and country club memberships. Top earners can make as much as $3 million–$4 million every year plus perks.

While college athletics may be big business, college athletes are still treated as amateurs by the NCAA, which is chartered as a nonprofit organization. As a result, player benefits are restricted. Athletic scholarships (which are offered on a renewable, yearly basis) do not cover all the expenses of attending school, leaving athletes with a gap of between $200 and $6,000 per school year to cover out of their own pockets. Often the demands of their sports make it impossible for them to supplement their incomes with part-time work. (Limited funds are available to athletes for special educational needs and emergencies, though it took a lawsuit to increase access to these monies.) Health care for athletes is also an issue.

(Continued)

(Continued)

Many players have to provide their own health coverage or fall under university plans that don't cover the cost of injuries caused by athletic participation, leaving some former athletes thousands of dollars in debt. Unlike coaches, the movement of players is restricted. They must forfeit a year of eligibility if they transfer schools.

The National College Players Association (NCPA), founded by former UCLA linebacker Ramogi Huma with the assistance of United Steelworkers, hopes to improve the financial standing (and safety) of college athletes. The organization claims to have pressured the NCAA into establishing a $10 million fund to assist former players, improving catastrophic health care coverage, and eliminating limits on the amount that players can earn from part-time jobs. It hopes to convince the NCAA to raise scholarship amounts, allow multiple-year scholarships, permit athletes to transfer one time without punishment, and provide better sports-related medical coverage. Other critics of the NCAA and its member schools promote more ambitious agendas. The Nebraska legislature passed a measure that would pay football players (though the bill was vetoed) and later considered a similar law. Some argue that players should receive a portion of the royalties generated by jersey sales and the use of their images in video games. Former players have sued the NCAA in order to receive payment for appearing in rebroadcasts of past contests.

Proponents of paying athletes argue that it isn't fair that players receive so little when colleges, coaches, merchandisers, the NCAA, and others benefit so much from their labor. They use such terms as *sweatshop* and *indentured servitude* to describe playing conditions and the plight of college athletes. In the current system players often suffer genuine financial and physical hardship. Right now it is the athletes who "pay to play." Pay-for-play advocates also take issue with what they see as the NCAA's hypocrisy. The organization says it wants to promote student-athletes but operates like a corporation instead. According to Ramogi Huma, "The NCAA says one of its principles is to protect the athlete from commercial exploitation, then they turn around and exploit players for their commercial gain."[1] Current limits on scholarship amounts also make players more susceptible to illegal gifts from boosters and gamblers.

Those who support the current system hold fast to the ideal of amateur athletics. Said former NCAA president Myles Brand, "The NCAA historically has been against pay for play. I couldn't agree more with that position. If you start paying student-athletes (other than assisting them through financial aid), you essentially ruin the integrity of the college game."[2] Others argue that current scholarships are generous compared to what other students receive and some players go on to highly lucrative pro careers. They note that most athletic programs lose money. Only a few sports generate surplus monies, but athletes in all sports would have to be compensated, which would be prohibitively expensive. Additional costs would mean that some minor sports would have to be cut from university athletic programs.

Imagine that you are a member of a special commission convened to determine if the NCAA should provide college athletes with additional benefits (e.g., larger scholarships, salaries, profits from merchandise). You should come out of your discussion with a decision (including which, if any, additional benefits you would propose) and a list of reasons for your decision.

Notes

1. Kriegel, M. (2009, July 25). *NCAA's video game stance is pure hypocrisy.* Retrieved from http://msn.foxsports.com/collegefootball/story/NCAA-video-game-stance-is-pure-hypocrisy

2. Whiteside, K. (2004, September 1). College athletes want cut of action. *USA Today*, p. 3C.

Sources

Carey, J., & Gardiner, A. (2008, January 30). Settlement gives aid to athletes. *USA Today*, p. 6C.

Ferguson, R. (2002, January 18). NCAA a "sweatshop," Steelworkers chief says. *Toronto Star*, p. E11.

Huma, R., Waters, T., & Staurowsky, E. J. (2009, March 26). *Scholarship shortfall study reveals college athletes pay to play.* Retrieved from http://www.ncpanow.org/releases_advisories?id=0009

Peterson, K. (2009, July 16). After injuries, college athletes are often left to pay the bills. *The New York Times*, p. A1.

Raissman, B. (2008, March 21). Brackets of millions, players net nothing. *Daily News*, p. 93.

Sack, A. (2008, March 7). Should college athletes be paid? *Christian Science Monitor*, Opinion, p. 9.

Upton, J., & Wieberg, S. (2006, November 16). Million-dollar coaches move into mainstream. *USA Today*, p. 1A.

Fostering Ethical Accountability

A group's success or failure is highly dependent on the behaviors of its individual members. Destructive behavior by just one person can be enough to derail the group process. Every team member has an ethical responsibility to take her or his duties seriously. The job of the leader, then, is to foster ethical accountability, to encourage followers to live up to their moral responsibilities to the rest of the group. A critical moral duty of group members is to pursue shared goals—to cooperate. Although this might seem like a basic requirement for joining a team, far too many people act selfishly or competitively when working with others. Those pursuing individual goals ignore the needs of teammates. For example, some athletes care more about individual statistics such as points and goals than team victories. Competitive individuals seek to advance at the expense of others. For instance, the ambitious salesperson hopes to beat out the rest of the sales group to earn the largest bonus.

Cooperative groups are more productive than those with an individualistic or competitive focus. Cooperative groups[5]

- are more willing to take on difficult tasks and to persist in the face of difficulties;
- retain more information;
- engage in higher-level reasoning and more critical thinking;
- generate more creative ideas, tactics, and solutions;
- transfer more learning from the group to individual members;
- are more positive about the task; and
- spend more time working on tasks.

In addition to being more effective, cooperative groups foster more positive relationships and cohesion between members. This cohesion reduces absenteeism and turnover while producing higher commitment and satisfaction. Members of cooperative groups also enjoy better psychological health (i.e., emotional maturity, autonomy, self-confidence) and learn important social and communication skills.[6] (I'll have more to say about group communication skills later in the chapter.)

As a leader, you can focus attention on shared goals by (1) emphasizing the moral responsibility members have to cooperate with one another, (2) structuring the task so that no one person succeeds unless the group as a whole succeeds, (3) ensuring that all group members are fairly rewarded (don't reward one person for a group achievement, for example), (4) providing feedback on how well the group and individuals are meeting performance standards, (5) encouraging individuals to help each other complete tasks, and (6) setting aside time for process sessions where the group reflects on how well it is working together and how it might improve.[7]

Creating a cooperative climate is also difficult when group members fail to do their fair share of the work. Social psychologists use the term *social loafing* to describe the fact that individuals often reduce their efforts when placed in groups.[8] Social loafing has been found in teams charged with all kinds of tasks ranging from shouting and rope pulling, to generating ideas and rating poems, to writing songs and evaluating job candidates. Gender, nationality, and age don't seem to have much impact on the rate of social loafing, although women and people from Eastern cultures are less likely to reduce their efforts.

A number of explanations have been offered for social loafing. When people work in a group, they may feel that their efforts will have little impact on the final result. Responsibility for the collective product is shared or diffused throughout the team. It is difficult to identify and evaluate the input of individual participants. The Collective Effort Model, developed by Steven Karau and Kipling Williams, is an attempt to integrate the various explanations for social loafing into one framework. Karau and Williams believe that "individuals will be willing to exert effort on a collective task only to the degree that they expect their efforts to be instrumental in obtaining outcomes that they value personally."[9] According to this definition, the motivation of group members depends on three factors: *expectancy,* or how much a person expects that her or his effort will lead to high group performance; *instrumentality,* the belief that one's personal contribution and the group's collective effort will bring about the desired result; and *valence,* how desirable the outcome is for individual group members.[10] Motivation drops if any of these factors are low. Consider the typical class project group, for example. Team members often slack off because they believe that the group will succeed in completing the project and getting a passing grade even if they do little (low expectancy). Participants may also be convinced that the group won't get an A no matter how hard they and others try (low instrumentality). Or some on the team may have other priorities and don't think that doing well on the project is all that important (low valence).

Social loafers take advantage of others in the group and violate norms for fairness or justice. Those being victimized are less likely to cooperate and may slack off for fear of being seen as "suckers." The small-group advantage can be lost because members aren't giving their best effort. Leaders need to take steps to minimize social loafing. According to the Collective Effort Model, they can do so by

- evaluating the inputs of individual members,
- keeping the size of work groups small,
- making sure that each person makes a unique and important contribution to the task,
- providing meaningful tasks that are intrinsically interesting and personally involving,
- emphasizing the collective group identity,
- offering performance incentives, and
- fostering a sense of belonging.

Resisting Groupthink and False Agreement

In addition to encouraging accountability on the part of individual members of the group, leaders must also help the group as a whole resist the destructive force of groupthink and false agreement.

Groupthink

Social psychologist Irving Janis believed that cohesion is the greatest obstacle faced by groups charged with making effective, ethical decisions. He developed the label *groupthink* to describe groups that put unanimous agreement ahead of reasoned problem solving. Groups suffering from this symptom are both ineffective and unethical.[11] They fail to (a) consider all the alternatives, (b) gather additional information, (c) reexamine a course of action when it's not working, (d) carefully weigh risks, (e) work out contingency plans, or (f) discuss important moral issues. Janis first noted faulty thinking in small groups of ordinary citizens (such as an antismoking support group that decided that quitting was impossible). He captured the attention of fellow scholars and the public through his analysis of major U.S. policy disasters such as the failure to anticipate the attack on Pearl Harbor, the invasion of North Korea, the Bay of Pigs fiasco, and the escalation of the Vietnam War. In each of these incidents, some of the brightest (and presumably most ethically minded) political and military leaders in our nation's history made terrible choices. (See Case Study 8.2 on page 305 for a contemporary example of the tragic consequences of groupthink.)

Janis identified the following as symptoms of groupthink. The greater the number of these characteristics displayed by a group, the greater the likelihood that members have made cohesiveness their top priority.

Signs of Overconfidence

- *Illusion of invulnerability.* Members are overly optimistic and prone to take extraordinary risks.
- *Belief in the inherent morality of the group.* Participants ignore the ethical consequences of their actions and decisions.

Signs of Closed-Mindedness

- *Collective rationalization.* Group members invent rationalizations to protect themselves from any feedback that would challenge their operating assumptions.
- *Stereotypes of outside groups.* Group members underestimate the capabilities of other groups (armies, citizens, teams), thinking that people in these groups are weak or stupid.

Signs of Group Pressure

- *Pressure on dissenters.* Dissenters are coerced to go along with the prevailing opinion in the group.
- *Self-censorship.* Individuals keep their doubts about group decisions to themselves.
- *Illusion of unanimity.* Because members keep quiet, the group mistakenly assumes that everyone agrees on a course of action.
- *Self-appointed mind guards.* Certain members take it on themselves to protect the leader and others from dissenting opinions that might disrupt the group's consensus.

The risk of groupthink increases when teams made up of members from similar backgrounds are isolated from contact with other groups. The risks increase still further when group members are under stress (due to recent failure, for instance) and follow a leader who pushes one particular solution. Self-directed work teams (SDWTs, described in more detail in "Focus on Follower Ethics: Self-Leadership in Self-Managed Teams") are particularly vulnerable to groupthink. Members, working under strict time limits, are often isolated and undertrained. They may fail at first, and the need to function as a cohesive unit may blind them to ethical dilemmas.[12]

FOCUS ON FOLLOWER ETHICS

SELF-LEADERSHIP IN SELF-MANAGED TEAMS

An estimated 90% of all U.S. firms employ self-directed work teams (SDWTs) or another form of self-managed groups.[1] An SDWT is made up of 6 to 10 employees from a variety of departments who manage themselves and their tasks. SDWTs operate much like small businesses within the larger organization, overseeing the development of a service or product from start to finish. SDWTs have been credited with improving everything from attendance and morale to productivity and product quality. In self-directed work teams, individual members have more responsibilities than they do in traditional groups where leaders make the decisions. Those in SDWTs are involved in additional tasks (e.g., staffing, evaluation, scheduling), and they have to develop new knowledge and skills to carry out these duties. Further, the ultimate success of the team now rests with followers, not leaders. In self-directed groups it is more important than ever that followers meet their ethical obligation to complete their work.

(Continued)

(Continued)

Business experts Christopher Neck and Charles Manz believe that self-leadership is key to living up to our duties as followers. Self-leadership is the process of exercising influence over our thoughts, attitudes, and behaviors and is key not just to our individual success as followers but to team success as well. According to Neck and Manz, "Self-leadership is just as important when you are working in a team as when you are working alone . . . In fact, only by effectively leading yourself as a team member can you help the team lead itself, reach its potential, and thus achieve synergy" (p. 82).

There are three key components to self-leadership. First, we need to lead ourselves to do unattractive but necessary tasks. Altering our immediate worlds and exercising direct control over the self can accomplish this objective. World-altering strategies include (1) using physical reminders and cues (notes, lists, objects) to focus our attention on important tasks; (2) removing negative cues, such as those that are distracting; (3) identifying and increasing positive cues (pleasant settings, music, etc.) that encourage us to undertake the work; and (4) associating with other people who reinforce our desirable behavior. Self-control strategies include observing, recording, and analyzing our use of desirable and undesirable behaviors; setting short- and long-term goals; determining our ultimate purpose; rewarding our achievements; and engaging in physical and mental practice to improve performance.

The second component of self-leadership is taking advantage of naturally rewarding activities. Some activities make us feel competent and in control and supply us with a sense of purpose. We don't need external motivation to get us to read a novel, for example, or to play a game of pickup basketball, knit, or paint, if we find these hobbies enjoyable. When we build natural rewards into our endeavors, we will be more likely to complete them. For instance, if we enjoy interacting with others, we can make sure that we leave time for informal talk during team meetings. We can also focus on the naturally rewarding aspects of our tasks instead of on the unpleasant aspects. Writing our part of a group paper for class, often perceived as a difficult chore, can be viewed instead as an opportunity to learn about a new subject and develop knowledge for a future career. In stressful situations, we can engage in emotional self-regulation through exercise, meditation, relaxing music, and other means.

The third component of self-leadership is shaping our psychological worlds or thought self-leadership. Thought self-leadership strategies include visualizing a successful performance (mental imagery); eliminating critical and destructive self-talk, such as "I can't do it"; and challenging unrealistic assumptions. For example, the mental statement "I must succeed at everything, or I'm a failure" is irrational because it sets an impossibly high standard. This destructive thought can be restated as "I can't succeed at everything, but I'm going to try to give my best effort no matter the task."

Note

Appelbaum, S. H., Bethune, M., & Tanenbaum, R. (1999). Downsizing and the emergence of self-managed teams. *Participation and Empowerment: An International Journal, 7*, 109–130.

SOURCE: Neck, C. P., & Manz, C. C. (2010). *Mastering self-leadership: Empowering yourself for personal excellence* (5th ed.). Upper Saddle River, NJ: Prentice Hall.

Irving Janis made several suggestions for reducing groupthink. If you're appointed as the group's leader, avoid expressing a preference for a particular solution. Divide regularly into subgroups and then bring the entire group back together to negotiate differences. Bring in outsiders—experts or colleagues—to challenge the group's ideas. Avoid isolation, keeping in contact with other groups. Role-play the reactions of other groups and organizations to reduce the effects of stereotyping and rationalization. Once the decision has been made, give group members one last chance to express any remaining doubts about the decision. Janis points to the ancient Persians as an example of how to revisit decisions. The Persians made every major decision twice—once while sober and again while under the influence of wine!

A number of investigators have explored the causes and prevention of groupthink.[13] They have discovered that a group is in greatest danger when the leader actively promotes his or her agenda and when it doesn't have any procedures in place (like those described in the last chapter) for solving problems. With this in mind, don't offer your opinions as a leader but solicit ideas from group members instead. Make sure that the group adopts a decision-making format before discussing an ethical problem.

There are two structured approaches specifically designed to build disagreement or conflict into the decision-making process to reduce the likelihood of groupthink.[14] In the devil's advocate technique, an individual or a subgroup is assigned to criticize the group's decision. The individual or subgroup's goal is to highlight potential problems with assumptions, logic, evidence, and recommendations. Following the critique the team then gathers additional information and adopts, modifies, or discontinues the proposed course of action. In the dialectic inquiry method, a subgroup or the team as a whole develops a solution. After the group identifies the underlying assumptions of the proposal, selected group members then develop a counterproposal based on a different set of assumptions. Advocates of each position present and debate the merits of their proposals. The team or outside decision makers determine whether to adopt one position or the other, integrate the plans, or opt for a different solution altogether. Both approaches can take more than one round to complete. For example, a team may decide to submit a second plan for critique or present several counterproposals before reaching a conclusion.

Charles Manz and his colleagues believe that self-managing work teams should replace groupthink with "teamthink." In teamthink, groups encourage divergent views, combining the open expression of concerns and doubts with a healthy respect for their limitations. The teamthink process is an extension of *thought self-leadership,* introduced in "Focus on Follower Ethics: Self-Leadership in Self-Managed Teams."[15] Like individuals, groups can improve their performance (lead themselves) by adopting constructive thought patterns—visualizing successful performances, eliminating critical and destructive self-talk, and challenging unrealistic assumptions.

Teamthink, like thought self-leadership, is a combination of mental imagery, self-dialogue, and realistic thinking. Members of successful groups use mental imagery to visualize how they will complete a project and jointly establish a common vision ("to provide better housing to the homeless," "to develop the best new software package for the company"). When talking with each other (self-dialogue), leaders and followers are particularly careful not to put pressure on deviant members, and at the same time, they encourage divergent views.

Teamthink members challenge three forms of faulty reasoning that are common to small groups. The first is all-or-nothing thinking. If a risk doesn't seem threatening, too many groups dismiss it and proceed without a backup plan. In contrast, teamthink groups realistically assess the dangers and anticipate possible setbacks. The second common form of faulty group thinking, described earlier, is the assumption that the team is inherently moral. Groups under the grip of this misconception think that anything they do (including lying and sabotaging the work of other groups) is justified. Ethically insensitive, they don't stop to consider the moral implications of their decisions. Teamthink groups avoid this trap, questioning their motivations and raising ethical issues. The third faulty group assumption is the conviction that the task is too difficult, that the obstacles are too great to overcome. Effective, ethical groups instead view obstacles as opportunities and focus their efforts on reaching and implementing the decision.

False Agreement

George Washington University management professor Jerry Harvey offers an alternative to groupthink based on *false agreement*.[16] Harvey believes that blaming group pressure is just an excuse for our individual shortcomings. He calls this the *Gunsmoke* myth. In this myth, the lone Western sheriff (Matt Dillon in the radio and television series) stands down a mob of armed townsfolk out to lynch his prisoner. If group tyranny is really at work, Harvey argues, Dillon stands no chance. After all, he is outnumbered 100 to 1 and could be felled with a single bullet from one rioter. The mob disbands because its members really didn't want to lynch the prisoner in the first place. Harvey contends that falling prey to the *Gunsmoke* myth is immoral because as long as we can blame our peers, we don't have to accept personal responsibility as group members. In reality, we always have a choice as to how to respond.

Professor Harvey introduces the Abilene paradox as an alternative to the *Gunsmoke* myth. He describes a time when his family decided to drive (without air conditioning) 100 miles across the desert from its home in Coleman, Texas, to Abilene to eat dinner. After returning home, family members discovered that no one had really wanted to make the trip. Each agreed to go to Abilene based on the assumption that everyone else in the group was enthusiastic about eating out. Harvey believes that organizations and small groups, like his family, also take needless "trips." An example of the Abilene paradox would be teams who carry out illegal activities that everyone in the group is uneasy about. Five psychological factors account for the paradox:

1. *Action anxiety.* Group members know what should be done but are too anxious to speak up.

2. *Negative fantasies.* Action anxiety is driven in part by the negative fantasies members have about what will happen if they voice their opinions. These fantasies ("I'll be fired or branded as disloyal") serve as an excuse for not attacking the problem.

3. *Real risk.* There are risks to expressing dissent: getting fired, losing income, damaging relationships. However, most of the time the danger is not as great as we think.

4. *Fear of separation.* Alienation and loneliness constitute the most powerful force behind the paradox. Group members fear being cut off or separated from others. To escape this fate, they cheat, lie, break the law, and so forth.

5. *Psychological reversal of risk and certainty.* Being trapped in the Abilene paradox means confusing fantasy with real risk. This confusion produces a

self-fulfilling prophecy. Caught up in the fantasy that something bad may happen, decision makers act in a way that fulfills the fantasy. For instance, group members may support a project with no chances of success because they are afraid they will be fired or demoted if they don't. Ironically, they are likely to be fired or demoted anyway when the flawed project fails.

Breaking out of the paradox begins with diagnosing its symptoms in your group or organization. If the group is headed in the wrong direction, call a meeting where you own up to your true feelings and invite feedback and encourage others to do the same. (Of course, you must confront your fear of being separated from the rest of the group to take this step.) The team may immediately come up with a better approach or engage in extended conflict that generates a more creative solution. You might suffer for your honesty, but you could be rewarded for saying what everyone else was thinking. In any case, you'll feel better about yourself for speaking up.

Promoting Enlightening Communication

Communication is the key to both the relationships between group members and the quality of their ethical choices. Shadowy groups are marked by ineffective, destructive communication patterns that undermine relationships while derailing the moral reasoning process. Healthier groups engage in productive or *enlightened* communication strategies that enable members to establish positive bonds and make wise ethical choices. Another responsibility of the leader, then, is to promote positive interaction between group members. Enlightening communication skills and tactics arise out of the pursuit of dialogue and include emotional intelligence; comprehensive, critical listening; supportive communication; productive conflict management; and argumentation.

Seeking Dialogue

The attitude we have toward other group members largely determines whether our interactions with them are destructive or productive. There are two primary human attitudes or relationships, according to philosopher Martin Buber: I–It and I–Thou.[17] Communicators in I–It relationships treat others as objects and engage in monologue. At its best, monologue is impersonal interaction focused on gathering and understanding information about the other party. At its worst, monologue manipulates others for selfish gain and is characterized by deception, exploitation, and coercion. (See Box 8.1

on page 288 for a particularly troubling form of monologue.) Participants in I–Thou (You) relationships, in contrast, treat others as unique human beings and engage in dialogue. Dialogue occurs between equal partners who focus on understanding rather than on being understood. Communication experts Kenneth Cissna and Robert Anderson identify the following characteristics of dialogue:[18]

- *Presence.* Participants in dialogue are less interested in a specific outcome than in working with others to come up with a solution. Their interactions are unscripted and unrehearsed.
- *Emergent unanticipated consequences.* Dialogue produces unpredictable results that are not controlled by any one person in the group.
- *Recognition of "strange otherness."* If dialogue is to flourish, discussants must refuse to believe that they already understand the thoughts, feelings, or intentions of others in the group, even people they know well. They are tentative instead, continually testing their understanding of the perspectives of other group members and revising their conclusions when needed.
- *Collaborative orientation.* Dialogue demands a dual focus on self and others. Participants don't hesitate to take and defend a position. At the same time, they care about the point of view of their conversational partners and about maintaining relationships. They focus on coming up with a shared, joint solution, not on winning or losing.
- *Vulnerability.* Dialogue is risky because discussants open their thoughts to others and may be influenced by the encounter. They must be willing to change their minds.
- *Mutual implication.* Speakers engaged in dialogue always keep listeners in mind when speaking. In so doing, they may discover more about themselves as well.
- *Temporal flow.* Dialogue takes time and emerges over the course of a group discussion. It is a process that can't be cut into segments and analyzed.
- *Genuineness and authenticity.* Participants in dialogue give each other the benefit of the doubt, assuming that the other person is being honest and sharing from personal experience. Although speakers don't share all their thoughts, they don't deliberately hide thoughts and feelings that are relevant to the topic and to the relationship.

By its nature, dialogue can't be forced. However, we can "open a space" for dialogue, increasing the chances it can occur.[19] Opening a space for dialogue involves (1) understanding the characteristics of dialogue, (2) being committed to I–Thou communication, (3) developing and constantly reflecting on our verbal and nonverbal communication skills, (4) responding to others as persons, and (5) being ready to engage in dialogue when others signal they are ready to enter the dialogue space. As leaders we should identify dialogue as the ethical ideal or standard for group interactions. Striving for dialogue acknowledges the intrinsic value of every group member and lays the groundwork for the enlightening communication strategies that follow. As group members, we are much more likely to listen and to support others when we treat them as equals whose experiences and opinions are just as valid as our own. Dialogue encourages healthy argument and conflict as well. Buber argued that the best example of the I–Thou relationship comes not when friends or intimates interact but when acquaintances profoundly disagree and yet remain in dialogue.[20] Confrontation tempts us to treat others like obstacles that need to be overcome so that we can win. Dialogue empowers us to remain genuinely present to fellow group members while holding fast to our own positions.

BOX 8.1 DISMISSIVENESS

Leaders sometimes claim that they are genuinely interested in the ideas of others when they are not. Rhetoricians Rob Anderson and Kenneth Cissna use the term *dismissiveness* to describe this unethical communication strategy. Dismissive speakers recognize the other person or argument but then claim that the other individual's position is really not worth consideration after all. Anderson and Cissna describe the attitude of the dismissive speaker this way:

> It's not simply that your position is weak, or that I disagree, or that you are wrong, or that you are unethical, or that you are ignorant or insensitive. It is that you are actually beneath response. Your points are self-defeating and patently absurd; they don't have the force necessary to stimulate reply. Yet I reply anyway, demonstrating my largess, my open-mindedness, my commitment to dialogue. I reply anyway, to dispense with the argument, characterizing it so that other audiences, less astute than I, will not be taken in.

Signs of dismissiveness include name-calling, mischaracterizing the positions of others, claiming that others aren't interested in dialogue, shifting the discussion to other topics, and being absolutely certain that one's position is right. Dismissiveness is common because communicators can be highly committed to their ideas, want to assert themselves, and, in some cases, seek to attack others. Politicians and talk show hosts engage in dismissive behaviors when they put opponents and callers in their place. Students may dismiss professors by claiming their classes are "worthless" and that the teachers are "too theoretical." Faculty, in turn, may dismiss students as "undisciplined" and claim that they "lack dedication" to their studies.

To avoid dismissing team members, which undermines the possibility of authentic dialogue, Anderson and Cissna suggest that we examine our motives. Do we claim we want dialogue but do so only to get what we want? Are we really interested in others' ideas or just pretending to be interested by acting sympathetic or open? Do we tell others that we want their feedback but then pay little attention to their thoughts, for example? Or do we say an idea is worthwhile without any intention of incorporating it into our plans? Only after we determine that we are truly willing to engage in dialogue can the process of I–Thou communication begin.

SOURCE: Anderson, R., & Cissna, K. N. (2008). Dismissiveness and dialogic ethics. In K. G. Roberts & R. C. Arnett (Eds.), *Communication ethics: Between cosmopolitanism and provinciality* (pp. 263–284). New York: Peter Lang.

Emotional Intelligence

Recognizing and managing emotions is essential to maintaining productive, healthy relationships in a group. Consider the negative impact of envy, for instance. Envy arises when people compare themselves to one another and fall short. They then experience resentment, hostility, frustration, inferiority, longing, and ill will toward the envied individual. Envy is common in organizations, which distribute assignments, raises, office space, and other resources unequally among members. However, this feeling may be even more frequent in teams because members know each other well and have more opportunity to engage in comparisons. Those who envy others in the group tend to reduce their efforts (see our earlier discussion of social loafing), are more likely to miss meetings, and are less satisfied with their group experience. The team as a whole is less cohesive and less successful.[21]

Experts assert that groups, like individuals, can learn how to cope with envy and other destructive feelings, and foster positive moods, through developing emotional intelligence. They also report that emotionally intelligent groups are more effective and productive.[22] Emotional intelligence consists of (1) awareness and management of personal emotions and (2) recognizing and influencing the emotions of others. Teams with a high emotional intelligence (EI) effectively address three levels of emotions: individual, within the team, and between the team and outside groups.[23] At the individual level, they recognize when a member is distracted or defensive. They point out when someone's behavior (e.g., moodiness, tardiness) is disrupting the group and provide extra support for those who need it. At the group level, EI teams engage in continual self-evaluation to determine their emotional states. Members speak out when the team is discouraged, for instance, and build an affirmative climate. They develop resources like a common vocabulary and rituals to deal with unhealthy moods. For example, one executive team set 10 minutes aside for a "wailing wall." During these 10 minutes members could vent their frustrations. They then were ready to tackle the problems they faced. At the intergroup level, EI teams recognize how other groups will respond to their efforts and strive to build positive relationships throughout the organization. They collaborate with other teams, for instance. Or they have someone from another department participate in the planning of a project that will require the help of that other division.

Raising team EI is an important leadership responsibility, which is accomplished largely through role modeling and establishing norms. As leaders, we must demonstrate our personal emotional intelligence before we can hope to improve the emotional climate of the group. Effective leaders display emotions that are appropriate to the situation, refrain from hostility, are sensitive to group moods, and take the lead in confronting emotional issues. Confrontation can mean reminding a group member not to criticize new ideas; phoning a member between meetings to talk about his or her rude, dismissive behavior; removing insensitive individuals from the team; calling on quiet members to hear their opinions; and bringing the group together to discuss its feelings of frustration or discouragement. Modeling such behaviors is critical to establishing healthy emotional norms or habits in the team, like speaking up when the group is discouraged or unproductive and celebrating collective victories. One list of group emotional norms can be found in Box 8.2.

BOX 8.2 GROUP EMOTIONAL NORMS

Norms That Create Awareness of Emotions

Interpersonal Understanding

1. Take time away from group tasks to get to know one another.

2. Have a "check-in" at the beginning of the meeting—that is, ask how everyone is doing.

3. Assume that undesirable behavior takes place for a reason. Find out what that reason is. Ask questions and listen. Avoid negative attributions.

4. Tell your teammates what you're thinking and how you're feeling.

Team Self-Evaluation

1. Schedule time to examine team effectiveness.

2. Create measurable task and process objectives and then measure them.

3. Acknowledge and discuss group moods.

4. Communicate your sense of what is transpiring in the team.

5. Allow members to call a "process check." (For instance, a team member might say, "Process check: Is this the most effective use of our time right now?")

Organizational Understanding

1. Find out the concerns and needs of others in the organization.

2. Consider who can influence the team's ability to accomplish its goals.

3. Discuss the culture and politics in the organization.

4. Ask whether proposed team actions are congruent with the organization's culture and politics.

Norms That Help Regulate Emotions

Confronting

1. Set ground rules and use them to point out errant behavior.

2. Call members out on errant behavior.

3. Create playful devices for pointing out such behavior. These often emerge from the group spontaneously. Reinforce them.

Caring

1. Support members: Volunteer to help them if they need it, be flexible, and provide emotional support.

2. Validate members' contributions. Let members know they are valued.

3. Protect members from attack.

4. Respect individuality and differences in perspectives. Listen.

5. Never be derogatory or demeaning.

(Continued)

(Continued)

Creating Resources for Working With Emotions

1. Make time to discuss difficult issues, and address the emotions that surround them.

2. Find creative, shorthand ways to acknowledge and express the emotion in the group.

3. Create fun ways to acknowledge and relieve stress and tension.

4. Express acceptance of members' emotions.

Creating an Affirmative Environment

1. Reinforce that the team can meet a challenge. For example, say things like "We can get through this" or "Nothing will stop us."

2. Focus on what you can control.

3. Remind members of the group's important and positive mission.

4. Remind the group how it solved a similar problem before.

5. Focus on problem solving, not blaming.

Building External Relationships

1. Create opportunities for networking and interaction.

2. Ask about the needs of other teams.

3. Provide support for other teams.

4. Invite others to team meetings if they might have a stake in what you are doing.

SOURCE: Condensed from Durskat, V. U., & Wolff, S. B. (2001, March). Building the emotional intelligence of groups, *Harvard Business Review*, pp. 80–90. Used by permission of the publisher.

Comprehensive, Critical Listening

We spend much more time listening than speaking in small groups. If you belong to a team with 10 members, you can expect to devote approximately 10% of your time to talking and 90% to listening to what others have to say. All listening involves receiving, paying attention to, interpreting, and then remembering messages. However, our motives for listening vary.[24] *Discriminative listening* processes the verbal and nonverbal components of a message. It serves as the foundation for the other forms of listening because we can't accurately process or interpret messages unless we first understand what is being said and how the message is being delivered. Tom and Ray Magliozzi of National Public Radio's *Car Talk* demonstrate the importance of discriminative listening on their weekly call-in program. They frequently ask callers to repeat the sounds made by their vehicles. A "clunk" sound can signal one type of engine problem; a "chunk" noise might indicate that something else is wrong.

Comprehensive listening is motivated by the need to understand and retain messages. We engage in this type of listening when we attend lectures, receive job instructions, attend oral briefings, and watch the evening weather report. *Therapeutic or empathetic listening* is aimed at helping the speaker resolve an issue by encouraging him or her to talk about the problem. Those in helping professions such as social work and psychiatry routinely engage in this listening process. All of us act as empathetic listeners, however, when friends and family come to us for help. *Critical listening* leads to evaluation. Critical listeners pay careful attention to message content, logic, language, and other elements of persuasive attempts so that they can identify strengths and weaknesses and render a judgment. *Appreciative listening* is prompted by the desire for relaxation and entertainment. We act as appreciative listeners when we enjoy a CD, live concert, or play.

Group members engage in all five types of listening during meetings, but comprehensive and critical listening are essential to ethical problem solving. Coming up with a high-quality decision is nearly impossible unless group members first understand and remember what others have said. Participants also have to critically analyze the arguments of other group members in order to identify errors (see the discussion of conflict and argumentation that follows).

There are several barriers to comprehensive, critical listening in the group context. In one-to-one conversations, we know that we must respond to the speaker, so we tend to pay closer attention. In a group, we don't have to carry as much of the conversational load, so we're tempted to lose focus or to talk to the person sitting next to us. The content of the discussion can also make listening difficult. Ethical issues can generate strong emotional reactions because they involve deeply held values and beliefs. The natural tendency is to reject the speaker ("What does he know?" "He's got it all wrong!") and become absorbed in our counterarguments instead of concentrating on the message.[25] Reaching an agreement then becomes more difficult because we don't understand the other person's position but are more committed than ever to our point of view.

Listening experts Larry Barker, Patrice Johnson, and Kittie Watson make these suggestions for improving listening performance in a group setting. Our responsibility as leaders is to model these behaviors and encourage other participants to follow our example.[26]

- *Avoid interruptions.* Give the speaker a chance to finish before you respond or ask questions. The speaker may address your concerns before he or she finishes, and you can't properly evaluate a message until you've first understood it.
- *Seek areas of agreement.* Take a positive approach by searching for common ground. What do you and the speaker have in common? Commitment to solving the problem? Similar values and background?
- *Search for meanings and avoid arguing about specific words.* Discussions of terms can keep the group from addressing the real issue. Stay focused on what speakers mean; don't be distracted if they use different terms than you do.
- *Ask questions and request clarification.* When you don't understand, don't be afraid to ask for clarification. Chances are others in the group are also confused and will appreciate more information. However, asking too many questions can give the impression that you're trying to control the speaker.
- *Be patient.* We can process information faster than speakers can deliver it. Use the extra time to reflect on the message instead of focusing on your own reactions or daydreaming.
- *Compensate for attitudinal biases.* All of us have biases based on such factors as personal appearance, age differences, and irritating mannerisms. Among my pet peeves? Men with Elvis hairdos, grown women with little girl voices, and nearly anyone who clutters his or her speech with "ums" and "uhs." I have to suppress my urge to dismiss these kinds of speakers and concentrate on listening carefully. (Sadly, I don't always succeed.)
- *Listen for principles, concepts, and feelings.* Try to understand how individual facts fit into the bigger picture. Don't overlook nonverbal cues such as tone of voice and posture that reveal emotions and, at times, can contradict verbal statements. If a speaker's words and nonverbal behaviors don't seem to match (as in expression of support uttered with a sigh of resignation), probe further to make sure you clearly understand the person's position.
- *Compensate for emotion-arousing words and ideas.* Certain words and concepts such as *fundamentalist, euthanasia, gay pride, terrorist,* and *fascist* spark strong emotional responses. We need to overcome our knee-jerk reactions to these labels (see our earlier discussion of emotional intelligence) and strive instead to remain objective.
- *Be flexible.* Acknowledge that other views may have merit, even though you may not completely agree with them.
- *Listen, even if the message is boring or tough to follow.* Not all messages are exciting and simple to digest, but we need to try to understand them anyway. A boring comment made early in a group discussion may later turn out to be critical to the team's success.

Defensive Versus Supportive Communication

Defensiveness is a major threat to accurate listening. When group members feel threatened, they divert their attention from the task to defending themselves. As their anxiety levels increase, they think less about how to solve the problem and more about how they are coming across to others, about winning, and about protecting themselves. Listening suffers because participants distort the messages they receive, misinterpreting the motives, values, and emotions of senders. On the other hand, supportive messages increase accuracy because group members devote more energy to interpreting the content and emotional states of sources. Psychologist Jack Gibb identified the following six pairs of behaviors that promote either a defensive or a supportive group atmosphere.[27] Our job as the group's leader is to engage in supportive communication, which contributes to a positive emotional climate and accurate understanding. At the same time, we need to challenge comments that spark defensive reactions and lead to poor ethical choices. ("Leadership Ethics at the Movies: *21*" describes one group caught up in defensive communication.)

Evaluation Versus Description

Evaluative messages are judgmental. They can be sent through statements ("What a lousy idea!") or through such nonverbal cues as a sarcastic tone of voice or a raised eyebrow. Those being evaluated are likely to respond by placing blame and making judgments of their own ("Your proposal is no better than mine"). Supportive messages ("I think I see where you're coming from," attentive posture, eye contact) create a more positive environment.

Control Versus Problem Orientation

Controlling messages imply that the recipient is inadequate (i.e., uninformed, immature, stubborn, overly emotional) and needs to change. Control, like evaluation, can be communicated both verbally (issuing orders, threats) and nonverbally (stares, threatening body posture). Problem-centered messages reflect a willingness to collaborate, to work together to resolve the issue. Examples of problem-oriented statements might include "What do you think we ought to do?" and "I believe we can work this out if we sit down and identify the issues."

Strategy Versus Spontaneity

Strategic communicators are seen as manipulators who try to hide their true motivations. They say they want to work with others yet withhold information and appear to be listening when they're not. This "false spon-taneity" angers the rest of the group. On the other hand, behavior that is truly spontaneous and honest reduces defensiveness.

Neutrality Versus Empathy

Neutral messages such as "You'll get over it" and "Don't take it so seri-ously" imply that the listener doesn't care. Empathetic statements, such as "I can see why you would be depressed" and "I'll be thinking about you when you have that appointment with your boss," communicate reassurance and acceptance. Those who receive them enjoy a boost in self-esteem.

Superiority Versus Equality

Attempts at one-upmanship generally provoke immediate defensive responses. The comment "I got an A in my ethics class" is likely to be met with this kind of reply: "Well, you may have a lot of book learning, but I had to deal with a lot of real-world ethical problems when I worked at the advertising agency." Superiority can be based on a number of factors, including wealth, social class, organizational position, and power. All groups contain members who differ in their social standing and abilities. However, these differences are less disruptive if participants indicate that they want to work with others on an equal basis.

Certainty Versus Provisionalism

Dogmatic group members (those who are inflexible and claim to have all the answers) are unwilling to change or consider other points of view. As a consequence, they appear more interested in being right than in solving the problem. Listeners often perceive certainty as a mask for feelings of inferior-ity. In contrast to dogmatic individuals, provisional discussants signal that they are willing to work with the rest of the team in order to investigate issues and come up with a sound ethical decision.

LEADERSHIP ETHICS AT THE MOVIES

21

Key Cast Members: Jim Sturgess, Kevin Spacey, Kate Bosworth, Laurence Fishburne, Aaron Yoo, Liza Lapira, Jacob Pitts, Josh Gad, Jack McGee

Synopsis: Loosely based on the true story of a group of MIT students who win millions at the blackjack tables in Las Vegas through an elaborate card counting system, the film stars Kevin Spacey as professor Micky Rosa, who recruits star student Ben Campbell (Sturgess) for his team of card cheats. Ben is from a working-class background and joins the group in order to pay for his medical school tuition. But he gets caught up in the glamour and financial rewards of his new role as a Vegas high roller and the thrill of beating the system as part of an elite team, which includes love interest Jill (Bosworth). Ben's overconfidence puts him in conflict with teammates and professor Rosa and threatens his future.

Rating: PG-13 for violence, sexual content, and partial nudity

Themes: defensive communication, groupthink, team leadership, affective conflict, integrity, greed, corruption, loyalty, betrayal

Discussion Starters

1. Why does Ben change his mind and join the team?

2. What forms of defensive communication do team members use? What evidence of groupthink do you see?

3. Why do group members engage in so much conflict?

Productive Conflict

In healthy groups, members examine and debate the merits of the proposal before the group, a task-related process that experts call *substantive (constructive) conflict.*[28] Substantive conflicts produce a number of positive outcomes, including these:

- Accurate understanding of the arguments and positions of others in the group
- Higher-level moral reasoning
- Thorough problem analysis
- Improved self-understanding and self-improvement
- Stronger, deeper relationships
- Creativity and change
- Greater motivation to solve the problem
- Improved mastery and retention of information
- Deeper commitment to the outcome of the discussion
- Increased group cohesion and cooperation

- Improved ability to deal with future conflicts
- High-quality solutions that integrate the perspective of all members

It is important to differentiate between substantive conflict and *affective (destructive) conflict,* which is centered on the personal relationships between group members. Those caught in personality-based conflicts find themselves either trying to avoid the problem or, when the conflict can't be ignored, escalating hostilities through name-calling, sarcasm, threats, and other means. (Complete the "Self-Assessment: Task/Relationship Conflict Scale" on page 300 to determine whether your group engages in substantive or affective conflict.) In this poisoned environment, members aren't as committed to the group process, sacrifice in-depth discussion of the problem in order to get done as soon as possible, and distance themselves from the decision. The end result? A decline in moral reasoning that produces an unpopular, low-quality solution.

Sometimes constructive conflict degenerates into affective conflict.[29] This occurs when disagreement about ideas is seen as an insult or a threat and members display anger because they feel their self-concepts are threatened. Others respond in kind. Members can also become frustrated when task-oriented conflicts seem to drag on and on without resolution. There are a number of ways that you as a leader can encourage substantive conflict while preventing it from being "corrupted" into affective conflict. Begin by paying attention to the membership of the group. Encourage the emergence of minority opinion by forming teams made up of people with significantly different backgrounds. Groups concerned with medical ethics, for example, generally include members from both inside the medical profession (nurses, surgeons, hospital administrators) and outside (theologians, ethicists, government officials). Individuals and subgroups that disagree with the majority cast doubt on the prevailing opinion and stimulate further thought. In the end, the majority generally comes up with a better solution because members have examined their assumptions and considered more viewpoints and possible solutions.[30]

Next, lay down some procedural ground rules—a conflict covenant—before discussion begins. Come up with a list of conflict guideposts as a group. "Absolutely no name-calling or threats." "No idea is a dumb idea." "Direct all critical comments toward the problem, not the person." "You must repeat the message of the previous speaker—to that person's satisfaction—before you can add your comments." Highlight the fact that conflict about ideas is an integral part of group discussion and caution against hasty decisions. Encourage individuals to stand firm instead of capitulating. If need be, employ the devil's advocate or dialectical inquiry tactics described earlier to build conflict into the discussion. This is also a good time to remind members of the importance of cooperation and emotional intelligence. Groups that emphasize shared goals view conflict as a mutual problem that needs everyone's attention. As a result, team members feel more confident dealing with conflict, and collective performance improves.[31] Teams that demonstrate high levels of EI are also more equipped to manage conflict and therefore perform better. In particular, if members can collectively control their emotions, they listen more closely to opposing ideas and seek the best solution without being upset when their proposals are rejected.[32]

During the discussion, make sure that members follow their conflict covenant and don't engage in conflict avoidance or escalation. Stop to revisit the ground rules when needed. Be prepared to support your position. Challenge and analyze the arguments of others as you encourage them to do the same. If members get stuck in a battle of wills, reframe the discussion by asking such questions as "What kind of information would help you change your mind?" "Why shouldn't we pursue other options?" or "What would you do if you were in my position?"[33] You can also ask participants to develop new ways to describe their ideas (in graphs, as numbers, as bulleted lists) and ask them to step back and revisit their initial assumptions in order to find common ground.

After the decision is made, ensure that the team and its members will continue to develop their conflict management skills. Debrief the decision-making process to determine whether the group achieved its goals, work on repairing relationships that might have been bruised during the discussion, and celebrate or remember stories of outstanding conflict management.[34]

SELF-ASSESSMENT

TASK/RELATIONSHIP CONFLICT SCALE

The following scale will help you determine if your team is engaged in affective or substantive conflict. Choose a problem-solving group from work or school and answer each of the following questions.

Very little						A great deal
1	2	3	4	5	6	7

1. How much friction is there among members in your group? _____

2. How much are personality conflicts evident in your group? _____

3. How much tension is there among members in your group? _____

4. How much emotional conflict is there among members in your group? _____

5. How often do people in your group disagree about opinions? _____

6. How frequently are there conflicts about ideas in your group? _____

7. How much conflict about the work you do is there in your group? _____

8. To what extent are there differences of opinion in your group? _____

Scoring: Add up your scores from Questions 1–4 and record the total below. The higher the score, the greater the level of affective conflict in your group. Add up your scores from Questions 5–8 and record the total below. The higher the score, the greater the level of substantive or task conflict in your team.

Affective conflict _____ out of 28   Substantive/task conflict _____ out of 28

SOURCE: Reprinted from A multi-method examination of the benefits and detriments of intragroup conflict by Karen A. Jehn. Published in *Administrative Science Quarterly* vol. 40, pp. 256–282, June 1995. © Johnson Graduate School of Management, Cornell University.

Engaging in Effective Argument

Making arguments is the best way to influence others when the group is faced with a controversial decision. That's why argumentative people are more likely to emerge as leaders.[35] An argument is an assertion or a claim that is supported by evidence and reasons. In the argumentation process, group members interact with each other using claims, evidence, and reasoning in hopes of reaching the best decision. They avoid personal attacks that characterize affective conflicts.

Argumentation in a small group is not as formal and sophisticated as a legal brief or a debate at a college forensics tournament. In more formal settings, there are strict limits on such things as how long arguers can speak, what evidence they can introduce, how they should address the audience, and how the argument should be constructed. Argumentation in a group is much less structured. No one enforces time limits for individual speakers, and members may interrupt each other and get off track. Nonetheless, when leading a group, you'll have to make sure the group carries out the same basic tasks as the members of a university debate team.[36]

The first task is to identify just what the controversy is about. All too often teams waste their time debating the wrong issues and end up solving the wrong problem. In Case Study 8.1, the controversy surrounds boosting benefits for athletes. The commission must determine its response to the following assertion: "The NCAA should provide college athletes with more benefits." The decision is *not* a referendum on the role of sports in American society or on whether the NCAA should be abolished (though some critics argue that it should be).

Once the controversy is clearly identified, you need to assemble and present your arguments. As I noted earlier, arguments consist of a claim supported by evidence and reasons. Back up your claim with examples, personal experience, testimonials from others, and statistics. Also, supply reasons or logic for your position. The most common patterns of logic include *analogical* (drawing similarities between one case and another, as we saw in Chapter 7), *causal* (one event leads to another), *inductive* (generalizing from one or a few cases to many), and *deductive* (moving from a larger category or grouping to a smaller one).

You could use all four types of reasoning if you believe that college athletes ought to be paid. You might note that college athletes are employees of the university and deserve the same benefits as other workers (analogical reasoning). You could argue that the current system drives up coaches' salaries while taking advantage of players (causal reasoning). You could illustrate the likely advantages of paying players by pointing to how this practice has helped Olympic athletes. They, too, used to be treated as amateurs but now can earn money from their sports (inductive reasoning). You might note that the push for more benefits for athletes is a natural outcome of the growth of college sports (deductive reasoning).

While you formulate your position, you need to identify and attack the weaknesses in the positions of other participants. This process is often neglected during group discussions. Group communication experts Dennis Gouran and Randy Hirokawa found that undetected errors are the primary cause of poor-quality decisions.[37] These errors include incomplete data, accepting bad information as fact, selecting only the information that supports a flawed choice, rejecting valid evidence, poor reasoning, and making unreasonable inferences from the facts. Be on the lookout for the common errors in evidence and reasoning found in Box 8.3. According to Gouran and Hirokawa, all groups make mistakes, but members of successful groups catch their errors and get the group back on track through corrective communication called *counteractive influence*.

BOX 8.3 COMMON FALLACIES

Faulty Evidence

> Unreliable and biased sources
>
> Source lacking proper knowledge and background
>
> Inconsistency (disagrees with other sources, source contradicts himself or herself)
>
> Outdated evidence
>
> Evidence appears to support a claim but does not
>
> Information gathered from secondhand observers
>
> Uncritical acceptance of statistical data
>
> Inaccurate or incomplete citation of sources and quotations
>
> Plagiarism (using the ideas or words of others without proper attribution)

Faulty Reasoning

> Comparing two things that are not alike (false analogy)
>
> Drawing conclusions based on too few examples or examples that aren't typical of the population as a whole (hasty generalization)

Believing that the event that happens first always causes the event that happens second (false cause)

Arguing that complicated problems have only one cause (single cause)

Assuming without evidence that one event will inevitably lead to a bad result (slippery slope)

Using the argument to support the argument (begging the question)

Failing to offer evidence that supports the position (non sequitur)

Attacking the person instead of the argument (ad hominem)

Appealing to the crowd or popular opinion (ad populum)

Resisting change based on past practices (appeal to tradition)

Attacking a weakened version of an opponent's argument (straw argument)

SOURCE: Inch, E. S., Warnick, B., & Endres, D. (2006). *Critical thinking and communication: The use of reason in argument* (5th ed.). Boston: Pearson.

Implications and Applications

- As a leader, you will do much of your work in committees, boards, task forces, and other small groups. Making ethical choices is one of a team's most important responsibilities. Your task is to foster the conditions that promote effective, ethical decisions.

- Because destructive behavior on the part of just one member can derail the group process, encourage participants to take their ethical responsibilities seriously. Promote commitment to shared goals and take steps to minimize social loafing.

- An overemphasis on group cohesion is a significant threat to ethical decision making. Be alert for the symptoms of groupthink. These include signs of overconfidence (illusion of invulnerability, belief in the inherent morality of the group), signs of closed-mindedness (collective rationalization, stereotypes of outside groups), and signs of group pressure (pressure on dissenters, self-censorship, illusion of unanimity, and self-appointed mind guards).

- The devil's advocate and dialectic inquiry methods are two ways to build in disagreement and reduce the likelihood of groupthink.

- Avoid false agreement or consensus by speaking out if you are concerned about the group's direction.

- A dialogic approach to communication, one that treats others as humans rather than as objects, lays the groundwork for productive group interaction.

- Leaders of emotionally intelligent groups model emotional regulation and encourage the development of positive norms that address the needs of individuals, the team, and outside groups.
- Expect to spend most of your time in a group listening rather than speaking. Model effective comprehensive, critical listening behaviors that overcome distractions, biases, and other listening barriers.
- Build a positive group climate through supportive messages that are descriptive, problem oriented, spontaneous, empathetic, focused on equality, and provisional.
- To improve problem solving, foster substantive or task-oriented conflict about ideas and opinions. Set ground rules to help the group avoid affective (relational) conflict involving personalities.
- Encourage effective argument based on clearly identifying the controversy, assembling and presenting arguments, and addressing the weaknesses of opposing arguments.

For Further Exploration, Challenge, and Self-Assessment

1. Interview a leader at your school or in another organization to develop a "meeting profile" for this person. Find out how much time this individual spends in meetings during an average week and whether this is typical of other leaders in the same organization. Identify the types of meetings she or he attends and her or his role. Determine whether ethical issues are part of these discussions. As part of your profile, record your reactions. Are you surprised by your findings? Has this assignment changed your understanding of what leaders do?

2. Brainstorm strategies for encouraging commitment to shared goals in a group that you lead or belong to. What steps can you take to implement these strategies?

3. Evaluate the level of social loafing in your group. What factors encourage members to reduce their efforts? What can you as a leader do to raise the motivation level of participants?

4. Have you ever been part of a group that was victimized by groupthink? Which symptoms were present? How did they affect the group's ethical decisions and actions? Does the Abilene paradox (false agreement) offer a better explanation for what happened?

5. Evaluate a recent ethical decision made by one of your groups. Was it a high-quality decision? Why or why not? What factors contributed to the group's success or failure? Which of the keys to effective ethical problem

solving were present? Absent? How did the leader (you or someone else) shape the outcome, for better or worse? How would you evaluate your performance as a leader or team member? Write up your analysis.

6. Develop a plan for becoming a better listener in a group. Implement your plan and then evaluate your progress.

7. Use the self-leadership strategies in "Focus on Follower Ethics: Self-Leadership in Self-Managed Teams" to develop a strategy for carrying out your team responsibilities.

8. Identify forms of faulty evidence and reasoning (as well as dismissive communication) in a public argument about an ethical issue. Draw from talk shows, newspaper editorials, speeches, interviews, debates, congressional hearings, and other sources. Possible topics might include national health care, the war in Afghanistan, stem cell research, illegal immigration, and reducing the national debt.

9. With other team members, develop a conflict covenant. Determine how you will enforce this code. Or as an alternative, complete the "Self-Assessment: Task/Relationship Conflict Scale" as a group and develop strategies for engaging in more substantive conflict.

10. Fishbowl discussion: In a fishbowl discussion, one group discusses a problem while the rest of the class looks on and then provides feedback. Assign a group to Case Study 8.1 or 8.3. Make sure that each discussant has one or more observers who specifically note his or her behavior. When the discussion is over, observers should meet with their "fish." Then the class as a whole should give its impressions of the overall performance of the team. Draw on chapter concepts when evaluating the work of individual participants and the group.

CASE STUDY 8.2

RESPONDING TO GROUPTHINK AND FAULTY REASONING AT NASA

On January 31, 2003, America's space program suffered its second shuttle disaster when the *Columbia* disintegrated on reentry into the Earth's atmosphere. All seven aboard died in the explosion. The accident occurred nearly 17 years to the day after the *Challenger* explosion. That disaster also took the lives of seven astronauts, including the first teacher headed into space.

(Continued)

(Continued)

Space shuttle *Columbia*'s troubles began when a piece of foam the size of a flat-screen television broke off the propellant tank and hit the spacecraft 82 seconds after liftoff. The debris struck with a ton of force and probably caused a 6- to 10-inch hole. This opening allowed superheated gas to enter the craft when it came back to Earth.

The day after the launch, NASA officials reviewed tracking videos. This footage showed the debris strike but didn't reveal any damage because the pictures couldn't pick up details smaller than 2 feet. Five days after the launch, the mission control team in charge of the *Columbia* flight first discussed the possibility that a piece of insulating foam might have damaged the shuttle's left wing. Mission project leader Linda Ham downplayed the likelihood that the shuttle had been seriously compromised. She pointed out that the group had earlier concluded that foam, which routinely comes off during shuttle launches, wouldn't do any significant damage. Foam damage was considered a minor maintenance problem that could be taken care of between trips.

Other engineers and managers at NASA were not convinced that the foam strike was insignificant. Bryan O'Connor, NASA's top safety official, ordered a hazard assessment. Those carrying out the assessment requested permission to ask for additional satellite images from the Pentagon to determine whether there was damage to the orbiting ship. Ham denied their request in part because the shuttle would have to slow in order to position the wing for a photograph. This maneuver would disrupt the mission. The hazard assessment group was then forced to depend on the conclusions of a team of Boeing engineers. These experts used a computer program that determined there was potential for "significant tile damage" but not a complete "burn-through." However, their analysis was flawed. The group's software was not designed for use in making in-flight decisions. Also, Boeing engineers assumed that the reinforced carbon material around the strike area was as damage resistant as the glassy tiles on the rest of the ship. It was not.

During the same period, low-level NASA engineers launched their own independent investigation. Their requests for photos were denied because they didn't come through proper channels. Senior structural engineer Rodney Rocha then drafted an e-mail pointing out the "grave hazards" caused by the foam. Sadly, he never sent the message to Ham, claiming, "I was too low down here in the organization, and she's way up here. I just couldn't do it."[1]

Meanwhile, members of the mission control team continued to express concern about possible damage to the shuttle but backed down when pressured by Ham. Dissenters lacked hard data to establish that the shuttle had been damaged. When the group met for the final time, engineers did not even discuss possible dangers to the shuttle. Instead, they talked about how eager they were to review the astronauts' launch day photos after the shuttle landed to determine exactly where the foam had come off the tank. Mission control informed the astronauts that debris had hit their craft. However, controllers said that the problem was "not even worth mentioning" except that a reporter might ask them about it.

After the explosion, the Columbia Accident Investigation Board, chaired by Admiral Harold Gehman (USN, retired), wrote a scathing report that placed much of the blame on NASA's culture. Board members accused the agency of becoming overconfident after years of flying safely. Safety, which was elevated to top priority after the first shuttle disaster, became less important as years passed and space budgets were cut. NASA administrator Sean O'Keefe and other top managers appeared more interested in keeping the shuttles flying in order to complete the space station by February 2004. Engineers also lost sight of the fact that a space shuttle is a highly risky experimental craft. Communication between teams, departments, and organizational levels broke down. Nobody, including the leaders of NASA, seemed clear about the agency's mission after the success of the manned moon landing and the unmanned Mars probes.

Although flawed culture drew most of the headlines describing the Columbia board's final report, groupthink and faulty reasoning were just as much to blame. Mission control team members displayed many groupthink symptoms. They rationalized that shredding foam was only a routine problem, and team leader Ham pressured dissenters. Individuals eventually kept their doubts to themselves and thus gave the appearance that everyone in the group solidly backed its conclusions. The hazard assessment task force and Boeing engineers fell prey to shaky logic. These groups relied on a flawed computer model and assumed that all materials covering the spacecraft were equally durable.

There is no guarantee that the Columbia crew could have been rescued even if NASA officials had recognized the danger. Shuttle astronauts had a limited amount of food, water, and air and couldn't go to the space station for repairs. Any attempt to launch a rescue shuttle would have endangered another crew, because the second shuttle would face the same risk of a

(Continued)

(Continued)

fatal foam strike as the first. Nonetheless, by falling victim to both group-think and faulty assumptions, leaders at NASA eliminated any chance that the *Columbia* crew would make it back to Earth safely.

NASA grounded the space shuttle fleet after the *Columbia* disaster and spent more than $1 billion trying to fix insulation problems. Foam damage continues to be an issue despite these efforts. *Discovery* shed several pieces of foam during the first shuttle flight after the *Columbia* crash, and its 2006 mission was nearly delayed after a small piece of foam fell off before launch. *Endeavour*'s heat shield was damaged during a 2007 liftoff and again in 2009.

Although foam damage remains a concern, the way in which NASA responds to this and other safety issues has changed dramatically. No longer are safety worries routinely dismissed as they were before *Columbia;* engineers don't have to prove that a part will fail in order to be heard. Instead, the shuttle program manager and other leaders encourage detailed discussion of safety problems and listen carefully. For example, when the shuttle *Endeavour* was gashed in 2007, the crew deliberately flipped the ship over as it orbited the space station, allowing the station crew to iden-tify the location and size of the gouge. The *Endeavour* astronauts also used a laser scanner attached to a robotic arm to inspect the damage. On the ground, more than 100 people worked on the analysis of the *Endeavour* gash. One team of engineers conducted computer simulations to predict what would happen upon reentry, and another group of engineers from a different research center double-checked the first team's work. During mis-sion management meetings, they reviewed the data and agreed that the gouge was not a threat. As a final precaution, engineers determined what would happen if they were wrong and some of the aluminum structure above the gash was lost. They decided that the *Endeavour* would still return safely. And it did.

As NASA prepares to replace the shuttle program with new spacecraft to take astronauts beyond the moon, there are indications that groupthink could reemerge as a problem at the agency. There have been complaints that the Constellation program, which will use larger rockets and space capsules, has been run with a "my way or the highway" attitude that ignores design flaws and possible safety issues. Then, too, there is pressure to keep the shuttles in the air well after they are to be retired. Plans are to ground the shuttles because they are unsafe for additional missions. U.S. astronauts would travel to the international space station on Soviet shuttles until the new spacecraft come online. However, powerful critics oppose this plan. For example, former senator John Glenn, the first American to orbit around Earth, told a congressional committee, "I never thought I would see the day when the world's richest, most powerful, most accomplished spacefaring nation would have to buy tickets from Russia to get up to our station."[2]

Discussion Probes

1. How much blame do you assign to those who questioned the safety of the *Columbia* mission but either kept their doubts to themselves or failed to communicate them to NASA's top management?

2. What advice would you give to group members (such as those on the mission control team) who have doubts but lack the evidence to support their position?

3. If you were the head of NASA, would you have launched a rescue shuttle if you had identified the damage to the *Columbia?* Why or why not?

4. Evaluate the steps NASA has taken to change its culture and to resist groupthink. Do you think the agency can continue its progress? Do you think progress is slowing? Can you suggest any additional strategies to make the agency less susceptible to future disasters?

5. Should the shuttle program be grounded as originally planned, or should it be continued until the new missile system can be developed?

6. What leadership and followership ethics lessons do you draw from this case?

Notes

1. Sawyer, K. (2003, August 24). Shuttle's "smoking gun" took time to register. *The Washington Post,* p. A1.

2. Schwartz, J. (2008, December 30). The fight over NASA's future. *The New York Times,* p. D1.

Sources

Barrett, J. (2003, July 18). *Q&A: Clearly there is a problem here.* Retrieved from http://www.newsweek.com/2003/07/17/q-amp-a-clearly-there-is-a-problem-here.html

Chang, K. (2007, August 20). Caution over damage to *Endeavour* illustrates changes at space agency. *The New York Times,* p. A12.

(Continued)

(Continued)

Glanz, W. (2003, August 27). NASA ignored dangers to shuttle, panel says. *The Washington Times*, p. A1.

Grose, T. K. (2003, September 1). Can the manned space program find a new, revitalizing mission in the wake of the *Columbia* tragedy? *U.S. News & World Report*, p. 36.

Hilzenrath, D. S. (2003, September 2). Rescue of *Columbia* a hindsight dream. *The Washington Post*, p. A8.

Johnson, J. (2007). Dinged up *Endeavour* returns. *Los Angeles Times*, p. A10.

Klotz, I. (2009, July 17). Space shuttle trips on hold as NASA probes debris woes. *The Gazette*, p. A13.

Lambright, W. H. (2008, March/April). Leadership and change at NASA: Sean O'Keefe as administrator. *Public Administration Review*, pp. 230–240.

Leary, W. E., & Schwartz, J. (2006, July 4). Shuttle launching set for today despite broken foam. *The New York Times*, p. A11.

Mishra, R. (2003, August 27). Probe hits NASA in crash of shuttle. *The Boston Globe*.

Sawyer, K. (2003, August 24). Shuttle's "smoking gun" took time to register. *The Washington Post*, p. A1.

CASE STUDY 8.3

INCENTIVES FOR ORGAN DONATIONS

Each year more than 6,000 Americans die while waiting for an organ transplant. More than half of those who need transplants perish before they get the kidneys, livers, or other organs they need. In the European Union, 15%–30% of patients die while awaiting transplantation. And the shortage is only going to get worse as the population ages. However, the need for organ donations is not limited to the West. Worldwide, 2 million people develop renal failure every year and must have a kidney transplant or ongoing dialysis treatment in order to survive.

Governments are trying a variety of forms of reimbursement to boost organ supplies, particularly of kidneys. Seventy-eight countries signed the Istanbul Declaration, developed by the Transplantation Society and the International Society of Nephrology, which specifies ethical reimbursements for living donors. These can include disability, life and health insurance, dialysis if the donor should need such treatment, and priority for future transplants. The Istanbul Declaration also opposes trafficking in human organs and "transplant tourism." In human organ trafficking, poor individuals in India, the Philippines, Pakistan, and elsewhere are often deceived or coerced into providing organs for international sale. In transport tourism, wealthy individuals travel to poorer nations to undergo transplant procedures.

Federal legislation in the United States currently forbids selling organs, but states can offer tax deductions for nonmedical expenses such as travel, lodging, and lost wages related to giving an organ. According to Sally Satel, a resident scholar at the American Enterprise Institute and a kidney transplant recipient, current incentives in the United States are "too timid." She suggests that donors receive in-kind payments like a down payment on a house or a contribution to a retirement fund. Two doctors from Yale University argue that people should have the right to control what happens to their bodies. They propose that donors charge $40,000 for organs, with a federal agency regulating costs and marketing. Critics claim, though, that selling organs favors the rich at the expense of the poor and can lead to serious abuses. Incentives also replace altruistic motives with selfish ones. According to the Institute of Medicine, offering financial incentives could "lead people to view organs as commodities and diminish donations from altruistic motives."[1] Yet, to this point altruism has not kept pace with the growing demand for organs. Noted a professor of surgery at the University of Minnesota, "At first glance, compensation for donors might appear repugnant. Yet to me, what is truly repugnant is the sad reality of patients dying and suffering while waiting for a kidney."[2]

Discussion Probes

1. What ethical principles can be applied when deciding whether or not to offer incentives to organ donors?

2. What values are in conflict in this case?

3. What kinds of reimbursement should be given to those who donate their organs?

4. Should donors be allowed to sell their organs? Be offered in-kind payments? Why or why not?

5. How should organs be allocated?

6. Would you become a transplant tourist if you needed a new organ and couldn't get one in your home country?

7. What leadership and followership ethics lessons do you draw from this case?

(Continued)

(Continued)

Notes

1. Jacoby, J. (2009, July 5). A deadly organ donor system. *Boston Globe,* Opinion, p. 9.
2. Creswell, A. (2008, August 9). Transplants trade at crossroads. *Weekend Australian,* Review, p. 15.

Sources

Cohen, L. R., & Undis, D. J. (2006, March/April). New solution to the organ shortage. *Saturday Evening Post,* p. 32.

Lister, S. (2006, February 16). Let people sell their kidneys for transplant, say doctors. *The Times (London),* p. 31.

Not for sale at any price. (2006, April 8). *The Lancet,* p. 1118.

Robertson, C. (2005, Spring). Organ advertising: Desperate patients solicit volunteers. *The Journal of Law, Medicine & Ethics,* pp. 170–174.

Satel, S. (2009, March 10). Kidney for sale: Let's legally reward the donor. *The Globe and Mail,* p. A17.

Slegers, M. (2008, December 8). Health: New directive aims to boost organ donation. *Europolitics.*

Suhaimi, N. D. (2008, November 9). Some have laws to offer compensation. *The Straits Times.*

Notes

1. Palmer, P. (1996). Leading from within. In L. C. Spears (Ed.), *Insights on leadership: Service, stewardship, spirit, and servant-leadership* (pp. 197–208). New York: Wiley, p. 2.

2. Rothwell, J. D. (1998). *In mixed company: Small group communication* (3rd ed.). Fort Worth, TX: Harcourt Brace.

3. Tropman, J. (2003). *Making meetings work: Achieving high quality group decisions* (2nd ed.). Thousand Oaks, CA: Sage, p. 196.

4. Dukerich, J. M., Nichols, M. L., Elm, D. R., & Voltrath, D. A. (1990). Moral reasoning in groups: Leaders make a difference. *Human Relations, 43,* 473–493; Nichols, M. L., & Day, V. E. (1982). A comparison of moral reasoning of groups and individuals on the "defining issues test." *Academy of Management Journal, 24,* 21–28.

5. Johnson, D. W., Maruyama, G., Johnson, R., Nelson, D., & Skon, L. (1981). Effects of cooperative, competitive, and individualistic goal structures on achievement: A meta-analysis. *Psychological Bulletin, 82,* 47–62; Johnson, D. W., & Johnson, R. (1989). *Cooperation and competition: Theory and research.* Edina, MN: Interaction Book Company; Johnson, D. W., & Johnson, F. P. (2000). *Joining together: Group theory and group skills* (7th ed.). Boston: Allyn & Bacon.

6. Johnson, D. W., & Johnson, R. (2005). Training for cooperative group work. In M. A. West, D. Tjosvold, & K. G. Smith (Eds.), *The essentials of teamworking: International perspectives* (pp. 131–147). West Sussex, UK: Wiley.

7. Johnson & Johnson (2000); Johnson & Johnson (2005).

8. Amichai-Hamburger, Y. (2003). Understanding social loafing. In A. Sagie, S. Stashevsky, & M. Koslowsky (Eds.), *Misbehaviour and dysfunctional attitudes in organizations* (pp. 79–102). New York: Palgrave Macmillan.

9. Karau, S. J., & Williams, K. D. (2001). Understanding individual motivation in groups: The Collective Effort Model. In M. E. Turner (Ed.), *Groups at work: Theory and research* (pp. 113–141). Mahwah, NJ: Erlbaum, p. 119.

10. Karau, S. J., & Williams, K. D. (1995). Social loafing: Research findings, implications, and future directions. *Current Directions in Psychological Science, 4,* 134–140; Williams, K. D., Harkins, S. G., & Karau, S. J. (2003). Social performance. In M. A. Hogg & J. Cooper (Eds.), *The Sage handbook of social psychology* (pp. 327–346). London: Sage.

11. Janis, I. (1971, November). Groupthink: The problems of conformity. *Psychology Today,* 271–279; Janis, I. (1982). *Groupthink* (2nd ed.). Boston: Houghton Mifflin; Janis, I. (1989). *Crucial decisions: Leadership in policymaking and crisis management.* New York: Free Press.

12. Moorhead, G., Neck, C. P., & West, M. S. (1998). The tendency toward defective decision making within self-managing teams: The relevance of groupthink for the 21st century. *Organizational Behavior and Human Decision Processes, 73,* 327–351.

13. See the following:

    Chen, A., Lawson, R. B., Gordon, L. R., & McIntosh, B. (1996). Groupthink: Deciding with the leader and the devil. *Psychological Record, 46,* 581–590.

    Esser, J. K. (1998). Alive and well after 25 years: A review of groupthink research. *Organizational Behavior and Human Decision Processes, 73,* 116–141.

    Flippen, A. R. (1999). Understanding groupthink from a self-regulatory perspective. *Small Group Research, 3,* 139–165.

    Jones, P. E., & Roelofsma, P. H. M. P. (2000). The potential for social contextual and group biases in team decision-making: Biases, conditions and psychological mechanisms. *Ergonomics, 43,* 1129–1152.

    Street, M. D. (1997). Groupthink: An examination of theoretical issues, implications, and future research suggestions. *Small Group Research, 28,* 72–93.

14. Cosier, R. A., & Schwenk, C. R. (1990). Agreement and thinking alike: Ingredients for poor decision. *Academy of Management Executive, 4,* 69–74; Schweiger, D. M., Sandberg, W. R., & Rechner, P. (1989). Experiential effects of dialectical inquiry, devil's advocacy, and consensus approaches to strategic decision making. *Academy of Management Journal, 32*(4), 745–772.

15. Manz, C. C., & Neck, C. P. (1995). Teamthink: Beyond the groupthink syndrome in self-managing work teams. *Journal of Managerial Psychology, 1*(1), 7–15; Manz, C. C., & Sims, H. P. (1989). *Superleadership: Leading others to lead themselves.* Upper Saddle River, NJ: Prentice Hall.

16. Harvey, J. (1988). *The Abilene paradox and other meditations on management.* New York: Simon & Schuster. See also Harvey, J. B. (1999). *How come every time I get stabbed in the back my fingerprints are on the knife?* San Francisco: Jossey-Bass.

17. Buber, M. (1970). *I and thou.* (R. G. Smith, Trans.). New York: Charles Scribner's Sons; Johannesen, R. L. (2002). *Ethics in human communication* (5th ed.). Prospect Heights, IL: Waveland, Ch. 4.

18. Cissna, K. N., & Anderson, R. (1994). Communication and the ground of dialogue. In R. Anderson, K. N. Cissna, & R. C. Arnett (Eds.), *The reach of dialogue: Confirmation, voice, and community* (pp. 9–30). Cresskill, NJ: Hampton.

19. Stewart, J. (2008). Cosmopolitan communication ethics: Understanding and action. In K. G. Roberts & R. C. Arnett (Eds.), *Communication ethics: Between cosmopolitanism and provinciality* (pp. 105–119). New York: Peter Lang.

20. Czubaroff, J. (2000). Dialogical rhetoric: An application of Martin Buber's philosophy of dialogue. *Quarterly Journal of Speech, 2,* 168–189.

21. Duffy, M. K., & & Shaw. J. D. (2000). The Salieri syndrome: Consequences of envy in groups. *Small Group Research, 31,* 3–23.

22. Goleman, D., Boyatzis, R., & McKee, A. (2002, Spring). The emotional reality of teams. *Journal of Organizational Excellence, 55–65*; Rapisarda, B. A. (2002). The impact of emotional intelligence on work team cohesiveness and performance. *The International Journal of Organizational Analysis, 10,* 363–370; Prati, L. M., Douglas, C., Ferris, G. R., Ammeter, A. P., & Buckley, M. R. (2003). Emotional intelligence, leadership effectiveness, and team outcomes. *The International Journal of Organizational Analysis, 11,* 21–40. Some examples in this section are taken from these sources.

23. Durskat, V. U., & Wolff, S. B. (2001, March). Building the emotional intelligence of groups. *Harvard Business Review,* pp. 80–90.

24. Wolvin, A. D., & Coakley, G. C. (1993). A listening taxonomy. In A. D. Wolvin & C. G. Coakley (Eds.), *Perspectives in listening* (pp. 15–22). Norwood, NJ: Ablex.

25. Johnson, J. (1993). Functions and processes of inner speech in listening. In D. Wolvin & C. G. Coakley (Eds.), *Perspectives in listening* (pp. 170–184). Norwood, NJ: Ablex.

26. Barker, L., Johnson, P., & Watson, K. (1991). The role of listening in managing interpersonal and group conflict. In D. Borisoff & M. Purdy (Eds.), *Listening in every-day life: A personal and professional approach* (pp. 139–157). Lanham, MD: University Press of America.

27. Gibb, J. R. (1961). Defensive communication. *Journal of Communication, 11–12,* 141–148. See also Borisoff, D., & Victor, D. A. (1998). *Conflict management: A communication skills approach* (2nd ed.). Boston: Allyn & Bacon, Ch. 2.

28. See the following:

Amason, A. C., Thompson, K. R., Hochwarter, W. A., & Harrison, A. W. (1995). Conflict: An important dimension in successful management teams. *Organizational Dynamics, 23*, 20–35.

Amason, A. C. (1996). Distinguishing the effects of functional and dysfunctional conflict on strategic decision making: Resolving a paradox for top management teams. *Academy of Management Journal, 39*, 123–148.

Bell, M. A. (1974). The effects of substantive and affective conflict in problem-solving groups. *Speech Monographs, 41*, 19–23.

Bell, M. A. (1979). The effects of substantive and affective verbal conflict on the quality of decisions of small problem-solving groups. *Central States Speech Journal, 3*, 75–82.

Johnson, D. W., & Tjosvold, D. (1983). *Productive conflict management*. New York: Irvington.

29. Kotlyar, I., & Karakowsky, L. (2006). Leading conflict? Linkages between leader behaviors and group conflict. *Small Group Research, 37*, 377–403.

30. Moscovici, S., Mugny, G., & Van Avermaet, E. (Eds.). (1985). *Perspectives on minority influence*. Cambridge, UK: Cambridge University Press; Maas, A., & Clark, R. D. (1984). Hidden impact of minorities: Fifteen years of minority influence research. *Psychological Bulletin, 95*, 428–445; Nemeth, C., & Chiles, C. (1986). Modeling courage: The role of dissent in fostering independence. *European Journal of Social Psychology, 18*, 275–280; Nemeth, C. J. (1994). The value of minority dissent. In S. Moscovici, A. Mucchi-Faina, & A. Maass (Eds.), *Minority influence* (pp. 3–15). Chicago: Nelson-Hall.

31. Alper, S., Tjosvold, D., & Law, K. S. (2000). Conflict management, efficacy, and performance in organizational teams. *Personnel Psychology, 53*, 625–642.

32. Jordan, P. J., & Troth, A. C. (2004). Managing emotions during team problem solving: Emotional intelligence and conflict resolution. *Human Performance, 17*, 195–218.

33. Roberto, M. A. (2005). *Why great leaders don't take yes for an answer*. Upper Saddle River, NJ: Wharton School Publishing.

34. Roberto.

35. Schultz, B. (1982). Argumentativeness: Its effect in group decision-making and its role in leadership perception. *Communication Quarterly, 3*, 368–375.

36. Infante, D., & Rancer, A. (1996). Argumentativeness and verbal aggressiveness: A review of recent theory and research. In B. Burleson (Ed.), *Communication yearbook 19* (pp. 319–351). Thousand Oaks, CA: Sage; Infante, D. (1988). *Arguing constructively*. Prospect Heights, IL: Waveland.

37. Gouran, D. S., Hirokawa, R. Y., Julian, K. M., & Leatham, G. B. (1993). The evolution and current status of the functional perspective on communication in decision-making and problem-solving groups. *Communication Yearbook, 16*, 573–576; Gouran, D. S., & Hirokawa, R. Y. (1986). Counteractive functions of communication in effective group decision making. In R. Y. Hirokawa & M. S. Poole (Eds.), *Communication and group decision making* (pp. 81–89). Beverly Hills, CA: Sage.

9

Creating an Ethical Organizational Climate

Bad ethics is bad business.

—Anonymous

Ethics has everything to do with management.

—Business ethics professor Lynn Sharp Paine

WHAT'S AHEAD

Leaders act as ethics officers for their organizations, exercising influence through the process of social learning and by building positive ethical climates. Healthy ethical climates are marked by zero tolerance for destructive behaviors, justice, integrity (ethical soundness, wholeness, and consistency), concern for process as well as product, structural reinforcement, and social responsibility. Important tools for building an ethical organizational climate include shared values, codes of ethics, and continuous ethical improvement.

The Leader as Ethics Officer

In the introduction to this text, I argued that ethics is at the heart of leadership. When we become leaders, we assume the ethical responsibilities that come with that role. Nowhere is this more apparent than in the organizational context. Examine nearly any corporate scandal—Enron, World Savings, Fannie Mae, WorldCom, HealthSouth, Galleon hedge funds, Guidant medical devices, Qwest—and you'll find leaders who engaged in immoral behavior and encouraged their followers to do the same. The same pattern can be found in the nonprofit and governmental sectors (e.g., ACORN, New Era Philanthropy, United Way, the British Parliament). On a more positive note, leaders are largely responsible for creating the organizations we admire for their ethical behavior.

Leaders are the ethics officers of their organizations, casting light or shadow in large part through the example they set.[1] Michael Brown and Linda Trevino draw on social learning theory to explain why and how ethical organizational leaders influence followers.[2] Social learning theory is based on the premise that people learn by observing and then emulating the values, attitudes, and behaviors of people they find legitimate, attractive, and credible. When it comes to ethics, followers look to their leaders as role models and act accordingly. Leaders are generally seen as legitimate, credible, and attractive because they occupy positions of authority with power and status. Ethical leaders build on this foundation. They increase their legitimacy by treating employees fairly and boost their attractiveness by expressing care and concern for followers. They enhance their credibility (particularly perceptions of their trustworthiness) by living up to the values they espouse. Such leaders are open and honest and set clear, high standards that they follow themselves.

Moral leaders make sure that ethics messages aren't drowned out by other messages about tasks and profits. They focus attention on ethics through frequent communication about values, mission, corporate standards, and the importance of ethical behavior. They reinforce follower learning by using rewards and punishments to regulate behavior, which makes it clear which actions are acceptable and which are not.

Trevino, Brown, and their colleagues distinguish between ethical leaders and those who are unethical, hypocritical, or ethically neutral.[3] The *unethical leader* falls short as both a moral person and a moral influence agent. This person casts one or more of the shadows described in Chapter 1 by bullying others, deceiving investors, acting irresponsibly, and so on. At the same time, the unethical leader clearly communicates that ethics don't matter; only results do. "Chainsaw" Al Dunlap was one such leader. As CEO of

Sunbeam he drove up the company's stock prices by eliminating thousands of jobs while inflating sales figures. The *hypocritical leader* talks a lot about ethical values but doesn't live up to the rhetoric. Prominent pastor Ted Haggard is an example of a hypocritical leader. As leader of the National Association of Evangelicals, he led public efforts to condemn homosexuality while he was carrying on an affair with a male prostitute.

The *ethically neutral leader* is not clearly seen as either ethical or unethical. This person doesn't send out strong messages about ethics and leaves followers unsure about where he or she stands on moral issues. Ethically neutral leaders appear to be self-centered and focus exclusively on the bottom line. Sandy Weill, former Citigroup CEO, typifies the ethically neutral leader. Weill stayed on the sidelines when it came to ethics, rewarding his managers according to their results. It was during his tenure that star analyst Jack Grubman continued to promote WorldCom and other telecom companies even as they were heading for bankruptcy. Hewlett-Packard's past CEO, Carly Fiorina, is another a leader who appeared to focus more on financial performance than on ethics.[4] During her tenure at HP the company lost its outstanding ethical reputation. Salespeople adopted questionable tactics to make their numbers, and financial analysts began to doubt the company's quarterly reports. Conflict over HP's merger with Compaq set the stage for a scandal involving board members after Fiorina departed. Under the direction of the board chair, private investigators spied on company directors and obtained information about journalists under false pretenses.

From their analysis of the four categories of ethical leadership, Trevino and her colleagues conclude that acting ethically is not enough. Executives must also ensure that employees know that they care (aren't just neutral) about ethics. Otherwise, followers will continue to focus on financial results without concern for ethics. Ethical leaders make ethical considerations a top organizational priority. They create positive ethical climates that promote moral behavior by leaders and followers alike. Identifying the characteristics of healthy ethical climates is the subject of the next section.

Ethical Climates

Ethical climate is best understood as part of an organization's culture. From the cultural vantage point, an organization is a tribe. As tribal members gather, they develop their own language, stories, beliefs, assumptions, ceremonies, and power structures. These elements combine to form a unique perspective on the world called the organization's culture.[5] How an organization responds to ethical issues is a part of this culture. Every organization faces a special set of ethical challenges, creates its own set of values and norms, develops guidelines for enforcing its ethical standards, honors particular ethical heroes, and so on. Ethical climate, in turn, determines what members believe is right or wrong and shapes their ethical decision making and behavior.

Management professors Bart Victor and John Cullen argue that ethical climates can be classified according to the criteria members use to make moral choices and the groups that members refer to when making ethical determinations.[6] Victor and Cullen identify five primary climate types. *Instrumental* climates follow the principle of ethical egotism. Ethical egotists make decisions based on selfish interests that serve the individual and his or her immediate group and organization. *Caring* climates emphasize concern or care for others. *Law and order* climates are driven by external criteria such as professional codes of conduct. *Rules* climates are governed by the policies, rules, and procedures developed in the organization. *Independence* climates give members wide latitude to make their own decisions. (To determine the ethical climate of your company or organization, complete the "Self-Assessment: Ethical Climate Questionnaire.")

Leaders would do well to know the particular ethical orientation of their organizations. To begin, each of the five climate types poses unique ethical challenges. Members of instrumental organizations often ignore the needs of others, whereas those driven by a care ethic are tempted to overlook the rules to help out friends and colleagues. Leaders and followers in law and order cultures may be blind to the needs of coworkers because they rely on outside standards for guidance. On the other hand, those who play by organizational rules may be blinded to societal norms. Independence produces the best results when members have the knowledge and skills they need to make good decisions.

Studies using the Victor and Cullen climate types suggest that self-interest poses the greatest threat to ethical performance.[7] Rates of immoral behavior are highest in work units and organizations with instrumental climates. Members of these groups are also less committed to their organizations. Caring (benevolent) climates promote employee loyalty. Rules climates discourage ethical misbehavior but don't encourage attachment to the organization. External laws and codes that are internalized into an organization's climate are positively linked with such outcomes as job satisfaction and psychological well-being.

SELF-ASSESSMENT

ETHICAL CLIMATE QUESTIONNAIRE

Instructions

Indicate whether you agree with each of the following statements about your company or organization. Use the scale below and write the number that best represents your answer in the space next to the item.

Completely false	Mostly false	Somewhat false	Somewhat true	Mostly true	Completely true
0	1	2	3	4	5

1. In this company (organization), people are mostly out for themselves. _1_

2. The major responsibility for people in this company (organization) is to control costs. _0_

3. In this company (organization), people are expected to follow their own personal and moral beliefs. _3_

4. People are expected to do anything to further the company's (organization's) interests, regardless of the consequences. _0_

5. In this company (organization), people look out for each other's good. _4_

6. There is no room for one's personal morals or ethics in this company (organization). _1_

7. It is very important to follow strictly the company's (organization's) rules and procedures here. _5_

8. Work is considered substandard only when it hurts the company's (organization's) interests. _0_

9. Each person in this company (organization) decides for him- or herself what is right and wrong. _1_

10. In this company (organization), people protect their own interest above other considerations. _1_

11. The most important consideration in this company (organization) is each person's sense of right and wrong. _4_

12. The most important concern is the good of all the people in the company (organization). _2_

13. The first consideration is whether a decision violates any law. _4_

14. People are expected to comply with the law and professional standards over and above other considerations. _5_

15. Everyone is expected to stick by company (organization) rules and procedures. _4_

16. In the company (organization), our major concern is always what is best for the other person.   _4_

17. People are concerned with the company's (organization's) interests—to the exclusion of all else.   _1_

18. Successful people in this company (organization) go by the book.   _5̸4_

19. The most efficient way is always the right way in this company (organization).   _3_

20. In this company (organization), people are expected to strictly follow legal or professional standards.   _5_

21. Our major consideration is what is best for everyone in the company (organization).   _3_

22. In this company (organization), people are guided by their own personal ethics.   _2_

23. Successful people in this company (organization) strictly obey the company (organization) policies.   _4_

24. In this company (organization), the law or ethical code of one's profession is the major consideration.   _4_

25. In this company (organization), each person is expected, above all, to work efficiently.   _4̸3_

26. It is expected that you will always do what is right for the customer and public.   _5_

Scoring

Caring Climate Score
Add up scores on items 5, 12, 16, 19, 21, 25, 26 =   (Range 0–35) _25_

Law and Code Climate Score
Add up scores on items 13, 14, 20, 24 =   (Range 0–20) _17_

Rules Climate Score
Add up scores on items 7, 15, 18, 23 =   (Range 0–20) _17_

Instrumental Climate Score
Add up scores on items 1, 2, 4, 6, 8, 10, 17 =   (Range 0–35) _5_

Independence Climate Score
Add up scores on items 3, 9, 11, 22 =   (Range 0–20) _9_

SOURCES: Cullen, J. B., Victor, B., & Bronson, J. W. (1993). The Ethical Climate Questionnaire: An assessment of its development and validity. *Psychological Reports, 73*, 667–674; used by permission. See also Victor, B., & Cullen, J. B. (1988). The organizational bases of ethical work climates. *Administrative Science Quarterly, 33*, 101–125.

Signs of Healthy Ethical Climates

There is no one-size-fits-all approach to creating an ethical climate. Rather, we need to identify principles and practices that characterize positive ethical climates. Then we have to adapt these elements to our particular organizational setting. Key markers of highly ethical organizations include zero tolerance for destructive behaviors, integrity, justice, a focus on process, and structural reinforcement. (For a list of the signs of unhealthy climates, see "Focus on Follower Ethics: The Seven Signs of Ethical Collapse" below.)

FOCUS ON FOLLOWER ETHICS

THE SEVEN SIGNS OF ETHICAL COLLAPSE

Arizona State University business ethics professor Marianne Jennings identifies seven signs that a company is in deep ethical trouble. Identifying these signs can keep us from joining a questionable organization, help us recognize whether our current organization is in danger, and encourage us to take steps as followers to stop the decline.

Sign 1: Pressure to Maintain Numbers

The first sign of ethical trouble is obsession with meeting quantifiable goals. Driven by numbers, companies overstate sales, hide expenses, make bad loans, and ship defective products. Nonprofits also feel the pressure to reach their goal numbers. Universities want to be ranked highly by *U.S. News and World Report* and other publications, so they may lie about graduation and placement rates. Charities, driven to achieve their fund-raising objectives, may make false claims about how many people they serve.

Sign 2: Fear and Silence

In every moral meltdown, there are indications that something is seriously amiss. For example, employees at Enron circulated a list titled "Top Ten Reasons Enron Restructures So Frequently." Item 7 on the list said, "To keep the outside investment analysts so confused that they will not be able to figure out that we don't know what we're doing." However, few challenge the status quo because those who do so are publicly shamed, demoted, or dismissed. Others don't want to believe that the organization is in trouble; still others are bribed into silence through generous salaries and loan packages.

(Continued)

(Continued)

Sign 3: Young 'Uns and a Bigger-Than-Life CEO

Some CEOs become icons who are adored by the community and the media (though often not by employees). Outsiders are loath to criticize the legendary CEO when everyone is singing his or her praises. The iconic CEO also surrounds him- or herself with loyal supporters who are often young and inexperienced. For example, CEOs brought in their sons and daughters to help them run AIG, Archer Daniels Midland, and Adelphia, all companies that ran afoul of the law.

Sign 4: Weak Board

The boards of companies on the verge of moral collapse are weak for a variety of reasons. They may have inexperienced members, be made up of friends of the CEO, or be reluctant to reign in a legendary CEO. Members may fail to attend meetings or devote the necessary time to their board roles. The board of HealthSouth is a case in point. HealthSouth (which engaged in Medicare and accounting fraud) was made up of company officers and outsiders who had contracts and other financial relationships with CEO Richard Scrushy and the firm. The HealthSouth board ignored lawsuits and federal investigations that indicated that the company was in trouble.

Sign 5: Conflicts

Conflicts of interest arise when an individual plays two roles and the interests of one role are at odds with those of the other role. Officers of the company are then tempted to profit at the expense of stockholders, employees, and others. That was the case with CFO Andrew Fastow of Enron, who made millions from the entities he designed to hide company debt.

Sign 6: Innovation Like No Other

Highly successful companies often believe that they can defy economic and business reality. They might have been the first in a new industry or be headed by an entrepreneurial leader who succeeded against all odds. Their arrogance convinces them that they can continually innovate themselves out of any tight spot. Instead, these groups and their leaders innovate themselves into moral trouble by inventing illegal accounting practices, tax evasion schemes, and faulty business models. Finova Group grew rapidly by making loans to small businesses and time-share properties turned down by other financial institutions. The firm could charge higher interest, generating greater margins. However, Finova soon had a portfolio full of bad loans. Rather than write these loans off, the company used creative accounting to hide these losses. In some cases, company officers even counted the poor loans as assets.

Sign 7: Goodness in Some Areas Atones for Evil in Others

A good many fallen organizations and leaders try to atone for their sins in one area by doing good in others. Tyco and Dennis Kozlowski, WorldCom and Bernie Ebbers, and Adelphia and John Rigas were all known for their charitable acts, giving to universities and local communities, contributing to disaster relief, encouraging employees to volunteer for service projects, and so on. In the case of endangered organizations, the motive for philanthropy is not serving the common good but soothing the conscience of those involved in fraud, insider trading, accounting tricks, and other misdeeds.

SOURCE: Jennings, M. M. (2006). *The seven signs of ethical collapse: How to spot moral meltdowns in companies... before it's too late.* New York: St. Martin's Press.

Zero Tolerance for Destructive Behaviors

Researchers report that organizations, like individuals, have their "dark sides." Some organizations, such as humanitarian relief agencies and socially responsible businesses, shine brightly. Others, such as corrupt police departments and authoritarian political regimes, are cloaked in darkness. Few of us will experience the oppression of truly dark organizations. However, most of us will experience the shadows cast by dark-side behaviors. These are destructive or antisocial actions that deliberately attempt to harm others or the organization.[8] Those who engage in such unethical behaviors are driven to meet their own needs at the expense of coworkers and the group as a whole. Common categories of misbehaviors include incivility, aggression, sexual harassment, and discrimination.

Incivility consists of rude or discourteous actions that disregard others and violate norms for respect.[9] Such actions can be intentional or unintentional; they include leaving a mess for the maintenance staff to pick up, sending a "flaming" e-mail, claiming credit for someone else's work, making fun of a peer, or inadvertently ignoring a team member on the way into the office. Incivility reduces employee job satisfaction, task performance, motivation, loyalty, performance, creativity, and willingness to cooperate.

Aggression refers to consciously trying to hurt others or the organization itself.[10] Aggressive behaviors can take a variety of forms, ranging from refusing to answer e-mails to swearing at coworkers to murder. Such behaviors can be categorized along three dimensions. They can be physical–verbal (destructive words or deeds), active–passive (doing harm by acting or failing to act), or direct–indirect (doing harm directly to the other person or indirectly through an intermediary and attacking something that the target values). Aggression does extensive damage to individuals and organizations. Victims may be hurt; experience more stress, which leads to poor health; become fearful, depressed, or angry; lose the ability to concentrate; and feel less committed to their jobs. Observers of aggressive incidents also experience more anxiety and have a lower sense of well-being and commitment. Performance at the organizational level drops as a product of the aggressive actions of employees. Workplace aggression reduces productivity while increasing absenteeism and turnover. Organizations become the targets of lawsuits and negative publicity.

Sexual harassment is a form of aggression directed largely at women.[11] Quid pro quo harassment occurs when targets are coerced into providing sexual favors in return for keeping their jobs or getting promoted. Hostile work environment harassment exists when job conditions interfere with job performance. Components of hostile working conditions include demeaning comments, suggestive gestures, threats, propositions, bribes, and sexual assault. The work performance of victims drops, and they may quit their jobs. Targets also suffer physically (headaches, sleep loss, nausea, eating disorders) and psychologically (depression, fear, a sense of helplessness).

Discrimination is putting members of selected groups, such as women, minorities, disabled employees, older workers, and homeless people, at a disadvantage. Such negative treatment is generally based on stereotypes and prejudice (e.g., older workers can't learn new skills, Hispanics are lazy). Because of the passage of antidiscrimination laws and changes in societal values, employment discrimination is generally expressed subtly through such behaviors as dismissing the achievements of people of color and women, avoiding members of low-status groups, and hiring and promoting those of similar backgrounds.[12]

Destructive behaviors are all too common in modern organizations. Twenty percent of one sample reported being the targets of uncivil messages in a given week. There were 15,000 incidents of violence resulting in time away from work in one 12-month period in the United States, and assaults and suicides account for 13% of all deaths on the job. Fifty to sixty percent of female students and employees report being the targets of harassing actions. Unemployment rates are significantly higher for minorities and women, and people of color continue to earn less than White men.[13]

Fortunately, leaders can significantly reduce the rate of destructive behaviors by actively seeking to prevent and control them. Moral leaders

1. Create zero-tolerance policies that prohibit antisocial actions. (We'll take a closer look at codes of ethics later in the chapter.) They insist on employee-to-employee civility, forbid aggression and sexual harassment, and prohibit discrimination. These policies also outlaw other unethical practices like lying to customers or paying kickbacks. (Case Study 9.2 on page 352 describes how one company adopted a zero-tolerance policy to eliminate bribery.)

2. Obey guidelines. As noted earlier, leaders are powerful role models. Zero-tolerance policies will have little effect if leaders do not follow the rules they set. Ironically, leaders are most likely to violate standards because they believe that they are exceptions to the rules (see the discussion of unhealthy motivations in Chapter 2). Furthermore, because they are in positions of power, leaders are freer to act uncivilly, to bully others, or to offer favors in return for sex.

3. Constantly monitor for possible violations. Destructive behavior may be hidden from the view of top leaders. Some managers are good at "kissing up and kicking down," for example. They act respectfully toward superiors while bullying employees and treating them with disrespect. Ethical leaders actively seek feedback from employees further down the organizational hierarchy. They conduct 360-degree reviews that allow employees to rate their supervisors and provide channels (human relations departments, open door policies) for reporting misbehaviors. Those who come forward with complaints are protected from retribution.

4. Move quickly when standards are violated. Ethical leaders recognize that failing to act sends the wrong message, undermining ethical climate. If left unchecked, incivility escalates into aggression. A culture of aggression forms when abusive members are allowed to act as role models. Victims of sexual harassment won't come forward if they think that their leaders won't respond. Patterns of discrimination perpetuate themselves unless leaders intervene.

5. Address the underlying factors that trigger destructive actions. Moral leaders try to screen out potential employees who have a history of destructive behavior. They also try to eliminate situational elements that produce antisocial action. Important contextual triggers include unpleasant working conditions, job stress, oppressive supervision, perceived injustice (see the discussion below), and extreme competitiveness.[14]

Justice

Treating people fairly or justly is another hallmark of an ethical organizational climate. Justice in the workplace takes three forms: distributive, procedural, and interactional. Ethical organizations strive to distribute outcomes like pay, office space, time off, and other organizational resources as fairly as possible. They use fair procedures or policies to make these determinations. Further, moral leaders treat people with dignity and respect and share information about how decisions are made.[15]

Perceptions of justice or injustice have been found to have powerful effects on the attitudes and behaviors of organizational members.[16] Those who believe that their organizations are just are generally more satisfied, committed, trusting, and accepting of authority. They are also more likely to engage in such moral behaviors as helping out other employees and reporting ethical violations to management. In contrast, perceptions of unfair treatment increase such withdrawal behaviors as neglecting job responsibilities, absenteeism, and quitting. Those who believe they have experienced injustice are also more likely to engage in dark-side behaviors like sexual harassment, incivility, and exacting revenge on coworkers or the organization as a whole. In addition, they are less likely to report ethical problems to management.

Strategies for promoting fairness or justice include the following:[17]

- Distribute pay and other benefits according to a well-structured system; explain how pay raises are granted.
- Provide other benefits (training, time off) to employees when they are asked to do more but the budget doesn't allow for raises.
- Offer clear explanations for how resources like budgets and space are distributed; tie decisions to organizational values and purpose.
- Base performance appraisal on job-related criteria; clarify standards and expectations in advance and allow for feedback.
- Involve followers in decision-making processes (grant them a significant voice).
- Allow employees to challenge or appeal job decisions.
- Deal truthfully with organizational members.
- Supply rationale for layoffs and firings; express sincerity, kindness, and remorse.
- Follow through on reports of ethical violations; punish wrongdoers.
- Offer public apologies for injustices and offer compensation to victims of injustice.

Integrity

Integrity is ethical soundness, wholeness, and consistency.[18] All units and organizational levels share a commitment to high moral standards, backing up their ethical talk with their ethical walk. Consistency increases the level of trust, encouraging members and units to be vulnerable to one another. They are more willing to share undistorted information, negotiate in good faith, take risks, share authority for making decisions, collaborate, and follow through on promises. Organizational productivity and performance improve as a result (see Chapter 6).

According to business ethicist Lynn Paine, managers who act with integrity see ethics as a driving force of an enterprise. These leaders recognize that ethical values largely define what an organization is and what it hopes to accomplish. They keep these values in mind when making routine decisions. Their goal? To help constituents learn to govern their own behavior by following these same principles. Paine believes that any effort to improve organizational integrity must include the following elements:[19]

There are sensible, clearly communicated values and commitments. These values and commitments spell out the organization's obligations to external stakeholders (customers, suppliers, neighbors) while appealing to insiders. In highly ethical organizations, members take shared values seriously and don't hesitate to talk about them.

Company leaders are committed to and act on the values. Leaders consistently back the values, use them when making choices, and determine priorities when ethical obligations conflict with one another. For example, former Southwest Airlines president Herb Kelleher put a high value both on the needs of his employees and on customer service. However, it's clear that his workers came first. He didn't hesitate to take their side when customers unfairly criticized them. Such principled leadership was missing at Arthur Andersen, which used to be one of the largest accounting firms in the country. Andersen accountants certified the financial statements of Qwest, Waste Management, Boston Chicken, Global Crossing, WorldCom, and the Baptist Foundation of Arizona, which were all found guilty of accounting fraud. They were reluctant to challenge the accounting practices of clients because they didn't want to lose lucrative consulting contracts with these organizations. Andersen's managing partners dissolved the firm after executives were convicted for obstruction of justice for shredding Enron documents.[20]

The values are part of the routine decision-making process and are factored into every important organizational activity. Ethical considerations shape such activities as planning and goal setting, spending, gathering and sharing information, evaluation, and promotion.

Systems and structures support and reinforce organizational commitments. Systems and structures, such as the organizational chart, how work is processed, budgeting procedures, and product development, serve the organization's values. (I'll have more to say about the relationship between ethics and structure later in the chapter.)

Leaders throughout the organization have the knowledge and skills they need to make ethical decisions. Organizational leaders make ethical choices every day. To demonstrate integrity, they must have the necessary skills, knowledge, and experience. Ethics education and training must be part of their professional development.

Paine and other observers warn us not to confuse integrity with compliance. Ethical compliance strategies are generally responses to outside pressures such as media scrutiny, the U.S. Sentencing Commission guidelines, or the Sarbanes–Oxley Act. Under these federal guidelines, corporate executives can be fined and jailed not only for their ethical misdeeds but also for failing to take reasonable steps to prevent the illegal behavior of employees. Although compliance tactics look good to outsiders, they frequently don't have a lasting impact on ethical climate.[21] Large firms typically have formal ethics strategies in place, including ethics codes and policies, ethics officers, and systems for registering and dealing with ethical concerns and complaints. However, all too often these programs have minimal influence on company operations. Policies are frequently not enforced; ethics officials may devote only a small portion of their time to their ethical duties; some complaint hotlines are rarely used. In addition, CEOs rarely talk to their ethics officers or communicate to employees about ethics. Many lower-level workers receive no ethics training at all in a given year.[22]

Process Focus (Concern for Means and Ends)

Concern for how an organization achieves its goals is another important indicator of a healthy ethical climate. In far too many organizations, leaders set demanding performance goals but intentionally or unintentionally ignore how these objectives are to be reached. Instead, they pressure employees to produce sales and profits by whatever means possible. Followers then feel powerless and alienated, becoming estranged from the rest of the group. Sociologists use the term *anomie* to refer to this sense of normlessness and unease that results when rules lose their force.[23] Anomie increases the likelihood that group members will engage in illegal activities and reduces their resistance to demands from authority figures who want them to break the law. (Turn to "Leadership Ethics at the Movies: *Glengarry Glen Ross*" for an example of employees driven to win at any cost.) Loss of confidence in the organization may also encourage alienated employees to retaliate against coworkers and the group as a whole.

Leaders can address the problem of anomie by making sure that goals are achieved through ethical means. False promises cannot be used to land accounts, all debts must be fully disclosed to investors, kickbacks are prohibited, and so on. They can also make a stronger link between means and ends through ethics programs that address all aspects of organizational ethical performance.

LEADERSHIP ETHICS AT THE MOVIES

GLENGARRY GLEN ROSS

Key Cast Members: Jack Lemmon, Alec Baldwin, Al Pacino, Ed Harris, Alan Arkin, Kevin Spacey

Synopsis: Chicago resort property salesmen find themselves in a high-stakes sales contest. The winner gets a Cadillac, the second-place finisher receives a set of steak knives, and the losers get fired. Desperate to keep their jobs, members of the sales force will do anything to close a deal, including using high-pressure tactics, lying to potential buyers, and stealing sales leads. Pacino stars as the office hot shot and Lemmon as Shelley, the down-on-his-luck agent convinced that he hasn't lost his sales touch. Based on the Pulitzer Prize–winning play of the same name.

Themes: anomie, unhealthy organizational climate, deception, abuse of power, unethical rewards, greed, antisocial behavior

Discussion Starters

1. What signs of an unhealthy ethical organizational climate do you see at this firm? Whom do you blame for creating this atmosphere?

2. Which unethical sales practice do you find most troubling?

3. Should Shelley be condemned, pitied, or both?

Structural Reinforcement

An organization's structure shouldn't undermine the ethical standards of its members, but as I noted in our discussion of integrity, it should encourage higher ethical performance on the part of both leaders and followers. Three elements of an organization's structure have a particularly strong impact on moral behavior:

1. *Monetary and nonmonetary reward systems.* Organizations often encourage unethical behavior by rewarding it.[24] Consider the case of the software company that paid programmers $20 to correct each software bug they found. Soon programmers were deliberately creating bugs to fix! Another software firm headquartered in Korea gave large incentives to salespeople for making lofty sales targets. This encouraged employees to misrepresent sales by reporting that customers had paid when they had not and by having fellow workers pose as clients. In one 9-month period, 70% of reported sales were fictitious.[25] A visit to the local 10-minute oil change shop provides another case of the impact of misplaced rewards. Some lube and oil franchises pay managers and employees based in part

on how many additional services and parts they sell beyond the basic oil change. As a consequence, unscrupulous mechanics persuade car owners to buy unneeded air filters, transmission flushes, and wiper blades. (Turn to Case Study 9.3 on page 355 for another example of a company that rewarded unethical behavior.) It is not always easy to determine all the consequences of a particular reward system. However, ethical leaders make every effort to ensure that desired moral behaviors are rewarded, not discouraged.

SOURCE: Dilbert: @Scott Adams/United Features Syndicate, Inc.

2. *Performance and evaluation processes.* Performance and evaluation processes must reflect the balance between means and ends described earlier, monitoring both *how* and *whether* goals are achieved. Ethically insensitive monitoring processes fail to detect illegal and immoral behavior and may actually make such practices more likely. As noted earlier, when poor behavior goes unpunished, followers may assume that leaders condone and expect such actions. Former giant brokerage house Salomon Inc. is a case in point. In the early 1990s, a government securities trader at the firm violated Treasury regulations and confessed to then CEO John Gutfreund. Gutfreund took no action against the rogue trader, in part because he was a star performer. Failure to swiftly punish this star employee enabled him to continue his criminal behavior and cost Salomon millions in fines and much of its stock and bond business.[26]

3. *Decision-making rights and responsibilities.* Ethical conduct is more likely when workers are responsible for ethical decisions and have the authority to choose how to respond. Leaders at ethical organizations do all they can to ensure that those closest to the process or problem can communicate their concerns about ethical issues. These managers also empower followers to make and implement their choices. Unfortunately, employees with the most knowledge are often excluded from the decision-making process or lack the power to follow through on their choices. Such was the case in the *Columbia* shuttle explosion profiled in Chapter 8. Higher-ranking NASA officials dismissed the concerns of lower-level managers.

Social Responsibility

Concern for those outside the organization is another sign of a healthy ethical climate. Ethical organizations recognize that they have obligations to their communities. For example, responsible corporations engage in "triple bottom line" accounting.[27] They evaluate their success not just on financial results but also on their social and environmental performance. Good corporate citizens send volunteers to Habitat for Humanity building projects, sponsor food drives, set up philanthropic organizations to give money to needy causes, and so forth.[28] At the same time, they address environmental problems by taking such steps as capping plant emissions, using recycled components, creating less toxic products, reducing oil consumption, and buying from environmentally friendly suppliers. For example, Starbucks incorporates social responsibility into its corporate values. One of its guiding principles is "sustaining coffee communities." Another is "contributing positively to communities and the environment." Individual stores are free to promote local charities through volunteer hours, store products, and cash contributions. Corporate headquarters supports literacy programs and disaster relief. To measure its progress, the firm commissions an annual social responsibility report that indicates whether the company is reaching its social goals.[29] (More examples of socially responsible corporations can be found in the discussion of corporate values to follow.)

Recognizing the legitimate claims of stakeholders is key to social responsibility. Stakeholders are any group affected by or having a stake in the organization's policies and operations. Organizational stakeholders might include shareholders, suppliers, competitors, customers, creditors, unions, governments, local communities, and the general public.[30] Stakeholder theorists argue that organizational leaders have an ethical obligation to consider such groups because they have intrinsic value and ought to be treated justly. Reaching out to these parties contributes to the common good of society.[31] Socially responsible organizations try to identify all stakeholders and their interests. They seek to be accountable to these groups, cooperating with them whenever possible and minimizing the negative impact of organizational activities. When needed, these organizations engage in dialogue with their critics, as Nike did after years of ignoring public outcry about conditions at its overseas suppliers. The firm invited human rights, labor, and environmental officials to company headquarters to discuss international worker issues.[32]

Climate-Building Tools

To build or create ethical organizational climates, leaders rely heavily on three tools: core values, codes of ethics, and ethical learning.

Discovering Core Values

Identifying and applying ethical values is an important step to creating a highly moral climate. Leaders promoting integrity first define and then focus attention on central ethical values. I noted in Chapter 3 that comparing responses on a standardized value list can be a way to clarify group and organizational priorities. In this section, I will introduce additional strategies specifically designed to reveal shared values, purposes, and assumptions.

Core Ideology

Management experts James Collins and Jerry Porras use the term *core ideology* to refer to the central identity or character of an organization. The character of outstanding companies remains constant even as these firms continually learn and adapt. According to Collins and Porras, "truly great companies understand the difference between what should never change and what should be open for change, between what is genuinely sacred and what is not."[33]

Core values are the first component of core ideology. (See Box 9.1 for some examples.) One way to determine whether a value is sacred to your organization is to ask, "What would happen if we were penalized for holding this standard?" If you can't honestly say that you would keep this value if it cost your group market share or profits, then it shouldn't show up on your final list. To determine core values, Collins and Porras recommend the Mars Group technique. In this approach, participants imagine they have been asked to re-create the very best attributes of their organization (school, business, nonprofit) on another planet. Groups are limited to 5–7 people since space on the rocket ship is limited. Group members work from personal to organizational values by considering these questions:

What core values (values that you would hold regardless of whether they were rewarded) do you personally bring to your work?

What values would you tell your children that you hold at work and that you hope they will hold as working adults?

If you woke up tomorrow morning with enough money to retire, would you continue to live with those core values? Can you envision them being as valid for you 100 years from now as they are today?

Would you want to hold these core values even if one or more of them became a competitive disadvantage?

If you were to start a new organization in a different line of work, what core values would you build into the new organization regardless of industry?

Groups summarize their conclusions and present them to others in the organization, comparing their values with those of other groups traveling on other spaceships.

Core purpose is the second part of an organization's ideology. *Purpose* is the group's reason for being that reflects the ideals of its members. Here are some examples of corporate purpose statements:[34]

To be the world's best staffing services company and to be recognized as the best. (Kelly Services)

To bring inspiration and innovation to every athlete in the world. (Nike)

To be the most powerful one-stop shop to connect people with the wonders of modern technology. (RadioShack)

To simply delight you . . . every day. (Sara Lee)

Dedication to the highest quality of customer service delivered with a sense of warmth, friendliness, individual pride, and company spirit. (Southwest Airlines)

Asking the "Five Whys" is one way to identify organizational purpose. Start with a description of what your organization does and then ask why that activity is important five separate times. Each "Why?" will get you closer to the fundamental mission of your group.

BOX 9.1 CORE VALUES

Eaton Corporation

- Make our customers the focus of everything we do
- Recognize our people as our greatest asset
- Treat each other with respect
- Be fair, honest, and open
- Be considerate of the environment and our communities
- Keep our commitments
- Strive for excellence

(Continued)

(Continued)

Levi Strauss

- Empathy—Walking in other people's shoes
- Originality—Being authentic and innovative
- Integrity—Doing the right thing
- Courage—Standing up for what we believe

Amgen Inc.

- Be science-based
- Compete intensely and win
- Create value for patients, staff, and stockholders
- Be ethical
- Trust and respect each other
- Ensure quality
- Work in teams
- Collaborate, communicate, and be accountable

Denny's

- Giving our best
- Appreciating others
- A can-do attitude

First Horizon National Corporation

- Exceptional teamwork
- Individual accountability
- Absolute determination
- Knowing our customers
- Doing the right thing

Charles Stewart Mott Foundation

- Act honestly, truthfully, and with integrity
- Treat every individual with dignity and respect
- Be responsible, transparent and accountable
- Benefit communities

SOURCES: Abrahams, J. (2007). *101 mission statements from top companies.* Berkeley, CA: Ten Speed Press; Kidder, R. M. (2004). Foundation codes of ethics: Why do they matter, what are they, and how are they relevant to philanthropy? *New Decisions for Philanthropic Fundraising, 45,* 75–83.

Your organization's purpose statement should inspire members. (Don't make high profits or stock dividends your goal because they don't motivate people at every level of the organization.) Your purpose should also serve as an organizational anchor. Every other element of your organization (business plans, expansion efforts, buildings, products) will come and go, but your purpose and values will remain.

Appreciative Inquiry

Appreciative inquiry (AI) is another effective tool for developing a shared understanding of ethical values. Participants in the AI process set out to discover the organization's "positive core" and use the group's strengths to guide individual and collective action.[35] Appreciative inquiry has been used in a variety of organizational settings to, for example, promote creativity and innovation, facilitate strategic planning, boost quality, and reduce employee turnover, as well as to improve ethical performance.

AI begins by choosing an affirmative topic, based on the assumption that what organizational members study will determine the kind of organizations they create. Asking positive questions ("What are our values?" "What does ethics mean to us?") elicits positive examples and achievements. Once the affirmative topic is selected, appreciative inquiry moves through four stages: discovery, dream, design, and destiny.

The discovery phase identifies "the best of what has been and what is." Interviews and brainstorming sessions highlight organizational achievements and important traditions. These could include stories of organizational heroes and how the organization lived up to its commitments during tough times or descriptions of the group's tradition of social responsibility. In the dream phase participants look to the future to ask, "What might be?" They develop a vision of the organization's ethical future, focusing on the group's ultimate purpose ("What is the world calling us to become?"). The design stage incorporates both the discovery and dream phases by describing exactly how the organization will look and act if it lives up to its values. This ideal organization integrates the positive core elements of the group into the dream created by participants. For example: a place where everyone can voice his or her concerns about unethical behavior without fear of punishment, or a place where commitment to the community takes precedence over short-term profits. In the last stage—destiny—participants collectively commit themselves to building the desired organization. They might design tactics for encouraging dissent, for instance, or develop new community outreach programs.

South African industrial/organizational psychologists Leon van Vuuren and Freddie Crous describe how one university department used appreciative inquiry to develop "an ethical way forward."[36] After identifying core ethical values and experiences during the discovery phase, department members identified four key themes during the dream stage. They then put these values in the form of propositions during the design phase. Their important propositions included "We are committed to personal growth and meaningful work," "We respect the uniqueness and contributions of others," and "We act with integrity supported by visible ethical leadership." Departmental members committed themselves to supporting these values, which were formalized in a code of ethics, during the destiny stage.

Codes of Ethics

Codes of ethics are among the most common ethics tools. Companies listed on the New York Stock Exchange and the NASDAQ are required to have them, and under the Sarbanes–Oxley Act, public firms must disclose whether they have a code for their senior executives.[37] Many government departments, professional associations, social service agencies, and schools have developed codes as well. Nevertheless, formal ethics statements are as controversial as they are popular. Skeptics make these criticisms:[38]

- Codes are too vague to be useful.
- Codes may not be widely distributed or read.
- Most codes are developed as public relations documents designed solely to improve an organization's image.
- Codes don't improve the ethical climate of an organization or produce more ethical behavior.
- Codes often become the final word on the subject of ethics.
- Codes are hard to apply across cultures and in different situations.
- Codes often lack adequate enforcement provisions.
- Codes often fail to spell out which ethical obligations should take priority, or they put the needs of the organization ahead of those of society as a whole.
- Adherence to codes often goes unrewarded.

The experience of Enron highlights the shortcomings of formal ethical statements. Company officials had a "beautifully written" code of ethics that specifically prohibited the off-the-books financial deals that led to its bankruptcy (see Chapter 1).[39] Unfortunately, these same executives convinced the board of directors to waive this prohibition.

Defenders of ethical codes point to their potential benefits. First, a code describes an organization's ethical stance both to members and to the outside world. Newcomers, in particular, look to the code for guidance about an organization's ethical standards and values. They learn about potential ethical problems they may face in carrying out their duties. Second, a formal ethics statement can improve the group's image while protecting it from lawsuits and further regulation. In the case of wrongdoing, an organization can point to the code as evidence that the unethical behavior is limited to a few individuals and not the policy of the company as a whole. Third, referring to a code can encourage followers and leaders to resist unethical group and organizational pressures. Fourth, a written document can have a direct, positive influence on ethical behavior. Students who sign honor codes, for example, are significantly less likely to plagiarize and cheat on tests.[40] (See Case Study 9.1 for a closer look at one form of academic cheating.) Employees in companies with formal codes of ethics judge themselves, their coworkers, and their leaders to be more ethical than workers in companies that don't have codes. Members of code organizations believe that their organizations are more supportive of ethical behavior and express a higher level of organizational commitment.[41]

There's no doubt that a code of ethics can be a vague document that has little impact on how members act. A number of organizations use these statements for purposes of image, not integrity. They want to appear concerned about ethical issues while protecting themselves from litigation. Just having a code on file, as in the case of Enron, doesn't mean that it will be read or used. Nonetheless, creating an ethical statement can be an important first step on the road to organizational integrity. Although a code doesn't guarantee moral improvement, it is hard to imagine an ethical organization without one. Codes can focus attention on important ethical standards, outline expectations, and help people act more appropriately. They have the most impact when senior executives make them a priority and follow their provisions while rewarding followers who do the same.

CASE STUDY 9.1

TURN IT IN OR TURN IT OFF?

Access to the World Wide Web makes plagiarizing much easier for students. They now have access to literally billions of written documents and can quickly cut and paste sentences or sections from these sources into their papers or submit entire documents as their own. According to one survey, 40% of students admit to cutting and pasting work from the Internet without citing the source. Approximately 77% believe online plagiarism is "not a serious issue."[1]

(Continued)

(Continued)

To catch cheaters, professors and universities are turning to plagiarism detection programs. These programs compare student work against databases to determine how much of a paper copies or paraphrases from other sources. Turnitin, which is a product of the iParadigms LLC, is the most popular plagiarism detection software. Turnitin not only draws upon popular databases and websites; it also compares submissions to its database of previously submitted student papers. The program highlights sections from other sources, and provides an estimated percentage of questionable material in a paper along with links to the original sources.

Over 9,000 colleges, universities, and high schools use Turnitin. Students typically submit their preliminary or final work to the site, which then provides a report to the instructor. Many teachers and professors are enthusiastic about the product. Not only does Turnitin catch violators, but its reports also serve as evidence to back up charges of plagiarism. Before Turnitin, many instructors were in the same position as the English teacher who said she "felt like I was losing the battle in terms of being certain that students were accountable for their own work."[2] There is evidence that plagiarism detection programs like Turnitin serve as deterrents, reducing instances of plagiarism. Plagiarism detection software can also be used as a teaching tool to highlight what plagiarism is and to reduce cases of inadvertent cheating.

A significant number of instructors and students are opposed to Turnitin. Princeton, for example, refuses to purchase the software. Some critics contend that the site violates students' rights by retaining their work (40 million papers so far) without paying them for their efforts, thereby enriching the owners of the company at their expense. Students also fear that their work may be released to the public if, say, iParadigms LLC is sold. Then, too, requiring class members to submit their papers to Turnitin and similar sites assumes that they are guilty until proven innocent and undermines trust between students and faculty. According to Teresa Fishman, director of the Center for Academic Integrity at Clemson University, "There is no reason to suspect that the students have cheated yet. To set that environment up where there is a presumption of guilt sets up an unhappy situation in the classroom."[3]

Imagine that your college or university is considering the use of Turnitin or another plagiarism detection program. What recommendation would you make to decision makers? Why? If your institution already has such a program in place, would you recommend that it be retained? Discontinued? Modified? Support your position.

Notes

1. MacMillan, D. (2007, March 13). Looking over Turnitin's shoulder. *Businessweek.* Retrieved from http://www.businessweek.com/technology/content/mar2007/tc20070313_733103.htm

2. Solochek, J. S. (2009, September 3). Web site helps Wiregrass Ranch High educators detect student plagiarism. *St. Petersburg Times,* p. 9.

3. Solochek.

Sources

Chao, C. A., Wilhelm, W. J., & Neureuther, B. D. (2009). A study of electronic detection and pedagogical approaches for reducing plagiarism. *The Delta Pi Epsilon Journal, LI,* 31–42.

Dye, J. (2007, September). To catch a cheat. *Econtent,* pp. 32–37.

Marklein, M. B. (2009, November 19). The case of the purloined term paper. *USA Today,* p. 10B.

Read, B. (2008, February 29). Anti-cheating crusader vexes some professors. *The Chronicle of Higher Education,* The Faculty, p. 1.

Righton, B. (2007, June 11). How not to catch a thief. *Maclean's,* p. 62.

Communication ethicist Richard Johannsen believes that many of the objections to formal codes could be overcome by following these guidelines:[42]

- Distinguish between ideals and minimum conditions. Identify which parts of the statement are goals to strive for and which are minimal or basic ethical standards.
- Design the code for ordinary circumstances. Members shouldn't have to demonstrate extraordinary courage or make unusual sacrifices in order to follow the code. Ensure that average employees can follow its guidelines.
- Use clear, specific language. Important abstract terms such as *reasonable, distort,* and *falsify* should be explained and illustrated.
- Prioritize obligations. Which commitments are most important to the client? The public? The employer? The profession?
- Protect the larger community. Don't protect the interests of the organization at the expense of the public. Speak to the needs of outside groups.
- Focus on issues of particular importance to group members. Every organization and profession will face particular ethical dilemmas and temptations. For instance, lawyers must balance duties to clients with their responsibilities as officers of the court. Doctors try to provide the best care while health maintenance organizations pressure them to keep costs down. The code should address the group's unique moral issues.
- Stimulate further discussion and modification. Don't file the code away or treat it as the final word on the subject of collective ethics. Use it to spark ethical discussion and modify its provisions when needed.

- Provide guidance for the entire organization and the profession to which it belongs. Spell out the consequences when the business or nonprofit as a whole acts unethically. Who should respond and how? What role should outside groups (professional associations, accrediting bodies, regulatory agencies) play in responding to the organization's ethical transgressions?
- Outline the moral principles behind the code. Explain *why* an action is right based on ethical standards (communitarianism, utilitarianism, altruism) like those described in Chapter 5.
- Encourage widespread input. Draw on all constituencies, including management, union members, and professionals, when developing the provisions of the code.
- Back the code with enforcement. Create procedures for interpreting the code and applying sanctions. Ethics offices and officers should set up systems for reporting problems, investigating charges, and reaching conclusions. Possible punishments for ethical transgressions include informal warnings, formal reprimands that are entered into employment files, suspensions without pay, and terminations.

Most codes of ethics address the following:[43]

- *Conflicts of interest.* Conflicts of interest arise when an employee benefits at the expense of the organization or can't exercise independent judgment because of an investment, activity, or association. Even the appearance of a conflict of interest is problematic.
- *Records, funds, and assets.* Organizations must keep accurate records and protect funds and other assets. Such records (including financial statements) must meet state and federal regulations.
- *Information.* In for-profit organizations, employees can be liable if they or even their families reveal confidential information that undermines performance or competitive advantage. In the public sector, codes of ethics encourage employees to share rather than to withhold information from the public.
- *Outside relationships.* This category addresses contact with customers, suppliers, competitors, contractors, and other outside individuals and organizations, and includes prohibitions against bad-mouthing the competition, price fixing, and the sharing of sensitive information.
- *Employment practices.* This category covers discrimination, sexual harassment, drug use, voluntary activities, and related human resource issues.
- *Other practices.* This category sets policies related to a variety of other topics, including health and safety, the use of technology, the environment, political activities, and the use of organizational assets for personal benefit.

If you're interested in developing or refining a code of ethics, you can use the examples in Box 9.2 as a model.

BOX 9.2 ETHICS CODES

A SAMPLER

Conflicts of Interest (Cummins Inc.)

All of Cummins's employees are expected to use nondiscriminatory practices throughout the supplier selection process. Every employee is expected to avoid any situation in which his or her interests (or those of his or her family) may conflict with the interests of the company. Every employee with a financial interest in any actual or potential supplier or customer must disclose that interest to his or her supervisor immediately and, if applicable, in his or her annual Ethics Certification Statement.

In general, employees should neither accept nor offer gifts to customers or suppliers unless the gifts are designated as part of a recognized business event.

Gifts exceeding U.S. $50 in value may be given or accepted only with the concurrence of an employee's supervisor. All gifts (except minor promotional token items) not reported and approved by the employee's supervisor must be reported annually on the Ethics Certification Statement.

Records, Funds, and Assets (Honeywell)

Honeywell's financial, accounting, and other reports and records will accurately and fairly reflect the transactions and financial condition of the company in reasonable detail, and in accordance with generally accepted and company-approved accounting principles, practices and procedures, and applicable government regulations.

Protecting Information (Coca-Cola)

Safeguard the company's nonpublic information, which includes everything from contracts and pricing information to marketing plans, technical specifications, and employee information.

Outside Relationships (Eaton)

We respect the rights of competitors, customers, and suppliers. The only competitive advantages we seek are those gained through superior research, engineering, manufacturing, and marketing. We do not engage in unfair or illegal trade practices.

(Continued)

(Continued)

Employment Practices (Cummins Inc.)

Treatment of Each Other at Work

Each employee will treat every other employee, every customer, every vendor, and all others met in the course of work with dignity and respect. Harassment of any type in the workplace will not be tolerated.

Other Practices (PPG Industries)

Political Activity Policy

1. Each employee is encouraged to participate in the electoral process at all levels of government by voting and supporting candidates and issues of his or her choice.

2. No employee shall, directly or indirectly, contribute or expend any of the company's money, property, services, or other things of value for any use prohibited by laws regulating the electoral process or the political activity of corporations.

SOURCES: Center for the Study of Ethics in the Professions at Illinois Institute of Technology. (2010). *Index of codes.* Retrieved from http://ethics.iit.edu/codes; The Coca-Cola Code of Business Conduct. Retrieved from http://www.thecoca-colacompany.com/ourcompany/business_conduct .html.

Continuous Ethical Improvement

The Need for Continuous Ethical Learning

Total quality management (TQM) describes a continuous improvement process designed to reduce product defects, improve response times, and eliminate waste. The TQM movement is founded on the belief that organizations, like individuals, learn through experience, observation, training, and other means. Although all organizations learn, some learn faster and more efficiently than others, a characteristic that gives them a competitive edge. Those that learn quickly produce better products in less time while responding to demographic shifts and technological advances. High-tech firms are particularly aware of the importance of rapid learning. They scramble to stay ahead in the development of memory chips, cell phones, software, and other products.

Organizations ought to be as concerned about continuous ethical improvement, what I'll call total ethical management (TEM), as they are about improving products and services.[44] Three factors should encourage ongoing ethical learning: risk, lingering ethical weaknesses, and change. Let's take a closer look at each.

Risk. As we've seen, serious ethical misbehavior can threaten the very survival of an organization. Accounting fraud is a quick path to corporate bankruptcy, malfeasance in government agencies leads to budget reductions, and contributions dry up when the leaders of social service agencies and religious groups live like royalty. Managerial misconduct (whether motivated by poor judgment or criminal intent) is now a leading cause of business crises. No type of organization, be it religious, humanitarian, business, government, or military, is exempt from ethical failure.

On a more positive note, there is evidence that moral organizations can be extremely effective, as noted in the introduction to this chapter. The Body Shop, Longaberger, Texas Instruments, Chick-fil-A, Ben & Jerry's, Tom's of Maine, Herman Miller, and ServiceMaster are highly successful as well as highly ethical. Shared values can increase productivity by focusing the efforts of employees and by encouraging supervisors to empower their subordinates. Having a good reputation attracts customers, clients, and investors and forms the basis for long-term relationships with outside constituencies.[45]

Ethical Weakness. Organizations can never claim to have arrived when it comes to ethical development. There will always be room for improvement. In addition, the same inconsistencies that plague individual leaders are found in the climate of entire organizations. Starbucks, which I cited earlier as a positive example, has been criticized for not paying coffee growers enough. Valuable rainforest has been destroyed in order to grow its coffee beans.

Change. Organizational leaders must recognize that they operate in constantly shifting environments. Competitors, suppliers, government regulations, and public tastes are always changing. Each change, in turn, brings new ethical challenges. Take the case of genetically altered foods. Opponents are raising moral objections to these products. They worry about their safety and their impact on the environment. Critics believe that biotechnology companies are putting the health of consumers and the future of native plants and animals at risk. Leaders of biotech companies must now publicly acknowledge and respond to these arguments.

Like the environments in which they live, organizations themselves are in a constant process of transformation. New employees join, divisions reorganize, companies become publicly owned, and products and services are added or dropped. Each change alters the ethical landscape. Consider the impact of a changing workforce, for instance. As more women and minorities join an organization, leaders need to focus more attention on diversity issues. They must consider such questions as "How do we make all individuals feel like valued team members?" "How do we ensure that everyone has an equal chance of being promoted, regardless of background?" "How far do we go to meet the needs of subgroups (working mothers, nonnative speakers, and religious minorities)?" (We'll start to develop some answers to these questions in the next chapter.)

Enhancing Organizational Ethical Learning

Ethical development, like other forms of organizational learning, is more likely under the right conditions. Key factors that spur organizational learning and continuous ethical improvement include the following.[46]

Scanning Imperative. Ethical learners look outside the immediate group for information. They continually scan the environment for emerging ethical issues that might affect the organization in the future. Global warming is one such issue. In just the past few years, organizations of all kinds have had to determine how they can reduce their carbon emissions. Ongoing learners monitor newspapers and trade journals to identify questionable industry practices and consider the ethical impact of entering a new market or introducing a new product (see the earlier discussion of genetically altered foods). In addition, moral leaders look closely at what other organizations do to prevent and to manage ethical problems. Organizational learning theorists call this process benchmarking. In benchmarking, groups identify outstanding organizations and isolate the practices that make them so effective. They then adapt these practices to their own organizations.[47]

Information on effective ethical practices can be found in a variety of sources. You may want to draw on these as you identify ethical benchmarks. Managerial texts and business ethics books include examples of moral and immoral behavior, sample ethics codes, and case studies. There are also two academic journals—the *Journal of Business Ethics* and *Business Ethics Quarterly*—devoted exclusively to ethics in the workplace. Information on corporate mission and values, social responsibility, academic cheating, religion and ethics, and other ethical topics can be found on a host of websites.

Performance Gap. A performance gap is the distance between where an organization is and where it would like to be. Martin Marietta is one example of an organization that recognized its ethical failings and took steps to correct them. The defense contractor, under investigation for improper billings in the mid-1980s, responded by highlighting its code of conduct, starting an ethics training program, developing a system for reporting ethical concerns, and rewarding executives for moral behavior. As a result, the company (which later merged with Lockheed) improved its compliance with federal regulations and reduced the number of ethical complaints filed by employees. The firm also prevented a number of potential crises stemming from bad management, safety problems, and discrimination.

Some organizations turn their moral failures into case studies. At West Point, Army instructors used the massacre of civilians at My Lai during the Vietnam War to teach ethical principles to cadets. Organizations don't have to wait for an ethical disaster to strike to identify performance gaps, of course. Ethics audits (surveys that measure employee perceptions of values and corporate behavior), ethics hotlines, and focus groups track the moral climate of the group as a whole. Ethics items on performance appraisal forms provide data on individual performance.

Climate of Openness. Openness is, first of all, the free flow of information. In open organizations, leaders make a conscious effort to reduce barriers of all kinds between individuals and units. In this environment, new ideas are more likely to develop and then to be shared throughout the group as a whole. Learning leaders put few restrictions on what can be shared, rotate people between divisions, set up forums for sharing ideas, and form multidepartment task forces. In addition, they create formal (company-wide forums, idea fairs) and informal (employee cafeterias, celebrations) settings where members can meet and share information about projects, procedures, and ethics.

Openness also refers to the type of communication that occurs between group members. In learning organizations, people engage in dialogue (see Chapter 8). They recognize that they can glean important information from anyone, regardless of status. When they interact, members treat others as equals and are more interested in understanding than in being understood. They work together to create shared meaning.

Ethical dialogue can be facilitated through designated dialogue sessions. In these gatherings, members meet to engage in open communication about moral questions. Dialogue sessions work best when attendees complete assigned readings in advance, meet in a quiet setting, convene at a round table or in a circle to emphasize equality, and suspend their opinions and judgments.[48]

Continuous Education. Continuous education reflects the organization-wide commitment to the never-ending process of learning. Organizations that value learning will make it a priority everywhere, not just in the training department. These groups (a) support on-the-job training (such as when an experienced worker helps a new hire resolve an ethical problem), (b) hold retreats, (c) encourage networking and dialogue, and (d) send people to conferences, classes, and workshops to learn more about ethics.

Involved Leadership. Leaders play a critical role in driving continuous ethical improvement. The key is hands-on involvement. Involved leaders are students. They encourage the learning of others by first learning themselves. If they want to promote diversity, for instance, they are the first to take diversity training. They continue to be involved in the learning process by interacting with followers, visiting job sites, and holding forums on ethical issues.

System Perspective. The system perspective refers to seeing the big picture, to recognizing that organizations are highly interdependent. Ongoing ethical learners try to anticipate the ethical implications of their decisions for those in other divisions. A big-picture leader may be tempted to "dump" an incompetent employee onto another department but recognizes that this strategy benefits her unit at the expense of another. The productivity of the organization as a whole suffers because this ineffective person is still on the payroll. With this in mind, she confronts the problem employee immediately. (See Box 9.3 for one example of an ethical learning strategy that addresses organizational systems.)

The open communication climate described earlier facilitates system thinking. Communicating across boundaries helps members develop a better understanding of the ethical problems faced by other units and learn how their actions may result in moral complications for others.

BOX 9.3 FRIENDLY DISENTANGLING

Boston College business ethics professor Richard Nielsen introduces "friendly disentangling" as an effective strategy for addressing problematic (unethical) organizational traditions. He describes this method as a form of action learning that both respects and criticizes ongoing tradition while pushing for reform. Friendly disentangling is based on four principles. First, there is good in everyone. Second, systems, not individuals, are the cause of many unethical behaviors. Third, others ought to be approached in a friendly, cheerful manner. Fourth, solving systems problems requires ongoing experimental learning.

To illustrate how friendly disentangling works, professor Nielsen describes how John Woolman, a 18th-century Philadelphia Quaker cloth merchant and activist, used this approach to convince farmers to abandon the use of slaves, and how Robert Greenleaf (see Chapter 6) employed this method to increase the percentage of Black managers at AT&T between 1955 and 1964.[1] The method incorporates the following four components:

1. *Develop a "we" relationship with others, and look for the source of the problematic behavior within "our" shared tradition system rather than in individuals.* Woolman assumed there was good even in slave owners. Greenleaf had worked for many years with managers at AT&T and reminded himself that these were basically good people working in a system that was biased against African Americans. He wanted to confront the problem of discrimination but do so in a cooperative manner.

2. *Approach those involved in a friendly manner and suggest that there may be problems in our shared tradition system.* Woolman was friendly and cheerful when he approached slaveholders and initiated dialogue about the problems with slavery. Greenleaf would express his appreciation and respect for managers, reminding them of his long-standing relationships with them before introducing the topic of racial bias in the AT&T organizational culture.

3. *Request help in disentangling a specific behavior from a troublesome assumption within the traditional system.* Colonial slave owners had been socialized to believe that Blacks were lazy. Woolman had to address this perception as well as their fear that rejecting slavery would also mean rejecting their parents and community. Greenleaf had to challenge the assumption that Blacks weren't suitable for management positions, which was reinforced by the fact that there were few Black managers. Few African American candidates applied for managerial openings because they knew that they were not likely to be promoted.

4. *Work with those who are agreeable to experiment with alternative behaviors.* Woolman and cooperative local Pennsylvania farmers experimented by freeing a few slaves to sharecrop. It soon became apparent that the sharecroppers were more productive than the slaves, demonstrating that Blacks could be as hardworking as Whites. Greenleaf instituted several experimental initiatives, including recruiting African Americans for management training programs and providing a wider variety of experiences to prepare them for leadership roles. As Blacks did well in these programs, more moved into management positions.

The efforts of both Woolman and Greenleaf paid off. By 1770 Colonial Quakers were forbidden to own slaves, and by 1800 Pennsylvania became the

(Continued)

(Continued)

first state south of New England to ban slavery. In a 10-year period before the passage of the Civil Rights Bill, the number of Black managers at AT&T increased from .5% to around 4.5%.

Note

1. Nielsen also uses the example of Pakistan's Chaudhry Muhammad Hussain to demonstrate how friendly disentangling is effective in non-Western societies. Hussain, a Muslim, brought together members of diverse religious and economic groups to improve the lives of farmers and build the Punjab yarn industry.

Sources

Nielsen, R. P. (1996). *The politics of ethics: Methods for acting, learning, and sometimes fighting with others in addressing ethics problems in organizational life*. Oxford, UK: Oxford University Press.

Nielsen, R. P. (1998). Quaker foundations for Greenleaf's servant-leadership and "friendly disentangling" method. In L. Spears (Ed.), *Insights on leadership* (pp. 126–144). New York: John Wiley & Sons.

Implications and Applications

- As a leader, you will serve as an ethics officer of your organization, exercising influence by the example you set for followers and by making sure that ethical messages aren't drowned out by messages about tasks and profits.
- Create a positive ethical climate that encourages moral decision making and behavior.
- Organizations have varying ethical orientations or ethical climates that affect their ethical decision making and behavior. Climates marked by self-interest are most likely to encourage unethical behavior.
- Combat the shadow side of organizational life by creating zero-tolerance policies for incivility, aggression, sexual harassment, discrimination, and other destructive actions.
- Create perceptions of organizational justice by distributing resources fairly, following equitable processes, and treating others with dignity and respect.
- Integrity develops through clearly communicated values and commitments, leaders who are committed to these values, application of the values to routine decisions, systems and structures that support organizational commitments, and members who are equipped to make wise ethical choices.
- Don't confuse compliance with integrity. Compliance protects an organization from regulation and public criticism but often has little impact on day-to-day

operations. Integrity is at the center of an organization's activities, influencing every type of decision and activity.

- Pay close attention to how your organization achieves its goals. Failure to do so will create anomie and undermine ethical performance.

- Reinforce ethical commitments in your organization through the design of monetary and nonmonetary reward systems, performance and evaluation processes, and allocation of decision-making authority.

- Ethical organizations recognize their obligations to their communities, demonstrating concern for social and environmental performance. Help your organization act in a socially responsible manner by honoring its ethical obligation to stakeholder groups.

- Shared values are essential to any healthy ethical climate. Encourage your organization to identify these values through the use of task forces, employee meetings, and other means.

- Useful codes of ethics can play an important role in shaping ethical climate. Make sure they define and illustrate important terms and address the problems faced by the members of your particular organization. View ethics statements as discussion starters, not as the final word on the topic of organizational morality.

- Risk, lingering ethical weaknesses, and constant change create a demand for continuous organizational ethical development.

- The ethical learning capacity of your organization will be determined by the presence or absence of such factors as scanning the environment, recognizing performance gaps, open communication, continuous education, involved leadership, and system thinking.

For Further Exploration, Challenge, and Self-Assessment

1. Select a well-known senior executive and determine whether this person should be classified as ethical, hypocritical, ethically neutral, or unethical. Provide evidence to support your conclusion.

2. Analyze the ethical climate of your organization. In your paper, consider the following questions: How would you classify its ethical orientation based on the "Self-Assessment: Ethical Climate Questionnaire"? Overall, would you characterize the climate as positive or negative? Why? What factors shape the moral atmosphere? What role have leaders played in its formation and maintenance? What steps does the organization take to deal with misbehaviors? Does the organization consider both means and ends? How does the group's structure reinforce (or fail to reinforce) espoused values and ethical behavior? What inconsistencies do you note? Write up your findings.

3. Discuss each of the following statements in a group or, as an alternative, argue for and against each proposition in a formal debate. Your instructor

will set the rules and time limits. Refer to the discussion of argumentation and Box 8.3 ("Common Fallacies") in the previous chapter for more information on constructing effective arguments.

Pro or con: Organizations are less ethical now than they were 10 years ago.

Pro or con: Formal codes of ethics do more harm than good.

Pro or con: Ethical businesses are more profitable over the long term.

Pro or con: Organizational values can't be developed; they must be uncovered or discovered instead.

Pro or con: An organization's purpose has to be inspirational.

Pro or con: An organization can change everything except its core values and purpose.

4. Write a research paper on one form of destructive behavior in the workplace. Conclude with suggestions to help leaders curb this type of behavior.

5. Compare and contrast an organization that has a climate of integrity with one that pursues ethical compliance.

6. Describe a time when you experienced anomie in an organization. What factors led to your feelings of powerlessness and alienation? How did anomie influence your behavior? As an alternative, reflect on a time when you felt you were treated unjustly in an organization. What factors led you to believe you were being treated unfairly? How did experiencing injustice influence your behavior?

7. Develop a shared set of values for your class using strategies presented in the chapter.

8. Evaluate an ethical code based on chapter guidelines. What are its strengths and weaknesses? How useful would it be to members of the organization? How could the code be improved? What can we learn from this statement?

CASE STUDY 9.2

ROOTING OUT CORRUPTION AT SIEMENS GLOBAL

For many years offering bribes was business as usual at Siemens Global, the giant German engineering firm. Siemens employees channeled payments to government officials, primarily in developing countries, in order to secure contracts. For example, Siemens paid at least $40 million in bribes to win the right to produce Argentina's national identity cards; $20 million to build power plants in Israel; $14 million to supply medical equipment in China; $14 million to construct rail lines in Venezuela; and $5 million to supply phone equipment in Bangladesh. The company also made secret payments to Saddam Hussein's Iraqi government to participate in the

United Nations–sponsored oil-for-food program. Bribes typically ranged from 5% to 6% of a contract's value, though they could go as high 40% in highly corrupt nations. So far investigators have identified a total of 2.1 billion euros in suspicious payments. Money that could have gone to roads, schools, and hospitals in needy areas went to dishonest government officials instead. Residents of poor countries paid more than they should have for power plants, highways, railways, and phone equipment.

Siemens executives covered up illegal payments by transferring money to foreign accounts in countries with lax banking regulations. They also funneled money to phony companies in nations where they were bidding for contracts. Local "consultants" then delivered the payoffs to officials, often using suitcases or bags stuffed with cash. Between 2001 and 2006, one midlevel executive supervised the payoff program (with an annual budget of $40 million–$60 million) to make sure that the payments were disguised and that employees didn't siphon off funds designated for foreign officials. Noted a spokesperson for German federal prosecutors, "Bribery was Siemens' business model. Siemens had institutionalized corruption."[1]

The illegal payment scheme was unearthed in 2006. Siemens, with annual sales of over 72 billion euros, paid $1.6 billion in fines in Germany and the United States (where it is listed on the New York Stock Exchange) and must spend another $1 billion to monitor its compliance to antibribery statutes. (The penalties would have been much higher, but the firm cooperated with U.S. investigators.) Siemens also had to pay $100 million to the World Bank to support anticorruption work and was banned from bidding on World Bank contracts for two years. Several German employees, including a former board member, have been convicted of fraud and other crimes, and hundreds more are under investigation.

The task of rooting out corruption at Siemens and restoring the company's reputation has been spearheaded by CEO Peter Loeschler, appointed as the firm's first non-German chief executive in 2007. The first step he took was to announce a zero-tolerance policy: "The approach was very simple—zero tolerance. From Day One, what I have clearly communicated to everyone is that we have a Zero-Tolerance policy that there is absolutely no grey zone and that Siemens stands for clean business everywhere, and at all times."[2] To implement this policy, CEO Loeschler

- removed half of the management board,
- selected the company's general counsel to be chief compliance officer and made him a member of the board,

(Continued)

- fired offenders even if they didn't violate local laws,
- centralized business functions to make it harder for individuals and divisions to operate illegally,
- established an amnesty program where employees could come forward with information without fear of punishment,
- adopted new antibribery rules,
- hired outside legal and financial investigators to identify suspicious payments,
- hired the cofounder of Transparency International to develop an anticorruption training program for employees,
- increased the compliance staff from 86 to 500, and
- created a web portal that employees can use to ethically evaluate their interactions with customers and consultants.

Siemens's chief ethics officer Peter Solmssen is cautiously optimistic about efforts to stamp out corruption. He believes that the firm has eliminated the system of bribes and kickbacks but admits, when it comes to unethical behavior, "it's never over."[3] Solmssen is right to be cautious. The anticorruption push faces significant obstacles. Some are cultural. Until 1999, bribery payments were legal (and tax deductible) in Germany. The German business culture is only recently becoming more transparent in response to regulatory and investor pressure from outside the country. Then, too, Siemens operates in a variety of countries, many of which tolerate bribery. The sheer size of Siemens poses its own set of difficulties. Over 400,000 employees have to accept the fact the firm has a new way of doing business.

Solmssen looks forward to the day that Siemens can shift its focus from rooting out corruption to creating a healthy company culture that depends "on a more values-based leadership where people don't need to look at the rule book, where they know intuitively what the right thing to do is."[4]

Discussion Probes

1. What should be the elements of a zero-tolerance ethics policy? Are any of these elements missing at Siemens Global?

2. Evaluate Siemens Global's efforts to root out corruption. Are there any other steps the organization should take?

3. Given the company's massive size and the scale of its corrupt activities, did it get off too easy? Should it have faced additional financial penalties?

4. How can Siemens move beyond compliance to develop a healthy ethical climate?

5. What leadership and followership ethics lessons do you take from this case?

Notes

1. Schubert, S., & Miller, T. C. (2008, December 21). Where bribery was just a line item. *The New York Times*, p. BU1.

2. James, K. (2008, May 24). Siemens' straight shooter. *The Business Times Singapore.*

3. Dougherty, C. (2008, October 7). The sheriff at Siemens, at work under Justice Dept's watchful eye. *The New York Times*, p. B11.

4. Dougherty.

Sources

Big victory against global bribery. (2008, December 17). *The Christian Science Monitor*, p. 8.

Gow, D. (2008, January 25). Siemens prepares to pay $2bn fine to clear up slush fund scandal. *The Guardian*, p. 34.

Landler, M., & Dougherty, C. (2008, February 19). Coming clean Germany breaks with its clubby business past. *The New York Times*, p. C1.

O'Reilly, C., & Matussek, K. (2008, December 16). Siemens settles bribery cases. *The Washington Post*, p. D2.

Prodham, G. (2008, June 10). A face-lift for corporate Germany. *The International Herald Tribune*, Finance, p. 14.

Siemens settles World Bank with $100 million for anti-fight corruption. (2009, July 6). *Africa News.*

CASE STUDY 9.3

THE FAILURE OF WASHINGTON MUTUAL

The closure of Seattle-based savings and loan association Washington Mutual (WaMu) was by far the biggest bank failure in the history of the United States. The nation's sixth largest bank, which at one point held $307 billion in assets, was seized by regulators and sold at a bargain price ($1.9 billion) to JPMorgan Chase in 2008. Chase agreed to assume WaMu's debt, which saved taxpayers from having to bail the firm out. Depositors were insured against losses, but WaMu stockholders were wiped out and 18,000 employees lost their jobs.

(Continued)

(Continued)

For decades Washington Mutual had an admirable track record. It had survived as a regional thrift for over a hundred years, weathering both the Great Depression and the savings and loan crisis of the 1980s. However, WaMu's ethical climate changed dramatically for the worse when under the leadership of Kerry Killinger, who became the company's CEO in 1990. CEO Killinger wanted to make WaMu the "Wal-Mart of banking" by offering mortgages and credit cards to lower- and middle-income individuals who could not get loans from other financial institutions. To achieve this goal, the firm began a rapid expansion program, buying other thrifts and opening hundreds of branches across the country.

Expansion also meant dramatically increasing loan volume and becoming a major player in the subprime mortgage market. Subprime loans are high risk/high margin. They go to consumers who normally couldn't qualify for home loans due to credit problems or inadequate income. Because they are risky, lenders can charge higher interest and fees. Washington Mutual, along with other major lenders like Countrywide and Wachovia, began to offer a variety of new mortgage products. These included (a) adjustable rate mortgages (ARMs) with low initial interest rates that then adjusted upward, (b) no-down-payment loans, and (c) flexible payment plans that allowed homeowners to determine how much to pay each month. Some borrowers took advantage of the new mortgage options to get into houses they otherwise couldn't afford, or to refinance their current residences, using their home equity to buy everything from swimming pools and new cars to expensive electronics. Some consumers never intended to pay their home loans back.

In 2003 WaMu announced its new advertising slogan, "The Power to Say Yes," which also became the firm's mantra. Just saying yes meant giving loans to just about everyone who asked for one, regardless of income, credit history, or ability to repay. Little or no documentation was required. In one case, for example, a mariachi singer applied for a loan, claiming earnings of $100,000 or more. To document his claim, the applicant provided a picture of himself, dressed in his mariachi costume, in front of his house. His application was approved.

According to senior mortgage underwriter Keysha Cooper, "At WaMu, it wasn't about the quality of the loans; it was about the numbers. They didn't care if we were giving loans to people that didn't qualify. Instead, it was how many loans did you guys close and fund?"[1] Cooper reports being pressured by brokers and supervisors to approve questionable loans. In one case, when she refused to OK a suspect loan application, she was put on probation and her manager signed off on the mortgage.

WaMu generously rewarded those who helped create high loan volume, further encouraging excessive risk and fraud. Realtors could receive "referral fees" of over $10,000 for steering clients to WaMu. Agents often did not mention this arrangement to home buyers or clearly explain the terms of the loans to borrowers. Brokers could earn $20,000–$30,000 off of a $500,000 mortgage, and top producers were sent on all-expenses-paid trips to Hawaii and other vacation destinations. Loan officers pushed variable-rate loans in particular because they generated higher fees for the officers and higher earnings for the firm. Between 2003 and 2006, the percentage of adjustable-rate mortgages at WaMu grew from 25% to 70% of new home loans. The stock price rose, and CEO Killinger reaped a windfall in bonuses. He received over $100 million during his tenure at Washington Mutual, the vast majority during the peak of the firm's subprime push.

Washington Mutual and its competitors operated under the faulty assumption that housing prices would continue to increase indefinitely (housing markets typically rise and fall). When housing prices declined in 2007–2008, subprime and then prime mortgage defaults soared, igniting the mortgage crisis. Millions had to abandon their homes because they couldn't afford rising payments, lost their jobs, or now owed more than their homes were worth. Wall Street investment banks (which bought bundles of subprime mortgages and sold them to overseas investors) had to be propped up by the federal government. The stock market crashed, and the world economy headed into a recession.

Washington Mutual was particularly hard hit by the mortgage crisis. The default rate on its subprime loans rose to over 27%, and financial losses mounted. As the firm's stock price tanked, Killinger was fired, and depositors withdrew $17 billion. The run on the savings and loan prompted its closure and sale. In just a few short weeks, "the giant lender that came to symbolize the excesses of the mortgage boom" was gone.[2]

Discussion Probes

1. What signs of an unhealthy, unethical climate do you see at Washington Mutual?

2. What similarities do you see between the WaMu story and other examples of corporate ethical failure?

3. How much responsibility do you place on homeowners for the mortgage crisis and the collapse of Washington Mutual?

(Continued)

(Continued)

4. Should Killinger return some of the millions he earned while at WaMu?

5. Do you think the mortgage crisis could have been predicted? If so, why did leaders fail to take action to prevent it?

6. What leadership and followership ethics lessons do you take from this case?

Notes

1. Morgensen, G. (2008, November 2). Was there a loan it didn't like? *The New York Times*, p. BU1.
2. Dash, E., & Sorkin, A. R. (2008, September 26). In largest bank failure, U.S. seizes, then sells. *The New York Times*, p. A1.

Sources

Dash, E. (2008, October 16). U.S. to examine actions of Washington Mutual. *The New York Times*, p. B12.
Farley, R., & Drobnic Holan, A. (2008, October 12). What caused crisis? No one thing. *St. Petersburg Times*, p. 1A.
Goodman, P. S., & Morgenson, G. (2008, December 28). Saying yes to anyone, WaMu build empire on shaky loans. *The New York Times*, p. A1.
Perry, E. (2009, September 26). A year after collapse, WaMu still haunts. *The Oregonian*, pp. B1, B9.
Simon, R. (2008, August 7). Lax lending standards extended well into 2007, report says. *The Globe and Mail*, p. B8.

Notes

1. See, for example, Grojean, M. W., Resick, C. J., Dickson, M. W., & Smith, D. B. (2004). Leaders, values, and organizational climate: Examining leadership strategies for establishing an organizational climate regarding ethics. *Journal of Business Ethics, 55*, 223–241; Gottlieb, J. Z., & Sabzgiri, J. (1996). Towards an ethical dimension of decision making in organizations. *Journal of Business Ethics, 15*, 1275–1285.

2. Trevino, L. K., Hartman, L. P., & Brown, M. (2000). Moral person and moral manager: How executives develop a reputation for ethical leadership. *California Management Reviews, 42*, 128–133; Trevino, L. K., Brown, M., & Pincus, L. (2003). A qualitative investigation of perceived executive ethical leadership: Perceptions from inside and outside the executive suite. *Human*

Relations, 56, 5–37; Brown, M. E., Trevino, L. K., & Harrison, D. (2005). Ethical leadership: A social learning perspective for construct development and testing. *Organizational Behavior and Human Decision Processes, 97*, 117–134; Trevino, L. K., & Brown, M. E. (2005). The role of leaders in influencing unethical behavior in the workplace. In R. E. Kidwell & C. L. Martin (Eds.), *Managing organizational deviance* (pp. 69–87). Thousand Oaks, CA: Sage; Brown, M. E., & Trevino L. K. (2006). Ethical leadership: A review and future directions. *The Leadership Quarterly, 17*, 595–616.

3. Trevino, Hartman, & Brown; Trevino, L. K., & Nelson, K. A. (2004). *Managing business ethics: Straight talk about how to do it right* (3rd ed.). Hoboken, NJ: Wiley, Ch. 9.

4. Johnson, C. E. (2008). The rise and fall of Carly Fiorina: An ethical case study. *Journal of Leadership & Organizational Studies, 15*(2), 188–196.

5. Pacanowsky, M. E., & O'Donnell-Trujillo, N. (1983). Organizational communication as cultural performance. *Communication Monographs, 5*, 126–147.

6. Victor, B., & Cullen, J. B. (1988). The organizational bases of ethical work climates. *Administrative Science Quarterly, 33*, 101–125; Victor, B., & Cullen, J. B. (1990). A theory and measure of ethical climate in organizations. In W. C. Frederic & L. E. Preston (Eds.), *Business ethics: Research issues and empirical studies* (pp. 77–97). Greenwich, CT: JAI; Cullen, J. B., Victor, B., & Bronson, J. W. (1993). The ethical climate questionnaire: An assessment of its development and validity. *Psychological Reports, 73*, 667–674.

7. Fritzsche, D. J. (2000). Ethical climates and the ethical dimension of decision making. *Journal of Business Ethics, 24*, 125–140; Peterson, D. K. (2002). The relationship between unethical behavior and the dimensions of the Ethical Climate Questionnaire. *Journal of Business Ethics, 41*, 313–326; Cullen, J. B., Parboteeah, K. P., & Victor, B. (2003). The effects of ethical climates on organizational commitment: A two-study analysis. *Journal of Business Ethics, 46*, 127–141; Sims, R. L., & Keon, T. L. (1997). Ethical work climate as a factor in the development of person–organization fit. *Journal of Business Ethics, 16*, 1095–1105; Trevino, L. K., Butterfield, K. D., & McCabe, D. L. (1998). The ethical context in organizations: Influences on employee attitudes and behaviors. *Business Ethics Quarterly, 8*, 447–476; Martin, K. D., & Cullen J. B. (2006). Continuities and extensions of ethical climate theory: A meta-analytic review. *Journal of Business Ethics, 69*, 175–194.

8. Griffin, R. W., & O'Leary-Kelly, A. M. (Eds.). (2004). *The dark side of organizational behavior*. San Francisco: Jossey-Bass; Mumford, M. D., Gessner, T. L., Connelly, M. S., O'Conner, J. A., & Clifton, T. (1993). Leadership and destructive acts: Individual and situational influences. *The Leadership Quarterly, 4*, 115–147.

9. Pearson, C. M., & Porath, C. L. (2004). On incivility, its impact and directions for future research. In R. W. Griffin & A. M. O'Leary-Kelly (Eds.), *The dark side of organizational behavior* (pp. 131–158). San Francisco: Jossey-Bass; Porath, C. L., & Erez, A. (2007). Does rudeness really matter? The effects of rudeness on task performance and helpfulness. *The Academy of Management Journal, 50*, 1181–1197.

10. Buss, A. H. (1961). *The psychology of aggression.* New York: Wiley.

11. Levy, A. C., & Paludi, M. A. (2002). *Workplace sexual harassment* (2nd ed.). Upper Saddle River, NJ: Prentice Hall.

12. Diboye, R. L., & Halverson, S. K. (2004). Subtle (and not so subtle) discrimination in organizations. In R. W. Griffin & A. M. O'Leary-Kelly (Eds.), *The dark side of organizational behavior* (pp. 404–425). San Francisco: Jossey-Bass.

13. Pearson, C. M., & Porath, C. I. (2005). On the nature, consequences and remedies of workplace incivility: No time for "nice"? Think again. *Academy of Management Executive, 19,* 7–18; U.S. Department of Labor Bureau of Labor Statistics. (2007, August 9). Retrieved from http://www.dol.gov/; Ilies, R., Hauserman, N., Schwochau, S., & Stibal, J. (2003). Reported incidence rates of work-related sexual harassment in the United States: Using meta-analysis to explain reported rate disparities. *Personnel Psychology, 56,* 607–651; Diboye & Halverson.

14. Baron, R. A. (2004). Workplace aggression and violence: Insights from basic research. In R. W. Griffin & A. M. O'Leary-Kelly (Eds.), *The dark side of organizational behavior* (pp. 23–61). San Francisco: Jossey-Bass.

15. Cropanzano, R., & Stein, J. H. (2009). Organizational justice and behavioral ethics: Promises and prospects. *Business Ethics Quarterly, 19,* 193–233.

16. Colquitt, J. A., Conlon, D. E., Wesson, M. J., Porter, C. O. L. H., & Yee, N. K. (2001). Justice at the millennium: A meta-analytic review of 25 years of organizational justice research. *Journal of Applied Psychology, 86,* 425–445; Fortin, M. (2008). Perspectives on organizational justice: Concept clarification, social context integration, time and links with morality. *International Journal of Management Reviews, 10,* 93–126; Trevino, L. K., & Weaver, G. R. (2001). Organizational justice and ethics program "follow-through": Influences on employee's harmful and helpful behavior. *Business Ethics Quarterly, 11,* 651–671.

17. Greenberg, J., & Wiethoff, C. (2001). Organization justice as proaction and reaction: Implications for research and application. In R. Cropanzano (Ed.), *Justice in the workplace* (Vol. 2, pp. 271–302). Mahwah, NJ: Lawrence Erlbaum; Folger, R., & Baron, R. A. (1996). Violence and hostility at work: A model of reactions to perceived injustice. In G. R. VandenBos & E. Q. Bulato (Eds.), *Violence on the job: Identifying risks and developing solutions* (pp. 51–85). Washington, DC: American Psychological Association; Reb, J., Goldman, B. M., Kray, L. J., & Cropanzano, R. (2006). Different wrongs, different remedies? Reactions to organizational remedies after procedural and interactional injustice. *Personnel Psychology, 59,* 31–64; Kickul, J. (2001). When organizations break their promises: Employee reactions to unfair processes and treatment. *Journal of Business Ethics, 29,* 289–307; Trevino & Weaver.

18. A number of authors use the term *integrity* to describe ideal managers and organizations. See the following:

>   Brown, M. T. (2005). *Corporate integrity: Rethinking organizational ethics and leadership.* Cambridge, UK: Cambridge University Press.
>
>   Pearson, G. (1995). *Integrity in organizations: An alternative business ethic.* London: McGraw-Hill.

Petrick, J. A. (1998). Building organizational integrity and quality with the four Ps: Perspectives, paradigms, processes, and principles. In M. Schminke (Ed.), *Managerial ethics: Moral management of people and processes* (pp. 115–131). Mahwah, NJ: Erlbaum.

Solomon, R. C. (1992). *Ethics and excellence: Cooperation and integrity in business.* New York: Oxford University Press.

Srivastva, S. (Ed.). (1988). *Executive integrity.* San Francisco: Jossey-Bass.

19. Paine, L. S. (1996, March–April). Managing for organizational integrity. *Harvard Business Review,* pp. 106–117.

20. Toffler, B. L., & Reingold, J. (2003). *Final accounting: Ambition, greed, and the fall of Arthur Andersen.* New York: Broadway.

21. McKendall, M., DeMarr, B., & Jones-Rikkers, C. (2002). Ethical compliance programs and corporate illegality: Testing the assumptions of the corporate sentencing guidelines. *Journal of Business Ethics, 37,* 367–383; Rockness, H., & Rockness, J. (2005). Legislated ethics: From Enron to Sarbanes-Oxley, the impact on corporate America. *Journal of Business Ethics, 57,* 31–54; Andreoli, N., & Lefkowitz, J. (2008). Individual and organizational antecedents of misconduct in organizations. *Journal of Business Ethics, 85,* 309–332.

22. Adobor, H. (2006). Exploring the role performance of corporate ethics officers. *Journal of Business Ethics, 69,* 57–75; Weaver, G. R., Trevino, L. K., & Cochran, P. L. (1999). Integrated and decoupled corporate social performance: Management commitments, external pressures, and corporate ethics practices. *Academy of Management Journal, 42,* 539–552; Weaver, G. R., Trevino, L. K., & Cochran, P. L. (1999). Corporate ethics practices in the mid-1990s: An empirical study of the Fortune 1000. *Journal of Business Ethics, 18,* 283–294; Lindsay, R. M., & Irvine, V. B. (1996). Instilling ethical behavior in organizations: A survey of Canadian companies. *Journal of Business Ethics, 15,* 393–407.

23. Cohen, D. V. (1993). Creating and maintaining ethical work climates: Anomie in the workplace and implications for managing change. *Business Ethics Quarterly, 3,* 343–358.

24. James, H. S. (2002). Reinforcing ethical decision-making through organizational structure. *Journal of Business Ethics, 28,* 43–58.

25. Dunn, J., & Schweitzer, M. E. (2005). Why good employees make unethical decisions. In E. W. Kidwell & C. L. Martin (Eds.), *Managing organizational deviance* (pp. 39–60). Thousand Oaks, CA: Sage.

26. Useem, M. (1998). *The leadership moment: Nine stories of triumph and disaster and their lessons for us all.* New York: Times Business, Ch. 7.

27. Panchak, P. (2002). Time for a triple bottom line. *Industry Week,* p. 7; Robins, F. (2006). The challenge of TBL: A responsibility to whom? *Business and Society Review, 111,* 1–14.

28. Kotler, P., & Lee, N. (2005). *Corporate social responsibility: Doing the most good for your company and your cause.* Hoboken, NJ: Wiley.

29. Information on the social responsibility audit called "Living Our Values" can be found on the Starbucks website (see http://www.starbucks.com/responsibility).

30. Buchholz, R. A., & Rosenthal, S. B. (2005). Toward a conceptual framework for stakeholder theory. *Journal of Business Ethics, 58,* 137–148; Sims, R. R. (2003). *Ethics and corporate social responsibility: Why giants fall.* Westport, CT: Praeger.

31. Donaldson, T., & Preston, L. E. (1995). The stakeholder theory of the corporation: Concepts, evidence, and implications. *Academy of Management Review, 20,* 65–91; Cooper, S. (2004). *Corporate social performance: A stakeholder approach.* Burlington, VT: Ashgate; Goodpaster, K. E. (1991). Business ethics and stakeholder analysis. *Business Ethics Quarterly, 1,* 53–27; Philips, R. (2003). *Stakeholder theory and organizational ethics.* San Francisco: Berrett-Koehler; Freeman, R. E., Harrison, J. S., & Wicks, A. C. (2007). *Managing for stakeholders: Survival, reputation, and success.* New Haven, CT: Yale University Press.

32. Zadek, S. (2004, December). The path to corporate responsibility. *Harvard Business Review,* pp. 125–132.

33. Collins, J. C., & Porras, J. I. (1996, September–October). Building your company's vision. *Harvard Business Review,* p. 66.

34. Kuczmarski, S. S., & Kuczmarski, T. D. (1995). *Values-based leadership.* Englewood Cliffs, NJ: Prentice Hall.

35. See, for example:

> Cooperrider, D. L, & Whitnes, D. (2005). Appreciative inquiry: A positive revolution in change. San Francisco: Berrett-Koehler.

> Lewis, D., Medland, J., Malone, S., Murphy, M., Reno, K., & Vaccaro, G. (2006). Appreciative leadership: Defining effective leadership methods. *Organization Development Journal, 24,* 87–100.

> Whitney, D., & Trosten-Bloom, A. (2003). *The power of appreciative inquiry: A practical guide to positive change.* San Francisco: Berrett-Koehler.

36. Van Vuuren, L. J., & Crous, F. (2005). Utilising Appreciative Inquiry (AI) in creating a shared meaning of ethics in organizations. *Journal of Business Ethics, 57,* 399–412.

37. Paine, L., Deshpande, R., Margolis, J. D., & Bettcher, K. E. (2005, December). Up to code. *Harvard Business Review,* pp. 122–133.

38. For more information on the pros and cons of codes of conduct, see the following:

> Darley, J. M. (2001). The dynamics of authority influence in organizations and the unintended action consequences. In J. M. Darley, D. M. Messick, & T. R. Tyler (Eds.), *Social influences on ethical behavior in organizations* (pp. 37–52). Mahwah, NJ: Erlbaum.

> Hatcher, T. (2002). *Ethics and HRD: A new approach to leading responsible organizations.* Cambridge, MA: Perseus.

> Mathews, M. C. (1999). Codes of ethics: Organizational behavior and misbehavior. In W. C. Frederick & L. E. Preston (Eds.), *Business ethics: Research issues and empirical studies* (pp. 99–122). Greenwich, CT: JAI Press.

> Metzger, M., Dalton, D. R., & Hill, J. W. (1993). The organization of ethics and the ethics of organizations: The case for expanded organizational ethics audits. *Business Ethics Quarterly, 3*(1), 27–43.

Trevino, L. K., Butterfield, K. D., & McCabe, D. L. (1998). The ethical context in organizations: Influences on employee attitudes and behaviors. *Business Ethics Quarterly, 8,* 447–476.

Wright, D. K. (1993). Enforcement dilemma: Voluntary nature of public relations codes. *Public Relations Review, 19,* 13–20.

39. Countryman, A. (2001, December 7). Leadership key ingredient in ethics recipe, experts say. *The Chicago Tribune,* pp. B1, B6.

40. McCabe, D., & Trevino, K. L. (1993). Academic dishonesty: Honor codes and other contextual influences. *Journal of Higher Education, 64,* 522–569.

41. Adams, J. S., Taschian, A., & Shore, T. H. (2001). Codes of ethics as signals for ethical behavior. *Journal of Business Ethics, 29,* 199–211; Valentine, S., & Barnett, T. (2003). Ethics code awareness, perceived ethical values, and organizational commitment. *Journal of Personal Selling & Sales Management, 23,* 359–367.

42. Johannsen, R. L. (2002). *Ethics in human communication* (5th ed.). Prospect Heights, IL: Waveland, Ch. 1.

43. Hopen, D. (2002). Guiding corporate behavior: A leadership obligation, not a choice. *Journal for Quality & Participation, 25,* 15–19.

44. For more information on the link between learning and organizational integrity, see Petrick, J. A. (1998). Building organizational integrity and quality with the four Ps: Perspectives, paradigms, processes, and principles. In M. Schminke (Ed.), *Managerial ethics: Moral management of people and processes* (pp. 115–131). Mahwah, NJ: Erlbaum.

45. Paine, L. S. (1997). *Cases in leadership, ethics, and organizational integrity: A strategic perspective.* Boston: Irwin McGraw-Hill, p. 1.

46. Learning factors taken from DiBella, A., & Nevis, E. C. (1998). *How organizations learn: An integrated strategy for building learning capability.* San Francisco: Jossey-Bass; DiBella, A. J., Nevis, E. C., & Gould, J. M. (1996). Organizational learning as a core capability. In B. Moingeon & A. Edmondson (Eds.), *Organizational learning and competitive advantage* (pp. 38–55). London: Sage.

47. Camp, R. C. (1989). *Benchmarking: The search for industry best practices that lead to superior performance.* Milwaukee, WI: Quality Press.

48. Brown, J. (1995). Dialogue: Capacities and stories. In S. Chawla & J. Renesch (Eds.), *Learning organizations: Developing cultures for tomorrow's workplace* (pp. 153–164). Portland, OR: Productivity Press.

10

Meeting the Ethical Challenges of Diversity

One may also observe in one's travels to distant countries the feelings of recognition and affiliation that link every human being to every other human being.

—Aristotle

Human beings draw close to one another by their common nature, but habits and customs keep them apart.

—Confucian saying

WHAT'S AHEAD

In this chapter, we examine the problems and opportunities posed by cultural and other differences. Leaders have an ethical obligation to foster diversity in their organizations. At the same time, they must master the ethical challenges of leadership in a global society. Ethical global leaders acknowledge the dark side of globalization and recognize the impact of ethical diversity. They understand the relationship between cultural values and ethical choices, seek ethical common ground, and develop strategies for making choices in cross-cultural settings.

Promoting Diversity in the Organization:
An Ethical Imperative

Globalization may be the most important trend of the 21st century. We now live in a global economy shaped by multinational corporations, international travel, the Internet, immigration, and satellite communication systems. Greater cultural diversity is one product of globalization. Non-Whites account for most of the population growth in the United States. In other industrialized nations, most new workers are immigrants or members of groups currently underrepresented in the workplace. Italy will need 350,000 new migrants each year to maintain its working-age population at 1995 levels, for example, and Germany will need 500,000. However, cultural diversity isn't the only reason that the workforce is becoming more heterogeneous. Women are participating in the labor force at historically high rates, no longer dropping out after marriage. Seventy-one percent of women with children under age 18 in the United States work outside the home; women account for 51% of those employed in management and professional occupations. Governments around the world have instituted laws that prohibit discrimination against racial minorities, women, gays and lesbians, individuals with disabilities, older workers, and others.[1]

In light of these trends, diversity expert Taylor Cox concludes that managing diversity is the core of modern organizational leadership. Cox and others define managing diversity or diversity management as taking advantage of the benefits of a diverse workforce while coping with the problems that can arise when people from different backgrounds work together. The goal is to enable all employees, regardless of ethnicity, age, gender, sexual orientation, or physical ability, to achieve their full potential and to contribute to organizational goals and performance.[2]

Researchers and organizational leaders have discovered that there are many benefits to a diverse workforce. Diverse organizations are more innovative, make better decisions (see our discussion of minority influence in Chapter 8), have lower absentee and turnover rates, attract higher-quality employees, improve their public image, and gain market share.[3] These benefits make the "business case" for encouraging diversity. However, the best reason for promoting diversity is that it is the right thing to do based on the ethical perspectives described in Chapter 5. In addition to doing more good than harm (utilitarianism), honoring differences recognizes the dignity of individuals (Kant), promotes justice (Rawls), and builds community (communitarianism). Helping followers of all kinds reach their full potential also reflects love of neighbor (altruism).

Although fostering diversity is an ethical imperative, there are significant barriers to carrying out this task. (See Case Study 10.1.) Prejudice, stereotypes, and ethnocentrism are important attitudinal obstacles. *Prejudice* is the prejudgment of out-group members based on prior experiences and beliefs. Prejudice is universal, but the degree of prejudice varies from person to person, ranging from slight bias to extreme prejudice such as that displayed by racist skinheads. Negative prejudgments can be dangerous because they produce discriminatory behavior. For instance, police in many urban areas believe that African Americans are more likely to commit crimes. As a consequence, officers are more likely to stop and question Black citizens, particularly young men, and to use force if they show the slightest sign of resistance.[4] (One leader struggling to overcome his prejudices is described in "Leadership Ethics at the Movies: *Gran Torino*.")

Stereotyping is the process of classifying group members according to their perceived similarities while overlooking their individual differences. For example, one persistent stereotype is that Asian Americans have strong technical but not managerial skills. As a result, some organizations are eager to hire Asian Americans as engineers but are reluctant to put them in managerial roles. Because of perceptual biases, stereotypes are particularly devastating to marginalized groups. The natural tendency is to blame our failures on outside factors and to attribute our success to internal factors. The opposite is true when we evaluate the behavior of low-status groups. When we fall short, we blame other people, bad luck, bad weather, and other external forces. When we succeed, we point to our knowledge, character, skills, motivation, and training. Conversely, when members of marginalized groups fail, it is their laziness, low intelligence, or poor character that is to blame. When they succeed, however, we give the credit to the help they get from others rather than to their individual skills and effort.[5]

Ethnocentrism is the tendency to see the world from our cultural group's point of view. From this vantage point, our customs and values then become the standard by which the rest of the world is judged. Our cultural ways seem natural; those of other groups fall short. A certain degree of ethnocentrism is probably inevitable.[6] Ethnocentrism can help a group band together and survive in the face of outside threats. However, ethnocentrism is a significant barrier to cross-cultural communication and problem solving. High levels of ethnocentrism can lead to the following problems:

- Inaccurate attributions about the behavior of those who differ from us (we interpret their behavior from our point of view, not theirs)
- Expressions of disparagement or animosity (ethnic slurs, belittling nicknames)
- Reduced contact with outsiders

- Indifference and insensitivity to the perspectives of members of marginalized groups
- Pressure on other groups to conform to our cultural standards
- Justification for war and violence as a means of expressing cultural dominance

Examples of ethnocentrism abound. For many years, the Bureau of Indian Affairs made assimilation its official policy, forcing Native Americans to send their children to reservation schools, where they were punished for speaking their tribal languages. Government officials in Australia kidnapped Aboriginal children and placed them with White families. In other instances, well-meaning people assumed that their values and practices are the only "right" ones. Many early missionaries equated Christianity with Western lifestyles and required converts to dress, live, think, and worship like Europeans or North Americans.

Organizations (often unconsciously) erect barriers to diversity through routine practices. These can include (1) inaccessible facilities that make it hard for people with disabilities to enter workplaces, movie theaters, churches, and other buildings; (2) long work weeks and evening and weekend hours, which increase stress for working mothers; (3) an emphasis on self-promotion, which makes people from cultures such as Japan that value modesty uncomfortable; and (4) informal networks that exclude minorities, women, individuals with disabilities, and others from information and contacts for promotion.[7]

CASE STUDY 10.1

RELIGIOUS CLOTHING IN THE CLASSROOM

Fostering diversity is far from easy. Evidence of that fact can be found in disputes over religious clothing in public schools. France, the Netherlands, and several German states ban female Muslim students from wearing headscarves, but districts in the United States generally allow the practice. However, the controversy is not limited to Muslim dress. Bans on religious clothing and jewelry can also include Sikh turbans, Jewish yarmulkes, Christian crosses, and conspicuous symbols of other faiths.

Those opposed to religious attire in the classroom are concerned that such clothing violates religious neutrality by promoting particular religious beliefs and can be a tool for evangelization, as in the case of a Christian teacher wearing a T-shirt emblazoned with a Bible verse. They worry that immigrants who wear traditional dress are not integrating into their new cultures. Some French leaders view burqas (which cover the body and the face) as symbols of sexual discrimination. They want to expand the religious clothing ban beyond the classroom to prohibit Muslim women from wearing burqas anywhere in public. Said French President Nicolas Sarkozy, "The burqa is not a religious sign. It is a sign of subservience, a sign of debasement. It will not be welcome on the territory of the French Republic."[1]

Proponents of religious clothing in public schools base their support on human rights and freedom of religion. The International Covenant on Civil and Political Rights states that "the freedom to manifest religion or belief" includes the "wearing of distinctive clothing or headcoverings."[2] Supporters argue that the freedom of religion extends into the schools, as long as such expression doesn't interfere with the rights of others. President Obama criticized French law prohibiting the wearing of body and face scarves in public schools. "It is important for Western countries to avoid impeding Muslim citizens from practicing religion as they see fit," he said, "for instance, by dictating what clothes a Muslim woman should wear."[3]

Students who want to wear religious attire to school but can't are forced to transfer to private schools or other districts. In some cases they continue their education in other countries. Teachers who defy religious clothing restrictions are denied employment or lose their jobs. Members of minority religions complain that bans on religious dress in the classroom further stigmatize them and subject them to more discrimination and abuse.

Discussion Probes

1. Should students be allowed to wear religious clothing to public school? Why or why not?

2. Should teachers be allowed to wear religious clothing to public school? Why or why not?

3. If you agree that religious clothing can be worn in the classroom, would you put any limits on what is acceptable?

4. At what point does freedom of religious expression become a form of evangelism?

5. What leadership and followership ethics lessons do you take from this case?

(Continued)

(Continued)

Notes

1. Thistlethwaite, S. B. (2009, June 27). Wearing faith on your sleeve. *The Washington Post,* p. B02.
2. Wu, A. C. (2008, January 30). Balancing rights and burqas. *The Washington Times,* p. A17.
3. Thistlethwaite.

Sources

Chrisafis, A. (2009, January 27). Veiled threats: Row over Islamic dress opens bitter divisions in France. *The Guardian,* International, p. 24.

Coyne, I. (2008, January 15). Turbans make targets, some Sikhs find. *The New York Times,* p. NJ1.

Erdem, S. (2008, February 7). Universities protest as MPs debate lifting headscarf ban. *The Times,* p. 38.

Hammond, B. (2009). Religious rule for teachers challenged. *The Oregonian,* pp. A1, A4.

Overcoming the barriers described here begins with addressing our attitudes. We can reduce our levels of negative prejudice, stereotyping, and ethnocentrism by committing ourselves to the following:

Mindfulness. In most routine encounters, we tend to operate on "autopilot" and perform our roles mechanically, without much reflection. When we're engaged in such mindless interaction, we're not likely to challenge the ethnocentric assumption that ours is the only way to solve problems. Mindfulness is the opposite of mindlessness. When we're mindful, we pay close attention to our attitudes and behaviors. Three psychological processes take place.[8]

The first is *openness to new categories.* Being mindful makes us more sensitive to differences. Instead of lumping people into broad categories based on age, race, gender, or role, we make finer distinctions within these classifications. We discover that not all student government officers, retirees, engineers, Japanese exchange students, and professors are alike.

The second psychological process involves *openness to new information.* Mindless communication closes us off to new data, and we fail to note the kinds of cultural differences I described earlier. We assume that others hold the same ethical values. In mindful communication, we pick up new information as we closely monitor our behavior along with the behavior of others.

The third psychological process is *recognizing the existence of more than one perspective*. Mindlessness results in tunnel vision that ignores potential solutions. Mindfulness, on the other hand, opens our eyes to other possibilities. For example, there can be more than one way to make and implement ethical choices.

Dignity and Integrity. Dignity and integrity ought to characterize all of our interactions with people of other cultures. We maintain our own dignity by confronting others who engage in prejudicial comments or actions; we maintain the dignity of others by respecting their views. Respect doesn't mean that we have to agree with another's moral stance. But when we disagree, we need to respond in a civil, sensitive manner.

Moral Inclusion. As we saw in Chapter 4, widespread evil occurs when groups have been devalued or dehumanized. This sanctioning process is called moral exclusion.[9] Exclusionary tactics include biased evaluation of women and minorities, hostility, contempt, condescension, and double standards (one for insiders, another for outsiders). Moral inclusiveness rejects exclusionary tactics of all kinds. If we're dedicated to inclusiveness, we'll apply the same rules, values, and standards to those outside our group as we do to our fellow group members.

Cosmopolitanism. The term *cosmopolitan* describes an attitude or a perspective that incorporates mindfulness, human dignity, and moral inclusion.[10] Cosmopolitans view themselves as citizens of the world with global obligations. If we adopt this perspective, we will honor the intrinsic value of all people, not just members of our immediate group, and will seek to establish a just global society. While maintaining our identification with a particular region or culture, we will not be bound by all of its values and customs. Instead, we will acknowledge our group's shortcomings while, at the same time, appreciating the value of other cultural approaches and recognizing that everyone shares an "essential humanity."[11]

By committing ourselves as leaders to mindful communication, the dignity of others, moral inclusion, and cosmopolitanism, we can reduce ethnocentrism and prejudice in the group as a whole. Using morally inclusive language and disputing prejudiced statements, for instance, improves ethical climate because followers will be less likely to attack other groups in our presence. However, if we don't speak out when followers disparage members of out-groups, the practice will continue. We'll share some of the responsibility for creating a hostile atmosphere. (For one list of skills essential to ethical cross-cultural communication, turn to "Focus on Follower Ethics: Personal Competencies for Establishing Cross-Cultural Relationships.")

In addition to addressing attitudes about diversity, we can initiate diversity programs. Diversity initiatives address the organizational obstacles to diversity described earlier, highlight the importance of diversity, prevent discrimination, and build diversity practices into routine processes and operations. Effective diversity initiatives include (a) the involvement of senior management (taking the lead in diversity projects, hiring consultants, participating in diversity training and programs); (b) education and training featuring seminars and workshops that help employees understand the value of a diverse workforce, overcome prejudice and discrimination, and develop the skills they need to lead multicultural teams; (c) creating diversity action plans for business units and the entire organization; (d) holding managers accountable for diversity results; (e) offering flexible work arrangements (telecommuting, job sharing, working at home, part-time employment) to accommodate the needs of diverse employees; and (f) providing career development opportunities for members of marginalized groups that increase the likelihood of promotion and entry into management.[12] (Complete the "Self-Assessment: Diversity Perceptions Scale" to determine your perceptions of the diversity climate of your organization and your level of comfort with diversity issues.)

LEADERSHIP ETHICS AT THE MOVIES

GRAN TORINO

Key Cast Members: Clint Eastwood, Bee Vang, Ahney Her, Christopher Carley, John Carroll Lynch

Synopsis: Retired autoworker Walt Kowalski (Eastwood) emerges as the unlikely hero in this story set in a racially mixed Detroit neighborhood. Walt, a racist Korean War veteran, particularly resents his new Hmong neighbors from Southeast Asia. As time passes, however, he discovers that he may have more in common with the Hmong than with his own family. Walt defends his neighbors from the local gang and becomes a mentor to Thao (Vang), the teen next door who had earlier tried to steal his prize 1972 Gran Torino in a gang initiation. Still burdened by guilt from his wartime experiences, Kowalski must decide how to respond when the gangbangers attack Thao and his sister Sue (Her).

Rating: R for violence and language

Themes: cultural differences, racism, ethnocentrism, cross-cultural leadership, character, the cycle of violence, guilt, altruism, moral decision making

Discussion Starters

1. How does Walt demonstrate prejudice, stereotyping, and ethnocentrism?

2. What does Walt share in common with his Hmong neighbors?

3. What accounts for Walt's conversion from bigot to cross-cultural hero?

Mastering the Ethical Challenges of Leadership in a Global Society

So far we've focused on our ethical obligation to foster diversity within our organizations. However, globalization means that we also have to master the ethical challenges of leading across national and cultural boundaries. Meeting these challenges begins with acknowledging the dark side of the globalization process and recognizing the impact of ethical diversity.

The Dark Side of Globalization

Supporters of globalization point to its benefits. Free trade produces new wealth by opening up international markets, they argue. At the same time, the costs of goods and services drop. Cheaper, faster means of communication and travel encourage unprecedented cross-cultural contact.[13] The greater flow of information and people puts pressure on repressive governments to reform.

Critics of globalization paint a much bleaker picture. They note that global capitalism encourages greed rather than concern for others. Ethical and spiritual values have been overshadowed by the profit motive. Local cultural traditions and the environment are being destroyed in the name of economic growth. The gap between the rich and the poor keeps growing.[14]

Debate over whether the benefits of globalization outweigh its costs is not likely to end anytime soon. This much is clear, however: As leaders, we need to give serious consideration to the dark side of the global society in order to help prevent ethical abuse. With that in mind, let's take a closer look at how leaders cast the shadows I outlined in Chapter 1 in a global environment.

The Global Shadow of Power

In the modern world, a leader's power is no longer limited by national boundaries. Increasing interdependence brought about by the integration of markets, communication systems, computers, and financial institutions means that the actions of one leader or nation can have a dramatic impact on the rest of the world. Pulitzer Prize–winning foreign affairs correspondent Thomas Friedman points to the collapse of Thailand's currency in 1997 as an example of just how integrated the international economy has become.[15] When the value of the Thai baht plunged, Southeast Asia went into a deep recession that drove down world commodity prices. The Russian economy, which is heavily based on exports of oil and other commodities, then collapsed. Investors sold off their holdings to cover their losses in Southeast Asia and Russia. This massive sell-off forced the Brazilian government to raise interest rates as high as 40% to retain economic capital. Some frightened investors sought safety in U.S. Treasury bonds, driving down interest rates and undermining the financial standing of many U.S. mutual funds and banks. The recent financial crisis is another case illustrating the interdependence of the global economic system. The recession started in the United States but quickly spread to other industrialized nations. Exporting countries like China received fewer orders for their products. The price of oil, at an all-time high before the slowdown, dropped dramatically as global economic activity slowed, lowering the income of oil-producing nations in the Middle East and elsewhere.

FOCUS ON FOLLOWER ETHICS

PERSONAL COMPETENCIES FOR ESTABLISHING CROSS-CULTURAL RELATIONSHIPS

Anthropologist Mikel Hogan identifies 14 personal competencies that are essential for ethical (mindful, respectful, inclusive) and effective communication with people of other cultural backgrounds. These abilities foster dialogue, productive conflict management, and effective problem solving in diverse groups. As a professor and trainer, Hogan has introduced these skills to organizational leaders but more often to students and employees in follower roles.

1. *Be nonjudgmental.* Turn off the natural tendency to negatively judge others who are different from you.

2. *Be flexible.* Adjust and then readjust to changing conditions as often as needed.

3. *Be resourceful.* Get the information and items you need to respond effectively to any cross-cultural situation.

4. *Personalize observations.* Express your feelings and ideas in a way that affirms that you recognize the other person as an individual, even though you may not share the same perspective. Use "I messages" ("I disagree") rather than "you messages" ("You are mistaken"). Demonstrate that you are listening.

5. *Pay attention to thoughts and feelings.* Monitor your interior reactions, which allows you to stay in charge of the situation and respond more effectively.

6 & 7. *Listen attentively/observe carefully.* Pay attention to the whole message, including nonverbal cures like tone of voice, gestures, and posture.

8. *Assume complexity.* Recognize that culturally diverse interactions involve differing perspectives and can lead to misunderstandings.

9. *Tolerate the stress of uncertainty.* Don't show irritation or annoyance in ambiguous, culturally diverse settings. Be aware that fear, anxiety, and frustration can interfere with your ability to communicate effectively.

10. *Have patience.* Remain calm in the face of the stress generated by diverse encounters.

11. *Manage personal biases.* Try to move beyond your perspective so that you can treat others respectfully, as unique individuals. Acknowledge that no one person is representative of an entire group.

12. *Keep a sense of humor.* Don't take yourself so seriously. Laugh at yourself when you make a cross-cultural blunder and at humorous moments in intercultural encounters.

13. *Show respect.* Express understanding of, and esteem for, those of other cultures.

14. *Show empathy.* Try to understand the other person's perspective— that individual's feelings, attitudes, and beliefs that are based on her or his cultural background.

SOURCE: Hogan, M. (2006). *The Four Skills of Cultural Diversity Competence: A Process for Understanding and Practice* (3rd ed.). Brooks Cole/Cengage.

SELF-ASSESSMENT

DIVERSITY PERCEPTIONS SCALE

Respond to each item by circling the appropriate number (1 = *strongly disagree*, 6 = *strongly agree*).

1. I feel that I have been treated differently here because of my race, gender, sexual orientation, religion, or age. (Reverse)

   1   2   3   4   5   6

2. Managers here have a track record of hiring and promoting employees objectively, regardless of their race, gender, sexual orientation, religion, or age.

   1   2   3   4   5   6

3. Managers here give feedback and evaluate employees fairly, regardless of employees' race, gender, sexual orientation, religion, age, or social background.

   1   2   3   4   5   6

4. Managers here make layoff decisions fairly, regardless of factors such as employees' race, gender, age, or social background.

   1   2   3   4   5   6

5. Managers interpret human resource policies (such as sick leave) fairly for all employees.

   1   2   3   4   5   6

6. Managers give assignments based on the skills and abilities of employees.

   1   2   3   4   5   6

7. Management here encourages the formation of employee network support groups.

   1   2   3   4   5   6

8. There is a mentoring program in use here that identifies and prepares all minority and female employees for promotion.

   1   2   3   4   5   6

9. The "old boys' network" is alive and well here. (Reverse)

   1   2   3   4   5   6

10. The company spends enough money and time on diversity awareness and related training.

   1   2   3   4   5   6

11. Knowing more about cultural norms of diverse groups would help me be more effective in my job.

   1   2   3   4   5   6

12. I think that diverse viewpoints add value.

   1   2   3   4   5   6

13. I believe diversity is a strategic business issue.

   1   2   3   4   5   6

14. I feel at ease with people from backgrounds different from my own.

   1   2   3   4   5   6

15. I am afraid to disagree with members of other groups for fear of being called prejudiced. (Reverse)

   1   2   3   4   5   6

16. Diversity issues keep some work teams here from performing to their maximum effectiveness. (Reverse)

   1   2   3   4   5   6

Scoring

This scale measures two dimensions—the organizational and the personal—each of which contains two factors as follows:

I. Organizational dimension
   a. Organizational fairness factor (Items 1–6)
   b. Organizational inclusion factor (Items 7–10)

II. Personal dimension
   c. Personal diversity value factor (Items 11–13)
   d. Personal comfort with diversity (Items 14–16)

Reverse scores on Items 1, 9, 15, and 16. Then add up your responses to all 16 items (maximum score 96). The higher your total score, the more positive your view of the diversity climate. Similarly, the higher your score on each of the item subsets described above, the more positive your perceptions on that factor.

SOURCE: Adapted from Mor Barak, M. (2005). *Managing diversity: Toward a globally inclusive workplace.* Thousand Oaks, CA: Sage, pp. 293–294. Used by permission.

Ethical leadership in the multinational context must take into account the potential, far-ranging consequences of every choice. Shadows fall when leaders forget this fact. For example, the U.S. government refused for decades to increase mileage requirements for trucks and automobiles, which contributed to global warming. Saudi Arabia's unwillingness to ban terrorist groups contributed to the World Trade Center and Bali bombings.

Concentration of power is a by-product of globalization that increases the likelihood of abuse. The United States is a case in point. Critics accuse the world's only superpower of throwing its political and military weight around. Corporations also wield great influence in the global marketplace. Multinational companies have more economic clout than many nations. According to one estimate, 53 of the world's 100 largest economies are corporations.[16]

The Global Shadow of Privilege

As noted earlier, globalization appears to be increasing, not decreasing, the gap between the haves and the have-nots. Between 1960 and 1995, the income gap between the world's richest and poorest people more than doubled.[17] So far, leaders of wealthy nations have been more interested in promoting the sale of their goods than in opening up their markets to poorer countries. Privileged nations also consume more, which leads to environmental damage in the form of logging, oil drilling, and mineral extraction. This damage has a disproportionate impact on the disadvantaged. Whereas the wealthy can move to cleaner areas, the poor cannot. Instead, poor citizens must deal with the loss of hunting and fishing grounds, clean air, and safe water.

Leaders will continue to cast shadows unless they take steps to make globalization more equitable. To do so, they must (a) put the common (international) good above private gain or self- or national interest, (b) create a global economy that recognizes the interconnectedness of all peoples and the importance of sustaining the environment, (c) practice restraint and moderation in the consumption of goods, and (d) seek justice and compassion by helping marginalized groups.[18]

The Global Shadow of Mismanaged Information

Deceit is all too common on the international stage. Nations routinely spy on each other for economic and military purposes and do their best to deceive their enemies. Businesses from industrialized countries frequently take advantage of consumers in economically depressed regions. Take the marketing of infant formula, for instance. Save the Children estimates that the lives of 3,800 babies could be saved every day if they were adequately breast-fed rather than bottle-fed.[19] Breast-fed babies are more resistant to disease and are less likely to sicken and die in impoverished countries where infant formula is frequently diluted or mixed with polluted water. As an added benefit, poor households could then spend their money on other pressing needs. Despite the adoption of the International Code of Marketing of Breast-Milk Substitutes in 1981, formula manufacturers continue to engage in a variety of deceptive sales practices, which have drawn the ire of health officials at the World Health Organization and in Bangladesh, Nigeria, the Philippines, and other developing nations. These practices include (a) claiming that baby formula is equal to or better than breast-feeding; (b) playing on women's fears that they won't produce enough milk; (c) representing healthy, thriving babies in television ads and on packaging, leaflets, and posters (many women in impoverished nations are particularly vulnerable to these images because they can't read); (d) disguising salespeople as health workers; and (e) gaining medical endorsement by providing free samples to hospitals and gifts to doctors.

In addition to casting shadows through deception, global leaders also cast shadows by withholding information. They don't feel as much obligation to share data about safety problems and environmental hazards with foreign nationals as they do with their own citizens. They are guilty of extracting information from poor countries, giving little in return. For example, clinical drug trials in developing countries produce data that go back to company headquarters in Europe or the United States. Weaker countries are given little support in their efforts to develop their own research facilities.[20]

The Global Shadow of Inconsistency

Economic and social disparities make it hard for leaders of multinational firms and nonprofits to act consistently. For instance, what are "fair" wages and working conditions in a developing nation? Do these workers deserve the same safety standards as employees in an industrialized country? Should drugs that are banned in the United States for their undesirable side effects be sold in countries where their potential health benefits outweigh their risks? Should a multinational corporation follow the stringent pollution regulations of its home country or the lower standards of a host nation? All too often global leaders answer these questions in ways that cast shadows on disadvantaged world citizens. They pay the bare minimum to workers in developing countries, pay less attention to safety and environmental problems in overseas locations, dump dangerous products they can't sell in their homelands, and so on.

The shadow of inconsistency grows deeper and longer when leaders ignore human rights abuses and cooperate with repressive regimes in order to benefit from the status quo. That appears to be the case with Unocal (a division of Chevron) and Total, a French petroleum company. They operate Myanmar's (Burma's) Yadana oil field that produces approximately 630 million cubic feet of natural gas annually.[21] The two companies pay the Burmese military government, one of the most repressive regimes in the world, hundreds of millions in taxes and revenues each year. Very little of that money helps the average citizen. At least 40% of the Burmese national budget goes to the military; only 2%–3% is devoted to health and welfare. As a result, the nation suffers from widespread poverty, inadequate medical care, and substandard education (fewer than half of all children attend primary school). Buddhist monks and others who protest against the government are promptly jailed. A group of Myanmar citizens successfully brought suit against Unocal in a U.S. court for human rights violations. The court found that the Burmese military used murder and rape to clear the way for the Yadana pipeline and forced citizens to construct it. While Unocal did not endorse the brutality, the firm benefited from the military's actions.

The Global Shadow of Misplaced and Broken Loyalties

Traditional loyalties are eroding in an integrated world. In the past, national leaders were expected to meet the needs of their citizens. Now, because their actions affect the lives of residents of other nations, they must consider their duties to people they may never meet. Failure to do so produces shadow in the form of environmental damage, poverty, hunger, and the widening income gap.

Broken loyalties cast shadows in a global society just as they do in individual leader–follower relationships. Many poorer world citizens feel betrayed by the shattered promises of globalization. Trade barriers remain in place, and special interests in wealthy nations continue to receive favored treatment. Economic exploitation adds to this sense of betrayal. Low labor costs drive the investments of many multinational companies. Executives at these firms are continually on the lookout for cheaper labor, so they transfer production to even more economically depressed regions.

The Global Shadow of Irresponsibility

Globalization increases the breadth of leaders' responsibilities because they are accountable for the actions of followers in many different geographic locations. Like local leaders, they can't be blamed for all the misdeeds of their followers. Yet they should be held to the same set of responsibility standards outlined in our discussion of the shadow side of leadership in Chapter 1. In order to cast light instead of shadow, global leaders must do the following:

1. *Take reasonable efforts to prevent followers' misdeeds.* Fostering a consistent, ethical organizational climate in every location can prevent many moral abuses. Integrity and a clear set of guiding values should be as characteristic of branch offices as they are of headquarters. This can be done by (a) clearly stating organizational values, (b) communicating these values to all branches through print and electronic media and training programs, (c) letting business partners know about standards, and (d) translating ethical behavior into performance standards and then evaluating followers based on those criteria.[22]

2. *Acknowledge and address ethical problems wherever they occur.* Geographic and cultural distance makes it easy for global leaders to deny responsibility for the misbehavior of followers. Subcontractors often get the blame for low wages and poor working conditions at foreign manufacturing facilities. More responsible firms acknowledge their duty to adequately supervise the activities of their contractors.

3. *Shoulder responsibility for the consequences of their directives.* Wise global leaders recognize that in trying to do the right thing, they might end up producing some unintended negative consequences. Take well-intentioned efforts to eliminate child labor, for instance. Removing children from the factory floor in developing countries can do significant harm. Poor children are an important source of income for their families. When fired from their manufacturing jobs, they often are forced into prostitution or begging. Levi Strauss realized that eliminating child laborers from its Bangladesh plants could do damage to both the children and their families. After identifying workers under age 14 (the international standard for child labor), company officials asked their contractors to remove these children from the production line while continuing to pay their wages. Levi Strauss covered the kids' school costs (tuition, uniforms, books) and agreed to rehire them when they reached age 14.[23]

4. *Admit their duties to followers.* Multinational leaders have obligations to all their followers, regardless of citizenship or ethnic and cultural background, and to the communities where they operate. Total, the French petroleum firm, claims that its purpose is to locate oil and it is not responsible for the actions of the Burmese government. Nevertheless, the company helps to underwrite an oppressive government that abuses its citizens.

5. *Hold themselves to the same standards as followers.* Leaders are not above the values, rules, and codes of conduct they impose on their global organizations. While they hold diverse followers to consistent standards, ethical leaders also live up to the same guidelines.

Leadership and Ethical Diversity

Along with taking stock of the potential moral pitfalls of globalization, leaders need to recognize that cultural diversity makes the always difficult process of ethical decision making even harder. Every ethnic group, nation, and religion approaches moral dilemmas from a different perspective. What is perfectly acceptable to members of one group may raise serious ethical concerns for another. Consider the differing responses to these common ethical problems.[24]

Bribery

Spurred by reports that ExxonMobil had paid $59 million to Italian politicians in order to do business in that country, Congress passed the Foreign Corrupt Practices Act of 1977, which forbids U.S. corporations from exchanging money or goods for something in return. Those guilty of bribery can be fined and sent to prison. Malaysia has even stricter bribery statutes, executing corporate officers who offer and accept bribes. On the other hand, bribery is a common, accepted practice in many countries in Africa, Asia, and the Middle East. In recognition of this fact, small payments to facilitate travel and business in less developed nations are permitted under the Corrupt Practices Act.

False Information

Mexico and the United States might be geographic neighbors, but citizens of these countries react differently to deception. In one encounter, American businesspeople were offended when their Mexican counterparts promised to complete a project by an impossible deadline. The Mexicans, on the other hand, viewed their deception as a way to smooth relations between the two sides while protecting their interests.

Intellectual Property Rights

Copyright laws are rigorously enforced in many Western nations but are less binding in many Asian countries. In fact, piracy is legal in Thailand, Indonesia, and Malaysia.

Gender Equality

Treatment of women varies widely. Denmark and Sweden have done the most to promote gender equality, whereas Japan and Saudi Arabia offer some of the stiffest resistance to women's rights. In Japan, women are expected to care for the home and are excluded from leadership positions in government and business. In Saudi Arabia, women (who must wear traditional garb) aren't allowed to drive or form relationships with non-Muslim men.

The challenges posed by cultural variables can discourage leaders from making reasoned moral choices. They may decide to cling to their old ways of thinking or blindly follow local customs. Cultural relativism ("When in Rome do as the Romans do") is an attractive option for many. Nevertheless, being in a new culture or working with a diverse group of followers doesn't excuse leaders from engaging in careful ethical deliberation. Just because a culture has adopted a practice doesn't make it right. Female circumcision may still be carried out in parts of Africa, but the vast majority of those in the West are appalled by this custom. Fortunately, we can expand our capacity to act ethically in a global society and brighten the lives of diverse groups of followers. To do so, we have to deepen our understanding of the relationship between cultural differences and ethical values. Then we need to search for moral common ground and identify strategies for making decisions in cross-cultural settings.

Cultural Differences and Ethical Values

Defining Culture

The same factors that make up an organization's culture—language, rituals, stories, buildings, beliefs, assumptions, power structures—also form the cultures of communities, ethnic groups, and nations. Cultures are comprehensive, incorporating both the visible (architecture, physical objects, nonverbal behavior) and the invisible (thoughts, attitudes, values). In sum, a culture is "the total way of life of a people, composed of their learned and shared behavior patterns, values, norms, and material objects."[25]

Several features of cultures are worth noting in more detail. These elements include the following:

- *Created.* Ethnocentrism would have us believe that ours is the only way to solve problems. In fact, there are countless ways to deal with the environment, manage interpersonal relationships, produce food, and cope with death. Each cultural group devises its own way of responding to circumstances.
- *Learned.* Elements of culture are passed on from generation to generation and from person to person. Cultural conditioning is both a formal and an informal process that takes place in every context—homes, schools, playgrounds, camps, games. The most crucial aspects of a culture, such as loyalty to country, are constantly reinforced. Patriotism in the United States is promoted through

high school civics classes, the singing of the national anthem at sporting events, flags flying on everything from pickup trucks to skyscrapers and giant construction cranes, and Fourth of July and Memorial Day programs.

- *Shared.* The shared nature of culture becomes apparent when we break the rules that are set and enforced by the group. There are negative consequences for violating cultural norms of all types. Punishments vary depending on the severity of the offense. For example, you might receive a cold stare from your professor when your cell phone goes off in class. However, you may face jail time if you break drug laws.
- *Dynamic.* Cultures aren't static but evolve. Over time, the changes can be dramatic. Compare the cultural values of the *Leave It to Beaver* television show with those found in modern situation comedies. The world of the Cleavers (a suburban two-parent family with a well-dressed, stay-at-home mom) has been replaced by portrayals of unmarried friends, single parents, blended families, and gay partners.

Ethical decisions and practices are shaped by widely held cultural values. Although each culture has its own set of ethical priorities, researchers have discovered that ethnic groups and nations hold values in common. As a result, cultures can be grouped according to their value orientations. These orientations help explain ethical differences and enable leaders to predict how members of other cultural groups will respond to moral dilemmas. In this section of the chapter, I'll describe two widely used cultural classification systems. I will also introduce a third approach specifically developed to explain moral similarities and differences across cultures. Before we examine the cultural classification systems, however, there are four cautions to keep in mind. First, all categories are gross overgeneralizations. They describe what most people in that culture value. Not all U.S. residents are individualistic, for example, and not all Japanese citizens are collectivists. However, *in general,* more Americans put the individual first, whereas more Japanese emphasize group relations. Second, scholars may categorize the same nation differently and have not studied some regions of the world (such as Africa) as intensively as others (Europe, Asia, and the United States). Third, political and cultural boundaries aren't always identical. For instance, the Basque people live in both France and Spain. Fourth, as noted earlier, cultures are dynamic, so values change. A society may change its ethical priorities over time.

Programmed Value Patterns

Geert Hofstede of the Netherlands conducted an extensive investigation of cultural value patterns.[26] According to Hofstede, important values are "programmed" into members of every culture. He surveyed more than 100,000 IBM employees in 50 countries and three multicountry regions to uncover these value dimensions. He then checked his findings against those of other researchers who studied the same countries. Four value orientations emerged:

Power Distance

The first category describes the relative importance of power differences. Status differences are universal, but cultures treat them differently. In high–power distance cultures (Philippines, Mexico), inequality is accepted as part of the natural order. Leaders enjoy special privileges and make no attempt to reduce power differentials; however, they are expected to care for the less fortunate. Low–power distance cultures (Ireland, New Zealand), in contrast, are uneasy with large gaps in wealth, power, privilege, and status. Superiors tend to downplay these differences and strive for a greater degree of equality.

Individualism Versus Collectivism

Hofstede's second value category divides cultures according to their preference for either the individual or the group. Individualistic cultures put the needs and goals of the person and her or his immediate family first. Members of these cultures see themselves as independent actors. In contrast, collectivistic cultures give top priority to the desires of the larger group (extended family, tribe, community). Members of these societies stress connection instead of separateness, putting a high value on their place in the collective. Think back to your decision to attend your current college or university. As a resident of Canada or the United States, you probably asked friends, high school counselors, and family members for advice, but in the end, you made the choice. In a collectivistic society such as Peru or Pakistan, your family or village might well have made this decision for you. There's no guarantee that you would have even gone to college. Families with limited resources can afford to send only one child to school. You might have been expected to go to work to help pay for the education of a brother or sister.

Masculinity Versus Femininity

The third dimension reflects attitudes toward the roles of men and women. Highly masculine cultures such as Japan, Venezuela, and Italy maintain clearly defined sex roles. Men are expected to be decisive, assertive, dominant, ambitious, and materialistic; women are encouraged to serve. They are to care for the family, interpersonal relationships, and the weaker members of society. In feminine cultures such as Finland, Denmark, and the Netherlands, the differences between the sexes are blurred. Both men and women can be competitive and caring, assertive and nurturing. These cultures are more likely to stress interdependence, intuition, and concern for others.

Uncertainty Avoidance

This dimension describes the way in which cultures respond to uncertainty. Three indicators measure this orientation: anxiety level, widely held attitudes about rules, and employment stability. Members of high–uncertainty avoidance societies (Greece, Portugal, Japan) feel anxious about uncertainty and view it as a threat. They believe in written rules and regulations, engage in more rituals, and accept directives from those in authority. In addition, they are less likely to change jobs and view long-term employment as a right. People who live in low–uncertainty avoidance cultures (Ireland, Sweden) are more comfortable with uncertainty, viewing ambiguity as a fact of life. They experience lower stress and are more likely to take risks such as starting a new company or accepting a new job in another part of the country. These people are less reliant on written regulations and rituals and are more likely to trust their own judgments instead of obeying authority figures.

Hofstede argues that value patterns have a significant impact on ethical behavior.[27] For example, masculine European countries give little to international development programs but invest heavily in weapons. Feminine European nations do just the opposite. High–uncertainty avoidance cultures are prone to ethnocentrism and prejudice because they follow the credo "What is different is dangerous." Low–uncertainty avoidance cultures follow the credo "What is different is curious" and are more tolerant of strangers and new ideas. Other researchers have joined Hofstede in linking value patterns to ethical attitudes and behavior.[28] They have discovered that members of feminine cultures are more sensitive to the presence of moral issues. Masculine/high–power distance/high–uncertainty avoidance countries are generally more corrupt, and their citizens are more likely to look to formal codes and policies for ethical guidance. Consumers from short-term orientation/low–power distance/low–uncertainty avoidance societies generally punish socially irresponsible firms.

Of the four value dimensions, individualism versus collectivism has attracted the most attention. Scholars have used this dimension to explain a variety of cultural differences, including variations in ethical behavior. Management professors Stephen Carroll and Martin Gannon report that individualistic countries prefer universal ethical standards such as Kant's categorical imperative.[29] Collectivistic societies take a more utilitarian approach, seeking to generate the greatest good for in-group members. Citizens of these nations are more sensitive to elements of the situation. To see how these orientations affect ethical decisions, let's return to the four dilemmas I introduced earlier in the chapter.

- *Bribery.* Payoffs tend to be more common in collectivistic nations and may be a way to meet obligations to the community. In some cases, there are laws against the practice, but they take a backseat to history and custom. Individualistic nations view bribery as a form of corruption; payoffs destroy trust and benefit some companies and people at the expense of others.
- *False information.* Individualists are more likely to lie in order to protect their privacy; collectivists are more likely to lie in order to protect the group or family. This accounts for the conflict between the Mexican and U.S. businesspeople described earlier. Mexicans, who tend to have a collectivistic orientation, promise what they can't deliver in order to reduce tensions between their in-group and outsiders. Americans (among the world's most individualistic peoples) condemn this practice as deceptive and therefore unethical. Individualists and collectivists also express disagreement differently. For instance, Germans and Americans don't hesitate to say no directly to another party. Japanese may answer by saying "That will be difficult" rather than by offering an out-and-out refusal. This indirect strategy is designed to save the face or image of the receiver.
- *Intellectual property rights.* Whereas individuals own the rights to their creative ideas in individualistic societies, they are expected to share their knowledge in collectivistic nations. Copyright laws are a Western invention based on the belief that individuals should be rewarded for their efforts.
- *Gender equality.* Resistance to gender equality is strongest in collectivistic nations such as Saudi Arabia and Japan. Women are seen as an out-group in these societies. Many men fear that granting women more status (better jobs, leadership positions) would threaten group stability. Individualistic nations are more likely to have laws that promote equal opportunity, although in many of these countries (such as the United States) women hold fewer leadership positions than men and continue to earn less.

In addition to shaping our moral choices, both individualism and collectivism create *ethical blind spots.* Being self- or group-focused can make us particularly susceptible to certain types of ethical abuses. See Box 10.1 for one list of the ethical problems associated with individualism and collectivism.

Project GLOBE

Project GLOBE (Global Leadership and Organizational Behavior Effectiveness) is an international effort involving 170 researchers who have gathered data from more than 17,000 managers in 62 countries. The researchers hope to better equip global managers by identifying the relationship between cultural values and effective leadership behaviors. Like Hofstede, the GLOBE researchers identify power distance, uncertainty avoidance, gender differentiation (masculinity and femininity), and individualism versus collectivism as important cultural dimensions. However, they extend Hofstede's list by including the following:[30]

In-Group Collectivism

This dimension describes the degree to which societal members take pride in their small groups, families, and organizations. In-group collectivism differs from Hofstede's collectivism dimension, which describes maintaining harmony and cooperation throughout society as a whole. Being a member of a family, a close group, or an employing organization is very important to members of in-group collectivist societies (Iran, India, China), and they have high expectations of other group members. People living in countries that score low on this dimension, such as Denmark, Sweden, and New Zealand, don't have similar expectations of friends and family.

BOX 10.1 ETHICAL DISADVANTAGES OF COLLECTIVISM AND INDIVIDUALISM

University of Illinois psychology professor Harry Triandis argues that there are ethical strengths and weaknesses associated with collectivism and individualism. In general, collectivism is better for interpersonal relationships but poses a danger when members deal with outsiders. Individualism promotes human rights, creativity, and achievement but undermines social connections. Some of the specific ethical disadvantages of collectivism and individualism are outlined here:

Ethical Disadvantages of Collectivism

Suppression of individual thought and innovation

Undermining of the self-esteem of some members

Encouragement of blind obedience to authoritarian groups and leaders

Harsh treatment of out-groups (e.g., discrimination, ethnic cleansing)

Human rights abuses

Wife beating and killing

Continual feuds between groups

Hoarding of information by the in-group

Ethical Disadvantages of Individualism

High crime rates

Selfishness and narcissism

Extreme competitiveness

Violence

Suicide and drug abuse

Aggression

Materialism

Lack of concern about the common good

SOURCE: Triandis, H. C. (1995). *Individualism and collectivism.* Boulder, CO: Westview, Ch. 7.

Assertiveness

Assertiveness is the extent to which a culture encourages individuals to be tough, confrontational, and competitive, as opposed to modest and tender. Spain and the United States rate high on this dimension; Sweden and New Zealand rate low. Those in highly assertive societies have a take-charge attitude and value competition. They are not particularly sympathetic to the weak and less fortunate. Members of less assertive cultures place more value on empathy, loyalty, and solidarity.

Future Orientation

This is the extent to which a society fosters and reinforces such future-oriented activities as planning and investing (Singapore, Switzerland, the Netherlands) rather than immediate gratification (Russia, Argentina, Poland).

Performance Orientation

This is the degree to which a society encourages and rewards group members for improving performance and demonstrating excellence. In places such as Hong Kong, Singapore, and the United States, training and development are valued, and people take initiative. Citizens prefer a direct communication style and feel a sense of urgency. In countries such as Russia, Italy, and Argentina, people put loyalty and belonging ahead of performance. They are uncomfortable with feedback and competition and put more weight on someone's family and background than on performance.

Humane Orientation

Humane orientation is the extent to which a culture encourages and honors people for being altruistic, caring, kind, fair, and generous. Support for the weak and vulnerable is particularly high in countries such as Malaysia, Ireland, and the Philippines. People are usually friendly and tolerant and may develop patronage and paternalistic relationships with their leaders. In contrast, power and material possessions motivate people in the former West Germany, Spain, and France. Self-enhancement takes precedence. Individuals are to solve their own problems; children are expected to be independent.

It is clear that differences on these values dimensions can cause some serious ethical conflicts. Those scoring high on in-group collectivism see no problem in hiring friends and family members even when more qualified candidates are available, a fact that will trouble those who believe that members of their in-groups should not expect preferential treatment (see the "Family Values or Nepotism?" scenario in Case Study 10.2 on page 402). People oriented toward the future will save and invest. They will condemn those who live in the moment and spend all they earn. Competition, direct communication, power, and personal advancement are applauded in assertive, performance-oriented, less humane groups. These elements are undesirable to people who put more value on harmony, cooperation, family, and concern for others. Those living in assertive, performance-oriented cultures are tempted to engage in unethical activities in order to succeed. The businesses they create are more likely to be focused on shareholders, profits, and results instead of on stakeholders and social responsibility.[31]

Although there is plenty of evidence of ethical diversity in the GLOBE study, there are also signs of common ethical ground. As I noted in Chapter 6, the GLOBE researchers discovered that many of the characteristics associated with transformational leadership—motive arouser, foresight, encouraging, dynamic, motivational, trustworthy, positive, confidence builder, communicative—are admired across cultures (though to varying degrees).[32] In another study, researchers from Florida Atlantic University, the University of Maryland, and Wayne State University analyzed the GLOBE data to determine whether there are aspects of ethical leadership that are important for effective leadership across cultures. Four attributes emerged, although the extent to which each is endorsed and how each is implemented differ across cultures.[33] Character and integrity (consistency, virtue) were rated as important, as were altruism, collective motivation (putting the interests of the group ahead of personal interests), and encouraging and empowering (helping followers feel competent). Taken together, these dimensions describe positive, people-oriented leadership that respects the rights and dignity of others. The fact that observers from many different cultural backgrounds agree on the attributes of ethical leadership suggests that there are common ethical standards shared by all cultures. We'll take a closer look at those standards later in the chapter.

Psychological Systems

University of Virginia moral psychologist Jonathan Haidt and others believe that to understand ethical diversity we first need to understand the psychological systems or foundations of morality. These mental foundations, which are part of our genetic makeup, enable humans to successfully live together in groups. Cultures shape how these systems are used, emphasizing one or more values over the others. Haidt compares these moral intuitions to taste buds. Nearly everyone is born with the same set of taste receptors. But each culture develops its own cuisine, which emphasizes different tastes.

Haidt identifies five foundations for our moral intuitions:[34]

1. *Harm/care.* All species are sensitive to suffering in their own offspring, but humans are also sensitive to suffering beyond the family and can feel sympathy for outsiders. Because groups are attuned to cruelty and harm, they generally approve of those who prevent or alleviate suffering and make virtues out of kindness and compassion. However, the other four moral foundations temper the amount of compassion that individuals in different cultures display.

2. *Fairness/reciprocity.* Reciprocity (paying back others) is essential for the formation of alliances between individuals who are not related to each other. All cultures have virtues related to justice and fairness. Yet, while some societies value individual rights and equality, a great many more groups do not.

3. *In-group/loyalty.* Trusting fellow in-group members and distrusting those who belong to other groups have been essential for human survival. As a result, most cultures create virtues out of patriotism, loyalty, and heroism, and some societies (Japan, for instance) put a high value on in-group cohesion. Even when the society as a whole doesn't emphasize loyalty, there are usually subgroups that do (e.g., the police and the military).

4. *Authority/respect.* Hierarchy is a fact of life in primate as well as human groups. While primates rely on brute strength to assert their dominance, people use such factors as prestige and deference. In many cultures followers feel respect, awe, and admiration for leaders and expect good leaders to act like wise parents.

5. *Purity/sanctity.* Only humans appear to feel disgust, which helps to protect the body against the transmission of disease through corpses, feces, vomit, and other possible contaminants. Purity has a social dimension as well. For instance, disgust can be felt for those with deformities or for those of lower social class, such as the untouchables in India. Members of most cultural groups disapprove of those individuals who are contaminated by lust, gluttony, greed, and uncontrolled anger.

The United States and many other Western nations largely focus on reducing harm and promoting autonomy. That is not the case in much of the rest of the world, however. In Brazil, morality is based on loyalty, family, respect, and purity, in addition to care. Confucian and Hindu values systems emphasize authority and stability. Muslim societies place a high priority on purity, which is reflected in the segregation of men and women and separation from infidels. Haidt urges leaders to keep all five moral systems in mind when dealing with diverse groups. We need to realize that although purity and authority may not be important to us, they are to a great proportion of the world's population. We must acknowledge and address these concerns. Unless we are dealing with a highly liberal Western audience, our ethical appeals will be most effective if they speak to loyalty, authority, and purity in addition to care and fairness.

Standing on Moral Common Ground

Confronted with a wide range of ethical values and standards, a number of philosophers, business leaders, anthropologists, and others opt for ethical relativism. In ethical relativism, there are no universal moral codes or standards. Each group or society is unique. Therefore, members of one culture can't pass moral judgment on members of another group.

I'll admit that, at first glance, ethical relativism is appealing. It avoids the problem of ethnocentrism while simplifying the decision-making process. We can concentrate on fitting in with the prevailing culture and never have to pass judgment. On closer examination, however, the difficulties of ethical relativism become all too apparent.[35] Without shared standards, there's little hope that the peoples of the world can work together to address global problems. There may be no basis on which to condemn the evil of notorious leaders who are popular in their own countries. Furthermore, the standard of cultural relativism obligates us to follow (or at least not to protest against) abhorrent local practices such as the killing of brides by their in-laws in the rural villages of Pakistan. Without universal rights and wrongs, we have no basis on which to contest such practices.

Cross-cultural research suggests that there might be moral commonalties when making ethical decisions. To determine if there are universal moral principles or a "moral grammar" built into the mental capacities of all humans, investigators use variations of the "trolley problem." In the trolley problem, an out-of-control trolley threatens to kill five people unless immediate action is taken. In one case, the trolley operator is incapacitated, and a passenger has to decide whether or not to throw a switch, diverting the vehicle to safety on a sidetrack (and saving the five passengers) but killing a pedestrian who happens to be standing on the rails. In the other case, someone standing by the tracks must decide whether or not to directly intervene by throwing another bystander into the path of the trolley to slow it down and save the five passengers.

One group of researchers collected responses to the trolley problem from 30,000 subjects in 120 countries.[36] There was widespread agreement across all national, religious, and education groups. By a significant margin, participants said they would throw the switch to save the trolley passengers but not throw someone onto the tracks to accomplish the same goal. Respondents reported that throwing a switch is an impersonal act, and they saw the death of the pedestrian as an unfortunate consequence. On the other hand, throwing a bystander onto the track is a deliberate, highly personal act that makes the victim a means to an end.

The trolley problem may be hypothetical, but it has parallels in real life. The American Medical Association believes that hastening death by withholding treatment is more acceptable than hastening death through a drug overdose. The medical group permits passive euthanasia for terminally ill patients (which is similar to throwing the trolley switch). However, the AMA opposes active euthanasia (which raises the same concerns as throwing a bystander onto the trolley track).

Research into the neurological basis of moral judgments is in the initial stages but suggests that, when it comes to ethics, there might some cultural unity to go along with cultural diversity. Additional evidence of ethical common ground comes from universal standards, which have enabled members of the world community to punish crimes against humanity and to create the United Nations and its Universal Declaration of Human Rights. In fact, responsible multinational corporations such as The Body Shop, Nike, and Starbucks adhere to widely held moral principles as they conduct business in a variety of cultural settings. In this final section, I'll describe four different approaches to universal ethics: a Global Ethic, Eight Global Values, the Global Business Standards Codex, and the Caux Principles. Any one of these approaches could serve as a worldwide standard. As you read each description, look for commonalties. Then decide for yourself which approach or combination of approaches best captures the foundational values of humankind.

A Global Ethic

Many of the world's conflicts center on religious differences: Hindu versus Muslim, Protestant versus Catholic, Muslim versus Jew. However, these hostilities didn't prevent 6,500 representatives from a wide range of religious faiths from reaching agreement on a global ethic.[37] A council of former heads of state and prime ministers then ratified this statement. Delegates of both groups agreed on two universal principles. First, every person must be treated humanely regardless of language, skin color, mental ability, political beliefs, or national or social origin. Every person and group, no matter how powerful, must respect the dignity of others. Second, "what you wish done to yourself, do to others" (or the Golden Rule). These two foundational principles, in turn, lead to the following ethical directives or imperatives:

- Commitment to a culture of nonviolence and respect for all life
- Commitment to a culture of solidarity and a just economic order (do not steal, deal fairly and honestly with others)
- Commitment to a culture of tolerance and truthfulness
- Commitment to a culture of equal rights and partnership between men and women (avoid immorality; respect and love members of both genders)

Eight Global Values

Rushworth Kidder and his colleagues at the Institute for Global Ethics identified eight core values that appear to be shared the world over. They isolated these values after conducting interviews with 24 international "ethical thought leaders."[38] Kidder's sample included United Nations officials, heads of state, university presidents, writers, and religious figures drawn from such nations as the United States, Vietnam, Mozambique, New Zealand, Bangladesh, Britain, China, Sri Lanka, Costa Rica, and Lebanon. Each interview ran from 1 to 3 hours and began with this question: "If you could help create a global code of ethics, what would be on it?" These global standards emerged:

- *Love:* Spontaneous concern for others, compassion that transcends political and ethnic differences
- *Truthfulness:* Achieving goals through honest means, keeping promises, being worthy of the trust of others

- *Fairness (justice):* Fair play, evenhandedness, equality
- *Freedom:* The pursuit of liberty, right of free expression and action, and accountability
- *Unity:* Seeking the common good; cooperation, community, solidarity
- *Tolerance:* Respect for others and their ideas; empathy, appreciation for variety
- *Responsibility:* Care for self, the sick and needy, the community, and future generations; responsible use of force
- *Respect for life:* Reluctance to kill through war and other means

Kidder and his fellow researchers don't claim to have discovered the one and only set of universal values, but they do believe that they have established ethical common ground. Kidder admits that the eight values are ordinary rather than unique, but the fact that the list contains few surprises is evidence these standards are widely shared.

The Global Business Standards Codex

Harvard business professor Lynn Paine and her colleagues argue that world-class corporations base their codes of ethics on a set of eight universal, overarching ethical principles.[39] Paine's group compiled these guidelines after surveying a variety of global and corporate codes of conduct and government regulations. The researchers offer their Global Business Standards Codex as a benchmark for those who want to conform to universal standards of corporate conduct.

I. Fiduciary principle. Act on behalf of the company and its investors. Be diligent and loyal in carrying out the firm's business. As a trustee, be candid (open and honest).

II. Property principle. Respect and protect property and the rights of its owners. Don't steal or misuse company assets, including information, funds, and equipment. Avoid waste and take care of property entrusted to you.

III. Reliability principle. Honor all commitments. Keep promises and follow through on agreements even when they are not in the form of legally binding contracts.

IV. Transparency principle. Do business in a truthful manner. Avoid deceptive acts and practices and keep accurate records. Release information that should be shared in a timely fashion but maintain confidentiality and privacy as necessary.

V. Dignity principle. Respect the dignity of all who come in contact with the corporation, including employees, suppliers, customers, and the public. Protect their health, privacy, and rights. Avoid coercion. Promote human development instead by providing learning and development opportunities.

VI. Fairness principle. Deal fairly with everyone. Engage in fair competition, provide just compensation to employees, and be evenhanded in dealings with suppliers and corporate partners. Practice nondiscrimination in both employment and contracting.

VII. Citizenship principle. Act as a responsible member of the community by (a) obeying the law, (b) protecting the public good (not engaging in corruption, protecting the environment), (c) cooperating with public authorities, (d) avoiding improper involvement in politics, and (e) contributing to the community (e.g., economic and social development, giving to charitable causes).

VIII. Responsiveness principle. Engage with groups (neighborhood groups, activists, customers) that may have concerns about the company's activities. Work with other groups to better society while not usurping the government's role in protecting the public interest.

The Caux Principles

The Caux Round Table is made up of business executives from the United States, Japan, and Europe who meet every year in Caux, Switzerland. Round Table members hope to set a world standard by which to judge business behavior. Their principles are based on twin ethical ideals. The first is the Japanese concept of *kyosei,* which refers to living and working together for the common good. The second is the Western notion of human dignity, the sacredness and value of each person as an end rather than as a means to someone else's end.[40]

> *Principle 1. The responsibilities of corporations: Beyond shareholders toward stakeholders.* Corporations have a responsibility to improve the lives of everyone they come in contact with, starting with employees, shareholders, and suppliers, and then extending out to local, national, regional, and global communities.

> *Principle 2. The economic and social impact of corporations: Toward innovation, justice, and world community.* Companies in foreign countries should not only create jobs and wealth but also foster better social conditions (education, welfare, human rights). Corporations have an obligation to enrich the world community through innovation, the wise use of resources, and fair competition.

> *Principle 3. Corporate behavior: Beyond the letter of law toward a spirit of trust.* Businesses ought to promote honesty, transparency, integrity, and keeping promises. These behaviors make it easier to conduct international business and to support a global economy.

Principle 4. Respect for rules: Beyond trade friction toward cooperation. Leaders of international firms must respect both international and local laws in order to reduce trade wars and to promote the free flow of goods and services.

Principle 5. Support for multilateral trade: Beyond isolation toward world community. Firms should support international trading systems and agreements and eliminate domestic measures that undermine free trade.

Principle 6. Respect for the environment: Beyond protection toward enhancement. A corporation ought to protect and, if possible, improve the physical environment through sustainable development and cutting back on the wasteful use of natural resources.

Principle 7. Avoidance of illicit operations: Beyond profit toward peace. Global business leaders must ensure that their organizations aren't involved in such forbidden activities as bribery, money laundering, support of terrorism, drug trafficking, and organized crime.

After spelling out general principles, the Caux accord applies them to important stakeholder groups. Leaders following these standards hope to (a) treat customers and employees with dignity, (b) honor the trust of investors, (c) create relationships with suppliers based on mutual trust, (d) engage in just behavior with competitors, and (e) work for reform and human rights in host communities.

Making Ethical Choices in Culturally Diverse Settings

The universal principles described in the last section play an important role when we are faced with making ethical decisions involving more than one culture. According to business ethicists Thomas Donaldson and Thomas Dunfee, we need to hold fast to global principles while we take local values into account.[41] Their Integrative Social Contracts Theory (ISCT) provides one set of guidelines for balancing respect for ethical diversity with adherence to universal ethical standards.

ISCT is based on the idea of social contracts—agreements that spell out the duties of institutions, communities, and societies. The theory is integrative because it incorporates two kinds of contracts: macrosocial and microsocial. *Macrosocial* contracts are broader and lay the foundation for how people interact with one another. The requirement that the government protect its citizens and the belief that employers should respect the rights of workers are examples of ideal contracts. *Microsocial* contracts govern the relationships between the members of specific groups (local towns, regions, nations, companies, professions). These contacts are revealed by the norms of the group. For example, those who participate in auctions must adhere to the norms of the auction community, which include revealing whether participants have the means to back up their bids and not interfering with others who are making bids. Community contracts are considered authentic or binding if members of the group have a voice in the creation of the norms, members can exit the group if they disagree with prevailing norms, and the norms are widely recognized and practiced by group members. Under these standards, prohibitions against free speech in countries ruled by repressive regimes would not be authentic because citizens had no say in creating these rules and can't leave the community if they want.

Local communities have a great deal of latitude or *moral free space* to create their own rules, and these norms should be respected whenever possible. An Indonesian manager participating in an Australian real estate auction should obey Australian auction norms, for instance. However, universal principles such as those described in the previous section (what Donaldson and Dunfee call *hypernorms*) take priority when global principles clash with community standards. Exploitation of workers (excessive hours, low pay, imprisonment, sexual abuse) might be the norm in some developing countries. But such practices should be rejected because they violate hypernorms that urge us to respect the dignity of other human beings, treat them fairly and humanely, and follow the Golden Rule.

To make decisions following ISCT guidelines, follow these steps:

1. Identify all relevant stakeholders or communities.

2. Determine whether these communities are legitimate (do they allow voice and exit by members?).

3. Identify authentic norms (those that are widely known and shared).

4. Determine whether the norms are legitimate (do not conflict with hypernorms).

5. Resolve any conflicts between legitimate norms. (If both sets of norms do not conflict with universal standards, go with the option that is dominant—the one accepted by the larger community.)

University of Louisiana professors J. Brooke Hamilton, Stephen Knouse, and Vanessa Hill (HKH) offer another set of guidelines for making choices in ethically diverse contexts. They provide six questions specifically designed to help managers at multinational enterprises (MNEs) make moral choices when corporate values conflict with business practices in the host country.[42]

The questions described below, which make up the HKH model, are designed to serve as a discussion/decision guide, not as a rigid set of steps. Managers don't have to come to a definite answer to one question before moving to another. They may return to earlier questions later and answer them differently.

1. *What is the Questionable Practice (QP) in this situation?*
   - In the initial stage of the HKH decision-making format, managers determine that the norms of the MNE clash with the norms of the local culture. At this point the disparity is labeled as "questionable" because it may involve cultural differences rather than ethical issues. The key is to come to a clear understanding of the nature of the conflict.

2. *Does the QP violate any laws that are enforced?*
   - If the QP violates laws of the home country (the U.S. Foreign Corrupt Practices Act, for example, or European Union prohibitions against bribery) or the host country, it should be discontinued.

3. *Is the QP simply a cultural difference, or is it also a potential ethics problem?*
   - A QP reflects a cultural difference if it "does not cause harm and appears to be that culture's legitimate way of achieving some worthwhile business or social outcome."[43] It rises to the level of a potential ethical issue if it creates harm or violates a universal global principle like treating people with respect and practicing the Golden Rule.

4. *Does the QP violate the firm's core values or code of conduct, an industry-wide or international code to which the firm subscribes, or a firmly established hypernorm?*
   - How managers answer this question will be determined by whether they believe that their companies are driven solely by the desire to comply with the law or whether they believe their firms are committed to ethical integrity instead (see Chapter 9). Compliance-driven firms are more likely to conform to local rules because they are primarily interested in following the law; survival is the core value. Integrity-driven firms have a higher standard. Managers at these firms judge local practices based on whether they conform to important corporate values (customer service, treating employees fairly) and such international guidelines as the Caux Principles and the Global Business Standards Codex.

5. Does the firm have leverage (something of value to offer) in the host country that allows the firm to follow its own practices rather than the QP?
   - Only managers at integrity-driven companies will ask this question, as managers at compliance-oriented firms will go along with local practices. If the firm can offer significant benefits like jobs, cash, training, and new

technology, it can better resist the pressure to engage in unethical activity and can negotiate a way to adapt to local customs without violating its core values. For instance, a large Western oil firm that values equal treatment of both genders may be able to leverage its power in a traditionalist Middle Eastern country to promote women to positions of organizational authority.

6. Will market practices in the host country improve if the firm follows its own practices rather than the QP in the host country marketplace?

   • A company without leverage will have to conform to customs of the home country or exit the market. However, if the firm has such leverage, it has an obligation to try to improve conditions in the countries in which it operates. Modeling respect for individuals, honest business practices, and concern for the environment can encourage local firms and other MNEs to do the same and result in better living and working conditions and a healthier economy.

You can practice your ability to make cross-cultural ethical choices by applying the steps of the ISCT and HKH models to Case Study 10.3 (page 404). This case highlights the difficult ethical choices facing American technology companies operating under a Communist regime.

Implications and Applications

- Fostering diversity is not just good business strategy; it is an ethical imperative for leaders.
- Prejudice, stereotypes, and ethnocentrism are barriers to diversity and lead to moral abuses. You can avoid casting shadows if you commit yourself to mindfulness, human dignity, moral inclusiveness, and cosmopolitanism.
- Acknowledging the dark side of globalization reduces the likelihood of ethical abuse on the world stage. As a leader in a global environment, you must take additional care to avoid casting shadows of power, privilege, mismanaged information, inconsistency, misplaced and broken loyalties, and irresponsibility.
- Cultural differences make ethical decisions more difficult. Nevertheless, resist the temptation to revert to your old ways of thinking or to blindly follow local customs. Try instead to expand your capacity to act ethically in multicultural situations.
- Understanding the relationship between cultural differences and ethical values can help you predict how members of another group will respond to moral questions.
- Two popular cultural value classification systems are Hofstede's programmed values (power distance, individualism versus collectivism, masculinity versus femininity, uncertainty avoidance) and the GLOBE cultural dimensions, which

include Hofstede's categories along with in-group collectivism, assertiveness, future orientation, performance orientation, and humane orientation.

- All humans seem concerned about care, fairness, loyalty, respect for authority, and purity, though cultures differ in the relative importance they put on each of these moral foundations, which leads to ethical conflicts. Keep all five psychological or moral systems in mind when dealing with diverse groups.

- Universal standards can help you establish common ground with diverse followers. These shared standards can take the form of religious commitments, global values, or world business standards.

- To make ethical decisions in cross-cultural settings, take both local values and global principles into account. Follow community norms except when they conflict with universal moral standards. As a business leader, make the most of your company's leverage in another country to improve local conditions.

For Further Exploration, Challenge, and Self-Assessment

1. Distribute the "Self-Assessment: Diversity Perceptions Scale" to other members of your organization and discuss your responses. What factors contributed to your organizational and personal perceptions? What can you do to boost your individual and collective scores?

2. Form groups and debate the following proposition: "Overall, globalization does more harm than good."

3. Pair off and brainstorm a list of the advantages and disadvantages of ethical diversity. What conclusions do you draw from your list?

4. Using the Internet, compare press coverage of an international ethical issue from a variety of countries. How does the coverage differ and why? Write up your findings.

5. Rate yourself on one or both of the cultural classification systems described in the chapter. Create a value profile of your community, organization, or university. How well do you fit in?

6. In a research paper, analyze the cultural values that likely influenced the ethical decision of a prominent leader.

7. Use the five psychological moral systems or foundations to explain an ethical conflict. Share your analysis with the rest of the class.

8. Write a response to the following: Is there a common morality that peoples of all nations can share? Which of the global codes described in the chapter best reflects these shared standards and values? If you were to create your own declaration of global ethics, what would you put on it?

CASE STUDY 10.2

ETHICAL DIVERSITY SCENARIOS

Family Values or Nepotism?

A number of companies in India will hire the children of employees once a child has completed his or her schooling. The firms honor this commitment even though more qualified applicants are available. This benefit is extremely valuable in a country where jobs are often hard to find. Also, many Indians believe that the West has allowed economic considerations to break up families. Although this practice is popular among employees, it would be considered nepotism in the United States and violates the principle of equal opportunity. The Equal Employment Opportunity Commission would fine U.S. companies for making such commitments.

As a manager, how should you react to Indian nepotism? Should you refuse to accept Indian companies as partners or suppliers unless they cease this practice?

SOURCE: Donaldson, T. (1996, September–October). Values in tension: Ethics away from home. *Harvard Business Review, 74,* 48–57.

Medical Treatment Policies

Your Europe-based clothing manufacturing company has plants in several sub-Saharan African countries. Your firm pays higher-than-average wages for the region and offers superior working conditions. However, the local media has been critical of your policy toward on-the-job injuries. If a European or other expatriate employee working at a plant gets hurt, he or she is taken to the local private hospital, which provides superior care. If a local worker sustains the same injury, he or she sees the company nurse or is taken to the local public hospital, which is poorly staffed and provides minimal care.

Your company's treatment of local employees is better than the practice of other manufacturers in the region, many of which do not have nurses on staff. Your medical policy has not kept locals from applying to work at your plants (you have a long list of applicants on file). Further, you can't attract expatriates to work at your facilities unless you offer high-quality medical care.

As human resources director, would you recommend that the company change its medical policies to provide the same care for local workers as it provides for expatriate employees?

SOURCE: Mitchell, C. (2003). *International business ethics: Combining ethics and profits in global business.* Novato, CA: World Trade Press.

Hazardous Material Labels

Governments in most industrialized countries require manufacturers to place safety labels on containers of hazardous materials and ban the importation of unmarked products. These labels inform users about the content of the materials, how to use them, and what to do in the case of an accident. Government authorities in many developing nations aren't as likely to require such labels. Managers who purchase unlabeled containers from vendors in developing countries may not be sure what they are buying but, even more important, are putting their employees at risk. Workers could harm themselves while using the products on a daily basis and don't know how to respond in the case of an accident involving the materials.

Requiring suppliers in poor nations to place safety labels on their containers significantly boosts their costs. They have to spend time and money to gather and communicate such information and may be annoyed by having to comply with what they perceive as "petty demands." A number of suppliers may seek out more accepting customers instead. The additional administrative costs are also passed onto the buyer, which can put the purchaser at a competitive disadvantage. Some purchasing managers try to lower their costs and maintain their relationships with suppliers by buying unlabeled materials for use in international facilities where safety labels aren't required.

As a purchasing manager in a multinational firm, would you require your suppliers in developing countries to label their hazardous materials? Would you use unlabeled hazardous materials in countries where the law allows?

SOURCE: Reynolds, S. J. (2003). A single framework for strategic and ethical behavior in the international context. *Business Ethics Quarterly, 13*, 361–379.

The Exiled President

You are a diplomat in a small Central American country. For years your home government has pushed for the development of stable democracies in Central America, hoping to end the military coups that once were common in the region. The latest democratically elected president in your host state came to office with a commitment to the poor. Within weeks of assuming the presidency, he threatened to nationalize the local holdings of several of your home nation's multinational corporations. He condemned your government (and those of several other Western countries) for engaging in "capitalist imperialism." The president's leftist policies angered local

(Continued)

(Continued)

business interests, and they soon drove him into exile with the help of the army. Military officers installed a new president who promised to be friendlier toward your nation. However, the new president has yet to set a timeline for holding elections. In the meantime, the exiled president, who still enjoys widespread support among the poor and working classes, wants to return to office. He has asked for help from the international community.

Would you recommend that your government support the deposed president's efforts to return to office? If so, what steps should it take?

SOURCE: Fictional case based on actual international events.

CASE STUDY 10.3

GOOGLE MEETS THE GREAT FIREWALL OF CHINA

The Chinese Internet market is exploding. In one decade the number of Chinese with access to the global Internet went from 80,000 to 130 million. To enter this lucrative market, American technology firms must participate in the Communist government's censorship program, which has been dubbed the "Great Firewall of China." The Chinese Communist government uses a variety of strategies to police websites and Internet traffic to determine whether users are breaking the law by defaming the government, divulging state secrets, or promoting separatist movements. Chinese officials ban such "subversive" material as government criticism, pornography, and information about Tibet, Taiwanese independence, and the Falun Gong religious sect. An estimated 30,000–50,000 human censors monitor Internet traffic and set up fake sites to catch offenders. Student volunteers steer university chat room discussions, and cartoon icons remind users of the Internet rules. Automatic censoring systems remove offensive chat room and bulletin board postings within minutes by detecting and then eliminating messages containing such words as *dictatorship, corruption,* or *truth.* Access to a number of websites is blocked, and users can only access portions of other sites. For example, a Chinese citizen may be able to visit an American university website but not be able to access material on a Chinese prodemocracy speaker sponsored by the university.

American firms have done their part to shore up the Great Firewall. Cisco Systems and Juniper Networks sell China's government networking hardware that enables officials to filter out content, allowing access to the

World Wide Web but only to information favorable to the Chinese government. Yahoo! screens content and de-lists websites like *The New York Times* and Human Rights Watch from its search engine and, until its recent merger with a Chinese provider, did so without notifying users. Yahoo! also gave Chinese authorities the e-mail address of a journalist who is now serving a 10-year prison term for sending material to a democracy website. MSN (Microsoft) censors words and removes blogs at the government's request.

From 2006 to 2010 Google supported China's censorship efforts, blocking content that Beijing deems controversial. For instance, Westerners using the search term *Tiananmen* might get images of protesters being overrun by tanks in 1989. In China, the same search would generate an image of a U.S. official posing for a snapshot in Tiananmen Square. The company's decision to censor appeared to contradict its motto to "do no evil" and undermined its efforts to provide unlimited access to information. Google justified its action by arguing that censorship is the lesser of two evils. "Filtering our search results clearly compromises our mission," the firm admitted. "Failing to offer Google search at all to a fifth of the world's population, however, does so far more severely."[1] Unlike some of its competitors, Google was transparent about its censorship efforts, notifying users that content had been blocked.

Critics, such as Reporters Without Borders, Amnesty International, and some members of Congress, took issue with Google's assertions. Human rights advocates pointed out that censorship violates the United Nations Universal Declaration of Human Rights by denying freedom of speech and information. Iowa Republican congressman Jim Leach argued that Google's actions turned it into a "functionary of the Chinese government."[2] California representative Tom Lantos (a Holocaust survivor) told Google, Yahoo!, and other Internet firms doing business in China, "While technologically you are giants, morally you are pygmies."[3] The Global Online Freedom Act (GOFA) was introduced in Congress to prohibit American companies from engaging in political censorship in Internet-restricting countries (Belarus, Cuba, Ethiopia, Iran, Laos, North Korea, the People's Republic of China, Tunisia, Vietnam), though it has yet to be passed.

In early 2010, after an attack on its computer systems allegedly originating in China, Google closed its Internet search service in mainland China and directed users to an uncensored search engine in Hong Kong. The Chinese government responded by accusing Google of violating its pledge to follow censorship laws and of collaborating with U.S. spy agencies. Chinese business partners began to cut off their relationships with Google.

(Continued)

(Continued)

China's Great Firewall will likely survive for the foreseeable future. Hopes were that censors would be overwhelmed by the flow of information generated by the rapid growth of computers, Internet cafes, social media, and blogs. However, increasingly sophisticated technology provided by U.S. firms makes it easier than ever for Chinese authorities to clamp down on Internet activity. Google's chief legal officer admitted that the company's attempts to loosen information access had failed and that censorship in China is more restrictive than ever. "Far from our presence helping to open things up," he lamented, "it seems that things are getting tighter for open expression and freedom."[4]

Discussion Probes

1. Google initially argued that filtering Internet content is less damaging than not being in the Chinese market. Do you agree?

2. Use the steps of Integrative Social Contracts Theory or the HTK decision-making process to determine whether American high-tech firms should participate in the Great Firewall of China. What do you conclude?

3. Should the U.S. government prevent U.S. technology companies from working with repressive regimes in China and elsewhere?

4. Is Internet access to information a human right or a privilege?

5. Is web censorship ever justified? What topics, if any, should be filtered?

6. What leadership and followership ethics lessons do you take from this case?

Notes

1. Grossman, L., & Beech, H. (2006, February 13). Google under the gun. *Time*.

2. Silla, B., Knight, D., & Fang, B. (2006, February 27). Learning to live with big brother. *U.S. News & World Report*.

3. Hamilton, J. B., Knouse, S. B., & Hill, V. (2007). Google in China: A manager-friendly heuristic model for resolving cross-cultural ethical conflicts. *Journal of Business Ethics, 86*, 143–157, p. 154.

4. Helft, M., & Markoff, J. (2010, January 14). In Google's rebuke of China, focus falls on cybersecurity. *The New York Times*, p. A1.

Sources

Benkert, G. G. (2008). Google, human rights, and moral compromise. *Journal of Business Ethics, 85,* 453–478.

Dann, G. E., & Haddow, N. (2007). Just doing business or doing just business: Google, Microsoft, Yahoo! and the business of censoring China's Internet. *Journal of Business Ethics, 79,* 219–234.

Einhorn, B. (2006, August 11). *Search engines censured for censorship.* Retrieved from http://www.businessweek.com/globalbiz/content/aug2006/gb200 60810_220695.htm

Farrell, K. (2008). Corporate complicity in the Chinese censorship regime: When freedom of expression and profitability collide. *Internet Law, 11,* 1, 11–21.

Levy, S. (2006, February 13). Google and the China syndrome. *Newsweek,* p. 14.

Ramstack, T. (2008, May 21). U.S. web services misused by oppressors. *The Washington Times,* p. C08.

The party, the people and the power of cyber-talk. (2006, April 29). *The Economist,* pp. 27–30.

Wiseman, P. (2008, April 23). In China, a battle over Web censorship. *USA Today,* p. 1A.

Notes

1. Mor Barak, M. E. (2005). *Managing diversity: Toward a globally inclusive workplace.* Thousand Oaks, CA: Sage; Konrad, A. M. (2006). Leveraging workplace diversity in organizations. *Organization Management Journal, 3,* 164–189; Scully, S. (2001, March 13). Minorities gain ground on whites in '00 census. *The Washington Times,* p. A1; Bureau of Labor Statistics. (2009). *Women in the labor force.* Retrieved from http://www.bls.gov/CPS/wlf-intro-2009.htm

2. Cox, T. (1993). *Cultural diversity in organizations: Theory, research and practice.* San Francisco: Berrett-Koehler; Cox, T. (2001). *Creating the multicultural organization: A strategy for capturing the power of diversity.* San Francisco: Jossey-Bass.

3. See the following:

> Hays-Thomas, R. (2004). Why now? The contemporary focus on managing diversity. In M. S. Stockdale & F. J. Crosby (Eds.), *The psychology and management of workplace diversity* (pp. 3–30). Malden, MA: Blackwell. Konrad.

> Koonce, R. (2001, December). Redefining diversity. *Training and Development,* pp. 22–28.

> Kossek, E. E., Lobel, S. A., & Brown, J. (2006). Human resource strategies to manage workplace diversity: Examining the "business case." In A. M. Konrad, P. Prasad, & J. K. Pringle (Eds.), *Handbook of workplace diversity* (pp. 53–74). London: Sage.

> Mor Barak.

4. Drummond, T. (2000, April 3). Coping with cops. *Time,* pp. 72–73.

5. Brown, R. (1995). *Prejudice: Its social psychology.* Oxford, UK: Blackwell; Fiske, S. T. (1998). Stereotyping, prejudice, and discrimination. In D. T. Gilbert, S. T. Fiske, & G. Lindzey (Eds.), *The handbook of social psychology* (Vol. 2, pp. 357–411). Boston: McGraw-Hill.

6. Gudykunst, W. B., & Kim, Y. Y. (1997). *Communicating with strangers: An approach to intercultural communication* (3rd ed.). New York: McGraw-Hill; Gudykunst, W. B. (2004). *Bridging differences: Effective intergroup communication* (4th ed.). Thousand Oaks, CA; Sage; Cox (1993), Ch. 13.

7. Cox (1993), Ch. 13.

8. Langer, E. J. (1989). *Mindfulness.* Reading, MA: Addison-Wesley; Langer, E. J. (1997). *The power of mindful learning.* Reading, MA: Addison-Wesley.

9. Opotow, S. (1990). Moral exclusion and injustice: An introduction. *Journal of Social Issues, 46*(1), 1–20.

10. Smith, W. (2007). Cosmopolitan citizenship: Virtue, irony and worldliness. *European Journal of Social Theory, 10,* 37–52; Maas, T., & Pless, N. M. (2009). Business leaders as citizens of the world. Advancing humanism on a global scale. *Journal of Business Ethics, 88,* 537–550; Appiah, K. A. (2006). *Cosmopolitanism: Ethics in a world of strangers.* New York: Norton.

11. Fine, R., & Boon, V. (2007). Introduction: Cosmopolitanism: Between past and future. *European Journal of Social Theory, 10,* 5–16, p. 6.

12. Mor Barak; Cox (2001); Morrison, A. M. (1996). *The new leaders: Guidelines on leadership diversity in America.* San Francisco: Jossey-Bass; Konrad.

13. Tavis, T. (2000). The globalization phenomenon and multinational corporate developmental responsibility. In O. F. Williams (Ed.), *Global codes of conduct: An idea whose time has come* (pp. 13–36). Notre Dame, IN: University of Notre Dame Press; Dunning, J. H. (2003). Overview. In J. H. Dunning (Ed.), *Making globalization good: The moral challenges of global capitalism* (pp. 11–40). Oxford, UK: Oxford University Press.

14. Muzaffar, C. (2002). Conclusion. In P. F. Knitter & C. Muzaffar (Eds.), *Subverting greed: Religious perspectives on the global economy* (pp. 154–172). Maryknoll, NY: Orbis; Ritzer, G. (2004). *The globalization of nothing.* Thousand Oaks, CA: Pine Forge; Dunning, J. H. (2000). Whither global capitalism? *Global Focus, 12,* 117–136.

15. Friedman, T. (2000). *The Lexus and the olive tree* (Expanded ver.). New York: Anchor.

16. Melloan, G. (2004, January 6). Feeling the muscle of the multinationals. *The Wall Street Journal,* p. A19.

17. Statistics taken from Singer, P. (2002). *One world: the ethics of globalization.* New Haven, CT: Yale University Press.

18. Muzaffar.

19. Richter, J. (2001). *Holding corporations accountable: Corporate conduct, international codes and citizen action.* London: Zed; Perez, J. (2006, December 4). Yellow pad: What the milk companies don't want you to know. *BusinessWorld,*

pp. 1–5; Moorhead, J. (2007, May 15). Milking it. *The Guardian*, p. 8; NAFDAC warns violators of BMS international code. (2007, August 7). *Africa News*.

20. Karim, A. (2000, June 23). Globalization, ethics, and AIDS vaccines. *Science*, pp. 21–29.

21. The mess that the army has made—Myanmar. (2005, July 23). *The Economist*, Special Report; Armitage, J., & Conde, B. (2007, October 19). Why the French are so keen to stay in Burma despite unrest. *The Evening Standard*, p. B34; Campbell, D. (2004, December 14). Energy giant agrees settlement with Burmese villagers. *The Guardian*, Foreign Affairs, p. 17.

22. Solomon, C. M. (2001). Put your ethics to a global test. In M. H. Albrecht (Ed.), *International HRM: Managing diversity in the workplace* (pp. 329–335). Oxford, UK: Blackwell.

23. Donaldson, T. (1996, September–October). Values in tension: Ethics away from home. *Harvard Business Review*, pp. 48–57.

24. Carroll, S. J., & Gannon, M. J. (1997). *Ethical dimensions of management*. Thousand Oaks, CA: Sage.

25. Rogers, E. M., & Steinfatt, T. M. (1999). *Intercultural communication*. Prospect Heights, IL: Waveland, p. 79.

26. Hofstede, G. (1984). *Culture's consequences*. Beverly Hills, CA: Sage; Hofstede, G. (1991). *Cultures and organizations: Software of the mind*. London: McGraw-Hill.

27. Hofstede, G. (2001). Difference and danger: Cultural profiles of nations and limits to tolerance. In M. H. Albrecht (Ed.), *International HRM: Managing diversity in the workplace* (pp. 9–23). Oxford, UK: Blackwell.

28. Husted, B. W. (1999). Wealth, culture and corruption. *Journal of International Business Studies, 30,* 339–359; Vitell, S. J., Nwachukwu, S. L., & Barnes, J. H. (1993). *Journal of Business Ethics, 12,* 753–760; Davis, J. H., & Ruhe, J. A. (2003). Perceptions of country corruption: Antecedents and outcomes. *Journal of Business Ethics, 43,* 275–288; Franke, G. P., & Nadler, S. S. (2007). Culture, economic development, and national ethical attitudes. *Journal of Business Research, 61,* 254–264; Williams, G., & Zinkin, J. (2008). The effect of culture on consumers' willingness to punish irresponsible corporate behaviour: Applying Hofstede's typology to the punishment aspect of corporate social responsibility. *Business Ethics: A European Review, 17,* 210–226.

29. Carroll & Gannon.

30. Javidan, M., & House, R. J. (2001). Cultural acumen for the global manager: Lessons from Project GLOBE. *Organizational Dynamics, 29,* 289–305; House, R. J., Hange, P. J., Javidan, M., Dorfman, P. W., & Gupta, V. (Eds.). (2004). *Culture, leadership, and organizations: The GLOBE study of 62 societies*. Thousand Oaks, CA: Sage.

31. Quigley, N. R., Sully de Luque, M., & House, R. J. (2005). Responsible leadership and governance in a global context: Insights from the GLOBE study. In J. P. Doh & S. A. Sumpf (Eds.), *Handbook on responsible leadership and governance in global business* (pp. 352–379). Cheltenham, UK: Elger.

32. Den Hartog, D. N., House, R. J., Hange, P. U., Ruiz-Quintanilla, S. A., & Dorfman, P. W. (1999). Culture-specific and cross-culturally generalizable implicit leadership theories: Are attributes of charismatic/transformational leadership universally endorsed? *The Leadership Quarterly, 10,* 219–257.

33. Resick, C. J., Hange, P. J., Dickson, M. W., & Mitchelson, J. K. (2006). A cross-cultural examination of the endorsement of ethical leadership. *Journal of Business Ethics, 63,* 345–359.

34. Haidt, J., & Bjorklund, F. (2008). Social intuitionists answer six questions about moral psychology. In W. Sinnott-Armstrong (Ed.), *Moral psychology (Vol. 2): The cognitive science of morality: Intuition and diversity* (pp. 182–217). Cambridge, MA: MIT Press; Haidt, J., & Graham, J. (2007). When morality opposes justice: Conservatives have moral intuitions that liberals may not recognize. *Social Justice Research, 20,* 98–116; Jacobs, T. (2009, May). Morals authority. *Miller-McCune,* pp. 47–55.

35. Talbot, M. (1999). Against relativism. In J. M. Halstead & T. H. McLaughlin (Eds.), *Education in morality* (pp. 206–217). London: Routledge.

36. Hauser, M. D., Young, L., & Cushman, F. (2008). Reviving Rawls's linguistic analogy: Operative principles and the causal structure of moral actions. In W. Sinnott-Armstrong (Ed.), *Moral psychology (Vol. 2): The cognitive science of morality: Intuition and diversity* (pp. 107–144). Cambridge, MA: MIT.

37. Kung, H. (1998). *A global ethic for global politics and economics.* New York: Oxford University Press; Kung, H. (1999). A global ethic in an age of globalization. In G. Enderle (Ed.), *International business ethics: Challenges and approaches* (pp. 19–127). Notre Dame, IN: University of Notre Dame Press; Kung, H. (2003). An ethical framework for the global market economy. In J. H. Dunning (Ed.), *Making globalization good: The moral challenges of global capitalism* (pp. 146–158). Oxford, UK: Oxford University Press.

38. Kidder, R. M. (1994). *Shared values for a troubled world: Conversations with men and women of conscience.* San Francisco: Jossey-Bass.

39. Paine, L., Deshpande, R., Margolis, J. D., & Bettcher, Kk. E. (2005, December). Up to code: Does your company meet world-class standards? *Harvard Business Review,* pp. 122–133.

40. Caux Round Table. (2000). Appendix 26: The Caux principles. In O. F. Williams (Ed.), *Global codes of conduct: An idea whose time has come* (pp. 384–388). Notre Dame, IN: Notre Dame University Press.

41. Donaldson, T., & Dunfee, T. W. (1994). Toward a unified conception of business ethics: Integrative social contracts theory. *Academy of Management Review, 19,* 252–284; Donaldson & Dunfee (1999). *Ties that bind: A social contracts approach to business ethics.* Boston: Harvard Business School Press.

42. Hamilton, J. B., Knouse, S. B., & Hill, V. (2008). Google in China: A manager-friendly heuristic model for resolving cross-cultural ethical conflicts. *Journal of Business Ethics, 86,* 143–157. See also Hamilton, J. B., & Knouse, S. B. (2001). Multinational enterprise decision principles for dealing with cross cultural ethical conflicts. *Journal of Business Ethics, 31,* 77–94.

43. Hamilton, Knouse, & Hill, p. 149.

11

Ethical Crisis Leadership

The key difference between a crisis-prone organization and one which is prepared is the emotional, intellectual, political, and ethical courage and strength of its top executives.

—Crisis experts Thierry Pauchant,
Ian Mitroff, and Gerald Ventolo

Nothing devastates the soul as much as a crisis.

—Ian Mitroff

WHAT'S AHEAD

This chapter examines ethical leadership in crisis situations. Crises are major unexpected events that pose significant threats to groups and organizations. They pass through three stages: precrisis, crisis event, and postcrisis. Ethical leaders have a series of tasks to carry out during each phase. Five ethical principles and strategies are essential to fulfilling these moral duties: assume broad responsibility, practice transparency, demonstrate care and concern, engage the head as well as the heart, and improvise from a strong moral foundation.

M anaging a crisis is the ultimate test of ethical leadership. Bankruptcies, hurricanes, political scandals, industrial accidents, school shootings, food-borne illnesses, oil spills, fraud, computer data theft, terrorist attacks, and other crisis events bring out the worst or best in leaders. Decisions must be made quickly under the glare of media scrutiny. Jobs, manufacturing plants, office buildings, planes, homes, and lives may have been lost. Entire organizations, groups, societies, and economic and political systems might be at risk. As we've seen throughout this text, leaders often fail to meet the ethical challenges posed by crises. At Enron, the British Parliament, and the Peanut Corporation of America, leaders sparked crises through their unethical behavior. For their part, leaders at AIG and the Jefferson County, Colorado, Sheriff's Office ignored widely held moral standards and values in response to crisis events. On the other hand, we have also seen how other leaders, like Greg Mortenson and executives at Siemens Global, coped effectively with crisis events. Their values become clearer; their moral commitments become greater.

This chapter introduces the ethical challenges posed by leadership in crisis, building on the foundation laid in earlier chapters. To ethically manage crisis events, you will need to draw upon concepts we have discussed previously—values, moral reasoning, ethical decision-making formats, group decision making, and ethical perspectives, to name a few. However, you will also need to understand the characteristics of crisis as well as the elements of ethical crisis management. Section 1 of this chapter provides an overview of the nature and stages of crises. It identifies important leadership tasks that must be carried out in each crisis phase. Section 2 identifies principles and strategies that equip leaders to ethically carry out these responsibilities.

Crisis: An Overview

A crisis is any major unanticipated event that poses a significant threat. Such events are rare (making them difficult to prepare for), they generate a good deal of uncertainty (their causes and effects are unclear), and they are hard to resolve (there is no set formula for determining how to act). Further, decisions about how to deal with a particular crisis must be made rapidly, and those outside the immediate group (customers, clients, suppliers, neighbors) are also impacted.[1]

The stress and anxiety generated by crises makes them particularly hard to manage in an ethical manner. Stress interferes with cognitive abilities. Individuals tend to narrow their focus to a just a few perspectives and alternatives. They often perceive the world less accurately and ignore important information. At the organizational level, stress prompts groups to delegate decision-making authority to a small team of top officials, limiting access to diverse viewpoints. Time limits also prevent talking to a variety of stakeholders. All of these factors subvert ethical reasoning and creative problem solving while increasing the likelihood that the needs of some stakeholders will be overlooked.[2]

Investigators divide crises into different types. These types can help leaders better prepare for, and respond to, crisis events. Groups and organizations will be more vulnerable to some types of crises than others. Manufacturers have to be highly concerned about product safety; coastal communities have to be ready for ocean storms. When disaster strikes, the nature of the crisis will also help to determine the course of action. Responding to the disruption of a work stoppage requires one set of strategies while responding to a computer security breach demands another.

Crisis management experts Matthew Seeger, Timothy Sellnow, and Robert Ulmer identify ten types of crisis.[3]

1. *Public perception:* negative stories about the organization's products, personnel, or services; negative rumors; blogs and websites

2. *Natural disasters:* tornadoes, hurricanes, mudslides, wildfires, blizzards, earthquakes, volcano eruptions

3. *Product or service:* product recalls, food-borne illnesses, concern about products and services generated by the media

4. *Terrorist attacks:* bombings, hijackings, abductions, poisonings

5. *Economic:* cash shortages, bankruptcies, hostile takeovers, accounting scandals

6. *Human resource:* workplace violence, strikes, labor unrest, discrimination, sexual harassment, school and workplace shootings, theft, fraud

7. *Industrial:* mine collapses, nuclear accidents, fires, explosions

8. *Oil and chemical spills:* tanker and railway spills, pipeline and well leaks

9. *Transportation:* train derailments, plane crashes, truck accidents, multivehicle pileups

10. *Outside environment:* collapse of financial systems, rising fuel prices, deregulation, nationalization of private companies, mortgage crisis

Ian Mitroff offers an alternative typology based on the intentions of those involved in the crisis event.[4] He notes that there has been a sharp rise in what he labels *abnormal accidents*—deliberate acts that are intentionally designed to disrupt or destroy systems. He contrasts abnormal accidents with *normal accidents,* those unintentional events that cause systems to break down. The Oklahoma City bombing, kidnappings, the release of nerve gas in a Tokyo subway, Enron's collapse, and cyber attacks on large corporations and the military would be examples of abnormal accidents. The *Exxon Valdez* oil spill, plane crashes, and mining disasters are normal accidents that reflect problems with routine operating procedures. Abnormal accidents are harder to prepare for, but modern organizations have no choice but to plan for them. For example, since most terrorist acts are aimed at private businesses, not the government, Mitroff argues business has to do its part to respond to terrorist threats. (See Case Study 11.1 for a closer look at one of the ethical issues raised by terrorism.) He also points out that even routine crises are becoming harder to deal with in an increasingly complex, interconnected society. When power went out on the East Coast in 2003, for instance, every organization in the region was impacted, and airline traffic throughout the whole country was disrupted.[5]

CASE STUDY 11.1

THE TERRORIST AND THE TICKING BOMB: ETHICAL LEADERSHIP IN SUPREME EMERGENCIES

Philosophers and ethicists use the term *supreme emergencies* to refer to situations where, many argue, normal rules should be set aside for extreme measures. For example, during World War II Winston Churchill ordered the bombing of German cities in order to defeat Hitler, which resulted in the deaths of 300,000 civilians and serious injury to an additional 780,000. The British prime minister determined that the threat justified killing noncombatants.

The War on Terror has renewed debate over whether there are ever times when extreme measures are morally justified. The "ticking bomb" scenario is often used to illustrate this dilemma. In the scenario, security forces have captured a suspect they believe has planted a bomb that will kill hundreds or thousands of people. Time is short, and the captive refuses to cooperate. Authorities must determine if they should use torture to get the suspected terrorist to reveal the location of the explosive device.

Opposition to torture is generally based on deontological grounds. Such interrogational techniques demean the value of human beings and treat people as a means to an end. Torture can do irreversible physical and psychological damage and violates basic human rights and international law.

However, when faced with the ticking bomb scenario, many of those who oppose torture in principle agree that torture is justified in this particular set of circumstances. They adopt a utilitarian approach, arguing that the likely positive consequences (saving many lives) justify the damage caused to one person. This logic has been used by the U.S. government to support the "enhanced interrogation" (torture) of prisoners in Iraq and Afghanistan as well as the "outsourcing" of suspects to countries like Egypt that place few restrictions on interrogation techniques.

Do supreme emergencies justify setting aside normal moral standards? Perhaps not. Many who died in Germany during World War II (including children) had little or no connection to the war effort. Utilitarian reasoning alone does not justify killing a greater number of people in Germany to save a smaller number of people in Great Britain. Then, too, there are other costs associated with killing innocent civilians. Some British officers felt that bombing nonmilitary targets violated their professional honor and failed to differentiate the Allies from Hitler. (The Nazis also engaged in the killing of civilians, on a much larger scale.)

British philosopher Bob Brecher takes issue with those who use the ticking bomb scenario to justify interrogational torture. He begins by pointing out the logical weaknesses of the hypothetical case. In reality, there likely wouldn't be enough time between the planting of the bomb and its detonation to detain and question a suspect. The prisoner may not know where the device is planted or be innocent. (Of 5,000 terrorist suspects detained without access to legal counsel in the two and a half years after 9/11, only 3 were charged with terrorist acts, and 2 of the 3 were later acquitted.) Eliciting the location of the explosive would take a skilled interrogator, and information gained through torture is notoriously unreliable. Many suspects are likely to say anything to get the torturer to stop. Those trained to resist torture would likely give false answers at first, further delaying discovery of the bomb.

Brecher also points out the long-term damage caused by interrogational torture. Such activity encourages the creation of a new profession—torturer—and of a society that tolerates such activity. He argues that who we are as civilized nations means that we cannot engage in torture of any kind. Further, there is no such thing as "torture lite." Those who have undergone even limited or focused torture aimed at eliciting information often never recover. Even innocent subjects of torture are humiliated, their wills broken.

(Continued)

(Continued)

Despite the concerns of Brecher and other critics, support for extreme measures in supreme emergencies appears to be widespread. Taxpayers continue to fund nuclear missile systems that would incinerate hundreds of thousands of civilians, for instance. Polls report that approximately one half of all Americans support the use of torture to gather information that protects the nation from further attacks.

Do you believe that extreme measures like killing civilians and interrogational torture are ever justified? Why or why not?

Sources

Alexander, L. (2000, Fall). Deontology at the threshold. *San Diego Law Review*, Rev. 893.

Brecher, B. (2007). *Torture and the ticking bomb.* Malden, MA: Blackwell.

Poll: U.S. split on torture. (2009, April 24). Retrieved from http://www.upi.com/Top_News/2009/04/24/Poll-US-split-on-torture/UPI-55341240631033/

Statman, D. (2006). Supreme emergencies revisited. *Ethics, 117,* 58–79.

Walzer, M. (1977). *Just and unjust wars: A moral argument with historical illustrations.* New York: Basic Books.

The Three Stages of a Crisis

Whatever the type, crises pass through three stages: precrisis, crisis event, and postcrisis.[6] In each stage leaders have a moral obligation to carry out particular tasks or functions.

Stage 1. Precrisis

Precrisis is the period of normalcy between crisis events. During this, the longest phase, the group or organization typically believes that it understands the risks it faces and can handle any contingency that arises. The temptation to become overconfident grows as the time between crises increases. Funding for backup data sites, disaster drills, training, and other types of crisis preparation may be cut, which increases the likelihood of another crisis. That was the case at NASA, for example (see Chapter 8). Safety was a top priority after the space shuttle *Challenger* crash but gradually became less of a priority over time. Other goals, like completing missions on time, took precedence, and safety concerns were dismissed. As a result, the *Columbia* shuttle exploded 17 years later.

Complacency isn't the only barrier to crisis prevention. Human biases (decision-making and judgment errors), institutional failures (organizational breakdowns in processing information), and special-interest groups (resistance from groups looking out for the interests of their own members) also derail crisis preparedness.[7] These factors are summarized in Box 11.1.

Ethical leaders in the precrisis stage help their groups detect possible trouble and develop strategies for managing crises should they strike. Crisis expert Stephen Fink uses the Greek word *prodromes* (which means "running before") to describe the warning signs that precede a crisis. Ignoring or downplaying these signs generally results in disaster.[8] Parents, school officials, and law enforcement officers had plenty of warning that Eric Harris and Dylan Klebold were threats, for example (Chapter 4), and officials in Pennsylvania were suspicious of Judge Ciavarella's courtroom practices long before the sentencing kids for cash scandal was exposed (Chapter 6).

Crisis management experts offer a variety of strategies for recognizing danger signs.[9] These include (1) environmental scanning (looking outward to the media and larger environment and inward to the organization for potential problems), (2) brainstorming potential weaknesses, (3) creating a crisis management plan for dealing with likely risks, and (4) establishing a reputation for integrity or credibility that will serve as a reservoir of goodwill when a crisis strikes. (Complete the "Self-Assessment: Crisis and/or Disaster Preparedness Scale" to determine your crisis readiness and that of your work organization.)

Crisis preparation pays off. Crisis-ready organizations are less likely to experience unexpected threats, suffer significantly less damage if such events do strike, and recover much more quickly.[10]

BOX 11.1 BARRIERS TO CRISIS PREVENTION

Human Biases

- Positive illusions that falsely convince decision makers that a problem doesn't exist or isn't severe enough to require action
- Interpreting events in an egocentric manner that favors the leader and the organization while blaming outsiders
- Discounting the future by ignoring possible long-term costs; refusing to invest resources now to prevent future crises

(Continued)

(Continued)

- Maintaining the dysfunctional status quo by refusing to inflict any harm (such as higher Social Security taxes) that would address a mounting problem (the danger that the Social Security system will become insolvent)
- Failure to recognize problems because they aren't vivid (they are not personally experienced as direct threats)

Institutional Failures

- Failure to collect adequate data due to (a) ignoring certain problems and discounting evidence, (b) the presence of conflicting information, and (c) information overload
- Information is not integrated into the organization as a whole because departments operate independently and managers maintain secrecy
- Members lack incentive to take action because they are rewarded for acting selfishly or believe that everyone agrees with current procedures
- Leaders fail to learn from experience or to disseminate lessons learned because information is not recorded or shared or because key organizational members are lost

Special-Interest Groups

- Impose social burdens (higher taxes, water pollution, high drug prices) in order to benefit themselves
- Blame complex problems on individuals rather than on systems that are at fault
- Oppose reform efforts

SOURCE: Bazerman, M. H., & Watkins, M. D. (2004). *Predictable surprises: The disasters you should have seen coming, and how to prevent them*. Boston: Harvard Business School Press. Reprinted by permission of Waveland Press, Inc. from Hackman, M. Z., & Johnson, C. E. Leadership: *A communication perspective*, p. 405. Long Grove, IL: Waveland press, Inc. 2009. All rights reserved.

Stage 2: Crisis Event

The second stage commences with a "trigger event" like an explosion, a shooting, or bankruptcy, and the recognition that a crisis has occurred. It ends when the crisis is resolved. Realization that a crisis has erupted sparks strong emotions like surprise, anger, fear, and disbelief. Confusion reigns as group members try to understand what is happening and worry about what will happen to the group and to themselves. At the same time, significant harm is done to people, property, and the larger environment, and the incident garners significant press coverage.

Ethical leaders play a critical role during this stage. They first recognize that a crisis has occurred and persuade others that the group is in grave danger. This is not always an easy task. During the financial crisis of 2009, for example, not everyone was convinced that the threat was great enough to justify government investment in banks and other financial institutions. Leaders then implement the crisis management plan, mobilize the crisis management team, and focus on damage control. Immediate threats to individuals, property, and the environment take priority. Leaders may need to redeploy staff and such resources as equipment, phone lines, and office space while cooperating with emergency personnel, government officials, neighborhood associations, the media, and other outside groups.

Leaders are also responsible for speaking on behalf of the organization. One person (typically the chief operating officer) should take the primary responsibility as spokesperson in the case of an emergency. This prevents conflicting messages and the spread of misinformation. Effective spokespeople go to the scene of the crisis, cooperate with the media, and provide accurate information. Those directly impacted by the crisis have particularly important information needs and should take top priority. They not only need to know what happened but also need to learn how to protect themselves. Potential victims of a flu epidemic need to be vaccinated, for example. City residents in the path of a tornado need to be warned to take shelter. Consumers need to learn of contaminated food products.

Stage 3: Postcrisis

Investigation and analysis take place during the third and final stage. Group members try to determine what went wrong, who was to blame, how to prevent a recurrence of the problem, and so on. This is also a period of recovery where ethical leaders try to salvage the legitimacy of the group or organization, help group members learn from the crisis experience, and promote healing.

The image of an organization generally suffers during a crisis as outsiders blame it for failing to prevent the disaster, causing harm, and not moving quickly enough to help victims. As a consequence, effective leaders convince the public that it has a legitimate reason to exist and can be trusted. The best way to rebuild an organization's image depends a great deal on the particular crisis and the past history of the group. If the organization is not at fault and has a good reputation, simple denial ("we are not at fault") may be sufficient. However, if the organization is to blame, it should admit responsibility, offer compensation to victims, and take corrective action by improving safety procedures, recalling products, and so forth.[11]

The second leadership task in the postcrisis stage is to encourage the group to learn from the experience lest it be repeated again. Organizational crisis learning takes three forms.[12] *Retrospective sensemaking* looks for causation, determining what members overlooked and identifying faulty assumptions and rationalizations that contributed to the disaster. Such processing broadens the group's base of knowledge and gives it more options for responding in the future. *Reconsidering structure* refers to making major changes in leadership, mission, organizational structure, and policies as a result of the disruption caused by the crisis event. For example, the Department of Homeland Security, made up of several existing government agencies, was created after the 9/11 attacks. *Vicarious learning* draws from the experiences of other groups and organizations, both good and bad. Some organizations illustrate what *not* to do while others serve as exemplary role models. Government response to Hurricane Katrina has emerged as a classic example of crisis *mis*management. Local and state officials were slow to order a mandatory evacuation and stranded poorer residents who didn't have cars. The Federal Emergency Management Agency (led by an unqualified manager) waited too long to implement emergency plans, and the president didn't get involved until days had passed. A House congressional committee investigating the disaster concluded that the government's response to Katrina was a "litany of mistakes, misjudgments, lapses, and absurdities."[13] There is also much to learn from how BP and the federal government mismanaged the oil spill off the coast of Louisiana.

The third leadership task in the postcrisis stage is to promote healing, which helps members move beyond the crisis. Healing begins with explaining what happened. A cause needs to be identified and corrective action taken. Corrective steps might include, for instance, strengthening levees after a hurricane and tightening computer security measures after data have been stolen. Forgetting, which is replacing feelings of stress, anxiety, and loss with positive emotions like optimism and confidence, is easier when such preventative measures have been put in place. Ethical leaders also shape the memories of what happened by honoring crisis heroes and by marking important anniversaries. If possible, they also foster a sense of renewal that sets aside blame and looks to the future and new opportunities.

SELF-ASSESSMENT

CRISIS AND/OR DISASTER PREPAREDNESS SCALE

This instrument measures how prepared you think you and your organization are for a natural disaster, a terrorist attack, an industrial accident, or another form of crisis. The higher your score (possible scores range from 21 to 84), the higher your level of perceived preparedness.

Instructions

Score each of the following as

1 = strongly disagree,   2 = disagree,   3 = agree,   4 = strongly agree.

Reverse scores where indicated.

1. I am very familiar with our building's evacuation plan.   1 2 3 4

2. It would be easy for a potentially threatening
   nonemployee to gain access to my workplace. (Reverse)   1 2 3 4

3. If my organization suffered a serious crisis, I might
   lose my job. (Reverse)   1 2 3 4

4. If my organization suffered a serious crisis, I would still
   get paid until we could reopen.   1 2 3 4

5. My organization has provided each employee with a basic
   emergency preparedness kit (e.g., flashlight, smoke mask).   1 2 3 4

6. The security at my workplace is adequate.   1 2 3 4

7. If a crisis occurred at my organization, I am familiar
   with the plan for how family members can get information
   on the status (e.g., safety) of their relatives.   1 2 3 4

8. In the event of an emergency or a disaster, I am familiar with my
   organization's plan to continue operations from another location. 1 2 3 4

9. All organization members are required to rehearse
   portions of our crisis plan (e.g., evacuation).   1 2 3 4

10. If my organization suffered a serous crisis,
    I would still have my job.   1 2 3 4

11. If my organization suffered a crisis, I would still be covered
by my organization's employee benefits (e.g., health insurance).   1 2 3 4

12. Security at my workplace has been significantly increased
since September 11, 2001.   1 2 3 4

13. I know where the nearest fire extinguisher is
to my desk/workstation.   1 2 3 4

14. If a crisis and evacuation occurred at my organization, I am
familiar with our plan on how to communicate with my fellow
employees from scattered or emergency locations
(e.g., cell phone numbers, websites, e-mail lists).   1 2 3 4

15. Most of our employees are familiar with my organization's
crisis/disaster plan.   1 2 3 4

16. As part of our emergency plan, customers and suppliers
would be able to contact us for information.   1 2 3 4

17. If my organization suffered a crisis/disaster, I would have
the data I need to do my job backed up at a remote site.   1 2 3 4

18. My organization offers to pay to have volunteer employees
trained in basic life support techniques (e.g., CPR, first aid).   1 2 3 4

19. My organization has contingency plans in place so our
customers would be covered if we suffered a disaster.   1 2 3 4

20. I know where the nearest emergency exits are
to my desk/workstation.   1 2 3 4

21. My organization's emergency plan has been coordinated
with local agencies (e.g., the fire department, hospitals).   1 2 3 4

SOURCE: Fowler, K. L., Kling, N. D., & Larson, M. D. (2007). Organizational preparedness for coping with a major crisis or disaster. *Business & Society*. Founded at Roosevelt University, 46, 100–101. Published by SAGE Publications, Inc.

Components of Ethical Crisis Management

As we saw in the previous section, ethical leaders have important tasks to carry out in each stage of crisis development. Theorists and researchers have identified five principles and/or strategies that equip them to fulfill these duties. Ethical leaders assume broad responsibility, practice transparency, demonstrate care and concern, use their heads as well as their hearts, and improvise from a strong moral foundation.

Assume Broad Responsibility

Responsibility is the foundation of ethical crisis leadership.[14] Preventing, managing, and recovering from crises all depend on the willingness of leaders and followers to accept their moral responsibilities. Society grants individuals and organizations significant freedom to make and carry out decisions. Such freedom means that people and groups are accountable for their actions. They have an ethical duty to prevent crises because such events do significant harm. The first step in preventing crises is to behave as a moral person. Since a great many crises (fraud, accounting scandals, embezzlement, sexual harassment) are the direct result of the immoral actions of leaders, eliminating these behaviors greatly reduces the group's exposure to scandal. Moral leaders also create healthy ethical organizational climates that have a low risk of moral failure and crisis (see Chapter 9).

In addition to engaging in, and fostering, ethical behavior, the responsible crisis leader fights against complacency, human biases, institutional weaknesses, special-interest groups, and other obstacles to crisis prevention. He or she commits the money and resources needed to identify, prevent, and manage trouble spots. This includes assigning groups to brainstorm potential weaknesses, investing in computer security, holding disaster drills, and creating crisis management plans. Leaders aren't the only ones who are responsible for crisis prevention, however. This duty extends to everyone who has a role, no matter how small, in anticipating such events. According to crisis prevention expert Robert Allinson, "Anyone who is in any way connected with a potential or actual disaster is responsible for its occurrence."[15] (Turn to Case Study 11.2 on page 436 for an example of how two low-level followers generated a major organizational crisis.)

Sadly, a significant number of organizations still fail to take their crisis prevention responsibilities seriously. A recent corporate survey revealed that, while the vast majority had crisis management plans, a significant portion (approximately one fifth) did not.[16] Case Study 11.3 on page 439 describes how one organization is resisting a crisis prevention effort.

SOURCE: Dilbert: @Scott Adams/United Features Syndicate, Inc.

If a crisis does erupt, leaders are obligated to mitigate the harm they and/or their followers cause to others through, for instance, deceptive advertising, fraud, or industrial accidents. A rapid response is key to fulfilling this ethical duty. Exxon continues to be used as a poor example of crisis management in large part because of its slow response to the grounding of the *Exxon Valdez*, which caused the largest oil spill up to that point in U.S. history. Then CEO Lawrence Rawl didn't get to the scene of the accident until 10 days after the spill, initial containment efforts were ineffective, and the firm denied at first that it had any responsibility for what happened.[17] More recently, executives at Toyota were slow to respond to sudden acceleration problems in their vehicles.[18]

When the immediate danger is past, leaders have an obligation to ensure that a similar crisis doesn't happen again and to assure the public of that fact. Their ethical duties include carrying out the postcrisis tasks noted earlier: rebuilding the group's image, helping members learn from the crisis, and promoting healing.

Crises broaden both the scope and the depth of a leader's ethical obligations. In a crisis, the breadth of a leader's responsibility greatly expands. New stakeholder groups are formed, including those who had no previous interest in the organization but are currently threatened as well as members of the general public who learn about the crisis event. Leaders may also need to go to extraordinary lengths (depth) to meet the needs of victims. Take the case of Marsh & McLennan Companies, for example. When the terrorist planes hit the World Trade Center in 2001, 295 of its employees were killed. Company officials at the professional services firm responded by creating a set of benefits and services for the families of those who died, which included assigning "relationship managers" to help each family get the help it needed, providing counseling services, enhancing salary and insurance benefits, setting up a victims' relief fund, and creating memorials for the victims.[19]

Practice Transparency

Like responsibility, transparency is another requirement placed on groups and organizations operating freely in society. We want governments to reveal the ways they spend our tax dollars, for instance, and require audited financial statements and annual reports from publicly held corporations. Failure to disclose information spawns abuses of power and privilege and makes it impossible for individuals to act as informed members of the community.[20] Transparency is key to exercising personal freedom and establishing healthy relationships between people, between people and organizations, and between organizations.[21] When crisis strikes, transparency takes on added significance.

Transparency begins with openness. When faced with the challenge of mismanaged information, the transparent leader tells the truth and avoids hiding or distorting information. A transparent group is open about its policies, compensation packages, safety measures, values, spending, positions on political issues, and so on. Leaders regularly share this information through websites, presentations, publications, press releases, and other means. Openness, in turn, is marked by candor and integrity. Ethical leaders are willing to share bad as well as good news, such as when earnings are down and construction plans have to be shelved. Johnson & Johnson's response to the Tylenol poisoning has become a "textbook" case of crisis management in part because of the firm's honesty. During the product tampering crisis, corporate officials initially denied that there was any potassium cyanide used in the manufacture of Tylenol.[22] Later, when leaders discovered that minute amounts of the chemical were used during testing at some facilities, it immediately released this information to the public. Such candor helped the company recover quickly from this abnormal accident.

Transparency also involves symmetry.[23] Symmetry refers to maintaining balanced relationships with outside groups based on two-way communication. Instead of imposing their will on others, organizations engaged in symmetrical relationships seek to understand and to respond to the concerns of stakeholders. They regularly interact with, and gather information from, customers, vendors, neighbors, activist groups, and others. Even more important, they act on these data, changing their plans as needed. For example, if neighbors strenuously object to the construction of a new product distribution facility, executives may find another location or modify the design of the building to meet the concerns of those living nearby. A study of excellent public relations programs found that the best public relations efforts—those that increase organizational effectiveness and benefit society—are based on symmetrical relationships with stakeholder groups.[24]

Crisis preparedness and trust are two positive by-products of transparency. Openness makes it less likely that leaders will engage in unethical behavior. As ethicist Jeremy Bentham noted, "The more strictly we are watched, the better we behave." Symmetry also serves as an early warning system. Partnerships foster two-way communication that will reveal if customers are having problems with products or services, if activist groups are offended by the organization's environmental practices, and so forth.

Stakeholders and the general public are more prone to trust organizations they perceive as open and give them the benefit of the doubt in crisis situations. As a consequence, these groups suffer less damage to their image, and regain their legitimacy more rapidly. For example, Pepsi was the victim of a hoax that started in Seattle. Consumers placed syringes in cans of Diet Pepsi and then complained to the media. The corporation's reputation for safety and quality, as well as its Seattle bottler's work in the community, helped Pepsi weather the crisis and recover quickly.[25]

Maintaining transparency is particularly difficult when a crisis is triggered. First, there are privacy concerns. Victims' families may need to be notified before information can be released to the press. Second, admitting fault can put the organization at a disadvantage in case of a lawsuit. Third, there may be proprietary information about, say, manufacturing processes and recipes, which should not be released to competitors. (Even the leading proponents of corporate transparency agree that businesses have a right to privacy, to security, and to control certain types of information.)[26] Fourth, uncertainty makes it difficult for an organization to determine what its course of action should be, and, as a result, to communicate concrete details to the public. Fifth, being specific may offend some stakeholders who feel that they have been treated unfairly. Sixth, making a commitment to a single course of action too soon may limit the group's ability to deal with the crisis.[27]

Some observers suggest that leaders in a crisis situation use *strategic ambiguity* as an alternative to transparency. In strategic ambiguity, communicators are deliberately vague, which allows them to appeal to multiple audiences.[28] For example, the promise to respond "forcefully" to a crisis is an abstract statement, which can be interpreted many different ways by stakeholders. It also leaves the door open for the group to choose a variety of possible strategies for managing the crisis event. If challenged, the leader can claim that she or he never made a specific commitment to particular stakeholder groups.

More often than not, however, strategic ambiguity is unethical, used to shift the blame and to confuse stakeholders while providing them with biased and/ or incomplete information. This appears to be the case with Jack in the Box.[29] In 1993, children in Washington state were sickened with *E. coli* poisoning after eating hamburgers at the firm's stores. Throughout the crisis Jack in the Box president Robert Nugent made use of ambiguous communication. He emphasized that there was a "potential" link between the illnesses and company food. He pointed to other possible contributors (including a food supplier) to the outbreak and claimed that the firm intended to follow state and federal regulations. (Later it was revealed that Jack in the Box had failed to adopt stricter state of Washington cooking times that likely would have prevented the outbreak.) The restaurant chain's response was unethical because it (a) favored the needs of internal stakeholders (employees, managers, shareholders) over external stakeholders (consumers, regulators) and (b) provided outsiders with incomplete and inaccurate information.

While the amount and type of information to be shared will vary with each crisis, the goal should always be to be as open as possible. Cooperate with the media and government officials, respond quickly to inquiries, provide detailed background information on the crisis, be honest about what happened, release information as soon as it is available, and be more concerned about meeting the needs of victims than about protecting organizational assets (see the discussion of compassion in the next section).

Rhetorician Keith Hearit illustrates how transparency can be practiced when communicating to stakeholders during a crisis. Hearit believes that, in order to be ethical, the group's explanation of events and response to public criticism must have the right manner and content.[30] *Manner* refers to the form of the communication, which needs to (1) be truthful (disclose relevant information that matches up with the reality of what happened); (2) be sincere (express true regret, reflect seriousness of the event and its impact, demonstrate commitment to taking corrective action and reconciling with stakeholders); (3) be timely (immediately after the event, in time to help victims deal with the damage); (4) be voluntary (not coerced but driven by moral considerations, seek reconciliation, humble); (5) address all stakeholders (speak to all who were wronged, not just a few groups); and (6) be in the proper context (available to all victims).

The *content* of the message is just as important as the form it takes. The ethical story of events

- clearly acknowledges wrongdoing;
- accepts full responsibility for what happened;
- expresses regret for the offense, the harm done, and failure to carry out responsibilities;
- identifies with the injured parties (both with their suffering and with the damage done to relationships);
- asks for forgiveness;
- seeks reconciliation with injured parties;
- fully discloses information related to the offense;
- offers to carry out appropriate corrective action; and
- offers appropriate compensation.

Demonstrate Care

Demonstrating concern has practical as well as ethical benefits. Nothing draws more public condemnation than a group that refuses to take responsibility for harming others, as in the case of the *Exxon Valdez*, or appears callous, as when NASA declared that there had been "an apparent malfunction" as millions watched the crash of the *Challenger* shuttle on television. (More recently, BP's

CEO was criticized after saying that he was anxious for the Gulf oil spill crisis to end because he would "like his life back." This remark appeared callous to the families of the 11 BP employees who were killed when a drilling rig exploded, triggering the massive leak.) Victims who have received adequate assistance are less likely to sue the organization later.

While it is in the interest of leaders and organizations to act in a compassionate manner for image and financial reasons, it is even more important to do so for ethical reasons. Altruism is an important ethical principle as we saw in Chapter 5 and is particularly relevant to crisis situations. Love of neighbor urges us to meet the needs of those threatened by crisis, no matter who they are. Victims deserve our help because of their status as human beings. (See "Leadership Ethics at the Movies: *Nanking*" for a particularly notable demonstration of altruism in crisis.)

Showing concern during a crisis goes well beyond addressing the physical and financial needs of victims. Those harmed by a crisis have significant emotional and spiritual needs too.[31] They may be overwhelmed with feelings of loss and grief as well as guilt for surviving when others did not. Their sense of security, meaning, and purpose is threatened. Posttraumatic stress disorder, where individuals periodically relive the terror, is common. Of course, victims aren't the only ones to experience many of these reactions. The triggering event, as noted earlier, generates surprise, anger, fear, and disbelief for crisis managers, other group members, and outside observers as well. For instance, the entire population of the United States felt threatened and disoriented during the terrorist attacks of 9/11.

The emotional and spiritual demands of crises mean that ethical leaders need to address the whole person during the crisis and postcrisis stages. They stay in constant communication with group members, calming their fears. They help followers regain their focus and emphasize the importance of community. They arrange for emotional and spiritual counseling and recognize that the whole organization may need to pass through a grieving process. Ethical leaders also recognize that, if the group is to heal, they must foster hope while honoring the past.

The ethic of care, introduced in Chapter 5, has been specifically applied to crisis management. The care ethic fosters crisis preparation because those concerned about others are more likely to take their complaints seriously and therefore are more alert to possible signs of trouble. Once they have identified prodromes, they are more likely to give voice to their concerns instead of exiting the organization.[32]

Concern for others can also prompt a group or an organization to go well beyond what the law or fairness requires when responding to a crisis. Consider the case of the San Ysidro, California, McDonald's shooting, for example.[33] On July 18, 1984, a lone gunman out to "hunt humans" shot

40 people at the restaurant (21 died). McDonald's was not at fault and was, in fact, a victim of the attack. But rather than declaring its innocence or decrying the unfairness of headlines blaming it for the carnage, McDonald's followed the "Horwitz Rule." Executive VP and General Counsel Don Horwitz told management: "I don't want you people to worry or care about the legal implications of what you might say. We are going to do what's right for the survivors and families of the victims, and we'll worry about lawsuits later."[34] (It could have been argued that providing help was evidence that McDonald's was in some way responsible for what happened.) The company then suspended its national advertising campaign out of respect for victims and their families, sent personnel to help with funeral arrangements, paid hospital bills, and flew in relatives to be with their families. Corporate executives sought the counsel of an important local religious leader, attended funerals, demolished the restaurant, and then donated the land to the city.

The steps taken by McDonald's in this instance weren't "fair" and devalued the rights of the firm. After all, the restaurant chain wasn't to blame, and yet its leaders spent millions suspending advertising, creating a fund for families of victims, demolishing the restaurant, donating the land, and so on. Driven by care, corporate officials kept their focus on responsibility to victims and the importance of acknowledging their pain. They listened to the community and worked hard at maintaining connections with local political, community, and religious groups.

▶ LEADERSHIP ETHICS AT THE MOVIES

NANKING

Key Cast Members: Woody Harrelson, Mariel Hemingway, Stephen Dorff, Rosalind Chao, John Getz, Jürgen Prochnow

Synopsis: This film describes the efforts of a group of Westerners to save the lives of nationals during the Japanese occupation of the Chinese capital of Nanking in 1937. It draws from the journals and letters of the expatriates (read by Harrelson, Hemingway, and other actors), war footage, and interviews with Chinese victims and Japanese victimizers. The victorious Japanese army beheaded, shot, and bayoneted thousands of captive soldiers as well as civilians (including infants and children) in the weeks after taking the city. They also raped thousands of Chinese women and girls. In the midst of the carnage, an unlikely coalition, led by a Nazi German businessman, an American

(Continued)

(Continued)

missionary, a surgeon, and the dean of a women's college, created a safe zone and managed to protect an estimated 250,000 refugees.

Rating: R for graphic images and descriptions of wartime atrocities

Themes: ethical crisis leadership, courage, compassion, evil, dehumanization, moral decision making, altruism

Discussion Starters

1. How did the Japanese dehumanize Chinese soldiers and civilians? What immediate impact did dehumanization have? What was the long-term impact of dehumanization on the Japanese soldiers who participated in the atrocities?

2. Why were the expatriates able to save 250,000 refugees? What price did they pay for their actions?

3. What components of ethical crisis management do you see in the story of the occupation of Nanking?

Engage the Head as Well as the Heart

Rational thought, problem solving, and other cognitive skills and strategies are important complements to care and compassion in ethical crisis management. Moral leaders respond with their heads as well as their hearts.[35] In particular, they are highly mindful and engage in strategic and ethical rational thinking. (Followers must also engage their heads as well as their hearts—see "Focus on Follower Ethics: Blowing the Whistle: Ethical Tension Points.")

Ethical crisis leaders, in addition to paying heedful attention themselves (see Chapter 10), create *mindful* cultures. University of Michigan business professors Karl Weick and Kathleen Sutcliffe argue that collective mindfulness is the key to creating "high-reliability organizations" (HROs).[36] HROs (emergency rooms, air traffic control systems, power plants) rarely fail even though they face lots of unexpected events. Attention to minor problems sets HROs apart from their less reliable counterparts. Unlike crisis-prone organizations that ignore minor deviations until they magnify into a crisis, HROs respond forcefully to the weakest signal that something is wrong.

Weick and Sutcliffe use the deck of an aircraft carrier to illustrate the characteristics of mindful cultures that prevent harmful crises from occurring. One naval crew member described an aircraft carrier this way:

> . . . imagine that it's a busy day, and you shrink San Francisco Airport to only one short runway and one ramp and one gate. Make planes take off and land at the same time, at half the present time interval, rock the runway from side to side, and require that everyone who leaves in the morning returns that same day. Make sure the equipment is so close to the edge of the envelope that it's fragile. Then turn off the radar to avoid detection, impose strict controls on radios, fuel the aircraft in place with their engines running, put an enemy in the air, and scatter live bombs and rockets around. Now, wet the whole thing down with sea water and oil, and man it with 20-year-olds, half of whom have never seen an airplane close-up. Oh and by the way, try not to kill anyone.[37]

Despite the dangers, very few carrier accidents occur because Navy leaders encourage five mindful practices. First, carrier crews are *preoccupied with failure*. Every landing is graded, and small problems like a plane in the wrong position are treated as signs that there may be larger issues like poor communication or training. Second, those who work on carriers are *reluctant to simplify*. Each plane is inspected multiple times, and pilots and deck crew communicate responsibilities through hand and voice signals and different colored uniforms. Third, carrier crews sustain continuous *sensitivity to operations*. Everyone on board is focused on launching and landing aircraft. Officers observe all activities and communicate with each other constantly. Fourth, people on carriers share a *commitment to resilience*. Their knowledge equips them to come up with creative solutions when unexpected events like equipment failures or severe weather occur. Fifth, carrier personnel demonstrate *deference to expertise*. Lower-ranking individuals can overrule their superiors if they have more expertise in, for example, landing damaged planes.

Leaders responding to crises also need to employ *ethical rationality*. Ethical rationality ties together research on business ethics, strategy, and crisis management. Rationality is defined as "a firm's ability to make decisions based on comprehensive information and analysis."[38] Rational firms and leaders (which are generally more successful) do a thorough job of scanning the environment and analyzing the information they gather. They are also able to quickly generate lots of alternative solutions and ideas.[39] At the same time, ethics is at the core of their corporate strategy.[40] Such organizations keep the needs of stakeholders in mind and are concerned about building a "good society." They make routine choices based on moral principles like utilitarianism and the Categorical Imperative.

Ethical rationality serves firms well in crisis management. They are less likely to experience crisis events because they continually scan the environment and analyze the data they collect. Leaders are not prone to act selfishly (e.g., lie, ignore stakeholder groups, hurt the environment) because they recognize that all stakeholders have intrinsic value and they are committed to the greater good. When a crisis is triggered, they have more information on hand and can rapidly generate and evaluate alternative courses of action under time pressures. Such firms have a clearer understanding of their stakeholder groups and how they might be impacted by crisis events. Further, ethically rational companies (and nonprofits) are more likely to make sound moral choices during a crisis because leaders are in the practice of incorporating ethical principles into routine decision making.

FOCUS ON FOLLOWER ETHICS

BLOWING THE WHISTLE: ETHICAL TENSION POINTS

Deciding to go public with information about organizational misbehavior can cause a crisis. Not only do whistle-blowers put their careers, health, and relationships at risk (see Chapter 2), they put their leaders, their coworkers, and the group as a whole in danger. Everyone suffers when the whistle blows. Employees lose their jobs, donations dry up, contracts are cancelled, stock prices decline, and so on. Followers must determine whether the benefits of going public (e.g., improving patient safety, protecting the public, eliminating waste and fraud) justify such wide-scale disruption. To make this determination, ethics professor J. Vernon Jensen argues that potential whistle-blowers must respond to a series of questions or issues that he calls "ethical tension points." We can use these questions as a guide if we are faced with the choice of going public or keeping silent. Jensen identifies the following as key ethical tension points in whistle-blowing:

- *What is our obligation to the organization?* Do conditions warrant breaking contractual agreements, confidentiality, and loyalty to the group?
- *What are our moral obligations to colleagues in the organization?* How will their lives be affected? How will they respond?
- *What are our ethical obligations to our profession?* Does loyalty to the organization take precedence, or do professional standards?

- *Will the act of whistle-blowing adversely affect our families and others close to us?* Is it fair to make them suffer? How much will they be hurt by our actions?
- *What moral obligation do we have to ourselves?* Do the costs of going public outweigh the benefits of integrity and feelings of self-worth that come from doing so?
- *What is our ethical obligation toward the general public?* How will outsiders respond to our message? Do the long-term benefits of speaking out outweigh any short-term costs (fear, anger, uneasiness)?
- *How will my action affect important values such as freedom of expression, truthfulness, courage, justice, cooperativeness, and loyalty?* Will my coming forward strengthen these values or weaken them? What values (friendship, security) will have to take lower priority?

SOURCE: Jensen, J. V. (1996). Ethical tension points in whistleblowing. In J. A. Jaksa & M. S. Pritchard (Eds.), *Responsible communication: Ethical issues in business, industry, and the professions* (pp. 41–51). Cresskill, NJ: Hampton.

Improvise From a Strong Moral Foundation

Dartmouth professor Paul Argenti interviewed corporate executives whose firms successfully weathered the World Trade Center terrorist attacks. One of the lessons of 9/11, according to Argenti, is that, during a disaster, managers must make quick decisions without guidance.[41] They are more likely to make wise choices if they are prepared. Preparation includes not only training and planning but also instilling corporate values. Employees of several undamaged Starbucks stores near Ground Zero kept their locations open even as the rest of outlets in the United States were closed for the day. They provided free coffee and pastries to hospital staff and rescue workers. Several people were saved when Starbucks workers pulled them inside, rescuing them from collapsing buildings. Leaders and followers at these stores were acting in accordance with one of the eight principles of the Starbucks mission statement, which is "Contribute positively to our communities and our environment." Employees at *The New York Times,* OppenheimerFunds, and Goldman Sachs also drew from their organizations' core ideology to continue to serve readers, customers, and clients.

The ability to ethically improvise is critical in a crisis because no amount of planning and practice can totally equip individuals for the specific challenges they will face during the crisis event. Unethical decisions, such as refusing to take action or responsibility, can cause significant harm and undermine the future of the group or organization. In addition, the crisis forces changes in priorities. Concern for profit must be set aside in favor of damage control and helping victims. The stakeholders who are normally most important (e.g., corporate stockholders and owners) take a backseat to those most directly impacted by events.

Successful improvisation requires that employees be empowered to act on their own initiative. They must not only know the moral course of action but also be able to act on their choices, like the Starbucks employees on September 11, 2001. Their decision to distribute free food and drinks cost Starbucks money, but corporate headquarters supported their actions.

A number of observers have noted that organizations, like individuals, have moral character.[42] They argue that virtuous organizations as well as virtuous people are more likely to make the right ethical choices under pressure. When crises strike, organizations must act quickly, and their response will reflect (or fail to reflect) their character. Those groups that ethically manage crises demonstrate such virtues as courage, compassion, optimism, humility, and integrity.

Richard Nielsen of Boston College and Ronald Dufresne of St. Joseph's University believe that crises can spur both individual and organizational character development.[43] The key is to engage in dialogue or conversation that is grounded in the ethical tradition of the group. The group then adapts to the crisis while protecting its essential values. Nielsen and Dufresne offer a four-step method (drawn from the work of Danish philosopher Søren Kierkegaard) for promoting collective character growth. They illustrate this "uplifting method" using a crisis caused by the death of a cancer patient at the Dana-Farber Cancer Institute in Boston. The patient died after receiving four times the prescribed amount of an experimental chemotherapy drug.

Step 1 of the uplifting method is to approach others in a friendly, open, and respectful manner. Dana-Farber Cancer Institute leaders were open and respectful with both the public and the press and candid about shortcomings that might have led to the drug overdose. Step 2 is to frame the problem or crisis as a conflict between "a potentially destructive environment and our internal tradition." Institute officials noted that the drive to generate grants through aggressive research had overshadowed the group's mission to treat patients. Step 3 is to consider alternatives based on ethical tradition while, at the same time, adapting tradition in light of possible solutions. Leaders at Dana-Farber implemented changes, like suspending some research, increasing treatment protocol training, and requiring more oversight of chemotherapy dosages. However, the organization did not suspend all cancer research. Step 4 is to adopt solutions that are informed by the group's ethical tradition but adjust them as needed. Dana-Farber administrators not only implemented the steps described above but also increased focus on the "total care" of cancer patients. All staff members (including researchers) work together to treat patients. At the same time, the institute also continues to look for cancer cures.

Implications and Applications

- A crisis, which is any major unanticipated event that poses a significant threat, will be the ultimate test of your ability to provide ethical leadership.
- Ten types of crisis include public perception, natural disasters, product or service, terrorist attacks, economic, human resource, industrial, oil and chemical spills, transportation, and outside environment.
- Deliberate attempts to disrupt or destroy systems (abnormal accidents) are on the rise, and you must help your group or organization prepare for them.
- All crises follow a three-stage pattern of development: precrisis, crisis event, postcrisis.
- Precrisis is the period of normalcy between crisis events. Ethical, effective leaders use this time to identify potential trouble spots and to prepare crisis management plans.
- The crisis event starts with a "trigger event" and the recognition that a crisis has occurred. This stage ends when the immediate crisis is resolved. During this phase ethical leaders identify the crisis, activate crisis management plans, and try to limit the damage.
- Postcrisis is a period of investigation and recovery. Moral leaders try to determine what went wrong and institute corrective measures. They also help the group salvage its reputation, engage in crisis learning, and begin the healing process.
- Responsibility is the ethical foundation for ethical crisis leadership. As a leader, you have a duty to try to prevent the harm caused by crises, to mitigate the damage caused by your group, to address the needs of all affected stakeholder groups, to take steps to prevent a similar event from happening again, to help the organization learn from the experience, and to foster renewal.
- In an emergency, make transparency your goal. As much as possible, be open with stakeholders and strive to maintain symmetrical relationships with these groups based on two-way communication.
- Altruism (care) should be the driving ethical principle during crisis events. Address the emotional and spiritual concerns of those impacted, not just their financial and physical needs. Go beyond what the law and justice require.
- As a leader, you will need to engage the head as well as the heart when responding to crises. Create a mindful culture that closely monitors and corrects even minor problems and deviations. Base decisions on information and analysis, as well as on moral values, in order to better anticipate and manage crisis events.

- No amount of preparation can prepare you and the rest of your group for every contingency, so you will need to ethically improvise. Successful improvisation draws on the core mission and values of your group or organization.
- Crises reveal the moral character of groups as well as individuals. Conversation grounded in the ethical tradition of the organization, which also adapts to the demands of the crisis, can spur collective character development.

For Further Exploration, Challenge, and Self-Assessment

1. Use the "Self-Assessment: Crisis and/or Disaster Preparedness Scale" to determine your readiness level and that of your organization. If possible, distribute the instrument to others in your organization and compare scores.

2. Form a team at your organization and create a crisis management plan.

3. Brainstorm a list of possible crises that could strike your college or university or a work organization with other students. Then select one of these events and outline a crisis management strategy for dealing with this situation. If time permits, assume the role of organizational leaders and conduct a mock press conference, using other members of the class as media representatives.

4. In a research paper, evaluate the crisis response of an organization using the ethical standards/strategies described in the chapter. Describe the events and provide an analysis. Include suggestions that would help the organization do a better job of ethical crisis management in the future.

5. React to the following statement: "Crises reveal the true character of an organization."

6. Create a case study that demonstrates how an organization was able to ethically improvise during a crisis event. Or, as an alternative, create a case study that demonstrates how an organization was able to learn from a crisis event.

7. In a group, come up with a list of guidelines for determining what to reveal and what to keep secret in a crisis.

CASE STUDY 11.2

TWO IDIOTS AND A VIDEO CAMERA: THE DARK SIDE OF SOCIAL MEDIA

Is there a dark side to social media like Facebook, MySpace, and Twitter? Just ask leaders at Domino's Pizza. A video posted on YouTube and other online sites showed a Domino's employee engaged in a variety of disgusting acts in a franchise kitchen while another worker, armed with a video camera, cheered him on. During the two and a half–minute video, employee Michael puts cheese up his nose and farts on a piece of salami before placing these items on a sub sandwich. Camera operator Kristy provides the commentary, saying at one point: "In about five minutes it'll be sent out delivery where somebody will be eating these, yes, eating them, and little did they know that cheese was in his nose and that there was some lethal gas that ended up on their salami. Now that's how we roll at Domino's."[1]

The impact of the footage was immediate and dramatic. The original video was seen nearly a million times before being taken down 48 hours later. (Copies of the video still draw considerable traffic, drawing more than a million additional hits and counting.) Stories on the Domino's video appeared in *The New York Times*, NBC, and other mainstream media. Perceptions of Domino's quality went from positive to negative hours after it was posted. Tweeters and bloggers filled cyberspace with comments like "Yuk. I'm never eating at Domino's again."

Operators of two sites where the video was posted alerted Domino's to its presence. Two Georgetown University students and a Kentucky computer consultant then used Google satellite images and other information to identify the location where the video was shot (Conover, North Carolina) and the two employees—Michael Setzer and Kristy Hammonds—who engaged in the "prank." Once she was identified, Hammonds posted a message apologizing for the video and claiming that the food was never delivered. However, Setzer and Hammonds were fired and charged with felony food tampering. (They may be sued by the company and face additional charges.)

Domino's officials opted at first for a limited response to the video, posting a statement on their website and responding to inquiries. They didn't want to prompt more people to view the clip and hoped to minimize further negative publicity. However, this strategy backfired. The chain was criticized for being unresponsive on blogs and tweets, and news of the video spread anyway. On the second day after the tape appeared, Patrick Doyle, head of U.S. operations, posted a video on YouTube apologizing and describing the company's quality efforts. He said he was "sickened" by the actions of the two individuals involved, reported that the Conover store had been sanitized, and pledged to review hiring practices to prevent another occurrence of such behavior. The firm also opened a Twitter account to answer questions from the public.

Domino's discovered that once a message gets out in one social forum, it quickly spreads to another. In just two days the Domino's prank had

(Continued)

become one of the hottest topics in cyberspace. "What we've learned is if something happens in this medium, it's going to automatically jump to the next," noted Domino's spokesperson Tim McIntyre. "So we might as well talk to everybody at the same time."[2] This incident served as a wake-up call, spurring the company to develop a more visible social media presence.

Marketers and public relations professionals criticized Domino's for its initial response but then praised the firm for its more aggressive reaction after the first day had passed. These experts encourage organizations to develop crisis management plans to deal with web attacks and urge them to continually monitor blogs, tweets, and other online messages to determine what is being said about them. Other effective tactics include developing Facebook, Twitter, and other social media sites; enlisting customers to help defend the image of the company; and responding instantly to attacks (at least reporting that the organization is investigating the problem).

Domino's cyber crisis also demonstrates that, in a digital world, followers can do significant damage to their organizations. "Two idiots with a video camera and an awful idea" were able to cripple a large, multinational corporation.[3] Leaders need to recognize that they are more vulnerable than ever to the actions of their employees. Followers have a moral obligation to consider the possible shadows they might cast through social media.

Discussion Probes

1. Is there anything that Domino's executives could have done to prevent this crisis?

2. How would you evaluate the crisis response of Domino's based on the five components of ethical crisis leadership presented in the chapter?

3. How active is your organization on social media? What have you learned from this involvement so far that can be applied to crisis prevention and management?

4. Do your organizational memberships (as a student, a worker, etc.) limit what you say or post online? What types of information do you hold back because of your ethical obligations as a follower?

5. Can you think of other examples of the "dark side" of social media? What do these cases have in common with this one?

6. What leadership and followership ethics lessons do you take from this case?

Notes

1. Clifford, S. (2009, April 16). Video prank at Domino's taints brand. *The New York Times,* p. B1.

2. Clifford.

3. Sarno, D., & Semuels, A. (2009, April 20). Internet: Tweets are an ally in crisis PR. *Los Angeles Times,* p. B1.

Sources

Beale, C. (2009, April 20). How Domino's execs were left looking like twits. *The Independent,* p. 46.

Dysart, J. (2009, June 12). The dark side of social media. *Utility Week.*

Evangelista, B. (2009, May 3). How Domino's case unfolded. *San Francisco Chronicle,* p. D1.

Gianatasio, D. (2009, April 15). *Domino's president issues video apology.* Retrieved from http://www.adweek.com/aw/content_display/news/agency/e3id3ff b6d5b9e0b9116ccc43b9768bb31f

Horvitz, B. (2009, April 16). Domino's nightmare holds lessons for marketers: Companies have to learn how to handle social-media attacks. *USA Today,* Money, p. 7A.

York, E. B. (2009, April 20). What Domino's did right—and wrong—in squelching hubbub over YouTube video. *Advertising Age.* Retrieved from http://adage.com/article?article_id=136086

Zerillo, N. (2009, April 20). Crisis forces Domino's to revamp social media plan. *PR Week,* p. 1.

CASE STUDY 11.3

BEACONS FOR CLIMBERS

Personal locator beacons are lifesavers for those lost or hurt on land or at sea. When activated, the devices, which are about the size of a cell phone or television remote, send a signal to an orbiting satellite that is then forwarded to search and rescue crews, fixing the exact location of victims. Armed with this knowledge, rescuers can focus their efforts and respond much more rapidly. This results in a much greater chance of survival and reduces the risks for searchers. More than 22,000 individuals (including 5,700 Americans) have been rescued using this tool. Locator beacons cost hundreds of dollars to buy but can be rented online or from REI and other outdoor stores.

(Continued)

While personal locator devices significantly reduce the risk for victims and rescuers alike, mountain climbers still consider them to be optional equipment. In 2006 three climbers without personal locator beacons were lost during a winter storm on Oregon's Mount Hood. Search and rescue teams spent days combing the mountainside in dangerous winter and avalanche conditions, recovering only one body. In 2009 another three climbers, who also declined to rent locator devices for $5 before heading up the mountain, lost their lives despite a massive rescue effort.

In response to these tragedies, county officials, state legislators, law enforcement officials, editorial writers, and many in the general public argue that locator devices should be required equipment for all (an estimated 10,000 people annually) who climb Mount Hood. To them, such a requirement is a commonsense measure that will save the lives of climbers and, perhaps, of searchers. Said one proponent of the locator requirement, "I think it's morally outrageous for people to climb and not use them because they put the rescuers at risk."[1] Beacon advocates point to the successful rescue of one group of Mount Hood climbers to demonstrate their effectiveness. Searchers followed their beacon signal to their snow cave in whiteout conditions.

Efforts to require locator devices are opposed by search and rescue groups. They fear that mandating beacons will encourage climbers to ignore training and other safety measures and take unnecessary risks. According to the Portland Mountain Rescue group website, "Contrary to what might seem common sense, we believe that mandating beacons actually increases risks for both climbers and the rescuers." The site goes on to say, "Any government mandate to carry these devices overstates their usefulness and creates an unwarranted reliance on technology and devalues the motivation to develop the proper safe traveling skills and planning for unexpected situations, thus leading to more rescues."[2] The organization notes that climbers carrying beacons have an unrealistic expectation of how soon they can be rescued, which may put searchers in greater danger.

Leaders of search and rescue organizations also fear that stranded climbers without beacons would hesitate to ask for help for fear of prosecution and that enforcing the law would be difficult. They point out that falls, rockslides, and avalanches cause many deaths. In many of these accidents, victims don't have time to activate the beacon signal. Climbers chafe at the thought that the government would tell them what to carry up the mountain. When weight is an issue, they want the freedom to determine what items to take and which to leave behind.

So far opponents have been successful in defeating attempts to require climbers to carry beacons. However, pressure to mandate the use of this tool builds every time climbers who spurn the devices are lost on Mount Hood.

Discussion Probes

1. What ethical values play an important role in this case?

2. What ethical duties do climbers have to rescuers? To their families? To the general public?

3. Is it unethical for climbers to refuse to carry locator devices? Why or why not?

4. Do you find any weaknesses in the logic of either side of the debate over requiring locator devices?

5. Based on the ethical crisis leadership principles/strategies presented in the chapter, should locator devices be required for mountain climbers? Why or why not?

6. What leadership and followership ethics lessons do you take from this case?

Notes

1. Duin, S. (2009, December 15). Mountain rescue and common sense. *The Oregonian*, p. B1.

2. PMR's position statement regarding mission to rescue 3 missing climbers on Mt. Hood and locator beacons. (2009, December 16). Retrieved from http://www .pmru.org/pressroom/headlines/20091213PMRStatementRegardingMissions.html

Sources

Fought, T. (2009, December 20). Ore. debates beacons for climbers. *The Boston Globe*, News, p. 26.

Johnson, R. (2008, April). Get saved anywhere. *Outdoor Life*, pp. 24–25.

Menke, S. M. (2004, February 20). NOAA: Rescues rising with satellite beacons. *Newsbytes*.

Tomlinson, S., & Graves, B. (2009, December 15). Radio beacons: Climbers, rescuers and politicians debate whether mountain locater units should be mandatory. *The Oregonian*, pp. A1, A10.

Yet again, rescuers search a silent mountain. (2009, December 15). *The Oregonian*, p. B8.

Notes

1. Pearson, C. M., & Judith, A. C. (1998). Reframing crisis management. *Academy of Management Review, 23*(1), 59–71; Fearn-Banks, K. (2007). *Crisis communications: A casebook approach* (3rd ed.). Mahwah, NJ: Lawrence Erlbaum.

2. Christensen, S. L., & Kohls, J. (2003). Ethical decision making in times of organizational crises: A framework for analysis. *Business & Society, 42,* 328–358.

3. Coombs, W. T. (1999). *Ongoing crisis communication: Planning, managing, and responding.* Thousand Oaks, CA: Sage; Seeger, M. W., Sellnow, T. L., & Ulmer, R. R. (2003). *Communication and organizational crisis.* Westport, CT: Praeger.

4. Mitroff, I. I. (2005). *Why some companies emerge stronger and better from a crisis.* New York: AMACOM.

5. For more information on the relationship between complexity and crises, see Perrow, C. (1999). *Normal accidents: Living with high-risk technologies.* Princeton, NJ: Princeton University Press.

6. Seeger, Sellnow, & Ulmer.

7. Bazerman, M. H., & Watkins, M. D. (2004). *Predictable surprises: The disasters you should have seen coming and how to prevent them.* Boston: Harvard Business School Press.

8. Fink, S. (2002). *Crisis management: Planning for the inevitable.* Lincoln, NE: Backinprint.com.

9. See, for example:

> Mitroff, I. I., Pearson, C. M., & Harrington, L. K. (1996). *The essential guide to managing corporate crises: A step-by-step handbook for surviving major catastrophes.* New York: Oxford University Press.
>
> Mitroff, I. I., & Alpsaian, M. C. (2003, April). Preparing for evil. *Harvard Business Review,* pp. 109–115.
>
> Mitroff, I. I., & Anagnos, G. (2001). *Managing crises before they happen: What every executive and manager needs to know about crisis management.* New York: American Management Association.

10. Fink; Lee, J., Woeste, J. H., & Heath, R. L. (2007). Getting ready for crises: Strategic excellence. *Public Relations Review, 33,* 334–336.

11. Coombs, W. T., & Holladay, S. J. (2004). Reasoned action in crisis communication: An attribution theory-based approach to crisis management. In D. P. Millar & R. L. Heath (Eds.), *Responding to crisis: A rhetorical approach to crisis communication* (pp. 95–115). Mahwah, NJ: Lawrence Erlbaum; Benoit, W. L. (2004). Image restoration discourse and crisis communication. In D. P. Millar & R. L. Heath (Eds.), *Responding to crisis: A rhetorical approach to crisis communication* (pp. 263–280). Mahwah, NJ: Lawrence Erlbaum.

12. Weick, K. E., & Sutcliffe, K. M. (2001). *Managing the unexpected: Assuring high performance in an age of complexity.* San Francisco: Jossey-Bass.

13. Harris, S., Smallen, J., & Mitchell, C. (2006, February 18). Katrina report spreads blame. *National Journal,* p. 38; A post-Katrina public flaying. *U.S. News & World Report,* pp. 62–64.

14. Seeger et al.

15. Allinson, R. E. (1993). *Global disasters: Inquiries into management ethics.* New York: Prentice Hall, p. 16.

16. Lee, Woeste, & Heath.

17. Fearn-Banks.

18. Whoriskey, P. (2010, March 19). Toyota resisted government safety findings: Automaker followed "game plan," escaped a broad early recall. *The Washington Post,* p. A01.

19. Greenberg, J. W. (2002, October). September 11, 2001: A CEO's story. *Harvard Business Review,* pp. 58–64.

20. Birkinshaw, P. (2006). Transparency as a human right. In C. Hood & D. Heald (Eds.), *Transparency: The key to better governance?* (pp. 47–57). Oxford, UK: Oxford University Press.

21. Lazarus, H., & McManus, T. (2006). Transparency guru: An interview with Tom McManus. *Journal of Management Development, 25*(10), 923–936.

22. Fearn-Banks.

23. Christiansen, L. T., & Langer, R. (2009). Public relations and the strategic use of transparency. In Heath, R. L., Toth, E. L., & Waymer, D. *Rhetorical and critical approaches to public relations II* (pp. 129–153). New York: Routledge.

24. Grunig, L. A., Grunig, J. E., & Dozier, D. M. (2002). *Excellent public relations and effective organizations: A study of communication management in three countries.* Mahwah, NJ: Lawrence Erlbaum; Grunig, J. E. (2001). Two-way symmetrical public relations: Past, present, and future. In R. L. Heath (Ed.), *Handbook of public relations* (pp. 11–30). Thousand Oaks, CA: Sage.

25. Fearn-Banks.

26. Lazarus & McManus.

27. Ulmer, R. R., & Sellnow, T. L. (2000). Consistent questions of ambiguity in organizational crisis communication: Jack in the Box as a case study. *Journal of Business Ethics, 25,* 143–155.

28. Eisenberg, E. M. (1984). Ambiguity as strategy in organizational communication. *Communication Monographs, 51,* 227–242.

29. Ulmer & Sellnow.

30. Hearit, K. M. (2006). *Crisis management by apology: Corporate response to allegations of wrongdoing.* Mahwah, NJ: Lawrence Erlbaum, Ch. 4.

31. See, for example:

   Hodgkinson, P. E., & Stewart, M. (1991). *Coping with catastrophe: A handbook of disaster management.* London: Routledge.

   Mitroff.

   Pauchant, T. C., & Mitroff, I. I. (1992). *Transforming the crisis-prone organization: Preventing individual, organizational, and environmental tragedies.* San Francisco: Jossey-Bass.

32. Simola, S. (2005). Concepts of care in organizational crisis prevention. *Journal of Business Ethics, 62,* 341–353.

33. Simola, S. (2003). Ethics of justice and care in corporate crisis management. *Journal of Business Ethics, 46,* 351–361.

34. Starmann, R. G. (1993). Tragedy at McDonald's. In J. A. Gottschalk (Ed.), *Crisis response: Inside stories on managing image under siege* (pp. 309–322). Detroit, MI: Visible Ink.

35. Witt, J. L., & Morgan, J. (2002). *Stronger in the broken places: Nine lessons for turning crisis into triumph.* New York: Times Books/Henry Holt.

36. Weick & Sutcliffe. See also:

> Roberts, K. H. (2006). Some characteristics of one type of high reliability organization. In D. Smith & D. Elliott (Eds.), *Key readings in crisis management: Systems and structures for prevention and recovery* (pp. 159–179). London: Routledge.

> Weick, K. E., & Roberts, K. H. (2006). Collective minds in organizations: Heedful interrelating on flight decks. In D. Smith & D. Elliott (Eds.), *Key readings in crisis management: Systems and structures for prevention and recovery* (pp. 343–368). London: Routledge.

37. Rochlin, G. I., LaPorte, T. R., & Roberts, K. H. (1987). The self-designing high-reliability organization: Aircraft carrier flight operations at sea. *Naval War College Review, 40*(4), 76–90.

38. Snyder, P., Hall, M., Robertson, J., Jasinski, T., & Miller, J. S. (2006). Ethical rationality: A strategic approach to organizational crisis. *Journal of Business Ethics, 63,* 371–383.

39. Eisenhardt, K. M. (1989). Making fast strategic decisions in high-velocity environments. *Academy of Management Journal, 32,* 543–576.

40. Hosmer, L. T. (1994). Strategic planning as if ethics mattered. *Strategic Management Journal, 15,* 17–34.

41. Argenti, P. (2002, December). Crisis communication: Lessons from 9/11. *Harvard Business Review,* pp. 103–109.

42. Sandin, P. (2009). Approaches to ethics for corporate crisis management. *Journal of Business Ethics, 87,* 109–116; Seeger, M. W., & Ulmer, R. R. (2001). Virtuous responses to organizational crisis: Aaron Feuerstein and Milt Cole. *Journal of Business Ethics, 31,* 369–376.

43. Nielsen, R. P., & Dufresne, R. (2005). Can ethical organizational character be stimulated and enabled? "Upbuilding" dialog as crisis management method. *Journal of Business Ethics, 57,* 311–326.

Epilogue

It's only fair to tell you fellows now that we're not likely to come out of this.

—Captain Joshua James, speaking to
his crew during the hurricane of 1888

Captain Joshua James (1826–1902) is the "patron saint" of the search and rescue unit of the U.S. Coast Guard. James led rescue efforts to save sailors who crashed off the shores of Massachusetts. When word came of shipwreck, James and his volunteer crew would launch a large rowboat into heavy seas. James would keep an eye out for the stricken vessel as his men rowed, steering with a large wooden rudder. During his career, he never lost a crewman or a shipwrecked person who had been alive when picked up. The captain's finest hour came during a tremendous storm in late November 1888. Over a 24-hour period, James (62 years old at the time) and his men rescued 29 sailors from five ships.

Philip Hallie, who writes about James in his book *Tales of Good and Evil, Help and Harm,* argues that we can understand James's courageous leadership only as an extension of his larger community. James lived in the town of Hull, a tiny, impoverished town on the Massachusetts coast. Most coastal villages of the time profited from shipwrecks. Beachcombers would scavenge everything from the cargo to the sunken ship's timbers and anchors. Unscrupulous people called "mooncussers" would lure boats aground. On dark, moonless nights, they would hang a lantern from a donkey and trick sea captains into sailing on to the rocks.

Unlike their neighbors up and down the coast, the people of Hull tried to stop the carnage. They built shelters for those who washed ashore, cared for the sick and injured, protested against shipping companies and insurers who

446 perienced captains and crews into danger, and had their lifeboat always at the ready. During the storm of 1888, citizens burned their fences to light the way for Captain James, his crew, and victims alike. According to Hallie,

> Many of the other people of Hull tore up some picket fences near the crest of the hill and built a big fire that lit up the wreck and helped the lifesavers to avoid the flopping, slashing debris around the boat. The loose and broken spars of a ruined ship were one of the main dangers lifesavers had to face. But the sailors on the wrecked ship needed the firelight too. It showed them what the lifesavers were doing, and what they could do to help them. And it gave them hope: It showed them that they were not alone.[1]

The story of Captain James and his fellow villagers is a fitting end to this text. In their actions, they embodied many of the themes introduced earlier: character; values; good versus evil; moral action; altruism; cooperation; transformational, authentic, and servant leadership; social responsibility; ethical crisis leadership; and purpose. The captain, who lost his mother and baby sister in a shipwreck, had one mission in life: saving lives at sea. Following his lead, residents took on nearly insurmountable challenges at great personal cost. They recognized that helpers often need help. By burning their fences, these followers (living in extremely modest conditions) cast a light that literally made the difference between life and death. But like other groups of leaders and followers, they were far from perfect. In the winter hurricane season, the village did its best to save lives. In the summer, pickpockets (helped by a corrupt police force) preyed on those who visited the town's resorts. The dark side of Hull shouldn't diminish the astonishing feats of Captain James and his neighbors, however. Hallie calls what James did during the storm of 1888 an example of "moral beauty."

> And moral beauty happens when someone carves out a place for compassion in a largely ruthless universe. It happened in the French village of Le Chambon during the war, and it happened in and near the American village of Hull during the long lifetime of Joshua James.
>
> It happens, and it fails to happen, in almost every event of people's lives together—in streets, in kitchens, in bedrooms, in workplaces, in wars. But sometimes it happens in a way that engrosses the mind and captivates memory. Sometimes it happens in such a way that the people who make it happen seem to unify the universe around themselves like powerful magnets. Somehow they seem to redeem us all from deathlike indifference. They carve a place for caring in the very middle of the quiet and loud storms of uncaring that surround—and eventually kill—us all.[2]

Notes

1. Hallie, P. (1997). *Tales of good and evil, help and harm.* New York: HarperCollins, p. 146.

2. Hallie, p. 173.

References

Abrahams, J. (2007). *101 mission statements from top companies*. Berkeley, CA: Ten Speed Press.

Adams, G. B., & Balfour, D. L. (1998). *Unmasking administrative evil*. Thousand Oaks, CA: Sage.

Adams, J. S., Taschian, A., & Shore, T. H. (2001). Codes of ethics as signals for ethical behavior. *Journal of Business Ethics, 29,* 199–211.

Addario, L., & Polgreen, L. (2009, March 23). In aid groups' expulsion, fears of more misery engulfing Darfur. *The New York Times,* p. A6.

Adobor, H. (2006). Exploring the role performance of corporate ethics officers. *Journal of Business Ethics, 69,* 57–75.

AIG bonuses; only part of the mess. (2009, March 19). *The Philadelphia Inquirer,* p. A14.

Alderman, H. (1997). By virtue of a virtue. In D. Statman (Ed.), *Virtue ethics* (pp. 145–164). Washington, DC: Georgetown University Press.

Alexander, C. (1999). *The* Endurance: *Shackleton's legendary Antarctic expedition.* New York: Alfred A. Knopf.

Alexander, J. A., Comfort, M. E., Weiner, B. J., & Bogue, R. (2001). Leadership in collaborative community health partnerships. *Nonprofit Management & Leadership, 12,* 159–175.

Alexander, L. (2000). Deontology at the threshold. *San Diego Law Review, Rev. 893.*

Alford, C. F. (1997). *What evil means to us.* Ithaca, NY: Cornell University Press.

Allen-Mills, T. (2009, March 9). Judges paid off to keep jails full in kids-for-cash scandal. *The Australian,* World, p. 12.

Allinson, R. E. (1993). *Global disasters: Inquiries into management ethics.* New York: Prentice Hall.

Allport, G. (1961). *Pattern and growth in personality.* New York: Holt, Rinehart & Winston.

Alper, S., Tjosvold, D., & Law, K. S. (2000). Conflict management, efficacy, and performance in organizational teams. *Personnel Psychology, 53,* 625–642.

Amason, A. C. (1996). Distinguishing the effects of functional and dysfunctional conflict on strategic decision making: Resolving a paradox for top management teams. *Academy of Management Journal, 39,* 123–148.

Amason, A. C., Thompson, K. R., Hochwarter, W. A., & Harrison, A. W. (1995). Conflict: An important dimension in successful management teams. *Organizational Dynamics, 23,* 20–35.

Amichai-Hamburger, Y. (2003). Understanding social loafing. In A. Sagie, S. Stashevsky, & M. Koslowsky (Eds.), *Misbehaviour and dysfunctional attitudes in organizations* (pp. 79–102). New York: Palgrave Macmillan.

Anand, V., Ashforth, B. E., & Joshi, M. (2004). Business as usual: The acceptance and perpetuation of corruption in organizations. *Academy of Management Executive, 18,* 39–53.

Anderson, R., & Cissna, K. N. (2008). Dismissiveness and dialogic ethics. In K. G. Roberts & R. C. Arnett (Eds.), *Communication ethics: Between cosmopolitanism and provinciality* (pp. 263–284). New York: Peter Lang.

Anderson, S., Cavanagh, J., Collins, C., Pizzigati, S., & Lapham, M. (2008). *Executive excess 2008.* Retrieved from http://www.faireconomy.org/files/executive_excess_2008.pdf

Andreoli, N., & Lefkowitz, J. (2008). Individual and organizational antecedents of misconduct in organizations. *Journal of Business Ethics, 85,* 309–332.

Annas, J. (2006). Virtue ethics. In D. Copp (Ed.), *The Oxford handbook of ethical theory* (pp. 515–536). Oxford, UK: Oxford University Press.

Appelbaum, S. H., Bethune, M., & Tanenbaum, R. (1999). Downsizing and the emergence of self-managed teams. *Participation and Empowerment: An International Journal, 7,* 109–130.

Appiah, K. A. (2006). *Cosmopolitanism: Ethics in a world of strangers.* New York: Norton.

Arendt, H. (1964). *Eichmann in Jerusalem: A report on the banality of evil.* New York: Viking.

Argenti, P. (2002, December). Crisis communication: Lessons from 9/11. *Harvard Business Review,* pp. 103–109.

Aristotle. (350 B.C.E./1962). *Nichomachean ethics* (Martin Ostwald, Trans.). Indianapolis, IN: Bobbs-Merrill.

Armitage, J., & Conde, B. (2007, October 19). Why the French are so keen to stay in Burma despite unrest. *The Evening Standard,* p. B34.

Armour, S. (2006, November 8). Employers look closely at what workers do on job. *USA Today,* pp. B1, B2.

Ashforth, B. E. (1997). Petty tyranny in organizations: A preliminary examination of antecedents and consequences. *Canadian Journal of Administrative Sciences, 14*(2), 126–140.

Ashmos, D. P., & Duchon, D. (2000). Spirituality at work: A conceptualization and measure. *Journal of Management Inquiry, 9,* 134–145.

Aspinwall, L. G., & Staudinger, U. M. (Eds.). (2002). *A psychology of human strengths: Fundamental questions about future directions for a positive psychology.* Washington, DC: American Psychological Association.

Avedlund, E. (2009). *Too good to be true: The rise and fall of Bernie Madoff.* New York: Portfolio.

Avolio, B. J., & Gardner, W. L. (2005). Authentic leadership development: Getting to the root of positive forms of leadership. *The Leadership Quarterly, 16*, 315–340.

Avolio, B. J., Gardner, W. L., Walumbwa, F. O., Luthans, F., & May, D. R. (2004). Unlocking the mask: A look at the process by which authentic leaders impact follower attitudes and behaviors. *The Leadership Quarterly, 15*, 801–823.

Avolio, B. J., & Locke, E. E. (2002). Contrasting different philosophies of leader motivation: Altruism versus egoism. *The Leadership Quarterly, 13*, 169–191.

Bad bosses drain productivity. (2005, November). *Training & Development*, p. 15.

Bad judges: No deal. (2009, August 6). *The Philadelphia Inquirer*, p. A01.

Bailon, R. R., Moya, M., & Yzerbyt, V. (2000). Why do superiors attend to negative stereotypic information about their subordinates? Effects of power legitimacy on social perception. *European Journal of Social Psychology, 30*, 651–671.

Baker, P. (2009, March 18). Adding pressure to Sudan, Obama will tap retired general as special envoy. *The New York Times*, p. A6.

Barbuto, J. E., & Wheeler, D. W. (2006). Scale development and construct clarification of servant leadership. *Group & Organization Management, 31*, 300–326.

Barker, L., Johnson, P., & Watson, K. (1991). The role of listening in managing interpersonal and group conflict. In D. Borisoff & M. Purdy (Eds.), *Listening in everyday life: A personal and professional approach* (pp. 139–157). Lanham, MD: University Press of America.

Baron, R. A. (2004). Workplace aggression and violence: Insights from basic research. In R. W. Griffin & A. M. O'Leary-Kelly (Eds.), *The dark side of organizational behavior* (pp. 23–61). San Francisco: Jossey-Bass.

Barrett, J. (2003, July 18). *Q&A: Clearly there is a problem here.* Retrieved from http://www.newsweek.com/2003/07/17/q-amp-a-clearly-there-is-a-problem-here.html

Barron, J., & Buettner, R. (2009, March 20). Scorn trails A. I. G. executives, even in their own driveways. *The New York Times*, p. A1.

Barry, D. (2008, September 15). On an infested river, battling invaders eye to eye. *The New York Times*, p. A13.

Barry, V. (1978). *Personal and social ethics: Moral problems with integrated theory.* Belmont, CA: Wadsworth.

Bartholomew, C. S., & Gustafson, S. B. (1998). Perceived leader integrity scale: An instrument for assessing employee perceptions of leader integrity. *The Leadership Quarterly, 9*, 143–144.

Bass, B. M. (1990). *Bass & Stogdill's handbook of leadership* (3rd ed.). New York: Free Press.

Bass, B. M. (1995). The ethics of transformational leadership. In J. Ciulla (Ed.), *Ethics: The heart of leadership* (pp. 169–192). Westport, CT: Praeger.

Bass, B. M. (1996). *A new paradigm of leadership: An inquiry into transformational leadership.* Alexandria, VA: U.S. Army Research Institute for the Behavioral and Social Sciences.

Bass, B. M., & Avolio, B. J. (1993). Transformational leadership: A response to critiques. In M. M. Chemers & R. Ayman (Eds.), *Leadership theory and research: Perspectives and directions* (pp. 49–80). San Diego, CA: Academic Press.

Bass, B. M., Avolio, B. J., Jung, D. I., & Berson, Y. (2003). Predicting unit performance by assessing transformational and transactional leadership. *Journal of Applied Psychology, 88*, 207–218.

Bass, B. M., & Steidlmeier, P. (1999). Ethics, character, and authentic transformational leadership behavior. *The Leadership Quarterly, 10*, 181–217.

Batson, C. D., & Thompson, E. R. (2001). Why don't moral people act morally? Motivational considerations. *Current Directions in Psychological Science, 10*, 54–57.

Batson, C. D., Thompson, E. R., & Chen, H. (2002). Moral hypocrisy: Addressing some alternatives. *Journal of Personality and Social Psychology, 83*, 330–339.

Batson, C. D., Van Lange, P. A. M., Ahmad, N., & Lishner, D. A. (2003). Altruism and helping behavior. In M. A. Hogg & J. Cooper (Eds.), *The Sage handbook of social psychology* (pp. 279–295). London: Sage.

Bauby, J. D. (1997). *The diving bell and the butterfly: A memoir of life in death.* New York: Vintage Books.

Bazerman, M. H. (1986). *Management in managerial decision making.* New York: Wiley.

Bazerman, M. H., & Watkins, M. D. (2004). *Predictable surprises: The disasters you should have seen coming and how to prevent them.* Boston: Harvard Business School Press.

Beale, C. (2009, April 20). How Domino's execs were left looking like twits. *The Independent*, p. 46.

Bedian, A. G. (2007). Even if the tower is "ivory," it isn't "white": Understanding the consequences of faculty cynicism. *Academy of Management Learning and Education, 6*, 9–32.

Bell, M. A. (1974). The effects of substantive and affective conflict in problem-solving groups. *Speech Monographs, 41*, 19–23.

Bell, M. A. (1979). The effects of substantive and affective verbal conflict on the quality of decisions of small problem-solving groups. *Central States Speech Journal, 3*, 75–82.

Bellah, N., Madsen, R., Sullivan, W. M., Swidler, A., & Tipton, S. M. (1991). *The good society.* New York: Vintage.

Belmonte, K. (2007). *William Wilberforce: A hero for humanity.* Grand Rapids, MI: Zondervan.

Benefiel, M. (2005). The second half of the journey: Spiritual leadership for organizational transformation. *The Leadership Quarterly, 16*, 723–747.

Benefiel, M. (2005). *Soul at work: Spiritual leadership in organizations.* New York: Seabury Books.

Benkert, G. G. (2008). Google, human rights, and moral compromise. *Journal of Business Ethics, 85*, 453–478.

Bennis, W., & Nanus, B. (2003). *Leaders: Strategies for taking charge.* New York: Harper Business Essentials.

Bennis, W. G., & Thomas, R. J. (2002). *Geeks and geezers: How era, values, and defining moments shape leaders.* Boston: Harvard Business School Press.

Benoit, W. L. (2004). Image restoration discourse and crisis communication. In D. P. Millar & R. L. Heath (Eds.), *Responding to crisis: A rhetorical approach to crisis communication* (pp. 263–280). Mahwah, NJ: Erlbaum.

Bentham, J. (1948). *An introduction to the principles of morals and legislation.* New York: Hafner.

Berman, D. K. (2008, October 28). The game: Post-Enron crackdown comes up woefully short. *The Wall Street Journal,* p. C2.

Bies, R. J., & Tripp, T. M. (1998). Two faces of the powerless: Coping with tyranny in organizations. In R. M. Kramer & M. A. Neale (Eds.), *Power and influence in organizations* (pp. 203–219). Thousand Oaks, CA: Sage.

Big victory against global bribery. (2008, December 17). *Christian Science Monitor,* p. 8.

Bilger, B. (2009, April 20). Swamp things; Florida's uninvited predators. *The New Yorker,* p. 80.

Bing, S. (2000). *What would Machiavelli do? The ends justify the meanness.* New York: HarperBusiness.

Bird, F. B. (1996). *The muted conscience: Moral silence and the practice of ethics in business.* Westport, CT: Quorum.

Birkinshaw, P. (2006). Transparency as a human right. In C. Hood & D. Heald (Eds.), *Transparency: The key to better governance?* (pp. 47–57). Oxford, UK: Oxford University Press.

Blackwell, T. (2009, September 30). Mandatory flu shots rile health workers; "invasive procedure." *National Post,* p. A8.

Blake, J. (2008, March 3). CNN special projects. *CNN International TV.* Retrieved from https://www.ikat.org/2008/03/03/cnn-special-projects/

Blasi, A. (1984). Moral identity: Its role in moral functioning. In W. M. Kurtines & J. L. Gewirtz (Eds.), *Morality, moral behavior, and moral development* (pp. 128–139). New York: Wiley.

Block, P. (1996). *Stewardship: Choosing service over self-interest.* San Francisco: Berrett-Koehler.

Bly, L. (2009, January 2). "Three Cups of Tea" author finds new mountains to climb. *USA Today,* p. 4D.

Boje, D. (2008). Critical theory approaches to spirituality in business. In J. Biberman & L. Tischler (Eds.), *Spirituality in business: Theory, practice, and future directions* (pp. 160–187). New York: Palgrave Macmillan.

Booker, K. (2001, May 28). The chairman of the board looks back. *Fortune,* pp. 63–76.

Bordas, J. (1995). Becoming a servant-leader: The personal development path. In L. Spears (Ed.), *Reflections on leadership* (pp. 149–160). New York: Wiley.

Bosch, X. (2003, July 5). UN agency sets out global rules for protecting genetic data. *The Lancet,* p. 45.

Brady, E., & Halley, J. (2009, February 24). The blowup over blowouts. *USA Today,* p. 1C.

Bratton, V. K., & Kacmar, K. M. (2004). Extreme careerism: The dark side of impression management. In W. Griffin & K. O'Reilly (Eds.), *The dark side of organizational behavior* (pp. 291–308). San Francisco: Jossey-Bass.

Brecher, B. (2007). *Torture and the ticking bomb*. Malden, MA: Blackwell.

Brissett, D., & Edgley, C. (Eds.). (1990). The dramaturgical perspective. In D. Brissett & C. Edgley (Eds.), *Life as theater: A dramaturgical sourcebook* (2nd ed., pp. 1–46). New York: Aldine de Gruyter.

Brown, D. J., Scott, K. A., & Lewis, H. (2004). Information processing and leadership. In J. Antonakis, A. T. Cianciolo, & R. J. Sternberg (Eds.), *The nature of leadership* (pp. 125–147). Thousand Oaks, CA: Sage.

Brown, J. (1995). Dialogue: Capacities and stories. In S. Chawla & J. Renesch (Eds.), *Learning organizations: Developing cultures for tomorrow's workplace* (pp. 153–164). Portland, OR: Productivity Press.

Brown, M. E., & Trevino, L. K. (2006). Ethical leadership: A review and future directions. *The Leadership Quarterly, 17,* 595–616.

Brown, M. E., Trevino, L. K., & Harrison, D. (2005). Ethical leadership: A social learning perspective for construct development and testing. *Organizational Behavior and Human Decision Processes, 97,* 117–134.

Brown, M. T. (2005). *Corporate integrity: Rethinking organizational ethics and leadership*. Cambridge, UK: Cambridge University Press.

Brown, R. (1995). *Prejudice: Its social psychology*. Oxford, UK: Blackwell.

Brown, R. P. (2003). Measuring individual differences in the tendency to forgive: Construct validity and links with depression. *Personality and Social Psychology Bulletin, 29,* 759–771.

Bruhn, J. G. (2001). *Trust and the health of organizations*. New York: Kluwer/Plenum.

Brune, T. (2009, March 19). Not his fault but now his problem. *Newsday,* p. A7.

Buber, M. (1970). *I and thou* (R. G. Smith, Trans.). New York: Charles Scribner's Sons.

Buchholz, R. A., & Rosenthal, S. B. (2005). Toward a conceptual framework for stakeholder theory. *Journal of Business Ethics, 58,* 137–148.

Burns, J. M. (1978). *Leadership*. New York: Harper & Row.

Burns, J. M. (2003). *Transforming leadership: A new pursuit of happiness*. New York: Atlantic Monthly Press.

Burton, J. P., & Hoobler, J. M. (2006). Subordinate self-esteem and abusive supervision. *Journal of Managerial Science, 3,* 340–355.

Buss, A. H. (1961). *The psychology of aggression*. New York: John Wiley & Sons.

Camp, R. C. (1989). *Benchmarking: The search for industry best practices that lead to superior performance*. Milwaukee, WI: Quality Press.

Campbell, D. (2004, December 14). Energy giant agrees to settlement with Burmese villagers. *The Guardian,* Foreign Affairs, p. 17.

Cannici, W. J. (2009). The Global Online Freedom Act: Combating American businesses that facilitate Internet censorship in China. *Internet Law.*

Carey, J., & Gardiner, A. (2008, January 30). Settlement gives aid to athletes. *USA Today,* p. 6C.

Carlson, D. S., & Perrewe, P. L. (1995). Institutionalization of organizational ethics through transformational leadership. *Journal of Business Ethics, 14,* 829–838.

Carroll, S. J., & Gannon, M. J. (1997). *Ethical dimensions of management*. Thousand Oaks, CA: Sage.

Carver, C. S., & Scheier, M. F. (2005). Optimism. In C. R. Snyder & S. J. Lopez (Eds.), *Handbook of positive psychology* (pp. 231–243). Oxford, UK: Oxford University Press.

Casarjian, R. (1992). *Forgiveness: A bold choice for a peaceful heart*. New York: Bantam.

Cauchon, D. (2009, December 1). Invasive carp threatens Great Lakes. *USA Today*, p. 17A.

Caudron, S. (1995, September 4). The boss from hell. *Industry Week*, pp. 12–16.

Caux Round Table. (2000). Appendix 26: The Caux principles. In O. F. Williams (Ed.), *Global codes of conduct: An idea whose time has come* (pp. 384–388). Notre Dame, IN: University of Notre Dame Press.

Cavanagh, G. F., & Moberg, D. J. (1999). The virtue of courage within the organization. In M. L. Pava & P. Primeaux (Eds.), *Research in ethical issues in organizations* (Vol. 1, pp. 1–25). Stamford, CT: JAI Press.

Center for the Study of Ethics in the Professions at Illinois Institute of Technology. (2010). *Index of codes*. Retrieved from http://ethics.iit.edu/codes

Central Asia Institute. (2009). *About CAI*. Retrieved from https://www.ikat.org/about-cai/

Chaleff, I. (2003). *The courageous follower: Standing up to and for our leaders* (2nd ed.). San Francisco: Berrett-Koehler.

Chan, A., Hannah, S. T., & Gardner, W. L. (2005). Veritable authentic leadership: Emergence, functioning, and impacts. In W. L. Gardner, B. J. Avolio, & F. O. Walumbwa (Eds.), *Authentic leadership theory and practice: Origins, effects and development* (pp. 3–41). Amsterdam, Netherlands: Elsevier.

Chan, S. P. (2009, May 6). Microsoft may not be done cutting jobs. *The Seattle Times*, p. A1.

Chan, W. (1963). *The way of Lao Tzu*. Indianapolis, IN: Bobbs-Merrill.

Chang, K. (2007, August 20). Caution over damage to *Endeavour* illustrates changes at space agency. *The New York Times*, p. A12.

Chao, C. A., Wilhelm, W. J., & Neureuther, B. D. (2009). A study of electronic detection and pedagogical approaches for reducing plagiarism. *The Delta Pi Epsilon Journal, LI*, 31–42.

Charges possible in outbreak. (2009, February 15). *Newsday*, p. A50.

The cheat sheet. (2009, July 9). *The Boston Globe*, p. G23.

Chen, A., Lawson, R. B., Gordon, L. R., & McIntosh, B. (1996). Groupthink: Deciding with the leader and the devil. *Psychological Record, 46*, 581–590.

Chernow, R. (2009, March 23). Madoff and his models; where are the snow jobs of yesteryear? *The New Yorker*, p. 28.

Chrisafis, A. (2009, January 27). Veiled threats: Row over Islamic dress opens bitter divisions in France. *The Guardian*, International, p. 24.

Chrislip, D. D. (2002). *The collaborative leadership fieldbook*. San Francisco: Jossey-Bass.

Chrislip, D. D., & Larson, C. E. (1994). *Collaborative leadership: How citizens and civic leaders can make a difference.* San Francisco: Jossey-Bass.

Christensen, L. T., & Langer, R. (2009). Public relations and the strategic use of transparency: Consistency, hypocrisy and corporate change. In R. L. Heath, E. L. Toth, & D. Waymer (Eds.), *Rhetorical and critical approaches to public relations II* (pp. 129–153). New York: Routledge.

Christensen, S. L., & Kohls, J. (2003). Ethical decision making in times of organizational crises: A framework for analysis. *Business & Society, 42,* 328–358.

Christians, C. G., Rotzell, K. B., & Fackler, M. (1999). *Media ethics* (3rd ed.). New York: Longman.

Christie, R., & Geis, F. L. (1970). *Studies in Machiavellianism.* New York: Academic Press.

Cissna, K. N., & Anderson, R. (1994). Communication and the ground of dialogue. In R. Anderson, K. N. Cissna, & R. C. Arnett (Eds.), *The reach of dialogue: Confirmation, voice, and community* (pp. 9–30). Cresskill, NJ: Hampton.

Ciulla, J. B. (2004). Leadership ethics: Mapping the territory. In J. B. Ciulla (Ed.), *Ethics: The heart of leadership* (pp. 3–24). Westport, CT: Praeger.

Clapp-Smith, R., Vogelgesang, G. R., & Avey, J. B. (2009). Authentic leadership and positive psychological capital: The mediating role of trust at the group level of analysis. *Journal of Leadership & Organizational Studies, 15*(3), 227–240.

Clark, K. (2001, December 31). Nothing but the plane truth. *U.S. News & World Report.*

Clifford, S. (2009, April 16). Video prank at Domino's taints brand. *The New York Times,* p. B1.

The Coca-Cola Company. (2010). *Code of business conduct.* Retrieved from http://www.thecoca-colacompany.com/ourcompany/business_conduct.html

Cohen, D. V. (1993). Creating and maintaining ethical work climates: Anomie in the workplace and implications for managing change. *Business Ethics Quarterly, 3,* 343–358.

Cohen, L. R., & Undis, D. J. (2006, March/April). New solution to the organ shortage. *Saturday Evening Post,* p. 32.

Colby, A., & Damon, W. (1992). *Some do care: Contemporary lives of moral commitment.* New York: Free Press.

Colby, A., & Damon, W. (1995). The development of extraordinary moral commitment. In M. Killen & D. Hart (Eds.), *Morality in everyday life: Developmental perspectives* (pp. 342–369). Cambridge, UK: Cambridge University Press.

Colle, Z. (2007, April 21). Evidence of cover-up key to Tillman hearings. *The San Francisco Chronicle,* p. A1.

Colle, Z., & Collier, R. (2007, April 25). Lawmakers see cover-up, vow to probe Tillman death. *The San Francisco Chronicle,* p. A1.

Collier, R., & Epstein, E. (2007, March 27). Tillmans assail Pentagon report. *The San Francisco Chronicle,* p. A1.

Collins, J. (2001). *Good to great.* New York: HarperBusiness.

Collins, J. (2001, January). Level 5 leadership: The triumph of humility and fierce resolve. *Harvard Business Review,* pp. 67–76.

Collins, J. C., & Porras, J. I. (1996, September–October). Building your company's vision. *Harvard Business Review*, pp. 65–77.

Colquitt, J. A., Conlon, D. E., Wesson, M. J., Porter, C. O. L. H., & Yee, N. K. (2001). Justice at the millennium: A meta-analytic review of 25 years of organizational justice research. *Journal of Applied Psychology, 86*, 425–445.

Comte-Sponville, A. (2001). *A small treatise on the great virtues: The uses of philosophy in everyday life.* New York: Metropolitan.

Connelly, S., Helton-Fauth, W., & Mumford, M. D. (2004). A managerial in-basket study of the impact of trait emotions on ethical choice. *Journal of Business Ethics, 51*, 245–267.

Conrad, C., & Poole, M. S. (1998). *Strategic organizational communication: Into the twenty-first century* (4th ed.). Fort Worth, TX: Harcourt Brace.

Coombs, W. T. (1999). *Ongoing crisis communication: Planning, managing, and responding.* Thousand Oaks, CA: Sage.

Coombs, W. T., & Holladay, S. J. (2004). Reasoned action in crisis communication: An attribution theory-based approach to crisis management. In D. P. Millar & R. L. Heath (Eds.), *Responding to crisis: A rhetorical approach to crisis communication* (pp. 95–115). Mahwah, NJ: Erlbaum.

Cooper, C. D., Scandura, T. A., & Schriesheim, C. A. (2005). Looking forward but learning from our past: Potential challenges to developing authentic leadership theory and authentic leaders. *The Leadership Quarterly, 16*, 475–493.

Cooper, S. (2004). *Corporate social performance: A stakeholder approach.* Burlington, VT: Ashgate.

Cooperrider, D. L, & Whitney, D. (2005). *Appreciative inquiry: A positive revolution in change.* San Francisco: Berrett-Koehler.

Cornwell, R. (2007, April 26). Secrets and lies: How war heroes returned to haunt Pentagon. *The Independent* (London).

Cosier, R. A., & Schwenk, C. R. (1990). Agreement and thinking alike: Ingredients for poor decision. *Academy of Management Executive, 4*, 69–74.

Countryman, A. (2001, December 7). Leadership key ingredient in ethics recipe, experts say. *The Chicago Tribune*, pp. B1, B6.

Coutts, M. (2009, January 27). Would Jesus run up the score? Christian school under fire for winning 100–0. *National Post*, p. A1.

Covey, S. (1989). *The seven habits of highly effective people.* New York: Simon & Schuster.

Cox, T. (1993). *Cultural diversity in organizations: Theory, research and practice.* San Francisco: Berrett-Koehler.

Cox, T. (2001). *Creating the multicultural organization: A strategy for capturing the power of diversity.* San Francisco: Jossey-Bass.

Coyne, I. (2008, January 15). Turbans make targets, some Sikhs find. *The New York Times*, p. NJ1.

Craigie, F. C. (1999). The spirit and work: Observations about spirituality and organizational life. *Journal of Psychology and Christianity, 18*, 43–53.

Creswell, A. (2008, August 9). Transplants trade at crossroads. *Weekend Australian*, Review, p. 15.

Cropanzano, R., & Stein, J. H. (2009). Organizational justice and behavioral ethics: Promises and prospects. *Business Ethics Quarterly, 19,* 193–233.

Crosariol, B. (2005, November 21). The diminishing allure of rock-star executives. *The Globe and Mail,* p. B12.

Crosby, B. C., & Bryson, J. M. (2005). A leadership framework for cross-sector collaboration. *Public Management Review, 7,* 177–201.

Cullen, D. (2009). *Columbine.* New York: Twelve.

Cullen, J. B., Parboteeah, K. P., & Victor, B. (2003). The effects of ethical climates on organizational commitment: A two-study analysis. *Journal of Business Ethics, 46,* 127–141.

Cullen, J. B., Victor, B., & Bronson, J. W. (1993). The ethical climate questionnaire: An assessment of its development and validity. *Psychological Reports, 73,* 667–674.

Curl, J. (2009, January 28). Blagojevich tapes aired at impeachment trial. *The Washington Times,* p. A08.

Czubaroff, J. (2000). Dialogical rhetoric: An application of Martin Buber's philosophy of dialogue. *Quarterly Journal of Speech, 2,* 168–189.

Dann, G. E., & Haddow, N. (2007). Just doing business or doing just business: Google, Microsoft, Yahoo! and the business of censoring China's Internet. *Journal of Business Ethics, 79,* 219–234.

Darley, J. M. (1996). How organizations socialize individuals into evildoing. In D. M. Messick & A. E. Tenbrunsel (Eds.), *Codes of conduct: Behavioral research into business ethics* (pp. 12–43). New York: Russell Sage Foundation.

Darley, J. M. (2001). The dynamics of authority influence in organizations and the unintended action consequences. In J. M. Darley, D. M. Messick, & T. R. Tyler (Eds.), *Social influences on ethical behavior in organizations* (pp. 37–52). Mahwah, NJ: Erlbaum.

Dash, E. (2008, October 16). U.S. to examine actions of Washington Mutual. *The New York Times,* p. B12.

Dash, E., & Sorkin, A. R. (2008, September 26). In largest bank failure, U.S. seizes, then sells. *The New York Times,* p. A1.

Davey, M. (2008, December 15). 2 sides of a troubled governor, sinking deeper. *The New York Times,* p. A1.

Davey, M. (2009, January 12). Uneasy times for Blagojevich and his colleagues. *The New York Times,* p. A13.

Davey, M. (2009, January 30). On his way out, Blagojevich makes a day of it. *The New York Times,* p. A1.

Davey, M. (2009, February 1). A governor's removal spurs (the latest) calls for political reform in Illinois. *The New York Times,* p. A16.

Davey, M. (2009, December 13). Be careful what you fish for. *The New York Times,* p. WK3.

Davis, J. H., & Ruhe, J. A. (2003). Perceptions of country corruption: Antecedents and outcomes. *Journal of Business Ethics, 43,* 275–288.

Day, L. A. (2006). *Ethics in media communications: Cases and controversies* (5th ed.). Belmont, CA: Wadsworth/Thompson.

De George, R. T. (1995). *Business ethics* (4th ed.). Englewood Cliffs, NJ: Prentice Hall.

Dean, J. W., Brandes, P., & Dharwadkar, R. (1998). Organizational cynicism. *Academy of Management Review, 23,* 341–352.

DeGroot, T., Kiker, D. S., & Cross, T. C. (2000). A meta-analysis to review organizational outcomes related to charismatic leadership. *Canadian Journal of Administrative Sciences, 17,* 356–371.

Den Hartog, D. N., House, R. J., Hanges, P. U., Ruiz-Quintanilla, S. A., & Dorfman, P. W. (1999). Culture-specific and cross-culturally generalizable implicit leadership theories: Are attributes of charismatic/transformational leadership universally endorsed? *The Leadership Quarterly, 10,* 219–257.

DePree, M. (1989). *Leadership is an art.* New York: Doubleday.

DePree, M. (2003). Servant-leadership: Three things necessary. In L. C. Spears & M. Lawrence (Eds.), *Focus on leadership: Servant-leadership for the 21st century.* (pp. 89–97) New York: Wiley.

Deresky, H. (2003). *International management: Managing across borders and cultures.* Upper Saddle River, NJ: Prentice Hall.

Devine, T., Seuk, J. H., & Wilson, A. (2001). *Cultivating heart and character: Educating for life's most essential goals.* Chapel Hill, NC: Character Development.

DiBella, A., & Nevis, E. C. (1998). *How organizations learn: An integrated strategy for building learning capability.* San Francisco: Jossey-Bass.

DiBella, A. J., Nevis, E. C., & Gould, J. M. (1996). Organizational learning as a core capability. In B. Moingeon & A. Edmondson (Eds.), *Organizational learning and competitive advantage* (pp. 38–55). London: Sage.

Diboye, R. L., & Halverson, S. K. (2004). Subtle (and not so subtle) discrimination in organizations. In R. W. Griffin & A. M. O'Leary-Kelly (Eds.), *The dark side of organizational behavior* (pp. 404–425). San Francisco: Jossey-Bass.

Dickson, D. M. (2009, July 31). Doing well—regardless; billions in bonuses paid employees despite losses. *The Washington Times,* p. A10.

Dirks, K. T. (1999). The effects of interpersonal trust on work group performance. *Journal of Applied Psychology, 84,* 445–455.

Donaldson, T. (1996, September–October). Values in tension: Ethics away from home. *Harvard Business Review,* pp. 48–57.

Donaldson, T., & Dunfee, T. W. (1994). Toward a unified conception of business ethics: Integrative social contracts theory. *Academy of Management Review, 19,* 252–284.

Donaldson, T., & Dunfee, T. W. (1999). *Ties that bind: A social contracts approach to business ethics.* Boston: Harvard Business School Press.

Donaldson, T., & Preston, L. E. (1995). The stakeholder theory of the corporation: Concepts, evidence, and implications. *Academy of Management Review, 20,* 65–91.

Doran, J. (2009, March 14). The biggest swindle in history. *The Irish Times,* Weekend, p. 2.

Dotlich, D. L., Noel, J. L., & Walker, N. (2008). Learning for leadership: Failure as a second chance. In J. Gallos (Ed.), *Business leadership* (2nd ed., pp. 478–485). San Francisco: Jossey-Bass.

Dougherty, C. (2008, October 7). The sheriff at Siemens, at work under Justice Dept's watchful eye. *The New York Times*, p. B11.

Dreazen, Y. J. (2008, December 26). Military finds an unlikely adviser in school-building humanitarian. *The Wall Street Journal*, p. A9.

Driscoll, J. W. (1978). Trust and participation in organizational decision making as predictors of satisfaction. *Academy of Management Journal, 21*, 44–56.

Drummond, T. (2000, April 3). Coping with cops. *Time*, pp. 72–73.

Duchon, D., & Plowman, D. A. (2005). Nurturing the spirit at work: Impact on work unit performance. *The Leadership Quarterly, 16*, 807–833.

Duffy, M. K., & & Shaw, J. D. (2000). The Salieri syndrome: Consequences of envy in *groups. Small Group Research, 31*, 3–23.

Duin, S. (2009, December 15). Mountain rescue and common sense. *The Oregonian*, p. B1.

Dukerich, J. M., Nichols, M. L., Elm, D. R., & Voltrath, D. A. (1990). Moral reasoning in groups: Leaders make a difference. *Human Relations, 43*, 473–493.

Dunn, J., & Schweitzer, M. E. (2005). Why good employees make unethical decisions. In E. W. Kidwell & C. L. Martin (Eds.), *Managing organizational deviance* (pp. 39–60). Thousand Oaks, CA: Sage.

Dunning, J. H. (2000). Whither global capitalism? *Global Focus, 12*, 117–136.

Dunning, J. H. (2003). Overview. In J. H. Dunning (Ed.), *Making globalization good: The moral challenges of global capitalism* (pp. 11–40). Oxford, UK: Oxford University Press.

Durskat, V. U., & Wolff, S. B. (2001, March). Building the emotional intelligence of groups. *Harvard Business Review*, pp. 80–90.

Dye, J. (2007, September). To catch a cheat. *Econtent*, pp. 32–37.

Eberly, D. E. (1994). *Building a community of citizens: Civil society in the 21st century*. Lanham, MD: University Press of America.

Eilperin, J. (2010, February 7). Fight over invasive species turns into fight over lesser of two evils. *The Oregonian*, p. A2.

Einearsen, S., Schanke Aasland, M., & Skogstad, A. (2007). Destructive leadership behavior: A definition and conceptual model. *The Leadership Quarterly, 18*, 207–216.

Einhorn, B. (2006, August 11). *Search engines censured for censorship*. Retrieved from http://www.businessweek.com/globalbiz/content/aug2006/gb20060810_220695.htm

Eisenberg, E. M. (1984). Ambiguity as strategy in organizational communication. *Communication Monographs, 51*, 227–242.

Eisenberg, N. (2000). Emotion, regulation, and moral development. *Annual Review of Psychology, 51*, 665–697.

Eisenhardt, K. M. (1989). Making fast strategic decisions in high-velocity environments. *Academy of Management Journal, 32*, 543–576.

Elangovan, A. R., & Shapiro, D. L. (1998). Betrayal of trust in organizations. *Academy of Management Review, 23*, 547–566.

Ellenwood, S. (2006). Revisiting character education: From McGuffey to narratives. *Journal of Education, 187*, 21–43.

Enright, R. D., Freedman, S., & Rique, J. (1998). The psychology of interpersonal forgiveness. In R. D. Enright & J. North (Eds.), *Exploring forgiveness* (pp. 46–62). Madison: University of Wisconsin Press.

Enright, R. D., & Gassin, E. A. (1992). Forgiveness: A developmental view. *Journal of Moral Education, 21,* 99–114.

Erdem, S. (2008, February 7). Universities protest as MPs debate lifting headscarf ban. *The Times,* p. 38.

Esser, J. K. (1998). Alive and well after 25 years: A review of groupthink research. *Organizational Behavior and Human Decision Processes, 73,* 116–141.

Etzioni, A. (1993). *The spirit of community: The reinvention of American society.* New York: Touchstone.

Etzioni, A. (Ed.). (1995). *New communitarian thinking: Persons, virtues, institutions, and communities.* Charlottesville: University Press of Virginia.

Etzioni, A. (Ed.). (1995). *Rights and the common good: A communitarian perspective.* New York: St. Martin's.

Etzioni, A. (1996). *The new golden rule: Community and morality in a democratic society.* New York: Basic Books.

Etzioni, A. (2006, July–September). A neo-communitarian approach to international relations: Rights and the good. *Human Rights Review,* pp. 69–80.

Etzioni, A. (2006, Summer). A communitarian approach: A viewpoint on the study of the legal, ethical and policy considerations raised by DNA tests and databases. *Journal of Law, Medicine & Ethics,* pp. 214–221.

Evangelista, B. (2009, May 3). How Domino's case unfolded. *San Francisco Chronicle,* p. D1.

Fairholm, G. W. (1996). Spiritual leadership: Fulfilling whole-self needs at work. *Leadership & Organization Development Journal, 17*(5), 11–17.

Farley, R., & Drobnic Holan, A. (2008, October 12). What caused crisis? No one thing. *St. Petersburg Times,* p. 1A.

Farrell, K. (2008). Corporate complicity in the Chinese censorship regime: When freedom of expression and profitability collide. *Internet Law, 11,* 1, 11–21.

Fearn-Banks, K. (2007). *Crisis communications: A casebook approach* (3rd ed.). Mahwah, NJ: Erlbaum.

Ferguson, R. (2002, January 18). NCAA a "sweatshop," Steelworkers chief says. *Toronto Star,* p. E11.

Fine, R., & Boon, V. (2007). Introduction: Cosmopolitanism: Between past and future. *European Journal of Social Theory 10,* 5–16.

Fink, S. (2002). *Crisis management: Planning for the inevitable.* Lincoln, NE: Backinprint.com.

Fiol, C. M., Harris, D., & House, R. J. (1999). Charismatic leadership: Strategies for effecting social change. *The Leadership Quarterly, 1,* 449–482.

Fisher, R., & Ury, W. (1991). *Getting to yes* (2nd ed.). New York: Penguin.

Fisher, S. (2007, September). Flying off into the sunset. *Costco Connection,* pp. 17–19.

Fisher, W. (1987). *Human communication as narration: Toward a philosophy of reason, value, and action.* Columbia: University of South Carolina Press.

Fiske, S. T. (1993). Controlling other people: The impact of power on stereotyping. *American Psychologist, 48,* 621–628.

Fiske, S. T. (1998). Stereotyping, prejudice, and discrimination. In D. T. Gilbert, S. T. Fiske, & G. Lindzey (Eds.), *The handbook of social psychology* (Vol. 2, pp. 357–411). Boston: McGraw-Hill.

Fitzpatrick, D. (2005, May 12). "Aw-shucks" president embodies Southwest style. *Pittsburgh Post-Gazette.*

Flescher, A. M., & Worthen, D. L. (2007). *The altruistic species: Scientific, philosophical, and religious perspectives of human benevolence.* Philadelphia: Templeton Foundation Press.

Fletcher, G. (1993). *Loyalty: An essay on the morality of relationships.* New York: Oxford University Press.

Flippen, A. R. (1999). Understanding groupthink from a self-regulatory perspective. *Small Group Research, 3,* 139–165.

Folger, R., & Baron, R. A. (1996). Violence and hostility at work: A model of reactions to perceived injustice. In G. R. VandenBos & E. Q. Bulato (Eds.), *Violence on the job: Identifying risks and developing solutions* (pp. 51–85). Washington, DC: American Psychological Association.

Fortin, M. (2008). Perspectives on organizational justice: Concept clarification, social context integration, time and links with morality. *International Journal of Management Reviews, 10,* 93–126.

Foster, R. J. (1978). *Celebration of discipline: The path to spiritual growth.* New York: Harper & Row.

Fought, T. (2009, December 20). Ore. debates beacons for climbers. *The Boston Globe,* News, p. 26.

Fowler, K. L., Kling, N. D., & Larson, M. D. (2007). Organizational preparedness for coping with a major crisis or disaster. *Business & Society, 46,* 100–101.

Franke, G. P., & Nadler, S. S. (2007). Culture, economic development, and national ethical attitudes. *Journal of Business Research, 61,* 254–264.

Freedman, S., Enright, R. D., & Knutson, J. (2005). A progress report on the process model of forgiveness. In E. L. Worthington, Jr. (Ed.), *Handbook of forgiveness* (pp. 393–406). New York: Routledge.

Freeman, R. E., Harrison, J. S., & Wicks, A. C. (2007). *Managing for stakeholders: Survival, reputation, and success.* New Haven, CT: Yale University Press.

French, R. P., & Raven, B. (1959). The bases of social power. In D. Cartwright (Ed.), *Studies in social power* (pp. 150–167). Ann Arbor: University of Michigan, Institute for Social Research.

Frey, B. F. (2000). The impact of moral intensity on decision making in a business context. *Journal of Business Ethics, 26,* 181–195.

Friedman, T. L. (2000). *The Lexus and the olive tree* (Expanded ver.). New York: Anchor.

Friedman, T. L. (2009, July 19). Teacher, Can we leave now? No. *The New York Times,* WK, p. 10.

Fritzsche, D. J. (2000). Ethical climates and the ethical dimension of decision making. *Journal of Business Ethics, 24,* 125–140.

From the complaint: "You just don't give it away for nothing." (2008, December 10). *The New York Times,* p. A32.

Fromm, E. (1964). *The heart of man: Its genius for good and evil.* New York: Harper & Row.

Fry, L. W. (2003). Toward a theory of spiritual leadership. *The Leadership Quarterly, 14,* 693–727.

Fry, L. W. (2005). Toward a theory of ethical and spiritual well-being, and corporate social responsibility through spiritual leadership. In R. A. Giacalone, C. L. Jurkiewicz, & C. Dunn (Eds.), *Positive psychology in business ethics and corporate responsibility* (pp. 47–84). Greenwich, CT: Information Age.

Fry, L. W., Vitucci, S., & Cedillo, M. (2005). Spiritual leadership and army transformation: Theory, measurement, and establishing a baseline. *The Leadership Quarterly, 16,* 835–862.

Garcia-Zamor, J. C. (2003). Workplace spirituality and organizational performance. *Public Administration Review, 63,* 355–363.

Gardner, J. (1995). Building a responsive community. In A. Etzioni (Ed.), *Rights and the common good: The communitarian perspective* (pp. 167–178). New York: St. Martin's.

Gardner, W. L., Avolio, B. J., Luthans, F., May, D. R., & Walumbwa, F. O. (2005). "Can you see the real me?" A self-based model of authentic leader and follower development. *The Leadership Quarterly, 16,* 343–372.

Garvin, D. A. (1993, July–August). Building a learning organization. *Harvard Business Review,* pp. 78–91.

Gaudine, A., & Thorne, L. (2001). Emotion and ethical decision-making in organizations. *Journal of Business Ethics, 31,* 175–187.

Geracimos, A. (2009, September 29). Health workers spurn flu shot; for some, jobs depend on it. *The Washington Times,* p. A1.

Gettleman, J. (2007, September 3). Chaos in Darfur on rise as Arabs fight with Arabs. *The New York Times,* p. A1.

Giacalone, R. A., & Jurkiewicz, C. L. (2003). Right from wrong: The influence of spirituality on perceptions of unethical business activities. *Journal of Business Ethics, 46,* 85–97.

Giacalone, R. A., & Jurkiewicz, C. L. (2003). Toward a science of workplace spirituality. In R. A. Giacalone & C. L. Jurkiewicz (Eds.), *Handbook of workplace spirituality and organizational performance* (pp. 3–28). Armonk, NY: M. E. Sharpe.

Gianatasio, D. (2009, April 15). *Domino's president issues video apology.* Retrieved from http://www.adweek.com/aw/content_display/news/agency/e3id3ffb6d5b9e 0b9116ccc43b9768bb31f

Gibb, J. R. (1961). Defensive communication. *Journal of Communication, 11–12,* 141–148.

Gilbert, J. A., & Tang, T. L. (1998). An examination of organizational trust antecedents. *Public Personnel Management, 27,* 321–338.

Gilligan, C. (1982). *In a different voice: Psychological theory and women's development.* Cambridge, MA: Harvard University Press.

Gioia, D. A. (1992). Pinto fires and personal ethics: A script analysis of missed opportunities. *Journal of Business Ethics, 11,* 379–389.

Glanton, D. (2009, February 8). Peanut recall puts town "in hot water." *Los Angeles Times,* p. A28.

Glanton, D. (2009, February 9). Ex-peanut plant workers tell of rats, filth, mold. *The Oregonian,* pp. A1, A4.

Glanz, W. (2003, August 27). NASA ignored dangers to shuttle, panel says. *The Washington Times,* p. A1.

Goldberg, M. (1997). Doesn't anybody read the Bible anymo'? In O. F. Williams (Ed.), *The moral imagination: How literature and films can stimulate ethical reflection in the business world* (pp. 19–32). Notre Dame, IN: University of Notre Dame Press.

Goleman, D., Boyatzis, R., & McKee, A. (2002, Spring). The emotional reality of teams. *Journal of Organizational Excellence,* pp. 55–65.

Gonzalez, J. (2009, January 9). Top execs still live like kings. *Daily News,* p. 6.

Goodman, E. (2002, October 6). Freeze-frame nation. *The Oregonian,* p. C3.

Goodman, P. S., & Morgenson, G. (2008, December 28). Saying yes to anyone, WaMu build empire on shaky loans. *The New York Times,* p. A1.

Goodpaster, K. E. (1991). Business ethics and stakeholder analysis. *Business Ethics Quarterly, 1,* 53–27.

Gorovitz, S. (Ed.). (1971). *Utilitarianism: Text and critical essays.* Indianapolis, IN: Bobbs-Merrill.

Gottlieb, J. Z., & Sabzgiri, J. (1996). Towards an ethical dimension of decision making in organizations. *Journal of Business Ethics 15,* 1275–1285.

Gouran, D. S., & Hirokawa, R. Y. (1986). Counteractive functions of communication in effective group decision making. In R. Y. Hirokawa & M. S. Poole (Eds.), *Communication and group decision making* (pp. 81–89). Beverly Hills, CA: Sage.

Gouran, D. S., Hirokawa, R. Y., Julian, K. M., & Leatham, G. B. (1993). The evolution and current status of the functional perspective on communication in decision-making and problem-solving groups. *Communication Yearbook, 16,* 573–576.

Gow, D. (2008, January 25). Siemens prepares to pay $2bn fine to clear up slush fund scandal. *The Guardian,* p. 34.

Graen, G. B., & Graen, J. A. (Eds.) (2007). *New multinational network sharing.* Charlotte, NC: Information Age.

Graen, G. B., & Uhl-Bien, M. (1998). Relationship-based approach to leadership. Development of leader–member exchange (LMX) theory of leadership over 25 years: Applying a multi-level multi-domain perspective. In F. Dansereau & F. J. Yammarino (Eds.), *Leadership: The multiple-level approaches* (pp. 103–158). Stamford, CT: JAI Press.

Graham, G. (2004). *Eight theories of ethics.* London: Routledge.

Greenberg, J., & Wiethoff, C. (2001). Organization justice as proaction and reaction: Implications for research and application. In R. Cropanzano (Ed.), *Justice in the workplace* (Vol. 2, pp. 271–302). Mahwah, NJ: Erlbaum.

Greenberg, J. W. (2002, October). September 11, 2001: A CEO's story. *Harvard Business Review*, pp. 58–64.

Greenhouse, S., & Rosenbloom, S. (2008, December 24). Wal-Mart to settle suits over pay for $352 million. *The New York Times*, p. B1.

Greenleaf, R. K. (1977). *Servant leadership*. New York: Paulist Press.

Griffin, R. W., & O'Leary-Kelly, A. M. (Eds.). (2004). *The dark side of organizational behavior*. San Francisco: Jossey-Bass.

Griswold, C. L. (2007). *Forgiveness: A philosophical exploration*. Cambridge, UK: Cambridge University Press.

Grojean, M. W., Resick, C. J., Dickson, M. W., & Smith, D. B. (2004). Leaders, values, and organizational climate: Examining leadership strategies for establishing an organizational climate regarding ethics. *Journal of Business Ethics, 55,* 223–241.

Grose, T. K. (2003, September 1). Can the manned space program find a new, revitalizing mission in the wake of the *Columbia* tragedy? *U.S. News & World Report*, p. 36.

Grunig, J. E. (2001). Two-way symmetrical public relations: Past, present, and future. In R. L. Heath (Ed.), *Handbook of public relations* (pp. 11–30). Thousand Oaks, CA: Sage.

Grunig, L. A., Grunig, J. E., & Dozier, D. M. (2002). *Excellent public relations and effective organizations: A study of communication management in three countries*. Mahwah, NJ: Erlbaum.

Guarino, M. (2009, December 29). Minnesota, Ohio join lawsuit against Illinois over Asian carp. *The Christian Science Monitor*. Retrieved from http://www
.csmonitor.com/USA/2009/1229/Minnesota-Ohio-join-lawsuit-against-Illinois-over-Asian-carp

Gudykunst, W. B. (2004). *Bridging differences: Effective intergroup communication* (4th ed.). Thousand Oaks, CA: Sage.

Gudykunst, W. B., & Kim, Y. Y. (1997). *Communicating with strangers: An approach to intercultural communication* (3rd ed.). New York: McGraw-Hill.

Guroian, V. (1996). Awakening the moral imagination. *Intercollegiate Review, 32,* 3–13.

Guth, W. D., & Tagiuri, R. (1965, September–October). Personal values and corporate strategy. *Harvard Business Review*, pp. 123–132.

H.R. 1577: To require the Secretary of the Treasury to pursue every legal means to stay or recoup certain . . . (2009, July 12). *GovTrack.us*. Retrieved from http://www.govtrack.us/congress/bill.xpd?bill=h111–1577

Hackman, M. Z., & Johnson, C. E. (2008). *Leadership: A communication perspective* (5th ed.). Prospect Heights, IL: Waveland.

Haidt, J. (2001). The emotional dog and its rational tail: A social intuitionist approach to moral judgment. *Psychological Review, 108,* 814–834.

Haidt, J. (2003). The moral emotions. In R. J. Davidson, K. R. Scherer, & H. H. Goldsmith (Eds.), *Handbook of affective sciences* (pp. 852–870). Oxford, UK: Oxford University Press.

Haidt, J., & Bjorklund, F. (2008). Social intuitionists answer six questions about moral psychology. In W. Sinnott-Armstrong (Ed.), *Moral psychology (Vol. 2): The cognitive science of morality: Intuition and diversity* (pp. 182–217). Cambridge, MA: MIT Press.

Haidt, J., & Graham, J. (2007). When morality opposes justice: Conservatives have moral intuitions that liberals may not recognize. *Social Justice Research, 20,* 98–116.

Hajdin, M. (2005). Employee loyalty: An examination. *Journal of Business Ethics, 59,* 259–280.

Halley, J. (2009, January 29). Lopsided games are often pointless. *USA Today,* p. 4C.

Hallie, P. (1979). *Lest innocent blood be shed: The story of the village of Le Chambon and how goodness happened there.* New York: Harper & Row.

Hallie, P. (1997). *Tales of good and evil, help and harm.* New York: HarperCollins.

Hamilton, J. B., & Knouse, S. B. (2001). Multinational enterprise decision principles for dealing with cross cultural ethical conflicts. *Journal of Business Ethics, 31,* 77–94.

Hamilton, J. B., Knouse, S. B., & Hill, V. (2009). Google in China: A manager-friendly heuristic model for resolving cross-cultural ethical conflicts. *Journal of Business Ethics, 86,* 143–157.

Hamilton, W. (2009, March 13). "Sorry" is not enough, Madoff's victims say. *Los Angeles Times,* p. A1.

Hamilton, W. (2009, July 31). Payouts lavish despite bailout. *Los Angeles Times,* p. A1.

Hammer, K. (2009, October 14). Asian carp just one flop away from Great Lakes. *The Globe and Mail,* p. A3.

Hammond, B. (2009). Religious rule for teachers challenged. *The Oregonian,* pp. A1, A4.

Hanna, S. T., Lester, P. B., & Vogelgesang, G. R. (2005). Moral leadership: Explicating the moral component of authentic leadership. In W. L. Gardner, B. J. Avolio, & F. O. Walumbwa (Eds.), *Authentic leadership theory and practice: Origins, effects and development* (pp. 43–81). Amsterdam, Netherlands: Elsevier.

Harris, G. (2009, January 31). Peanut plant recall leads to criminal investigation. *The New York Times,* p. A17.

Harris, G. (2009, February 12). Peanut foods shipped before testing came in. *The New York Times,* p. A24.

Harris, J. (2009, October 16). Retail giant finds its green religion. *National Post,* p. FP12.

Harris, S., Smallen, J., & Mitchell, C. (2006). February 18). Katrina report spreads blame. *National Journal,* p. 38.

Hart, D. K. (1992). The moral exemplar in an organizational society. In T. L. Cooper & N. D. Wright (Eds.), *Exemplary public administrators: Character and leadership in government* (pp. 9–29). San Francisco: Jossey-Bass.

Hartocollis, A., & Chan, S. (2009, October 23). Flu vaccine requirement for health workers is lifted. *The New York Times,* p. A30.

Harvey, J. B. (1988). *The Abilene paradox and other meditations on management.* New York: Simon & Schuster.

Harvey, J. B. (1999). *How come every time I get stabbed in the back my fingerprints are on the knife?* San Francisco: Jossey-Bass.

Harvey, P., Martinko, M. J., & Gardner, W. L. (2006). Promoting authentic behavior in organizations: An attributional perspective. *Journal of Leadership and Organizational Studies, 12,* 1–11.

Hatcher, T. (2002). *Ethics and HRD: A new approach to leading responsible organizations.* Cambridge, MA: Perseus.

Hatzfeld, J. (2005). *Machete season: The killers in Rwanda speak* (L. Coverdale, Trans.). New York: Farrar, Straus and Giroux.

Hauser, M. D., Young, L., & Cushman, F. (2008). Reviving Rawls's linguistic analogy: Operative principles and the causal structure of moral actions. In W. Sinnott-Armstrong (Ed.), *Moral psychology (Vol. 2): The cognitive science of morality: Intuition and diversity* (107–144). Cambridge, MA: MIT.

Hays, K. (2007, May 24). Linda Lay files against forfeiture. *The Houston Chronicle,* Business, p. 3.

Hays-Thomas, R. (2004). Why now? The contemporary focus on managing diversity. In M. S. Stockdale & F. J. Crosby (Eds.), *The psychology and management of workplace diversity* (pp. 3–30). Malden, MA: Blackwell.

Healy, B., & Syre, S. (2009, July 6). Uneasy times for the Shapiro family. *The Boston Globe,* Metro, p. 1.

Hearit, K. M. (2006). *Crisis management by apology: Corporate response to allegations of wrongdoing.* Mahwah, NJ: Erlbaum.

Heflick, R. (2005, December 9). Forgiving Josef Mengele. *Der Spiegel.*

Held, V. (2006). The ethics of care. In D. Copp (Ed.), *The Oxford handbook of ethical theory* (pp. 537–566). Oxford, UK: Oxford University Press.

Henriques, D. B. (2009, June 30). Madoff, apologizing, is given 150 years. *The New York Times,* pp. A1, B4.

Hercules, B. (Producer), & Pugh, C. (Producer). (2005). *Forgiving Dr. Mengele* [Documentary]. Available from First Run Features, The Film Center Building, 630 Ninth Ave., Suite 1213, New York, NY 10036, or from firstrunfeatures.com.

Higgs, M. (2009). The good, the bad and the ugly: Leadership and narcissism. *Journal of Change Management, 9,* 165–178.

Hilzenrath, D. S. (2003, September 2). Rescue of *Columbia* a hindsight dream. *The Washington Post,* p. A8.

Hodgkinson, P. E., & Stewart, M. (1991). *Coping with catastrophe: A handbook of disaster management.* London: Routledge.

Hodgson, G. (2009, August 12). Eunice Kennedy Shriver; mental health campaigner who founded the Special Olympics. *The Independent,* Obituaries, p. 26.

Hoffman, M. (2000). *Empathy and moral development: Implications for caring and justice.* Cambridge, UK: Cambridge University Press.

Hofstede, G. (1984). *Culture's consequences.* Beverly Hills, CA: Sage.

Hofstede, G. (1991). *Cultures and organizations: Software of the mind.* London: McGraw-Hill.

Hofstede, G. (2001). Difference and danger: Cultural profiles of nations and limits to tolerance. In M. H. Albrecht (Ed.), *International HRM: Managing diversity in the workplace* (pp. 9–23). Oxford, UK: Blackwell.

Hogan, M. (2007). *Four skills of cultural diversity competence: A process for understanding and practice* (3rd ed.). Belmont, CA: Thomson.

Hoge, W. (2007, September 7). Sudan officials and rebels to discuss peace in Darfur. *The New York Times*, p. 12.

Hollander, E. P. (1992, April). The essential interdependence of leadership and followership. *Current Directions in Psychological Science*, pp. 71–75.

Hood, J. N. (2003). The relationship of leadership style and CEO values to ethical practices in organizations. *Journal of Business Ethics, 43*, 263–273.

Hopen, D. (2002). Guiding corporate behavior: A leadership obligation not a choice. *Journal for Quality & Participation, 25*, 15–19.

Hornstein, H. A. (1996). *Brutal bosses and their prey.* New York: Riverhead.

Horvitz, B. (2009, April 16). Domino's nightmare holds lessons for marketers: Companies have to learn how to handle social-media attacks. *USA Today*, Money, p. 7A.

Hosmer, L. T. (1994). Strategic planning as if ethics mattered. *Strategic Management Journal, 15*, 17–34.

House, R. J., Hange, P. J., Javidan, M., Dorfman, P. W., & Gupta, V. (Eds.). (2004). *Culture, leadership, and organizations: The GLOBE study of 62 societies.* Thousand Oaks, CA: Sage.

Howell, J., & Avolio, B. J. (1992). The ethics of charismatic leadership: Submission or liberation? *Academy of Management Executive, 6*, 43–54.

Hubbartt, W. S. (1998). *The new battle over workplace privacy.* New York: AMACOM.

Hughes, C. (2008, November 21). Pirates: We want pounds 17M within 10 days . . . or else. *The Mirror*, p. 31.

Huma, R., Waters, T., & Staurowsky, E. J. (2009, March 26). Scholarship shortfall study reveals college athletes pay to play. Retrieved from http://www.ncpanow.org/releases_advisories?id=0009

Husted, B. W. (1999). Wealth, culture and corruption. *Journal of International Business Studies, 30*, 339–359.

Ilies, R., Hauserman, N., Schwochau, S., & Stibal, J. (2003). Reported incidence rates of work-related sexual harassment in the United States: Using meta-analysis to explain reported rate disparities. *Personnel Psychology, 56*, 607–651.

Ilies, R., Morgeson, F. P., & Nahrgang, J. D. (2005). Authentic leadership and eudemonic well-being: Understanding leader–follower outcomes. *The Leadership Quarterly, 16*, 373–394.

Illinois yields to NCAA, will retire mascot. *The Washington Post*, p. E02.

Inch, E. S., Warnick, B., & Endres, D. (2006). *Critical thinking and communication: The use of reason in argument* (5th ed.). Boston: Pearson.

Infante, D. (1988). *Arguing constructively.* Prospect Heights, IL: Waveland.

Infante, D. A., & Rancer, A. S. (1982). A conceptualization and measure of argumentativeness. *Journal of Personality Assessment, 46*, 72–78.

Infante, D., & Rancer, A. (1996). Argumentativeness and verbal aggressiveness: A review of recent theory and research. In B. Burleson (Ed.), *Communication yearbook 19* (pp. 319–351). Thousand Oaks, CA: Sage.

Jacobs, T. (2009, May). Morals authority. *Miller-McCune*, pp. 47–55.

Jacoby, J. (2009, July 5). A deadly organ donor system. *Boston Globe*, Opinion, p. 9.

James, H. S. (2000). Reinforcing ethical decision-making through organizational structure. *Journal of Business Ethics, 28*(1), 43–58.

James, K. (2008, May 24). Siemens' straight shooter. *The Business Times Singapore*.

Janis, I. (1971, November). Groupthink: The problems of conformity. *Psychology Today*, pp. 271–279.

Janis, I. (1982). *Groupthink* (2nd ed.). Boston: Houghton Mifflin.

Janis, I. (1989). *Crucial decisions: Leadership in policymaking and crisis management.* New York: Free Press.

Janis, I., & Mann, L. (1977). *Decision making.* New York: Free Press.

Jaramillo, F., Grisaffe, D. B., Chonko, L. B., & Roberts, J. A. (2009). Examining the impact of servant leadership on sales force performance. *Journal of Personal Selling & Sales Management, 24*(3), 257–275.

Javidan, M., & House, R. J. (2001). Cultural acumen for the global manager: Lessons from Project GLOBE. *Organizational Dynamics, 29,* 289–305.

Jehn, I. A. (1995). A multi-method examination of the benefits and detriments of intragroup conflict. *Administrative Science Quarterly, 40,* 256–282.

Jennings, M. M. (2006). *The seven signs of ethical collapse: How to spot moral meltdowns in companies . . . before it's too late.* New York: St. Martin's Press.

Jensen, J. V. (1996). Ethical tension points in whistleblowing. In J. A. Jaksa & M. S. Pritchard (Eds.), *Responsible communication: Ethical issues in business, industry, and the professions* (pp. 41–51). Cresskill, NJ: Hampton.

Johannsen, R. L. (1991). Virtue ethics, character, and political communication. In R. E. Denton (Ed.), *Ethical dimensions of political communication* (pp. 69–90). New York: Praeger.

Johannsen, R. L. (2002). *Ethics in human communication* (5th ed.). Prospect Heights, IL: Waveland.

Johnson, C. E. (1997, Spring). A leadership journey to the East. *Journal of Leadership Studies, 4,* 82–88.

Johnson, C. E. (2000). Emerging perspectives in leadership ethics. *Proceedings of the International Leadership Association,* pp. 48–54.

Johnson, C. E. (2000). Taoist leadership ethics. *Journal of Leadership Studies, 7,* 82–91.

Johnson, C. E. (2002). *Enron's ethical collapse: Lessons from the top.* Paper delivered at the National Communication Association convention, New Orleans, LA.

Johnson, C. E. (2003). Enron's ethical collapse: Lessons for leadership educators. *Journal of Leadership Education, 2.* Retrieved from http://www.fhsu.edu/jole/issues/JOLE_2_1.pdf

Johnson, C. E. (2007). Best practices in ethical leadership. In J. A. Conger & R. E. Riggio (Eds.), *The practice of leadership: Developing the next generation of leaders* (pp. 150–171). San Francisco: Jossey-Bass.

Johnson, C. E. (2007). *Ethics in the workplace: Tools and tactics for organizational transformation.* Thousand Oaks, CA: Sage.

Johnson, C. E. (2008). The rise and fall of Carly Fiorina: An ethical case study. *Journal of Leadership & Organizational Studies, 15*(2), 188–196.

Johnson, C. E., & Hackman, M. Z. (1997). *Rediscovering the power of followership in the leadership communication text.* Paper presented at the National Communication Association convention, Chicago.

Johnson, D. W., & Johnson, R. (1989). *Cooperation and competition: Theory and research.* Edina, MN: Interaction Book.

Johnson, D. W., & Johnson, R. (2000). *Joining together: Group theory and group skills* (7th ed.). Boston: Allyn & Bacon.

Johnson, D. W., & Johnson, R. (2005). Training for cooperative group work. In M. A. West, D. Tjosvold, & K. G. Smith (Eds.), *The essentials of teamworking: International perspectives* (pp. 131–147). West Sussex, UK: Wiley.

Johnson, D. W., Maruyama, G., Johnson, R., Nelson, D., & Skon, L. (1981). Effects of cooperative, competitive, and individualistic goal structures on achievement: A meta-analysis. *Psychological Bulletin, 82,* 47–62.

Johnson, D. W., & Tjosvold, D. (1983). *Productive conflict management.* New York: Irvington.

Johnson, J. (1993). Functions and processes of inner speech in listening. In D. Wolvin & C. G. Coakley (Eds.), *Perspectives in listening* (pp. 170–184). Norwood, NJ: Ablex.

Johnson, J. (2007). Dinged up Endeavour returns. *Los Angeles Times,* p. A10.

Johnson, J., & Orange, M. (2003). *The man who tried to buy the world: Jean-Marie Messier and Vivendi Universal.* New York: Portfolio.

Johnson, M. (1993). *Moral imagination: Implications of cognitive science for ethics.* Chicago: University of Chicago Press.

Johnson, R. (2008, April). Get saved anywhere. *Outdoor Life,* pp. 24–25.

Jones, A. (2006, October 17). Judge vacates Lay's conviction. *The Wall Street Journal.* Retrieved from http://blogs.wsj.com/law/2006/10/17/judge-lake-vacates-kenneth-lays-conviction/

Jones, A. (2009, January 7). Executives on trial: Enron's Skilling to be resentenced. *The Wall Street Journal,* p. C7.

Jones, L. B. (1996). The path: Creating your mission statement for work and for life. New York: Hyperion.

Jones, P. E., & Roelofsma, P. H. M. P. (2000). The potential for social contextual and group biases in team decision-making: Biases, conditions and psychological mechanisms. *Ergonomics, 43,* 1129–1152.

Jones, T. M. (1991). Ethical decision making by individuals in organizations: An issue-contingent model. *Academy of Management Review, 15,* 366–395.

Jonsen, A. R., & Toulmin, S. (1988). *The abuse of casuistry: A history of moral reasoning.* Berkeley: University of California Press.

Jordan, P. J., & Troth, A. C. (2004). Managing emotions during team problem solving: Emotional intelligence and conflict resolution. *Human Performance, 17,* 195–218.

Jourdan, G. (1998). Indirect causes and effects in policy change: The Brent Spar case. *Public Administration, 76,* 713–770.

Judge, W. Q. (1999). *The leader's shadow: Exploring and developing executive character.* Thousand Oaks, CA: Sage.

Jurkiewicz, C. L., & Giacalone, R. A. (2004). A values framework for measuring the impact of workplace spirituality on organizational performance. *Journal of Business Ethics, 49,* 129–142.

Kant, I. (1964). *Groundwork of the metaphysics of morals* (H. J. Ryan, Trans.). New York: Harper & Row.

Kanter, R. M. (1979, July–August). Power failure in management circuits. *Harvard Business Review,* pp. 65–75.

Kanungo, R. N. (2001). Ethical values of transactional and transformational leaders. *Canadian Journal of Administrative Sciences, 18,* 257–265.

Kanungo, R. N., & Conger, J. A. (1990). The quest for altruism in organizations. In S. Srivastra & D. L. Cooperrider (Eds.), *Appreciative management and leadership* (pp. 228–256). San Francisco: Jossey-Bass.

Kanungo, R. N., & Mendonca, M. (1996). *Ethical dimensions of leadership.* Thousand Oaks, CA: Sage.

Karau, S. J., & Williams, K. D. (1995). Social loafing: Research findings, implications, and future directions. *Current Directions in Psychological Science, 4,* 134–140.

Karau, S. J., & Williams, K. D. (2001). Understanding individual motivation in groups: The Collective Effort Model. In M. E. Turner (Ed.), *Groups at work: Theory and research* (pp. 113–141). Mahwah, NJ: Erlbaum.

Karim, A. (2000, June 23). Globalization, ethics, and AIDS vaccines. *Science,* pp. 21–29.

Katz, F. E. (1993). *Ordinary people and extraordinary evil: A report on the beguilings of evil.* Albany: State University of New York Press.

Kekes, J. (1991). Moral imagination, freedom, and the humanities. *American Philosophical Quarterly, 28,* 101–111.

Kekes, J. (2005). *The roots of evil.* Ithaca, NY: Cornell University Press.

Kellerman, B. (2004). *Bad leadership: What it is, how it happens, why it matters.* Boston: Harvard Business School Press.

Kellerman, B. (2008). Bad leadership—and ways to avoid it. In J. V. Gallos (Ed.), *Business leadership* (pp. 423–432). San Francisco: Jossey-Bass.

Kellerman, B. (2008). *Followership: How followers are creating change and changing leaders.* Boston: Harvard Business School Press.

Kelley, R. (1992). *The power of followership.* New York: Doubleday/Currency.

Kelley, R. (1998). Followership in a leadership world. In L. C. Spears (Ed.), *Insights on leadership: Service, stewardship, spirit and servant-leadership* (pp. 170–184). New York: Wiley.

Keltner, D., Langner, C. A., & Allison, M. L. (2006). Power and moral leadership. In D. L. Rhode (Ed.), *Moral leadership: The theory and practice of power, judgment, and policy* (pp. 177–194). San Francisco: Jossey-Bass.

Kennedy, D. (2004). *The dark side of virtue: Reassessing international humanitarianism.* Princeton, NJ: Princeton University Press.

Kennedy, H. (2009, March 17). Enough is enough! *Daily News (New York)*, p. 6.

Kernis, M. H. (2003). Toward a conceptualization of optimal self-esteem. *Psychological Inquiry, 14*, 1–26.

Kickul, J. (2001). When organizations break their promises: Employee reactions to unfair processes and treatment. *Journal of Business Ethics, 29*, 289–307.

Kidder, R. M. (1994). *Shared values for a troubled world: Conversations with men and women of conscience.* San Francisco: Jossey-Bass.

Kidder, R. M. (1995). *How good people make tough choices: Resolving the dilemmas of ethical living.* New York: Fireside.

Kidder, R. M. (2004). Foundation codes of ethics: Why do they matter, what are they, and how are they relevant to philanthropy? *New Decisions for Philanthropic Fundraising, 45*, 75–83.

Kidder, R. M. (2005). *Moral courage.* New York: William Morrow.

King, S., Biberman, J., Robbins, L. & Nicol, D. M. (2007). Integrating spirituality into management education in academia and organizations: Origins, a conceptual framework, and current practices. In J. Biberman & M. D. Whitty (Eds.), *At work: Spirituality matters* (pp. 243–256). Scranton, PA: University of Scranton Press.

Kipnis, D. (1972). Does power corrupt? *Journal of Personality and Social Psychology, 24*, 33–41.

Kirkland, R. (2002). Self-fulfillment through selflessness: The moral teachings of the Daode Jing. In M. Barnhart (Ed.), *Varieties of ethical reflection: New directions for ethics in a global context* (pp. 21–48). Lanham, MD: Lexington.

Kiuchi, T., & Shireman, B. (2002). *What we learned in the rainforest: Business lessons from nature.* San Francisco: Berrett-Koehler.

Klenke, K. (2005). The internal theater of the authentic leader: Integrating cognitive, affective, conative and spiritual facets of authentic leadership. In W. L. Gardner, B. J. Avolio, & F. O. Walumbwa (Eds.), *Authentic leadership theory and practice: Origins, effects and development* (pp. 43–81). Amsterdam, Netherlands: Elsevier.

Klotz, I. (2009, July 17). Space shuttle trips on hold as NASA probes debris woes. *The Gazette*, p. A13.

Knouse, S. B. (2001). Multinational enterprise decision principles for dealing with cross cultural ethical conflicts. *Journal of Business Ethics, 31*, 77–94.

Kohlberg, L. A. (1984). *The psychology of moral development: The nature and validity of moral stages* (Vol. 2). San Francisco: Harper & Row.

Kohlberg, L. A. (1986). A current statement on some theoretical issues. In S. Modgil & C. Modgil (Eds.), *Lawrence Kohlberg: Consensus and controversy* (pp. 485–546). Philadelphia: Palmer.

Kolp, A., & Rea, P. (2006). *Leading with integrity: Character-based leadership.* Cincinnati, OH: AtomicDog.

Konrad, A. M. (2006). Leveraging workplace diversity in organizations. *Organization Management Journal, 3*, 164–189.

Koonce, R. (2001, December). Redefining diversity. *Training and Development*, pp. 22–28.

Kossek, E. E., Lobel, S. A., & Brown, J. (2006). Human resource strategies to manage workplace diversity: Examining the "business case." In A. M. Konrad, P. Prasad, & J. K. Pringle (Eds.), *Handbook of workplace diversity* (pp. 53–74). London: Sage.

Kotler, P., & Lee, N. (2005). *Corporate social responsibility: Doing the most good for your company and your cause.* Hoboken, NJ: Wiley.

Kotlyar, I., & Karakowsky, L. (2006). Leading conflict? Linkages between leader behaviors and group conflict. *Small Group Research, 37,* 377–403.

Kotter, J. P. (1990). *A force for change: How leadership differs from management.* New York: Free Press.

Kouwe, Z. (2009, June 30). Waiting to see Madoff, an angry crowed is disappointed. *The New York Times,* pp. B1, B5.

Kouzes, J. M., & Posner, B. Z. (2003). *Credibility: How leaders gain and lose it, why people demand it.* San Francisco: Jossey-Bass.

Kouzes, J. M., & Posner, B. (2007). *The leadership challenge* (4th ed.). San Francisco: Jossey-Bass.

Krakauer, J. (2009). *Where men win glory: The odyssey of Pat Tillman.* New York: Doubleday.

Kramer, R. M., & Tyler, T. R. (Eds.). (1996). *Trust in organizations: Frontiers of theory and research.* Thousand Oaks, CA: Sage.

Kriegel, M. (2009, July 25). *NCAA's video game stance is pure hypocrisy.* Retrieved from http://msn.foxsports.com/collegefootball/story/NCAA-video-game-stance-is-pure-hypocrisy

Krieger, F. (2009, May 28). Owners turn to kidnap and ransom cover. *Lloyd's List,* p. 9.

Kuczmarski, S. S., & Kuczmarski, T. D. (1995). *Values-based leadership.* Englewood Cliffs, NJ: Prentice Hall.

Kung, H. (1998). *A global ethic for global politics and economics.* New York: Oxford University Press.

Kung, H. (1999). A global ethic in an age of globalization. In G. Enderle (Ed.), *International business ethics: Challenges and approaches* (pp. 19–127). Notre Dame, IN: University of Notre Dame Press.

Kung, H. (2003). An ethical framework for the global market economy. In J. H. Dunning (Ed.), *Making globalization good: The moral challenges of global capitalism* (pp. 146–158). Oxford, UK: Oxford University Press.

Labaton, S. (2009, June 11). Treasury to set executives' pay at 7 ailing firms. *The New York Times,* p. 1.

Lambright, W. H. (2008, March/April). Leadership and change at NASA: Sean O'Keefe as administrator. *Public Administration Review,* pp. 230–240.

Landler, M., & Dougherty, C. (2008, February 19). Coming clean Germany breaks with its clubby business past. *The New York Times,* p. C1.

Lang, D. L. (1991). Transformational leadership is not charismatic leadership: Philosophical impoverishment in leadership continues. *Human Resource Development Quarterly, 2,* 397–402.

Langer, E. J. (1989). *Mindfulness.* Reading, MA: Addison-Wesley.

Langer, E. J. (1997). *The power of mindful learning*. Reading, MA: Addison-Wesley.

Lapsley, D. K., & Hill, P. L. (2008). On dual processing and heuristic approaches to moral cognition. *Journal of Moral Education, 37*, 313–332.

Larrabee, M. J. (Ed.). (1993). *An ethic of care: Feminist and interdisciplinary perspectives*. New York: Routledge.

Layton, L. (2009, January 29). Every peanut product from Ga. plant recalled. *The Washington Post*, p. A01.

Layton, L. (2009, April 3). FDA hasn't intensified inspections at peanut facilities, despite illness. *The Washington Post*, p. A04.

Layton, L. (2009, May 28). House calls for closer watch on food supply. *The Washington Post*, p. A17.

Lazarus, H., & McManus, T. (2006). Transparency guru: An interview with Tom McManus. *Journal of Management Development, 25*(10), 923–936.

Leader of Darfur peacekeeping mission resigns. (2009, August 26). *The New York Times*, p. A10.

Leary, W. E., & Schwartz, J. (2006, July 4). Shuttle launching set for today despite broken foam. *The New York Times*, p. A11.

Lee, J., Woeste, J. H., & Heath, R. L. (2007). Getting ready for crises: Strategic excellence. *Public Relations Review, 33*, 334–336.

Leslie, L. Z. (2000). *Mass communication ethics: Decision-making in postmodern culture*. Boston: Houghton Mifflin.

Levy, A. C., & Paludi, M. A. (2002). *Workplace sexual harassment* (2nd ed.). Upper Saddle River, NJ: Prentice Hall.

Levy, S. (2006, February 13). Google and the China syndrome. *Newsweek*, p. 14.

Lewis, C. S. (1946). *The great divorce*. New York: Macmillan.

Lewis, D., Medland, J., Malone, S., Murphy, M., Reno, K., & Vaccaro, G. (2006). Appreciative leadership: Defining effective leadership methods. *Organization Development Journal, 24*, 87–100.

Lindsay, R. M., & Irvine, V. B. (1996). Instilling ethical behavior in organizations: A survey of Canadian companies. *Journal of Business Ethics, 15*, 393–407.

Lipman-Blumen, J. (2005). *The allure of toxic leaders: Why we follow destructive bosses and corrupt politicians—and how we can survive them*. Oxford, UK: Oxford University Press.

Liptak, A. (2002, April 18). Judge blocks U.S. bid to ban suicide law. *The New York Times*, p. A16.

Lisman, C. D. (1996). *The curricular integration of ethics: Theory and practice*. Westport, CT: Praeger.

Lister, S. (2006, February 16). Let people sell their kidneys for transplant, say doctors. *The Times* (London), p. 31.

Lowe, K. B., & Kroeck, K. G. (1996). Effectiveness correlates of transformational and transactional leadership: A meta-analytic review. *The Leadership Quarterly, 7*, 385–425.

Lowenheim, N. (2009). A haunted past: Requesting forgiveness for wrongdoing in international relations. *Review of International Studies, 35*, 531–555.

Lubit, R. (2002). The long-term organizational impact of destructively narcissistic managers. *Academy of Management Executive, 18,* 127–183.

Ludwig, D. C., & Longenecker, C. O. (1993). The Bathsheba syndrome: The ethical failure of successful leaders. *Journal of Business Ethics, 12,* 265–273.

Maag, C. (2008, December 23). Illinois impeachment panel hears of fund-raising. *The New York Times,* p. A20.

Maak, T. (2007). Responsible leadership, stakeholder engagement, and the emergence of social capital. *Journal of Business Ethics, 74,* 329–343.

Maak, T., & Pless, N. M. (2006). Responsible leadership: A relational approach. In T. Maak & N. M. Press (Eds.), *Responsible leadership* (pp. 33–53). London: Routledge.

Maak, T., & Pless, N. M. (2006). Responsible leadership in a stakeholder society—A relational perspective. *Journal of Business Ethics, 66,* 99–115.

Maak, T., & Pless, N. M. (2009). Business leaders as citizens of the world: Advancing humanism on a global scale. *Journal of Business Ethics, 88,* 537–550.

Maas, A., & Clark, R. D. (1984). Hidden impact of minorities: Fifteen years of minority influence research. *Psychological Bulletin, 95,* 428–445.

MacFarquhar, N. (2009, August 28). As Darfur fighting diminishes, U.N. officials focus on the south of Sudan. *The New York Times,* p. A4.

MacIntyre, A. (1984). *After virtue: A study in moral theory* (2nd ed.). Notre Dame, IN: University of Notre Dame Press.

MacMillan, D. (2007, March 3). Looking over Turnitins's shoulder. *Businessweek Online,* p. 6.

Maggin, A. (2009, March 27). Person of the week: Greg Mortenson. *ABC News.*

Making the food supply safer. (2009, August 10). *The Oregonian,* p. A10.

Mallon, T. (1997, June 15). *In the blink of an eye.* Retrieved from http://www.nytimes.com/books/97/06/15/reviews/970615.mallon.html

Manz, C. C., & Neck, C. P. (1995). Teamthink: Beyond the groupthink syndrome in self-managing work teams. *Journal of Managerial Psychology, 1,* 7–15.

Manz, C. C., & Sims, H. P. (1989). *Superleadership: Leading others to lead themselves.* Upper Saddle River, NJ: Prentice Hall.

Marklein, M. B. (2009, November 19). The case of the purloined term paper. *USA Today* p. 10B.

Martin, J., & Powers, M. E. (1983). Truth or corporate propaganda: The value of a good story. In L. R. Pondy, P. J. Frost, G. Morgan, & T. C. Dandridge (Eds.), *Organizational symbolism* (pp. 93–107). Greenwich, CT: JAI Press.

Martin, K. D., & Cullen, J. B. (2006). Continuities and extensions of ethical climate theory: A meta-analytic review. *Journal of Business Ethics, 69,* 175–194.

Martin, R. (2009, September 17). Health care staff: Vaccinate thyself. *St. Petersburg Times,* p. 1A.

Mathews, M. C. (1999). Codes of ethics: Organizational behavior and misbehavior. In W. C. Frederick & L. E. Preston (Eds.), *Business ethics: Research issues and empirical studies* (pp. 99–122). Greenwich, CT: JAI Press.

Maugh, T. H., & Engel, M. (2009, February 7). FDA says firm lied about peanut butter. *Los Angeles Times,* p. A1.

May, D. R., Chan, A. Y. L., Hodges, T. D., & Avolio, B. J. (2003). Developing the moral component of authentic leadership. *Organizational Dynamics, 32,* 247–260.

May, D. R., & Pauli, K. P. (2002). The role of moral intensity in ethical decision-making: A review and investigation of moral recognition, evaluation, and intention. *Business & Society, 41,* 84–117.

Mayer, R. C., & Gavin, M. B. (2005). Trust in management and performance: Who minds the shop while the employees watch the boss? *Academy of Management Journal, 48,* 874–888.

Mayers, D., Bardes, M., & Piccolo, R. F. (2008). Do servant-leaders help satisfy follower needs? An organizational justice perspective. *European Journal of Work and Organizational Psychology, 17*(2), 180–197.

Mazzetti, M. (2009, April 10). Navy's standoff with pirates shows U.S. power has limits. *The New York Times,* p. A1.

McAuliff, M., & Kennedy, H. (2009, March 19). Give it back! AIG's chief begs execs. *Daily News,* p. 7.

McCabe, D., & Trevino, K. L. (1993). Academic dishonesty: Honor codes and other contextual influences. *Journal of Higher Education, 64,* 522–569.

McCauley, C. D., & Van Velsor, E. (Eds.). (2004). *The Center for Creative Leadership handbook of leadership development* (2nd ed.). San Francisco: Jossey-Bass.

McCoy, K. (2009, March 4). Madoff clients' lawsuits look to others for recompense. *USA Today,* p. 1B.

McCoy, K. (2009, July 10). Madoff won't appeal sentence. *USA Today,* p. 3B.

McCrummen, S., & Tyson, A. S. (2009, April 13). Navy kills 3 pirates, Rescues ship captain. *The Washington Post,* p. A01.

McCullough, M. E., Pargament, K. I., & Thoresen, C. E. (2000). The psychology of forgiveness: History, conceptual issues, and overview. In M. E. McCullough, K. I. Pargament, & C. E. Thoresen (Eds.), *Forgiveness: Theory, research, and practice* (pp. 1–14). New York: Guilford.

McCullough, M. E., Sandage, S. J., & Worthington, E. L. (1997). *To forgive is human: How to put your past in the past.* Downers Grove, IL: InterVarsity Press.

McFaddon, R. D. (2009, January 16). All 155 aboard safe as crippled jet crash-lands in Hudson. *The New York Times,* p. A1.

McKendall, M., DeMarr, B., & Jones-Rikkers, C. (2002). Ethical compliance programs and corporate illegality: Testing the assumptions of the corporate sentencing guidelines. *Journal of Business Ethics, 37,* 367–383.

McLean, B. (2009, March 14). If only there were a Madoff to blame for the meltdown. *The Guardian,* p. 30.

McNeil, D. G., & Zrack, K. (2009, September 21). New York health care workers resist flu vaccine rule. *The New York Times,* p. A18.

Meilander, G. (1986). Virtue in contemporary religious thought. In R. J. Nehaus (Ed.), *Virtue: Public and private* (pp. 7–30). Grand Rapids, MI: Eerdmans.

Melloan, G. (2004, January 6). Feeling the muscle of the multinationals. *The Wall Street Journal,* p. A19.

Menke, S. M. (2004, February 20). NOAA: Rescues rising with satellite beacons. *Newsbytes.*

The mess that the army has made-Myanmar. (2005, July 23). *The Economist,* Special Report.

Messick, D. M., & Bazerman, M. H. (1996, Winter). Ethical leadership and the psychology of decision making. *Sloan Management Review, 37*(2), 9–23.

Metaxas, E. (2007). *Amazing grace: William Wilberforce and the heroic campaign to end slavery.* San Francisco: Harper San Francisco.

Metzger, M., Dalton, D. R., & Hill, J. W. (1993). The organization of ethics and the ethics of organizations: The case for expanded organizational ethics audits. *Business Ethics Quarterly, 3*(1), 27–43.

Michaelson, A. (2009). *The foreclosure of America: The inside story of the rise and fall of Countrywide Home Loans, the mortgage crisis, and the default of the American dream.* New York: Berkley Books.

Microsoft will not seek overpaid severance. (2009, February 23). TECHWEB.

Milloy, R. E. (2000, June 21). 2 sides give 2 versions of facts in Waco suit. *The New York Times,* p. A14.

Mirvis, P. H. (1997). "Soul work" in organizations. *Organization Science, 8,* 193–206.

Mishra, R. (2003, August 27). Probe hits NASA in crash of shuttle. *The Boston Globe.*

Mitchell, C. (2003). *International business ethics: Combining ethics and profits in global business.* Novato, CA: World Trade Press.

Mitchell, S. (1988). *Tao te ching.* New York: Harper Perennial.

Mitroff, I. I. (2005). *Why some companies emerge stronger and better from a crisis.* New York: AMACOM.

Mitroff, I. I., & Alpsaian, M. C. (2003, April). Preparing for evil. *Harvard Business Review,* pp. 109–115.

Mitroff, I. I., & Anagnos, G. (2001). *Managing crises before they happen: What every executive and manager needs to know about crisis management.* New York: American Management Association.

Mitroff, I. I., Pearson, C. M., & Harrington, L. K. (1996). *The essential guide to managing corporate crises: A step-by-step handbook for surviving major catastrophes.* New York: Oxford University Press.

Moore, S. (2009, April 19). F.B.I. and states vastly expanding databases of DNA. *The New York Times,* p. A1.

Moore, S. (2009, May 12). In a lab, an ever-growing database of DNA profiles. *The New York Times,* p. D3.

Moorhead, G., Neck, C. P., & West, M. S. (1998). The tendency toward defective decision-making within self-managing teams: The relevance of groupthink for the 21st century. *Organizational Behavior and Human Decision Processes, 73,* 327–351.

Moorhead, J. (2007, May 15). Milking it. *The Guardian,* p. 8.

Mor Barak, M. E. (2005). *Managing diversity: Toward a globally inclusive workplace.* Thousand Oaks, CA: Sage.

Morgan, D. (2009, August 16). Democratic dissenters. *The Oregonian,* p. D5.

Morgensen, G. (2008, November 2). Was there a loan it didn't like? *The New York Times,* p. BU1.

Morrell, M., Capparell, S., & Shackleton, A. (2001). *Shackleton's way: Leadership lessons from the great Antarctic explorer.* New York: Viking.

Morris, J. A., Brotheridge, C. M., & Urbanski, J. C. (2005). Bringing humility to leadership: Antecedents and consequences of leader humility. *Human Relations,* pp. 1323–1350.

Morrison, A. M. (1996). *The new leaders: Guidelines on leadership diversity in America.* San Francisco: Jossey-Bass.

Morrow, L. (2003). *Evil: An investigation.* New York: Basic Books.

Mortenson, G. (2009). *Stones into schools: Promoting peace with books, not bombs, in Afghanistan and Pakistan.* New York: Viking.

Mortenson, G., & Relin, D. O. (2006). *Three cups of tea: One man's mission to promote peace . . . one school at a time.* New York: Penguin Group.

Moscovici, S., Mugny, G., & Van Avermaet, E. (Eds.). (1985). *Perspectives on minority influence.* Cambridge, UK: Cambridge University Press.

Moss, M. (2009, February 9). Peanut case shows holes in food safety net. *The New York Times,* p. A1.

Moss, M., & Martin, A. (2009, March 6). Food safety problems elude private inspectors. *The New York Times,* p. A1.

Moxley, R. S., & Pulley, M. L. (2004). Hardships. In C. D. McCauley & E. Van Velsor (Eds.), *The Center for Creative Leadership handbook of leadership development* (2nd ed., pp. 183–203). San Francisco: Jossey-Bass.

Mozes-Kor, E., & Wright, M. (1995). *Echoes from Auschwitz: Dr. Mengele's twins: The story of Eva and Miriam Moses.* Terre Haute, IN: CANDLES.

Mulligan, T. S. (2006, May 26). The Enron verdicts. *Los Angeles Times,* p. A1.

Mumford, M. D., Gessner, T. L., Connelly, M. S., O'Conner, J. A., & Clifton, T. (1993). Leadership and destructive acts: Individual and situational influences. *The Leadership Quarterly, 4,* 115–147.

Murphy, J. G. (2003). *Getting even: Forgiveness and its limits.* Oxford, UK: Oxford University Press.

Muzaffar, C. (2002). Conclusion. In P. F. Knitter & C. Muzaffar (Eds.), *Subverting greed: Religious perspectives on the global economy* (pp. 154–172). Maryknoll, NY: Orbis.

NAFDAC warns violators of BMS international code. (2007, August 7). *Africa News.*

Nakashima, E. (2006, September 28). Between the lines of HP's spy scandal. *The Washington Post,* Tech News. Retrieved from http://www.washingtonpost.com/wp-dyn/content/article/2006/09/27/AR2006092701304.html

Nakashima, E. (2008, April 21). From DNA of family, a tool to make arrests. *The Washington Post,* p. A01.

Nanus, B. (1992). *Visionary leadership.* San Francisco: Jossey-Bass.

Narvaez, D. (2006). Integrative ethical education. In M. Killen & J. G. Smetana (Eds.), *Handbook of moral development* (pp. 717–728). Mahwah, NJ: Erlbaum.

Narvaez, D., & Lapsley, D. K. (2005). The psychological foundations of everyday morality and moral expertise. In D. K. Lapsley & F. C. Power (Eds.), *Character psychology and character education* (pp. 140–165). Notre Dame, IN: University of Notre Dame Press.

Nash, L. L. (1989). Ethics without the sermon. In K. R. Andrews (Ed.), *Ethics in practice: Managing the moral corporation* (pp. 243–257). Boston: Harvard Business School Press.

Nash, L. L. (1990). *Good intentions aside: A manager's guide to resolving ethical problems*. Boston: Harvard Business School Press.

Neck, C. P., & Manz, C. C. (2010). *Mastering self-leadership: Empowering yourself for personal excellence* (5th ed.). Upper Saddle River, NJ: Prentice Hall.

Nemeth, C., & Chiles, C. (1986). Modeling courage: The role of dissent in fostering independence. *European Journal of Social Psychology, 18,* 275–280.

Nichols, M. L., & Day, V. E. (1982). A comparison of moral reasoning of groups and individuals on the "defining issues test." *Academy of Management Journal, 24,* 21–28.

Nielsen, R. P. (1996). *The politics of ethics: Methods for acting, learning, and sometimes fighting with others in addressing ethics problems in organizational life.* New York: Oxford University Press.

Nielsen, R. P. (1998). Quaker foundations for Greenleaf's servant-leadership and "friendly disentangling" method. In L. Spears (Ed.), *Insights on leadership* (pp. 126–144). New York: John Wiley & Sons.

Nielsen, R. P., & Dufresne, R. (2005). Can ethical organizational character be stimulated and enabled? "Upbuilding" dialog as crisis management method. *Journal of Business Ethics, 57,* 311–326.

Noddings, N. (2003). *Caring: A feminine approach to ethics and moral education.* Berkeley: University of California Press.

Northouse, P. (2010). *Leadership: Theory and practice* (5th ed.). Thousand Oaks, CA: Sage.

Not for sale at any price. (2006, April 8). *The Lancet,* p. 1118.

O'Fallon, M. J., & Butterfield, K. D. (2005). A review of the empirical ethical decision-making literature: 1996–2003. *Journal of Business Ethics, 59,* 375–413.

O'Reilly, C., & Matussek, K. (2008, December 16). Siemens settles bribery cases. *The Washington Post,* p. D2.

Olmsted, K. S. (2009). *Real enemies: Conspiracy theories and American democracy, World War I to 9/11.* Oxford, UK: Oxford University Press.

Opotow, S. (1990). Moral exclusion and injustice: An introduction. *Journal of Social Issues, 46,* 1–20.

Oswick, C. (2009). Burgeoning workplace spirituality? A textual analysis of momentum and directions. *Journal of Management, Spirituality and Religion, 6,* 15–25.

Owner won't talk. (2009, February 12). *Newsday,* p. A08.

Pacanowsky, M. E., & O'Donnell-Trujillo, N. (1983). Organizational communication as cultural performance. *Communication Monographs, 5,* 126–147.

Padilla, A., Hogan, R., & Kaiser, R. B. (2007). The toxic triangle: Destructive leaders, susceptible followers, and conducive environments. *The Leadership Quarterly, 18,* 176–194.

Paine, L. S. (1996, March–April). Managing for organizational integrity. *Harvard Business Review*, pp. 106–117.

Paine, L. S. (1996). Moral thinking in management: An essential capability. *Business Ethics Quarterly*, 6, 477–492.

Paine, L. S. (1997). *Cases in leadership, ethics, and organizational integrity: A strategic perspective*. Boston: Irwin McGraw-Hill.

Paine, L., Deshpande, R., Margolis, J. D., & Bettcher, K. E. (2005, December). Up to code. *Harvard Business Review*, pp. 122–133.

Palmer, P. (1996). Leading from within. In L. C. Spears (Ed.), *Insights on leadership: Service, stewardship, spirit, and servant-leadership* (pp. 197–208). New York: Wiley.

Panchak, P. (2002). Time for a triple bottom line. *Industry Week*, p. 7.

Park, A. (2009, October 19). It's a jab or your job. *Time*, p. 55.

The party, the people and the power of cyber-talk. (2006, April 29). *The Economist*, pp. 27–30.

Pauchant, T. C., & Mitroff, I. I. (1992). *Transforming the crisis-prone organization: Preventing individual, organizational, and environmental tragedies*. San Francisco: Jossey-Bass.

Paulus, D. L., & Williams, K. M. (2002). The dark triad of personality: Narcissism, Machiavellianism, and psychopathy. *Journal of Research in Personality*, 36, 556–563.

Pearson, C. M., & Judith, A. C. (1998). Reframing crisis management. *Academy of Management Review*, 23(1), 59–71.

Pearson, C. M., & Porath, C. L. (2004). On incivility, its impact and directions for future research. In R. W. Griffin & A. M. O'Leary-Kelly (Eds.), *The dark side of organizational behavior* (pp. 131–158). San Francisco: Jossey-Bass.

Pearson, C. M., & Porath, C. I. (2005). On the nature, consequences and remedies of workplace incivility: No time for "nice"? Think again. *Academy of Management Executive*, 19, 7–18.

Pearson, G. (1995). *Integrity in organizations: An alternative business ethic*. London: McGraw-Hill.

Peck, M. S. (1983). *People of the lie: The hope for healing human evil*. New York: Touchstone.

Peddie, S. (2009, March 24). Top AIG execs return bonuses. *Newsday*, p. A03.

Perez, J. (2006, December 4). Yellow pad; what the milk companies don't want you to know. *BusinessWorld*, pp. 1–5.

Perez-Pena, R. (2008, December 10). Governor threatened Tribune over criticism, prosecutors says. *The New York Times*, p. A33.

Perrow, C. (1999). *Normal accidents: Living with high-risk technologies*. Princeton, NJ: Princeton University Press.

Perry, A. (2007, March 19). A war without end gets worse. *Time*.

Perry, A. (2007, May 7). How to prevent the next Darfur. *Time*.

Perry, E. (2009, September 26). A year after collapse, WaMu still haunts. *The Oregonian*, pp. B1, B9.

Peters, T. (1992). *Liberation management*. New York: Ballantine.

Peterson, C., & Seligman, M. E. P. (2004). *Character strengths and virtues: A handbook and classification*. Oxford, UK: Oxford University Press.

Peterson, D. K. (2002). The relationship between unethical behavior and the dimensions of the Ethical Climate Questionnaire. *Journal of Business Ethics, 41,* 313–326.

Peterson, K. (2009, July 16). After injuries, college athletes are often left to pay the bills. *The New York Times,* p. A1.

Petrick, J. A. (1998). Building organizational integrity and quality with the four Ps: Perspectives, paradigms, processes, and principles. In M. Schminke (Ed.), *Managerial ethics: Moral management of people and processes* (pp. 115–131). Mahwah, NJ: Erlbaum.

Petrou, M., & Savage, L. (2006, December 11). Genocide in slow motion. *Maclean's,* pp. 35–41.

Petruno, T. (2009, July 9). SEC division chief to resign. *Los Angeles Times,* p. B5.

Petry, C. (2010, January 22). Chicago locks will stay open, Supreme Court rules. *Metal Bulletin.*

Pfeffer, J. (1992, Winter). Understanding power in organizations. *California Management Review, 34*(2), 29–50.

Philips, R. (2003). *Stakeholder theory and organizational ethics*. San Francisco: Berrett-Koehler.

Pile, J. (2009, May 29). *Piracy: Murky waters to navigate.* Retrieved from http://free .financialmail.co.za/report09/deneysmay09/bden.htm

Piliavin, J. A., & Chang, H. W. (1990). Altruism: A review of recent theory and research. *American Sociological Review, 16,* 27–65.

Pilkington, E. (2009, March 7). Jailed for MySpace parody, the student who exposed America's cash for kids scandal. *The Guardian,* International, p. 21.

Pless, N. M. (2007). Understanding responsible leadership: Role identity and motivational drivers. *Journal of Business Ethics, 74,* 437–456.

Pless, N., & Maak, T. (2009). Responsible leaders as agents of world benefit: Learnings from "Project Ulysses." *Journal of Business Ethics, 85,* 59–71.

PMR's position statement regarding mission to rescue 3 missing climbers on Mt. Hood and locator beacons. (2009, December 16). Retrieved from http://www.pmru.org/ pressroom/headlines/20091213PMRStatementRegardingMissions.html

Pogatchnik, S. (2010, March 14). Abuse scandals hit Catholic Church across Europe. *The Oregonian,* p. A11.

Police targeting people for their DNA. (2009, November 24). *The Independent,* News, p. 6.

Poll: U.S. split on torture. (2009, April 24). Retrieved from http://www.upi.com/ Top_News/2009/04/24/Poll-US-split-on-torture/UPI-55341240631033/

Pollard, C. W. (1996). *The soul of the firm*. Grand Rapids, MI: HarperBusiness.

Porath, C. L., & Erez, A. (2007). Does rudeness really matter? The effects of rudeness on task performance and helpfulness. *The Academy of Management Journal, 50,* 1181–1197.

Potter, R. B. (1972). The logic of moral argument. In P. Deats (Ed.), *Toward a discipline of social ethics* (pp. 93–114). Boston: Boston University Press.

Powers, C. W., & Vogel, D. (1980). *Ethics in the education of business managers.* Hasting-on-Hudson, NY: Institute of Society, Ethics and the Life Sciences.

Prati, L. M., Douglas, C., Ferris, G. R., Ammeter, A. P., & Buckley, M. R. (2003). Emotional intelligence, leadership effectiveness, and team outcomes. *The International Journal of Organizational Analysis, 11,* 21–40.

Price, T. L. (2006). *Understanding ethical failures in leadership.* Cambridge, UK: Cambridge University Press.

Prodham, G. (2008, June 10). A face-lift for corporate Germany. *The International Herald Tribune,* Finance, p. 14.

Puffer, S. M., & McCarthy, D. J. (2008). Ethical turnarounds and transformational leadership: A global imperative for corporate social responsibility. *Thunderbird International Business Review, 50,* 304–314.

Puzzanghera, J., Simon, R., & Kristof, K. M. (2009, June 11). Financial crisis; plans to rein in exec pay announced. *Los Angeles Times,* p. B1.

Quigley, N. R., Sully de Luque, M., & House, R. J. (2005). Responsible leadership and governance in a global context: Insights from the GLOBE study. In J. P. Doh & S. A. Sumpf (Eds.), *Handbook on responsible leadership and governance in global business* (pp. 352–379). Cheltenham, UK: Elger.

Raissman, B. (2008, March 21). Brackets of millions, players net nothing. *Daily News,* p. 93.

Rampersad, A. (1997). *Jackie Robinson.* New York: Alfred A. Knopf.

Ramstack, T. (2008, May 21). U.S. web services misused by oppressors. *The Washington Times,* p. C08.

Ransley, C., & Spy, T. (Eds.). (2004). *Forgiveness and the healing process: A central therapeutic concern.* New York: Brunner-Routledge.

Rapisarda, B. A. (2002). The impact of emotional intelligence on work team cohesiveness and performance. *The International Journal of Organizational Analysis, 10,* 363–370.

Rawls, J. (1971). *A theory of justice.* Cambridge, MA: Belknap.

Rawls, J. (1993). Distributive justice. In T. Donaldson & P. H. Werhane (Eds.), *Ethical issues in business: A philosophical approach* (pp. 274–285). Englewood Cliffs, NJ: Prentice Hall.

Rawls, J. (1993). *Political liberalism.* New York: Columbia University Press.

Rawls, J. (2001). *Justice as fairness: A restatement* (E. Kelly, Ed.). Cambridge, MA: Belknap.

Read, B. (2008, February 29). Anti-cheating crusader vexes some professors. *The Chronicle of Higher Education,* The Faculty, p. 1.

Reave, L. (2005). Spiritual values and practices related to leadership effectiveness. *The Leadership Quarterly, 16,* 655–687.

Reb, J., Goldman, B. M., Kray, L. J., & Cropanzano, R. (2006). Different wrongs, different remedies? Reactions to organizational remedies after procedural and interactional injustice. *Personnel Psychology, 59,* 31–64.

Recession, broken promises posing health disaster. (2009, July 20). *The Globe and Mail*, p. A1.

Reeves, E. (2007, Summer). Genocide without end? The destruction of Darfur. *Dissent*, pp. 9–13.

Rego, A., & Pina e Cunha, M. (2008). Workplace spirituality and organizational commitment: An empirical study. *Journal of Organizational Change Management, 21*(1), 53–75.

Resick, C. J., Hange, P. J., Dickson, M. W., & Mitchelson, J. K. (2006). A cross-cultural examination of the endorsement of ethical leadership. *Journal of Business Ethics, 63*, 345–359.

Rest, J. R. (1986). *Moral development: Advances in research and theory.* New York: Praeger.

Rest, J. R. (1993). Research on moral judgment in college students. In A. Garrod (Ed.), *Approaches to moral development* (pp. 201–211). New York: Teachers College Press.

Rest, J. R. (1994). Background: Theory and research. In J. R. Rest & D. Narvaez (Eds.), *Moral development in the professions: Psychology and applied ethics* (pp. 1–25). Hillsdale, NJ: Erlbaum.

Rest, J. R., & Narvaez, D. (1991). The college experience and moral development. In W. M. Kurtines & J. L. Gewirtz (Eds.), *Handbook of moral behavior and development* (Vol. 2: Research, pp. 229–245). Hillsdale, NJ: Erlbaum.

Rest, J., Narvaez, D., Bebeau, M. J., & Thoma, S. J. (1999). *Postconventional moral thinking: A neo-Kohlbergian approach.* Mahwah, NJ: Erlbaum.

Reynolds, S. J. (2003). A single framework for strategic and ethical behavior in the international context. *Business Ethics Quarterly, 13*, 361–379.

Reynolds, S. J. (2006). Moral awareness and ethical predispositions: Investigating the role of individual differences in the recognition of moral issues. *Journal of Applied Psychology, 91*, 233–243.

Richter, J. (2001). *Holding corporations accountable: Corporate conduct, international codes and citizen action.* London: Zed.

Ricks, D. (2009, January 22). Salmonella scare spreads. *Newsday*, p. A10.

Righton, B. (2007, June 11). How not to catch a thief. *Maclean's*, p. 62.

Ritchey, W. (2009, January 14). Bush pushed the limits of presidential power. *Christian Science Monitor*, p. 11.

Ritzer, G. (2004). *The globalization of nothing.* Thousand Oaks, CA: Pine Forge.

Roberto, M. A. (2005). *Why great leaders don't take yes for an answer.* Upper Saddle River, NJ: Wharton School.

Roberts, K. H. (2006). Some characteristics of one type of high reliability organization. In D. Smith & D. Elliott (Eds.), *Key readings in crisis management: Systems and structures for prevention and recovery* (pp. 159–179). London: Routledge.

Robertson, C. (2005, Spring). Organ advertising: Desperate patients solicit volunteers. *The Journal of Law, Medicine & Ethics*, pp. 170–174.

Robins, F. (2006). The challenge of TBL: A responsibility to whom? *Business and Society Review, 111*, 1–14.

Rochlin, G. I., LaPorte, T. R., & Roberts, K. H. (1987). The self-designing high-reliability organization: Aircraft carrier flight operations at sea. *Naval War College Review, 40*(4), 76–90.

Rockness, H., & Rockness, J. (2005). Legislated ethics: From Enron to Sarbanes-Oxley, the impact on corporate America. *Journal of Business Ethics, 57*, 31–54.

Rogers, E. M., & Steinfatt, T. M. (1999). *Intercultural communication.* Prospect Heights, IL: Waveland.

Roloff, M. E., & Paulson, G. D. (2001). Confronting organizational transgressions. In J. M. Darley, D. M. Messick, & T. R. Tyler (Eds.), *Social influences on ethical behavior in organizations* (pp. 53–68). Mahwah, NJ: Erlbaum.

Ronnow, K. (2008). Educate girls, change the world. *Journey of Hope,* pp. 21–26.

Ronnow, K. (2009, March 23). *Mortenson receives Star of Pakistan.* Retrieved from http://www.bozemandailychronicle.com/news/article_ccff0e98–0c8e-5fc9–857d-b5a639ef7a25.html

Rosanas, J. M., & Velilla, M. (2003). Loyalty and trust as the ethical bases of organizations. *Journal of Business Ethics, 44*, 49–59.

Rosenfeld, P., Giacalone, R. A., & Riordan, C. A. (1995). *Impression management in organizations: Theory, measurement, practice.* London: Routledge.

Rothwell, J. D. (1998). *In mixed company: Small group communication* (3rd ed.). Fort Worth, TX: Harcourt Brace.

Royce, J. (1920). *The philosophy of loyalty.* New York: Macmillan.

Ruschman, N. L. (2002). Servant-leadership and the best companies to work for in America. In L. C. Spears & M. Lawrence (Eds.), *Focus on leadership: Servant-leadership for the twenty-first century* (pp. 123–139). New York: Wiley.

Russell, R. F., & Stone, A. G. (2002). A review of servant leadership attributes: Developing a practical model. *Leadership & Organization Development Journal, 23*(3), 145–157.

Sachs, J. (2007, May 27). Sharing the wealth. *Time,* p. 81.

Sack, A. (2008, March 7). Should college athletes be paid? *Christian Science Monitor,* Opinion, p. 9.

Salmonella shipped. (2009, February 7). *Newsday,* p. A09.

Sandin, P. (2009). Approaches to ethics for corporate crisis management. *Journal of Business Ethics, 87*, 109–116.

Sanford, N., & Comstock, C. (Eds.). (1971). *Sanctions for evil.* San Francisco: Jossey-Bass.

Saporito, B., Calabresi, M., Duffy, M., Newton-Small, J., Schere, M., Thompson, M., . . . Zagorin, A. (2008, March 30). *How AIG became too big to fail.* Retrieved from http://www.time.com/time/business/article/0,8599,1886275,00.html

Sarno, D., & Semuels, A. (2009, April 20). Internet; Tweets are an ally in crisis PR. *Los Angeles Times,* p. B1.

Satel, S. (2009, March 10). Kidney for sale: Let's legally reward the donor. *The Globe and Mail,* p. A17.

Saulny, S. (2008, December 11). Calls for governor to quit in scandal on Senate seat. *The New York Times,* p. A1.

Savage, D. G. (2010, January 13). Scanners put privacy against security. *Los Angeles Times,* p. A11.

Sawyer, K. (2003, August 24). Shuttle's "smoking gun" took time to register. *The Washington Post,* p. A1.

Scelfo, J. (2007, May 14). Accidents will happen. *Newsweek,* p. 59.

Schmit, J. (2009, April 27). Broken system hid peanut plants' risks. *USA Today,* p. 1B.

Schmit, J., & Weise, E. (2009, January 29). Peanut butter recall grows. *USA Today,* p. 1B.

Schrag, B. (2001). The moral significance of employee loyalty. *Business Ethics Quarterly, 11,* 41–66.

Schriesheim, C. A., Castor, S. L., & Cogliser, C. C. (1999). Leader-member exchange (LMX) research: A comprehensive review of theory, measurement, and data-analytic practices. *The Leadership Quarterly, 10*(1), 63–114.

Schubert, S., & Miller, T. C. (2008, December 21). Where bribery was just a line item. *The New York Times,* p. BU1.

Schultz, B. (1982). Argumentativeness: Its effect in group decision-making and its role in leadership perception. *Communication Quarterly, 3,* 368–375.

Schwartz, J. (2008, December 30). The fight over NASA's future. *The New York Times,* p. D1.

Schweiger, D. M., Sandberg, W. R., & Rechner, P. (1989). Experiential effects of dialectical inquiry, devil's advocacy, and consensus approaches to strategic decision making. *Academy of Management Journal, 32*(4), 745–772.

Scully, S. (2001, March 13). Minorities gain ground on whites in '00 census. *The Washington Times,* p. A1.

Seeger, M. W., Sellnow, T. L., & Ulmer, R. R. (2003). *Communication and organizational crisis.* Westport, CT: Praeger.

Seeger, M. W., & Ulmer, R. R. (2001). Virtuous responses to organizational crisis: Aaron Feuerstein and Milt Cole. *Journal of Business Ethics, 31,* 369–376.

Seib, C. (2009, March 16). Investors who made money from Madoff try to prevent clawback in aid of victims. *The Times,* p. 46.

Seiler, S. (2009). *Developing responsible leaders.* Paper presented at the International Leadership Association Conference, Prague, Czech Republic.

Sendjaya, S., & Sarros, J. C. (2002). Servant leadership: Its origin, development, and application in organizations. *Journal of Leadership and Organization Studies, 9*(2), 57–64.

Seston, A. (2006, December 6). AIDS day draws attention to epidemic. *The Daily Cardinal.*

Shared sacrifice? Not for these airline executives. (2006, February 2). *USA Today,* p. 14A.

Shockley-Zalabak, P., Ellis, K., & Winograd, G. (2000). Organizational trust: What it means, why it matters. *Organizational Development Journal, 18,* 35–47.

Shriver, D. W. (1995). *An ethic for enemies: Forgiveness in politics.* New York: Oxford University Press.

Shriver, D. W. (2001). Forgiveness: A bridge across abysses of revenge. In R. G. Helmick & R. L. Peterson (Eds.), *Forgiveness and reconciliation: Religion, public policy, & conflict transformation* (pp. 151–167.) Philadelphia: Templeton Foundation Press.

Sibon, J. (2009, March 13). Did he work alone? Questions over fraudster's family unanswered. *The Daily Telegraph*, City, p. 5.

Siemens settles World Bank with $100 million for anti-fight corruption. (2009, July 6). *Africa News*.

Silla, B., Knight, D., & Fang, B. (2006, February 27). Learning to live with big brother. *U.S. News & World Report*.

Simola, S. (2003). Ethics of justice and care in corporate crisis management. *Journal of Business Ethics, 46,* 351–361.

Simola, S. (2005). Concepts of care in organizational crisis prevention. *Journal of Business Ethics, 62,* 341–353.

Simon, R. (2008, August 7). Lax lending standards extended well into 2007, report says. *The Globe and Mail*, p. B8.

Simoncelli, T. (2006, Summer). Dangerous excursions: The case against expanding forensic DNA databases to innocent persons. *Journal of Law, Medicine & Ethics,* pp. 390–397.

Sims, R. L., & Keon, T. L. (1997). Ethical work climate as a factor in the development of person–organization fit. *Journal of Business Ethics, 16,* 1095–1105.

Sims, R. R. (2003). *Ethics and corporate social responsibility: Why giants fall.* Westport, CT: Praeger.

Singer, P. (2002). *One world: The ethics of globalization.* New Haven, CT: Yale University Press.

Slegers, M. (2008, December 8). Health: New directive aims to boost organ donation. *Europolitics.*

Smith, D. H. (1993). Stories, values, and patient care decisions. In C. Conrad (Ed.), *The ethical nexus* (pp. 123–148). Norwood, NJ: Ablex.

Smith, J. Y. (2009, August 12). The Olympian force behind a revolution. *The Washington Post,* p. A07.

Smith, M. E. (2006). Let's make the DNA identification database as inclusive as possible. *Journal of Law, Medicine & Ethics,* pp. 385–389.

Smith, P. K., Jostmann, N. B., Galinsky, A. D., & van Dijk, W. W. (2008). Lacking power impairs executive functions. *Psychological Science, 19*(5), 441–447.

Smith, T. (1999). Justice as a personal virtue. *Social Theory & Practice, 25,* 361–384.

Smith, W. (2007). Cosmopolitan citizenship: Virtue, irony and worldliness. *European Journal of Social Theory, 10,* 37–52.

Snyder, C. R., & Lopez. S. J. (2005). *Handbook of positive psychology.* Oxford, UK: Oxford University Press.

Snyder, P., Hall, M., Robertson, J., Jasinski, T., & Miller, J. S. (2006). Ethical rationality: A strategic approach to organizational crisis. *Journal of Business Ethics, 63,* 371–383.

Solochek, J. S. (2009, September 3). Web Site helps educators detect student plagiarism. *St. Petersburg Times,* p. 9.

Solomon, C. M. (2001). Put your ethics to a global test. In M. H. Albrecht (Ed.), *International HRM: Managing diversity in the workplace* (pp. 329–335). Oxford, UK: Blackwell.

Solomon, R. C. (1990). *A passion for justice: Emotions and the origins of the social contract.* Reading, MA: Addison-Wesley.

Solomon, R. C. (1992). *Ethics and excellence: Cooperation and integrity in business.* New York: Oxford University Press.

Son, H. (2009, June 19). AIG tries to keep a low profile. *The Boston Globe,* Business, p. 7.

Southwest Airlines. (2009). *Officer biographies: Colleen C. Barrett, president emeritus.* Retrieved from http://www.southwest.com/swamedia/bios/colleen_barrett.html

Spears, L. (1998). Introduction: Tracing the growing impact of servant-leadership. In L. C. Spears (Ed.), *Insights on leadership* (pp. 1–12). New York: Wiley.

Srivastva, S. (Ed.). (1988). *Executive integrity.* San Francisco: Jossey-Bass.

Stanley, D. J., Meyer, J. P., & Topolnytsky, L. (2005). Employee cynicism and resistance to organizational change. *Journal of Business and Psychology, 19,* 429–459.

Starmann, R. G. (1993). Tragedy at McDonald's. In J. A. Gottschalk (Ed.), *Crisis response: Inside stories on managing image under siege* (pp. 309–322). Detroit, MI: Visible Ink Press.

Statman, D. (2006). Supreme emergencies revisited. *Ethics, 117,* 58–79.

Staub, E. (1989). *The roots of evil: The origins of genocide and other group violence.* Cambridge, UK: Cambridge University Press.

Stein, R. (2009, September 26). Mandatory flu shots hit resistance. *The Washington Post,* p. A01.

Sternberg, R. J. (2002). Smart people are not stupid, but they sure can be foolish. In R. Sternberg (Ed.), *Why smart people can be so stupid* (pp. 232–242). New Haven, CT: Yale University Press.

Stevens, D. (2006, May 18). Forgiving Dr. Mengele: Letting go of the death camps in "Forgiving Dr. Mengele." *The New York Times,* p. E5.

Stewart, D. R. (2006, June 1). Southwest staff "family": The airline's corporate culture is tied to its success. *Tulsa World.*

Stewart, J. (2008). Cosmopolitan communication ethics: Understanding and action. In K. G. Roberts & R. C. Arnett (Eds.), *Communication ethics: Between cosmopolitanism and provinciality* (pp. 105–119). New York: Peter Lang.

Story, L. (2008, December 18). Wall St. profits were a mirage, but huge bonuses were real. *The New York Times,* p. A1.

Street, M. D. (1997). Groupthink: An examination of theoretical issues, implications, and future research suggestions. *Small Group Research, 28,* 72–93.

Sucher, S. J. (2008). *The moral leader: Challenges, tools, and insights.* London: Routledge.

Sudan: Be tough on Al-Bashir, activists tell Obama. (2009, September 14). *Africa News.*

Suhaimi, N. D. (2008, November 9). Some have laws to offer compensation. *The Straits Times.*

Sullivan, J. (2009, February 12). Audit outlines high fees, spending. *The Philadelphia Inquirer,* p. A01.

Sullivan, J. (2009, February 27). Class-action suit filed in corrupt judges case. *The Philadelphia Inquirer,* p. A01.

Sullivan, J. (2009, March 14). Report submitted in juvenile-detention scandal. *The Philadelphia Inquirer,* p. B01.

Swardson, A. (2007, March 11). A tale of courage, told in a blink of an eye. *The Washington Post,* p. A01.

Talbot, M. (1999). Against relativism. In J. M. Halstead & T. H. McLaughlin (Eds.), *Education in morality* (pp. 206–217). London: Routledge.

Tam, H. (1998). *Communitarianism: A new agenda for politics and citizenship.* New York: New York University Press.

Tangney, J. P. (2000). Humility: Theoretical perspectives, empirical findings and directions for future research. *Journal of Social and Clinical Psychology, 19,* 70–82.

Tavis, T. (2000). The globalization phenomenon and multinational corporate developmental responsibility. In O. F. Williams (Ed.), *Global codes of conduct: An idea whose time has come* (pp. 13–36). Notre Dame, IN: University of Notre Dame Press.

Tenbrunsel, A. E., & Messick, D. M. (2004). Ethical fading: The role of self-deception in unethical behavior. *Social Justice Research, 17,* 223–236.

Tepper, B. J. (2000). Consequences of abusive supervision. *Academy of Management Journal, 43*(2), 178–190.

Terez, T. (2001, December). You could just spit: Tales of bad bosses. *Workforce,* pp. 24–25.

Thistlethwaite, S. B. (2009, June 27). Wearing faith on your sleeve. *The Washington Post,* p. B02.

Thoma, S. J. (2006). Research on the defining issues test. In M. Killen & J. G. Smetana (Eds.), *Handbook of moral development* (pp. 67–91). Mahwah, NJ: Erlbaum.

Thomas, E., Smalley, S., & Wolfee, R. (2008, December 22). Being Rod Blagojevich. *Newsweek,* p. 30.

Thomas, G. (2000, January 10). The forgiveness factor. *Christianity Today,* pp. 38–43.

Thompson, G. (2009, October 18). Sudan's critics relieved that Obama chose a middle course. *The New York Times,* p. A10.

Thoresen, C. E., Harris, H. S., & Luskin, F. (2000). Forgiveness and health: An unanswered question. In M. E. McCullough, K. I. Pargament, & C. E. Thoresen (Eds.), *Forgiveness: Theory, research and practice* (pp. 254–280). New York: Guilford.

Throw it out: A court decision limits the scope of police DNA databases. (2008, December 4). Retrieved from http://www.economist.com/node/12726053

Timmons, M. (2002). *Moral theory: An introduction.* Lanham, MD: Rowman & Littlefield.

Tims, D. (2010, February 17). Bob gives Red Mill to workers. *The Oregonian,* pp. A1, A5.

Tivnan, E. (1995). *The moral imagination.* New York: Routledge, Chapman, and Hall.

Toffler, B. L., & Reingold, J. (2003). *Final accounting: Ambition, greed, and the fall of Arthur Andersen.* New York: Broadway.

Tomlinson, S., & Graves, B. (2009, December 15). Radio beacons: Climbers, rescuers and politicians debate whether mountain locater units should be mandatory. *The Oregonian,* pp. A1, A10.

Toor, S. R., & Ofori, G. (2009). Ethical leadership: Examining the relationships with full range leadership model, employee outcomes, and organizational culture. *Journal of Business Ethics, 90,* 533–547.

Totaro, P. (2009, June 20). After the MP blitz, a $4m blackout. *Sydney Morning Herald,* International News, p. 15.

Tourish, D. (2008). Challenging the transformational agenda: Leadership theory in transition? *Management Communication Quarterly, 21,* 522–528.

Tourish, D., & Pinnington, A. (2002). Transformational leadership, corporate cultism and the spirituality paradigm: An unholy trinity in the workplace? *Human Relations, 55,* 147–172.

Trevino, L. K., & Brown, M. E. (2005). The role of leaders in influencing unethical behavior in the workplace. In R. E. Kidwell & C. L. Martin (Eds.), *Managing organizational deviance* (pp. 69–87). Thousand Oaks, CA: Sage.

Trevino, L. K., Brown, M., & Pincus, L (2003). A qualitative investigation of perceived executive ethical leadership: Perceptions from inside and outside the executive suite. *Human Relations, 56,* 5–37.

Trevino, L. K., Butterfield, K. D., & McCabe, D. L. (1998). The ethical context in organizations: Influences on employee attitudes and behaviors. *Business Ethics Quarterly, 8,* 447–476.

Trevino, L. K., Hartman, L. P., & Brown, M. (2000). Moral person and moral manager: How executives develop a reputation for ethical leadership. *California Management Reviews, 42,* 128–133.

Trevino, L. K., & Nelson, K. A. (2004). *Managing business ethics: Straight talk about how to do it right* (3rd ed.). Hoboken, NJ: Wiley.

Trevino, L. K., & Weaver, G. R. (2001). Organizational justice and ethics program "follow-through": Influences on employee's harmful and helpful behavior. *Business Ethics Quarterly, 11,* 651–671.

Trevino, L. K., & Weaver, G. R. (2003). *Managing ethics in business organizations: Social scientific perspectives.* Stanford, CA: Stanford University Press.

Triandis, H. C. (1995). *Individualism and collectivism.* Boulder, CO: Westview.

Tronto, J. C. (1993). *Moral boundaries: A political argument for an ethic of care.* New York: Routledge.

Tropman, J. (2003). *Making meetings work: Achieving high quality group decisions* (2nd ed.). Thousand Oaks, CA: Sage.

Troyer, J. (2003). *The classical Utilitarians: Bentham and Mill*. Indianapolis: Hackett.

Turner, N., Barling, J., Epitropaki, O., Butcher, V., & Milner, C. (2002, April). Transformational leadership and moral reasoning. *Journal of Applied Psychology*, 87, 304–311.

U.S. Department of Labor Bureau of Labor Statistics. (2007, August 9). Retrieved from http://www.dol.gov/

Ulmer, R. R., & Sellnow, T. L. (2000). Consistent questions of ambiguity in organizational crisis communication: Jack in the Box as a case study. *Journal of Business Ethics*, 25, 143–155.

Upton, J., & Wieberg, S. (2006, November 16). Million-dollar coaches move into mainstream. *USA Today*, p. 1A.

Urbina, I. (2009, March 28). Despite red flags about judges, a kickback scheme flourished. *The New York Times*, p. A1.

Useem, M. (1998). *The leadership moment: Nine stories of triumph and disaster and their lessons for us all*. New York: Times Business.

Valentine, S., & Barnett, T. (2003). Ethics code awareness, perceived ethical values, and organizational commitment. *Journal of Personal Selling & Sales Management*, 23, 359–367.

Van Vuuren, L. J., & Crous, F. (2005). Utilising Appreciative Inquiry (AI) in creating a shared meaning of ethics in organizations. *Journal of Business Ethics*, 57, 399–412.

Varachaver, N. (2004, November 15). Glamour! Fame! Org charts! *Fortune*, pp. 76–85.

Vecchio, R. P. (1982). A further test of leadership effects due to between-group variation and in-group variation. *Journal of Applied Psychology*, 67, 200–208.

Velasquez, M. G. (1992). *Business ethics: Concepts and cases* (3rd ed.). Englewood Cliffs, NJ: Prentice Hall.

Verhovek, S. H. (1993, April 22). Death in Waco: F. B. I. saw the ego in Koresh, but not a willingness to die. *The New York Times*, p. A1.

Vetelson, A. J. (2005). *Evil and human agency: understanding collective evildoing*. Cambridge, UK: Cambridge University Press.

Victor, B., & Cullen, J. B. (1988). The organizational bases of ethical work climates. *Administrative Science Quarterly*, 33, 101–125.

Victor, B., & Cullen, J. B. (1990). A theory and measure of ethical climate in organizations. In W. C. Frederic & L. E. Preston (Eds.), *Business ethics: Research issues and empirical studies* (pp. 77–97). Greenwich, CT: JAI Press.

Vitell, S. J., Nwachukwu, S. L., & Barnes, J. H. (1993). *Journal of Business Ethics*, 12, 753–760.

Waddock, S. A., & Graves, S. B. (1997). The corporate social performance–financial performance link. *Strategic Management Journal*, 18, 303–319.

Waldman, D. A., Bass, B. M., & Yammarino, F. J. (1990). Adding to contingent-reward behavior: The augmenting effect of charismatic leadership. *Group and Organizational Studies*, 15, 381–394.

Waller, J. (2007). *Becoming evil: How ordinary people commit genocide and mass killing* (2nd ed.). Oxford, UK: Oxford University Press.

Waltman, M. A., Russell, D. C., Coyle, C. T., Enright, R. D., Holter, A. C., & Swoboda, C. M. (2009). The effects of a forgiveness intervention on patients with coronary artery disease. *Psychology and Health, 24*(1), 11–27.

Walumbwa, F. O., Avolio, B. J., Gardner, W. L., Wernsing, T. S., & Peterson, S. J. (2008). Authentic leadership: Development and validation of a theory-based measure. *Journal of Management, 34*(1), 89–126.

Walzer, M. (1977). *Just and unjust wars: A moral argument with historical illustrations.* New York: Basic Books.

Warnke, G. (1993). *Justice and interpretation.* Cambridge: MIT Press.

Washington, R. R., Sutton, C. D., & Field, H. S. (2006). Individual differences in servant leadership: The roles of values and personality. *Leadership & Organization Development Journal, 27,* 700–716.

Wayne, L. (2005, March 8). Boeing chief is ousted after admitting affair. *The New York Times,* p. A1.

Weaver, G. R., Trevino, L. K., & Cochran, P. L. (1999a). Corporate ethics practices in the mid-1990s: An empirical study of the Fortune 1000. *Journal of Business Ethics, 18,* 283–294.

Weaver, G. R., Trevino, L. K., & Cochran, P. L. (1999b). Integrated and decoupled corporate social performance: Management commitments, external pressures, and corporate ethics practices. *Academy of Management Journal, 42,* 539–552.

Webster, P. (1997, March 7). Memoir unlocks medical enigma. *The Guardian,* p. 15.

Weick, K. E., & Roberts, K. H. (2006). Collective minds in organizations: Heedful interrelating on flight decks. In D. Smith & D. Elliott (Eds.), *Key readings in crisis management: Systems and structures for prevention and recovery* (pp. 343–368). London: Routledge.

Weick, K. E., & Sutcliffe, K. M. (2001). *Managing the unexpected: Assuring high performance in an age of complexity.* San Francisco: Jossey-Bass.

Weidlich, T., & Calkins, L. B. (2006, October 24). Skilling jailed 24 years. *National Post,* p. FP1.

Weise, E. (2009, April 2). Nuts. *USA Today,* p. 1B.

Weise, E., & Schmit, J. (2009, February 10). Health risks may reach far beyond reported victims. *USA Today,* p. 1A.

Werhane, P. (1999). *Moral imagination and management decision-making.* New York: Oxford University Press.

West, H. R. (2004). *An introduction to Mill's utilitarian ethics.* Cambridge, UK: Cambridge University Press.

White, B. J., & Prywes, Y. (2007). *The nature of leadership: Reptiles, mammals, and the challenge of becoming a great leader.* New York: AMACOM.

Whiteside, K. (2004, September 1). College athletes want cut of action. *USA Today,* p. 3C.

Whitney, D., & Trosten-Bloom, A. (2003). *The power of appreciative inquiry: A practical guide to positive change.* San Francisco: Berrett-Koehler.

Whoriskey, P. (2010, March 19). Toyota resisted government safety findings: Automaker followed "game plan," escaped a broad early recall. *The Washington Post,* p. A01.

Wilkinson, T. (2003, January 21). To fight terror, Montanan builds schools in Asia. *Christian Science Monitor*, USA, p. 1.

Williams, G., & Zinkin, J. (2008). The effect of culture on consumers' willingness to punish irresponsible corporate behaviour: Applying Hofstede's typology to the punishment aspect of corporate social responsibility. *Business Ethics: A European Review, 17*, 210–226.

Williams, K. D., Harkins, S. G., & Karau, S. J. (2003). Social performance. In M. A. Hogg & J. Cooper (Eds.), *The Sage handbook of social psychology* (pp. 327–346). London: Sage.

Williams, R., & Johnson, P. (2006). Inclusiveness, effectiveness and intrusiveness: Issues in developing uses of DNA profiling in support of criminal investigations. *Journal of Law, Medicine & Ethics, 34*, 234–247.

Wilmers, R. G. (2009, July 27). Where the crisis came from. *The Washington Post*, p. A19.

Wilmot, W. W., & Hocker, J. L. (2001). *Interpersonal conflict* (6th ed.). New York: McGraw-Hill Higher Education.

Wilson, P. (2009, May 16). Dark day for British parliament. *Weekend Australian*, World, p. 11.

Wiseman, P. (2008, April 23). In China, a battle over Web censorship. *USA Today*, p. 1A.

Witt, J. L., & Morgan, J. (2002). *Stronger in the broken places: Nine lessons for turning crisis into triumph*. New York: Times Books/Henry Holt.

Wolvin, A. D., & Coakley, G. C. (1993). A listening taxonomy. In A. D. Wolvin & C. G. Coakley (Eds.), *Perspectives in listening* (pp. 15–22). Norwood, NJ: Ablex.

Women in the labor force. (2009). Retrieved from http://www.bls.gov/CPS/wlf-intro-2009.htm

Woodruff, P. (2001). *Reverence: Renewing a forgotten virtue*. Oxford, UK: Oxford University Press.

Worthington, E. L., Jr. (2005). Initial questions about the art and science of forgiving. In E. L. Worthington (Ed.), *Handbook of forgiveness* (pp. 1–13). New York: Routledge.

Wright, D. K. (1993). Enforcement dilemma: Voluntary nature of public relations codes. *Public Relations Review, 19*, 13–20.

Wu, A. C. (2008, January 30). Balancing rights and burqas. *The Washington Times*, p. A17.

Yet again, rescuers search a silent mountain. (2009, December 15). *The Oregonian*, p. B8.

York, E. B. (2009, April 20). What Domino's did right—and wrong—in squelching hubbub over YouTube video. *Advertising Age*.

York, G. (2009, July 20). Recession, broken promises posing health disaster. *The Globe and Mail*, p. A1.

Yukl, G. (2009). *Leadership in organizations* (7th ed.). Upper Saddle River, NJ: Prentice Hall.

Yurtsever, G. (2006). Measuring moral imagination. *Social Behavior and Personality, 34,* 212–213.

Zablocki, B. D. (2000). What can the study of communities teach us about community? In E. W. Lehman (Ed.), *Autonomy and order: A communitarian anthology* (pp. 71–88). Lanham, MD: Rowman & Littlefield.

Zadek, S. (2004, December). The path to corporate responsibility. *Harvard Business Review,* pp. 125–132.

Zerillo, N. (2009, April 20). Crisis forces Domino's to revamp social media plan. *PR Week,* p. 1

Zhang, U. (2009, February 14). Peanut corporation files for bankruptcy. *Wall Street Journal Abstracts,* p. A3.

Zhu, W., May, D. R., & Avolio, B. J. (2004). The impact of ethical leadership behavior on employee outcomes: The roles of psychological empowerment and authenticity. *Journal of Leadership and Organizational Studies, 11,* 16–26.

Zimbardo, P. G. (2005). A situationist perspective on the psychology of evil. In A. G. Miller (Ed.), *The social psychology of good and evil* (pp. 21–50). New York: Guilford.

Zimbardo, P. G. (2007). *The Lucifer effect: Understanding how good people turn evil.* New York: Random House.

Zinnbauer, B. J., & Pargament, K. I. (2005). Religiousness and spirituality. In R. F. Paloutzian & C. L. Park (Eds.), *Handbook of the psychology of religion and spirituality* (pp. 21–42). New York: Guilford.

Zyglidopoulos, S. C. (2002). The social and environmental responsibilities of multinationals: Evidence from the Brent Spar case. *Journal of Business Ethics, 36,* 141–151.

Index

About the Author

Craig E. Johnson (PhD, University of Denver) is professor of leadership studies and director of the Doctor of Business Administration program at George Fox University in Newberg, Oregon. He teaches undergraduate and graduate courses in leadership, ethics, and management. Previously he served as chair of the university's Department of Communication Arts. Johnson is the author of *Ethics in the Workplace: Tools and Tactics for Organizational Transformation* (also published by Sage) and coauthor, with Michael Z. Hackman, of *Leadership: A Communication Perspective.* His research findings, instructional ideas, and book reviews have been published in the *Journal of Leadership Studies,* the *Journal of Leadership and Organizational Studies,* the *Journal of Leadership Education, Academy of Management Learning and Education, The International Leadership Journal, Communication Quarterly, Communication Reports,* and other journals. Johnson has led and participated in service and educational trips to Kenya, Rwanda, New Zealand, China, Brazil, and Honduras, and has served in volunteer leadership roles in several nonprofit organizations.

SAGE Research Methods Online

The essential tool for researchers

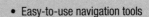